Peregrine Books
The Left in Britain 1956–68

In Hungary in 1956 Stalin's tanks blew apart the Left in the rest of the world. Old complacences were shattered, while new parties, new ideas and events brought a new militancy. The ferment continued for a decade and burst out in 1968 in Paris and across much of the world.

This book tells the story of those years in Britain, The New Left, CND, student politics, civil rights and a transformed trade union movement can all be seen springing up from that initial catastrophic break-up. David Widgery has written a lucid and exciting narrative of a time when the Left seemed invincible on the streets and impotent everywhere else. Each of his chapters is extensively illustrated by documents, pamphlets and articles showing how working-class movements combined with middle-class writers to bring about a completely changed understanding of what it now means to be 'on the Left'.

David Widgery is a doctor of medicine and has worked on various underground and socialist newspapers, including *Oz* which he edited after the imprisonment of its former editors on conspiracy charges in 1971.

The Left in Britain 1956-68

DAVID WIDGERY

PENGUIN BOOKS

Penguin Books Ltd, Harmondsworth,
Middlesex, England
Penguin Books Inc., 7110 Ambassador Road,
Baltimore, Maryland 21207, U.S.A.
Penguin Books Australia Ltd, Ringwood,
Victoria, Australia
Penguin Books Canada Ltd,
41 Steelcase Road West, Markham, Ontario, Canada
Penguin Books (N.Z.) Ltd,
182–190 Wairau Road, Auckland 10, New Zealand

First published 1976

Made and printed in Great Britain by
Hazell Watson & Viney Ltd,
Aylesbury, Bucks
Set in Monotype Times Roman

To the memory of
Victor Serge 1890–1947
Syndicalist, Bolshevik, Trotskyist

Contents

8   *Contents*

Men fight and lose that battle, and then the thing they fought for comes about in spite of their defeat, and when it comes, turns out to be not what they meant and other men have to fight for what they meant under another name. (WILLIAM MORRIS)

Mind you, political progress is not made after the fashion of a Corydon-Phyllis dance, jigging along, so to speak, with pipes (or say cigarettes) in our mouths, through pleasant places with the sun shining over us. But there's another side; it's very hard, very hard; we get mixed up in disputes among ourselves or about one thing and another and can't keep a straight line for the great thing, even if all of us know what that is. (TOM MAGUIRE)

I have undergone a little over ten years of various forms of captivity, agitated in seven countries and written twenty books. I own nothing. On several occasions a press with a vast circulation has hurled filth at me because I spoke the truth. Behind us lies a victorious revolution gone astray, several abortive attempts at revolution, and massacres in so great numbers as to inspire a certain dizziness. And to think it's not over yet. Let me be done with this digression; those were the only possible roads for us. I have more confidence in mankind and the future than ever before. (VICTOR SERGE)

Foreword

The idea for this book came when I woke up, nearly smothered under a shale of *Labour Workers* and *China Reconstructs*. A bookshelf had collapsed. I was living in a room three-quarters filled with heaps of the leaflets, pamphlets and newspapers of the far Left which I had bought from bookshop back rooms and hauled out of litter bins after demonstrations. Like a lot of people who decided they were Marxists in the middle sixties, I couldn't escape the feeling that I was in a political orphanage. So I had collected a bedroom museum of left-wing literature in an attempt to unravel my own political parentage. Fascinated and repelled I pored over unspeakably bitter polemics, marvelled at the Declarations of International Executive Committees, cross-checked Internal and External Bulletins and tried to marry them all up with what little fact and history there is of the modern labour movement. Along the way I found out that the authors of the polemical savageries were actually quite good friends, the International Executive was actually a couple of blokes in Clapham and that nobody reads Internal Bulletins much anyhow.

This amateur research also convinced me that these grubby, despised and ridiculed sheets, typed and printed by the authors themselves and hawked hand to hand down the teeming alleys of the sectaries, actually offered, for all their bombast and low comedy, a more penetrating view of how modern capitalism operates than several hundred Professors of Sociology (Marxist or otherwise), Fleet Street editorialists, TV news-readers and other ignorant experts. It taught me how little is known about the achievements and the organization of the post-war working class and the ideas of the men and women who lead it. And it forced me to face up to the obscurings rendered by the Left itself, not just the straightforward dishonesties of Stalinism and the almost deliberate owlishness of the New Left (in both its young-intellectuals-really-concerned-about-the-quality-of-life phase and its present Super-Marxist era) but the distortions present in the orthodox-Trotskyist version of things. So to enable me to spring-clean my room with a clear conscience, I have tried to cut away from the mounds of yellowed news-print writing that will show something of how the working-class move-ment woke up, after forty years of hibernation. The aim is to rescue the tracts, manifestos and analyses of the far Left from the contempt and restricted currency with which official society would like to treat them. It also means making available again participants' accounts of their own struggles, told in their own words with as little doctoring as possible. It's a working manual to be consulted, dipped into and passed on in the hope it will be of some help in the re-assembling of the modern revo-lutionary workers' movement. In fact because such a small group of people actually find written words convincing I half wish that it wasn't a book at all but some species of talking poster which might express what the modern socialist movement feels like from within – its humour and music and oratory and colours and the intellectual sensations of its mentors and inventors, the autumn and granite of E. P. Thompson, the whiskey and ice of Alasdair MacIntyre or the hurdy gurdy of Tony Cliff.

I am resigned to the fact that most 'professional' readers (members of revolutionary organizations including my own) will feel ill-served by this book. I can only declare that I have made the best effort I am capable of to be non-sectarian. I wish to give no comfort whatsoever to those tyros, theorem-provers and stamp-collectors who prefer a rote-learnt and pointless quarrel about something that happened in Korea when they were in nappies to the real problems of the present. Such people are the political equivalents of drivers going through a town centre using only their rear-view mirrors, and deserve the same fate. What I do regret is that the book reflects the pre-1968 Left's complete lack of interest in the particular situations of women and immigrants. Any reader who has become political through Women's Liberation, the Gay Liberation Movement and the immigrant and anti-racist organizations (movements whose political potential in modern capitalist society is still underestimated by many over-orthodox Marxists) will be justifiably shocked by how far these causes were excluded from the terms of left-wing debate in the fifties and sixties. The author of the successor to this volume will have to redress the balance by tracing the uneasy patterns of attraction and repulsion between the movements which resisted sexual and racial oppression alone and the more tra-ditional Marxist parties and groups.

Nonetheless this book will be worth the effort if my curiosity about the recent history of the revolutionary Left makes other people, at present just bewildered, curious too. And the writers of the original articles reprinted here will be satisfied if their words are still pungent and immediate enough to make socialists today. An attempt to sketch the outline of events so close to us runs many risks. It will be worthwhile if it shows how profoundly past battles shape the present terrain, if it can demonstrate that tank invasions and atom bombs and Labour Government wage freezes don't just repeat themselves for ever and ever, that they bring into being new forces, forces which sometimes sour and sometimes vanish, but which, organized, have the potential power to abolish the system of warfare and wage labour for good.

To assemble this book has been difficult. It has been fitted into time snatched from meetings, articles and *Socialist Worker* selling and earning a living as a doctor. It has been lost on the top of the 38 bus and shuffled through by Special Branch men who said they were looking for a bomb. The political ideas which underlie the socialist sub-scholarship are owed largely to Tony Cliff, Mike Kidron and Nigel Harris and their theoretical and editorial work in the *IS* journal, though I ought to add this book in no way represents official International Socialism policies. I have been given the run of several private collections, Bill Kaye, Julian Harber, and David Phillips being particulary long-suffering. For being inspiring, or helpful or just telling good stories, I would like to thank Adrian Perry, Mike Seifert, Ben Birnbaum, Anna and Ross Pritchard, Nigel Fountain, John Hoyland, Bob Rowthorn, Chris Harman, Eleanor Thornycroft, Jim Higgins, Neil Ascherson, Gery Lawless, Kate Williams, John Birtwhistle, Logie Barrow, Amanda Sebestyen, Chris Pallis, Stacy Marking, Ken Weller, Roger Cox, Jim Scott, Bobby Campbell, Duncan Hallas, Dorothy and Edward Thompson, Marsha Rowe and Steven Bodington. Peter Sedgwick inspired the project, Neil Middleton and David Duguid from Penguins kept me at it, Val Clarke turned some extremely messy drafts into glistening manuscripts and re-wrote passages she disagreed with, Sheila Rowbotham peeled oranges, made rude remarks, wrote file cards for newspapers and put up with them and me. Joe Cocker, the Stones and Messrs Glaxo and Nescafé kept me awake to write it finally in the two weeks in August 1972 when the dockers freed the Pentonville Five.

Bethnal Green Hospital
1 *May* 1973   David Widgery

Acknowledgements

Acknowledgement is made to the following authors, publishers and groups for permission to reprint material in this book previously published. Edward Thompson for 'Through the Smoke of Budapest'.* Granada Publishing for Brian Behan's 'Russian Inventions' and 'The South Bank Struggle' from *With Breast Expanded*, published by MacGibbon & Kee. Bob Potter and the editors of *Solidarity* for 'Special Work'. Peter Fryer for 'The Wortley Hall Conference'. Lawrence Daly for 'The Fife Socialist League'. Edward Thompson and John Saville for 'A Communist Salute'. Martin Grainger and the editor of the *Newsletter* for 'We Marched Against Britain's Death Factory'. Edward Thompson and John Saville for 'Beyond the Bomb'. Allison & Busby for 'Seeking a Revolution' from *Left, Left, Left* by Peggy Duff. Mike Kidron and the editor of *International Socialism* for 'No Bombs and No Illusions'. Peter Sedgwick and the editor of *International Socialism* for 'The Two New Lefts'. Bob Potter and the editor of the *Newsletter* for 'How to Fight the Service Slashes'. The editor of *Socialist Worker* for 'Carron, the Noble Knight' by Geoff Carlsson. Ken Weller and *Solidarity* for 'Fords: Some Lessons'. Mike Kidron and the editor of *International Socialism* for 'Labour's Party'. Stacy Marking for 'Trade-Unionism in Despair'. *Solidarity* for 'Crossman at King Hill'. Paul Foot for 'The Golden Boys'. Bob Rowthorn for 'They're Our Enemies, That's the Key Point'. Nigel Harris and the editor of *International Socialism* for 'The Loneliness of the Left'. Alasdair MacIntyre for 'The Strange Death of Social Democratic England'. Jim Prescott for 'Not Wanted on Voyage'. The Centre for Socialist Education for Lou Lewis's 'The Struggle at Mytons'. The Roberts–Arundel Strike Committee for 'The Story of the Strike'. The London Industrial Shop Stewards' Defence Committee for 'Smash The Freeze, Fight Unemployment'. Pete Gold and the editor of *Socialist Worker* for 'May Day – Give Your Guv'nor That Choking Feeling'. Jim Higgins and the editor of *Socialist Worker* for 'A Day with the Leadership'. The editors of *Solidarity* for 'The Seymour Hall Conference'. Colin Barker for 'The Pilkington Strike'. The editor of the *Agitator* for 'The Fords Strike'. The editor of *Socialist Worker* for 'I'd Like to Shake the Liver

* E. P. Thompson wishes to state that his political position remains, in general, that of the *May Day Manifesto* (1968), and that he is in radical disagreement with the selection and interpretation of the recent history of the Left presented in this book.

out of Him'. Walter Kendall for 'Why Workers' Control'. Alex Glasgow for 'The Socialist ABC'. Laurie Flynn for 'The This-Sideness of Our Thinking'. Chris Harman for 'Why We Fought the LSE'. Mike Gonsalves for 'There's Something Wrong with Essex'. Pete Latarche for 'Hull Demands "One Man – One Vote"'. Mike Rosen for 'To Sir, Without Love'. Shelia Rowbotham for 'Cinderella Organizes Buttons'. Nigel Fountain for 'On from Grosvenor Square (Part 73)'. The editor of *Idiot International* for 'Nothing So Romantic'. Maurice Brinton and Geoff Richman have also given permission for extracts from their pamphlets in the text of Chapter 8.

Every effort has been made to trace copyright holders but in those cases where this has not been possible the publishers would be interested to hear from those not acknowledged. Laurie Flynn, Colin Barker and Bob Rowthorn have asked to register that they have developed their positions from those extracts republished here. The editor regrets the refusal of *Labour Monthly* to reprint several articles, which has had the effect of underpresenting Communist Party writers.

Introduction: Farewell, Grosvenor Square

The story of the British Left from the 1956 split in the Communist Party up till the growth and disintegration of the Vietnam Solidarity movement is the record of a political adolescence. And who can review his own adolescence without an embarrassed blush or an amused smile at follies recognized as such too late? Not all of it will have been folly, of course: but even what was ardent and delightful is now revealed as without issue, harbouring from the outset the contradictions that would dissolve or defeat its hope. *Where have all the flowers gone?* sang the marchers; and, in pacific elegy, *Where have all the soldiers gone?* And now, a few years later, where have all the marchers gone? The years of my own biological teens were haunted, not by politics, but by the fear and joy of God: a God who would reckon each jet of sperm from my myriad masturbations and, on the day of judgement, present me with the final account. 'SEE WHAT YOU'VE DONE!' God would thunder at me, shaking His sage head and pointing to the great transparent bag, filled to the brim with futile sex-juice, a glistening mass many times my own size. The moment before I was to be hurled into this vat of sin, the spermatozoa released themselves from the goo and pranced before me in swarms of thousands, heads agape and reproachful, chanting 'WASTE! WASTE' in piping voices. Nowadays it is the memory of political waste which summons a reckoning of time mis-spent: the sperm-dance is performed by hordes of young heads, waving the banners of causes either (like Ban the Bomb) lost or (like Vietnam) won by other agencies than our protest. A generous but possible estimate of the largest CND march, the one from Aldermaston and Wethersfield into Trafalgar Square at Easter 1961, is of a final turnout of 100,000 participants. The great Vietnam solidarity demo of October 1968 took the whole width of Central London's streets under marchers' control; the Press scare about impending violence and the known record of the Metropolitan Police on these occasions meant that nobody could have come on the march without a realistic fear of trouble on the way; and the occasion drew, at a fair approximation 100,000 participants. But it was not the previous hundred thousand grown up by seven and a half years. In terms of personnel, the demonstrating Left of Britain simply did not cumulate. Witness not merely the great mass mobilizations but the countless local marches, occupations, conventions, moods and manias: in 1970, to take one single issue, direct-action episodes, supported by the mass of students, took place in one third of British universities following the disclosure of political file-material kept by the authorities on both teachers and taught at the University of Warwick. If the movements generated in these successive waves had possessed any capacity to educate in wider political horizons, the United Kingdom would now have a permanent cadre of several hundred thousand left-wing activists. In fact, most of the people whose middle-class manifestations are described in this book are now leading very quiet lives. And the apparently radical alignment of their actions and beliefs, from march to sitdown, college occupation to insurrectionary newspapers, was a temporary excitement within a liberalism whose subsequent career was to be indistinguishable from that evoked in the least militant of their generation. The only *dramatis personae* who can be identified as recurring from the scenes of the Left in the late fifties right along to the sixties *and* the seventies consist of two sorts of people: militant trade-unionists and active (usually Marxist and usually card-carrying) revolutionaries.

The other movements have seen an inversion of Christ's Law of the Proportions of Backsliding ('One of you twelve will betray me'); in the end, at best, there has been one solid burgher for the city of radical politics to every eleven hundred, or eleven thousand, tourists. The incorrigible stayers of Socialism got used to the passing scene, and anticipated the dereliction of the multitudes. All the more precious became the newcomer who was going to remain true: we learnt to snatch the chosen from the uncircumcised throng and to concentrate our attachments on him or her with the marks of the honesty that is strength; but more often than not, to our great sadness, we picked the wrong one.

Hence the strange age-distribution of the radical middle-class Left, that pyramid of the years crammed in its lower echelons by massed banks of eager Youth, thinning sharply to a tip at which a few veterans in their thirties, and an even fewer who were any older, looked at one another and then down and away into their rival factions of juniors. It was a distribution both statistically abnormal – for in the population as a whole the proportion of the elders was steadily rising – and subjectively pathological. It was possible to think, 'All these marvellous young people' at the first, second or even third Aldermaston or Young

Socialist march, but by the seventh or ninth, when it became obvious that these were different young people each time, the effect was less rejuvenating. How hollow now seems the announcement of the United Secretariat of the Fourth International that an 'international mass youth vanguard' was on its way to us in the run-up to the seventies. The youth movement was, increasingly over the years, a movement of students or near-students, reflecting but also distorting, through their upbringing in an elitist enclave, the pressures and demands of their generation. Each intake of the youth rebellion graduated into separate experiences of career, home, family, never again to re-assemble. Soon to be dispersed by the same competition and mobility which had socialized them for a while in a common privileged setting, the class of '58, of '68, of '72 reacted with a precocious consciousness to the first great horror of the world that came its way, to the Bomb, to the Vietnam war, to Ireland, and to the truncheon-swinging police. Its crowds swirled across streets and newsreels, related through a zigzag causality to other crowds, other issues: tenants, rent increases; workers, redundancies and wages; black people, discrimination and rotten jobs. The Instant Left was abstract, brave, verbally fluent and powerless. The working-class protest was concrete, cautious, verbally stereotyped and often successful. The student and middle-class movement was not (as some of its theoreticians argued) 'the little motor that sets the big motor turning'; it was symptomatic rather than effective, the stormy petrel whose appearance is a sign that the real storm is about to come. The stormy petrel does not cause the storm which it precedes; its movement towards the watchers is caused by the storm ahead of which it flies, not vanguard but herald. There are those who have told us that the petrel, that gallant little bird, is really the storm: they suffer from bad eyesight.

If the movements have gone, and if both the leaderships and the ranks which staffed them have nearly all vanished from political activity, can anything be said for the effectiveness of the British independent Left over 1956 to 1968? It will be easy for any reader from the established radical and revolutionary groupings to mock the incoherent and Utopian assemblies that were the forerunners of today's Socialism. In 1974 we have an official national student body, the NUS, aligned with left policies to the great terror of the liberal media, the leadership for its militancy contested within a spectrum ranging from radical to Trotskyist. Over most of the period described in this book, control of the NUS was firmly in the grip of right Labour or arrant conservative careerists, some of them conniving with the overseas operations of the

Central Intelligence Agency of the United States Government. The
NUS took no part whatever in the mass episodes of demonstration
and direct action that embraced thousands upon thousands of young
students. How was the transition effected and what was its nature?
Basically, what the non-unionized student movement did was to create
precedents for the unionized, breaks in the long tradition of inertia and
acquiescence; while the personnel and the issues disappeared, the
structures of aspiration and action remained. It was the nutty, bedraggled conclaves with no future, the Radical Student Alliance, the
Revolutionary Socialist Student Federation, even the defunct NALSO
(the Labour Left student organization in permanent war with Transport House) that dragged the entirely misnamed National Union of
Students – which for most of its existence was no more than the annexe
to a travel bureau – into this century of revolution. The same process
of pressure and infiltration, shifts in agitational style, followed by
collapse, followed by a further shift, took place at the local student
base in the universities and institutions; college life, that coagulated
ground of deference and insecurity, piled with obsequious sods of
ideological clay in which nothing could grow except a BA (Hons)
degree, was broken down finely by the repeated tilling of innumerable
small hoes, duplicated incitements left on canteen tables, arid debates
among veterans from last year's demo, electrifying spates of demagogy
by enraged psychopaths, sudden midnight fucks with the wrong person
and desperate unposted letters to the right one, besieged occupations,
paranoid stashings of dope in unfindable hidey-holes, the slow learning
of organization, reliability, discipline, presence.

A similar role was performed for the general political movement by
the fertilizing, founding New Left of yesteryear. We scattered brazen
images across the land, gryphon and giraffe ideas which had legs and
wings, to fly through windows and run up and down walls into the
people's houses, seizing the bodies of the sleepy sons and dutiful
daughters, waking up the neighbours into marches and outcries: penetrating, eventually, into those cages of mind-annulling repetition, the
workplaces.

The contrast from then to now is evident in the very nature of a
demonstration. People simply gawped and gaped at the first public
CND marchers; we were external to the public upon the pavements,
and for much of the time conscious that we would be viewed and
judged as an alien force. We were adventists, witnesses like those of
Jehovah, prepared to face the contumely of the world in the cause of
our imperative, a many-headed version of the eccentric little bloke

with the sandwich-board saying PREPARE TO MEET THY DOOM. And now there simply is no longer a public which is exterior to demonstration and visible mass action. Everybody is within the constituency of possible political crowds: miners with their picket armies; anxious parents protesting for zebra crossings; villagers on the streets against juggernaut lorries; nurses massed in the irresistible appeal of mercy's uniform; tenants blown together from a thousand separate dwellings by moneylenders and bailiffs; pensioners, council clerks, civil servants, dockers, Fenians, Fabians, teachers, schoolkids, binmen, clothing workers, and, still as ever, students, students, students. There are still the uninvolved on the side-walks, temporary consumers or permanent petty-bourgeois, chronic incapables of the private domestic patch and the 57 varieties of bewildered individualism. But nowadays, even the Right has learned to marshal its collectives for the streets, the headlined housewives striking against strikers, the bigoted pecksniffs of the anti-Abortion Lobby, the Festival of Pharisees, the State's own parades of armed might in the environs of Heath Row to announce that was done in Bogside can be done here. Demonstration has demonstrated its own necessity so demonstratively that we even have the counter-demonstration and the counter-counter-one: those who started the long trek to the Nuclear Weapons Research Establishment in 1958 have a lot to answer for. We got people into the habit: twenty and even ten years ago you knocked nervously at the council house door with a leaflet and remarked, as if advertising a jumble-sale for the Buddhists, 'Er, we do have this, well, demonstration coming up, if you'd like to hear ... Ah no, well cheerio'; and now the woman who opens the door will take the leaflet and say, 'Thanks, luv, see you at t'demo then.' It wasn't all our fault, it has something to do with the crisis of the capitalist system and the squeeze on wages and the pressures of de-colonization, the arms race, the credibility gap and whatever else you have. But it had to be got going: a task performed, thanklessly at the time, by knots of dishevelled enthusiasts, some of whom still survive into organized campaigning activity to reap the reward of a public response denied to many of their comrades who became dispirited.

Goodbye Rudi Dutschke, farewell Grosvenor Square, it's a long, long way to Aldermaston and nobody's there. The passing of the Golden Horde of the middle-class Left symbolizes a distinct set of transitions peculiar to the fate of Britain in the late fifties and the sixties. Political demands do not become salient, urgent, agitable material solely or even primarily because of their own star quality as issues which *ought* to excite the general interest. In the heyday of CND the general interest was excited by the awareness that the existence of human civilization and life on earth was imperilled by nuclear armaments and nuclear strategies, that our rulers had contingency plans for the extermination of everybody save themselves (who were to be secure from fall-out in their deep concrete shelters), and that a mistaken signal from a monitoring screen, reading a flight of missiles for a flight of ducks, could detonate World War Three. These ultimate horrors reigned over the world even before the arrival of CND and its successors, and still hold good now that the anti-nuclear movements have been dispersed from the field. The Polaris submarines and their rivals in the killer-packs of the Soviet fleet patrol under the ocean surface, the annihilation of cities in their torpedo-tubes; the H-Bomb airplanes are still in the skies over all the twenty-four hours; the deliverers of death hidden in silos maintain their targeting scrupulously, replaced only by other teams that take over when they sleep; we are still dependent for our lives and the lives of our children on the sane, sober judgement of the authors of Indochina's murder, Czechoslovakia's invasion, the torturers' regime in Chile and the suppression of all readable Russian literature. But the type of movement which could at one time capture and canalize public consciousness on the nuclear issue demanded not only the issue but also a social setting, an economic conjuncture, a given point in history. The movement began in a Britain that had *de facto* lost its position in the international Big League, but had not yet forgotten its Great Power aspirations. Unilateralism, the marchers' insistence that Britain should 'give a lead to the world', was the product of a moment in political history when this country stood divested of Empire and as yet unclad in a European mantle. The accusation from the Right that CND stood for a 'little England' mentality was profoundly unfair, since the movement was internationalist, directed against power-blocs abroad and towards fraternal campaigns within those blocs. But its internationalism still expressed a sense of active mission which would be impossible to re-kindle in a Britain already in relative decline during the boom years of the late sixties and now, within the gloomy economic context of the mid-seventies, manoeuvring desperately for solvency. The dating of this internationalism can be seen precisely in its demand that Britain *break with* its military alliances and form a new 'neutralist' bloc with the less-aligned nations. 'Britain', white missionary Britain, still maintains its identity within this foreign-policy revolution: whereas the first essential requirement of present-day internationalism is that we transcend ethnic barriers within Britain itself, in the battle against racism in daily employment and living. The response to Enoch Powell's anti-black speeches of 1968 revealed the precariousness of the decent liberal sentiments which the Left had taken for granted as existing in the majority. Echoing Karl Liebknecht's old slogan 'The enemy is at home', the Campaign had sought to alert its public to the responsibilities of the home government. None of us knew – as we should have known – that the enemy was not only in Whitehall, the rocket-range and the stockbroking belt but actually in our midst, at home in an almost literal sense. CND fought bravely for an internationalism whose validity would one day be tested in the advent of a determined anti-nuclear government. The internationalism of today's Left is at stake every day: it requires *immediately*, for any expression of itself at all, not as a handy culmination that will complete the work, the development of mass working-class sensitivities capable of fighting the chauvinist poison in production, housing, education, ideology and manners. For its own survival, the Left can no longer stand outside the factory gates, it must be inside; it can defer its moral absolutes no longer into the gestures of a future government, it must project them, defend them and uninterruptedly expand them now.

The first New Left of Britain, that formed by the collision and fusion of the two world-wide shock waves of Suez and Hungary, entered the Campaign for Nuclear Disarmament and perished with the host from which it fed. Invisible within the great marches that wound around and through the metropolis, there lay a conscious general staff for a wider social transformation, a small mobile headquarters not for this action, nor for the next engagement, but the total war that is the politics of Socialism. Peggy Duff (the Organizing Secretary of the Campaign for its entire active phase) concludes that 'in one way, CND did them (the New Left) no good. It swallowed them up as a political force in Britain.' The 1956–60 vintage of the independent Left was one of extraordinary potential, numbering many thousands of experienced cadres from the Communist Party crisis, hundreds of Labour Lefts bursting from their Party prison, contingents of determined and defiant pacifists and, within a short while, the Children's Crusade of teenagers from all classes, sensitized to the reality of war and violence through contact with conscript brothers and the proximity, over most of their conscious lifetime, of compulsory military service. When in 1961 I arrived, in my capacity as a Child Guidance Centre psychologist, in the playground of a girls' school for Educationally Sub-Normal Pupils and found the CND emblem painted (incorrectly) on an exterior wall, I knew at last that the campaign had penetrated society. As an initial rally-point CND was wonderful: but as a training-ground for a permanent commitment to radical politics, it was/a dreadful failure. The sophisticated militants from the New Left embroiled themselves in high diplomacy or counter-electoral strategy around the Labour Party, they remained glued to foreign policy, they refused to educate the ranks of the Campaign either in general Socialist theory or in the sordid practicalities of mass action around immediate bread-and-butter questions. And, truth to tell, the CND rankers did not want to be educated like this: 'there were too many people in CND who disliked and distrusted politics and too few with the will or the capacity to transform the movement into a different and more political entity.' Thus once again Peggy Duff, who in her memoir of CND points to the 'escapism' of foreign-policy campaigns which 'can wrap themselves up in their single issues and in the purity of their pacifist concerns, ignoring the essential links between repression and arms, between imperialisms and the arms race, between liberation, revolution, and peace'. While its grass-roots success and the sheer creativity of many of its participants remain unparalleled before or since in British politics, the basic model of the anti-nuclear campaign was that of the pressure-group trying to right a specific injustice, like the campaign to abolish hanging before it, and the campaign to abolish the slave-trade before that, and the abortion-reform lobby of recent years. CND could not even shift its concerns and resources towards action on the Indochina war, even though a moral fervour which takes to the streets in opposing the possible annihilation of London but remains paralysed in the face of the actual obliteration of Vietnam is surely rather suspect. And the very conception of single-issue activity in which the Campaign was rooted reflects an over-intellectual, over-ideologized vision of influence and power. The rest of politics does not stand still while you push on the question that you have selected as the supreme topic. Issues are levers which take persons and movements another step on their development (or their death) and which, once used for that purpose, must be left to go rusty.

The range of differing tactics and philosophies that operated in the anti-nuclear movement from 1958 to 1963 formed only an apparent diversity: all the contenders, however disputatious factionally, were addicts of the same brand, the single-issue blockbuster. By the time the Vietnam Solidarity Campaign came in the later sixties, sophistication had extended to the encouragement of 'links' between issues that could be seen as related to one another. According to the Theory of Links (whose proponents loomed no less large in the International Socialists than in the other left organizations around VSC) the main task of revolutionaries in their work around the war was to point to the connections between foreign-policy and domestic urgencies, among military, economic and political realities that were normally presented as separate. Dialectical materialists are trained to believe that everything is connected with everything else, and over long years have become adept at rising from the back of the hall after the speaker has finished with an eloquent complaint that something vital has been left out, an omission which conclusively proves the idiocy, idealism, mechanism, Menshevism and general bankruptcy of the speaker himself, the chairman and the sponsoring organization. The Vietnam campaign in Britain was the first one in which Marxist revolutionaries had to drop the role of interlocutor and critic, and themselves assume the responsibilities whose abdication they had denounced in others. It was a crucial experience for the revolutionary Left; their speakers now had to extend the issues of the campaign without diluting its impact or competing with the role of a more general political organization; the tortuous tactical debates and nerve-racking diplomacies of a pluralistic 'umbrella', the containment or expulsion of ultra-left splinters, the finesse of choosing and executing a date and route for a major demo – once the prerogative of the despised liberal elders of the nuclear campaign – became, quite suddenly, our hot potato. Virtually on the eve of the October 1968 demonstration in London – an event heralded in Press and TV alarums with rumours of violence, riot, and insurrection and better-authenticated reports of police practice in crowd-smashing at their training-ground in Hendon – the VSC awoke to the fact that no arrangements had been made for stewards or marshals, and asked the International Socialists to organize the control of the manifestation. After an inadequate gaggle of us had received our briefing and our NCO's armbands in a dingy hall above a pub, the clandestine Chief Steward, an unattached Greek nationalist working at the time around IS, turned to me on the stairs and said: 'We're going to be *massacred.*' The event, for good or ill, proved to be peaceful, as the fuzz desisted from the main body of demonstrators. As the thousands filed into Hyde Park, the YCL speaker orated, and Tariq Ali was his usual self, and then after all that there was the opportunity, if ever, for the IS speaker to Draw the Lessons and Show the Links and Point the Way Forward. But, overwhelmed by the occasion, he produced an endless burble: 'This is a wonderful demonstration . . . never seen anything like it . . . and the crowds are still coming in . . . this is really tremendous . . .' It was a fitting expression of the general tone of anticlimax.

The Vietnam campaigners were for their own part quite receptive to the generalization of their politics beyond its initial entry-point. The year of the NLF's Tet offensive was also that of France's semi-revolution of workers and students, of Prague's liberalizing springtime and Stalinizing autumn; on the home front yet another flock of starry-eyed Social-Democrats were learning the bitter truths of Labourism's betrayal, looking for the real meanings of the words that had been tarnished by Wilson, and for other words with fresh meanings. Gone was the old liberal campaign's desperate concern to be unsullied, to keep faith with the vicars and the MPs: after all, there were now no vicars or MPs around. During the unofficial and illegal seamen's strike of 1960 the speech of an anti-nuclear campaigner at an open-air rally in Liverpool could be cut short with a shush-shush from the chairman because he mentioned the sailors' march, in defence of the jailed Paddy Neary and against the tyranny of shipowner and union boss, that was taking place in the city on the same day. During the later shipping strike of 1966 it was a Trafalgar Square mass rally of the seamen themselves that cheered Bertrand Russell when he came down to give fraternal good wishes from the Vietnam movement and to say that it was all one struggle. It was not often that the orbits of working-class planet and student comet came near one another in this phase. But in future years the link between foreign and trade-union issues, demonstrator and striker, high-minded altruist and class-conscious egoist would cease to be a matter of verbal advocacy and analysis and become a part of common experience in the labour and socialist movement. Lenin's vision of the Russian revolution was that it depended on a link – the *smychka*, he called it – between the working class and the poorer peasantry. The British Left had in its attitude towards students and graduates something of Bolshevism's ambivalence towards the peasantry, at once part of the toiling masses and a layer of the petty-bourgeoisie, even conceivably a mainstay of capitalism: but, along with the ambiguity and uncertainty, came a determination that the worker student *smychka* must be maintained.

The development of the *smychka* in Britain was certainly not a synchronous process whereby campus and factory ignited in simultaneous combustion. Industrial unrest proceeded under its own momentum: days lost in strikes and lock-outs per 100 union members moved to 113 in 1968–72 (from 30 in 1960–67 and 38 in 1952–59); the percentage of union members involved in stoppages followed a straight progression, from 8 per cent in 1952-59 through 12 per cent in 1960–67 to 16 per cent in 1968–72, at approximately the proportion of strikers among the organized work-force during the peak of militancy in this century from 1901 to 1925. The number of workers per dispute is also climbing, and the duration of strikes is getting longer: the epoch of the short, sharp stoppage in which a small key section of highly organized and strategically placed workers won a quick victory as a precedent for themselves and for others is now clearly over. But the style and manner of militancy increasingly partook of a new experimentalism and confidence, particularly in the rise of the factory occupation as a form of pressure against redundancies – over 100 of these seizures occurred between March 1971 and the mid-1974 – and in the avalanche upheavals, here one moment and gone without trace the next, that shook hitherto backward industries and dormant sections of workers in this period.

Strikes and lock-outs, UK: short summary of annual averages from officially recorded figures*

Annual averages in relation to union membership	1901–25	1952–59	1960–67	1968–72
Disputes per **10,000** union members	c. 2.00	2.34	2.37	2.65
Aggregate day lost per **100** union members	c. 290	38	30	113
Workers involved per **100** union members	c. 16	8	12	16
Averages per dispute				
Duration (days)	c. 18	5	2½	7
Number of workers involved	c. 850	327	506†	609

The above extracted from a detailed analysis of strike trends to be summarized in John Westergaard and Henrietta Resler, *Class in Contemporary Britain* (forthcoming).

The exuberance of this working-class revolt, its insistence on expanding within its local base and squeezing the opportunities there to the full, followed closely on a wider cultural revolution of protest and Your Own Thing, manifested as much in May events in France and in the hippie-politics alliance in the United States as in any happenings nearer home. As the worker movement summated locally and nationally to the grand climax of direct action that liberated five dockers from Pentonville, shattered the Tories' intransigence before the miners and

* Official records understate industrial conflict by excluding, not only very small disputes, but also 'political' strikes and industrial action short of strikes (e.g., go-slow, working to rule, overtime bans).

† A 'freak' average – raised to a high level by the exceptional scale of strikes in only one year (1962, when there was one very large national dispute), whereas in all other years of the period the averages ranged from 280 to 370 only.

reduced Heath's bluster of early 1974 to a deflated departure from office, the student movement lost its heroic altruism and abstraction: students now fought their own battles, not those of others, no longer for the great liberal causes but for the gritty indispensables of everyday existence: higher grants, lower rents, payment for postgraduates, union recognition, fair academic assessment. Just as the euphoria of the old student-based radicalism had been the harbinger of an expansive buoyancy in the demands of workers, employees and tenants, so the new bread-and-butter militancy of the NUS and its local affiliates bespoke a necessary change in priorities: with inflation rampant and the job-market retrenched, the traditions of rebellion that had been constructed in the clouds had to find their proof, or else their refutation, here on earth. In 1972–4, while the experienced structures of organized manual labour held back or were constrained by their leadership, it was the white-collar and professional sections of trade-unions, the teachers, local government workers, nurses and hospital staff who were able to make a similar movement from new, sometimes barely existent traditions or organization to a forthright challenge against *de facto* wage-cuts and attendant worsenings of the conditions of toil. The ideals of the masochistic devotee to duty, of the loyal public servant, of dear Mr Chips who slaves on pushing his pupils through their certificates, of our Wonderful Nurses Doing a Grand Job, Bless Them (but don't pay them), have suffered as sharp an erosion as the high principles of the mass sit-down and the marathon teach-in. Who can afford, nowadays, to be noble?

The old issues, spearheaded by zealous crusaders with one guiding, mobilizing *idée fixe*, have gone with the boom that was, and with them the forms of organization that could satisfy their clientele. When the customers moved on, they moved into straight Marxism, an open-ended structure that could handle new issues and areas as they arose, or into a domestic, job-centred radicalism around one or other of the white-collar professions, or out of it all, into 'relationships' (i.e., three other people and the TV) and the quiet life. On the whole, among activists and former activists the experience of the fifties and sixties seems to have produced a permanent inoculation against any involvement in the Labour Party. The party was very much part of the scene of left debate in the late fifties, with the great Bomb controversy, the Clause Four battle among rival ideologues (for in those days the Right as well as the Left cared to spell out philosophies and programmes), and the heated sectarian forum that was the Young Socialists. While the Left is now past its maximum period of retraction from the party – in 1970 some of us, in keeping with a widespread mood among working-class electors, argued unsuccessfully in the Marxist groups for a boycott of the ballot – there is no chance that the militants will extend their endorsement of Labour to any greater loyalty than the act of voting for Wilson on the mainly negative grounds of knocking the Tories and the Liberals. Transport House may regard this indifference of revolutionaries as no loss: but the revolutionary Left has come to fulfil the role laid down prophetically for the older New Left by E. P. Thompson: 'the bureaucracy will hold the machine: but the New Left will hold the passes between it and the younger generation.' A positive Social-Democratic revival has been blocked off, not least through the antics of Wilson and his minions both in office and in opposition, but also because alternative Socialist traditions have been revitalized, have in fact become available for masses of people, especially those with any inkling of enthusiasm, to flirt with, to mess about with, perhaps even to embrace wholeheartedly.

Even the odd Labour Minister is not immune from the temptations of dalliance with ideas whose very attractiveness stems from their long serious relationship with Socialism's steadies. For there is every reason to believe that Mr Benn really is taken by the charms of workers' control and a militant-gradualist perspective on Socialist advance drawn variously from the late Robert Owen, the late G. D. H. Cole and the late Salvador Allende. The sectarian Left are quite wrong to see Bennery as yet another of Mr Wilson's many rubber faces: Mr Wilson, no less than Mr Jenkins and Mr Rees-Mogg, detests Benn's New Left language and is worried by it. There is a long, definite and traceable genealogy of anti-capitalist policies and prescriptions for industry, running from the early Utopian Socialists through the Marxists and the Industrial Unionists and the Syndicalists into the Guild Socialists, latterly bandied around the Trotskyist and academic Left, preserved in formalin in the documentation and discussion of the Institute for Workers' Control, diluted in half-measures and conference rhetoric by Jack Jones, Hugh Scanlon and other high union officers, whom the Institute imagines to be its allies, mixed in with rival programmes for the co-determination of private industry by joint boards of trade-unionists and capitalists and served up as such in official Labour Party policy, whittled further (in order to appease business fears of anything approaching Socialism) by the fraction of the Labour Party – a distinctly unrepresentative sample of its members – that actually runs the Government, and then postponed indefinitely for any actual legislation because of the crowded Commons timetable, the minority status of the

Labour Government, and, irrespective of other circumstances, the independence of the Parliamentary Party. Benn's expansionary proposals for nationalization are the surfacing of a Left undercurrent in this confused tradition.

Normally, at each stage whereby the concepts of workers' control are transmitted onward into a further bureaucracy, of trade-union hierarchs or careful academics or expensive Cabinet ministers, their content is sensibly modified till it no longer has a cutting edge which can be turned against the system by any actual group of workers that needs to exercise control over its problems. But Benn's insistence that large and profitable firms rather than failing lame ducks are eligible for State takeover, and his sympathy for the producers' co-operative as a means of keeping the workers' jobs in bankrupt enterprises, amount to a timely resuscitation of reformist Socialism of a type which would have been recognizable in most of the parties of the Second International before a neo-capitalist or a technocratic liberalism became their dominant creed. Benn is not a solitary swallow: apart from the other Ministers and Under-Secretaries with a left Social-Democrat disposition there is the intriguing emergence of the Labour Party's National Executive Committee as the Second Consul of the new Wilson administration, vetting, vetoing and consulting with its own sub-committees and those of the T U C whenever a promise of future legislation is to be drafted. The bonds between an incumbent Labour Government and the extra-parliamentary institutions of Labour have never been as close as now: and, in the context of the anti-capitalist politics of some of the watchdogs both inside and outside the Government, we can speak of Labour's own New Left as a force to be reckoned with.

But, having reckoned with it, we must at once discount it. The bourgeoisie may tremble, or make a show of trembling, before the name of Benn: as Trotsky commented when Hitler went into hysterics on hearing a speculation that the exiled man of October might prove to be the real victor of the Second World War, 'They fear revolution, and give it a man's name.' In the case of Benn they have given it a veritable misnomer, for the Government's proposals for a National Enterprise Board are no more than a continuation of the programme for a State Holding Company outlined in the 1969 NEC document 'Labour's Economic Strategy', where the new institution is explicitly modelled 'along the lines of the Italian IRI', the State-enterprise conglomerate founded under Mussolini and developed under Christian Democracy without any noticeable butchery of business leaders. The proposed Planning Agreements for the largest companies 'designed to bring an end to the "trench warfare" that has existed between the two sides of industry and break down the remoteness in the relationship between Government and industry' (*Labour Weekly*, 23 August 1974) have already been welcomed by the *Guardian* and *The Times*. If the present proposed dose of State capitalism is more than the Tories and the CBI can at present stomach, we may be sure that, by the General Election of 1984 (that is, if there still are General Elections in 1984), they will claim to have thought of the whole idea in the first place. The well-known process of bureaucratic transmutation of leftist slogans, from expropriation to nationalization, from nationalization to public ownership, from public ownership to national enterprise, from Tom Mann to Lord Robens, has already buffered Britain from any risk of a Socialist progression under the Labour Party. The moderate programmatic shift leftwards was the very least that could occur given the deterioration of the economy and private capital's failure to invest: the complacency of the Gaitskell–Crosland–Jenkins–Jay programme *Industry and Society*, which stated that 'the Labour Party recognizes that, under increasingly professional managements, large firms are as a whole serving the nation well' and proposed that the State should become an equity stockholder (not a manager) in private industry to give the community 'the opportunity of participating in the almost automatic capital gains of industry', would nowadays be impossible.

The party's movement towards industrial Statism was a halting, fumbling response to the storm-warnings of coming economic collapse signalled in the payments crisis of the first Wilson Government. It did not proceed from any mobilization of the Left within the constituencies or union delegations. For there was no recurrence of the Bevanite Left revolt during the 1964–70 government, nor in the opposition period afterwards. In betraying the party's hopes, the Wilson cabinet also ravaged its flesh and poisoned its circulation, as droves of constituency workers moved out of activity in disillusionment. It is useless now for the left ministers and union leaders to consecrate to the old cults of Socialism a party whose fabric is still in fundamental human and ideological disrepair. Even if Benn and Jones were attempting to preach a more vigorous gospel, they would be addressing a very thin congregation. Outside the party the mass of the electorate, watching their own hands tighten over belts, cynical and disengaged towards all politicians, has no interest in the rivalry between ex-revisionists and ex-anti-revisionists, neo-Gaitskellites and neo-Bevanites jousting from on high. Circuses have no pull when there is such a widespread and intense preoccupation with bread.

The middle-class New Left has finished. Labour's New Left will not begin. What then of Socialism's future, in a Britain now leading the deceleration of the world capitalist economy in the same spirit of stoicism with which it long ago presided over the system's more expansionary destinies? The politics of liberal enthusiasm and of social-democratic reform have elapsed. Class-politics, in this heartland of emnity founded on industrial division, remains as ever, has indeed become more powerful. The rank-and-file movement of workers in industry and public service was long advocated by International Socialists and others, as a means both of organizing against employer and State tactics and of supplanting the weak and bureaucratized leaderships of trade unions. This movement has now begun to make a serious appearance. For many years a revolutionary political organization like IS could function only in a propangandist or narrowly servicing relation to the active elements of trade-unionism. Fifteen years ago, one sold the organization's paper outside the meetings called by larger, grander bodies and built an essentially morale-boosting local group for isolated and highly theoretical revolutionaries. The Liverpool group at this time, for example, included a garrulous french-polisher, a couple of dropouts from the ILP, a mathematics lecturer, and an affable joiner of immense hostile intransigence against any involvement in the Labour Party, who once denounced Stan Newens, then a comrade of the same sectarian persuasion, as 'basically a Social Democrat'; the joiner's name, by the way, was Eric Heffer. Five years ago, one lobbied any conceivable trade-union activist to buy Tony Cliff's exposé of productivity deals, *The Employers' Offensive*, became a specialist in bonus schemes and manning agreements, and tried to integrate worker-recruits into an IS ambience whose meetings were dominated at worst by gurus, groupies, hairies or routinist hacks, and at best by keen young folk without a regular industrial base. A good many trade-unionists survived the ordeal, infiltrating a structure that was supposed to be ready to receive them but in practice had to undergo its own transformation, with the establishment of factory branches and a constant pressure from head office to face outwards, before it could start to become a workers' organization. Rank-and-file work in industry is now open to Socialist revolutionaries, as never since the twenties. In November 1973 the *Socialist Worker* Industrial Conference in Manchester drew an audience of nearly three thousand, with speakers from mining, the docks, the fire service, telecommunications, engineering, chemicals, construction, print, teaching, Pilkingtons, Fine Tubes, LIP in France, and IS itself. Twenty-three industrial fractions met briefly during the day, a foretaste of the founding convention of the Rank-and-File Movement which took place in the following spring.

A Marxist organization, conceived as a micro-splinter of the Left in inauspicious circumstances during the Korean war, a reject from Cold War pressures and Trotskyist acrimony, has now found itself endowed with unaccustomed powers and unprecedented dimensions. The International Socialists acquired their hegemony in that vacuum of the Left that opened out suddenly in 1968 as the wake from Enoch Powell's racist bombshells. Winning its organizational spurs within largely student or white-collar campaigns but with a long record of work among shop stewards in manufacturing industry, the IS now faces the problem of extending its serious but – in the context of capitalist power – small implantation inside the heavy brigades of the labour movement. The last era of the independent Left, from 1956 to roughly 1970, can be termed the Age of Minorities. The strength of a radical demonstration, whether numbered in hundreds, or in scores of thousands, reflected the ingathering of local weaknesses, tiny powerless groups who in their own terrain were unable to win the mass of people around them except perhaps in the temporary euphoria of one college or one workshop. The great mobilizations of the sixties were compounded as an assemblage of these manifold minorities, the Left seemed to be everywhere precisely because it enjoyed a stable mass support nowhere, its quick local industrial victories during the boom epoch of labour-shortage and wage-drift risked a certain thinness in the loyalty of workers to stewards and ensured that a nationwide solidarity of strikers in any industry would be rare, an untested weapon. When the test came, in the wave of redundancies and productivity deals that purged the economy in the late sixties, or in the outburst of worker-racism around Powell's speeches, the stewards and the left militants usually found themselves isolated under fire, dazed by the enemy's capacity to hit deep into their shop-floor base. The middle-class Left in its various campaigns swung from action to inertia, paying the price of the exhausted forerunner but leaving a residue of cadres for future contests. In the coming era of mass unemployment, general job-insecurity and inflation-led cuts in real wages, the defensive traditions of the Age of Minorities must be junked as so much garbage, and recycled. The ground formerly occupied by middle-class radicalism and working-class Labourism lies naked to all comers, susceptible to any new thrust that emerges after the collapse of old party loyalties, open to the opportune probings of the Nationalists and Liberals, to the temptations of the fascisms whether latent or blatant, and to the activity of a realistic and courageous Marxism. For revolutionary Socialists it now has to be the Age of Majorities: the majorities which have to be won, in factory after factory, workplace after workplace, in every cell of social and economic organization, to ensure that the workers, be they of the blue collar or the white, do not have to bear across their own hides the lash of capital's retrenchment. The policy demands of this majority-winning process cannot be uniform, cannot be drafted by committees meeting behind the backs of those whose livelihoods are at stake in the real struggle. Socialist cadres must keep one step ahead of their constituency, two or three steps at the most, and generate their slogans from what can be seen as the next link in the chain of solidarity. In 1973, for example, any trade-unionist who raised the demand of Threshold Agreements was well to the right of the wages programme that could be seriously fought for, in terms both of the amounts to be obtained and the criteria to be used in making effective claims. Threshold Agreements were in any case the standby of the Heath government to try and offset organized militancy. In mid-1974, however, the ability to obtain a Threshold Agreement, in the face of employer resistance and government reluctance, became in the worsening economic situation an important valid test of organized militancy. There are, in general, no specific 'transitional demands' for the present period of working-class consciousness. Any demand which unites workers and takes them forward together is to that extent transitional. Some of these demands are roughly foreseeable but by no means all. Nobody knew, for example, that the abolition of pay-beds would become the marshalling-point of direct action among health-service workers.

The requirements of an age of majorities mean that every socialist must engage, as the first call on his or her time and energy, in mass work within a real rank and file. This is, incidentally, one more reason why the committed revolutionary or radical will be unable to support the Labour Party in any other way beyond attendance at the polling-booth: if he has his priorities right, he will simply have no time for electoral canvassing. The calendar of class-struggle does not keep step with the dissolution and re-election of Cabinets: if we are truly within the orbit of our mates, the pull of their gravitation will guide our path more readily than that of the politician's planet. As well as being too disillusioned to work for Wilson, we shall be, and should be, too busy.

The acquisition of active, campaigning roles by Socialists within a local constituency should ideally present few difficulties. In theory that is what militant socialism is all about. But practically the transition is likely to be somewhat painful. We have all fled from the tasks of the Socialist campaigner, into the peculiar satisfactions of the prophet or the administrator, the minimal shop steward or the archetypal student leader, the paper-selling wanderer or the paper-reading follower: these postures are so much less demanding, so much more fulfilling in the short term, than the role of the active ferment among a group of people who see us every working day, know us by name and face and will call us to account for every word and action. When Nicolas Krasso, a young Hungarian Marxist who was a disciple of Lukács, saw the necessity in late 1956, after the Russian occupation, of convening all the revolutionary workers' councils of Greater Budapest into one assembly, he and a few student friends passed the word among the factories of the city. Clandestinely and circumspectly under the gaze of the patrolling tanks of the USSR, the workers' delegates made their way to the meeting-place, a hall in an electric-lamp factory on the outskirts, where Krasso was asked, on trying to enter: 'What are *you* doing here? You're not a worker.' The suspicious question was in large part misconceived (for of course revolutionary student groups have every right to try and meet worker groups) but not entirely so. The questioner was also asking: What role are you playing here? Define it, please. He was asking, too: Who are you accountable to, where do you come from? In effect, the older New Left defined their own roles out of any existence in relation to the type of workers' movement that we have today. One cannot arrive on the scene as a theoretician or publicist and say, 'Look, workers, here I am.' Workers are particularly suspicious of people from Marxist groups who show up only when there is some excitement at a factory in the form of a strike, and are nowhere to be seen during the many periods, some of them amounting to years, when the activity of the working class falls short of open strike action. Nor can one play the part of the adept servitor of trade-unionism, the technician of facts and figures who just happens to have more time to do research for the shop floor. The Socialist must join the workers' movement as a trade-unionist in his own right, with card, rule-book and box of anti-management tricks, undergoing the same problems of skill and morale in leadership as those he is addressing. His politics must be open: not regurgitated by the yard into every resolution with a practical content, but visible to everyone, displayed on his lapel rather than tucked away behind it. The crowning aim of the Age of Majorities is to construct, within the working class, a majority of conscious Socialists. Every act, every demand in revolutionary mass work must be subordinated to that first and final aim.

The road that runs from the capturing of active minorities to the securing of real majorities has very few signposts. Most of those that we have show us, as Rosa Luxemburg remarked, the way *not* to go. But it is clear that the way forward lies through a sharpening polarization of society, whose coming is not the creation of Socialists – even though it forms their greatest opportunity – but the product of an anarchic social system based on competitive profit. The extremisms are now on the agenda, and the middle position of moderation has to balance itself more and more precariously in relation to those extremes, and to become somewhat more extreme itself, on both the Left and the Right. It is important that we should not be deterred or gulled by the threat of right-wing violence, whether from the State or from extra-parliamentary quarters. No process of radicalization has ever taken place in any nation without a corresponding threat of radical Rightism. But it would be wrong to raise the perspective of a repetition of the thirties. The forces of the Left are far better organized and more powerful than in the thirties. Europe entered the decades of fascism in the grip of massacre's nightmare following the First World War, its petty bourgeoisies inflamed by despair, its labour movements crushed or worn down in a contracting market. The working class of this country has no memory of any major defeat. Its organization into trade unions has proceeded, in a heavy impetus of expansion and amalgamation, without respite since 1940. While the horizons of its economic expectations are still narrower then those of American and Continental labour, its appetites are zestful, its confidence unimpaired. The organized workers have at present little to fear from any counter-movement of the individualist middle classes, since the former professions are themselves now enrolled in trade unions with militant habits and a TUC alignment. Even from the universities the worst that the workers can fear is from the dons, for in the event of a re-run of 1926, the students of the present day will not be seen driving the trams but harassing the scabs. And the labour movement has new regiments of its own whom it has scarcely begun to muster, whom indeed it has often caused to turn back from its recruiting offices because it was known the reception there would be frosty: the blacks, the Asians, the migrants from Europe, and the women. In impending polarization, these millions can be won to a Socialist mass movement. The relaxation of manners and rules among younger people has produced an anti-authoritarian complex which, while far from constituting an arm of Socialist militancy, produces a numerous reserve of benevolent neutrals for any future punch-ups with established authority. For the moment the proper response to a hint of military takeover or paramilitary violence is to say: how very interesting and very salutary if they try anything on. Let them just dare.

But such a response should be only momentary. To engage in a public mental rehearsal of the scenarios of civil confrontation is merely to repeat the follies of the retired Blimps, who delight in the drafting of contingency plans as a recompense for the fact that nobody any more is offering them actual contingencies to deal with. Contingencies there indeed are, and scenarios, but they contain well-tried actors with familiar faces: government, employers, TUC, top union officials, the Special Patrol Force of the Metropolitan Police, the established political parties. Both the pace and the scope of the developing social confrontation in Britain are virtually unknown quantities. Whole phases from the classical drama of revolution and counter-revolution could be extended over years, telescoped into days, skipped completely, turned round into anticlimax or become aborted into a further period of stalemate (alias 'consensus'). And, while the actors of the ruling classes and the controlling elites are already listed in the cast, the agencies of working-class struggle, of rank-and-file mobilization, remain obscure in their character and their possible composition. If the resources of the British Left are stronger than in the thirties, it is because then they were pitiful, . nfinitesimal. Today the forces of capital and of labour both suffer from a discrepancy between their state of organization and their state of morale: but the contradiction is slanted in an opposite direction within the two camps. The centralized organization and planning capacity of the ruling class and its State compensates for their loss of political conviction, economic confidence and general *savoir faire*. By contrast, the working class is buoyant and potentially highly assertive: but its organization is in fairly poor shape, and its leadership appalling both in structure and in staffing. The national trade-union bureaucracies of both Left and Right are vying in a contest for the lowest public profile: with the exception of the passively conducted miners' strike just before the election of Wilson, no major section of manual workers has engaged in a serious official action since the great upheavals of 1972. The unions' honeymoon with the Labour Government is a passionless repetition of the first fling of 1964–7; observers stationed around the bridal suite of the Hotel Social Compact so far report little evidence of action, not even the noise of smashing crockery, This in an epoch of looming redundancies, soaring home-costs, and washed-out wages, when bacon and beef were first appreciated as delicacies. Further down the hierarchy of labour, several hundred thousand shop-stewards are looking at their pay-conscious workmates, at their quiescent union superiors and at the chances that now arise for substantial wage improvements with the repeal of the Industrial Relations Act and the end of Tory incomes policy. Those mass actions that have already occurred – such as the wave of strikes in Scotland and the national bakers' strike – have been forced forward in the teeth of union head-office opposition, even from the 'Lefts' of the TGWU and AUEW; in the recent period, some unions less cemented in the 'Social Contract' psychology than the main TUC hierarchs have been able to push past their obstruction, and it may be that some of the smaller unions will play a vanguard role in the opposition to wage-restraint. On the political Left, the membership of the Communist Party of Great Britain slumbers on, counting left MPs as it snores, its parliamentary dreams only temporarily disturbed by the sad news of the crushing of an identical electoral strategy in Chile. The more recent news of the Portuguese Communist Party's entanglement with the military regime has set off no qualms whatever in Britain's Communists: there had been no debate, no analysis, no sense of any parallel between the trust of the Chilean Left in the progressive military and the perilous coalition in Lisbon. While the CPGB will continue to recruit, it will also continue to refuse political training to its members: politics are no longer in command there, not even Stalinist politics, and in the coming stresses we can expect from the CP little or no initiative except from a few capable individuals.

It is thus in a political and economic context of mounting urgency, with an alarmingly small accumulation of any resources whatever from the previous massive investments of Left tradition, that socialists must gauge their next responsibilities. Short of an accelerated pre-revolutionary situation, a 1917 of Imperial Russia or 1936 of Republican Spain, which can at present be ruled out from any working perspectives, the expansion which any Marxist organization can envisage in its activities and recruitment must be modest by comparison with the seriousness of its goals. Boiled down to the proportions of immediately realizable possibility, the revolutionary work in the Age of Majorities means increasing the nucleus of politically minded workers in a pit or depot from around two to around six; selling *Chingari*, the Socialist monthly produced in Urdu and Punjabi, to those Asians who are confident enough to take its programme to heart; building a trade-union base in a shift of sixty women without previous experience of organization; winning a vote in a union branch for firm policies against wage-restraint; systematically working over a street on a council estate, finding the few workers there who will be already predisposed towards Socialist attitudes, and forming a political, not simply a sociable, relation with them; in a hostile workshop, with management keen to fire troublemakers and a frightened or apathetic labour-force, it will mean finding one other person with whom to discuss the next step, without risking exposure by breaking cover. There will also be the big jobs and the central occasions, the industry-wide gathering of stewards, the physical cordon against fascist marchers, the delegate conference of revolutionaries waging a fraternal polemic on perspectives, taking the decisions and dispersing to implement them. But the age of the majorities, unlike that of the minorities without a base, consists for the most part of a cellular, even molecular chain-building. It is the march of the spermatozoa into the eggs, the duplication, over and over again, of specialized cells, the use of tiny living templates for the growth of a new organism. A lot of the other sperms from older days have been and gone, quite a few of the eggs got flushed away down the loo, but it wasn't all a wank or a waste. Because enough little cells got fertilized, as we know now, to achieve the beginnings of a generation. A generation equipped to enter the decisive political battles of the next decade, battles that will either advance the cause of the workers by gigantic strides or else throw them back in a terrible retrogression.

February 1975   Peter Sedgwick

Chapter 1
The Double Exposure:
Suez and Hungary

BILL: The Affair of the Lone Banana, Chapter Two. With the banana secreted on his person, Neddie Seagoon arrived at the Port of Guatemala where he was accorded the typical Latin welcome to an Englishman.

MORIARTY: Hands up, you pig swine.

SEAGOON: Have a care, Latin devil – I am an Englishman. Remember, this rolled umbrella has more uses than one.

MORIARTY: Oooo!

SEAGOON: Sorry. Now, what's all this about?

MORIARTY: It is the revolution – everywhere there is an armed rising.

SEAGOON: Are you all in it?

MORIARTY: Right in it – you see, the united anti-socialist neo-democratic pro-fascist communist party are fighting to overthrow the unilateral democratic united partisan bellicose pacifist cobelligerent tory labour liberal party.

SEAGOON: Whose side are you on?

MORIARTY: There are no sides – we are all in this together.

('The Affair of the Lone Banana', Goon Show No. 104, BBC Home Service, October 1954)

After the uprising on June 17th
The Secretary of the Authors Union
Had leaflets distributed in the Stalinallee
Which said that the people
Had forfeited the government's confidence
And could only win it back
By redoubled labour. Wouldn't it
Be simpler in that case if the government
Dissolved the people and
Elected another?

(*The Solution*, BERTOLT BRECHT)

The fifties were a decade of social peace; for the old a blessed relief, for the young a total bore, for the revolutionary a hopeless paradox. The economy was almost audibly humming, the Tories were visibly beaming. An immense change of gear in capitalism, which the war had finalized, seemed cemented into the shape of the Welfare State. For Tory and social democrat alike an extended state role in industry and a constant trade-union presence in government were the basis of a new political status quo. At the Ministry of Labour, Lord Monckton was pliable and generous to the trade-union knights and, more importantly, on the shop floor full employment enabled the local shop stewards to bump up the nationally negotiated wage rates by as much again. Strikes were abrupt and usually successful, employers finding it cheaper to pay up than to fight the unions. In fact there was a general and perhaps welcome decline in 'politics' as a way of seeing the world or altering it, an adoption of compromise as a way of life. Those who thought we'd never had it so good were rather more convincing than the socialist stalwarts who saw a slump in every redundancy and the revolution in every dole queue. The *Daily Express* philosophy, though morally appalling, seemed to make more sense than that of the *Daily Worker*. Although in the older working-class territories of Yorkshire and the North living patterns remained very similar to those of pre-war days, in the rich Midlands and South-East things had really changed. Working-class families were smaller and more mobile – increasingly people left their older relatives to set up homes of their own in the new towns and the new estates Macmillan had been so successful in building. With the working-class nuclear family went the nuclear car, the front-room TV set and a whole litter of consumer durables.

It is not the case that the working-class was bribed by corrupting fridges and reactionary motor mowers into voting Tory or somehow bamboozled into thinking, as the Labour Right did, that capitalism had mysteriously vanished. But there was a widespread sense of relief at the outcome of the war and the apparently successful transition to peace, reaching a climax in that curious revival of working-class patriotism and royalist nostalgia which found its focus somewhere between Stanley Matthews, Queen Elizabeth the Second and Denis Compton. The bee-keeping Edmund Hillary clambered to the summit of Mount Everest on the very morning half a million royalists packed London's streets for the Coronation. The fruity reverence of Richard Dimbleby echoed over the world's airwaves. But within this sweet mid-fifties doze there were nightmares.

It was the young, bemused by their parents' burial in a cathode haze and unaware that the shopping centre was built over a bomb-site, who stirred first. The 1944 Education Act, which opened higher education to the working-class scholarship boys, was beginning to have results. But if it saved the upwardly mobile meritocrat from the scrapheap of the Secondary Modern, it did not always purchase his loyalty. The bulge of grammar-school louts who, as I did, apparently spent most of the late fifties arranging Brylcreemed coils on top of spotty foreheads and saving up for an electric bass guitar were in fact to turn out an awkward squad.

For there was something incongruous about educational equality without any alteration in the inequality of property. For every Joe Lampton who was getting out of the working class fast, there was a Jimmy Porter who had been given ideas by the Sixth Form and Penguin books but couldn't stand the bourgeoisie. For a short period, before they were absorbed *en bloc* into the literary star system, these grammar-school dead-end kids expressed an intense, if purely literary, revolt. The year 1956 saw the publication of *The Outsider* and the stage production of *Look Back in Anger*. The Angry Young Men's underdog snobbery and highly focused egotism (most blatant and religious in Colin Wilson) expressed the depth of their own social isolation. But it still punctured the serenity of the arty middle class. In political terms they drifted, without exception, to the far Right without actually changing their views very much. Unlike the American beats, whose pursuit of the orgiastic was a collective project, the British Angry Young Men had no real connection with the rebels they inspired (Danny Cohn-Bendit is really Lucky Jim fourteen years later), and so denounced them instead.

These literary delinquents had their parallel in the deviant working class. In the 1956 'Rock and Roll Riots' the kiss-curled middleweight Bill Haley was to unearth a new form of working-class revolt. Teds were a generation of moneyed juveniles who took the new prosperity seriously. Instead of trying to impress boss or parent or teacher, they impressed each other, with speed and noise and clothes and bikes. And rock, which George Melly, who ought to know, described as 'screw and smash music' and the 'Any Questions' panel described as 'the logical progression of jungle music'. Teds were a warning that the calm of Two-Way Family Favourites and Coronation tea caddies would not last for ever. But the dark gremlins who came out bopping in the cinemas got really rough treatment from the police. At the Elephant and Castle post-war kids found out how shallow the new freedom was, that Britain may have been 'Shakin' All Over' but there was to be no dancing in the aisles.

The post-war Left was too busy looking in vain for the old conflicts in the old places to notice these new cultural warnings. The Labour Party leadership was busy demonstrating its expertise at containing its socialist minorities. The Bevanites, less radical than the Socialist League but well to the left of the Tribunites in the sixties, were finally forced into the Labour Party fold and were there made to accept the bi-partisan anti-communism of the reformists, for the sake of reforms, of course. The Communist Party was still pursuing its worthy solidarities with the Eastern bloc, only now with increasingly little gratitude from the Russians. But this internationalism had a shrunken and formal meaning internationally and the blind faith of an uncritical defence of the Kremlin still acted to paralyse the Party's political faculties. The Trotskyist Left was operating within the Labour Party to little visible effect, continuing its clandestine, rigorous and narrow internal debates about Russia and international economics, while conducting intricate splits and quarrels in which it would seem ideas were more often used to assail rivals than to explain what was going on.

But if the Labour Party, Communist Party and the Trotskyists were all, in their various ways, disorientated and becalmed in the fifties, re-duced to fighting paper battles and defending outmoded loyalties, they possessed a formidable organized working-class base. The Labour Party consisted of tens of thousands of active working-class people, not simply a five-yearly election apparatus. And the Labour Left differed from the revolutionaries in method rather than aim. They wanted the end of the capitalist system and acknowledged the class struggle, but attempted to express and resolve it in Parliament. The Communist Party, now larger and looser than it had ever been, was a powerful force in the factories, pits and quays. If its Marxism was doc-trinaire and Russified, the Party still provided a working-class political education and an industrial organization for many thousands of workers. Even the Trotskyist groups, although more important for the ideas and the traditions they transmitted than the activity they could undertake, were a small but genuine part, despite the Communists' efforts, of the British Labour movement. Their membership was over-whelmingly of industrial workers, many of whom had spent their life in the Communist movement and some of whom still had positions of real influence in the trade unions. And the theorists of British Trot-skyism, Cliff from Palestine, Healy from Ireland, James from the West Indies, all with remarkable qualities of their own, somehow stamped it with an unorthodoxy which was to give it great strength. And for all varieties of socialist, the invasion of Hungary and Suez and the crisis in both the Western and the Communist blocs they manifested were of enormous importance. Although Britain is commonly regarded as something of a backwater in the revolutionary movement, the 1956 crisis was to have a critical impact, antedating the formation of an independent Left in other countries by some years and setting intellectual and organizational precedents which have been highly influential.

EAST OF EDEN

The Suez adventure was the last major direct intervention against a Third World successor regime. Its execution was sordid and incompetent. It was to result in the end of Eden, the first public rift in the NATO entente, a blasting asunder of the unspoken alliance of both front benches on foreign policy and popular working-class demonstrations which were on a new scale and militancy. And it was to illuminate the new and more discreet way modern imperialism was being forced to operate in the 'post-colonial' era.

Classical, pith-helmeted British imperialism had been able to treat its conquered colonies as virtual plantations. The native economy was wrenched into line with the British needs for raw material and markets. Primary products were extracted by an unskilled and brutally treated native work-force. Reliable princes and helpful sheiks, remnants of a feudal structure, were maintained, partly to frustrate and squash local businessmen. The trade operation was clothed in a system of colonial government and the British Government provided the personnel to run and police these states as well as subsidizing the boats, trains and planes which removed their wealth.

The twentieth century has seen a continual process of modification in this pattern, in which an apparent loosening, even striking-off, of the shackles has actually masked a more intensive exploitation. In the post-war period Britain dismantled much of the machinery of Empire, the visible trappings of state conquest, partly in response to the pressure which the nationalist movements were able to exert during the Second World War. The decline in importance of raw products, the rise of the nationalist movements, above all the post-war dominance of larger and fewer giant super-firms which eclipsed and replaced the banks by fusing in themselves technique, manufacture and finance, had made old-model imperialism based on the direct control of the subject state a dispensable liability. The trade mission replaced the Governor's residence. As Mike Kidron puts it, 'capitalism has undergone a transformation which enabled it to withstand, however unwillingly, the loss of its colonies, without disaster, without indeed much dislocation or discomfort;

which has enabled it, in most cases, to work, however grudgingly, for the relatively peaceful transfer of stewardship to a local ruling class'.*

The transfer of stewardship in Egypt proved particularly grudging and extremely explosive. An important wing of the Tory Party, the Suez Group, were reluctant to relinquish the zones the British Army occupied at the end of the desert war and wanted an armed colonial presence in the Near East. Their reasons were military. They still, ludicrously, wanted Britain to rule the waves. After Indian independence ('the scuttle' Churchill had called it) the Indian Army was no longer theirs. But they believed a real British force could stay in Suez. Eden, who had replaced Churchill as Prime Minister and whose entire 'brilliant' career had been in foreign affairs, was obsessed with the assembly of pacts. Realizing that oil extraction was the diplomatic key, he tried to tie Egypt into a stabilizing pro-British pact and preferred tankers to gunboats. But the decision was taken for them when a group of radical army officers executed a *coup d'état* in Egypt in 1951. Far from entering a rigged British alliance, Nasser was concerned to revive the mythical Arab nation in a new unity between Arab leaders, both sheiks and socialists, under his leadership. And he also began to experiment with the politics of 'non-alignment', effectively getting the Russians to bid against the West for his political support and his country's oil. For oil was the key. In general the Western capitalist nations were less and less dependent on raw materials. In particular, Britain's enforced isolation during the war had obliged her to find synthetic substitutes for colonial raw products. But this made oil of enhanced importance, both supplanting coal as an energy source and being increasingly used for synthetic fibres and plastics as well as fuel.

Oil companies took almost one-third of British overseas investment and the Americans were making a major attack on the traditional British domination of the Near Eastern oil fields. Eden, frustrated by Nasser and with strikes mounting for the first time at home, began to reveal the last-ditch colonialist who lay just beneath the suave diplomat. The Egyptians had the temerity to purchase arms from Czechoslovakia, the Templar Mission in Jordan collapsed and then Hussein, the young King of Jordan, a traditionally British sphere, dismissed the British commander of his British-trained army. Eden saw stars, made one of the worst speeches in Parliament since Randolph Churchill collapsed from tertiary syphilis, and, with considerable foresight, swore to his

* Michael Kidron, 'Imperialism: Highest Stage But One', *International Socialism*, 9.

under-secretary, Nutting, 'Nasser's got to go, it's either me or Nasser.'*

Eden was being pushed towards war from three directions. His own back-benchers could scent imperial grape-shot and liked what they smelled. The arrest and deportation of Makarios, symbol of resistance to the British in Cyprus, was greeted with jubilation by them. The French, themselves embedded in a losing attempt to hang on to Algeria, whose national rebels were strengthened by Nasser's new pan-Arab enthusiasm, wanted a punitive raid on Egypt. And in Israel Ben-Gurion returned from his sheep to argue for a 'preventive' war to expand Zionist territory into Egypt. On 26 July Nasser announced his intention to nationalize the canal his people had constructed.

The following weeks were to see Eden's film-star glamour, which had always teetered on the obsessional and the openly vain, disintegrate into a parody of arch-imperialism. Despite the virtual climb-down of the Egyptian negotiator, Fawzi, at the United Nations, Eden activated a plot rigged up between French, Israelis and Britain whereby the Israelis, who had been deliberately provoking a response on the Jordan border, would launch an invasion of Egypt. This France and England, in their role as wise imperial parents, would halt by 'enforcing a cease-fire', enabling them to reassert control over Egypt and replace Nasser. As it turned out the wise parents, who could anyway barely conceal their suspicion of each other, were clearly exposed as wicked uncles. The Israelis achieved their objectives far too quickly, with the invasion armada still halfway between Malta and Port Said. And Britain issued its ultimatum to both sides to retire to ten miles each side of the Suez Canal at a stage of the battle when this in fact amounted to an order for the Israelis to advance forty miles and the Egyptians to pull back about eighty. Nasser had anyway blocked the canal by sinking eighty ships across it – ruining whatever strategic aim the operation ever had. Dulles, who was using an anti-colonial rhetoric to enable US firms to replace British in the Middle East, broke publicly with the British. Macmillan, one of the most ardent supporters of the adventure, ratted on Eden, operating his own first-in first-out rule. To French fury, Eden called a cease-fire with troops twenty-five miles from Port Said and a hurriedly assembled U N force was sent in. Giles cartoons became obsessed with sheiks in Cadillacs and G Is with oil tankers.

In Britain opposition to this blatant mixture of bully and bluff was slow to develop. The Parliamentary Labour Party had joined in condemnation of Nasser's nationalization. In *Tribune*, Bevan conceded the

*Anthony Nutting, quoted in *The Day Before Yesterday* by Alan Thompson, Sidgwick & Jackson, London, 1971, p. 124.

Egyptians' abstract right to nationalize but didn't like them actually doing so ... 'It must not be all take, Colonel Nasser.'* As the leadership edged towards the extreme centre, the Left inched right to occupy the newly vacated positions. The invasion produced immediate revulsion. British military intervention strikes an old and still intact nerve on the Left. But Labour's protest centred on the tactlessness of not using the UN; Noel-Baker demanded that Swedish and Swiss troops should set up 'a broad neutral zone around the frontiers of Israel'.† Bevan saw the invasion as wrong because it 'stains the reputation of this country irremediably. How can we hold our heads up in the councils of the world after this?' Fenner Brockway felt 'the striking feature of this outburst of feeling was the protest of morally moved people who would have never dreamed of associating themselves with the Left. I had five shocked letters from Eton College masters.'‡

This enthusiasm for the UN was sheer self-deception. The UN was clearly dominated by those who financed it and quite unwilling to override the national interests of the big powers. Had it been willing it was unable: South Africa swallowed up South-West Africa in the teeth of UN resolutions and recommendations, France boycotted and ignored Afro-Asian recommendations on Algeria in 1955 and 1957, so in 1956 Britain was to ignore the UN 'six requirements' and veto the Security Council's cease-fire vote. As the journal *International Socialism* put it, 'to pretend otherwise, that the United Nations are a power in its own right, or might become one – as the Left in this country do, from Transport House to *Tribune*, Canon Collins to *Peace News* – is to confuse piety with politics. It is to confuse the Great Powers' thieves' kitchen in New York with their soup kitchen annexe; and to suppose that internationalism is measured by the size of the queue.'§

Labour's parliamentary performance was a sickly mixture of rectitude and utopianism. But if the *Manchester Guardian*, John Foster Dulles and Aneurin Bevan, and the Eton staff-room were to be variously appalled by the tastelessness of Eden's gunboat diplomacy, the popular response was more vigorous. Energetic street fighting erupted in Trafalgar Square, with ballbearings rolled under police horses' hooves, not by long-haired armed strugglers but trade-unionists and their wives, in raincoats and ties, who were at first unprepared for the panicky police attack which seemed to echo Eden's own loss of nerve.

---

*Aneurin Bevan, *Tribune*, 10 August 1956.

†Philip Noel-Baker, *Hansard*, 31 October 1956.

‡Fenner Brockway, *Outside the Right*, Allen & Unwin, 1963, p. 158.

§'The Grand Illusion', Editorial, *International Socialism*, 16, Spring 1964.

But before very long there was small change and lighted cigarettes flying through the air towards the police horses and the hallowed cry of 'Where are the marbles?' – the thirties were not that quickly forgotten. The Labour Party arranged a number of meetings on the anodyne slogan of 'Law not War' and this slogan dominated the banners of its massive Trafalgar Square rally. Leftist dissenters opted for 'Out with Eden' rather than solidarity with Nasser. The Government was therefore never near being driven from office. Eden was replaced months later with discreet talk of gall bladders. The boat he took to New Zealand to convalesce travelled via the Panama Canal. But if the Labour Party seemed still capable of capturing foreign policy dissent, a more serious shock was to hit the Left, tearing away from the small British Communist Party a chunk large enough to alter decisively the balance of power on the Left and begin to move its internationalism towards something more than 'Peace Committee' pieties and appeals to UNO's knowhow.

HUNGARY

The Hungarian Revolution was the most important of a cluster of working-class uprisings in Eastern Europe in the mid-fifties. Building workers in East Germany had spontaneously struck over alterations in wage differentials in 1953, three months after Stalin's death. And three years later the Polish, Hungarian and Bulgarian workers were in turn spontaneously to challenge their own police, armies and governments. In each case the risings were subdued by concessions on wages and conditions, by Russian tanks, or by both. But the political shock-waves from Poznan and Budapest were to have a shattering effect on the Western Communist Parties. For not only were Communists obliged to watch their own leaders and writers twist the Russian invasion into some triumph of socialist internationalism, but they were to see the bewildered Russian machine-gunners shooting down not clerical fascists but socialist factory workers organized in Workers' Councils and conducting the longest general strike in European history. The shock was unrepeatable, coming as it did in a time when the whole belief-system of High Stalinism was already under stress through the disclosures of Khrushchev's 'Secret Speech'. And it was to release from the Communist Party into a world of new political opportunities, political personnel, from left social democrats to crypto-Trotskyists, who were to exert a shaping influence on the socialist consciousness which arose in the sixties.

As part of the carve-up of Europe agreed between Churchill, Stalin and Roosevelt at Yalta, the Western powers had consigned the Balkans to the embrace of Russia, whose army had swept back the occupying Nazi divisions. In all of these countries the old order, often virtually feudal and always very right-wing, had disintegrated. But the forces of the Left were also very weak. In Hungary itself, the Communist Party had been virtually eliminated when Bela Kun's Soviet Republic was crushed in 1919. Rumania's Communist Party was tiny, Albania's founded only in 1941, the Bulgarian party, strong in the twenties, was driven underground in 1934. All the Eastern parties had suffered not only police and legal attacks in their own countries but the summary execution by Stalin of very many of those leaders who had fled for refuge to Moscow. And the Stalin–Hitler pact, disorientating enough for British Communists, was a literal disaster in Czechoslovakia and the Nazi-occupied countries.

So although in Yugoslavia and Albania Communists actually came to dominate the partisan resistance to Hitler, only in Czechoslovakia did they command real working-class support. This meant that the governments installed by the Russians came to power, not by the self-activity or active choice of Polish or Czech workers, but by permission of the Red Army. As Mose Pijade of the Yugoslav Communist Party was able to sneer, 'certain heads of other parties . . . arrived in their free countries in places with pipes in their mouths, and . . . for four years, four times daily, vainly called on the masses to struggle via radio, while we won our freedom with arms in our hands'.* And with the exception of Yugoslavia and later Albania, the state by which they governed in the factory and the school was centralized and repressive and their economies dominated by Russia's needs. The Russian economy, with much of its heavy industry in ruins, systematically siphoned off the wealth of the newly 'liberated' Eastern bloc. About twelve million tons of Polish coal, for example, went annually to Russia at a price which was less than 8 per cent of the world market price, and was paid for, not in the form of Russian credits or products, but by transfer of German reparations due to Russia. Bulgarian tobacco was bought cheaply by Russia and subsequently re-sold in Western Europe at four times the price. Czech factories were used to make shoes from Russian leather.†

* Quoted in T. Cliff, 'Background to Hungary', *Socialist Review*, reprinted in *A Socialist Review*, International Socialism, 1965, p. 228.

† See T. Cliff, *Russia, a Marxist Analysis*, International Socialism, 1964, Chapter 9.

The degree of control exerted by the Russians and their fear that there might be attempts to assert independence from Russia and Comecon is indicated by the fates of the leading ministers in the post-war governments. Tito, who successfully broke out of the Soviet orbit in 1948 by decentralization and increasing trade with the West, was denounced as a fascist agent throughout the world.* And a series of trials led to the arrest and execution of many real or imagined 'Titoites'. These included Kostov and Slansky, Secretaries of the Bulgarian and Czech Parties, and Rajk and Clementis, Foreign Ministers in Hungary and Czechoslovakia – all executed – and Gomulka, the Polish Party Secretary, and Kardelj and Ana Pauker, the Yugoslavian and Rumanian Secretaries, who were imprisoned.

Stalin's death marked the end of the purges but in no way slackened the economic hoops which bound the Russian empire together. The rulers were allowed autonomy only provided they remained subordinate to the Russian economy as far as industrial output was concerned. But by 1956, ten years of relatively uninterrupted recovery and expansion of heavy industry had brought with it a need for alteration and reform within the economic and thence the political system. The colossal expansion of heavy industry which was the driving aim of the Plan was achieved at the expense of working-class living standards and had caused a complete dislocation of light industry and agriculture. Grain production and housing construction were particularly wasteful. Informal working-class resentment, expressed in the factories in absenteeism, low-quality work and self-inflicted wounds, acted to worsen the economic crisis.

By the fifties an increasingly vociferous group of the bureaucracy began to argue that economic reform (a shift towards light industry and consumer goods and an introduction of incentives) was necessary if the system was to keep going. They also pressed for a political liberalization, for use of the carrot rather than the stick, and this pressure was naturally stronger in East Europe than Russia itself. In Hungary in the years immediately prior to 1956 a very severe balance-of-payments crisis highlighted the failure to achieve balanced growth and strengthened national and liberalizing elements in the apparatus. Imre Nagy was actually promoted from Minister of the Interior to replace Rákosi in 1953 by the Russians and applied quite vigorous reforms. But he

---

* A book on the subject by James Klugmann called *From Trotsky to Tito* was hailed by the present editor of the *Morning Star* in *Communist Review*: 'Every active Communist should buy this book, read it, study it'; and it was introduced into party educational classes. In 1956 it was retracted by the Executive Committee.

moved too quickly for the Kremlin, who halted this experimental liberalization after twenty-two months.

But the effects of the uncertainty and the tentative rearrangements within the apparatus extended beyond it. The weakening of police rule and partial easing of censorship were necessary if the reformers, from Khrushchev himself right through to Dubček, were to outflank the conservatives and the generals. But free discussion continually threatened to spill over from artists, journalists and students into the working class and overflow from a relatively safe assertion of middle-class intellectual freedom into the extremely explosive application of the same ideas in the factory. The Petöfi Circle was formed as a centre of debate on liberalization by student members of the Young Communist League. Odd copies of the *Literary Gazette* appeared inside the factories. The administration was indecisive, unable to return to hardline repression (the Russians had sacked Rákosi in July when he returned from Moscow intent on purging the Writers' Union) yet unable (unlike Gomulka) to retain a hold over the spread of ideas. Workers and students alike were increasingly sliding out of the control of the Hungarian Government. On 23 October a massive demonstration in Budapest moved on spontaneously to the main radio station to have their demands broadcast. On their way they dismantled a twenty-six-foot bronze statue of Stalin, leaving only his boots behind. But at the radio station, the secret policemen opened sub-machine-gun fire on the demonstrators. The Hungarian Revolution had begun.

For the next four months a stand-up battle was to be fought between the Russian rulers and their liberal and conservative allies in Budapest and the workers and intellectuals of Hungary. It was to require two invasions by Russian tanks, the second a merciless obliteration of whole areas of working-class Budapest, the deaths of 30,000 Hungarians, the majority said by the hospitals to be young factory workers, wave after wave of arbitrary arrests, the dissolution of the Writers' and the Journalists' Union, the erasure of the Workers' Councils and the granting of comparatively gigantic wage rises to extinguish the revolt. But despite the obedient slander of the Hungarian Revolution as a fascist and counter-revolutionary attempt to reintroduce the landlords and priesthood, every moment of the revolution actually bears witness to the reverse. The rising was a classical spontaneous general strike organized by Workers' Councils federated in a Central Workers' Council meeting under the noses of the Russians in a Budapest electric-light factory. The fighting was popular in character, based on captured weapons, improvised tactics and ruthless vengeance for the despised secret police, who were sometimes hanged in the street with money left, untouched, in their mouths to symbolize their betrayal.

But the Russian soldiers, who in some cases had been told they were going to Germany to fight fascism, were encouraged to desert, some joining the Hungarians and many more being sent back to Russia for insubordination. Political prisoners were released, and the Councils operated control over production, notably of weapons, radios and fuel, with a mastery which contrasted totally with the wasteful inefficiency of the Plan. The period was certainly complex, moving from gaiety and release to sudden savagery and including strong anti-Russian elements and considerable peasant hostility to the state farms, but its content was profoundly socialist. It was those who blew it to bits with their artillery and their executions who were the enemies of socialism.

KING STREET

In Britain the Hungarian crisis had a shattering impact on Communists already disorientated by the secret Khrushchev speech on Stalin's crimes which had reached them via the *Manchester Guardian*. There had been previous crises based on the indigestibility of Russian actions. As early as 1924, Arthur Read, who had been expelled from Oxford University with R. P. Dutt for publishing a Communist magazine, *Free Oxford*, whose contributors included Carpenter, Varga and Radek, had led objections to the British Party's condemnation of Trotsky's book *The Lessons of October*. And although Read himself disappeared from politics he did influence Harry Wicks, who was to go on to encounter the American supporter of Trotsky, J. P. Cannon, at a Moscow cadre school. Cannon had acquired a translation of the criticism of Bukharin's *Draft Programme of the Communist International*, which Trotsky wrote in exile in Alma Ata in 1927. Wicks returned to England to lead the first of a series of groups of Communists to leave or more often be expelled from the Communist Party in the thirties for advancing criticism of Stalin and Comintern policy. And after the war there was considerable internal disquiet about Russia, especially over the whereabouts of several British Communists who had disappeared in Russia, including Len Winnicott, a veteran of the Invergordon Mutiny, Rose Cohen and Edith Bone. These inquiries had always been contained by the Party leadership's claim to special information obtained from their personal Russian connections.

There certainly were a small number of individual leaders of the Communist Party who deliberately lied, withheld information, knowingly slandered Marxist critics and ruthlessly expelled those who asked awkward questions (all presumably privately justified in the name of some Marxist truth actually more demanding than truth). But the duplicity of King Street full-timers which clearly did exist explains very little about the intensity and the durability of rank-and-file Communist involvement with Russia. For that loyalty, slowly drained of a real political meaning but pursued nevertheless, was a symbol of the whole decline in the meaning of Marxism as a revolutionary method within the Western Communist movement. For it was the obligation to defend the Soviet Union without reservation which enforced the doctrinal rigidity, the decline in controversy and lack of independence on all other matters. Not only had the heroism of the Russian soldiers in the Second World War acted to counter-balance any criticisms of Stalin's earlier methods in Spain and Germany, but the swift development of the Cold War and particularly the Korean War again acted to stifle and postpone the nagging doubts. The spirit of '*Non paseran*' had taken hold of the Party's intelligence. The uphill slogging work of defending the Russians, passing motions for increased East–West trade, distributing the friendship society periodicals, and organizing the crowning glory of a 'progressive tour' physically linked British Communists to the fact of socialism. Although the work of the Party in Britain was slow, routine and not particularly revolutionary, it attained a heightened meaning within the context of the achievements of the 'Socialist Camp', farms and swimming pools and art galleries which could actually be visited and touched. As for those on the Right who argued that the cost in terms of loss of liberty was too great, well, that was anti-working-class liberalism (it often was) and anyway atrocity stories were never true (only in Stalin's case they were).

To critics on the Left a more ruthless attitude was required because their criticisms were cast within the half-familiar Marxist tenets.

It was as if 'Trotskyism' was a species of mental ailment standing in relation to Marxism as the stoats and the weasels stood to the comfortable security of Toad Hall. And unlike the badgers of the *New Statesman* and the moles of *Tribune* these weasels and stoats were not arguing about the state of the herbaceous border but squatting in the stables and laying claim to the dining hall. They denied the very facts that the Communist Party depended on. Therefore, the theoreticians of the Party, tutored by Stalin, had to argue that there was a necessary affinity between all political theories critical of Russia, that Trotsky's Bolshevik criticisms necessarily developed into fascist activities. Criticism of Toad could lead nowhere save to acts of political murder, poisoning and sabotage against his mansions. So persuasive was Stalin's mythological power (particularly to middle-class intellectuals afflicted by the blend of class guilt and messianic pretension which often seems to arise within socialist groups) that a whole belief system was actually structured around the mustachioed butcher. His writings, which now read as stingy platitudes, were inflated into theoretical advances on the level of the writings of Marx and Engels. The vast, murderous and highly inefficient apparatus with which he ruled Russia was acclaimed as a triumph of popular democracy by the very people who still read Marx on the Paris Commune and Lenin on the State and Revolution in their education classes. A physical scientist as eminent as Bernal could write as late as 1953, with a straight, indeed positively pious, face, 'Stalin's achievement is something greater than the building up and defending of the Soviet Union, greater even than the hope for peace and progress he gave the whole world. It is that his thought and his example is now embodied in the lives and thoughts of hundreds of millions of men, women and children; it has become an indissoluble part of the great human tradition.'*

Such was the degree of self-delusion and such were the pressures of the Cold War that Communists would actually read the entire transcript of the Moscow Trials, annotate it in the margin and believe every word. Only the combined shock of the Russian invasion and the Khrushchev speech were enough to prise open the assumptions British Communists had locked themselves into.

The special force of Hungary on the British Party was also due to the intellectual courage of workers and intellectuals in the Communist Party willing to run the gauntlet of the multiple political, disciplinary and emotional weapons at the disposal of King Street. Peter Fryer, the *Daily Worker*'s correspondent in Hungary, whose despatches had been discontinued by the paper after the second day, was a vital eyewitness, able to challenge for the first time the leadership's monopoly over information from the East. His book *Hungarian Tragedy* conveyed the horror and bewilderment of a life-long Communist at what the Russians were doing and refuted in detail the apologetics of the *Daily Worker*. A quite separate group of dissidents in Yorkshire were active before the invasion in the publication of an internal discussion bulletin, the *Reasoner*. Their journal was a result of the Khrushchev speech and the cascade of discussion which had been let loose in *World News* and the *Daily Worker* throughout the summer of 1956, and resulted in the setting-up of a Commission on Inner Party Democracy. This was ex-

*J. D. Bernal, 'Stalin as Scientist', *Modern Quarterly*, Summer 1953.

panded in July as a further concession (only four out of fourteen of the original team were not dependent on the Communist Party for their living). The editors of the *Reasoner* were both graduates in history but were political activists in strong Communist branches at Halifax and Hull, both specialists in working-class history and teaching in the Workers' Educational Association. There is a strong sense at class and history and a certain Halifaxness in their bulletins, with an implied appeal to obligation towards dissident fellow intellectuals in the Soviet bloc.

None of this prevented their vigorous denunciation simply because they were intellectuals. There was much talk of 'a petty bourgeois outlook, so bankrupt of positive content', and other Marxist swearwords came from the Executive Committee. Joan Simon was to argue that in times of crisis certain Party intellectuals unconsciously act as 'purveyors of bourgeois ideas which corrupt the class consciousness of the proletariat'.* This view of consciousness would seem to be nearer to spirit possession than Marxism and inclines one to speculate where exactly the wife of the Professor of Education at Leeds University gets her ideas from.

It became clear that the free debate sanctioned after Khrushchev's speech was getting out of hand and an increasingly defensive Communist Party took to making official statements in reply to letters, forbade critics to sign as a group (although this was allowed for letter writers encouraging loyalty to the Party) and suspended the editors of the *Reasoner* for the publication of an unauthorized journal (although the editor of *Labour Monthly*, R. P. Dutt, has been publishing the views of social democrats and non-Communists for half a century under Communist Party auspices). The Executive Committee invoked Rule 27, the Communist Party's Catch-22, a rule which entitled them to interpret all the other rules as necessary. By 1957 the mini-liberalization had been put into reverse gear and in the 25th (Special) Conference the Party leadership, who allowed no factions and published a recommended list of Executive Committee candidates, steamrollered the remaining opposition which had centred round the minority report of the Inner Party Democracy Committee. While the minority report was rather ambiguous, it clearly stood for a new political independence in relation to Russia and would have continued a debate which would have necessarily challenged the King Street bureaucrats. It was heavily defeated. One of the most moving moments was the interruption of

* Joan Simon, letter to *World News*, Vol. IV (23 February 1957), pp. 125–6, cited in Neal Wood, *Communism and British Intellectuals*, Gollancz, 1959, p. 211.

Andrew Rothstein, who claimed, with a remarkable expertise in selective inaccuracy, that the decline of the Russian Social Democratic party between 1907 and 1911 was due to the fact that Russian workers were 'bewildered or confused by the groups of backboneless and spineless intellectuals who have turned in upon their own emotions and frustrations to rend the Party instead of using their capabilities to rally workers around it'. This nauseating piety was interrupted by Johnny McLoughlin, a London Communist with a real working-class following in the car industry, who bellowed with great accuracy, 'You are the enemy, you lying old swine.'

Immediately after the Conference 'A Political Letter to Members' was issued arguing that the main danger to the Party, after 'a debate done in the face of a tremendous attack by the class enemy', was 'revisionism' (a word whose extreme ambiguity must lead to its great popularity among Marxist bureaucrats: it usually means 'thinking differently from me'). Branches were ominously instructed that 'there should be the most comradely discussion with members who may have queries or criticisms concerning the particular decisions of the Congress and these should be collectively considered so that unity is reached on the basis of the decisions of the Congress'. It warned sternly that 'It is harmful to give assistance to Trotskyist and anti-Party people who will try to cover up their aims by the participation of one or two Communists as sympathetic contributors to journals or conferences whose main political content is anti-Communist and anti-Party.' And it ended ominously, ordering 'Urgent attention to regular Marxist education'.

These precautions reflect the scale of the disgust and the disillusion with the Communist Party. Clearly a large part of the slump in membership and *Daily Worker* sales was due to portions of an inactive paper membership finally drifting out of politics. But the resignation of some of the most active party members had been more painful. A total of eleven journalists left the *Daily Worker*. The Young Communist League membership plummeted from 3,500 in 1955 to 1,387 in 1958. In Leeds a stormy report-back meeting rejected the Special Conference report. Jim Roche, city trade-unionist, resigning after twenty-seven years' membership, argued that 'the leadership has exhibited all the worst features of a rigid uncompromising bureaucracy' and the events of 1956 demonstrated that 'The Communist Party is now a self-perpetuating bureaucracy which not only interprets rules, it also makes them.' Don Renton, a leader of a strong dissident focus in Nottingham, stressed that his resignation was forced because of the manifest duplicity of the leadership and the extent of the control of the full-timers. And Dick Nettleton, who had been a leader of the 1939 Metro-Vickers strike, a youth member of a delegation to China and a Manchester organizer, introduced a new and important element in his resignation letter, shock at the Russians' nuclear test on 21 April 1957, one of the dirtiest explosions ever. The *Reasoner* Group had continued to publish, producing a quarterly Marxist-humanist journal, the *New Reasoner*, with an expanded editorial board but still Halifax-based. They were to sponsor conferences and pamphlets and for a period operate as a fiercely independent grouping within the maelstrom of competing Marxist sects who uneasily eyed each other and their prey in forum gatherings.

One of the most famous of these multi-sectarian meetings was the New Left summer camp, at which almost all of the warring factions were present and on their best behaviour under canvas. Peter Sedgwick, who spent the conference in bed with an asthma attack and thus shared a room with the visiting speakers, recalls that Michael Stewart (then a Labour Leftist, soon to become Labour Foreign Secretary and the most servile apologist for American policy) folded his clothes very neatly and said only four precise words: 'Good evening' and 'Good morning', Brian Behan of the Socialist Labour League and South Bank Strike delivered a long poetic monologue on the possible existence of God, and Tony Cliff recruited him from his sick bed to International Socialism.

The most immediately successful of the sectarian groupings was The Club, a hardened nucleus of Trotskyists who had captured the remnants of the Revolutionary Communist Party and had been associated with *Socialist Outlook*, a front magazine issued during the Bevanite era with Trotskyist sponsorship. Unpopular even within the microcosmic world of British Trotskyism, they were to show great organizational cunning if little political ability. For the Trotskyists were, for once, in a commanding position. They of anyone had the right to say 'I told you so'. As the monolith of Stalinism unfroze they were increasingly able to show that Trotsky's writings, especially after he was expelled from Russia, were in essence accurate. In particular the timely publication of a new translation of one of Trotsky's clearest works, *The Revolution Betrayed*, was to make available a Marxist explanation of the crisis within Marxism. Some delegates experienced an almost physical response on reading the new edition, opportunely published by The Club, of a book which they had been encouraged to treat as a species of political pornography. Healy and Banda, the leaders of

The Club, personally visited every dissident who published a critical letter in the debate, usually leaving a copy of *The Revolution Betrayed*. Their converts were invited to remain in the Party and fight to the end. And Peter Fryer was made the editor of a new weekly socialist newspaper under, it only slowly became apparent, their effective control.

The *Newsletter* was a fine piece of working-class journalism with a fresh and honest voice, a flair for news within the Labour movement and a readability unusual on the Left. 'We have no sectional axe to grind,' it announced. It energetically campaigned against racial discrimination and organized street meetings and paper sales in the streets of Notting Hill Gate after the murder of Kelso Cochrane by fascist-organized race rioters. The *Newsletter* may have been only a small weekly, but its robust reporting and its sympathy with the rank-and-file point of view against both employer and union leadership guaranteed a generous reception by the strikers in Covent Garden, the London Docks, Paisley Threadmills and Harland and Wolffs. Its strike bulletins for the London busmen and the building workers of the South Bank were received with the gratitude and generosity which trade-unionists in dispute always show for honest working-class journalism. For a couple of years the *Newsletter* swung the industrial initiative away from the Communist Party, and the paper's first rank-and-file conference, despite heavy attacks by the Fleet Street and King Street press, brought together delegates representing a real body of working-class influence, debating the tactics for revolutionary trade-unionism in an atmosphere which had been gone for twenty years in the Communist Party. In London the *Newsletter*, with the aid of Brian Behan's magical oratory, captured the loyalty of an informal grouping of Irish building industry militants who having been syndicalists in the Communist Party proceeded to be syndicalists in the Socialist Labour League. Lawrence Daly, a militant in the mining industry whose Fife Socialist League effectively replaced the Communist Party, and an independent at the 1958 Conference, saw it as 'representing a definite new stage in the development of a militant socialist movement in Britain. It gathered together a surprisingly large number of youthful delegates from industry who are ready for a fighting lead in the struggle for radical social change.' And of the Communist denunciations of the conference, he wondered, 'When will the *Daily Worker* ever take seriously its slogans about working-class unity?'* A proposal to form a political party was made at the meeting but heavily defeated.

But this hopeful alliance of industrial militants seeking a new net-

* Lawrence Daly, quoted in the *Newsletter*, November 1958.

work of solidarity, political activists fed up with the Communist Party and Trotskyists who had been in political mothballs for twenty years, was not to last. The openness, free debate and non-sectarian spirit which had been so attractive was revealed to be a temporary expedient. Without explanation and apparently by a process of political magic it was revealed that the *Newsletter* was not actually a paper for rank-and-file workers but was controlled by The Club. On 6 December 1958, G. Healy openly joined its board. By February 1959 the *Newsletter* was talking of 'the *Newsletter*'s predecessor *Socialist Outlook*' and announced they were to set up an organization whose 'provisional' National Secretary was to be G. Healy. The Socialist Labour League, as it was called, seemed at first to be in the *Newsletter*'s non-sectarian tradition, genuinely anxious to begin piecing together the fragments from the shattered Communist Party and finding a real footing in the modern class struggle. At a time when the Communist Party was still attacking the Campaign for Nuclear Disarmament, the *Newsletter* had joined the Aldermaston March with banners proclaiming 'Ban the Bomb. Black the Bases'. The small token industrial action taken by building workers, on Pat Arrowsmith's initiative, in Stevenage against nuclear armaments was enthusiastically welcomed. 'Spokesmen of the League suggested informal discussions with the Direct Action Committee . . . to work out common policy for common action,' announced the *Newsletter*, beaming.

But on 5 September 1959 it was announced that Fryer, 'owing to illness, was unable to continue his duties' and it later became clear that having had his name and newspaper cynically used to relaunch The Club he had been hounded to the point of nervous collapse. The former modesty and accuracy of the *Newsletter* went with him. The First Conference of the Socialist Labour League had been billed as 'At the very least . . . a milestone; there are signs that it might even be a watershed.' But by November 'British Labour is heading for its greatest crisis since 1926', by December it was 'the end of an era for British social democracy' and in January 1960 'a new era of political understanding in which the Marxists will have their greatest opportunity of all time'. It came as no great surprise, then, to find the Second Conference of the SLL, which actually revealed a marked decline in influence, hailed as '"The finest conference ever of the Marxist movement in Britain". This was the feeling voiced on all sides by delegates and visitors to the Second National Conference of the SLL.' Those interested in irony might have noted that, in the *Newsletter*'s estimation, 'the most heated discussion' in the 1959 conference had been a two-hour debate over whether the National Secretary would have the right of summary expulsion. The conference was to approve such action 'where the breach of discipline is so grave that the circumstances must be made known to the working class immediately'. Over the next year a succession of ex-Communists, workers and intellectuals alike, who had looked to the SLL for a new political future, were to leave or be expelled. The *Newsletter* was to fall back to fortnightly, and the League was to lose the respect and the *élan* which for a brief period it had commanded in the labour movement. Increasingly the organization was to be known for its vanity, its venom and its valiant hawking of its ever more frequent and strident periodicals. It effectively ceased to produce any theoretical work after the collapse of *Labour Review*, acquiring the habit instead of serialized exposures of its fellow Marxists' misdeeds, denouncing them with such an evident hatred that it must have left little emotion for the capitalist class.

The other main grouping on the revolutionary Left was the International Socialists, who had been more or less obliged to set up in business in 1951 after having been abruptly expelled en bloc by the leadership of what remained of the Revolutionary Communist Party. The RCP had been led till 1949 by Jock Haston, the ex-merchant seaman whose improvisatory ability and sense of humour had been tested to the limit during the war (his skill at fiddling Paper Control in order to finance and print vigorous denunciations of the imperialist war were especially admired). The post-war years had been immensely complicated for the rapidly dwindling groups of Trotskyists, whose ability, minus the Old Man, to distinguish workers' state from capitalist state and boom from slump was being severely taxed. Several RCP members, looking at Russia after the war, had begun to suggest that, although all property was nationalized by the state in the Soviet Union, since at least 1928 there was no way workers could really control the state, which was effectively operated by a class of managers. Ray Challinor, an ex-Bevin boy then working as a Manchester engineer, argued this case in the discussion journal *Left* in 1947, and Tony Cliff, a Palestinian revolutionary who had languished in Ireland during the war, published a long internal document on the theory of state capitalism in 1948, with innumerable statistics and Russian source material. Relatively little attention was given to Cliff's view that his theory developed Marxist ideas about what had happened in Russia helpfully. A fairly fraternal debate about Russia became an expelling issue only much later, during the Korean war, when Cliff and Co. argued that Marxists should be attacking the British and American invading forces rather than supporting the North Korean regime and the Russians. At the time *Socialist Outlook* had nothing but praise for North Korea and Cliff and his supporters were expelled on various charges, in some cases *in absentia* and without a hearing.* The importance of this particular debate was not solely for the archivist and those of a Biblical inclination. The intellectual effort of explaining quite how the liberating and life-giving ideas of the Marxist pioneers had ended in a society so profoundly exploitative as Russia was in itself also an active reassertion of revolutionary springs at the base of Marxism. And having committed one heresy against the doctrine of official Trotskyism, and having been therefore formally excommunicated, the socialist sinners were able to proceed to new endeavours with a clear conscience. *Socialist Review*, the monthly journal which the group of twenty-five or so just managed to produce, was able to take a long cool look at many other myths of the Left and do theoretical work of some originality and importance.

During the 1950s the International Socialist group was still too small to have much impact, was fairly marginally involved in trade-union disputes and viewed the SLL's growth with a good deal of ill-concealed envy. *Socialist Review* was followed in 1960 by a more ambitious journal, *International Socialism*, which had a strong emphasis on workers' control, Marxist economics and political theory and continued to attract to it socialists who were dissatisfied with the intellectual thinness of much of post-war Marxism. To begin with it attempted to be both the magazine of a grouping which was still evolving and a more general forum. Independent socialists like Ken Coates, Bob Pennington and Chris Pallis who had been expelled from the SLL co-existed on the IS journal for an uneasy period. Pallis was to found a libertarian Marxist grouping – Solidarity – based on the ideas of Paul Cardan, whose libertarian-Marxist critique of modern capitalism had a considerable appeal to Marxists browned off with the 'Old Left' in all its guises and gave certain imaginative hints about the form revolts in modern capitalism would take.

But by 1960 the political tremors of Hungary had settled. The Communist Party, still covered with a heavy layer of dust, had survived and had begun to recover its industrial initiative once it became clear that

---

*Those who now argue that the state-capitalist theory is a deliberate watering-down of socialist ideas in response to the anti-Communist feeling during the Korean war (such as Tariq Ali in *The Coming British Revolution* and Teresa Hayter in *Hayter of the Bourgeoisie*) are therefore crediting Cliff with gifts of foresight amounting almost to prophecy.

there was no real alternative community of militants outside it. The
SLL continued operations, and were particularly active in the Young
Socialists, but on a smaller and still more sectarian scale. Political
attention had swung back to the unilateralist battle in the Labour
Party and CND. The period of intense emotional and political tur-
bulence was followed by one of retrenchment. The revolutionary Left
had had its ideas confirmed by history itself and had thereby been able
to break out of its extreme isolation and in some cases even develop its
ideas. The sixties were to see the old revolutionary questions asked
again, but this time not in Hungary but closer to home.

Through the Smoke of Budapest:
Edward Thompson

Stalinism has sown the wind, and now the whirlwind centres on Hungary. As I write the smoke is still rising above Budapest.

It is true that dollars have also been sown in this embittered soil. But the crop which is rising will surely not turn out to be the one which Mr Dulles expected – some new Syngman Rhee for Eastern Europe, backed by a fraudulent Chancellory and a Papal Junta?

By an angry twist of history, it seems that the crop is coming up as students', workers' and soldiers' councils, as 'anti-Soviet' soviets.

I do not know how things will be when this is published. Will Russian troops withdraw soon enough to prevent the country from being engulfed in waves of nationalist fury and anarchy? Will a new, honest government of Communists and others succeed in wresting calm from the passions of the moment – calm enough to ensure some justice, more mercy, and that the will of the people finds expression?

It is all that we dare hope for. But – leaving aside such groups of counter-revolutionaries as there must have been – those youths and workers of Budapest who first threw up barricades against the Soviet tanks, surely they did not wish to embrace the 'American Century'? Nor can they then, unless in desperation, have found comfort in the hypocritical appeal to the Security Council of governments blooded to the elbow from their exploits in Kenya, Cyprus, Algeria – and now Egypt.

No chapter would be more tragic in international socialist history, if the Hungarian people, who once before lost their revolution to armed reaction, were driven into the arms of the capitalist powers by the crimes of a Communist government and the uncomprehending violence of Soviet armies.

And so I hope that the Communist Party, my party, will regain the support of the working people. But *where* is my party in Hungary? Was it in the broadcasting station or on the barricades? And *what* is it? Is it a cluster of security officials and discredited bureaucrats? Or is it a party 'rooted in the people' of town and countryside, capable of self-purification and new growth?

We will read the answer in its actions. I hope we will hear less about 'rooting out' this and that, 'ruthlessly smashing' this and that, and more about learning from the people, serving the people, and honouring Communist principle.

I know that our Hungarian comrades will recall the prayer of their great patriot, Kossuth, over one hundred years ago:

Send, O God! the genial rays of the sun, that flowers may spring from this holy blood, that the bodies of my brethren may not perish in lifeless corruption ... As a free man, I kneel on the fresh graves of my brethren. Sacrifices like these sanctify the earth; they purge it of sin. My God! a people of slaves must not live on this sacred soil, nor step on these graves!. ...

*

It is time that we had this out. From start to finish, from February onwards, our leadership has sided (evasively at times, perhaps) with Stalinism.

This is not to say that they have defended the memory of Stalin, or seriously questioned the dishonest attempt to make one man a scapegoat for the sins of an historical epoch.

On the contrary, they have run two lines of argument. First, all 'wrong things' (which we 'could not know about') were associated with the influence of one man in Russia, and the 'cult' of his 'personality'; second, Stalin's theory was admirable but (unknown to us) an alarming gap grew up between his theory and his practice.

Convenient arguments, these, for our leadership: since they absolve us from all responsibility for having passed 'wrong information' and justified 'wrong things': since they absolve them from all need to drive out the influence of Stalinism upon their own theory and practice, and that of our Party.

But there *is* one 'wrong theory' of Stalin's which we are licensed to criticize: the theory of the intensification of the class struggle. All right, let us look at it. The theory derives, in fact, from Lenin – thrown out in a fluid situation of revolutionary crisis, and, like so much else, wrested out of context by Stalin and turned into a stone axiom:

Certain comrades interpreted the thesis on the abolition of classes, the establishment of a classless society and the dying out of the state, to mean justification of laziness and complacency, justification of the counter-revolutionary theory of the subsiding of the class struggle and the weakening of state authority. Needless to say, such people cannot have anything in common with our Party. These are either degenerates, or double dealers, who must be driven out of the Party. The abolition of classes is not achieved by subduing the class struggle but by intensifying it. The state will die out not by the weakening of state authority, but by strengthening it to the utmost necessary for the purpose of finally crushing the remnants of the dying classes and for organizing defence against the capitalist environment ...

(STALIN, Report to January 1933 Plenum, *CPSU (B)*)

Take out this one 'wrong theory' and this whole passage falls apart, and shows itself to be corrupt. The theory of the all-powerful, centralized state is wrong – our comrades in Poland and Yugoslavia are proving this in life. The attitude towards the role of the Party, and towards party comrades, is wrong.

And the Stalinist theory of the dictatorship of the proletariat is wrong. Once again, Stalin made out of Lenin's words a stone axiom:

> The dictatorship of the proletariat is the domination of the proletariat over the bourgeoisie, untrammelled by law and based on violence and enjoying the sympathy and support of the toiling and exploited masses.

(STALIN, *Foundations of Leninism*)

As we learn from Hungary, such a dictatorship need not for long command the sympathy of the toiling masses: nor would it do in Britain. This is indeed a far cry from Engels' definition of the 'two infallible expedients' which distinguish this phase of transition: election to all positions by universal suffrage, with the right of recall residing in the electors: and all officials to receive workers' wages (Introduction, *Civil War in France*).

And the identification of all disagreement, all opposition, all hesitation, with 'objective' counter-revolution is wrong. It permeates Stalin's writings and the *History of the CPSU (B)* (upon which a generation of our full-timers have received their education) from end to end. 'The opposition has ideologically broken with Leninism . . . and has objectively become a tool of counter-revolution against the regime of the proletarian dictatorship.' 'To attain victory, the Party of the working-class, its directing staff, its advanced fortress, must first be purged of capitulators, deserters, scabs and traitors' (*CPSU (B)*, 289, 360).

And the military vocabulary of Stalinism is wrong, and strange and offensive to the ears of the British working class.

And the attitude to discussion is wrong. This should have been clear when, in 1931, Stalin branded the editors of a journal which had permitted a discussion of certain pre-war theories of Lenin, for 'rotten liberalism', for 'stupidity bordering on crime, bordering on treason to the working class'. 'Slander must be branded as such and not made the subject of discussion.'

And the theory of the Party is wrong, the theory that 'the Party becomes strong by purging itself', the theory of the Party's paternal, self-appointed mission and infallibility, the 'cult of the Party' which submerges all loyalty to people, to principle, to the working class itself in loyalty to the Party 'iron discipline'.

And the mechanical theory of human consciousness is wrong: the theory that historical science 'can become as precise a science as, let us say, biology': the subordination of the imaginative and moral faculties to political and administrative authority is wrong: the elimination of moral criteria from political judgement is wrong: the fear of independent thought, the deliberate encouragement of anti-intellectual trends amongst the people is wrong: the mechanical personification of unconscious class forces, the belittling of the conscious process of intellectual and spiritual conflict, all this is wrong:

The superstructure is created by the basis precisely in order to serve it and actively help it to take shape and consolidate itself, to actively strive for the elimination of the old watchword basis, together with its superstructure.

(STALIN, *Marxism in Linguistics*)

Desperately the old superstructure rallies to the defence of the basis that gave rise to it.

(JAMES KLUGMAN, *Basis and Superstructure*)

All these theories are not altogether wrong. But they are wrong enough to have brought our movement into international crisis. And it was mechanical idealism such as this, mounted on Soviet tanks, which fired through the smoke at the workers and young people of Budapest.

*

Stalinism is socialist theory and practice which has lost the ingredient of humanity. The Stalinist mode of thought is not that of dialectical materialism, but that of mechanical idealism. For example:

if the passing of slow quantitative changes into rapid and abrupt qualitative changes is a law of development, then it is clear that revolutions made by oppressed classes are a quite natural and inevitable phenomenon.

Hence the transition from capitalism to Socialism and the liberation of the working class from the yoke of capitalism cannot be effected by slow changes by reforms, but only by a qualitative change of the capitalist system, by revolution.

Hence, in order not to err in policy, one must be a revolutionary, not a reformist.

(STALIN, *Dialectical and Historical Materialism*)

The gap between Stalinist theory and practice is inherent in the theory. 'Truth is always concrete,' wrote Lenin: but from the fluid movement of Lenin's analysis of particular social realities, Stalin plucked axioms. Stalinism is Leninism turned into stone.

Instead of commencing with facts, social reality, Stalinist theory starts with the idea, the text, the axiom: facts, institutions, people, must be broken to conform to the idea. Wheat is grown in hothouses to 'prove' a scientific theory: novels are written to 'prove' the correctness of the Party line: trials are faked to 'prove' the 'objective' treason of the victims.

Stalinist analysis, at its most degenerate, becomes a scholastic exercise, the search for 'formulations' 'correct' in relation to text but not to life. And how often is this 'correct formulation' poised mid-way between two deviations, one to the left, one to the right? 'To the question, which deviation was worse? Comrade Stalin replied: "One is as bad as the other ..."' Do the real choices of life present themselves in this mechanical way?

'He had completely lost consciousness of reality,' declares Khrushchev. And he was not alone. This gap developed everywhere. It was this gap which defied Khrushchev's analysis: 'Not only a Marxist-Leninist but also no man of common sense can grasp how it was possible to make whole nations responsible for inimical activity.' Precisely so. But this is the irony of Stalin's career. Emerging as the most 'realistic', the 'strongest' Marxist, he limited his vision to the single task of holding and extending the power of the Soviet State. Tearing his severe, textual path through unprecedented complexities and dangers he allowed one part of reality to escape him – the thoughts, prejudices, aspirations, of living men and women. Stalinism is at the opposite pole to common sense.

*

But never free from the restraint of common sense: rather, the Stalinist oscillates between the axiom and 'realpolitik': dogmatism and opportunism. When the axioms cease to produce results, a 'mistake' is 'recognized': Khrushchev's speech is made: the tanks withdraw from Budapest. But the theory is little changed. For Stalinism prevents a serious critique from emerging within the borders of its rule. And we, outside these borders, have also failed.

Stalinism was not 'wrong things' about which 'we could not know', but distorted theories and degenerate practices about which we knew something, in which, to some degree, we shared, and which our leadership supports today. Who does not know that our moral atrophy, our military vocabulary and structure, our paternalist outlook upon the people and their organizations, our taste for disseminating 'wrong information', our fear of popular initiatives independent of our guidance, our dislike of criticism, our secrecy and occasional bad faith with our friends – all these have crippled our propaganda, isolated us, and robbed our work of its right reward? And who does not know that it was our rank-and-file that was tainted least with these things, and our leadership most?

Our leaders do not wish to discuss this because they do not wish to change. At heart, they have always feared the 'thaw'. Their hearts lie with Soviet tanks. After all, tanks are mechanical things, which will answer to controls and can consolidate power. 'Marxism-Leninism' is safe with them. But if people take initiative into their own hands . . . it is too great a risk.

And on the other side of the smoke, what do we hope for from the people of Poland, the workers and students of Budapest, when their wounds are healed and their national pride assuaged? First, I hope, a new respect for *people*, permeating the whole of society, its institutions, its social relations. And then, a new respect for truth, for principle. A democracy which does not limit its action within narrow limits defined by a paternal Party, pronouncing anathema on all who stray outside, but one based on real confidence in the people's initiatives. A new understanding of the continuity of human culture. And finally, a new internationalism, based (among socialist countries) upon true independence and respect: and (among Communist Parties) upon truthful exchanges and fraternal controversy – exchanges in which the membership, by personal and published contact, can take part.

*

The Polish and Hungarian people have written their critique of Stalinism upon their streets and squares. In doing so, they have brought back honour to the international Communist movement. These revolutions have been made by Communists: not it is true by those who arrogated to themselves all wisdom and authority, but by Communists just the same. Wherever this wind of Stalinism has been sown, Communists have also sown good socialist seed. The crop of human brotherhood will prevail, when the winds have passed away.

I recall a 'Christmas message' from my brother, which he wrote after meeting Communist partisans, in December 1943:

There is a spirit abroad in Europe which is finer and braver than anything that tired continent has known for centuries, and which cannot be withstood. You can, if you like, think of it in terms of politics, but it is broader and more generous than any dogma. It is the confident will of whole peoples, who have known the utmost humiliation and suffering and who have triumphed over it, to build their own life once and for all.

It is the crime of Stalinism that it crabbed and confined this spirit, while many of those who are now greeting, with complacent self-approval, the exploits of the Polish and Hungarian peoples, themselves were feeding Stalinism with each strident anti-Communist speech, with the rearmament of Germany, with each twist of the Cold War.

Stalinism confined this spirit, but it was never killed. Today it walks abroad again, in full daylight, on Polish streets. It was present on the Budapest barricades, and today wrests with anarchy for the future of Hungary. Never was there a time when comrades of ours were in so great need of our solidarity, in the face of the blind resistance of Stalinism, the black passions of reaction.

This socialism of free people, and not of secret speeches and police, will prove *more* dangerous to our own imperialism than any Stalinist state. Its leaders will make mistakes enough, but not such 'mistakes' as destroy their own honour and the good name of the party.

We British Communists have a right and duty to greet our comrades in these lands of reborn principle.

Shame on our leaders for their silence!

Greetings to the Polish people! Honour to the working people, and students, who shed their blood at Budapest! May they regain mastery over their own future, and curb the mob passions unloosed by their ordeal!

And may it prove that Communist need never fire on Communist again!

1 November 1956.

(Abridged from 'Through the Smoke of Budapest', published in the *Reasoner: A Journal of Discussion*, ed. E. P. THOMPSON and JOHN SAVILLE, final issue, November 1956)

Russian Inventions:
Brian Behan

Now, after ten years in the Communist Party, we seemed no larger. All we did was hold our own. Our membership never went above thirty thousand, and this was only kept up by frantic recruiting drives in which, like the runner on the escalator, we kept running like mad just to stay in the same place. And yet in the union we were making great strides. I was now the London Delegate to our annual conference. Our positions on the Executive Committee were increasing. This, I used to think, was due to workers' love and respect of what we did on the jobs. In fact, it was partly that and partly because we had an election machine that our opponents lacked. Any similar gang of fanatics could have been equally successful.

Outside the unions, no one paid us the slightest attention. I stood as local Communist candidate and received precisely 181 votes. I felt bad about this until I noticed that nearly all our candidates received about the same. I have since concluded that this is the mathematical average of loonies in each area in Britain. I once said this to a Communist, and he said, 'No it's not. I got 190.'

People just didn't trust us. First there came the Russian brides; the refusal of the Russians to allow Russian wives of Englishmen to rejoin them in Britain. This seemed so heartless that even I couldn't justify it. Then came Tito's break with Stalin, and our whole world went topsy-turvy again. Tito became a running dog of the Imperialists, complete with blood dripping from inch-long fangs. To all who doubted we had the one line: 'You are believing the lies of Imperialism.' I came to blows with two of my best friends over the Korean war.

It seemed fantastic that our party was among the best fighters for workers' rights everywhere, except in Russia. 'Why haven't the workers in Russia got the right to strike?' No answer. 'Why aren't they free to leave their jobs as and when they please?' No answer.

'Is it true that the Communists are fiddling votes in the ETU?' This last was the hardest to bear. I, Simon Pure, had refused even to accept the increased delegation fees in my own union. The thought of Communists actually fiddling votes made me ill. I determined to fight, however hard it might be. I began to speak up on the Executive Committee. I found my first opportunity around the case of Dr Edith Bone.

'I value one hair on an old woman's head more than I do the whole Hungarian Government.'

Not a sound came from the rest of the Executive. Harry Pollitt had his hands clasped together, sitting up on a slightly raised platform.

'I want to know why we did nothing to save this woman from seven years' imprisonment. If it is true that we knew nothing, then we stand exposed as idiots. Everyone else knew.'

John Gollan hastened to reassure the Executive. Small, thin, tubercular, he had a magically interesting voice. It was as though all his personality had run into his mouth. Resting one knee on his chair, he said, 'It's simply not true that we knew nothing. Some of us have been trying for years to get some satisfaction from the Hungarian Embassy. But we simply didn't get anywhere.'

It's no accident that the Scotch form the biggest part of the leadership of the British Communist Party. You only have to live in a place like Partick in Glasgow, to know why the residents provide more Communists per head of the population than anywhere else. Never have I seen anywhere such acres of grey granite blocks specially built to house the wage slaves. At least the slums we lived in in Dublin were hand-me-downs from the rich. So if we lived in squalor it was grand squalor. Our rooms were large and lofty. Our plastered ceilings works of art. Our door had an old duke's head for a knocker, while the one beside it had a rampant lion holding the knocker in his jaws. In Glasgow I saw my first 'Single end'. A little cubby hole scooped out of the wall, in which lived a man and four children. Right along the Clyde stretch mile after mile of these barrack blocks. It frightened me, because I had never really seen the effects of industrialization before. The more prosperous English only supply the secondary leadership of the Communists. Pollitt was largely a historical accident. A large, fat, well-fed English tradesman, whose son went to Cambridge.

Now he signalled me to speak again. 'I want to know, then, who these comrades were who knew Dr Bone was in jail.' After a moment, Gollan did a count. 'There was Dutt, Pollitt and myself.' He sat down as though to banish the idea. 'Then,' I went on, 'the position is even more disgraceful. To know that the woman was in jail, and do nothing about it.'

I was interrupted by Gollan. 'That again, comrades, is simply not true.' He had an earnest method of delivery which almost convinced you black was white. As he spoke he bent a long, thin hand out like a man stroking whiskers. 'We did everything we could to get Mrs Bone released. Comrade Pollitt and I made representations, time and again, to the Hungarian Embassy, without any success. Comrade Pollitt raised this and other cases in Moscow last year. You must remember that this was at the height of the cold war. We didn't want to give our enemies anything on a plate!'

'Even so,' I argued, 'that's no excuse. You should have informed this Executive, and run a public campaign in the *Daily Worker*. Look at how the workers would have respected us now if we had. How can anybody respect people who leave their own comrades to rot in jail, and say nothing about it.'

In front, someone scoffed. This angered me. 'I see nothing at all funny about the fate of a woman who has been a Communist all her life. Even if she wasn't, we should have done everything possible to get her out.' Still no reaction came from the rest. My tirade rolled on. 'We talk so much about the dignity of the individual and how we are out to elevate our working class. How can anyone take us seriously after this. They can hear a woman on the radio tell how she had spent seven years in solitary confinement in a so-called Communist country, for no reason whatever. Will they ever trust us when they know we did nothing to help her?'

This had no effect either. Not a single one of the thirty members of the Executive opened his mouth. And yet, individually, they were as pleasant a crowd as you could meet. Indeed, some of them held their posts as trade-union leaders on the basis of a bluff, hearty, hail-fellow-well-met attitude, that certainly had nothing on the surface, at least, to do with stony cold cells. Others were learned men, lecturers in their universities, some contributors to the leading cultural magazines. And yet here around the bones of one old lady they were dumb. In pursuit of an abstract political concept they were capable of defending the most monstrous barbarities. I knew, because I was one of them and had defended wickedness on the same basis. I had eliminated the individual from the centre of things, and substituted the machine. The aim, the goal, all else was secondary. Indeed, I had taken pride in my ability to subordinate things to the needs of the party. Now at least I was determined to do something. I pressed a resolution.

'I want this executive to publicly condemn the imprisonment of Dr Edith Bone.' The vote was thirty-two against my resolution, one for. Then I tried another tack.

'I want this executive to deplore the conduct of the three comrades in keeping this a secret from the rest of the executive.'

Again thirty-two votes to one.

That night I told my wife I intended resigning from the Executive.

(From *With Breast Expanded*, McGibbon & Kee, London, 1964, pp. 146–9)

Special Work:
Bob Potter

Reading M. B.'s review of *Ultra-Leftism in Britain*, by Betty Reid, reminded me of some experiences I had in the Communist Party twelve to fifteen years ago.

I had joined the CP in 1952 as a member of Clapham North Branch. The Secretary was a civil servant named Douglas Moncrieff. Filled with the enthusiasm of all new recruits, I was equally active in the YCL, and was soon to be elected Secretary of the Wandsworth Branch.

For several years I was one of the few stalwarts who kept the organization going, planning the weekly branch meetings, distributing literature, speaking on street corners, etc., etc.

Early in 1954 Douglas Moncrieff approached me regarding some 'special work' for the Party. He had been co-opted on to a secret security committee, headed by Betty Reid, and answerable only to the Party Secretariat. Its job was to investigate alleged increasing Trotskyite infiltration.

I was asked to go to the open-air meetings held each Saturday afternoon on Clapham Common, especially those addressed by one John Burns (yes, the one and only G. H.), and take a series of photographs of the audience. The exposed films would be sent to King Street for developing, and I would be re-imbursed for the cost of the films.

The object of the exercise was never detailed. I declined.

A year later I joined London Transport as a bus conductor and was posted to Battersea Garage. Within weeks an industrial branch of the CP had been formed, with myself as secretary. Within six months we had ten members, were producing a monthly six-page bulletin, which sold over one hundred copies each edition, and I was running as a Communist candidate in the local elections, sponsored by the bus branch.

At that year's Area Conference (I don't think the same local organization functions today) the Area Secretary, Joe Bent, singled out Battersea Garage bus group as a shining example for all to follow.

Meanwhile, there was considerable dissension in the Party nationally on the issue of democratic centralism. Comrades at all levels were complaining of the lack of open discussions. The dissatisfaction was such that the leadership was forced to act, and a special commission was set up to inquire into 'Inner-Party Democracy'. All were encouraged to submit statements to the commission. 'Address your comments to the Commission Chairman, Betty Reid!'

To me, the appointment of Betty Reid, Chief of the Secret Security Committee, to a responsible post on this particular body was a blatant insult to the membership. I put this point of view to the bus branch, and we passed a unanimous resolution demanding the removal of Betty Reid. Together with Fred Whelton, I was instructed to carry this resolution to the next Area Committee meeting.

The Area Committee agreed the matter should be placed on the agenda of the next Area membership meeting.

Then, at the eleventh hour we were approached by Peter Maxwell, Area Chairman. The matter had been re-discussed by the 'Area Secretariat', who had referred the matter to Party Centre (in the person of Bill Laughlan). To hold a public discussion on the Party Security Organization would do irreparable damage to the Party. Permission to discuss it before the Area membership was withdrawn, and we were warned against trying to raise it under 'any other business'.

Fred and I reported back to the bus branch. We all resigned from the Communist Party.

A month or two later the workers of Budapest took up arms against *their* Betty Reids, and all over the world millions more left the ranks. But apparently Betty Reid goes marching on with her ever decreasing little band of followers.

(From *Solidarity*, Vol. 6, No. 2, 13 November 1969)

The Wortley Hall Conference:
Peter Fryer

Opening the conference of Socialist Forums held at Wortley Hall, near Sheffield, on 27–28 April, KEN ALEXANDER said it was not an attempt to set up a new political party, but a means by which those on the Left in the Labour movement could exchange ideas on policy and organization.

Ex-Communist Party members of fairly recent vintage, 'rebel' Communists, Labour Party members and representatives of other groups were present. He appealed for a certain amount of restraint to be shown.

MARXISM UNIMPAIRED

PROFESSOR HYMAN LEVY, whose subject was 'Why Marxism is Unimpaired', said Marxism was in a process of development. In that sense he was a 'revisionist'. But there were certain principles which had not been subject to change. . .

MERCIA EMMERSON (Islington) said one of the things that made her join the Communist Party was the recognition of working-class values, that there was no such thing as absolute values. The danger lay in a party regarding itself as the fount of wisdom and condemning those who questioned that as 'objectively' counter-revolutionary. Were there not absolute humanitarian values? The 'traitor' of today was rehabilitated twenty years afterwards.

JIM ROCHE (Leeds) said the working class needed truth. Marxism had been distorted by those who denied it to them. He believed there were proletarian values – on the question of blacklegs for example. There were standards of proletarian conduct that had been distorted.

KEN COATES (Nottingham) said Marxism was inseparable from struggle. Therefore the task of those present was to go forward to build a Marxist party. It could not be done today or tomorrow. The Communist Party leaders had betrayed exactly the things they claimed to uphold: they had impaired the most fundamental value of Marxism, the class struggle, because they were prepared to make a deal.

RAYA LEVIN (London) said that to the extent the Soviet Union had not achieved a classless society to that extent the moral values of the proletariat had been distorted. A Marxist analysis of the Soviet Union involved an analysis of why a classless society had not been achieved there.

PETER WORSLEY (Hull) said that for a long time it was denied that there were any contradictions in the Soviet Union, but they had to start analysing what the contradictions were. He looked at Marxism as a tool. But there had not been much Marxist analysis in the last few decades. 'The sort of analysis that Deutscher and Trotsky have made, the kind of new fresh analysis we must make of the class changes in our own country: these things have hardly been touched on,' he said. 'There has just been a repetition of what Lenin said fifty years ago, and an acceptance of the Soviet handout – except for people like Trotsky.' They must start from the beginning and make a critical re-analysis.

TOM KAISER (Sheffield) said the officials of the Communist Party were prepared to see their organization disintegrate rather than give up power. They thought they knew what was best for the mass of the people.

ADRIAN GASTER (Wolverhampton) thought that what happened in the Soviet Union was inevitable, but agreed that their task was to analyse what went on there and find out the practical limits which would condition the kind of socialism we got here.

JOHN DANIELS (Nottingham) said one of the things he had learned was to study the sources, including Trotsky, who devoted a great deal of attention to finding a Marxist explanation of developments in the Soviet Union. They must study not only the rise of the Stalinist bureaucracy but the rise of all bureaucracies in the Labour movement.

DICK GOSS (London) said things went wrong in Russia not because they lacked beautiful ideals but because they oversimplified their economic tasks and did not take the best from capitalism.

ALAN LAMOND (London) said the question of the dictatorship of the proletariat and the theory of the state had also to be examined. On many points of fact and interpretation Marxists had been wrong and other people right. Marxism had proved to be a defective tool in the analysis of history in the past forty years. He did not think the Trotskyist interpretation of the Soviet experience was correct – 'nor is their current policy'. The most crucial of all was the relationship of Marxism to its institutions. Democratic centralism was based on the idea that a Marxist party should be a supreme institution. If the attempt was made to put the principles of Marxism in the hands of a new party they would get stagnation.

H. KENDALL (London) said Professor Levy seemed to have adopted a kind of double standard which allowed him under no circumstances to attack what was wrong in the Soviet Union when it was wrong, but only afterwards.

BERT WYNN (Derbyshire) said their biggest mistake as Marxists had been to dogmatize about the breakdown of capitalism, instead of paying due regard to the victories the British working class had already won because of its strength.

JACK BRITZ (London) said Lamond had given no reasons for Marxism being wrong. They could all sit back and agree about historical materialism, but what about the class struggle under capitalism? What about the state machine?

HAROLD SILVER (Hull) said that by denying fundamental humanist concepts and by supporting the Soviet Union without knowing the full facts, Communists had cut themselves off from the possibility of acting in a truly Marxist way.

ERIC HEFFER (Liverpool) said in order to protect the interests of the bureaucracy in the Soviet Union the Stalinists had been prepared to hold back the class struggle in country after country throughout the world. 'Let us get down to the real task of rebuilding the movement, particularly in Britain, so that we can create a genuine Marxist movement,' he said.

JOHN SAVILLE (Hull) said they must stop talking hot air and build a body of Marxist ideas that meant something to the British working class. That implied studying our own working-class movement and its history, about which far too little was known. 'We have not done anything yet to analyse our economy over the last thirty years. There is nobody here who can give an analysis of exactly how the working class are robbed by the Welfare State. We have not started yet to apply our Marxist tools of analysis to our contemporary society.'

M. HAMILTON (Leeds) said Professor Levy should have stated exactly what he meant by Marxism. Marxism was both a body of theory and a method. The fundamental concept of Marxism was the application of scientific method to the problems of society. 'A scientist never says his scientific method is wrong. You test your theories in practice. In so far as it is possible to apply the scientific method to the problems we are faced with that is the only way we can tackle it.'

Replying to the discussion, Professor Levy said it was a peculiar thing that the conference had concentrated on ethical issues. This was a symptom both of the type of gathering and of the situation in which they met. 'You must not ask too much of Marxism in predicting the course of events,' he added.

LESSONS OF THE STALIN ERA

Opening a discussion on 'Lessons of the Stalin Era' another speaker stressed the importance of a fresh study of the history of the Soviet Union and of the Communist International.

'If we have a feeling of solidarity with the Soviet people,' the speaker concluded, 'we cannot show them better than by very honestly and frankly coming out over such things as the events in Hungary. The spirit of the October Revolution is inseparable from a policy of evaluating in an independent Marxist way what is happening there and speaking our minds quite independently.'

JERRY DAWSON (Merseyside Unity Theatre) said dependence on the Soviet Union was best illustrated in the field of culture. How many people had been alienated by the slavish following of Zhdanov?

T. COWAN (London) thought there was a danger of putting Trotsky on a pedestal.

HAROLD RUBEN (London) said Gollan used the word 'revisionism' as a term of abuse. But Stalinism itself was an integral, well-knit system of revisionism. It was a revision of the heart of Marx and Lenin on the nature of the state. This was seen best in Hungary, when the worst condemnation of *Pravda* was that the workers' councils had come into collision with the state power. This contemptuous attitude to the working class was the political basis of Stalinism. Its ideological basis was the Big Lie. Its philosophical basis was the substitution of idealism for materialist dialectics.

G. HEALY (London), who said he was expelled from the Communist Party twenty-one years ago for opposing the Moscow trials, called on those who had come into opposition to Stalinism more recently to have a little patience with the enthusiasm of anti-Stalinists of an earlier vintage. 'This is the season for reading books, not burning them,' he said. 'Let us have no label-sticking in advance. Let us get rid of demagogy. Don't put anybody on a "pedestal". Read and study. Examine every point of view.'

Declaring his support for the defence of the Soviet Union against its capitalist enemies, JACK GALE (Leeds) said the real way to defend the Soviet Union was to face up to what was wrong, analyse it and put it in its context: the socialist basis of the economy.

JEFF BARKER (Birmingham) felt there was a danger of throwing the baby out with the bathwater. He was not convinced that the methods used in the Soviet Union to build socialism might not turn out to be historically justified.

JOHN ST JOHN (London) said the cult of the individual was closely tied up with the cult of the party. They needed Marxist analysis of the present as well as the past; there were going to be increased conflicts in the Soviet Union. 'There are forces arising out of the technical and social developments of the Soviet Union which are going to do the job. These people are our allies,' he declared.

DAVID WOOD (Nottingham) said the lecturer had tended to discuss too much what might have been. They must take notice of the tremendous material and cultural achievements of the USSR. He was prepared to give much of the credit for the change in the balance of class forces in the world to the much-maligned Stalin.

JOHN FAIRHEAD (London) said Communists had neglected work on behalf of the colonial liberation movements.

MARTIN FLANNERY (Sheffield) said the economic basis of socialism had been laid in the Soviet Union despite all the bad things that had happened. Khrushchev's revelations had been forced by the movement of the Soviet people, who were 'going to force a lot of other things'. The main failing of the Soviet leadership was a lack of faith in the working class.

In reply, the lecturer said the Soviet bureaucracy was not a ruling class, it had not come to power in the way that ruling classes do. While the bureaucracy might not submit without some rather sharp fights, and it might come to some kind of political revolution, there was no scope for a social revolution.

'This is at the basis of our whole attitude of friendship, plus criticism of the Soviet authorities,' he added.

'We must associate ourselves with the majority of the Soviet people who are struggling by many means, political, literary and others, to bring about an all-important adjustment in the nature of Soviet society.'

WINNING SOCIALISTS

A discussion on 'Winning Socialists' and the future of the Socialist Forum movement was opened by four speakers who had done much to build the movement and organize the conference: Pauline Harrison (Sheffield), Joe Young (London), Lawrence Daly (Fife) and Tom Kaiser (Sheffield).

PAULINE HARRISON said there were 136 people at the conference, about 60 of them from Yorkshire, about 30 from London and about 30 from Lancashire and Cheshire.

JOE YOUNG said the Forum movement had a big part to play, between the opposite poles of Welfare Statism and Stalinism, in the rethinking that the Left needed to engage in. 'We need a kind of movement which is the opposite of the dogmatic approach, of a "line",' he said.

LAWRENCE DALY said they all agreed that the objective was socialism. The question was: what kind of socialism? He believed firmly that the Communist Party was absolutely right to propound the idea of 'The British Road to Socialism'. But it never had the intention of carrying it out. They could not solve their problems by going back to Lenin or anybody else. It was living thinkers who had to supply the answers to today's problems. Emotional fanaticism expressed in a sectarian form was one of the biggest obstacles to the advance of socialism.

TOM KAISER opposed the formation of anything that would resemble a new political party. The role of the Forums was not to create a new centre of political power but to stimulate a new climate of socialist opinion. They would thereby stimulate activity through the whole Labour movement. This was more important than membership or the search for a mass party.

PETER FRYER (London) said a new Marxist party would be premature – a vanguard with no one following it. He believed that Marxists should enter the Labour Party because that was where the workers were, and where experience in leadership could be gained. At the same time the Forums had an important part to play in the field of ideas and controversy.

ROYDEN HARRISON (Sheffield) said there was only one decision the conference should take, and that was that the discussion should go on. The Forum movement needed a journal. The editorial boards of the two Forum journals, published in London and Sheffield, had met and agreed to amalgamate.

RALPH SAMUEL (London) said the Forums could not be primarily concerned with what happened in the Communist Party. The sooner the Forum movement had within it Left Labour people who were militant and did not give in to Fabianism the sooner it would get away from this type of introspection. They should integrate themselves as much as possible with the Labour left wing.

EDWARD THOMPSON (Halifax) said they must start from real people: the British people, the colonial peoples, the whole of humanity under the threat of world war. Their political positions were not derived from the statement of principles alone. 'For us to set up Forums which ignore people who think themselves socialists is to cut ourselves off from hundreds of thousands of people. Therefore I think the Forums must orientate themselves towards the Labour movement.' There were hundreds of forms of activity which did not depend on joining a party or taking up an attitude.

RAYMOND CHALLINOR (Stoke-on-Trent) said the question was how best they could influence members of the working class. They must have some publication which reflected their common views. Only through an interchange of ideas could they hope to break down the barriers which past sectarianism had raised.

PADDY MACMAHON (London) said the interests of the working-class comrades and the intellectual comrades must fuse. Both had a contribution to make. It was wrong to think that the workers were not interested in ideas. Unless the Forums made provision for the participation of industrial workers they would not win them. They must continue to iron out their differences and so build an effective movement. The working class did not look on parties as hobbies, they looked on them as tools to help them achieve their class aims. The Forums should try to help the ferment of discussions going on inside the Communist Parties.

JOHNNIE MCLOUGHLIN (West Ham) said this gathering arose on the anvil of world communism. It was the first large attempt to create a really organized movement of the 'Marxist anti-Stalinist Left'. The key question was the conquest of power by the working class. He himself remained in the Communist Party because he believed that in that party was the largest number of people who could deal hammer-blows at the capitalist system. The Labour Party had not got and could not have factory organization. The Communist Party branch at Briggs was of great value to the workers there. The workers' movement could be built only on clarity of ideas. He thought a Marxist workers' party would be built, and he believed that it still could be done within the Communist Party. 'I urge comrades to fight within the party,' he added.

MICHAEL SEGAL (London) said that there was a danger of having nothing at all within a couple of months if they did not organize. On the other hand if they adopted a programme and formed a party there was a danger of becoming one more little sect, and he was not interested in that. They should set up a national liaison committee and prepare for a further conference attended by elected representatives from all over the country – a national conference of the Left to discuss the whole range of problems that concerned the British working class.

MERCIA EMMERSON suggested that industrial comrades and economists form a study circle to thrash out a Marxist analysis of the development of present-day capitalism, and produce a sort of discussion pamphlet. Perhaps the Trotskyists could also contribute. 'If we cannot contribute this original thinking we are doomed,' she said.

The proposal for the setting-up of a national co-ordinating committee was carried unanimously.

Winding up the conference, John St John said there was general agreement that they did not want to set up a new party. But even if they did not have a platform there might emerge a recognized viewpoint, just as the Left Book Club had a viewpoint in the thirties.

Referring to the 'wonderful spirit of co-existence' which had manifested itself at the conference, Mr St John quoted Galileo as saying that the art of doubt was the only progressive art. That was something they might take to heart.

Between the various groups of Trotskyists, the various vintages of ex-Communists, there could be agreement – or at least friendly discussion. The proceedings had given them reason to be hopeful and encouraged.

A vote of thanks to the organizers of the conference was moved by Edward Thompson.

(From the *Newsletter*, 10 May 1957)

The Fife Socialist League:
Lawrence Daly

The defection of 10,000 members (30 per cent of the total) from the British Communist Party in 1956–8 is already described as 'the revolt of the intellectuals'; sometimes by those same historians who claim that the intellectuals formed only a tiny minority of the CP's membership!

The contradiction is obvious. The bulk of the dissenters were industrial workers, though their dissent was more articulately expressed by those intellectuals (John Saville, E. P. Thompson, Christopher Hill, etc.) who were determined that the Party must abandon its blind loyalty to the Soviet leaders. In industrial West Fife the CP admitted a drop of 25 per cent in membership. Not the least of King Street's crimes was the fact that most of them vowed 'never again' and disappeared from political life. Others believed that the CP's betrayal of socialist principles made the need for a genuine socialist organization all the more urgent. They looked at the Labour Party and, in West Fife at least, could not see any possibility of its being won for a socialist programme.

In most areas it was aged and declining. Young people would simply not join it. It was firmly in the grip of a right wing which supported NATO and the Bomb. Its MP, W. W. Hamilton, had drafted for it the only constituency party resolution on the 1954 Labour Party Conference agenda supporting German rearmament. Economy cuts were enforced by Labour-controlled local authorities to help Attlee's increased armaments programme in 1951, and after.

In these circumstances we decided that the formation of a Fife Socialist League was necessary to conduct analytical, educational and propaganda work, free from the restrictions imposed by the Labour and CP machines. The foundation meeting was held in February 1957, but informal discussions and activities had been taking place since June 1956. In December 1956 we had organized a public meeting for Peter Fryer in the mining town of Lochgelly, and we sold his book, *Hungarian Tragedy*, and his pamphlet, *The CP and Hungary*. In August, I and another ex-member had addressed a packed meeting of miners in Lochore on the reasons for our resignation. We had read, sold and discussed the three issues of the *Reasoner* in 1956 and felt attracted by its ideas, more so than by P. Fryer's subsequent *Newsletter*, which eventually became the open organ of the Trotskyist Socialist

Labour League. In March 1957 we adopted a League constitution which declared the building of democratic socialism to be our basic aim. For the next twelve months we were very much pre-occupied with the continued crisis in the CP, using the *New Reasoner* and, to a lesser extent, the *Newsletter*, to develop our case.

As the 1958 local elections approached, however, we began to look seriously at the possibility of an electoral challenge to the Labour/Communist tradition in the heart of the West Fife coalfield. My own division, Ballingry, the largest in the country, seemed the natural choice. I had already been defeated twice by Labour, as a Communist candidate, in straight fights, but had obtained a big vote. We invited a number of workers and housewives, who had never belonged to any political party, to assist us and we received an encouraging response. We entered the fray to the jeers of both the Labour and Communist Parties. A new CP candidate was also standing. The Labour County Councillor jubilantly forecast an overwhelming victory, thinking that the Left vote was hopelessly split. The CP reached the same conclusion and accused us of giving the right wing a walk-over. Opinion in the League was divided. The trained dialectitians cautiously forecast either a narrow defeat or (less likely) a narrow victory. The 'inexperienced' new recruits declared that we would win comfortably. The result was astounding. The League got 1,085 votes, Labour 525, and the CP 197. The CP could console itself with the knowledge that it took the District Council seat from Labour by a narrow margin in a straight fight and that it had brought off the double in another village a few miles away.

This demonstrated not only the depth of the workers' disgust with the Labour Party but also their readiness to choose an alternative where Tory candidates could not reap the advantage from a split vote.

Since May 1958, the League has held a public meeting in Ballingry every six months, on council affairs, at which I report back and invite suggestions and criticism. Prior to the meeting we issue to every tenant a bulletin indicating some of the councillor's work over the previous six months and spot-lighting problems that still require to be solved. We realized, of course, that nothing less than a total socialist offensive on a national scale was needed if the future of the people of Fife was to be assured. We had fought the election on a policy which demanded unilateral nuclear disarmament, extended public ownership and more democracy in local government. For this reason we felt it necessary to develop our association with those socialists gathered around the *New Reasoner*. And for the same reason we decided to contest the West Fife constituency in the 1959 General Election. We held pit-head meetings in protest against the Nagy execution in June 1958, and felt no qualms about opposing the CP, which had held the seat from 1935 to 1950, and had been the only 'Left' alternative to date. We appealed to our friends of the New Left to give us their assistance, and many of them did so, financially and otherwise. (Their reasons have been outlined by John Saville in *New Reasoner* No. 10.) Others considered that in principle they could not support a fight against the Labour Party, especially since it might help the Tories.

Many electors in West Fife had the same doubts, though a Tory victory in the constituency was virtually impossible as the anti-Tory vote was usually three to one. Swamped by its opponents numerically and financially, the League nevertheless fought with tremendous enthusiasm. Its members and its new friends, students, lecturers, etc., campaigned alongside each other in a spirit of mutual understanding and dedication. Against Toryism and the acquisitive society; against Gaitskellism and NATO; against King Street and mental servitude. We received a friendly reception from the electors. 4,886 of them overcame their 'split vote' fear and supported the League. We displaced the CP, its vote in this one-time stronghold going down to 3,828. Despite Labour's 25,000 votes, the Labour Party knew that only the presence of a Tory candidate prevented a much stronger expression of the West Fife people's opposition to the MP and the policies he has supported. Since the election, Mr Hamilton has announced his conversion to unilateralism, while reaffirming his constitutional loyalty to Mr Gaitskell! Winds of change blow in strange corners.

In December 1959, the League adopted new rules raising full membership fees to 6d. weekly and permitting associate membership for socialists outside Fife at 10s. per year. Associates have no voting power but receive League publications free, are kept informed of activities and can participate in all policy discussions by attendance at meetings or by correspondence. In February 1960, the first number of the *Socialist*, the League's monthly journal, appeared. In March a policy declaration was adopted which restated our support for unilateralism, public ownership, industrial democracy and self-government for Scotland in Scottish Affairs. Visiting speakers in recent months have dealt with the Mining Crisis (Ken Alexander), Scottish Self-Government (Hamish Henderson), Revolution (E. P. Thompson) and Unilateralism (Mervyn Jones). On Saturday, 7 May, a League contingent participated in the all-Scottish unilateralist demonstration through the streets of Glasgow. We are selling *New Left Review*, New Left Pamphlets including *Britain without the Bomb*, and other New Left literature.

The recent municipal election results in West Fife emphasize the need for a rapid growth of the League. In militant Cowdenbeath, the 'Independents' have taken control because the workers can no longer tolerate Labour Group bureaucracy. In Lochgelly, expelled Labour candidates topped the poll against official Labour candidates, in a split which arose over personalities rather than policies, but the expulsions were condemned as 'dictatorship' by the voters. (These towns are just outside the West Fife constituency.) In the smaller mining villages this trend may express itself next year in support of local CP candidates at the triennial County and District elections, or, in those villages where there has never been a 'Communist' tradition, 'Independents' will be encouraged to come forward. The League hopes to meet the situation with a number of candidates. During the summer months we aim to conduct socialist propaganda throughout the area by leaflet and open-air meetings. We made a start recently with pit-head and street meetings on the Sharpeville massacre and the Boycott. We are, of course, acutely conscious of our weakness, in size, organization, finance and political clarity. But we are striving to overcome these difficulties and are confident of doing so, in discussion and action, together with our growing number of friends in the New Left. Our electoral support, so far, encourages us in the belief that we represent the future of the socialist movement in Fife.

(From the *New Left Review*, No. 4, July–August, 1960)

A Communist Salute:
Edward Thompson and John Saville

We are, in origin, a Communist journal: a journal of the democratic Communist opposition. We have readers, not only in Britain but scattered across the world, who have come with us along the same tradition.

When we commenced publication, in our duplicated form in 1956, the Communist movement was in a shambles of intellectual disgrace and moral collapse. Some observers saw our journal as a last bridge by which deluded innocents might evacuate the illusions of Marxism, and 're-habilitate' themselves in conventional capitalist politics. Who knows? A Crossman, a Dennis Healey, a Strachey or a Stephen Spender of the future might be found among our ranks.

We never looked for that kind of re-habilitation. Rather, we sought to re-habilitate the rational, humane and libertarian strand within the Communist tradition, with which men of great courage and honour – from Tom Mann to Ralph Fox – have been identified; a tradition which the elect of King Street have brought into shifty disrepute.

We never thought of our journal as a bridge. We thought, perhaps, at first, of it as a last stand amid a general rout. Since that time we have altered some opinions. We tend to see 'Marxism' less as a self-sufficient system, more as a major creative influence within a wider socialist tradition.

But we still have no desire to disown our debt to the Communist tradition. For all its confusion, its mixed motives, its moral amnesia and doctrinal arrogance, it was the major carrier of humanist aspirations in Britain in the thirties and early forties; it brought professional and industrial workers into a kind of association unique in the labour movement at that time; and it stimulated forms of organization and collective intellectual endeavour from which the younger generation of socialists may still be able to learn.

We would like to feel that this journal has been, not the bridge for an evacuation, but the point of junction at which this valid part of the Communist tradition has been transmitted to a new socialist generation which did not have to face the dilemmas of the thirties and the forties, and which is, perhaps, a little too scornful of those who did.

And since our tradition merges now with this younger socialist tradition, and will no longer appear as something distinct, we take, for the last time, a Communist leave of our old comrades:

A salute to our Polish comrades, who found the way, and who set alight once more the humanist flame within the Communist world!

A salute to Tibor Dery, still in his Hungarian gaol!

A salute to Wolfgang Harich, imprisoned in East Germany!

A salute to our French comrades who have taken their places in building the French New Left!

A salute to those comrades in Britain who have fought with us every inch of the way!

To adapt the words of Tom Mann, we hope to grow more dangerous as we grow more old.

(Editorial in the last issue of the *Reasoner* before its amalgamation with the *Universities and Left Review* into the *New Left Review*, Spring, 1960)

Revolutionary Traditions: Tony Cliff

Now, first of all, I'll not be as short as all that, I'm sorry to say. Second of all, there's quite a danger that I'll cover many things that everybody knows, but still I think they'll have to be summed up and I think there are three reasons that personally I'm terribly interested in this subject. Reason number one is simply the fact that we moved into much more activism and there'll be a danger that we'll become mindless militants. It's true that theory without action is sterile, but activity without theory is blind. Reason number two is simply that the British labour movement has such terrible traditions as regards theory that it's very important to fight against this tradition. Third of all because on the left we are quite an attractive proposition, there's really no competition, so to say, people would join us because there is nothing better so to say, and when reading letters by Roger Cummings and Ignatius Tsong it looks as if people didn't know that there was thirty years of a debate on the subject of socialism in one country, as if the whole thing was dead, and it becomes absolutely clear that these things will have to be hammered up on the question of really what our traditions are. Starting from this point I must make clear about the question of traditions. Traditions sound as though they are a subject for a Conservative Party conference. Now the truth is this, that when you look at Marxism, if Marx and Engels defined in the *Communist Manifesto* the Communists as those that generalized the movement and the experience of the working class over time and over countries, then of necessity the question of tradition is central to it. We have to learn that the Paris commune of 1871, the lessons of the Paris Commune, are as alive today in 1967 as they were in 1871, but of course, because the truth is always concrete and because Marxism therefore has always to be bloomin' concrete, always practical, has to change all of the time. Unless it changes it's bloomin' dead, and that's why on the one hand you have to stick to tradition but on the other hand you have to stick to growth. This dialectical relation is central to the whole thing. Those that simply speak in the name of tradition are bloody useless, because what really happens happened like the German Social Democrats in 1914 – they quoted Marx and Engels from 1848. Marx and Engels said in 1848, said, 'Yes, we in Germany should carry the battle against Tsarist Russia,' and the Social Democrats got up in 1914 and said, as Marx and Engels said, 'We have to carry the battle against Tsarist Russia' and that's why they supported the war in 1914. And you find the same experience repeats itself with the Mensheviks in Russia quoting Marx and Engels, that the backward countries have to follow in the footsteps of the advanced countries, as Marx said in the introduction of the first volume of *Capital*, and so on and so on and so on. In other words the danger of tradition is the danger of death; on the other hand the danger of no tradition is also death, because the whole idea of Marxism is really the idea of generalization from the experience of the struggle. Therefore what I will say about the IS Group's tradition is a very simple one – is that in reality we have changed all the time, and thank heaven for that. How much we owe to people that came before us is fantastic and as well when I quite often say 'When you sit on the shoulders of a giant you see quite far', and I think you'd also look quite tall, and this is really what happens and our basic ideas are taken really from an old old revolutionary tradition and this is what I'll try to develop now.

I'll try to go through every idea that we're talking about and try to show the roots – where did it come from? Well, let's start from when we broke from traditional Trotskyism. Now we broke on one simple thing on the Russian question. This was the central issue of the time. Now what did we accept from Trotsky? We accepted from Trotsky first of all that the working class is the agent of the socialist revolution, that the working class is the subject, not the object, but the subject of the socialist revolution, that the criterion to every change in society is what role the working class is playing actively in it. That's what was so idiotic in the letter of Ignatius Tsong and Roger Cummings, because they didn't ask what was the role of the workers. I don't care whether the workers have a high standard of living or a low standard of living. It's important what the workers are doing in the whole game. What is their role, that's the first thing that we took from Trotsky straight. The second thing we took from Trotsky straight is opposition to all rising bureaucracies. Thirdly we took from Trotsky the theory of the impossibility of socialism in one country. The fact that the pressure of world capitalism distorts development in every workers' state. In this case the Russian Workers' State. We also accepted from Trotsky the question of the international nature of the revolution. Those things we accepted from him. Now what were the defects, where we didn't agree – and it is quite important to see to what extent you are growing on the shoulders of somebody quite tall. Because the thing is this, there's a danger that somebody makes a picture and you afterwards come and make a stroke next to the picture; he makes a picture, a beautiful picture, of something – a tree – and you come and make a stroke next to it and say, 'Look how original I am, my good God! everything started from me, look at the stroke. Wasn't it original?' Yes, but there was also a tree in the picture, remember that, and I'm not suddenly speaking in the name of modesty – I'm not modest at all but coming simply to have a sense of historical proportions and historical perspective. Now what we thought was wrong with Trotsky was this, that if it was true that the working class was the agent of the socialist revolution then the form of property is a bloody stupid criterion for deciding whether a state is a workers' state or not, because the worker as an active element in society doesn't give a damn about the form of property. What the worker as an active agent cares about is the relations in production, in other words what place the worker is in the process of production; whether the worker comes to a state enterprise like the railways or private enterprise like ICI it doesn't come in relation to it as regards the form of property. But he doesn't come and say I sell you my labour power because it is private, or in the other case I will sell you my labour power because it is the state. No, no. The form of property doesn't appear at all to the working class as an active agent in society and therefore he says the form of property is not a criterion that decides the nature of the state. Trotsky was not consistent enough in his own criteria of approach. Second of all, planning is not a criterion of judging the nature of the state because the question is who is being planned and who is doing the planning, not simply planning in the abstract if you speak about in terms of active agency of the working class, and therefore we say quite simply that the form of property shouldn't decide whether Russia is a workers' state or not a workers' state. Third of all, if we speak about internationalism then international capitalism not only distorts but international capitalism determines the laws of motion of the economy in every chunk of the international economy. What I mean by that, I mean that perhaps the pressure of Marks and Spencer over the Co-op is not only distorting the internal relations of the Co-op, but dictating the basic decisions of the Co-op, from wages policy, to advertising policy, to all the rest of it. And that's why we came and said, 'It's not good enough to come and say Russia is distorted under the pressure of world capitalism,' we have to come and say, 'What are the laws of motion of the economy of Russia when you look at world capitalism as the decisive one?' and we said quite simply that the decisive thing that accumulation is the motive force in every economy in the world including the Russian economy. Above all in the Russian economy, because of its backwardness and therefore of its incapacity to face world capitalism unless it imitates world capitalism. This is the payment of backwardness when it faces something much mightier than them. You see that many of those things are simply elementary things. The comrades have heard it and perhaps my summing up is not very useful, but I think it is quite important to be absolutely clear to what extent we really started from a developed idea that started long before us. For years and years and years the Bolshevik Party fought on the question of workers' power and then the question of workers' control and the question of the distortions and the fight against bureaucracy etc. and to what extent our development was a development of the same thing and not simply starting without any roots and without any connection with the past, and of course the central thing is quite simply that we came to the conclusion that workers' control is the decisive thing in evaluating a workers' state. That workers can get many many things from the top, they can get reforms, the cow can get extra grass, the farmer can give her extra hay. One thing the farmer will never give is the control over the shed. This has to be taken, and therefore a workers' state is a state where the workers control their destiny. It cannot be given to them, they have to do it themselves. Once you abolish the element of workers' control you abolish the essence of the workers' state. This was really the first theoretical thing we were faced with and we are still with it, and when we are faced with new phenomena and new backward countries in the process of industrialization we use the same criterion and the same general approach, and therefore for us it is not a surprise when what happened to Nkrumah, whatever happens in China, it is not a surprise we use the same basic method. The question of the international nature of capitalism, the question of the laws of motion of capitalism that emphasizes the capital accumulation to subordinate everything to it, and the fact that workers' power cannot exist unless you change completely the rules of the game, the whole rules of the economy etc.

From this we went to another problem: you know we are not living in Russia and whether you like it or not we can't face straightforward in conflict with the Russian rulers because we are not facing them. What we are facing are the rulers of the West. Now here we face a very difficult problem. You see, by tradition, the Marxist tradition was a very simple one. We had slumps every ten years from 1817 onwards – 1827, 1837, 1847/8, 1857 and so on. We had slumps every time and we were absolutely convinced that the slumps would become deeper and the booms would become shallower. Came the end of the Second World War we had to face the simple fact, what to say. Should we say like practically all the Marxists, in inverted commas or not in inverted commas, said that the slump was around the corner. For example, the *Daily Worker* spoke of a million unemployed. You read *Tribune* when the Tories won in 1951, 'millions of unemployed – the thirties are repeated – coming back because of the victory of the Tories'. Then of course there were even the funniest ones of course were the Revolutionary Communist Party, the predecessor of the SLL. They came in 1945 with a very clear statement saying that anybody who believes that there will be only three million unemployed in the immediate future is suffering from reformist illusions, in other words it won't be three million it will be much more. If you say only three millions you are completely whitewashing capitalism. And Gerry Healy wrote you need a, the workers need an alarm clock. What for? To get up in the morning to run to the labour exchange. Now this was not the historical fact, this was one perspective. There was another perspective we could face. Simply what the right wing said at the time and the ex-left wing in the form of John Strachey and Harold Laski and G. D. H. Cole. Now in the thirties like good British empiricists what happened yesterday, what happened today will happen tomorrow but more emphasized. You see because quite naturally they know from experience that a boy aged ten is stronger than a baby aged one and a man aged twenty is stronger than a boy aged ten they should have drawn a simple conclusion that a man aged 100 must be as strong as Samson. Now British empiricism prevents them from doing that. They know that people die at the age of 100 or a little bit earlier. But in the case of British capitalism the picture is different. Therefore in the thirties everything was terrible, unemployment, fascism, war, etc. You read the Strachey: capitalism means war, capitalism means fascism, capitalism means unemployment. Marvellous clear consistent picture. Then, thanks to good old Adolph Hitler, or I don't know exactly whom, we got full employment in 1939 and children of the war and this is a fact, British children who grew during the war were much better fed than the children who grew during the thirties. So the picture changed now. Today is pink, tomorrow pinker. Tomorrow will be nicer than today. Capitalism is not in decline any more, everything is marvellous in the garden. So we faced a very serious theoretical problem on the one hand: we couldn't accept a thing that is breaking straightaway into your face that there are five or six or seven million unemployed in the streets. Simply statistics deny it.

(From a speech at Wortley Hall, Sheffield, 22 April 1967, to an aggregate meeting of the International Socialism group)

Chapter 2
Don't You Hear
The H-Bombs' Thunder?

(1)
Don't you hear the H-bombs' thunder
Echo like the crack of doom?
While they rend the skies asunder
Fall-out makes the earth a tomb.
Do you want your homes to tumble,
Rise in smoke towards the sky?
Will you let your cities crumble,
Will you see your children die?

Chorus:
Men and women, stand together.
Do not heed the men of war.
Make your minds up now or never,
Ban the bomb for evermore.

(2)
Tell the leaders of the nations
Make the whole wide world take heed
Poison from the radiations
Strikes at every race and creed.
Must you put mankind in danger,
Murder folk in distant lands?
Will you bring death to a stranger,
Have his blood upon your hands?

(3)
Shall we lay the world in ruin?
Only you can make the choice.
Stop and think of what you're doing.
Join the march and raise your voice.
Time is short; we must be speedy.
We can see the hungry filled,
House the homeless, help the needy,
Shall we blast, or shall we build?

('The H-Bombs' Thunder', words by JOHN BRUNNER. Tune: 'Miners' Life
    Guard')

I gave a letter to the postman,
He put it in his sack.
But by early next morning
He brought my letter back.
        She wrote upon it,
Return to Sender.
Address unknown.
No such number.
No such zone.

('Return to Sender', ELVIS PRESLEY. No. 1 in the top 20 during the Cuban
    missile crisis)

The Campaign for Nuclear Disarmament was born not with a bang but with a whimper. People rejecting nuclear weapons on principle had been unsuccessfully pottering around for at least ten years before the campaign took off in 1958 with the Cold War almost over. Nuclear power had been brandished against the already surrendering Japanese cities of Hiroshima and Nagasaki in 1945 as half-experiment and half-demonstration of a new era of American power. And from 1947, until Russia herself exploded her first bomb in 1953, Communist-led peace movements organized energetic campaigns to outlaw nuclear weapons, obtaining over one million British signatures for the Stockholm peace appeal.* Within the Labour Party the Left's most successful challenge to the platform was on the issue of rearmament of West Germany, that uphill and mutedly anti-imperialist battle which dogged the fifties. This campaign revived the older loyalties of the Popular Front and anti-fascism in Bevanite bosoms and was often successful in wielding big constituency and union block votes against the leadership's Cold War wrath. Sixty-two Labour MPs defied the whip in voting against the 1955 Defence White Paper which openly committed Britain to building its own 'independent nuclear deterrent' (probably making official a decision taken by Attlee long before 1948). And even after Bevan's defection to the Gaitskell establishment, what remained of the Bevanites, grouped now in Victory for Socialism, continued to denounce the bomb their ex-leader had embraced.

Quite separate from this marshalling of foreign-policy disloyalty within the Labour Party there existed a far older pacifist and religious objection to nuclear weaponry as an extreme example of the general horror of war. At its most likeable it was the sombre decency of *Peace News*, then a vegetarian tabloid with a Quaker emphasis on active witness. At its worst it was the dog-collared sanctimoniousness of broad-

*The *Daily Worker* has however the dubious honour of being the only British newspaper to call for the use of nuclear bombs in the Second World War. The *Worker* also welcomed editorially the Hiroshima–Nagasaki explosions. (See Ray Challinor, 'Zig-zag: The Communist Party and the Bomb', *Socialist Review*, October 1954.) Orthodox Trotskyists were also enthusiastic about nuclear weapons. If exploded by degenerate or deformed workers' states, this was felt to be of assistance in 'defending socialist property relationships'. A correspondence on this subject in *Tribune* is reproduced in *Socialist Review*, March 1961. One group of Trotskyists argue that nuclear warfare would indeed enhance the chances of building socialism: see, for example, *The Mineworker*; *For Workers' Control of the Mining Industry on the Anti-Capitalist Programme* (organ of the Militant and Revolutionary Miners' Group, Mineworkers' International), 'The Inevitability of the Nuclear War and its Social Consequences', by Tom Fitter, Westoe NUM, Co. Durham. Several sarcastic songs have been written on this subject.

church Anglicanism, with its barely concealed moral smugness and its taste for ethic posturing and nasal pieties. At certain fascinating points this ethical tradition has run across the revolutionary socialist tradition (Tom Mann, for example, was a vegetarian until 'the recognition that however widely food reform might be diffused, it would never provide a cure for the economic evils I deplore').

But the Independent Labour Party, whose fierce commitment to the Glasgow class struggle had in early days co-existed with its non-conformist, teetotal and ethical socialist sniffyness, was now vegetating in abstract utopianism. Fenner Brockway's somewhat saintly anti-imperialism and his taste for personal negotiations with the leaders of various ex-British colonies were about all that remained of its revolutionary socialist origins. And Dick Shepherd's Peace Pledge Union, whose adherents were required to swear 'I renounce war and will never sanction another one', once a mass organization, had been decimated by the Second World War, in which many pacifists eventually elected to serve. But it had been under PPU auspices that small attempts at direct action were taken by pacifists at Aldermaston, Porton and Mildenfield in the early fifties. And these tiny sit-ins, code-named Operation Gandhi, were the first evidence that the rather limp pacifist tradition of the thirties had turned towards active opposition to war preparations.

The people who founded CND were a perfect blend of labour and Anglican traditions; its Chairman, the pious cleric John Collins, its Secretary, the capable Bevanite organizer Peggy Duff. But the ideas of Operation Gandhi were what, to the Canon's and the Duff's horror, took command of the supporters of the Campaign and swung it, ten years after seventy PPU demonstrators had first sat-in for a few hours in a South Wales army camp, towards an open clash with the state.

The first committee of CND expressed its political ideas. It was to be a lobby of barely radical big-wigs to form an élite pressure group. Collins thought it would be over soon; Clive Jenkins said, 'If we could get the people to do this, it would be a three or six month job.' But the strange alliance which presented itself to the public at the Central Hall on 17 February 1958 had struck political gold. Peggy Duff booked and filled four overflow halls. When A. J. P. Taylor, having described with lurid relish the effect of a nuclear explosion, asked 'Is there anyone here who would want to do this to another human being?' there was a complete hush until he yelled, to thunderous applause, 'Then why are we making the damned things?' Prophetically and quite against the platform's wishes, about a thousand steamed-up members of the audience rushed on Downing Street after the meeting chanting 'Ban the bomb' and 'Eden must go' (he had actually resigned twelve months ago).

The extraordinary scale of the support for such an unlikely leadership as the bombastic don Taylor and the woolly Yorkshire popularist Priestley is a conundrum. The bomb was certainly an extraordinarily powerful symbol, the stupid beauty of its fluffy cloud hovering over its appalling explosive power on impact, and its harvest of leukaemia, still-births and congenital deformities. Most terrifying was the legacy of fallout, that silent, invisible radiation slowly mounting in bone strontium and milk calcium as the tests went on. In the *New Reasoner*, Edward Thompson wrote: 'Strontium 90 is a merciless critic; it penetrates alike the specious rhetoric about a "free community of nations", the romantic longueurs of imperialism in retreat, the flatulent composure of the Fabian "social engineer", the bluff incompetence and moral atrophy of the "political realists".'[*]

It was the facts, until then successfully held back and hidden by ambiguous civil servants and muzzled scientists, which were CND's most effective canvassers. First the realization that the H-bomb was not just a bigger bang but a totally different kind of weapon. Then the slow realization of the immensity of what had actually happened at Hiroshima, spurred by Robert Jungk's book, James Cameron's reporting, John Hoyland's 'Youth Against the Bomb' wall poster, the Committee of 100 leaflet of a Hiroshima-born child too horrible for any printer to reproduce in full. Then, under CND prodding, the full scale of the deception of 'civil defence', that ludicrous assembly of unfilled sandbags and radioactive baked beans, became known. Nor was this process confined merely to exposure journalism. Spies for Peace demonstrated that the country was dotted with 'regional seats of government', bomb shelters for top people, to enable them to administer the charred remains of those of us who stayed on top. And despite Peggy Duff's attempt to wave people on to refreshments at Knowl Hill, thousands of Easter marchers actually visited a brick and metal nuclear bomb shelter deep in the pretty Berkshire countryside.

CND had such emotional power because it forced people to face what they and their leaders would rather they didn't. It proved that near village greens were neat grey buildings calmly constructing atom bombs. That behind barbed wire those cheery GIs were guarding control panels where officers were poised over buttons which could

---

[*] Edward Thompson, 'The New Left', *New Reasoner*, 9, Summer 1959.

explode everything. CND managed to persuade all sorts of people that they actually could hear the H-bombs' thunder. And when Bertrand Russell, his lower jaw set into a permanent scowl, said in Trafalgar Square that we would be lucky to be alive in a year's time, the new urgency convinced.

Within weeks of its foundation, CND had found the perfect vehicle for its organized fervour, its awkward mix of gaiety and grimness. It was the Aldermaston March, that moving *tableau vivant* of the Left in the late fifties. To watch it saunter down the grassy Berkshire hills that led into Reading, or across the sandy pine-forested Sunday stretch, was to watch a moving diagram of different traditions which, while apparently jostling amiably and swapping sandwiches, were actually rival contenders for influence in the re-awakening socialist movement. At the front strode the detachments from the high estates of Church, Parliament and Trade Unions, the weary priests, wooden MPs, perhaps a dapper trade-union official talking to an actress. But behind, despite the systematizing efforts of marshals who had each year more complicated instructions to tidy people into colours and regions, the march soon broke down into some sort of political time machine where Woodcraft Folk marched between Mothers Against War and the Esperantists, where Community Party banners of re-armament vintage borne by fierce ladies in sensible shoes swept past stove-in top hats, and where ancient embroidered trade-union banners jousted with tin billies tied to overfilled rucksacks. Within the march were contending moral centres, the decent rain-coated trudge of the Constituency Labour Parties acting to counter-balance the flagrant, be-banjoed hordes of gothic beats (who were always called anarchists by everybody, to the great annoyance of the proper anarchists). The Young Communist League still maintained cultural hegemony over rival youth politicos despite the glares of the Trots marshalling well-drilled Young Socialist squaddies on the final day. But anyway both had a weather eye open for that much anticipated combination of art student and marquee. (I once emerged from a rest-heap in Kidwells Park holding the hand of a girl with red hair and black stockings and green eyes. We hung on all the way to Slough, too surprised to say much and spent the rest of the march avoiding each other.)

At regular intervals there would be a formal tilt between the forces of chaos and revolution and those of order and progress. Peggy Duff in the blue Co-op loudspeaker van would make school-mistressy remarks at the expense of anarchists attempting to take over the Head of the March (as it was known, rather like the Head of the River), while

Quakers and Communists quietly attended to their vacuum flasks and dabbed their blisters. Behind the march swept an unruly group of stragglers who took lorries to the front of the march when no one was looking. Behind them came the conscience of the march, expressing the inherent decency of the organizers, the Elsan and Litter Team, dismantling bogs and forking litter with glum masochism. For, as the 'Advice to Marchers' instructed, 'Don't do anything or wear anything that will distract the attention of the world from the great issues with which we are concerned.'

Alongside it, pick-up trad bands blasted out variations of 'The Saints' and 'Oh, Didn't He Ramble', usually with so little unanimity about time signature as to make the business of being in tune quite superfluous. Although somewhere in the centre a determined figure, often on cornet, could be found remorselessly blazing away at his own authorized version of the tune. Every idiom produces its own sectarianism, and what Gerry Healy is to Trotskyism and John Mayall to blues, so the cornet was to revivalism. Elsewhere folk with guitars casually strummed the chords they had been perfecting since the last Aldermaston. Young Socialist members made up bawdy rhymes about their rivals and church-trained voices sang the CND hymnal in parts. The March was a student movement before its time, mobile sit-in or marching pop festival; in its midst could be found the first embers of the hashish underground and premature members of the Love Generation as well as cadres of forthcoming revolutionary parties.

Through the informal network of CND twined the flowering of poetry, or rather the jovialities of Pete Brown, the horn-rimmed visions of Horovitz, and the agonizing of Mitchell (the Beat Betjeman), whose public poetry readings of the early sixties, especially around *New Departures* magazine, were an early step towards the revival of political art in post-war Britain. The all-women meetings (excluding male reporters) of Women Against the Bomb were a first signal of the revival of a liberal feminism. It was the unavoidable meeting point between the old loyalists of Labour and Communist Parties and the quarrelsome sectaries of a new Left, a breeding ground for every tendency on the Left and a paper seller's delight.

To parents who were suspicious about politics anyway it offered a decent British sort of protest. What other political campaign would distribute a leaflet instructing you to 'carry with you on the March, in a bag or haversack; a mackintosh coat and hat. Eating utensils and a MUG. Some food or money to buy it. AND DON'T FORGET THE MUG!' and actually have a Medical Officer who advised: 'Do wear sensible shoes. Do paint your feet with surgical spirit or methylated spirits for a week before the march, but remember that the best training for your feet is plenty of walking.' To young people it promised access to a forbidden zone of promiscuity and abandon and offered a unique chance to thunder up Whitehall screaming defiance at parent, policemen and Parliament. And up and down the country CND branches flowered and fell, often throughout their lifespan entirely unknown to Carthusian Street. Behind hundreds of lapels and on thousands of railway bridges, CND signs were stuck. On Tyneside, 200 young workers met weekly to sing CND folksongs and wear red and black neck scarves actually purchased from the Scout Shop. Organized anarcho-syndicalism restarted in Teesside around a CND-based North-East Anarchist Federation, and Glasgow Young Socialists sent their coach loads to Falcon Field each year, once, in the new mood of protest, hurling inadequate southern pie and chips back at the proprietors of a certain motorway café on the way. It was this unofficial, defiant, often disowned, young rank and file of CND which took naturally to the ideas of direct action which were to dominate the activists after the hammering of unilateralists in the Labour Party and it is very often veterans of these marches who staff the newer political groups which arose out of its and other ashes.

CND AND LABOUR PARTY

The initial rush of CND's ideas almost swamped the Labour Left. And quite quickly CND re-focused the forces of opposition in the Labour Party, gave them a new target and new arguments. Since CND leadership still saw its politics in terms of getting sensible CND-influenced people to the levers of power and was staffed by many veteran Labour lefties, the Labour Party was the obvious political target. In 1958, as CND's political arc continued to rise at phenomenal rates and the first March made the Campaign a national force, the Labour Party came out with a weak statement on defence policy which came under fire from a medley of unilateralist resolutions, probably independently instigated by militants who belonged to both CND and the Labour Party, but due mainly to the astonishing independent growth of the Campaign. As early as 1957 unilateralist motions were commanding support in Conference. That year, such a motion had been seconded by Viv Mendleson, a Socialist Labour League supporter from a Labour Party branch led by Trotskyists, and soon to be hammered out of shape by Transport House for its pains. By 1959, 102 of the 428 resolutions were unilateralist and the platform was coming close to defeat on some aspects of defence extras like bases, over-flying patrols and testing, which found their way onto the agenda. But critics were still muted by the proximity of the election, which delayed and concealed the depth of unilateralist feeling.

After the catastrophic electoral performance by Labour in 1959 the gloves were off. In union after union, spiked by resentment of Gaitskell's self-righteous ineptitude, unilateralist resolutions were passed, often in unions which had been involved in the surge of industrial unrest which followed the slackening of the Tory boom in 1957. The thaw in the unions was probably accomplished by a relatively few officials putting the arithmetic of the block vote into reverse gear and aided by a good deal of passive sympathy among their members towards the mood, if not the political details, of CND. This process gathered speed and weight when the Communist Party announced itself converted to unilateralism in May 1960. Until then, in pursuit of the party line that unilateralism destroyed unity and split the 'peace forces', militants like Abe Moffet were to be found speaking in favour of the official right-wing TUC/Labour Party line against a CND resolution moved by Bert Wynn of the Derbyshire miners. The 1958 Labour Party unilateralist resolution from the Fire Brigade Union was also crushingly defeated by Communist Party administered block votes. But by June 1960 even the General and Municipal Workers' Union had passed a unilateralist resolution. (Peggy Duff likened this to the Daughters of the American Revolution burning their draft cards.) Although this decision was reversed by the efforts of a tireless Tom Williamson and a custom-built Labour Party statement on a 'non-nuclear club' which was promptly abandoned once the vote was reversed, it was clear that in the 1960 Labour Party Conference the block vote was, for once, to add stature to the Left.

The debate itself was an anti-climax. Frank Cousins' speech was especially nerveless. It was Gaitskell, under full frontal attack, who fought. And it was actually Gaitskell, with his own branch of pious obstinacy and his highly effective speech pledging himself to 'Fight, fight and fight again' to reverse the decision, who won at Scarborough. For the victory floodlit the ambiguities of the CND coalition which had almost accidently achieved it. The left MPs and union leaders were surprised by winning, dumbstruck by the venom of Gaitskell's reply and undecided about their next move, but with little stomach for defending an extreme left position. *Tribune*, while enthusiastically hailing CND, had never lost its fascination with Summitry. Crossman designed and Foot and Cousins supported a compromise plan (the Crossman–Padley Initiative) which merely modernized nuclear strategy, retaining NATO and tactical weapons. Having constructed a bridge back to NATO, the Tribunites proceeded to express great indignation when people actually crossed it. The haughty conscience of the *New Statesman* and the incurably élitist *Tribune* both preferred the false unity of anti-Gaitskellism, which led them to support the NATO enthusiast Wilson in the party election for leader, to arguing out the logic of unilateralism.

For in fact the Right won back much support by being clearly more willing than CND itself to spell out the implications of unilateralism. Britain banning the bomb meant the end of NATO. This meant the dissolution of British military allegiance to America, which meant an attack on the domestic economic system from which the alliance arose. And that was something that very few people in CND would face. As Peggy Duff puts it, 'they were basically very British, conservative and rather naïve. They thought banning the bomb was a fairly simple matter and they never recognized the revolution in British politics that it required. They wanted to get rid of the bomb, leave NATO and abandon the American alliance without upsetting the pattern of life in Sutton, Totnes, or Greenwich, SE3.'* For the bomb, as well as being a human and moral issue, was a class and political one. It was not just the supreme symbol of an immoral society, it was part of the logic of a social system in which vast technical power was placed in the political control of competitive, aggressive and uncontrolled ruling classes. The only real alternative to mass murder under class rule was workers' control and popular self-government, and, in the here and now, a real attempt to show the connection between the fight against the bomb and the fight against the boss. But at the time, with such industrial militancy as there was moving away from formal politics rather than towards it, those who insisted on these unpalatable truths were treated as vague utopians or gritty cranks.

The CND leadership, in the name of realism but in a spirit of evasion, began to back down from the firm anti-NATO position forced on them by the Campaign rank and file in 1959. Unilateralism became increasingly viewed by leading Campaigners as some sort of magnificently decent gesture by Britain, who would recover her long-lost moral authority by withdrawing from the web of nuclear terror and lead a flock of newly independent nations to Nirvana. The old Imperial

*Peggy Duff, *Left, Left, Left*, Allison & Busby, 1971, p. 131.

Lion would turn out as a fairy godmother after all. This mood extended from Cousins' 'make England great again' speeches to the *New Left Review*'s tremulous conviction that the 'log-jam' of the Cold War could be deftly unpicked by a British lumberjack's initiative. Phrases were invented to solve the problem. 'Positive neutralism' and 'non-alignment' conjured up pictures of purified small nations. Yugoslavia and Ghana, India and Algeria perhaps might ascend a new non-nuclear path to redemption, spurning the primrose paths of both Kremlin and Pentagon, and conducted by the Good Shepherdess Britannia. It was the politics of a religious water colour and was a tribute more to CND's generosity of sentiment and Sunday-school upbringing than its political acumen. Ten years later a clearer view of modern imperialism and the experience of Cuba, Vietnam and Czechoslovakia have again and again demonstrated how even after some form of revolution it is almost impossible to break clean of the economic clasp of the world powers and their alliances.

Perhaps realizing this at the time, and spurred by CND's utter disorientation in the terrifying week of the Cuba crisis, some strategists within the Campaign began in intention 'realistic' but in practice rightward-drifting experiments with short-term diplomacy. Stuart Hall, who had argued against an anti-NATO commitment within the New Left Club in 1959, on a train from Hull to London produced three interim demands: the withdrawal of nuclear weapons from all territories outside the USA and the USSR, a test-ban treaty and priority for the UN – an attempt, as he claimed, to combine 'utopianism and practicality'. This was extended by the executive to include virtually all CND demands, with the significant exception of withdrawal from NATO, and called 'Steps Towards Peace'. As CND dithered, dreamed or retreated according to taste, Gaitskell, whooped on by the press, begun to demonstrate his grip over the Labour Party's iron apparatus and flabby heart. The Party's political machine, with the enthusiastic support of the Transport House machine-minders, missed no opportunity to damage and weaken the unilateralist cause, from the refusal to endorse parliamentary candidates like Ernie Roberts to the muzzling of Young Socialist branches.

A crucial unofficial organizing arm was the Campaign for Democratic Socialism (CDS), a grouping of frank revisionists, actually founded in annoyance at Gaitskell's backing down on Clause 4, and thus even to his right. It is only now becoming clear the extent to which leading Labour Party revisionists were supported by agencies and foundations under the control of the Central Intelligence Agency. It would not appear that the Labour Right and Gaitskell had actually expected to be defeated on defence again in 1961 and to have to resign. But the hard men of CDS realized not only could he win the return bout on defence but he could use the flush of such a victory to guarantee the permanent right to the M Ps to ignore the Labour Party Conference, to push the Labour Party further away from even the most modest socialist programme and to triumphantly reassert his leadership. Their campaign to reverse the union votes aimed quite specifically at political nobbling – as Bill Rodgers put it daintily 'helping to equip those members of trade unions who wanted to speak at their conference to do so with a certain amount of information behind them'.* Besides actual bribery, CDS organizers could make use of anti-Cousins and anti-T & G feeling in other unions and promise patronage to Labour Party supporters increasingly thirsty for office as Macmillan's effortless confidence begun to disintegrate. Above all, they could appeal for 'unity', which means in the Labour Party 'voting as the leaders tell you to'. Gaitskell won back with confidence in 1961 despite a valiant rearguard action at Conference itself led by Duff. And Gaitskell celebrated his victory and vented his spleen by the skilful proscription of the paper *Keep Left* in the Young Socialists, the disbandment of supporting branches and the attempted expulsion of Russell and his co-sponsors of the World Peace Congress. When heckled in Glasgow by an alliance of Scottish Trots, YCLers and apprentices, Gaitskell called CND 'peanuts'. (Within a week two shipyard apprentices Bobby Campbell and Jim Scott, wrote a political song about the peanuts outburst which was received with rapture by the Gorbals Young Socialists and sung widely in the town. In London a Peanuts Club was opened by CNDers which runs to this day. When interrogated by a Labour Party inquiry as to why they walked out *en masse*, the Scots apprentices disarmingly replied they had all suddenly wished to use the lavatory.)

DIRECT ACTION

The recoil from Labour Party fixated politics among the young hard core of CND started long before Gaitskell's Conference victory. The meaning of the 'Fight, fight and fight again' speech was for them the end of pressure-group politics. The Campaign had argued, explained, pleaded and left the roads of Berkshire as clean as they would want to find them. And when they had finally successfully climbed through the

* William Rodgers, quoted in *The Day Before Yesterday*, by Alan Thompson, Sidgwick & Jackson, 1971, p. 209.

obstacle race of Labour Party democracy, Gaitskell told them to fuck off, told them that the Scarborough vote would be ignored and reversed and that they were peanuts. What is more, the Cuba crisis had further rubbed CNDers' faces in their own ineffectuality when things seemed more urgent than ever before. A few devout constitutionalists anxious to bang their heads on some lost deposits begun to field independent Ban the Bomb candidates. But among the activists of the campaign the initiative swung emphatically in 1961 to direct action under the leadership of the Committee of 100.

Civil disobedience covers a multitude of sins against the state, from mutiny to income-tax refusal. And its pioneers in post-war Britain had originated from those ethical extremists, much reviled by secular socialists, who believe that one should abstain from evil, even if the actual refusal to purchase South African fruit or brown in Spanish sunshine or eat sheep's kidney is, in itself, quite ineffectual. But Operation Gandhi had begun a reinterpretation, by a new generation of pacifists, of the tradition of moral abstention. The Direct Action Committee had soon parted company with CND, insisting that civil disobedience against nuclear weapons must involve an active, but nonviolent, interruption of the process of war-making. Ralph Schoenman, a somewhat bizarre enthusiast for the civil rights sit-ins sponsored in the American deep south by the National Association for the Advancement of Coloured Peoples, was to advance the tactic in the London Left Club. And when the Committee of 100, whose committee of arty bigwigs camouflaged some very determined politicos, led 4,000 people to sit down outside the Ministry of Defence on 18 February, it was clear they had taken the initiative away from the Canon. There were trade-union delegations, including representatives from the South Wales area National Union of Miners, all the left-wing groups and Lord Russell himself, the last of the Edwardian Enlightenment, who drawing-pinned a pungent denunciation of nuclear war on the front door of the Ministry. Then 'like some diminutive elfin emperor he walked away,' Jeff Nuttall recalls. 'His face was grim and gothic. A tousled youth in jeans and combat jacket careened down the pavement to the kerb and roared in hoarse cockney "Good ol' Bertie" and Russell's face swathed itself in beatific glee like a child with a very special present.'* On 29 April, 2,000 sat down along Whitehall and this time 826 were arrested and fined £1, providing the public with its first exhibition of that great sixties cameo: the stout policeman perspiring over the limp protester.

*Jeff Nuttall, *Bomb Culture*, Paladin, 1970, p. 50.

In June a demonstration in the Holy Loch proved a tougher affair, with Scots unilateralist workers thumping it out with much less restrained police, while Pat Arrowsmith's kayak bobbed between the parked nuclear submarines. The mood was still however one of sacrifice, a symbolic attempt on the state, out of disgust for nuclear wars. But it was clear that the Committee was raising the stakes of protest and taking with them many Ban the Bombers whose despair, frustration and disgust at conventional party politics prepared them to take political risks. And this represented a real break with liberal habits of thought and a growing realization that the state which exploded bombs in the Pacific also operated prison cells in Pentonville. While the Thoreau-variety active-pacifists still pushed the line of 'filling the jails', the anarcho-syndicalists' group based on the magazine *Solidarity* and other more revolutionary thinkers around the Committee revelled in the mood of illegality and were clearly aiming higher, delighted to have finally outwitted the sectarian plotting of the pacifists. For really the Committee of 100 was pioneering the confrontation theory, later to be re-invented by Cohn-Bendit's 22 March Committee and the German students. For each new demonstration by the 100 goaded the authorities into abandoning their humane and tolerant mask and lashing out to reveal their real nature. The Tories could embrace Collins but they would have to jail Russell.

Against the backdrop of the Berlin crisis, the police made pre-emptive arrests of thirty-three members of the Committee who were, ironically for pacifists, bound over under an Act of 1361 to keep the peace. The majority refused and were sentenced to two months in jail. This guaranteed the success of the now illegal demonstration in Trafalgar Square. Fifteen thousand attended, thousands sat down and stayed put. As dusk fell there was a moment's realization of the possibilities of mass power but also of its impotence if it simply waited to be carted away; 1,314 were arrested. In December a much more ambitious attempt was made to organize regional demonstrations against US bases, notably Wethersfield in Essex. This time the authorities arrested six Committee full-timers under the Official Secrets Act and had the air base plastered with signs, wire fences, special courtrooms, three thousand police and soldiers. And still several thousand demonstrators passed the threatening signs in the direction of the dimly outlined bombers, in a heavy mist, as if reclaiming the land for humans. The sentences meted out to the Wethersfield Six were the first taste of a new judicial viciousness against political dissent which was to become more familiar. The state could push the stakes up higher still. The advance of the Committee of 100 had been blocked off just as completely as had the drive of the unilateralists in the Labour Party.

Increasingly what was left among the younger supporters of CND was a real bitterness which came after their deepest emotions and constant political energies over three years had been constantly thwarted and mangled. In a very short space of time the super cynic Jimmy Porter, John Osborne's trad-playing hero in *Look Back in Anger*, who knew that there were no good causes left, had become David Mercer's hero Colin in the TV trilogy *The Generations*, the exhausted Committee of 100 organizer, devoured by his idealism and ending shot and symbolically crucified on the Berlin Wall. It was a time when young people grew old rather fast.

A LONG TIME DYING

CND was a long time dying. For years after the Campaign was effectively over, the March persisted, assembling each Easter out of the force of habit and duty. A determined but mutually unacknowledged alliance of Christians and Communists, both stern organizers, gave CND a strange longevity. But by 1963 mass campaigning energy had been sucked behind Harold Wilson and the Labour Party as the 'realistic' way to do something about the bomb. And when disillusion with Wilson came, it centred around British support for the Vietnam war and was expressed through the openly revolutionary Vietnam Solidarity Campaign, initiated by, amongst others, the redoubtable Ralph Schoenman. CND remained aloof from the VSC. In fact, YCND, *Peace News* and *Anarchy* all had ethical objections to the gigantic 27 October 1968 Vietnam demonstration. CND did experience a belated boom in 1967 with the release of the almost-banned film *The War Game* made by Peter Watkins, a petrifying reconstruction of what nuclear explosion would mean, which single-handed extended the Campaign's lifespan several more years. But in the same year Peggy Duff, CND's apparatus-woman, left the Campaign to join an international benevolent trust.

The Committee of 100, seen by the more sensible revolutionaries as a strictly ad-hoc grouping, disintegrated even faster. The nearest it came to capturing mass opinion within CND was during Peter Cadogan's 'March must decide' campaign on the 1963 Aldermaston, which attempted to canvass for a more militant finale. It ended with the Metropolitan Police, with the assistance of the CND marshals, boxing the most suspect marchers in a complete cordon and collectively frogmarching them through central London. And the Committee's independent initiatives, despite a flurry of regional activity like the mock-auction of the V-bomber base at Marham in Norfolk, were over by 1964. The VIPs vanished and the organization became reduced to the whims, and they were many, of its full-time secretary, Peter Cadogan, himself financed by a radical industrialist who manufactured locks for briefcases. Cadogan liquidated himself in September 1968 into a committee for extra-parliamentary action by the professional classes onto which Jo Grimond, the ex-Liberal leader, was invited.*

As the time passed, the unchanging CND platform speakers (the faces may have been different but the politics were the same) got less and less popular with the Trafalgar Square audience. The political balance of power was changing quite fast and changing outside CND. I have a vivid memory of seeing a huge *Tribune* banner wending its way through the giant office blocks of Victoria, carried by a ten-year-old boy and a greying lady bent double by the weight of unsold copies of the paper, like an awful warning from *Pilgrim's Progress*. The growing bands of the revolutionary Left on the march, whose lack of manners and lack of devotion to the cause did not endear them to the Christians or the Communists, shouted at Labour Left orators, sold each other their publications and arranged splinter marches to new areas of struggle *en route* – the Czech Embassy in 1968 and the Springer Press office in the *Daily Mirror*'s Holborn building after the shooting of Dutschke in 1969. The very tactics which CND had pioneered throughout the world, the peace march, the nuclear-disarmament badge, non-violent resistance, were rejected by them as liberal safety valves, now safely institutionalized by the state. Even the sit-down, which had once seemed to press close to revolution, was a formality, a ritual between police and protester which wasted both's time. The reflex action of sitting down the moment anything happened had become a near-obsessional form of self-restraint. Demonstrators would charge at high speed towards a police cordon but seconds before impact on blue serge would squat instead and get trodden on. When the Spies for Peace march eventually arrived at the Littlewick Green secret bomb shelter, having broken through barbed wire and fences to get to it, it immediately, despite a fine speech by Bob Rowthorn and a lot of Glaswegian cursing about middle-class liberals, proceeded to sit down, like several hundred large soft mushrooms, in clumps around the entrance, and wait until a large force of police arrived.

The Times, 13 September 1968, 'Dying Committee of 100 Leaves Brave New Heir'.

And until the last, CND's supporters insisted on limiting their protest to the bomb rather than the whole social order that spawned it.
Even in its heyday it was handicapped in connecting outwards to other,
deeper, struggles, by its own assumptions about political change. The
focus on the bomb was both a tremendous strength and a terrible weakness, forcing the Campaign to reach other issues through the political
keyhole of nuclear weapons rather than by opening the door. Its
strange mixture of utopianism and practicality spread wide but never
penetrated. Those working-class battles that were going on were inaccessible despite the tours of George Clark's caravan and Pat Arrowsmith's sheer grit. The working class were approached mainly via their
trade-union leaders. As people asked two boilermakers carrying a
banner saying '1,000,000 engineers oppose the bomb', 'Where are the
other 999,998?' The business of translating the high principles of international diplomacy to the small chips of class struggle proved too much
for the Campaign.

Still, it is part of CND's political achievement that it was the last
movement of its kind to be dominated by the Labour Left. For CND
had schooled a generation of young people entering left politics, taught
them to re-ink a Roneo, edit a magazine, hold a street meeting, rush a
police cordon and not get caught. Nuttall described the end for him:

They said on the plinth it had been the biggest of the marches. We marched
on from Trafalgar Square to Grosvenor Square and sat in the road. There
were some noisy exchanges with the police. Now we are sitting in a pub
sharing two half-pints between five. All but me are teenagers. They are
cynical teenagers. It wasn't easy to climb out of despair and try the old
moralities. They are cynical, sophisticated kids. It hasn't come easy, addressing
banal brown envelopes, systematic door-to-dooring throughout the previous
year. We sit in the pub and the dusk lights fall across their faces. They have
sacrificed a lot, have come out of the vital protective shells of isolation. They
have walked three days and risked arrest again and again. They have been
ignored again, snubbed. In the half-lit pub I can see profound hatred for the
organized world instil itself in their very flesh like poison.*

*Nuttall, op. cit.

The Duty to Rebel:
Alex Comfort

For many years now, and most evidently since last year, the salient new factor in the politics of Europe has been the growing discontent of ordinary men and women with the policies of inhumanity; of anger and disillusion with compromises, double talk and cruelty, and with the complete lack of principle which has become the rule in government since Hitler.

In Russia, and in the other Communist countries, reason has been genuinely in revolt; and scientists there have rebelled, and rebelled effectively, against the abuse of science, as the younger generation is rebelling against Stalinism. The atomic scientist Kapitza spent years under house arrest for refusing to work on atomic bombs.

In Germany, physicists have declared that they will not lend themselves to the development of nuclear weapons.

I choose scientists as examples, not because they have any greater moral duty to rebel against folly than others, but because in Britain and America they have been culpably slow to do so; among the public at large there is growing anger and apprehension all over Europe at the risks which are being run, and the absence of good faith among those who are running them.

However much this discontent is exploited for electoral purposes, I do not see the parties today giving an answer to the hundreds of people, of all persuasions, who are asking what they, individually, can do to reassert the rule of sanity.

That is the function of the campaign which we are launching here tonight: to make every individual reassume the moral responsibility for opposing public insanity. The issue is one for direct action by every one of us.

We are not at the mercy of the Government, nor of events, nor of the policy of other nations, nor of the world situation, if we are prepared as a public to be sufficiently combative.

I would remind you that once already in the last two years we have seen public opinion assert itself on a moral issue through the sheer force of unorganized indignation. The response which we have received from you tonight is of that same order.

Within the coming weeks we intend to raise throughout the country a solid body of opposition to the whole strategy of moral bankruptcy and ceremonial suicide which the hydrogen bomb epitomizes, to all the mentally under-privileged double-talk by which it has been justified.

I would urge every one of us at this meeting to go home determined to become a living focus of that opposition. Some of us are going to march to Aldermaston on Good Friday, whether the Minister of Works likes it or not. Some of us live in areas which have been selected to receive American guided missile bases.

The Government is intensely anxious about public reaction to those bases, and is trying to keep their location secret.

If there are no local committees in your area, keeping their eyes open for base building activity, form one. If there is no focus for public opposition to nuclear tests and nuclear weapons in your district, in your church, among your neighbours, become one. If you are not already exerting pressure on your Member, on the Prime Minister, on the Press, on any scientists involved in unethical projects whose addresses you can get, begin to do so now, by letter and by lobbies.

It is high time we held some atomic tests of our own – in Downing Street.

Much has been said about a summit conference. Sanity is always hardest to restore at the summit – the air there is rarefied. It seems to affect the brain. We can reassert it at the base.

The people must take over – you must take over. The leaders of all the parties are waiting, as they always wait on any issue of principle, to follow public opinion. We can coerce them.

Gaitskell and Bevan say they will not abandon the H-bomb unilaterally. If they were here tonight, they would see that in this issue their party is abandoning them unilaterally.

We can make Britain offer the world something which is virtually forgotten – moral leadership. Let us make this country stand on the side of human decency and human sanity – alone if necessary. It has done so before. If it does so again I do not think we need fear the consequences.

(From a speech to the founding meeting of CND at the Central Hall, Westminster, 17 February 1955)

We Marched against Britain's Death Factory: Martin Grainger

The first day of the great march to Aldermaston was in many ways the least representative of all. Between Friday and Monday the column gradually acquired a different composition and a very different temper.

It departed, garbed in many colours, under a pale spring sun. There was music and much affable good cheer. At this stage hecklers would probably not have received the treatment given them three days later at Aldermaston.

The music and good humour persisted. But as the days went by seriousness and purpose increased in giant strides. The attitude of the millionaire press must have come to many young marchers as their first lesson in political what's what.

The London crowds showed us a mixture of amusement and friendliness. There was little open encouragement but no hostility. They seemed impressed by our numbers.

The column was at this stage still taking stock of itself, appreciating its various ingredients, reading with curiosity the inscriptions on its own banners – all with a certain tolerant satisfaction.

It held all kinds of people, united in their abhorrence of nuclear war and in their determination to 'do something' about it.

'Nuclear disarmament' was the sole wording on many of the posters. But how? The proposed solutions varied widely.

'Ban the bomb,' said some inscriptions, appealing to some unspecified Pope or Caesar. 'Talks not tests,' demanded others. 'Love your enemies,' proclaimed yet another.

Readers of the *Newsletter* and of *Socialist Review* marched under banners saying: 'Black the bomb. Black the bases.' This was the road to effective action.

Pacifists and religious people seemed the biggest organized groups. But the largest element of all seemed to be unorganized, non-religious, non-pacifist and non-political – in the sense of being highly suspicious of all political parties' attitudes on the crucial issues.

The efficiency with which the march had been organized was evident from the outset. It depended on an intense solidarity among the marchers, and this developed as the march went on.

Luggage was entrusted to total strangers, food was shared and lifts were thumbed as easily as if transport had been a socialized service in a socialist society.

The self-organizing ability of ordinary people with a genuine unity of purpose was very obvious.

Up to the Albert Memorial we were a procession. By the time we had reached Turnham Green the marchers had learned they had a mobile canteen, their own film unit . . . and a Marxist contingent.

One of the best meetings of the march was held on the very first night in the open air, in a Hounslow side street. The use of the Town Hall had been refused by the Tory-dominated council.

Reference was made from the platform to the possibility of industrial action. Mention of the actions of the German trade unions drew the greatest applause heard at any meeting of the march.

Easter Saturday saw the column reduced to its hardest and most determined core. Snow, rain and sleet fell continuously from Hounslow to Slough.

Banners were few. They had to be protected. The demonstrators could get soaked: what they stood for had to be preserved intact.

Soon after London Airport the march took to winding country lanes, the dripping hedges sole witnesses, for several miles, of its ordeal.

We reached Slough, wet and footsore. Tea in the Methodist chapel was much appreciated. Fenner Brockway took the pulpit. Many took off their shoes.

Then the rain stopped for an hour or two. We walked out of Slough in great spirits, heavily escorted by a police cordon on either side.

The Slough district committee of the Amalgamated Engineering Union had joined the march, with an enormous banner. An Electrical Trades Union banner had appeared. The *Newsletter* contingent, its posters held high, marched right behind these detachments.

The pavements were packed with late shoppers and sightseers. We marched past them, shouting 'No work on H-bombs – no work on rocket bases!' Our slogans were taken up by other marchers near us. Many pamphlets were sold.

When the trade-union banner-bearers left the procession, on the outskirts of Slough, we gave them a lusty cheer. Between Slough and Maidenhead it began to rain again. The police escort melted away.

The high light on Sunday was the entry into Reading. Ian Mikardo and a group of Labour councillors were waiting for us under the railway bridge at the city boundary.

Our contingent greeted them with a full blast: 'Black the bomb – black the bases!'

The column went on through the working-class districts of the town. It was good to see emblems of the march prominently displayed in many windows overlooking our route. Sales of the *Newsletter* pamphlet were particularly brisk along this stretch.

The column came to a halt in the crowded market place, bending round on itself in the shape of a letter U.

As our group, towards the tail of the column, passed the front half we were cheered and applauded. The whole square heard the slogans of the *Newsletter* comrades ringing out.

Reading Labour Party held a meeting that evening in the Town Hall. It was packed. We obtained permission to sell our literature from the official stall, and brisk sales took place outside, too.

Ian Mikardo outlined the differences of opinion within the Labour Party on the question of unilateral nuclear disarmament.

Michael Scott spoke of the need for civil disobedience when institutions ceased to fulfil the aspirations of the majority of the people. He was loudly clapped. There were shouts demanding industrial action.

Monday, the final day, saw our numbers increase several-fold. We were gaining a new sense of strength. Sections of the Reading Labour movement had joined us.

The column now stretched, through country lanes, far out of sight. It took over an hour to pass by. At the midday break we distributed our leaflet. Everyone accepted it and read it.

After a further tiring stretch we reached our objective at last. The final mile was walked in complete silence, along the very edge of the heavily wired perimeter of the Atomic Weapons Research Establishment.

Many must have been surprised by the immensity of the enclosed area and struck by the brutal contrast between the dark, dense forest of rich pine through which we had just marched and the planned waste land of man-made structures with which we were suddenly confronted.

It all had a nightmarish quality. Here was the ultimate reality we had marched against.

Here it was in all its silent horror: those turf-covered mounds of too-geometrical proportions, those metal and concrete pill-boxes of weird but doubtless eminently functional design, those chimneys projecting from ground level, that eerie artificial lake, with its 'No Bathing' signboard and its solitary swan, those unnaturally scattered buildings of utterly incongruous form and size.

Here it lay behind two strong wire trellises, behind a necklace of 'Danger' signs, behind boards soberly stating that police dogs patrolled the perimeter.

Its purpose was the death of men, women and children – and nothing else. It had no redeeming features. It was evil incarnate. It was the final refuge of their class rule, the iron fist inside their velvet glove.

Here it lay, inaccessible, miles from anywhere, mysterious, malevolent, murderous. Here was the sinister factory of death built for the ruling class by their Labour lackeys, built in the last resort for waging war on what was left of the first workers' state in history . . .

The final meeting took place in a large hedged-in field, to which access could be gained only through an opening just wide enough to admit three or four cows walking side by side.

Into this peaceful meadow there streamed several hundred cars of all shapes and sizes, covered with posters and slogans, and several thousand tired, proud and determined marchers, the vast majority of them young and still in fighting spirit.

They were loudly cheered by the crowd of spectators massed on either side of the gate.

And then it happened. What neither fatigue, nor the rigours of the weather, nor the gibes of the capitalist press could achieve was accomplished by the leaders of the demonstration themselves.

Of all the speeches delivered in those four days, the ones at the last meeting were the most inept, and the most out of touch with the feelings of the marchers.

This militant and magnificent march ended in a veritable orgy of stale platitudes from the platform. Having refused access to the microphone to a rank-and-file viewpoint from among the marchers themselves, the 'leaders' allowed the demonstration to break up without outlining any effective or coherent course of action.

People just drifted away in hundreds. They even had to be appealed to, from the platform, not to disperse before the 'final resolution' had been put.

The appeal was not very successful. People persisted in drifting away. They had heard it all so many times before.

The final resolution was put, in an almost indecent hurry, to a thinning core of listeners numbering perhaps a quarter of those who had earlier thronged the field. The others had departed. But the last word will be theirs.

(From the *Newsletter*, 12 April 1958)

Against All Bombs:
Ken Weller

The campaign in Britain against nuclear weapons is beginning to turn towards the working class. As it does so, it will create an increasing challenge to the capitalist state.

This marks a development both in the activities and in the consciousness of the Campaign. It is a genuine turn to the masses of ordinary workers, not to the bureaucracies of the Labour and trade-union movements. Already as a result of this emphasis, we have seen the beginnings of industrial action against the Bomb. Workers directly involved have refused to handle nuclear cargoes. Others have held token strikes.

More and more people in the campaign are seeing the deeper implications of working class action against the Bomb. The class which dominates production controls society. It decides policy and, despite the democratic façade, enforces it through its State apparatus. Until the ordinary people are free in production, they cannot have any effective say in the decisions of war and peace, life and death. Only a society with inhuman relations in production would produce these monstrous weapons.

But the USSR has the same monstrous weapons. Should not this be different if your society was fundamentally different from ours? We know that the means of production are nationalized. But Marx himself insisted that it is the 'relations of production' (the relations between men and men at work) which determine the class nature of society. The property relations might reflect these relations of production or might serve to mask them ...

From this viewpoint, the USSR has essentially the same relations of production as Britain or America. The Russian worker has to wake up in the morning when the alarm clock rings. The time is not of his own choosing. Someone else has decided *what* he shall produce, *how much*, and *at what cost* to himself. Has he chosen to produce Sputniks rather than butter?

Both East and West management makes all the plans, and seeks to reduce the worker to a standard unit in them. It consciously removes variety and decision-making from his job, and subjects him to the ruthless tempo of the machines.

In Marxist terms, he is alienated. And any opposition to this system brings him up against the forces of the State, which, again, are beyond his control.

Is this a State that is 'beginning to wither away from the moment of the Revolution'? Or is it the kernel of the socialist programme that has withered away?

In Britain our protests bring us up against our State forces too. When a mass demonstration tried to immobilize the NATO base at Wethersfield last December, six of our members were gaoled for long periods. Many others have been arrested on similar demonstrations.

We have also protested against the Russian H-tests, which threaten workers all over the world with 'socialist' leukaemia. Our bourgeois police have protected your Embassy against us, and arrested hundreds of demonstrators.

Our struggle is the struggle for new relationships in production and in society. Both East and West, privileged minorities protected by their State machine manage production and parcel out the social product. They try and protect these privileges against greedy neighbours.

That is what the H-bomb defends. But workers can gain nothing from protecting their own workers against others. We must have faith only in ourselves, in our ability to transform society. We extend our hand in solidarity with the working people of Russia, over the heads of our rulers and yours. We have already taken up this struggle; it is yours too. Together we must ACT – OR WE SHALL PERISH TOGETHER.

WORKERS OF THE WORLD UNITE!

(Abridged text of a leaflet printed in Russian and distributed in Red Square, Moscow, by supporters of the Industrial Subcommittee of the Committee of 100)

Beyond the Bomb:
Edward Thompson and John Saville

At last it is beginning to move. The frozen formations of the Cold War era are beginning to break up. The response of the electors at Rochdale (where both Labour and Liberal advocated British renunciation of the bomb) and the rapidly gathering success of the Campaign for Nuclear Disarmament: these are signals of a new temper among the people.

All talk of sweeping socialist advances in the next few years is unrealistic unless it starts from this premise: *there is no way forward until the international deadlock is broken.*

For years both Right and Left have covertly regarded the Cold War as one of political and economic attrition which will end only when one of the two giants cracks up. The Right has speculated upon revolt or collapse behind the 'Iron Curtain'. The Left has awaited the classical slump which would awaken old-style revolutionary responses among the Western working class. The Trotskyists have hoped for a coincidence of both. All views led to a common conclusion: the British people must wait for something to happen, somewhere else, for some other nation to move first.

Now we are coming to understand that our destiny need not be left indefinitely in American or Russian (or Polish or Hungarian) hands. It is now our turn to move. Our turn because, paradoxically, the stalemate of the two giants has increased our room for manoeuvre. Our turn because, despite Alsatian dogs and Civil Service purges, the ravages of the Cold War have left our democratic processes relatively unclogged and the main fabric of our civil liberties intact; our radical tradition can still stir with unexpected vigour, where its American counterpart is scattered in disarray and is still re-grouping after the assault of McCarthyism; our labour movement is united, where the French movement lies temporarily disabled between the thorough-going treason of Mollet and the stagnant stalinism of Thorez. Our turn because the world waits for someone to move, and – with an election in the offing – there is a chance for our people to intervene.

This mood, as it grows, will be exhilarating. For the first time for years, our people will feel that it is in their power to influence world events. But how is this to be done? Popular imagination has seized upon the gesture of renouncing the H-bomb. To this, Mr Bevan in the House of Commons on 20 February has once again returned a frosty politician's answer. Delivering for a second time his metaphor of diplomatic nudity, he continued:

We could not possibly throw aside all our allies, all our obligations, all our friends, and negotiate with other nations without Great Britain having any friends anywhere in the world. You cannot repudiate the possession of the H-bomb and still shelter under our allies having the H-bomb. The case I am putting is that we ought not to renounce the H-bomb on high moral grounds because that contains implications going far beyond the bomb itself.

The argument is too thin. Is India without friends? Has Yugoslavia gained or lost influence by asserting a measure of independence of the two blocs? Which friends does Mr Bevan wish to keep? The diplomatic corps of Washington and the Quai d'Orsay? Or the uncommitted Bandung powers in Asia, the labour movements of Western Europe, and the people of Eastern Europe who are thirsting for some initiative which will at one and the same time relax international tension and slacken the military and strategic pressures of stalinism?

Who has proposed that Britain should renounce the H-bomb, only to shelter behind American rocket bases? The fig-leaf which Mr Bevan holds onto so desperately turns out to be – not the H-bomb at all – but NATO and the American alliance. And it is clear that in this respect opponents of the bomb must answer Mr Bevan's case. If Britain is to take the initiative in ending the deadlock – and if the campaign against the nuclear peril is to unite moral fervour with political realism – we must indeed go 'far beyond the bomb itself'. We must make a choice between NATO and the unmapped policy of positive neutrality . . .

We have twelve months, and perhaps less, to work out a policy 'beyond the bomb' and to press it forward. The Left has a particular responsibility. Social advance at home, and internal relaxation in the Communist countries, are both tied to this one problem. If we want the Polish compromise to broaden into democracy, if we want the embittered labour movements of Western Europe to find a new direction and unity, if we want to create the preconditions for further advance at home – then we must persuade Britain that it is time to 'do it herself'.

(Editorial from the *New Reasoner*, Spring 1958)

Seeking a Revolution:
Peggy Duff

For it wasn't then a nice, cosy, minority movement. It wasn't a collection of well-meaning people seeking limited reforms like capital punishment abolition or abortion reform. It was much more than the stage army of the good grown rather larger than usual. It wanted a revolution – and there were times when it marched up Whitehall and when, as on 17 September, it sat in Trafalgar Square, when the smell of revolution was in the air, insistent, compulsive and heady, like Paris in May 1968.

But it frightened its own leadership, scared the politicians stiff, and ranged against itself all the careful, unimaginative, conservative forces of all the establishments, including its own. They fought it, and fought it, and fought it again, and beat it.

It didn't last. How could it? It came up against all the hard inanities and harsh realities of politics. It had no programme, no ideology, no plans for alternative policies, let alone alternative governments. 'What splendid people they are,' said the press. 'What a pity that what they want is so unrealistic.'

So the march changed. It failed to get what it wanted either through marching, through the Labour Party, through civil disobedience, through Voters' Veto, through independent candidates, through any of the strategies marchers advocated. Frustration turned it in on itself. It ran furiously across roads, shouted at itself, barred its own passage, trumpeted at M Ps who tried to speak, and yet persisted long after many of the early marchers and most of the big names had stopped turning up. Some lost heart. Some learned to live with the bomb. Many stayed at home when a Labour Government came to power. Some carried the black and cherry banners of the anarchists. Some went on trying.

For it was OK to have a rather colourful carnival gathering of sincere but misguided moralists – but when great trade unions fell under its spell, when it started to win votes at Labour Party Conferences, when it really became a threat to the powers-that-be, enough was enough.

So they fought it and beat it. Not only the Tories, but the 'Socialists'; the Gaitskells, the Wilsons, the Healeys, the Stewarts, the democratic socialists, the bright young technocrats seeking power, accepting megaton and megadeath, the monstrous doctrine of nuclear-power politics. They fought it and won.

Then, year after year, they congratulated themselves that it was dead, that unilateralist resolutions had vanished from conference agendas, that Labour Party and trade-union banners had disappeared from the march. They didn't notice that when it died something died, too, in the Labour Party. 'Mr Gaitskell,' said Christopher Driver in his book *The Disarmers* (1964), 'virtually completed a process which had already taken almost fifty years: he turned a party of protest into a party of power.' He also made it almost indistinguishable from the Conservative Party and created the same political dilemma, the same unspeakable lack of choice, as in the United States. If CND declined, at least protest has survived and is putting forward new roots and invading new constituencies – which is more than can be said for social democracy. 'The man recovered of the bite, the dog it was that died.'

(From *Left, Left, Left*, Allison & Busby, London, 1971, pp. 143–4)

No Bombs and No Illusions:
Mike Kidron

The H-bomb is still there. So are the men who are prepared to use it. And if we remind ourselves of the monstrous crime against humanity which our Government so steadfastly contemplates committing, we may at times become pessimistic about the effects of our activities. If we do, we are making a grave mistake. We are quite right to shed our illusions. Passing resolutions inside the Labour Party will not of itself end the bomb. Nor will mass civil disobedience. But we should merely be exchanging one set of illusions for another if we therefore concluded that passing resolutions or taking part in civil disobedience is simply useless.

We are at a stage in political history at which old forms of organizations are crumbling. In five years time the Labour Party and the trade unions will have had to face the new gap between political and industrial action. The limits of parliamentarianism will have become much plainer. Sharper forms of struggle will develop outside Parliament. The habitual responses of both bureaucracy and rank-and-file will have become irrelevant. But we cannot go home and wait until this has happened. It is our responsibility to see that the central issues by means of which people define their action are those of the H-bomb and its essential connection with the social order of capitalism. What do we have to do to achieve this?

For the moment we have to continue mobilizing all the forces which are available for the struggle for unilateralism. *All* the tasks which we have undertaken remain relevant. Passing resolutions in the Labour Party is not undertaken simply to capture a disintegrating political machine. It is to reintegrate wherever we can on unilateralist and socialist principles. Work in the unions is not a failure because trade-unionists remain so non-political. We have to create political nuclei in the trade unions precisely to meet and withstand the trend. Sitting down in Trafalgar Square or at USAF bases is not justified only if the Americans thereupon fly home. It makes visible a form of revolt around which young people can regroup for the next advance.

The word must therefore be: no counsels of despair to replace our illusions of the past. But instead, we must educate ourselves, and this in an understanding of how we cannot get rid of the H-bomb without dealing with the social forces which create it. Education in socialism has to become a first priority for the Campaign against the Bomb.

(From 'Notes of the Quarter', *International Socialism*, 8, Spring, 1962)

Chapter 3
The Two New Lefts:
Peter Sedgwick*

... the Clubs and discussion-centres will be places beyond the reach of the interference of the bureaucracy, where the initiative remains in the hands of the rank-and-file ... Their influence will pervade the Labour Movement, as the Campaign is coming to pervade it; but because this influence derives from ideas it will elude administrative control. The bureaucracy will hold the machine; but the New Left will hold the passes between it and the younger generation.

(EDWARD THOMPSON, *New Reasoner*, Summer 1959)

I am not, I think, betraying a closely-guarded state secret when I say that the movement which once claimed to be 'The New Left' (and with which Wright Mills identified himself) has now, in this country, dispersed itself both organizationally and (to some extent) intellectually. We failed to implement our original purposes, or even to sustain what cultural apparatus we had. What purposes the review which now bears its name will fulfil remains to be seen.

(EDWARD THOMPSON reviewing Wright Mills in *Peace News*, 29 November 1963)

THE OLD NEW LEFT

From the spring of 1957 until around the summer of 1961, a British political movement which became known as the 'New Left' flourished hectically, before entering a fatal decline. In its prime, during the four years that followed the outrages of late 1956 upon Hungary and Egypt, the movement displayed an expansive and apparently tireless dynamism, accumulating an imposing set of political properties and insignia, the tokens and titles of an estate of presumable substance. There was the building, for instance, situated a stone's throw from Marx's old rooms in Soho, whose various floors were given over to the multiform functions of the New Left's cultural apparatus; its nether storeys housed

*This chapter first appeared in *International Socialism*, 17, August 1964.

the Partisan, 'London's left-wing coffee house' (a similar establishment opened later in Manchester), whose dramatic brutalist decor and white megawatt downglare diffused a curious alienation-effect upon the customers; the basement was more subdued, though still Spartan enough, a dining-room and resort for poetry and folk-song; the first floor began life as the frantic publicity HQ for the first Aldermaston march and subsequently became an odd little socialist library, full of literary garbage from the thirties, review copies of books just out, exchange copies of fraternal publications, and some true incunabula of Left lore. Here meetings and at least one exhibition (a heaped conspectus of cuttings and souvenirs from the thirties) took place. The uppermost floor held the editorial-cum-administrative office for the publications and groupings of the movement; the latter included the Universities and Left Review Club (1957–8; re-christened New Left Review Club from 1959 on), which used to attract hundreds to weekly lectures and discussions in the larger basements of central London, and further regular meetings were held by such autonomous sections as the Education, History of Socialism, Left Scientists, Social Priorities and Literature groups, the International Forum, and the London Schools Left Club, a self-governing unit for youngsters still at school. Between thirty and forty local Left Clubs ran on a modest scale outside London, mostly either in the South-East or in the industrial North (including Scotland). Sporadically through these years, there were hopes and hints of an informal New Left International, small but alive and identifiable. The Universities and Left Review Club's *Cry Europe* meeting, which packed St Pancras Town Hall on Bastille Day 1958, united on its platform representatives of the West German anti-nuclear mass campaign and the French neutralist Left, spokesmen from the crushed Hungarian revolution and the rising anti-fascist generation of Spain, and staff members from the established Left and liberal press (*Observer*, *New Statesman*, *Herald*). And all through its existence, the New Left sensed that it had allies abroad: the French PSU, the Italian PSI, the flickering Marxist revisionism of Eastern Europe, and the entire gamut of sociologue radicalism in the United States from Wright Mills to Riesman, were all announced (or else announced themselves) as fraternal delegates in the thronged convention of ideas that met in permanent session, with a limitless agenda, up to the crisis of the movement. From the rostrum of the Universities and Left Review Club, Isaac Deutscher prophesied to his eager audience that the coming decade would be known to posterity as 'the Red Sixties'; the slogan was taken up, made into the title of a pamphlet that was endorsed by a score of Labour

MPs. The society that published the pamphlet, a keen left Labou₁ grouping known as Victory for Socialism, was later to be taken over by disillusioned Bevanites, and in 1964 announced its own suspension 'in the interests of Party unity'. At the time, however, the prophecy had an alluring gleam.

While the extent of the New Left's actual influence is still far from clear, its news-value for the British intelligentsia was unmistakeable. The names of many of its writers became currency in that quotidian swapping of trends and trading of significances that weekend reviewers and columnists conduct, so to speak, within the temple of the arts. Between the organs of the Congress for Cultural Freedom and of the New Left a continuous sniping contest developed, and no volume of social-democratic theorizing was complete without a patient demolition of the latest arguments against capitalism offered by this neo-Marxist young set. A professor devoted all of three broadcast talks to the examination of the movement's political philosophy, and to the reproof of its 'vestigial Bolshevism'. While the political objectives of the New Left (e.g. unilateralism, workers' control) received little or no publicity outside the committed dissident press, its cultural analysis of capitalism and the mass media were much more widely acceptable. R. H. S. Crossman, to take the most sensational instance, reviewing Raymond Williams' *The Long Revolution* on the editorial page of the *Guardian*, called it 'undeniably the first book to break through the thought barrier of socialist ideas . . . the book I have been waiting for since 1945'. Explorations in cultural sociology were regarded by most of its critics as the proper province of the New Left, and as its chief source of intellectual strength; the politics were a strident intrusion, perhaps even symptomatic of an old-Marxist faction within the group that was taking the more sensitive, innocent youngsters for a ride. All the same, within these limitations the New Left enjoyed a run of fashionable publicity of a kind that has in Britain rarely been the privilege of aspiring revolutionary formations. In a diffuse way, too, it benefited from the lustre of a few of its more notable artistic and academic contributors, mascots or idols for the occasion who provided an assuring link with the insurgent literature of the late fifties or with the world of solid scholarship. The allegiance of these writers to the New Left was usually a secondary loyalty at the most (except in the case of C. Wright Mills), but their presence in its pages anchored the movement firmly in the world of discourse that it shared with the accredited media, and helped to generate the sense, common among the Left intelligentsia of its time, that here was a setting for social action that drew together and marshalled the deepest, most authentic radical concerns of the day.

Not the faintest murmur of this movement now remains. To be sure, a journal titled *New Left Review* is still edited from the Soho address from which the old crusade was organized, and the roll of 'New Left Clubs and Groups', amounting to some forty local sections, until recently filled an entire page of each issue. *NLR*'s original editors and contributors still (in many cases) write articles in the independent left-wing press and books under the imprint of general publishers; although their names now scarcely ever appear in the review which they founded. The kremlinologically inclined observer, comparing the present editorial board of *NLR* with its forerunner, will not fail to note that only one name, that of a poet domiciled in the United States, survives from the former central committee of twenty-six that had emerged from the various ordeals of amalgamation and accretion in the formative period from 1957 onwards. Even the few symbols of continuity turn, on closer examination, into indices of change; the New Left now only occupies the top floor of the Soho building, the Partisan and the Left Book Centre having long vanished, and scarcely any of the listed clubs and groups have as much as a paper existence. The largest assembly that can be mustered under the New Left banner is a literary discussion circle that meets at a London pub. On a broader plane, the international affiliations and contacts of the movement have expired, or fragmented out of recognition. The French and Italian Lefts are consumed in their own dissensions, the Marxist revisionism of the Soviet bloc has been worn out or squeezed out – and the more recent schisms of world Communism, in China and Rumania, have proved ignoble in spirit and devoid of ideas. On both sides of Europe, the idealist absolutes projected after 1956, by Hungary, Suez and Algeria, have grown dim, and enthusiasms are tranquillized by rising dosages of technological renewal, expert planning and governmental power.

Within the press of the British intelligentsia the New Left has ceased to function as a desirable subject. It has left the realm of relevant matter occupied by Beatles, computers, Harold Wilson, polystyrene, Pop art and bentwood furniture, and entered instead the limbo populated by Rosicrucians, diesel-engine maintenance, syndicalism, married life and Omar Khayyam. It might, of course, be argued that a socialist movement is better off for being in, as it were, a state of cultural illegality. In the present condition of the Left in Britain, a review printed in around four thousand copies (the present scale of *NLR*) could be much more significant than one (like *NLR* at its outset) with double the circulation and possibly a diluted clientele. Be this as it may, the change of scale certainly reflects a qualitative change in the aims of the New Left, not simply a loss or retreat.

The origins of the Old New Left (for some such discrimination must now be made) were closely linked with a set of conditions operating in temporary coincidence on the British radical-intellectual scene from 1956 onwards. Each element in this conjuction formed an interest within the movement and held a claim on its attention. There was, for instance, a post-Stalinist lobby; part of the New Left's history is of the evolution of a substantial section of it from an opposition within the British Communist Party to an unattached Marxism which could, at its best, ask searching questions of its less revolutionary colleagues. One of the components of the merger that created *New Left Review* in early 1960 was a quarterly journal named the *New Reasoner*, edited by two Yorkshire-based labour historians, John Saville and Edward Thompson, who had run a duplicated opposition bulletin (the *Reasoner*) as members of the Communist Party in that interval of agonized reappraisal in 1956 between the denunciation of Stalin and the destruction of Hungary's revolution. The *New Reasoner*'s broad responsibility was felt towards the Labour movement, but it maintained a dissident-Communist identity of sorts until the time of its amalgamation into *NLR*. It would perhaps be more accurate to say that with the merger the *New Reasoner* gave up certain formal attributes of ex-Communism, for instance its tendency to lapse into roll-calls of the Marxist great (from William Morris through Tom Mann to Christopher Caudwell) and its conscious bond with the Marxist dissent (in any case now defunct) of Eastern Europe. It brought into the fusion far more than it shed: an explicit commitment to class-struggle, an iteration of the role of human agency as against impersonal historic process (be it gradual or cataclysmic), a devotion to relatively punctilious habits of work.

The claim exerted by this tendency overlapped largely with the demands of a different source: the theoretically inclined sector of the Labour Left. Until the foundation of the New Left's publications, the militant wing of the Labour Party had lacked any organ which could stabilize and generalize its mode of action beyond the level of transient, reflex response. Only the Right and Centre of the party (through the work of Crosland, Strachey and various Fabian essayists) could claim any attempt at a pondered overview of British society or world economics. During the Gaitskell ascendancy in British Labour politics, the New Left engaged in a series of detailed studies in the structure of modern capitalism, the pattern of world trade and the record of Labour Parliamentarism. These empirical analyses could be seen to run in parallel with other discussions at both a more philosophical and a more tactical level. Ranged behind the close factual studies lay nuanced dissertations on work and alienation (often with the character, as one unkind critic put it, of a 'U' trailer advertising an 'A' thesis). In the front rank, advancing from the main body of massed data, thrust a bristling programmatic array: common ownership under workers' control, unilateral nuclear disarmament, neutralism in foreign policy, a new leadership for Labour. A quirk of fate has answered the last of these demands; a failure of nerve has caused the others to evaporate. The Labour Left no longer desires an independent theoretical base with an outspoken socialist platform. The sole residuary of the Old New Left's tactical heritage is its *Socialist Wages Plan*, a piece of bureaucratic Utopianism envisaging the control of wages by a committee of Government, TUC and employers, first published in 1959 and recently offered once again for the attention of the incoming Wilson Administration in the latest issue of *New Left Review*.*

These were the twin political elements of the primeval New Left: a utopian pole and (as it has turned out) a Machiavellian, romanticism and realpolitik rubbing off on one another, reflecting back and forth, crossing and fusing at peaks of intensity upon platform or pavement, before separating out, and at last burning out. The confrontation of these extremes took place as much within individuals as between them (even though one can think of people prominent in the Old New Left who were either almost-pure romantics or else unmistakeable realpoliticians); perhaps the most direct argument between the poles took place over the tactical question of support for independent electoral candidates (such as the Fife Socialist League). This, as it turned out, was resolved in a characteristic manner (at the Left Clubs conference in 1960) by deciding that 'variations in local conditions' were such that no general advice could be given; this was true enough, except that most of the local variation was inside the New Left itself. By and large, however, politics functioned as a single claim within the councils of the movement, as against the pretensions of its chief rival, which may be called Socio-Culture.

Socio-Culture was compounded of two sorts of item: there were specimens of personal creative work, whether poems, plays, paintings, films or critical essays, which were felt to be successful in manifesting, within the terms of their genre, some vision or insight relevant to a 'socialism at full stretch'. These were at first grouped under the catch-

*See John Hughes, 'An Economic Policy for Labour', *New Left Review*, 24, March–April 1964.

all slogan of 'commitment'; although the term was shortly dropped as an embarrassment, the subject-matter persisted on and off for years. This material bears re-reading after the lapse of time less than any other feature of Old New Left writing: bitsy or self-indulgently prolix by turns, its nose embedded in the furrow of literary vogue, incapable of either the long look back or the sideways swoop into neglected byways.

The other main arm of Socio-Culture lay in the exploration of the cultural mass media and their effects on popular moral and social consciousness. With the exception of its evidence to the Pilkington Committee (set up by the Government in 1960 to advise on the future of radio and TV), the New Left performed very little empirical work of its own in this field. Rather it theorized upon the role of the mass media in a class-divided society, and on the relationship between a critique of the media and the overall socialist case against capitalism. This concern was most evident in the journal *Universities and Left Review* (founded in Oxford, early 1957; merged into *NLR*, early 1960) and was given its fullest rationale in the work of Raymond Williams. What Williams finally offered was the replacement of a conflict model of society (of the sort which has been traditional among socialists and even radical reformers) with a communications model, in which the unity of humankind is primordially broken, not by the clash of rival social interests, but by blockages and faulty linkages in moral perception. Society is conceived as a kind of mental organism whose warring faculties, in the shape of sectional or partial value-systems, eventually, if effortfully, knit together in a single communications net or 'common culture'. Williams' style is peculiarly idiosyncratic and cloudy, so much so that it can have had scarcely any following in detail. Once exposed to view in its most extended form (*The Long Revolution*), the argument was at once subjected to stringent criticism in the pages of *New Left Review* by Edward Thompson. However, embryonic variants of the approach were common enough in New Left circles from the outset, particularly among contributors to *ULR*. Williams's model, indeed, grants a distinct positive role to the working-class movement, as the carrier of the collective, democratic values which form the main alternative in tradition to the hierarchical bourgeois norms of competition and 'service'. Other moral critics associated with the group tended to leave no scope for any active influence to emerge from below against the enervating effects of TV, the press and the domestic machines. Raymond Williams acted at times as a lucid and invaluable corrective to this paralysed vision of victimhood, in which the working class was sited always at *the receiving end* of transmission from an alien agency, whether as the objects of survey research, the beneficiaries of welfare and planning proposals, or the consumers of shoddy cultural goods. And yet the whole effect of the sociocultural mode, whether in its overweening or its plebeian variety, was subversive of political activism. This is not to deny that individual cultural critics became engaged in pamphleteering or public demonstration as the call of duty arose; only to indicate that the social approach which they were evolving left no place either causally or functionally for the operation of struggle.

Witness the New Left's evidence to the Pilkington Committee:

The task of the Pilkington Committee is, first to define a philosophy of communication in modern society, and then to apply it, with vigour and skill, to the particular problems which face us now. But it must be added that no reshaping of the present structure, by itself, will suffice. In the end, the quality of the service provided will depend on the critical awareness of the audience, the sense of responsibility on the part of those who serve that public, the conditions in which that service is received and the cultural life of society as a whole. Each of these has its roots deep in the *educational* structure (my italics – P.S.) of our society and the Pilkington Committee should not be inhibited from making these wider connections in its Report, because of its terms of reference.*

Briefly put, it's all in the mind, you know. And the solidarity primarily expressed is with the programmers and transmitters: wrongheaded as they may be, it is with these that the dialogue is conducted, to them that the bright ideas are tendered.

What emerges most strikingly from a retrospect of this section of the New Left is its distillation of the false consciousness of the middle-class meritocracy. The myth which the Leftish professional man most enjoys is to the effect that corruption lies about him everywhere *except* in his own element. The factory worker, the salesman, the stockbroker, the brigadier are all enslaved by virtue of their actual social functions, which are part of the machinery of class society. But the career worlds of the cultural media, of education (especially higher or further education) and of social welfare are commonly believed to be intrinsically classless or neutral agencies, floating with an eagle eye around the social pyramid but never integrally located within it. As an absent-minded host will deal out coffee-cups to the assembled guests, only to discover finally that he has forgotten one member of the company, namely himself, so the professionalized radical appoints himself as observer and dispenser to society within his speciality, a role with which he is so

* *New Left Review*, 7, January–February 1961.

wholly identified that he can never view it externally. Since his duties may be sponsored by one of the many collectivist or corporate institutions whose advertisements for pensionable posts occupy whole pages of his favourite weeklies, he is apt to believe that these or kindred bodies constitute a locus for progressive advance against the vulgarities of commerce: BBC as against independent TV, planning department as against speculator's sprawl, liberal studies as against barbarity, the sociologist's or economist's peephole into the bourgeois ant-heap. Over the last few years it has become more and more evident that the socio-cultural preoccupations of the New Left were not after all coursing heriocally against the stream, but instead have been, in the broadest sense, with it. 'We are full of confectionery and short of hospitals; loaded with cars and ludicrously short of decent roads; facing an educational challenge of major proportions, yet continuing a limited class system of schools'; these sentiments could have come today from a liberal newspaper editorial commenting on the latest batch of governmental reports, or from a party political broadcast on behalf of Transport House. (Actually they are from a New Left article of January 1960.) The components of socialist humanism, lovingly turned out, oiled and assembled in the comradely arsenals of yesteryear, are flung back at us in monstrous dispersion from the target areas on the other side.

Nor should this be entirely surprising. The institutionalization of the avant-garde, which has reached the perfection of a mechanized process in the visual arts, is today established in a wide variety of material. The repeated transformation of radical preferences (in theatre, film, TV, folksong, satire) into reigning norms, the increasingly frantic tempo and turn-over of critical acclaim, the apparently ever-shortening lag between debut and recognition, recognition and popularization: these arise from the cultural demands of an expanding selectively educated stratum which requires the installation around itself of an entire furniture of novelty to stand in lieu of, and partly in opposition to, the more genteel spiritual upholstery upon which the pre-war educated classes had reclined. So, too, in the realm of social ideas there is particular scope for the generation of trend-setting, trail-blazing, mess-clearing attitudes and programmes which have an inherent appeal to those middle sections of the community whose professional position is intimately bound up with the direction of public spending. A limited collectivism, a readiness to listen to experts and accept planning, is built into the consciousness of this social segment; current Labour Party style is indeed an attempt to trap and canalize this bias for electoral purposes. The Old New Left was of course more radical in many of its prescriptions than Harold Wilson – but in its social and cultural class-appeal it belonged half-consciously to the same programmatic family.

POLICIES

The diversity of the New Left's origins was reflected in the logic of its discourse. In this Federative People's Republic of the mind, all the constituent territories were egocentrically equal; all proclamations were posted in the several tongues side by side (laced with an official *lingua franca* combining features both of mandarin and demotic idiom), and massive verbal contingents from the separate duchies marched past in separate formation for a review which rapidly became a show of ceremonial unity rather than of fighting strength. Legislatively, the votes of the member-states were balanced within an implicit veto system, so that the metropolitan interest (analytic, socio-cultural, theatre-going) could never outweigh the provincial (romantic, movement-oriented, Club-brandishing), the reformist spirit was always countervailed by the revolutionary (and *vice versa*), and the intelligentsia always had the same ration of seats at the round table as the working-class Left (whose quota was seldom if ever taken up, though, by actual personnel). Dissent was never suppressed, but simply co-opted, usually settling thereafter into a voluntary silence. For, despite all divergences, the movement was agreed upon its basic enemies (capitalism, communism, philistinism) and was able to cohere, at least for a long period, through the cement of militant success. New autonomous oblasts constantly announced their accession and joined the march-past, a Left Club one month, a social critic the next; and the whole procession knew that it moved in time with the millionfold footsteps of a vast phantom army of potential fellow-travellers, that up-and-coming fresh, vigorous race of recruits against the effete, whose name is Youth. 'The bureaucracy will hold the machine; but the New Left will hold the passes between it and the younger generation.'

For Youth was more than another partner in the bloc of claims, it was the banner of the whole confederacy, the source of positives – authenticity of feeling, breadth of response, suspicion of establishment – for activator and analyst alike. However, the brilliance with which the cultural anthropologists of the New Left reported on the folkways of the young was in the end hopeless: the only section of young people among whom the movement made any progress was its own further-educated juniors. The Young Socialists, a solidly proletarian body, remained unscathed by New Left ideas. Among the thousands of youngsters who marched with CND the New Left never established an independent socialist presence. It is, of course, dauntingly difficult to make contact with a world as self-enclosed and as self-regarding as that of adolescence. But virtually every other left-wing tendency in Britain has made some showing in this respect, sometimes (it is true) by disreputable methods of intellectual manipulation. The New Left 'captured' youth in a purely mental fashion, by recording the detail of the teenage masquerade, by placing its nonconformity as 'the distorted moral response to a bureaucratic age' (as Stuart Hall put it in one of his superb pieces in this field), by annexing it into its world of honorary allusions. 'Only connect' was, one suspects, a favourite motto within the editorial reaches of the group; the New Left became trapped in the mass of its contemporary connections, unable to break through the web and connect with anything outside.

No less serious was the effect of the polymorph structure of the movement upon the ideas produced by it. The federal budget drained the regional ideological coffers, the official pidgin swamped each hardy vernacular. Much of the Old Left's writing displayed an inspirational public-relations flabbiness, designed to reassure rather than to discuss. A whole range of arguments were pre-empted by formulae which disarmingly included all candidates in the list of first-class honours. 'It is not a case of *either* this *or* that. We must, at every point, see both – the surge forward *and* the containment, the public sector *and* its subordination to the private, the strength of the trade unions *and* their parasitism upon capitalist growth, the welfare services and their poor-relation status.'* The additive logic of the New Left's idea-structure equally prevented its proclaimed loyalty to the Labour movement from functioning as an *over-riding* commitment. The general feeling in the organization was that everybody did their bit, and some people happened to have an industrial bit; whereas, for example, 'the class struggle for the secondary modern teacher lies in the fight for the comprehensive school and the social principles behind that'.† Only C. Wright Mills, a lone voice from abroad, argued for the repudiation of 'the labour metaphysic' (i.e., the idea of the working class as the historic agency of change), in his 'Open Letter to the New Left'.‡ For the rest, the New Left tended to invoke the Labour movement as the

*Edward Thompson, *New Left Review*, 3, May–June 1960.
†Stuart Hall in *Universities and Left Review*, 7, Autumn, 1959.
‡*New Left Review*, 5, September–October 1960.

framework within which it operated, without giving any theoretical primacy to the economic processes which define Labour, or to the struggles, in the first place industrial, out of which the social character of the movement is constantly renewed. *NLR* was from its inception intended to be 'both the product of the socialist movement and the point at which this movement is re-produced';* the trajectory of socialism is, however, by no means that of a merry-go-round in which each specialized hobby-horse rotates into view by turns. The economic antagonism in production, insufficient and incomplete as it is by itself, is still the ground for all other forms of socialist activity, the permanent reservoir for socialist politics.

This view is as implicit in the origins of the British Labour Party (parliamentary reformism) as it is in any Marxist teaching. It makes sense to try and fuse socialist ideas with the institutions of a working-class movement; but not to attempt to add industrial campaigning to a political movement of the intelligentsia. Of the few 'industrial comrades' with whom the New Left could claim any persistent contact, a high proportion were full-time trade-union officers. Shop stewards and rank-and-file worker militants were rarer here than in any left-wing grouping in Britain. This extraordinary defect in composition could not be corrected (as some of us tended to believe) by a more class-aware, more responsible orientation on the part of the New Left leadership. It was inherent in the terms of the group from its outset, in the Clubs no less than the *Review*; Fabian organizational forms cannot accommodate working-class (let alone revolutionary) politics.

Something should be said on the foreign policy advocated by the New Left. 'Positive neutralism' is a watchword seldom heard today on the British left-wing scene. Its viability was undermined by the Chinese invasion of India and the growing direct Soviet–US confrontation; its honour was put in question by Conor Cruise O'Brien's exposé of UN machinations in the Congo; its public expediency as a slogan has lapsed through the amalgamation, in foreign policy and defence, of Labour's Parliamentary Left and Right. (Three years ago, Konni Zilliacus was temporarily excluded from the Parliamentary Labour group for publishing an article attacking the Gaitskellite leadership in the international Communist Party journal *Problems of Peace and Socialism*; a recent issue of the same magazine carried an article by him eulogizing official Labour policies, with a by-line from the Prague editors noting that the views expressed in it were entirely personal.) It is difficult now to recollect how sacrosanct was the formulation of 'positive neutralism'

*Edward Thompson in *New Left Review*, 1.

in the New Left milieu of 1960–62. The phrase explicitly went beyond a policy of opposition to nuclear war preparations in the Soviet and US power-blocs; it implied an unyieldingly positive attitude to the existing neutral powers of the underdeveloped world. For Peter Worsley, indeed, commenting on the Belgrade neutralist conference in the twelfth issue of *NLR*,* the 'emergent peoples' were 'the makers of a new synthesis which may contain the germs of a shared and enriched world-culture'; a synthesis which apparently without further ado incorporated their own rulers, since these governments were in New Left sociology uniquely exempt from any analysis in the terms of bureaucracy, élite or class. For David Ross, writing in the same issue, the conference was 'by and large the nearest thing we have ever seen to a gathering of our sort of people in power'. Ghost-written gems from the Belgrade rostum could be quoted *in extenso* as the pronouncements of authenticated spokesmen for their peoples; Sudan's General Abboud, Prince Sihanouk, Marshal Tito, Emperor Selassie and Osagyefo Nkrumah stood at the summit of New Left diplomacy, the international Popular Front that answered the domestic indiscriminacy of ideas, the unchallenged bearers of the Common Culture. Castro's Cuba was an early candidate for the 'new synthesis' of the organic Third World: 'Elections and party government is [*sic*] seen now as a rupturing of the transitional period, slowing down its pace and altering its style. It would formalize the system and fracture the fraternity between people and leaders formed in the revolutionary war. With the memory of Batista's electoral hoax fresh in their minds, the Cuban poor regard elections as a bureaucratic postponement of the revolution.'†

The deformations of the Cuban revolution were ascribed exclusively to Cold War pressure; conversely, neutralism in foreign affairs was assumed to be a stimulus to healthy socialist development, without any further consideration of domestic social facts that might militate for or against a radical outcome. Thus Peter Worsley invokes 'the immense pressure Britain could generate, in alliance with India, Ghana, Yugoslavia, and backed by the uncommitted countries, for world peace and active neutrality', and remarks that 'most of these uncommitted nations are countries which could, under such stimulus, move towards socialism ... India, Austria, Israel, Indonesia, Ghana, to name but a few ...' (*Out of Apathy*, p. 136). The incongruity of this coalition was surpassed by the conclusion by a New Left pamphlet that the European Free

*November–December 1961.

†Stuart Hall and Norm Fruchter, 'Notes on the Cuban Dilemma', *New Left Review*, 9, May–June 1961.

Trade Association, which includes Portugal as well as Britain, Austria, Switzerland and the Scandinavian governments, was 'fundamentally a neutralist bloc' (*Britain's Crisis and the Common Market*, 1961). This was indeed the diplomacy-in-exile of an ideal Republic: fantasies of statecraft, hallucinated expediencies, clouded the social vision of the New Left and inflated its self-importance. The language of Positive Neutralism, New Powers, and Emergent Peoples was about as illuminating as the rival rhetorics of Free World, Camp of Peace, Western Values and Proletarian Internationalism.

DECLINE

The confederate New Left fell apart in the autumn of 1961; the explosion was characteristically muffled. No statement was ever published on the differences around *NLR* which were brought to a head shortly before the retirement of the editor Stuart Hall and the radical reorganization of the movement. The arguments were conducted out of sight, through the medium of discreet conventicles and duplicated factional documents. And the content of the debate was mostly internal to the New Left, over matters of tone rather than of detail. Nobody got up, as far as one knows, to query the advocacy, in *A Socialist Wages Plan*, of 'the re-allocation of labour between firms by propulsion rather than attraction' (in English: don't pay them more, sack them), or to denounce *NLR*'s tactical silence on the mass Civil Disobedience campaigns. For a long time there had been mounting dissatisfaction in the clubs with the lack of priorities evident in the content of the review. It had become little more than an image-conscious disc-jockey of political and cultural LPs cut outside its own ambit, its heterogeneity rationalized by a listing of the various 'audiences' and 'concerns' in which it was supposed to have a footing. Edward Thompson became the chief spokesman for that section of New Left opinion that was eager for a more activist and purposeful approach; after six months of argument up and down the country, the journal was re-structured. Instead of a large and amorphous editorial board (which in practice had left the running of *NLR* to a metropolitan in-group with ill-defined responsibilities, subject to overwork and drift), the review was entrusted to a small team of four with a mandate to re-establish New Left journalism as a serious source of ideas. The projected series of New Left Books was written off, having in two years produced one collection of essays and one literary-critical reprint from the United States. Little was to be heard henceforth of the Left Clubs.

By a mixture of design and default, *NLR* shortly became the preserve of a younger wave of New Left writers, most of whom had been involved in the production of *New University*, a student socialist journal edited from Oxford. Their elders on the New Left Board, lacking even a token editorial function, dispersed to catch up on their research, emigrate, help run CND, or just vanish. With the organizational passing of the Old New Left, whatever was distinctive in its ideas has perished also. The New New Left cadres in CND have formed no exception and offered little resistance to the processes of dissipation and dilution that have been visibly at work in the anti-nuclear movement as a whole, reflected in Bertrand Russell's turn from mass campaigning to personal diplomacy and research sponsorship, in the withdrawal of Labour's MPs from CND's Executive ('I am sure these Labour members feel that a CND connection might be a serious embarrassment during the election'*), and in the recurrent moves by the *moderantiste* wing of the Campaign to disown direct-action initiatives (Committee of 100, Spies for Peace) and play down the full unilateralist case. Stuart Hall co-authored the CND Executive's 'intermediate' policy statement of 1962, of which Canon Collins could later confess, in the mood of retrospect occasioned by his resignation from the chairmanship: '. . . we must never seem to be departing from our basic policy. It was, perhaps, our failure in this respect which led to the poor reception by the bulk of the Campaign of the "Steps Towards Peace" programme.'† John Rex, author of *NLR*'s main unilateralist pamphlet *Britain Without the Bomb*, produced for the Aldermaston March of 1960, can now write: 'What we can do realistically is to lay emphasis on stopping the spread of control, and if this is our aim the notion of unilateralism is entirely irrelevant. We have to see to it that those who are in a position to influence strategic thinking come out clearly for confining possession and control of the deterrent to Russia and America. Precisely because Mr Wilson is ambiguous on this we must make sure that he commits himself against the MLF.'‡ Attitudes such as this are, in fact, the dominant tendency in British socialism today. The role that is most commonly sought after is nothing more than that of the Left Centre to the Centre-Left.

Political initiative is directed not down to the grass-roots, but upwards, influencing the ambiguous leaders, strengthening and supporting their progressive, collectivist leanings. In this scheme, the medium of

*J. B. Priestley in the *New Statesman*, 26 October 1963.
† *Sanity*, May 1964.
‡ *Peace News*, 24 April 1961.

political advance is the Centre-Left, a body of persons who have influence, and possibly even administrative power, but lack gumption and consistency and are subject to the wrong pressures. The Left Centre has (it believes) the gumption and the principle, but not the influence; its job is to apply the right pressure at selected points so that the Centre-Left will swing towards policies which, however limited, will in the long run have delayed radical effects. The tactic has a built-in propensity to retreat from a public, campaigning role, or else the public campaign becomes an adjunct to the localized lobby at the top. The pressurizer is himself under pressure to reduce the most salient features of his own identity, to keep silence about any basic differences in purpose that might be thought to exist between himself and the object of his exertions. His public aim, after all, is not to supplant, but only to supplement, the part played by the influential Centre-Left.

At the moment, there are four or five socialist publications in Britain whose politics fall within Left-Centre/Centre-Left terms. Their outstanding characteristics are their militant reticence (or, in moments of daring, reticent militancy), their mastery of oblique, Aesopian language, and their protective colouring, viz., their total refusal to differentiate themselves from the main lines of official Labour policy. The monthly *Union Voice*, sponsored by a galaxy of constituency activists, union officials and *marxisants*, issues a Defence Broadsheet replete with quotes from Dennis Healey, George Brown and Harold Wilson; on unilateralism it is silent, and its qualms about NATO are expressed conditionally ('build up the United Nations so that it can take over from NATO'). When Wilson commits Parliamentary Labour to support of the oil war in Aden, *Tribune* quietly deplores 'hasty statements' of this ilk, until shamed into a more outspoken protest by its scandalized readers' letters. In the columns of *The Week*, a news analysis for socialists with far-Left backing, may be discerned a tougher stance, set in reported rather than direct speech, visible in the interstices between paste-ups. The new bi-monthly *International Socialist Journal*, whose slate of contributors overlaps markedly with that of *NLR*, seems to have been conceived as a theoretical meeting-ground for French, Belgian, Italian and British Left-Centre tacticians; and the annual *Socialist Register*, a volume of essays edited by two stalwarts of the Old New Left, John Saville and Ralph Miliband, while much more traditional in its independent-socialist tone, maintains a sober, silently aloof tenor that is in distinct contrast to the aggressive intellectual presence that burst from the pages of *Out of Apathy*.

The present development of *New Left Review* must be seen within this context of general caution and dependence, which runs deeper than the mere tactical conformity of Election Year. The previous management of the review was committed to the establishment of an independent cultural apparatus that could both challenge and elude the grasp of the Party bureaucracy. Now that this hope has failed, any successor movement of socialist intelligentsia must find a fresh rationale. From its beginning, the New Left has been concerned to define its limits, and to achieve the maximum intellectual density within those limits; its sponsors possess a unitary and homogeneous political culture, which they have maintained editorially without sentiment or mercy, preferring the risks of exclusiveness to the flaccid hospitality of their forerunners. As a consequence, the new *NLR* has succeeded in fulfilling the first duty of any serious political tendency: it has survived intact. The retrenched and concentrated politics of the present editorial team has given a wide berth to the impressionistic social journalism that marked *ULR*. We have been spared the sociologist's escapade into youth-leadership, the essay on the political significance of Beatlemania, complete with Twist photographs for Marxist voyeurs. We hear no more of the corroding effects of mass media and status objects; indeed, the captive consumer may now, in certain favoured circumstances, be numbered among the positives of socialist theory:

... the communications network in Cuba – transport, telecommunications, and newsprint – was very highly developed; in some sectors it had effectively reached saturation point. This sophisticated system of communication provided the indispensable *technical* pre-conditions for the astonishing mobilization of 1959–60. The absence of a political party was compensated by a television, radio and transport system which allowed immediate, electric contact between the revolutionary leadership and the working people of Cuba.*

The strength of *NLR* for the last two years has lain in its richly documented structural and historical studies of metropolitan and colonial societies, studded with Sartrean logic and gallicized syntax. (There have been occasional attempts to copy the typographical style of *Les Temps Modernes*.) Its cadres are partisans of 'rigour' (a key word in New Left deliberations not long ago), adept in the swift global interconnection and the dialectical surprise move. They lack nostalgia; when they survey the past, it is with a time-machine's traverse, plotting the orbit of elements in the historical ensemble, rather than registering sensuously the impact of men and events. They have never had to

*Robin Blackburn, 'Sociology of the Cuban Revolution', *New Left Review*, 21, October 1963.

'work through' a distorted loyalty: and so there is in them none of the energy of conscious rejection, no streak of puritan vigilance against the enemy within. They are not so much uprooted (the common fate of the mobile intellectual) as rootless. Whereas the other New Left had preserved a notional or umbilical link between itself and extra-intellectual sources of action in British society, this is an openly self-articulated, self-powered outfit, an Olympian *autogestion* of roving postgraduates that descends at will from its own space onto the target-terrains of Angola, Persia, Cuba, Algeria, Britain ...

For all its purism and scholarship, *NLR* is now committed, at least on paper, to an activist and Marxist philosophy, in which struggle is acknowledged as the engine of social change, and economic levers are seen as operating at a more fundamental level of potency than cultural influences. Only, the forms of struggle which are picked out for attention and commendation are not those of an industrial working-class movement; they are predominately either agrarian or technocratic, depending on whether an underdeveloped or an advanced society is under scrutiny. In its analyses of the 'Third World', *NLR* has dropped the neutralist endorsement of regimes by foreign policy alone, and maintains a more selective sympathy with those governments and movements which combine drastically radical domestic objectives with a mass rural social base. There is some variation among contributors as to the number and nature of 'peasant-based socialisms' that may be affirmed. For one writer, China has 'her distinctive variant of socialism' in the underdeveloped world, along with the 'royal socialism' of Cambodia, the 'democratic centralism' of Guinea and the 'African socialism' of Ghana and Mali.* The editorial team's standpoint is much more definitely *Fidelista*, with Cuba and Algeria taken as the most instructive models for social change, and Ghana, the UAR and Zanzibar as the exemplars of promise for the development of African socialism.†

Within this variance of assertion, certain silences are constant: never is any concern voiced for the fate of political democracy in the new regimes, or for the autonomy of trade unions; the vacillations of favoured Front leaders are never mentioned in print, and the corporatist features of their programmes and methods of appeal are ignored. This is not simply the old silence of the 'Friends of the Soviet Union', the factual mythology of bemused fellow-travellers; it is much

*Quotations and ascriptions are from Keith Buchanan, 'The Third World', *New Left Review*, 18, January–February 1963.

†See the review of Fenner Brockway's *African Socialism* in *New Left Review*, 24, March–April 1964.

more like the present silence of the intelligent Labour Left, confronted with an oracular parliamentary leader who (it is felt) may jump in any of several possible directions, some more progressive than others. (The early fixation of American liberals upon Kennedy was very similar.) The single-Front regimes of Castro, Ben Bella, Nasser and Nkrumah are the colonial analogue to the Centre-Left; the leader at the wheel is kept to the revolutionary course either by the discreet comments of the Left Centre inside the vehicle or by the encouraging bravos of Marxist bystanders. The most striking (and successful) instance of this approach is of course the part played by M. Michel Pablo (Raptis), formerly the secretary of the Fourth International, as a key economic consultant to Ben Bella, but others have accepted the same role. (Consider the implications of Ben Bella's: 'I am now so unreservedly committed to the Left that any opposition to me is necessarily counter-revolutionary.'*) Recently, too, Khrushchev has elevated Nasser's Egypt from the 'state-capitalist' status to which it had been hitherto consigned by Soviet theorists, and spoken of its 'advance on the road of socialist development'; the incipient mass Front, the Arab Socialist Union, is declared to be 'a political organization of the people' in which, presumably, the Egyptian Communists will play their part. ('It must be presumed that persecution of Communists has become a thing of the past . . . there are no stauncher fighters for progress and socialism than the Communists.'†)

Here then is a socialism which puts out no press, organizes no party, supports no strikes, rallies no class, carries no banner, articulates no ideology; its work is only to exhort and endorse the initiatives of the guiding directorate, and (where possible) to enter the inner circle of the latter's confidence. And, this is an absolutely reasonable terminus for a certain kind of socialist approach; if socialism is not bound up in its very nature with the achievement of democracy by an actual working class, there is not the slightest ground for withholding support from any agency whatsoever, no matter how militaristic, mystical or totalitarian, that conducts sweeping measures of statization and planning.

Jacobin in its inclinations towards the 'Third World' of radical scarcity, the New Left veers towards Fabian methods nearer home. The socialist potential of 'Third World' dictators lies in the extent of their readiness to expropriate the expropriators and make a sharp, decisive break with the ancient order; for British purposes, however, socialism

---

*To a *New Statesman* correspondent, 5 June 1964.

†From Khrushchev's radio speech on his return from the UAR, summarized in *Soviet Weekly*, 4 June 1964.

can be satisfactorily defined as 'democratically accountable social control over the big aggregates of capital'* and the permeation of planning methods into capitalism is thought to offer the best opportunity for militant socialist advance at a later stage. Thus Barbara Castle (widely tipped as a member of the next Labour Cabinet) can write that 'In Britain, as in France, the serious pursuit of planning will edge us towards more fundamental decisions about property – and therefore about power – than may seem obvious when we first start out on the road.'† This is sometimes put as the strategy of 'structural reforms', a sort of creeping takeover bid by the state against the private sector that will, at a certain point, perhaps through an exposé of capitalist obstructionism, clear the air for an explicit inauguration of socialism.

The initial agency of socialization need not, it seems, even be a government of Labour. Gaullist neo-capitalism is seen by one contributor as a 'compromise', 'an abandonment by capitalism of crucial prerogatives to the state' in which 'capitalism, in short, is attempting to preserve its position by the use of socialist techniques';‡ the same author notes the contemporary 'introduction of mechanisms *of a socialist nature* [Mallet's own italics] into the heart of capitalist economy'. Equally the work of structural reform may, as in Italy, be initiated by a socialist-liberal-clerical coalition, though more of this will be said a little later.

The programmatic consequences of the New Left's permissiveness towards gradualism are rather interesting. In the sphere of social ownership, no New Left writer has in the last two years singled out any particular area of private industry for nationalization – with the exception of steel and road haulage (the one firmly and the other tentatively booked for state ownership by official Labour policy), and, in one recent tantalizing editorial aside, the contraceptive industry. (This may be contrasted with the lengthy shopping-list of industries and firms given in the Old New Left's industrial policy document of 1957, *The Insiders*; the difference reflects the new mood of a Left convinced that Labour's further plans for social ownership may be safely left up Harold Wilson's sleeve, where they are assumed to reside.) On the other hand, *NLR* has been eloquent in its purveyance of detailed suggestions for indirect state limitation of monopoly power, and for the organization of an economic Civil Service. In offering these pro-

* John Hughes, 'An Economic Policy for Labour', *New Left Review*, 24, March–April 1964.

† 'The Lessons of French Planning', *New Left Review*, 24, March–April 1964.

‡ Serge Mallet in *New Left Review*, 19, March–April 1963.

posals, it has never considered the implications raised by the remarkable record of adaptability which British capitalism has been able to show in the face of governmental intervention, its long-standing capacities both of evasion and of fusion, when confronted with a rival social challenge. Although the success of a probing, 'edging', state-interventionist strategy must remain at least problematic, the New Left (both Old and New) has not hesitated to propose the incorporation of the trade unions into the future machinery of planning. In this respect the time-scale of its policy priorities is revealing; the direct extension of the public sector by nationalization is (except for the case of steel) indefinitely postdated, but the introduction of 'incomes policy', the creation of 'conditions under which the trade unions and their members can be expected to accept only modest increases in money wage terms', is urged 'without delay' upon 'a Labour Government, working from its existing economic and social policy commitments'.*

A similar sense of relative urgencies, as between incomes planning and nationalization, seems to have gone into Thomas Balogh's pamphlet *Planning for Progress*; Balogh is both an economic adviser to the Labour Party and a contributor to *NLR*. In effect, the economic bargaining-power of the working class is being mortgaged to a hopeful blueprint. The protestations of New Left writers in favour of 'workers' control' rest upon a suspect distinction between the control of wages and the control of conditions, the former being hived off for statized determination, the latter being left for the shop-stewards to practise in 'encroachment' at factory level. In fact, of course, in many industries the power of the trade-union movement at shop-floor level is inseparable from its ability to enforce improvements in locally determined rates of pay; and many improvements in conditions cost money, as a sort of social wage inside the factory. Nothing could be more calculated to undermine the 'power at the base' which the New Left is committed to defending than this bureaucratic buffering of working-class self-activity.

In all this, the New Left is almost consciously acting as a dynamizing Left Centre to the putative Centre-Left of Wilson, Callaghan, etc. What is particularly staggering is its failure to imagine that it might be out-manoeuvred; pursuing a tactic of total theoretical entry, all its eggheads have marched into the single basket of Left reformism, and are now busily appealing to the waverers outside, especially in the trade-union movement, to jump in as well. But the unknown factor in Left-reformist strategy lies not only in the possibility of sabotage or enticement from

* John Hughes, op. cit.

the business world. Equally doubt-provoking is (a) the immense responsibility that would attach to the leadership in a campaign of administrative encroachment; combined with (b) the desperate unlikelihood of any foreseeable Labour Cabinet that would answer to the part. The successful management of an encroaching, creeping revolution in an advanced capitalist society must surely demand qualities of intransigence and tactical brilliance at the top far in excess of the human resources on call in, let us say, a proletarian insurrection or the industrialization of a peasant territory. (After all, what makes a structural reform structural, and not simply any old reform, is not anything in its content, but precisely its timing in an unfolding militant strategy – no more socialist than the nationalization of coal (or of cars, as in France, or of petrol, as in Italy) unless it was followed through).

Are such qualities of militant intelligence really much in evidence in the Parliamentary Labour Party? The Old New Left thought not: 'Most of the people at the top of the Labour Party are professional politicians, very much at home in the conventions of capitalist politics. These are a very bad and untrustworthy sort of people. We all know this, but some fetish about "unity" prevents us from saying it. We should say it now since – being professional politicians and sensing which way the wind blows – some of them may start to try out a leftish "image" in their speeches.'* A trifle overpersonalized, perhaps, but well said. Labour's possible Front Bench has not changed very much since then. The addition of a radical Fabian here or a shifty middleman there is not going to make all that much difference – particularly if Mr Wilson fulfils his object of enlarging the powers of Premiership into something approaching those of Presidency. '*How can we prevent the Wilson Administration,*' asks *NLR* rhetorically, '*from going down in history as the involuntary renovator of capitalism, and ensure that it takes its place as the government which irreversibly inaugurates the transition to socialism?*' The simple, straight answer is that we can't (though there are other, more modest, mostly welfare functions for a Labour government, and certainly plenty of work for a clear-sighted Left); if we pretend more than this, we risk being transformed into apologists for measures which shackle working-class initiative without having the faintest relevance to a socialist transition. Militant Left-reformism is actually, in the Britain of 1964, as 'millennial', 'utopian', 'heroic' and 'romantic' as its proponents have supposed revolutionary Marxism to be.

We do not have to look far back for a practical demonstration of the

* Edward Thompson, *New Reasoner*, Autumn, 1959.

pitfalls that await even a dynamic gradualism based on an inadequate political vehicle. Italy has afforded a pioneering instance in the 'Opening to the Left', a strategy whereby an erstwhile independent socialist formation (the PSI) undertook to support a Centre-Left coalition in the hope of initiating structural, socializing reforms that would go beyond a neo-capitalist modernization. Three articles in *New Left Review* have commented on the evolution of this perspective. In the beginning, ambitious euphoria:

'At this decisive moment of Italian political history, the PCI remained faithful to its policy of "presence". Refusing the trap of a facile sectarianism, it announced a conditional approval of the Centre-Left formula, based on the declared belief that the "Opening to the Left" could set in motion a political dynamic which would shift the whole political centre of gravity in Italy decisively to the Left.'*

A more guarded, hedged approval followed, as the strategy progressed:

'I consider that a temporary alliance with the DC cannot be refused *a priori*, since it may be useful for the achievement of certain specific reforms. The condition of such an alliance, of course, should be that it is not a permanent option.'†

The final note, however, was one of bitter hindsight: 'Nenni may have wanted to do a number of things, and thought he could do them, but in fact, once he was captured he could do nothing.'‡

A good epitaph should be committed to memory: it may be useful for another tombstone.

* Perry Anderson, *New Left Review*, 13–14, January–April, 1962.

† Lelio Basso, 'The Centre-Left in Italy,' *New Left Review*, 17, Winter, 1962.

‡ Jon Halliday, 'The New Italian Socialist Party', *New Left Review*, 24, March–April 1964.

Chapter 4
That Was the Affluence That Was:
The Industrial Struggle from
1956 to 1964

The Talking Union Blues

Now, if you want higher wages let me tell you what to do,
You got to talk to the workers in the shop with you,
You got to build you a union, make it strong,
And if you all stick together, boys, it won't take long.

You'll get shorter hours ... better working conditions ...
holidays with pay ... take your wife and kids to the seaside ...

Now it ain't that simple, so I'd better explain,
Just why you've got to ride on the union train,
'Cause if you wait for the boss to raise your pay –
You'll all be waiting to Judgement Day.

All be buried ... gone to heaven ... St Peter'll be the shop
steward then ...

Now you know you're underpaid, but the boss says you ain't.
He speeds up the work 'till you're ready to faint.
You may be down and out but you ain't beaten,
You can hand out a leaflet and call a meeting.

Talk it over ... speak your mind ... decide to do something
about it ...

'Course, the boss may persuade some poor damn fool,
To go to your meeting and act as his tool.
But you can always tell a scab, though, that's a fact,
He's got a yellow streak running down his back.

He doesn't have to scab ... he'll always get along ... on
what he takes out of blind men's cups ...

You got a union now and you're sitting pretty,
Put some of the boys on the steering committee.
The boss won't listen when one guy squawks,
But he's got to listen when the union talks.

He'd better . . . be mighty lonely . . . if everybody decided to
walk out on him.

Suppose they're working you so hard it's just outrageous,
And they're paying you all starvation wages.
You go to the boss and the boss will yell –
'Before I'd raise your pay I'd see you all in hell.'
Well, he's puffing a big cigar, feeling mighty slick,
'Cause he thinks he's got your union licked,
But he looks out the window and what does he see –
A thousand pickets and they all agree.

He's a bastard . . . unfair . . . slavedriver . . . bet he beats his
own wife . . .

Now boys, you've come to the hardest time,
The boss will try to break your picket line.
He'll call out the police, the Brigade of Guards,
Tell you it's a crime to hold a union card,
They'll raid your meetings, hit you on the head,
They'll call everyone of you a goddam red.

Un-British . . . Moscow agents . . . Saboteurs . . . Even the kids.

Well up in Fylingdales here's what they found. Up at Coventry here's what
they found and out at Dagenham here's what they found: – And all over
England here's what they found. That if you don't let red-baiting break you
up, and if you don't let race hatred break you up, and if you don't let going
without break you up . . . You'll win . . . What I mean is take it easy but take
it . . . You'll win.

(An English version of the Almanac Singers talking blues. Published in *Songs
of Hope and Survival*, Hackney YCND)

The fifties opened in the sunshine of the biggest boom British capitalism
had yet experienced. One economist estimates 'the system as a whole
has never grown so fast for so long as since the war – twice as fast
between 1950 and 1964 as between 1913 and 1950, and nearly half as
fast again as during the generation before that'.* But by the end of the

* Michael Kidron, *Western Capitalism since the War*, Weidenfeld & Nicolson,
1968, p. ix.

decade even this most prosperous sun was sinking in the horizon, casting the first shadows of the unemployment, the incomes policy and the legal attack on the trade unions which were to dominate the trade-union movement in the sixties. But in this brief holiday in the fifties a certain amount of political hay was made. The Labour Party Right were in their element. 'Capitalism,' wrote their leading intellectual, 'has been reformed almost out of recognition. Despite occasional minor recessions and balance-of-payments crises, full employment and at least a tolerable degree of stability are likely to be maintained. Automation can be expected steadily to solve any remaining problem of under-production. Looking ahead, our present rate of growth will give us a national output three times as high as now in fifty years – an increase capable of sustaining not only a generous rise in home living standards, but also a level of investment in the under-developed areas fully as high as they can physically accommodate.'* The uninspiring yes-men who sat comfortably on top of the Trades Union Congress felt the same. The General Council contributed its own exhibit to the Production Exhibition (subtitled 'Investing in Success') at Olympia in 1956. It included a rather poor papier-mâché likeness of Ned Ludd, apocryphal leader of the Luddites, with, as the TUC magazine *Labour* put it, 'other symbols of the days that have gone, as a reminder of what the workers' attitude to the new ideas might be if the unions had not grown strong and efficient'.

It seemed as if the dark conditions of the thirties had somehow been turned inside out, that the grinding misery of unemployment, stagnation and poverty had been permanently inverted into work, growth and prosperity. Skilled workers could now choose work and confidently change employers without fear of getting stranded out on the dole. The appetite for labour was keen enough to bring women workers and immigrants into the work-force from their sinks and villages.† At work, wages went steadily up and up, managements invariably preferring to settle and shrug off the cost onto increased prices. And since prices rose at a slow 2½ per cent, these wages bought a real increase in living standards. Outside the works, cycle racks were replaced by car parks. In the kitchen, the glutinous taste of Ministry of War recipes and austerity cooking was finally taken off the tongue by new supermarket foods and foreign recipes. And on the trade-unionist's bookshelf, the thick-paged, orange-bound Left Book Club editions about Ellen

---

* Anthony Crosland, *The Future of Socialism*, Cape, 1956, revised edn 1964.

† Immigration from the West Indies reached a peak in 1958–60 and in 1963–4 for Asians, almost precisely in time with the jobs available.

Wilkinson's Jarrow battles and Strachey's forecasts of collapse had been replaced by shiny Penguin books with titles like *The Affluent Society* and *Room at the Top*.

The causes of post-war full employment are still debated, even as it ebbs away before the eyes of economists who seem as baffled by its going as its coming. It certainly was not the result of the wisdom of Maynard Keynes and his American disciple Alvin Hansen. Keynesian deficit budgeting may have contributed to ending the mass unemployment of the thirties, mainly because Keynes made a convincing theoretical case for doing what liberal economists knew was the correct action anyway. But government spending was not the cause of the exceptionally low levels of post-war unemployment. Nor was it the 'age of planning' so enthusiastically hailed by O-level Civics masters and *Guardian* leader writers. It seems the grim probability that the spectacular economic growth of the fifties was in fact mortgaged to the gigantic increase in state spending on armaments, that H-bombs stopped dole queues. Whatever its cause, at the time the boom seemed as never-ending as the slump had appeared in the thirties. Professional politicians assumed that, since there was no longer any poverty or unemployment, all that remained to argue about was how most efficiently to run the economy. The skin-thinness of this view is now quite apparent. But even at the height of the boom itself it was still the case that the affluence was unevenly spread and whole groups, the old, the disabled, the fatherless, those with large families, had been clean passed by. And at the height of boom, the machinery and the underlying principles of welfare established in 1945 were being quietly trimmed away, both in their immediate value and their universality of application. And it should also have been clear that the share workers took of the wealth they produced had advanced not one iota. Nevertheless there was a steady annual growth of real income until as late as 1967 and an evaporation of chronic unemployment. And this shifted the very assumptions on which the trade-union movement had rested.

The barons of the TUC were delighted. Their memoirs tell of a fighting youth, the battles of the thirties, the rewards of power and now the need for responsibility. For the symbols if not the substance of power had been granted to them. Trade-unionists appeared on the Boards of State Corporations and in the Honours List. They were conveyed in limousines to sit in panelled committees with the Government (only six joint committees before the war but eighty-one by 1954). They commanded respect even from Tory politicians. 'If I want to talk to the Minister, I just pick up that telephone,' a leading trade-unionist reported.* They were received in evening dress at banquets to the applause of the *Daily Express* and the occasional catcall from their members. And from its splendid new premises, the TUC Research Department, equipped with brains trained at the very best colleges, tendered elaborate annual reports to the Government. It seemed like the end of extremism. Enoch Powell and the right-wing Tories, and the Communist union leaders, still barred from the General Council and denouncing wage restraint, had both been left gathering dust on the political shelf, while the new union of Labour and Capital was vigorously pursued below. The Right was determined to eliminate from trade-unionism any element which actually challenged the *status quo*, and this era of semi-permanent understanding had affected Communists in the union leadership as well. Their politics were those of soldiering on, occasionally brandishing ideological souvenirs, but in no sense providing a coherent alternative to the new consensus. The natural inclination of trade-union full-timers, uncontrolled by an alert rank and file, to try to raise themselves within existing society acted on the Left as well as the Right. Communist officials in the ETU, for example, after fifteen years in office found themselves obliged to manipulate the postal franking dates of branch electoral returns in order to guarantee their re-election. And in *Labour Monthly*, the Communist publication, the procession of Left-inclined union leaders, while striking militant stances and urging the defeat of the right wing, had nothing real to say to their own members' new problems.

Not that there were not members or problems. But increasingly the rank-and-file union members who created and sustained the unions had peeled away from the glossy surface of official trade-unionism. In the paper battles of the Labour Party Conference and the TUC, trade-unionists were marshalled in huge batches, accounted for down to the last digit. But the contours of the real movement in the workshop were less angular. Beneath the noses of the great men discussing grand strategy at Blackpool were the militants debating the small coinage of the branch, the problems of overtime, automation and equal pay. For, in reality, trade-union organization had come to depend increasingly on a relatively small number of militants operating on the local level. The shop stewards who led these struggles were not so much antagonistic to union brass as independent of it. At the union centre the full-timers led their annual waltz with the employers' association to establish a

* Martin Harrison, *Trade Unions and the Labour Party since* 1945, Allen & Unwin, 1960, p. 294.

national rate throughout the industry. But the real value of the wage packet tended to depend on bargains struck locally between shop stewards, lay officers elected in the plant, and equivalent managers. For, ironically, payment by results, the piecework system introduced by employers to bypass trade-unionism, had been pushed into reverse. In strongly unionized plants, daily detailed bargaining over different jobs, changes in setting, various bonuses and special payments jacked up the wage until it towered over the basic rate formally agreed at the national level. Close comparison between different grades of skill enabled the lower paid to continually hitch their earnings upwards. Stewards could often memorize and calculate comparative rates down to the last farthing with arithmetical expertise which would leave a lot of professional mathematicians or dart players standing. Shop-floor control over the speed at which a job was done meant that workers actually controlled the flow of production and could effectively decide their overtime and actual working hours by bunching work together or slowing it right down. 'In disputes over prices there is one thing that is never discussed: the speed at which a job is to be done. We will discuss basic engineering problems such as maintaining certain finishes and dimensions, but not those of speeds and feeds. The reason is simple: the company must not be allowed to assert direct control over the speed at which a worker does his job. He must remain sole arbiter of that. It is part of his control over his working environment. The firm doesn't like this, of course, and would prefer so-called scientific studies, etc., to determine rates, rather than what comes down fundamentally to a clash of individual strengths.'* More workers went on strike more frequently, but the stoppages were abrupt, unofficial and usually quickly settled. Some stoppages were almost momentary, sorted out before even the steward, far less the union officials, knew about them. And the strikes were more often over issues of conditions and control than strict cash issues. What became known in the sixties as 'wage drift' originated here in the rank and file's wage push.

This type of bargaining encouraged the spread and strengthening of the shop-steward system, which became more advanced in British factories than in any other industrial country, but tended to discourage the 'political' aspect of trade-unionism. Resolution-mongering in the Labour Party and the Trades Councils was often ignored. Workers who were the leaders of militancy on the factory floor often failed to turn up at geographically based branch meetings. While a great majority of

* From 'The Convenor', a personal account of work by a Communist convenor in the Coventry district, *New Left Review*, 48, March–April 1968.

unionists voted in the annual election of their shop steward, very few would follow national union elections very closely. This agnosticism about politics in general and militancy about trade-unionism in particular was most marked in the Midland car industry. A convenor of stewards in Birmingham talking, after the Tories regained the town in 1959, about his members' militancy in the works, said, 'The trouble is they just don't link it up with politics and the way they vote.'*

But, in a sense, indifference and cynicism towards official parliamentary 'politics' was quite sensible. Your shop steward could do more for you than your MP and you could replace him the moment he ceased to represent your interests fully. The instinct to exert control over work rather than be dominated by it went deeper than the five-yearly motion of voting. And this drive for control continually pressed militant trade-unionism into highly political questioning of the management's god-given right to manage. In a strongly organized factory in a high-wage district, like the ENV gear-producing plant in Willesden, North London (site of the first International Socialist factory branch) stewards effectively banished the nominal managers of the factory from the floor running of the factory. Not only did the workers win good wages and conditions, including equal pay for women, but various informal institutions run by workers – cut-price shops, bars and cafés – sprang up. Informal watch-repairing and fancy metal work took place under the nose of the bosses.† The stewards in such a factory had to be finely tuned to the real needs of their workmates, hold regular works meetings and develop imaginative tactics for tying together the multitude of different grades of workers in the highly differentiated labour processes under their roof. They were also a key link in an informal network of militancy, able to give immediate donations from their funds to fellow workers in dispute and organize regular shop-floor whip-rounds in support of prolonged strikes. A similar range and scale of activities was studiously documented by the Court of Inquiry held into the Briggs body-plant dispute, who noted with apparent bewilderment that 'it appears for many years the shop stewards have come together as a sort of *corps d'élite* known as the shop stewards' committee, which is comprised of all the shop stewards in the plant'.‡ Among the activities dis-

* Dennis Butt, 'Men and Motors', *New Left Review*, 3.

† See Joyce Rosser and Colin Barker, 'A Working Class Defeat; The ENV Story', *International Socialism*, 31.

‡ 'Report of a Court of Inquiry into the Causes and Circumstances of a Dispute at Briggs Motor Bodies Ltd, Dagenham', HMSO, April 1957, Cmnd 131. Cited by Ken Coates and Anthony Topham in *Industrial Democracy in Great Britain*, MacGibbon & Kee, 1968, p. 210.

dainfully documented is 'the sale of Templegate lottery tickets of value £16,150. Prizes amounting to £9,339 12s. were paid out of this sum; £2,066 11s. went as "commission to Shop Funds" for the incidental expenses of shop stewards on union business, upwards of £1,900 was spent on various forms of strike activity, the printing of leaflets, donations to strikes outside Briggs, etc. . . .' The Committee was also discovered to 'publish once a month or once in two months a periodical called the *Voice of Ford Workers*, priced 2d., with a circulation of roughly 10,000'. This kind of activity was probably far more widespread than either Government inquiries, or for that matter the Marxist Left, realized.

But its existence increasingly led to rebukes from the official leadership. In 1956 Vincent Tewson, then TUC General Secretary, was to deplore the fact that 'among the selfish are those few who think they can do better on their own than acting in concert with their own union'. In 1960 a TUC General Council official referred to combined committees of shop stewards as 'a challenge to established union arrangements' aiming 'to usurp the policy-making functions of unions'. Communist stewards from Sheffield and Dagenham convening a national engineering shop stewards' conference banned by the AEU Executive had credentials suspended. The ENV stewards, for their part, felt 'the union outside was of very little importance; indeed in general the stewards only had recourse to the union officials as a "face-saver"'.

The relationships were actually much more complicated than the standard picture of corrupt leadership thwarting the real desires of a restive but betrayed rank and file so beloved of left-wing folklore. There was instead in the late fifties an uneasy stalemate subtly different within each union. The union leadership, with its head office, headed notepaper, briefcases and seaside conferences, was able to hold the balance between the employers and those actually struggling. They provided the symbolic unity represented by the union card, a union magazine which no one read, and occasionally vital financial aid. But since the struggles themselves were isolated, split up in time and space, so that at any particular time only a small number of people were involved, there was seldom a crisp widespread breach between militants and leadership. Rather the two sides stalked each other round and round in circles, the bureaucrats disliking the stewards' independence but seldom able openly to attack militant organization lest they had nothing left to sell to the employers, the militants scornful of their leadership but still unable to dispense with or actually challenge them.

For there was little in the mid-fifties acting to weld together politically the stewards in their localities.

But 1956 was to mark the end of golden boom and the beginning of a series of probing attacks by the employers on the positions of strength hollowed out by workers. The winter of 1956–7 was the first serious recession and brought with it a quite sharp bout of unemployment. This faltering in the British economy's growth was in some ways inevitable. Although, by previous British standards, the level of capital investment was high, it was clearly inadequate to face the 'economic miracles' of Germany and later Japan. Britain, which had been at first artificially shielded from the sharpening competition from its European competitors, whose factories were physically devastated, now was exposed to head-on competition. America, whose clear dominance over the world capitalist system was clearly established after the war, was less and less willing to support Britain as a junior economic partner. And British manufacturers themselves were increasingly exporting their cash, finding their capital forced abroad by the strength of the British working class. The disintegration of the Empire was also beginning to affect the home economy adversely. The pound, the sterling area and the City, remnants of the high noon of imperialism, which had acted as a buffer against trade rivals in pre-war conditions, now tended to act as a brake on growth. And the determination of the City of London to remain world financial centre increased Britain's trading vulnerability. For, as Chancellor after Chancellor was to find, as soon as the economy starts to expand out of a recession, its propensity to suck in imports forces another cutback which in turn depresses investment.

The 1956–7 recession served as a warning to Government and trade-unionists that things could not drift on interminably. The Monckton Era of an infinitely co-operative Minister of Labour was to change into sterner directives from the Government on wages. Since the thirties the Tories had seesawed ideologically between the old Liberal championing of the rule of the market and independent trade-unionism and corporatist enthusiasm for state planning and Government intervention. The dominant emphasis, despite Tory appeals to principle, depended almost entirely on the audience and situation, Tory rank-and-file getting to this day full-blooded economic *laissez-faire* while trade-union leaders and big industrialists are told of the virtues of collaborating in the national interest. But in 1956 the Tories tended to pursue both tacks simultaneously and experimentally. In the summer of 1967, Thorney-croft attempted to launch an incomes policy by setting a guiding light for wage increases. This was rejected by the Cabinet, but they revived instead an old Tory notion, pioneered by Macmillan in the thirties, of 'impartial authorities' designed to look independent of the Government and implicate union leadership in defining and adjudicating on national industrial problems. The first attempt was a three-man Council on Prices, Productivity and Incomes, soon known as the Three Wise Men, and without any real power. In 1958 the Cohen Council, asked to investigate 'independently' price stability, came to the conclusion that 'no one should be surprised if it proves necessary that unemployment should go somewhat further'. And in 1961, Selwyn Lloyd was persuaded to make the most serious attempt yet at integrating the trade unions into national policy with the National Economic Development Council. As he said, 'you can't talk publicly about things like restrictive practices and so on, but I felt it was very necessary to have some kind of private forum – a private meeting place – with an independent secretariat so that the other side would have confidence that it wasn't a government-controlled thing: where one could discuss seriously the obstacles to growth, and the ways we could promote economic efficiency and expansion'.* Lord Boyle recalls Mac's enthusiasm: '... the idea of NEDC sent him right back to his old Middle Way enthusiasms. I was struck by how tremendously effectively he took it through the Cabinet.'†

This new gusto for planning did not cramp traditional Tory economic style. A heavily deflationary budget in September 1957 forced the bank rate up to the unheard-of level of 7 per cent. And a relatively new weapon in the Tory armoury was its direct control over the wages of Government employees. Increasingly, national agreements were being settled by threatened or actual strike action and set-piece battles were fought out in single industries which set the level of national rises generally. The year 1956 had seen the first national action by engineers since the lock-outs of 1897 and 1922. In this dispute the employers were anxious to negotiate the removal of 'restrictive practices' and wanted a court of inquiry to begin this. The union began a national strike which was called off after only twenty-four hours by the casting vote of Lord Carron. The big leap in strike figures in 1957 was started by the March strikes by shipbuilders and continued by a major battle by London transport workers against the Government's 'guiding light' in May and June of the same year; 50,000 bus crew members were on official strike from 14 May to 20 June and they were supported by 2,500 meat trans-

* Selwyn Lloyd, quoted in *The Day before Yesterday*, by Allan Thompson, Sidgwick & Jackson, 1971, p. 187.
† Edward Boyle, quoted in *The Day before Yesterday*, p. 187.

port drivers, 4,000 Smithfield market workers, 3,500 cold-store workers and up to 20,000 dockers. The vigour of rank-and-file solidarity, especially between busmen and the dockers, was ignored by an entirely unprepared and hostile TUC General Council, which on 4 June refused to extend the strike.

It seems clear the Tories quite carefully isolated the busmen and their leader Cousins, the notorious opponent of restraint. They had settled with the railwaymen and miners, public-sector workers whose claims fell due at the same time, with generous increases of 3 and 4 per cent. Despite the verbal decorations these outcomes were clear breaches of Government wages policy, *The Economist* describing the railwaymen's settlement as 'for the country, a partial economic defeat'. But it left the Government free shrewdly to exploit the isolation and lack of power of the bus men and women. The showdown paid off by damping down wage demands and the Tories were not the only ones to register this. In important pioneer Labour pleas for incomes policy, Michael Stewart and Rex Winsbury noted approvingly, 'the small average size of subsequent wage increases in 1958 and much of 1959 seems to have been in large measure due to the psychological climate created by the failure of the bus strike'.* Indeed the crushing of the busmen in 1958 was to become a symbol of how strong government sets the workers an example by making a deliberate plan to crack a strike in the public sector. The *Economist* was nostalgically to advise Harold Wilson, eight years later in far worse economic difficulties, 'The only way to achieve an incomes policy in 1966 is going to be by outfacing the trade unions on some big national wages struggle in the same way as Mr Amory and Mr Macleod achieved about eighteen months of effective incomes policy in 1958–9 by outfacing Mr Cousins' London bus strike in May 1958.'

It was really only the seven-week official stoppage of all ten print unions, first in the provincial printing firms and then, when the ink supplies stopped, the Fleet Street dailies, in pursuit of their keynote claim for a 10 per cent wage increase and forty-hour week which broke bodily through the standstill with an eventual 4½ per cent settlement.

The rising spike of unemployment in the 1956 recession did not go unchallenged either. The industries in structural decline, often with strong Communist Party membership, had tended to react by organiz-

* M. Stewart and R. Winsbury, 'An Incomes Policy for Labour', Fabian Tract 350, 1963, p. 23. Cited in T. Cliff and C. Barker, *Incomes Policy, Legislation and Shop Stewards*, London, Industrial Shop Stewards Defence Committee, 1966, p. 66.

ing propaganda campaigns to attract more investment to their areas. A North East Lancashire campaign based on the spinning town of Nelson was carried out in 1958 with lobbies of Trades Councils and Parliament and a bus touring the north-east dockland with the banner 'Lancashire Today, You Tomorrow'. Aircraft workers lobbied Parliament and there was strike action against local unemployment and engineering redundancy on the north-east coast, in Dundee and on the Clyde, and in the newer towns of Coventry and Crawley. The strikes in the car industry were vigorously pursued with the support of the big-six committee (now renamed the National Motor and Ancillary Trades Shop Stewards Committee) and under the intransigent slogan 'No redundancy, we are not accepting it'. These strikes provided the first major test of workers' capacity to resist an industry-wide challenge, and were a clear warning of the difficulties ahead. In successive weeks in April 1958 APV Crawley, Standard works in Coventry and the Birmingham Norton factory struck against redundancies. The Coventry strike was over 3,000 jobs lost by the introduction of new automated tractor machinery and involved 11,000 workers. It was settled in two weeks on union advice and failed to gain anything except a £15 handshake for the sacked workers. The much smaller Norton strike in a newly organized factory over dismissal of twenty-eight men lasted thirty weeks and was only reluctantly given the most half-hearted official support, the union, for example, refusing to black goods even though exhibition workers had themselves refused to handle the Norton stand at Olympia. The Crawley settlement was perhaps the most successful and significant, the workers winning the right of consultation at shop-steward level, the right of discussion with management of possible alternative work-sharing or short-time work and the right to be retained on the payroll until a new satisfactory job was found.

But in general campaigns against redundancy remained small, easily isolated and relatively unsuccessful. The majority of workers were unwilling to join in sympathy over an issue they saw as someone else's problem. With overtime worked by 1,375,000 workers in manufacturing alone and with job mobility high, solidarity was slow arising. And the very rudimentary economic analysis offered by most of the Marxist groups was little help either. To workers who had never known the thirties the arguments of Harry Finch, the Norton convenor, in his widely read pamphlet that 'The brutal fact in this situation is that the 6,000 sacked BMC workers, the first list of 3,000 Standard workers . . . plus all the smaller redundancies are the beginning of mass unemployment' were not very convincing.* The tendency to see the first and short-lived recession as in fact the beginning of a major thirties-type crisis actually limited the Left to a constant reinterpretation of the present through the images of the past. For it was simply not true – yet – that 'All the Tory Party has to offer the workers is hunger, poverty, dole queues and imperialist adventures like the Suez affair', as Peter Fryer forecast in his book *The Battle for Socialism*. They also had on offer Tommy Steele, ITV and the end of conscription.

Indeed, to read the majority of the Left journals of the era it is scarcely possible to believe that the Tories actually thundered home in the 1959 election, so hectic are the denunciations of the Labour Right, the tributes to the rank and file's barely suppressed revolutionary enthusiasm and the descriptions of the imminence of an immediate return to Jarrow and the Hunger Marches. In *Labour Monthly*, Palme Dutt was so riled by the Tory walkover he lost his temper with the entire 'lukewarm, bedraggled, humdrum Britain of the 1950s'. For although most of the industrial disputes of the late fifties contain elements which uncannily prefigured the much sharper clashes of the sixties, probably the most prophetic disputes were those relatively small but ominous cases where a combination of trouble-shooting employer, militant-hounding union leadership and official inquiry set about the business of systematically weeding out rank-and-file trade-unionists.

For increasingly it became clear to the shrewder employer, the shop-steward-spotting sociologist and the cold-warring newspaper editor alike that wage drift and shop-floor power could be eradicated only by an actual shift of class power in the factory. The jawboning of Tory ministers about the need for responsibility in industrial relations, signatures of union leaders on national declarations of restraint, even statutory Government freezing of national pay awards, were meaningless unless there was a real shift of power on the shop floor. Management had to regain control of their work-places. In the chilly words of the pioneer of this school of industrial relations, Allan Flanders, 'more and more managements seem to me to be becoming aware that the labour situation has drifted dangerously far and that they are faced with the need to re-establish control over their own workers'. For the fifties saw the discovery of the shop steward as scapegoat for the nation's ills. 'Some shop stewards,' said the President of the National Union of Manufacturers, 'are an excrescence on trade unions.' Lord Carron, whose

* Harry Finch, 'The Fight Against Redundancy', published by Norton Motors Strike Committee, 1956. Cited in Michael Kidron, 'Policy for Redundancy', *Socialist Review*, December 1956.

personal dictatorship over his own union was increasingly unstable (in 1960 a large minority of his own National Committee voting to prevent his presidential speech being printed as a record in the union journal), felt the same: 'These men are werewolves who are rushing madly towards industrial ruin and howling delightedly at the foam on their muzzles which they accept as their only guiding light.' Johnny McLoughlin, a convenor at Dagenham, was publicly pilloried by Fleet Street as if he had been guilty of eating several children alive rather than simply a militant steward in a car factory. In that classic of Ealing snobbery *I'm All Right Jack*, Peter Sellers gave us Bro. Fred Kite, his mouth always open, his finger always wagging, his brother stewards always staring at him vacantly, and his members continually entering and leaving the factory gate. And in *The Angry Silence* the shop steward is issued with his political orders from an expressionless horn-rimmed commissar from London.

Militant employers took their cue. On the massive South Bank site where the Shell building was being erected by McAlpines and where some particularly gifted militants were working, 125 workers were sacked and the rest locked out in a brutal old-fashioned management attack which ended with the strike leaders serving long gaol sentences. What was new was the open and ugly collaboration of the leaders of the building unions concerned with McAlpines. No one was very surprised that the *Financial Times* had advised a lock-out aimed at re-employing 'a slightly altered labour force from which the worst militants have been weeded out'. But it was a shock to find the *Daily Worker* saying: 'Keep union rules or get out, trouble-makers are told.'

Again, in London Airport, to the rejoicing of the *Daily Mail* and *Common Cause*, a leading militant was sacked and his own union, under the direction of Carron, refused support for a strike over his re-instatement. And at Ford in 1962, the end of a protracted duel led to the successful expulsion of twenty-two shop stewards and put trade-unionism in the car factories on the defensive for the next six years. It is little wonder that the *Newsletter*'s rank-and-file conference so enthusiastically welcomed the charter's demands for the democratization of the union, the re-election of officers and the guarantee of rank-and-file control at all levels. The famous demand that union officials should have their smart saloon cars replaced by a van carrying union recruiting posters on its sides and a loudspeaker for addressing mass meetings on its roof has lived long after the conference's disintegration. It was clear that re-commencement of hostility by the employers and Government would end the uneasy truce between union leadership and its militant members.

And at the Esso refinery at Fawley, near Southampton, the very first productivity deal, custom-built to sap the shop-floor control on which the stewards' strength hinged, was signed in July 1960. The Esso package deal offered an astronomical immediate wage increase in return for the acceptance of a newly designed Blue Book covering work procedure. And as section after section of workers were painfully to discover in the sixties, the oil workers found that the initial glow of the cash increase soon faded. Seven years later Fawley workers had plummeted from their position as the highest-paid workers in the area to the bottom of the Southampton wage rates in big industry.

And besides the probing attacks of a few employers and the invention of new bargaining techniques to out-fox the stewards, it was also apparent that some more formal long-term legal solution would be required to undermine the unofficial movement further and to strengthen the employers' and unions' grip over industrial workers.

In June 1958 a group of Conservative lawyers produced a pamphlet called *A Giant's Strength*, advocating that trade unions should register with the Friendly Society register and there should be state powers to limit strikes. 'The need is,' rasped The *Economist* with its customary candour, 'for what union leaders will no doubt call, indignantly, a charter for blacklegs.' And more prophetic still came the eve of election words of Samuel Brittain, dissatisfied still with the Tory efforts: 'Paradoxically one of the strongest economic arguments for a Labour Government is that, beneath the layers of velvet, it might prove more prepared to face a showdown in dealing with the unions.'

But taking on the working class and a showdown with the unions was to take more doing than City-page editors could imagine. If Samuel Brittain had thought back to St Pancras in 1960 he could have reminded himself of the imagination, the organizing capacity and the strength of solidarity which the working-class movement still commanded. When Don Cook and Arthur Rowe were evicted from their council flats by a force of 400 policemen and twenty-eight bailiffs, a rocket signal brought railmen off the stations, had Irish building workers marching across London, brought the women of St Pancras onto the streets brandishing frying pans and ended in a pitched street battle between tenants and the police and a Government ban on demonstration throughout the area. An independent tenants' movement, aided by Communists and Labour Party members who put their loyalties to fellow workers before their party obligations, had created a little insurrection in Central London. The bailiffs' report on Arthur Rowe's eviction reported, '. . . the flat proved a tough nut to crack. The original door had been removed and a bulkhead lined with steel plates six inches thick fastened in its place, buttressed with heavy baulks of timber. The windows too were firmly secured with thick planks. Work commenced on the door, but no impression was made. Attention was then turned to the window and a hole made, through which the defendant kept up a steady stream of bottles . . .'* British workers were to prove equally uncooperative when Harold Wilson began the attempt to evict them from the positions of strength they occupied.

*County Court Officer, *Journal of the County Court Officers Association*, 21 October 1960, quoted in Ian Macdonald, 'Housing – the Struggle for Tenants' Control', *International Socialism*, 33, Summer 1968.

A Draft Charter of Workers' Demands: The Newsletter Conference

We, the delegates to the national industrial rank-and-file conference called by the Editorial Board of the *Newsletter* on 16 November 1958, submit the following Charter of workers' demands for the consideration of the members and leaders of the British working-class movement.

In our opinion, only a policy such as is here outlined can solve the problems that are now arising in industry in a way which will be in the true interests of working men and women, and which will help forward the fight for a socialist reconstruction of society.

*

We have considered the problem of *unemployment*. What sterner condemnation could there be of the capitalist system than its inability to provide work for all who need it?

Half a million are idle in this country at this moment. And many of the machines that should be enriching the lives of all of us are idle too.

There are a million families whose bread-winner is either out of a job or on short time. Millions more are seriously worried about the danger that soon they also will be out of work.

The unemployment figure is rising by 30,000 a month – and share values are rising too.

In our opinion the time to fight unemployment is now, while the greater part of our class is still in the factories.

We must fight unemployment before it grows any more – above all, by refusing to the employer the right to hire and fire at will.

WE DEMAND:

1. The sharing of all available work without loss of pay.
2. Solidarity action with all sections resisting sackings.
3. A national protest campaign led by the Trades Union Congress and Labour Party, including a one-day national stoppage against unemployment.
4. No discrimination against coloured workers.
5. Solidarity between unemployed workers and those in work to prevent the use of unemployed men as blacklegs.
6. Protection of shop stewards: all strikes against victimization to receive the full backing of the union concerned.

Believing that even with a militant fight against unemployment this problem cannot be solved within the framework of capitalist society, we have considered the problem of *nationalization.*

The root cause of unemployment lies in the private ownership for private profit of the means of production.

To remove an industry from the incompetent and greedy hands of profiteers is the way to ensure jobs and decent living standards for the men who work in it.

One of the biggest lessons of the South Bank dispute is that there is no need for McAlpine.

Equally, one of the biggest lessons of the BOAC dispute is that there is no need for d'Erlanger and men of his class.

The nationalization we envisage is nationalization *under workers' control.*

WE DEMAND:

1. The nationalization by the next Labour Government of the engineering, shipbuilding, building and textile industries and of the land of the big landowners.
2. No compensation to the former owners of these industries.
3. No representatives of big business to have a say in the running of these industries.
4. Control of these industries to be in the hands of democratically elected workers' councils.

*

Another problem we have considered is that of *the Labour Party.* We state without hesitation that the main thing wrong with the Labour Party today is that it is controlled by a junta of middle-class Fabians and full-time trade-union officials.

The rank-and-file in the trade unions and local Labour Parties no longer have a say in determining the policy of the party.

We recall that the basic aim of the Labour Party, as laid down in its 1918 constitution, is to work for the social ownership of the means of production.

The right-wing leaders have abandoned this aim. Only the rank-and-file can bring the party back to its original purpose and restore the socialist vision and energy of the pioneers of our movement.

The Tory Government can be defeated, and a Labour Government pledged to socialist policies elected, only if the industrial workers in particular bring back a fighting spirit to the Labour Party, and turn local parties into organs of working-class struggle.

WE APPEAL TO INDUSTRIAL WORKERS:

1. To enter the Labour Party as delegates to local parties from their trade-union branches.
2. To fight for the adoption of militant socialist policies and for the restoration of democracy within the party.
3. To make the local parties campaign centres in the industrial struggle, that will give the utmost moral and material help to all workers in dispute in their particular locality.

*

Last but not least, we have considered the problem of *the trade unions*. For many years the control of the unions has been passing into the hands of full-time paid officials.

In many unions these officials have in practice replaced the elected officials, and are taking decisions that are in violation of the constitutions and policies of their unions.

There is a growing division between the mass of trade-union members and the leaders.

We are firmly opposed to the creation of new trade unions or of any sort of 'breakaway' organizations whatever.

We believe, on the contrary, that the rank-and-file have the power, and the responsibility, to restore trade-union democracy, so that the unions can be better equipped to defend their members.

We believe that the employers' offensive makes more and more urgent the development of solidarity action among trade-unionists, regardless of whether a struggle is labelled 'official' or 'unofficial'.

Disputes must be judged, not by the label some full-time official attaches to them, but by the demands of the workers engaged in struggle.

We believe that the creation of links between workers, in the same and in different industries, in the form of solidarity action committees and similar rank-and-file bodies, can powerfully assist the restoration of trade-union democracy.

WE DEMAND:

1. No appointment of trade-union officials, but their periodical election, with the right of recall.
2. Salaries, expenses and delegation fees of union officials to be deter-

mined by the average wages of the members of that union.

3. An end to the practice of squandering union funds on large motor-cars without indication on them of who owns them. Union officials to travel in cheap, economical vans, carrying loudspeaker equipment for factory-gate and other meetings, and with the name of the union prominently displayed.

4. Annual policy-making conferences of the rank-and-file in all unions.

5. Direct rank-and-file representation at the Trades Union Congress and Labour Party annual conference. National full-time officials not to form part of the delegations at these gatherings.

6. Fullest consultation with the membership in formulating, presenting and fighting for demands, and in the acceptance of settlements.

7. Complete opposition by the trade-union movement to courts of inquiry, which are simply designed to prevent the winning of wage demands, and are now being used more and more to draw the teeth of the shop stewards' movement.

8. Prosecution of wage demands with the utmost energy, proper preparation of the membership and the broadest possible unity in action of the trade union forces against the employers.

9. A vigorous campaign for 100 per cent trade-unionism to seal up all gaps in organization.

*

Our demands, we are well aware, do not cover every one of the problems with which the British workers are faced today. But if the demands that we have advanced in this Charter were won, the Labour movement would be in far better shape to meet and beat back the offensive of the employing class.

Our demands are in line with the original constitutions and aims of the trade unions and of the Labour Party.

The pioneers who built our movement did so without the help of Consul cars, knighthoods or fat salaries.

They built our movement despite imprisonment and exile in Botany Bay. They made big sacrifices.

Today we need to recapture something of the spirit of the old days.

The job of the Labour movement is to fight the employers. This job cannot be done if the movement gets too 'respectable', but only if it regains its original purpose and militancy.

(The programme adopted at the November 1958 *Newsletter* rank-and-file Conference, drafted by Brian Behan, reprinted in the *Newsletter*, 8 November 1958)

The South Bank Struggle:
Brian Behan

In 1959 I went to work on the South Bank for the second time. This time my old lion looked out, while the Shell building was stacked three hundred feet up in the air.

Here, one of the biggest building disputes in history was to be fought out, a dispute that began with the sacking of two thousand men.

All round the edge of the crater the draglines lifted their iron necks and then sent their teeth darting down like a great buzzard's beaks. Remorselessly they tore at the ground like a pack of hungry hyenas round the body of an elephant. Deeper and deeper grew the cavity until it began to look like the great arsehole of all creation. Then into it climbed the carpenters and steelfixers; on platforms ninety feet below ground they shored up the avenging clay with struts of timber and steel. Then from a swan-like crane, with its rider perched one hundred and fifty feet up, comes an endless golden, thick, creamy porridge that will set rock hard and carry the monster on its back. I only had eyes for organization. Four thousand men, five years a-building. Link them to the Isle of Grain, the Atomic Power Station at Bradwell, and you had an army of 12,000. Imagine 12,000, enough to run a newspaper, buy a loud-speaker van or to cost over £100,000 a week if they all went slow together.

My mate was talking, 'By the way, I am the scaffolder's steward, and this is a ticket job.'

I just growled – part of my plan was to lie low and then emerge like a ravening lion. I would pretend hatred of all things union. 'Well,' he went on, 'we aren't too hard on new starters. We give them a couple of weeks, but if you aren't in by then, out you go.'

Now we had to go down the hole. Our task was to run a scaffold round the bottom for the chippies. Vast, like a canyon floor, there was still no room. In an area of twenty feet a crane was dropping sections of a concrete blow pipe. Behind us, welders were sticking a steel frame together before sinking it for all time. In front, the bucket of a digger was dropping thirty feet before it came up, raking and tearing out mouthfuls of clay and stones. Above us, in a ring round the edge, about thirty diggers all rocked back and forth, eating like giant pterodactyls. By half past four it was dark. But still the earth got no slumber. Bank after bank of searchlights lit up the hard frosty air; sparks from a welder's torch lit up his face, like a steel-helmeted Ku Klux Klan mask. A tremendous air of seething activity gripped the meanest tea boy. A big navvy, wearing a huge sombrero, is shouting McAlpine's Fusiliers:

> Get out in the morning, stripped to the skin,
> And earn your bonus for Darky Fin.
> And then down the glen rode McAlpine's men,
> With their fife and drum behind them.
> It was in the pub they drank their sub
> And it's in the spike you'll find them.
> They drank their sub, they drank their beer,
> They drank it with good cheer.
> And now we are on the road again.
> God damn and blast the beer.

'Hey, Ginger,' a man calls up to me, 'did you have it in last night?' I laughed, because in fact I had. Here on the South Bank of the Thames at Waterloo, Mac's men wrestled and fought with that great bear earth while sergeant death stretched his fingers round every throat. Four men died before that silly roof was stuck on, like a clown's hat on top of a grizzly bear's head. Then the hooters wailed and wailed. They screamed out against the death of a man crushed under the wheels of a wagon in the murky half-light. Work stops. What man can think of work looking in the face of death? Death is the only equalizer. A falling man will be smashed no matter how strong. The men stream off out the gates, leaving the jibs of cranes swinging silently pointing towards the moon. It's not the firm's fault, but they are blamed just the same. The men know that even if the firm are blameless it is always their own kind who lie crushed and mangled beneath the planner's beams.

The following day the man is gone and all but forgotten. A warm sun stretches the back, and makes it tingle with life. Bonus is on the agenda again. How much have we to come for last week? How much can we earn for next? It is true the bonus clerk is on the fiddle? What a poxy lot of targets! How can you make anything when you have to pay for the services of the crane? Why doesn't the bloody union draw up targets and get the employer to agree to them before the bastard job starts? 'Too busy poncing about talking politics. What has politics got to do with the likes of you and me. It's a load of ballsology really.' 'I've a good mind not to pay the swine any more. All they do is make for coffee shops and drink tea.'

'Listen, have you heard the one about the queer teddy bear. No? Well, he threw his paw across the table.'

'Very funny. Give us up a few lengths of four by two. Here comes that ticket-steward again. I reckon he lives in that office, but we have to carry him. You know it all comes out of our bonus.'

'Listen, if there's any more trouble on this job I'm pulling out. Strike, strike, strike all the time. Look, we lose more time over meetings. We have a meeting nearly every day now. The firm won't stand for it you know.'

'No?'

'Not likely. Do you think they're going to have a load of Commies run this job? That's all they are, you know.'

'Who?'

'The stewards, of course, who do you think I mean, you dozey 'aporth?'

'I hear the firm is going to sack the lot.'

'I shouldn't wonder if it's true, they're bound to have a sort out. Things can't go on like this.'

In a big office overlooking Hyde Park another discussion is taking place.

'Are you sure there is nothing else we can do?'

'Nothing, old boy. I can assure you we have the union's O.K. on this, they know what we have to deal with.'

'I still wonder if we are doing the right thing. We never seem to tell the men anything. No wonder they believe the first loud mouth they hear.'

'Look here, old chap, that's hardly fair, after all, we pay union rates and conditions. But we are in the grip of trained agitators.'

'H'm, I wish it was all as simple as that. If we did our job, what could they find to agitate about? If only you had accepted my profit-sharing and consultation scheme.'

'Look here, my dear fellow, we can't go back over that again. We have been building for years without any trouble like this.'

'But all our men are casual, they have no status, we take them on one job and lose them when it's finished. No wonder they don't feel particularly loyal to us.'

I am at home when the telegram comes – 'Come to site. All 2,000 being sacked Friday.' The sun was shining on the crowded meeting when I got there. A union official was telling the men there was nothing the union could do. 'We will watch the situation when the site re-opens, with a view to stopping victimization.'

Another official feels that eventual public ownership of the industry is the only answer, though this same gentleman has, in my hearing, denounced British Railways, root and crop. Nationalization-cum-State

Capitalism – what a solution; our present employers are not big and bold enough. We must have the employer to end all employers.

At the stewards' meeting they debate what to do ... I say, either fight or do nothing, what can we lose if we fight? We decide to fight. Alone now, no union backing, nothing. We turn savage. We determine to 'black Mac'. We are resolved that the site will not open without us. Feverishly now we prepare. First a conference of all building trade workers. Then a leaflet – fifty thousand of them putting our case, *Mac Produces Nothing*. Then a penny broadsheet with banner headings, photos, the lot. Our conference is held in the Holborn Hall, the attendance is varied. Dockers, bus drivers, builders, all listen to our case. Speaker after speaker praises our decision to stand and fight. I speak.

'If you really are with us in spirit, then be with us in the flesh next Monday morning, when Mac prepares to re-open.'

The delegates are silent. After all, it means the loss of a day's pay, the possibility of upsetting a not-so-bad governor. I press the point. 'Let us put a human wall round the site so that not a mouse will get through.'

On Monday I go to the site. Only a handful of men have turned up. My heart sinks, but I grab a poster and start walking up and down a very thin, skimpy line.

Then, just before eight o'clock, we hear the skirl of a bag-piper. From out of the mouth of Waterloo Station come the men of Abbey Wood Housing Site. Behind them the men from the building of the power station in Belvedere. Then over Waterloo Bridge come the lads from the *Daily Mirror* site. In five minutes we are the centre of a happy, excited throng, laughing and cat-calling to each other. Now our pickets are ten, twenty, thirty deep, and it's an honour to carry a poster. At eight o'clock the hooters blow, calling for work to begin. Not a single man goes in. A chorus of roars go up proclaiming that this day, at least, is ours.

It is the third week of the battle. Now the 'politicos' are appearing more openly, circling and mincing, trying to importune 'likely contacts'. One of them, so small that the sleeves of his raincoat hang down over his hands, rubs his hands over his sore eyes that make him look like a bull terrier, and mutters, 'There will be buckets of blood, yes, buckets of blood.' Yet he cringes when he passes John Law. He will live, like the Voyeur, through the actions of others.

It is early morning on the fourth week. Van after van pulls up under Waterloo Bridge. Out of them spill an endless stream of the lads in blue. Clattering down the embankment comes a patrol of mounted police. Their great haunched animals wheel and stamp in the road. Now comes a line of motor bikes, roaring round, making a complete circle. 'Paddy wagons' are now lining up, their attendants dropping their steps ready for their first customers. Swiftly the police spread out till they line every inch of the road. Our mass picket is pressed back, and slowly the gates yawn open to admit all those who have a mind to enter. Then we see what's afoot. A coach comes belting down the road. At first we see it's empty, and wonder why all the fuss about an empty coach. Then someone spots it. A cry goes up. 'The dirty, scabby bastards. They're lying down on the floor so we can't see them.'

Suddenly I feel afraid. What is there about us to terrify anyone. Surely we are the brotherhood of love? Imagine me in that coach. Shouldn't a man be free to do what he likes, work or not? Is our dictatorship any less evil than the employer's? But now the pickets start to shake and bend the line of police. The Inspector is screaming at the coach driver not to slow down, but to get to hell inside. Too late, the coach is stuck trying to angle its long body round the gate. Now the line of police is broken, and strikers' hands reach up to pull the driver out. Then a copper shouts over a walkie-talkie, 'Clear the gates.' Like cowboys at a rodeo the mounties ride in. Swiftly they isolate one group from another. Then they start picking out the leaders. Reaching down, they seize one man by the hair of the head and gallop off. Van after van is filled with struggling pickets. I sit in front of a broken-nosed bobby, who looks as though he's going to have me in a minute. I watch him very carefully. One thing I am sure of, the moment he comes at me I'm going to boot him good and proper. Another bobby comes in, his face split with the side edge of a picket poster. He doesn't exactly look as though he would 'suffer little children to come unto him'. Suddenly I realize what's wrong. There's not a single political fanatic in the coaches. They are waging the class war from the bottom of the Bridge café. If we peep through the slats we can see that violent struggles are still raging outside. But then suddenly everything falls silent. For the first time in five weeks we hear the triumphant roar of master dragline as he opens his mouth to begin devouring the earth as though nothing at all had happened.

(From *With Breast Expanded*, MacGibbon & Kee, 1964, pp. 152–7)

How to Fight the Service Slashes:
Bob Potter

The bus strike has ended in defeat for the London busmen. This is now obvious to all. After six weeks of solidarity which were an example to the whole working class, the London Transport Executive has pushed through the first set of service cuts.

By the end of January there will be 10 per cent fewer buses on the London streets. For the travelling public this means more waiting and longer queues. For the busmen it means longer hours and harder work. But the busmen will be no better off financially. The LTE expects that average earnings of crews will be the same in the coming winter as they were last winter, 'if not a few coppers less'.

This in spite of the 8s. 6d. award to central London drivers and conductors. The increase will be lost in the reduction of Sunday working and overtime. (The LTE hopes to do away with overtime altogether in the new year, as it is too expensive.)

The 14,000 'forgotten men' have been forced to accept a miserable 5s. and redundancy has hit the inside staffs – so far, the LTE has stated that 600 of these men are no longer required. How has it been possible for the LTE and the Tory Government to deliver such a powerful blow against the busmen? There is only one possible answer: bad trade-union leadership.

On Sunday, 4 May, the day before the strike began, Frank Cousins, speaking in Birmingham, argued that 'we are not taking on the Government'. Here was the blueprint of defeat. It is common knowledge that the busmen were not fighting Sir John Elliott. They were fighting the Tory Government. Elliott being only the paid instrument of that Government. If Cousins had developed the battle against the real opponents of the working class, the results would have been very different.

Other sections of the Transport and General Workers' Union should have been involved immediately: an approach should have been made to the rank-and-file railwaymen: the offer of support from the Electrical Trades Union should have been accepted. The Underground system would thus have been stopped. In a word, only industrial and political extension of the strike could have ensured victory.

Is it correct to lay the blame for the failure to do this on the shoulders of the TGWU general secretary?

I think it is, for it was he who won the vital delegate conference against the extension in the TGWU. He spoke before and after the debate, and he promised that he had other proposals to offer the delegates – proposals which were never forthcoming.

In this sense, the vote of the delegates against extension was largely a vote of confidence in Cousins. An extension to other sections in the first week would have had unanimous support, and would have brought speedy victory. It is true that the Trades Union Congress General Council was not prepared to help. But did anybody with any knowledge of these knights of the Labour movement expect otherwise?

These people are entrenched in the capitalist system. They are the fifth column of the Tory Party and the bitter enemies of trade-unionists. And Cousins, by opposing extension, was playing their game. Indeed the reason why Cousins did not use the platform at the recent TUC to expose the General Council's reactionary role was that if he had done so he would have shed light on the part he himself played.

The lessons of the strike must be learned by all. We must not make the same mistakes again.

FIRST, we should realize that no section of the Labour movement can win its demands – even limited demands – in isolation.

The employers work together and they work with the active support of the Tory Government. Only a counter-offensive by Labour can defeat this alliance.

SECONDLY, we must have no confidence in the officials who sit on the TUC General Council.

These people, with their fat pay packets, knighthoods and television appearances, are isolated from their members, and are more concerned with maintaining their positions and their 'respectability' than in leading the workers against the bosses.

THIRDLY, it is impossible to separate industrial battles from political battles. The Tories are determined to smash the trade unions and drive down the workers' living standards. The Rent Act has taken a good £1 from the pay packets of many of us.

These are political attacks, and must be met with vigour by the entire Labour movement.

FOURTHLY, there is a need for a rank-and-file movement among all sections of workers – a movement capable of giving effective and militant leadership.

There is not a job in the country that has deteriorated so much in pay and conditions in the last two decades as has the bus job.

If we continue to leave it to the paid officials, what will it be like twenty years from now?

That is why we busmen who support the *Newsletter* hope that busmen will be well represented at the national industrial rank-and-file Conference at the Holborn Hall on Sunday, 16 November.

(From 'Busmen's Special', supplement to the *Newsletter*, September 1958)

Carron, the Noble Knight: Geoff Carlsson

William Carron, ex-president of the Amalgamated Engineering Union, died last week with most of his life's work unfulfilled, although his influence still dominates the thinking of many of his colleagues in the trade-union hierarchy.

He above all typified the 'respectable' trade-unionist. His loyalty to the Labour Government, combined with an ability to understand the employers' problems, were his greatest attributes. His unswerving hostility to militants who fought to improve their standards of living was appreciated and rewarded by the bosses and their servants who hold political office.

In 1963, he was appointed a Director of the Bank of England and in the same year Her Majesty graciously knighted him for his services to trade-unionism. (Who better qualified to judge these services than the Queen, who has herself lodged a claim for a considerable increase, though no unofficial action is yet contemplated by her?)

As a reward for 'his conspicuous work within the church and constant witness to Roman Catholic principles in everyday life' that other great judge of trade-unionists, the Pope, appointed Sir William a Knight of the Order of Chivalry of St Gregory the Great. Many other honours were accorded him, culminating in perhaps the most apt for a working-class 'champion' – a life peerage in 1967 allowing him to take his place in the Upper Chamber where so many anti-union decisions have been passed.

He was outspoken against opponents. 'Saboteurs' was his term for those who opposed the government's Incomes Policy. Describing militants in the motor industry, he likened them to 'werewolves who are rushing madly towards industrial ruin and howling delightedly at the foam on their muzzles'.

He constantly tried (not without some success) to destroy the democratic structure of the AEU, to lengthen the term of office of officials, and to have others appointed instead of being subject to election. At the Labour Party Conference he frequently ignored the decisions of the union's policy-making body and cast the vote of 800,000 members contrary to union conference decisions. He blatantly described such action as 'Carron's Law'. In his blind hatred of Communism, Carron was quite prepared to use the same Stalinist methods which he so vociferously opposed.

Carron is dead. The opponents of the Incomes Policy have multiplied and those who support the 'werewolf' policy of 'do it yourself' to improve wages and conditions have increased considerably. It would seem that workers now place more reliance on their own actions than allowing noble Lords and bankers to handle their problems. It is the finest answer that can be given to those officials inside the AEF and other unions who aspire to follow the example of Sir William.

He will be missed by those who look for a paradise in the next world. For those who are concerned with building a better life now, let it be remembered that Carron's Law still holds good for many who still hold office within the trade unions.

(From the *Socialist Worker*, 14 December 1969)

Fords: Some Lessons:
Ken Weller

INTRODUCTION

For the moment, Dagenham is quiet. The wildcats have been tamed, Patrick Hennessy and his American executives rule the roost, Ford is king. This article attempts to describe what happened there.

Between October 1962 and April 1963, a struggle took place which ended in seventeen leading militants being left on the cobbles. Several of these men were blacklisted and unable to find work in their own trade for well over a year.

The struggle showed in a very clear way the absolute conflict of interests between workers and 'their' trade-union leaders, and the similarity of interests between these leaders and management.

What happened at Ford's closely followed a pattern well established in recent years. From Handley Page to Shell Mex House, from BLSP to Ford, the charade has been played again and again, with exactly the same end result: destruction of job organization.

Yet every time the situation arises again, the entire Left repeats its old well-worn slogans: 'Make the strike official'; 'Press your union Executive for action now'; 'BLANK is better than BLANK,* he won't let us down'. (They always do.) If half the energy had been put into helping the men carry out the struggle themselves, a few more disputes would be won.

Although most of the events at Ford's took place several years ago, we offer no apology for discussing them now. No other full analysis has been written, and many of the facts are only just beginning to emerge. The lessons are timeless.

THE BACKGROUND

Everyone knows that Ford has had a long and troubled labour relations history. The management at Ford's claim that 100,000 man-hours were lost in disputes in 1960, 184,000 in 1961, 415,000 in 1962. Following the

---

*For BLANK read Cousins, Roberts, Hill, Berridge, Paynter, Lowthian, etc. according to your particular political affiliations.

defeat of the men, the figures dropped to 3,400 man-hours lost in 1963 and 60,000 in 1964.*

The management calculated that in 1962 each worker at Dagenham, excluding the Paint, Trim and Assembly Division, lost fifteen man-hours due to disputes, compared with thirty minutes per man per year at the fourteen other Ford plants in Britain. In the Paint, Trim and Assembly Division the figure was seventy-eight hours per man per year. The overwhelming majority of time lost in disputes was due to overtime bans rather than to walkouts or strikes.

A detailed breakdown of the thirty-two disputes which took place between 28 May and 19 July 1962 was made in the September 1962 issue of *Ford Worker*, the paper of the Shop Stewards' Committee. Of the thirty-two disputes, twenty-eight were overtime bans and none of the remaining four exceeded an hour in length.†

Not a single dispute at Ford's since the war has been 'official'. The trade union officials have even signed a long series of agreements which have had the effect of undermining shop-floor struggles. For example on 14 August 1958 they signed an agreement which read:

The Achievement of Efficiency of Operations

The Trade Unions and the Company agree on the need:
1. to achieve efficient production by all reasonable means;
2. for the introduction of labour-saving machines and methods;
3. for the Company to transfer employees from one job or department to another, as may be desirable having in mind continuity of employment and flow of production.

It is not part of the duty of any Shop Steward whose constitution and duties are defined in the Procedure Agreement to deal with such matters in the Shop, but he may refer them for consideration by the Works Committee.‡

*Information from evidence given to the 'Jack Court of Inquiry' by L. T. Blakeman, their Labour Relations Manager. (See *Report* – Cmnd 1999, p. 11). Figures for 1963 and 1964 were given to us directly, if unwittingly, by the Labour Relations Department at Dagenham.

†Incidentally, of the thirty-two disputes, only nine were on wages questions. The remainder were about speed-up, supervisors and chargehands 'working with the tools', allocation of overtime, transfers of labour, reduction in the supply of protective clothing. Bescoby and Turner (in the May 1961 issue of *Manchester School*) estimate that 40 per cent of disputes at Fords were over what they called 'management questions', such as individual dismissals and arrangements of working hours. In my view the proportion is much higher.

‡From *Agreements and Conditions of Employment – Hourly Paid Workers* (commonly known as the 'Blue Book'), published by the Ford Motor Company, July 1964, p. 32.

This agreement signed away the right of shop-floor negotiations on nearly all the vital questions of 'managerial rights'. It is therefore no coincidence that over half the 'incidents' at Ford's were on just these questions.

Another agreement which was actually signed on the same day as the above was the 'Briggs Standardization Agreement'. This gave away many advantages which had been achieved by shop-floor negotiation at the better organized and more militant factory of Briggs Motor Bodies, originally a separate company but amalgamated with Fords in 1953 (it is now called the Metal Stamping and Body Division).

The proposal to standardize conditions had been bitterly opposed by the Briggs shop stewards, right from the start. For example, between February 1954 and May 1955 there had been 288 'incidents' at Briggs. Between August 1955 and March 1957 there were 234 more. Many of these were caused by attempts of the Ford management to introduce 'backstairs standardization'. This prolonged struggle culminated in the sacking of Johnnie McLoughlin, the bell-ringing shop steward.*

It is interesting to note that all the agreements referred to in this article were signed by officials of all the twenty-two negotiating unions at Fords, without regard to whether they were 'left' or 'right'. They were signed by 'Bill' Carron of the AEU, Douglass of BISAKTA and Jim Matthews of the NUGMW representing the 'right' – and by Ted Hill of the Boilermakers and Frank Haxell, late of the ETU (and the Communist Party), representing the 'left'.

Two other incidents further illustrate the activities of the trade-union leaders. The first was the October 1961 forty-hour week agreement, which had the effect of reducing the tea-break. The men refused to accept this and *unofficially* continued to take the old tea-break. After a dispute lasting until March 1962, during which the management vainly tried to implement the agreement, they eventually conceded defeat.†

The second example was the 'secret' Halewood deal signed early in 1960 between the management, the NUGMW and the AEU. In this

---

*This struggle was in many ways a blueprint of the big dispute later. Here, too, the union officials stepped in to stop immediate action by the men, by promises of 'official action' – later. In this case also the militant was suspended while negotiations continued . . . and continued . . . and continued, with the end result that all initiative was lost and the issue was dead. In this case also there was a 'Court of Inquiry', which also came to the conclusion that the sacking should stand. In this case also the unions 'reluctantly' decided that no action should be taken (in spite of the fact that the AEU had held a strike ballot which voted 1,118 to 429 for such action).

†See *Solidarity*, vol II, No. 3.

agreement, the two unions agreed to lower substantially wage rates for workers at Halewood, in return for preferential facilities provided to the unions by the management, in relation to recruiting members. This, incidentally, was a clear violation of previous agreements, signed by the same union leaders, for a single national wage scale for Ford workers. When news of the agreement leaked out, the other union leaders were up in arms. Their livelihoods were threatened! The plan nevertheless went ahead, but the TGWU was included in the carve-up. The scheme was actually introduced, but its operation defeated by the massive *unofficial* overtime bans at Halewood in March 1962.*

CARRON AND THE MILITANTS

Another aspect of the attitude of certain officials has been the campaign of vilification, both within and outside the union structure, against the shop stewards' committees. For example, William Carron (now Lord Carron), President of the AEU, made a statement to the *Sunday Dispatch* (now defunct) on 24 February 1957, at the height of the McLoughlin crisis. He said:

For a long time now, subversive elements have been at work at Briggs. Last year alone, there were 200 stoppages at the plant. In my view these subversive types were responsible for most, if not all, of them.

We find the same man writing in the *Ford Bulletin* (the paper of the Ford Motor Company) on 3 August 1962, right in the middle of negotiations which led to the later 'trouble', an article entitled 'Where is the Enemy?' He wrote:

The old need for unbridled militancy rapidly diminished with the reduction of our immediate major social and industrial problems.

One still finds pockets of militancy which are inspired by motives that cannot be accepted as being based purely on trade-union principles.

These motives spring from attempts to change the system of government we have in the United Kingdom and would attempt to replace this system with one that has been rejected in Parliamentary and Local Government elections by an overwhelming majority of opinion.

Disruptive tactics with political ambition as a source of inspiration will not contribute to the further well being of our citizenship or, for that matter, our membership, which depend entirely in these modern years on the produce of our factories and workplaces.

Carron made it quite clear that he regarded *his* enemy as the 'militants', not the bosses. We agree with his diagnosis.

*See *Solidarity*, vol. II, No. 9.

What lessons emerge from this record? Quite simply, that any appeal to, or reliance on, the union executives for 'support' against agreements which they themselves have signed is rather misplaced. So are appeals for 'help' in protecting militants against attacks in which the union leaders actively participate.

THE STORY OF THE STRUGGLE

The first act in the drama came early in 1962, when the trade unions put in for a wage increase. Let us tell the story in the words of W. B. Beard, OBE, Chairman of the Ford National Negotiating Council.*

... They [the Ford management] were not prepared to consider any wage improvement until they had a firm assurance that these unofficial walkouts were discontinued and the procedure observed. They argued that if there was difficulty with the procedure, then the proper method was to amend it, but there had been no attempt on the part of a relatively small number of individuals to operate the agreement at all. Indeed, they just walked out on the job and as a result not only was production stopped, but many who were entitled to consideration of a wage increase were paid off, because production had been halted. Side by side with this there was the general slackening in the demand for cars, and orders which they were unable to complete for they had missed the market. They also referred to work in some cases being off-standard. There was indeed a stalemate and the firm were clearly determined to exercise their function of management.

It was also clear that we as an NJNC† could not justify the walkouts which had taken place and it was equally clear that until the firm received assurances that this body had some control of their members, no progress was possible. Here then was a deadlock, which somehow had to be broken. After thinking over this position for some time, I suggested to the management that perhaps a small committee could meet them quite unofficially‡ and informally discuss the problems of industrial relations with no holds barred, in order to make progress. We had three meetings and suggestions were made by both sides, some of which were subsequently amended, to provide for closer contact between NJNC, the local full-time official and the men in the shop.

The final result was agreement on proposals by the full NJNC which it is hoped will eventually make for better industrial relations. In addition a joint statement was agreed which will be given to every employee dealing with the problems which have arisen and the agreement reached by the two sides of industry.

* From the November 1962 issue of the *United Patternmakers Association Journal.*
† The National Joint Negotiating Council, representing the management and twenty-two unions.
‡ Tut! Tut!

Buried in Beard's immortal prose is the story of how, in return for a 3d. an hour increase, the NJNC signed an agreement on 12 October 1962 which gave the Ford management carte blanche to 'deal' with the militants. The significant section of the agreement reads:*

> *The Trade Unions recognize the right of the Company to exercise such measures as are expressed within the Agreements against employees who fail to comply with the conditions of their employment by taking unconstitutional action.* They have stated, however, and the Company has acknowledged, that the Trade Unions shall not be required to share the responsibility of Management in taking action against employees who breach agreements. The Trade Unions, however, reserve the right to examine such cases.†

Five days later Bill Francis, deputy Convenor of the PTA plant, was sacked. He was discharged for holding a report-back meeting, during the lunch break, but on the Company's premises. This had been going on at Fords for years.

Immediately large numbers of workers stopped work. Next day there was a shift meeting and 3,000 men voted virtually unanimously to stay out until Francis was reinstated. Next day, 19 October, a mass meeting of the PTA plant voted 5,317 to 6 to stay out. The men were solid. At a further mass meeting on 23 October, 5,801 men voted for continuing the strike against 79 who voted to go back.

THE UNION OFFICIAL

Wee fat full-time union official
waistcoat bursting with status
Thirty years off the tools
grovels at the bosses' table
looking for a handout
for a dram
to give him strength
to climb on the workers' backs.

At this stage the men were on top. Victory was within their grasp. They had stopped production at a time when it was vital to the Company that as many vehicles be produced as possible. All the signs showed that the Company was prepared to compromise in order to get production moving again. But the trade unions had still to act . . .

*See *Solidarity*, vol. II, No. 7.
†From *Agreements and Conditions of Employment – Hourly Paid Workers*, p. 15.
(My emphasis throughout – K. W.)

BACK TO WORK

On 25 October, the Ford NJNC voted to recommend their members to return to work. This was put to a mass meeting on the 26th. The men voted for a return to work after they had had the clearest possible statement from 'their' officials that there would be no victimization. Kealey (TGWU) and O'Hagan (Blast Furnacemen) claimed that they had received such an assurance from Blakeman, the Company's Labour Relations Manager.* However, the point is without importance since it is clear that the Company had already made up its mind. That very same day they posted letters to their employees which stated:

As the future of the Company and its employees depends upon its operations being on an efficient and competitive basis, there will only be employment available for those who are prepared to observe the rules, regulations and agreements; and also to cooperate with the Company in removing all restrictive and bad practices.

The letter went on to say that only those who received such letters and signed them signifying their acceptance of the conditions therein would be re-employed.

The 'letter' led to scenes which hadn't been witnessed in England since the thirties. The pamphlet *What's Wrong at Fords* (published by the Fords Shop Stewards' Committee) graphically described the situation:

The Company servicemen patrolled the gates and only allowed entry to people who had signed. The letter was scrutinized and the member directed to the department he was to work in. Many members were sent to strange shops where they had no idea what had been the customary speeds, local agreements, etc. Before starting work the member was interviewed by the foreman and told how much work he would have to do and 'to watch his step' for there were thousands outside the gates.

In fact supervisors were so zealous and provocative in the use of their newly acquired powers (in many cases using them to settle old scores) that on 15 November the Industrial Relations staff at Fords had to issue a warning letter to all supervisors because of the threat of further trouble in the plant. The letter said:

* As late as June 1963 the report of the National Executive of the NUVB to the Annual Policy Conference of that union had emphasized that 'the men were persuaded to return to work and the Company promised that there would be no victimization'.

The Company has done its best to make it clear all along that we are always prepared to meet the unions – and go on meeting them – until we have jointly secured an end to the disruptions and unofficial actions to which we have been subjected.

We have always sincerely believed that our problems – and we are always going to have problems – can only be solved in close cooperation with the unions.

Everybody has made it clear how little they want to strike. It is now up to all of us to strive for harmony and good understanding inside and outside the factory.

In the meantime it is obvious that a very heavy responsibility rests upon all supervisors who must be scrupulously fair in all their dealings. They must make every effort to secure goodwill and respond to it – and show a real understanding of any problem which may arise.

The overwhelming mass of our employees have demonstrated their loyalty to the Company and the time to prove to them that their loyalty is valuable to themselves and to the Company is now. So although your job requires you to be firm, you must be fair, and always take the trouble to find out.

> MANAGER: Someone who can take three hours off for lunch without seriously disrupting production.

OFFICIAL STRIKE ACTION 'DEFERRED'

On 31 October, the officials met again. They agreed to 'defer a decision on action until some of the points at issue were clarified'. A further meeting with the management was held on 5 November, where because of the 'tough' attitude of the employers, strike notices were issued for 18 November. The officials were, of course, not uninfluenced by the equally 'tough' attitude of the men, who in many cases only remained at work because of the firm and repeated promises of 'official action'.

On 5 November, the NJNC again decided to defer strike action, after the Company had agreed that the sacked men would be considered as 'suspended' and that they should receive a payment of £7 10s. a week while negotiations continued. On 19 November, this 'ex gratia' payment was increased to £11 a week. At the same time the Shop Stewards' Committee set up a fund to bring the victimized men's income up to their normal wage.

In the meantime, the Shop Stewards' Committee had come to rely more and more on the National officials. A statement issued by the

Shop Stewards' Committee early in November is a good example. It reads:

Our trade unions have realized that if the Company is allowed to get away with this wholesale victimization of good trade-unionists, if they can throw out any worker who stands up for his rights and refuses to be treated like a machine, then effective trade-unionism will soon be buried at Fords. That is why our National officials are insisting that everyone shall be taken back and that no one shall be victimized.*

On 20 November, a meeting of the Ford Joint Shop Stewards' Committee passed a resolution which in effect placed them in a position of absolute reliance on the 'goodwill' of the officials of the unions. The resolution which was formulated, moved and supported by leading Communist Party members, including Kevin Halpin,† read in part:

2. Bearing in mind the decisions of yesterday, each union must insist on all back immediately. Failing agreement on any individual, the union should refer the case to the NJNC on the basis of previous declarations to take action if all members are not taken back.
3. Insist that National officials refute the statement made by the Company on the future of members in the plants.
4. That we insist that stewards should be allowed to function in the plant and operate all the customary agreements and we ask the National officials to ensure that this happens.‡

Ironically, on the same day (20 November) the management also declared its common cause with the union leaders. In a factory 'Notice' they declared:

At yesterday's meeting of the NJNC, the Company informed the Trade Unions of its determination to maintain law and order, normal working conditions, and efficient operation in the Company's plants. The Company stated that employees who indicated by word or action that they were not prepared to observe the Agreements and the Company's rules and regulations would not be retained in employment, nor would the Company continue to employ men who by their actions showed that they were solely interested in achieving disruption.

The Company also emphasized that 'wildcat strikes' would not be tolerated in future. Employees who went out on unofficial strike, and who are retained

* From *What This Fight Is All About*, an undated leaflet issued by the Ford Shop Stewards' Committee.

† For a more detailed analysis of the role of the Communist Party and of the Shop Stewards at Fords, see the article 'What's Wrong at Fords' in *Solidarity*, vol. II, No. 11.

‡ Appendix C to *What's Wrong at Fords*, published by the Ford Joint Shop Stewards' Committee.

in employment, would be liable to lose a significant proportion, if not all, of the merit money that they might be receiving.

These measures are designed to restore the joint authority of the unions and the Company, and to combat the activities of those employees who have no loyalty to either.

The number of victimized men still without work was gradually reduced. Ford re-hired some of them and others found alternative work. Only seventeen men were left out. On 31 January 1963, the unions again 'deferred' strike action (this time until 18 February), although Les Kealey of the TGWU was still mouthing rather tired threats of official strike action. In a statement issued by Region No. 1 of the TGWU (on 13 February), Kealey wrote:

Should we not arrive at a just settlement with the Company prior to 18 February, then without doubt the whole of the TGWU membership at Dagenham will withdraw its labour.

As 18 February approached, militancy grew, not only within the plant, but even amongst workers not directly affected; for example the Central Bus Committee of London Transport proposed that no bus services should be run along the mile-long approach to the works. This proposal was endorsed by mass meetings of the bus garages affected.

THE JACK COURT OF INQUIRY

By pure coincidence on 18 February the Minister of Labour appointed a Court of Inquiry 'into the causes and circumstances of a dispute between the Ford Motor Company Ltd, Dagenham, and members of the trade unions represented on the trade union side of the Ford NJNC'. To make sure that the Court of Inquiry didn't deliberate in an 'atmosphere of coercion', strike action was again 'deferred' until after the publication of the Court's findings.*

The Court's findings were published on 3 April 1963. They contained nothing new: virtual 100 per cent condemnation of the Joint Shop Stewards' Committee and all its works, compliments to union officials, advice to them on how they should establish their control at Dagenham, etc. Even one or two minor criticisms of the Company were thrown in, to provide a façade of fairness.†

*For more information on the Jack Court of Inquiry, see *Solidarity*, vol. II, No. 9, and also 'Report of Jack Court of Inquiry', HMSO, Cmnd 1999, April 1963.

†It has been said that history repeats itself first as tragedy then as farce. About

Immediately after the publication of the Jack findings, the Company ended its 'ex gratia' payments to the seventeen. The final fiasco came when the T G W U held a mass meeting of its members to decide whether they were in favour of strike action. Les Kealey, the main speaker, made his position quite clear. There would be no strike action unless there was an 'overwhelming' vote in favour. After seven months of defeat within the factory, after a Court of Inquiry, after speed-up, intimidation and slander, after no less than five separate 'deferments', and after a very large exodus of workers from Fords who were not prepared to accept the worsening of conditions,* only a small majority of workers voted for strike action. This allowed Kealey to call the strike off.

Inside the factory the defeat was a bitter experience. Many militants had been taken back on the basis that they would not be shop stewards. Many others had to 'keep their heads down'. The mobility of the remaining stewards was greatly restricted. The lines were speeded-up to a literally man-killing pace† and in this way older men were forced out

---

eighteen months after the report of the Jack Court, a Commission was set up by the Motor Industry Joint Study Group to 'inquire into Labour relationships at the Morris Motors Ltd (Cowley) plant, with particular reference to recent stoppages of work, which within the past year totalled 254, accounting for approximately three-quarters of a million man-hours lost'.

The report of the Commission went on to say that the stewards . . . 'have allowed themselves to lose faith in, and even become cynical about, not only management policy and competence, but also management attitudes and the existing means of handling disputes, including the agreed procedure'. The commission also found that 'when District officials are called in, it is customarily at the request of management'. The Commission recommended a return to procedure and the greater intrusion of District and Divisional officials into the affairs of the factory with a corresponding weakening of the autonomy of the shop stewards. This report and its recommendations were agreed to unanimously by all ten members of the commission, which included H. G. Barratt (Confederation of Shipbuilding and Engineering Unions), G. H. Doughty (DATA), Les Kealey (TGWU), A. Roberts (NUVB) and Sir William Carron of the AEU. Management was represented by five leading managers in the motor industry, one of whom was (surprise! surprise!) L. T. Blakeman, Labour Relations Manager of Fords, Dagenham. Trade union leaders and management were now cooperating in the open, instead of secretly, as at Dagenham!

* Fords has increased production in the region of 30 per cent. For example in the cushion shop the increase had been 37 per cent. In the week ending 16 November 1962, 209 men asked for their cards, many times the normal wastage for that time of year. The process continued for months.

† See 'Murder at Fords' (*Solidarity*, vol. IV, No. 4).

of the factory.* The trade-union officials virtually took over factory negotiations. Steps were taken to by-pass the shop-steward-dominated Joint Works Committee.† The wages at Fords became the lowest in the motor industry, and the profits the highest: £1,200 per year per employee. 'Everyone' was happy: the trade-union officials had increased facilities in the plant and a nice office of their own to work in. The Company ruled the roost. Collaboration had paid off. Meanwhile the men were driven into the ground.

CONCLUSIONS

Amongst the many lessons to be learned from the Ford defeat, a turning point in post-war labour history, was the cumulative effect of the apologetic and defensive attitudes which *everyone* (even the men themselves) adopted towards the militants and towards unofficial action. The arguments put forward against the sackings by the officials, whether 'left' or 'right', were that the sacked men were *not* militants . . . and therefore should not have been sacked. The only valid argument, and the one that would have rallied massive support, was that the men *were* militants, and for that reason had to be defended. Even the shop stewards' committee's main emphasis was that the sacked men were 'respectable, loyal, long-service employees'. The real issue (the defence of job organization) was thus played down.

The Court of Inquiry consisted of an urbane discussion between Professor Jack, the trade-union officials and the management ‡ on the best way to emasculate the shop stewards. For example Les Kealey (TGWU) said in his evidence to the Court (*Daily Telegraph*, 6 March 1963):

'My personal view is that Dagenham would be a happier place if the shop stewards were representatives of the unions the workers belong to. The problem now is how to get it altered' . . . Mr Kealey said the difficulty was in finding a tangible way of setting about it. One of the things he thought they could do was to try to stop the finance . . . 'It is contributed mostly by our members twice a year through Christmas and Derby draws. We ought to be persuading our members not to take part in this to the extent they do'.

* See 'After the Ford Defeat' (*Solidarity*, vol. IV, No. 2) and 'Too Old at Fifty' (*Solidarity*, vol. IV, No. 3).

†See 'The Path of Struggle' (*Solidarity*, vol. III, No. 10).

‡The men themselves, about whom presumably the Inquiry was concerned, were not represented.

Even the shop stewards' committee was at best on the defensive. For example, one of its statements read:

We regret, as any trade-unionist must, that there have been unofficial stoppages because they show there is a gap between the members and the union officials. We also feel that if National officials had taken a stronger attitude on some of the outstanding problems there would be less cause for strikes.*

It is this sort of attitude which has placed the control over the destinies of men on the job in the hands of people with entirely different, indeed opposing, interests: the trade-union leaders. There are four parties to any dispute: the state, the management, the labour bureaucrats . . . and the men. And it is the Ford workers, on their jacks, who will solve their own problems. This is what the Ford struggle emphasized. *Every gain at Fords was by the unofficial action of the men alone. Every defeat was the joint work of the management, trade-union bureaucrats and state.*

Never again must car workers leave the initiative in the hands of trade-union officials. They must build up their own, independent strength. They must tell both management and officials where to stuff their agreements. The only way to win is to build up really massive strength *within* the factory, with strong links with workers in other factories in the group, whether at home or abroad, and with workers in the car industry generally. There is good reason to believe that some Ford workers have learned this lesson.

Here's to the next time!

(From *What Happened at Fords* by Ken Weller (AEU) and Ernie Stanton (NUVB), Solidarity Pamphlet No. 26, consisting of reprints of three articles previously published in *Solidarity* in 1965)

* *What's Wrong at Fords*, published by Fords Joint Shop Stewards' Committee, p. 5.

Chapter 5
Let's Go with Labour:
The Labour Government 1964-70

I always felt that the Labour Party – don't misunderstand me when I say it –
has got something in common with an old stage-coach. I do not mean that it
is out of date, but if it is rattling along at a rare old speed most of the passengers
are so exhilarated, and some so seasick, that they don't start arguing.

(HAROLD WILSON)

I am really sorry to see my countrymen trouble themselves about politics.
House of Commons and House of Lords appear to me to be Fools; they
seem to me to be something Else beside human life.

(WILLIAM BLAKE)

Harold Wilson's emergence as Leader of the Labour Party after the
sudden and extravagantly mourned death of Hugh Gaitskell was
greeted with jubilation by the parliamentary Left. He was neither a
Gaitskellite nor overtly anti-Communist. Although the old Bevanites
may have distrusted his ambitiousness, he had some of Bevan's flair
for attacking the Tories. It was vaguely remembered that he had resigned from the Attlee Government . . . something principled-sounding
to do with prescription charges. Accordingly his fairly copious right-
wing utterances were regarded simply as camouflage protecting his
Bevanite bunkhouse from aerial attacks by Gaitskell's whips. His
rather less frequent radical remarks on Clause 4 and arms to South
Africa were magnified to unrecognizable dimensions.

Wilson, having mesmerized the Left, was able to proceed along a
programme at least as right-wing as Gaitskell's but untroubled by the
traditional Left's objections. The H-bomb did not disappear from the
face of the earth, but it certainly vanished from the pages of *Tribune*.
The Labour Party's quite explicit retreat from its internationalist neo-
principles on immigration policy went unmarked. Indeed it is difficult
not to see in an exhausted Bevanite Left an element of willed self-
deception, for a decade and a half of losing elections had made them

grateful for small political mercies. The dispirited Gaitskellites were equally thankful for Wilson's uncanny skill at re-uniting the warring Party leadership around a diffuse, modern-sounding radicalism. And Labour now actually looked as if it stood a chance against the seedy muddle of crooked osteopaths, Soviet attachés and slumlords which was ending the Tory Party's once self-confident rule. The earnest white-coated figure of Wilson busy mixing foaming test tubes to pre-cipitate the New Britain was in its way more convincing an image than the skull-like stare and tweed rompers of the 14th Earl of Home.

Even the worldly and professionally cynical editor of *Private Eye*, which had succeeded in making undergraduate humour a national commodity, was not immune. 'Consciously or not,' he has revealed, 'the satire movement had been working with Wilson to undermine the fuddy duddies.'* For, when pitched against the incompetent non-chalance of the Tories, Wilson's urgency and enthusiasm for efficiency and science had a hopeful side. At the time it was not obvious that these technological slogans would produce their own technological scandals: Ronan Point, the tower block which fell down; T. Dan Smith, the symbol of the new municipality-boss, discovered up to his thighs in local government corruption; Concorde, the flying white elephant whose development costs alone could rehouse Glasgow and Liverpool but will instead hoist businessmen to New York in time for Martinis before lunch.

What now seems most apparent about Wilson's political ideas is their extraordinary shallowness. He is the master-diplomat of the phrase, capable of abusing the meaning of fairly ordinary words so they become, in the ears of a swooning Labour Party, a new catechism. Now the speeches of Wilson with their vistas of purpose, opportunity, modernity with 'every pub as its own Parliament-in-miniature'† are just so many ghostly corridors. For the talk of modernization quite misunderstood the real social dimension of the changes briskly referred to. Instead science was seen as a sort of classless detergent cleansing away grimy restrictive practices and managerial incompetence to leave 'a society sparkling with opportunity'.

For in fact, whether led by Brown, Wilson or Foot, British social democracy would have come to power in a capitalism which did require a modernization of its class relationships. The system itself, rather than the people who worked for it, required drastic reforms if it were to survive in an increasingly competitive world economy. The traditional party of the bourgeoisie had showed itself incapable, through excessive

---

* Richard Ingrams, *The Life and Times of Private Eye*, Penguin Books, 1971, p. 18.
† In fact it proved more a case of Parliament as a pub-*en-masse*.

short-term greed, aristocratic inertia and general weariness, of pursuing those aims. And the more intelligent industrialists and the more far-seeing journals of business opinion saw clearly that a Labour Party which believed 'that on the whole we think that the big firms are serving the nation well' might do better at 'clearing the dead wood out of the boardroom' than a visibly wormy Tory Party. In fact, Wilson was able to utilize the Labour Party's special relationship with the trade-union officials to enforce a wages policy infinitely more damaging to working-class living standards than Lloyd's attempts. For in the context of British capitalism in the sixties even the quasi-radical aspects of Wilson's programme were in practice turned into their opposite. Wilson's opposition to the independent deterrent actually acted to dovetail British armed forces still closer with American imperial strategy. His opposition to Tory imperialism tailored our foreign policy to fit the needs of our American co-exploiter better. The expansion of higher education produced not liberated minds but trained personnel to lead the New, Competitive Britain. As History, that greatest of all Marxists, slowly peeled the socialist stickers off Wilsonism, what emerged as his aim was a shiny corporate state with a working class more closely integrated, more intensely exploited and more closely disciplined at the work-place than ever before.

But if Wilson had out-manoeuvred or absorbed the Bevanites in the leadership there was a more intransigent Left still reposing within the Labour Party. The academic Labour Left were in general to demonstrate the same gullibility as their parliamentary colleagues, vying with each other to submit bright ideas to the forthcoming Labour Government. The proud pioneer of incomes policy, John Hughes, was to argue with a straight face that 'The policies that have been outlined are designed to produce an economy that is progressively more efficient and uses its resources more rationally than the one we have been used to.'* And the grouping of Left trade-union officials and Labour Party Marxists who produced the weekly socialist news service *The Week* and the *Voice of the Unions*† argued that it ought to be possible for the trade unions to insert certain demands, like workers' control and opening the books, in return for accepting incomes policy. This strategy was given a theoretical rationale with different emphasis by

* John Hughes, 'The British Economy; Crisis and Structural Change', *New Left Review*, 21, March–April 1964.

† This included somewhere within it the nucleus which was to blossom into the International Marxist Group, the official British affiliate of the Paris-based Fourth International, as well as the directors of the Institute for Workers' Control.

Ernest Mandel, Andre Gortz and other advocates of 'structural reform' as a mode of aggressive trade-unionism in neo-capitalism. And although in Britain the conditional wage-freezers were not to get far beyond the seminar their attempts illustrated the dilemma of the Marxist Left in the early sixties.

For since Lenin's strictures on the early Communists who wished to ignore the Labour Party, British Marxists have been especially sensitive in their political attitude to this unique party. At least since the Second World War, Communist strategy has been based on a political and industrial alliance with the Labour Left, effectively the forty or so MPs identified with *Tribune* and their trade-union supporters, with the aim of parliamentary majority based on a Labour-Party-with-socialist-policies and including some Communist Members of Parliament. The Marxists, descended from the Trotskyist Revolutionary Communist Party which led an independent but less than successful life from 1944 to 1949, could probably all deliver a brilliant Marxist diatribe against this 'British Road' to socialism in their sleep. But they were a great deal more successful at denouncing the Communist Party than providing an organizational alternative to it. They too were pinioned to the Labour Party, only not by choice but rather as a consequence of reformism's strength and their own weakness. Although supporters of the *Newsletter*, *Socialist Review* and the other entry papers were directly involved in industrial disputes and the anti-nuclear struggles, it was natural in the fifties and early sixties for the constituency parties to be the focus for working-class political ambitions. However strongly its leadership was rejected, the Labour Party was considered the place in which to engage the political attention of workers and to grapple with existing class-consciousness. The ethics of entrism is a specialist subject in itself, but the fact of the matter is that until the late sixties it had proved impossible for a revolutionary group to escape successfully the gravitational field of social democracy and take up an orbit of its own. And even after the Socialist Labour League was founded and proscribed, much of its activity was still directed to Labour Party branches and the Young Socialist movement.

The Young Socialists indicate clearly the uneasy relationship which existed between the revolutionaries and the bureaucrats of the Labour Party. The YS, the Labour Party's third attempt at a youth section, was founded in 1960. From its beginning it was clear that, if left to their own choice, young socialists would support revolutionary ideas rather than Transport House orthodoxy. In fact the very rapidly growing and solidly working-class YS became an intense centre of Marxist debate in the early sixties. For the first year *Keep Left*, a YS paper in sympathy with the SLL, made most of the running. Its editor, Roger Protz, had made a spectacular resignation from the official Transport House youth paper *New Advance* during the first annual conference, declaring in a duplicated handout: 'The NEC is the editor of *New Advance*, not me. I carry out their wishes. They have produced a paper FOR Young Socialists, not OF Young Socialists.'* *Keep Left* was followed by *Rebel*, a paper which resulted from an amalgamation of the London and Liverpool YS papers *Rebel* and *Rally* produced by young supporters of International Socialism with the initial support of many other tendencies, and run by readers' meetings. The official Labour Party found very considerable difficulty in unearthing Young Socialists prepared to defend official policy and concentrated instead on manoeuvring against *Keep Left*, *Young Guard* and their supporters. In the course of their campaign there were rigged intrigues, summary expulsions, ejections by police and skilled attempts to exploit lack of unity among the Left. For there was within the YS a passionate and bitter intra-Marxist debate about the role of revolutionary leadership and the nature of Russia, its bomb and its bloc, as well as a vigorous concerted attack on Gaitskell and the Shadow Cabinet's politics.

However, all these groups campaigned for Labour in the 1964 election, adopting some variant of the old Trotskyist slogan 'Labour to Power' (the-better-to-expose-itself). The SLL's weekly paper the *Newsletter*, whose 'long-awaited two-colour issue' was deemed by its editorial board a 'great advance in the history of the world revolutionary movement', proferred a variety of advice.† On 14 March 1964, it was suggested that 'Labour must win the middle class by nationalizing

---

*Roger Protz, quoted in 'The Young Socialists: Labour's Lost Youth' by Mike Coggins, Fred Lindop, Hackney, 1965, p. 10. Protz, who has edited at some time or other most of the left-wing papers in Britain and has run *Socialist Worker* since its inception in 1968, was at this time a newly demobbed lance-jack from the Signals whose previous job was for D. C. Thomson comics. He got the job of editing *New Advance* mainly because of his innocence and ignorance of left-wing politics: 'When I told Transport House the last book I had read was *A Passage to India* they gave a visible sigh of relief.'

†These superlative statements perhaps need not to be taken too literally. The Sixth Conference of the SLL in 1964 was described as 'truly the most youthful and serious congress which has convened in Britain since the war'. Of the 28 November recall Conference, it was said: 'There has never been in the history of the British movement such a lively and thoughtful discussion.' The Third International Conference of the International Committee was 'beyond doubt the most impressive conference of our movement since the founding conference in the summer of 1938' etc., etc.

monopolies'; a few weeks later it was 'Mods and rockers must unite to clear out the Tories'. And at a meeting in Leeds Art Gallery on 28 March, Cliff Slaughter declared: 'We have to prepare a big fight against the re-introduction of conscription which will be used to decimate the youth movement.'

The International Socialists argued more modestly that 'Capital in Britain has raised problems of economic growth and structural change which the Tories are unable to, but which a Labour Government conceivably might, solve. The attempt – whether by imposing a wage freeze, speeding labour "mobility", or whatever – is bound to harm working-class interests. This would not be a conspiracy, since the leadership agrees with both diagnosis and cure. Equally it is not a programme to "socialize" British capitalism. What it does offer is a perspective in which an increasing number of workers might be affected by political decisions taken in their name, might be prepared to question those decisions actively and concert their activities around a coherent programme. Rather than ask of a future Labour Government to act in ways we know to be unrealistic, socialists should be directing their energies to the point of production where the real and ascribed interests of workers are bound to collide.'*

But despite the heavy weight of their own reservations there is little doubt that left-wing activists had something to do with Wilson's election victory. Students and CND members canvased energetically, Labour winning its first seat ever in Sussex, thanks, the new MP thought, to the efforts of the Young Socialists on polling day. There was a real, if temporary, enthusiasm among the politically active; the shop stewards at Fords Dagenham, for example, broke down the constituencies plant by plant and reckon they won four or five Tory marginals in Essex over to Labour. In fact the 1964 Labour vote was still less than the total that lost them the 1951 election and nearly a quarter of voters abstained. The Tory defeat actually depended on small shifts in loyalty in the commuter belt. Nevertheless Labour was in power at last. The *Observer* breathlessly introduced us to our new leaders. George Brown 'singled out as energizer of industry in Labour's New Britain; fits the bill', Dick Crossman 'erratic, brilliant, exasperating and engaging', Ray Gunter 'vital link between Wilson and unions. Second only to Nye Bevan in Welsh *hywl* (oratorial uplift). Innocent, round, apple-cheeked face; sharp, salty commonsense mind', Peter Shore 'lean-jawed and wiry economist, best mind in Transport House.

* *International Socialism*, 17, Summer 1964.

Pragmatic, forward-looking radical . . .' The *Sunday Times* interviewed Roy Jenkins in an official car as the Household Cavalry sprang to attention. '"Tell me honestly, do you enjoy all this?" "Well . . ." said Mr Jenkins, and smiling a winningly frank smile, "Well . . . yes." ' A friend of Callaghan reported that 'Since he became Chancellor he has changed. He tried not to but he can't help it. He's got an aura about him. He's started waving to people as if they were cheering him in the street instead of as if they were just people, if you get my meaning.' Crossman, brilliant mind, exasperating, etc., 'has been offering friends rides in *his* car, like a child showing off a new toy'.

The first hundred days of the Labour Government proved a political anti-climax and were spent soothing Capital's nerves and blowing socialist kisses into the future. An extreme sloth surrounded such subjects as capital gains tax, steel nationalization, Rent Act repeal and 'the nationalization of urban building land' which Wilson had promised an esctatic audience at Leeds Town Hall. It was more urgent to assure Zurich and Washington that it was business as usual and to sponge the fevered brow of the Ordinary Share Index. The radical pledges that were not entirely abandoned, like the housing target or the abolition of public schools, were either introduced only to be reversed again later on, like the removal of prescription charges, or carried out in a form which completely altered their content, like the Race Relations Act, used extensively by the police to prosecute Black militants, or the Rent Act, whose landlord-dominated assessment boards frequently increased rather than cut rent. Even such traditional ideological shuttlecocks as steel nationalization took on an altered meaning. The old socialist case for nationalization as a means of extending working-class political power had been effectively destroyed by workers' experience of the Attlee nationalization. Now what the steel unions wanted in practice was job security. But Wilson's White Paper, though decorated with the old-fashioned rhetoric of public ownership, actually followed another logic, that already begun by the private steel managers in their attempts to scale-up investment and unit-size to compete with the steel giants of Japan, Holland and America. Nationalization under Wilson was once again simply changing the name plates, giving an extremely generous collective golden handshake to the old private owners but leaving the profitable little bits at the end of the steel manufacturing pipeline in their hands. For the steel workers the operation was a massive irrelevancy, except in so far as it actually worsened the job situation.

On foreign policy, from which the Labour Left had tended to derive its definition in the post-war period, Wilson showed an almost embarrassing zeal in carrying out every American whim. He gave unequivocal support to the US bombing of North Vietnam as well as to the smaller but no less sordid colonial murdering in Aden, Malaysia and the Yemen. Buccaneer fighters were duly despatched to Verwoerd in South Africa. Despite the rhetorical flourishes against racialism, when a real choice actually presented itself the Cabinet enthusiastically tightened anti-immigration controls. Soskice proved himself, almost inconceivably, a more reactionary Home Secretary than Henry Brooke.

But in the election campaign of 1966, Wilson was still able to excuse his record on the basis of 'the Tory inheritance' and the smallness of his majority. Despite an obsessional concern with the strength of sterling, his speeches could still stress working-class reforms – the repeal of the Rent Act, abolition of prescription charges, comprehensive schools, council housing, poor relief – and get away with it. The Parliamentary Left, which had also used the smallness of Wilson's majority as an excuse for its own inaction, entered the election with a passion which was not shared by many electors. *Tribune*'s exultant election-day spread asked, 'Who doesn't want a landslide? We see you, Desmond Donnelly, with your *Spectator* pals – well, here it comes and you'll be buried in steel ... Pensions up, Rent Act security, Unemployment down, Prescription Charges off, who cares! We do ... and so do millions ... now, for bigger advances, VOTE LABOUR.' The Fleet Street press and the industrialists, viciously against Labour in 1964, were strangely silent, and the election was probably won on further middle-class shifts to Labour. But if the estimate of *Militant*, a Marxist paper published by Labour Party members, that the vote was 'an indication of a pre-revolutionary period in British society' was a fraction extravagant, Wilson's politics had been given a clear mandate by the working class as a whole. Except for the Marxists, who had a professional interest in Wilson's betrayals, disillusion was slow arising within the Labour Party and the anguished letters of resignations published in *Tribune* were few, heralds of the future rather than the real thing. *Tribune*'s readers were still more often moved to put pen to paper to denounce the paper's soapflake-mild criticisms of Wilson. The intellectual Left was isolated, mournful, demoralized. Socialist academics, together with members of various Left groups, attempted to start, or rather revive, that perpetual dream of socialist academics, a national network of Marxist classes for workers, this time to be called the Centre for Socialist Education. But the workers showed their customary lack of enthusiasm for socialist lecturers, the impressive list of sponsors proved incapable of actually organizing anything and the Centre was quietly amalgamated with the Institute for Workers' Control after a few promising publications and meetings. In the summer of 1966 a group of university socialists convened by stalwarts of the old New Left began the work which was to lead to the publication on 1 May 1967 of the Mayday Manifesto and the launching of a 'self-organizing self-financing socialist intellectual organization', the Mayday Manifesto Group. Their analysis was certainly a most coherent, closely argued and prettily written account of Wilsonism, sold briskly and was reprinted in an enlarged edition as a Penguin book. But the Group's declared aim to make an organized intervention into Left politics, implicit in the issue of a manifesto, was less successful. The manifesto's practical suggestions ranged from the plaintive to the vague, and its organization scarcely survived its launching meeting in the Central Hall, packed out with sectarian posses, rows of hopeful Communists, a hostile paper-selling squadron from the SLL, IS building shop stewards lounging against the back wall looking supercilious. At the close of the meeting at least a third of the audience streaked to the door to sell their various periodicals with much muttered greeting and cursing. It came as no great surprise that the first speaker from the floor came to bury not to praise, denouncing the platform vigorously for 'having no representative of the working class' on it.

She had of course a real point. The vacuum on the Left was glaringly apparent, but there was not, yet, a mass opposition to Wilson, whether on Vietnam, racialism or incomes policy, to fill it. For the process by which working-class people moved away from the Labour Party was not a clear-cut detonation of a whole slab of old loyalty but rather a general crumbling-away of commitment to Labour Party politics. And this slow unlearning took place, especially in the trade unions, in a multitude of separate trenches rather than a grand set-piece battle. Socialist intellectuals, in some cases even more isolated from working-class realities than they would care to admit, had a natural tendency to expect mass working-class disillusion to follow the rapid tempo of their own. Marxist publications like *The Week* also tended to telescope the political process, arguing in May 1967 that 'the significance of the vote against the Government is that it marks the formal end of Wilson's domination over the Labour Party which has completely confused the Left for some three years or more', only to report that the paper was closing in February 1968 because 'It has been felt that the original aim of the journal, that of becoming the expression of an organized Left inside the Labour Party and trade unions, is unlikely to be achieved in the near future. The main reason being that the mass left-wing opposition to right-wing policies of the Labour leadership – which we all expected in 1964 . . . has not materialized.'

For in fact, history-making intervention, mass left-wing opposition or alternative leaderships were, except in the columns of their own publications, not within the reach of the still tiny revolutionary Left. To attempt to span, virtually single-handed, the vacuum on the Left was to risk being torn completely out of shape. For the vacuum resulted from an immense but silent shift within the Left: the rightward movement of social democracy away from even the most meagre reformism and a corresponding move by the Communist Party to adopt the position newly vacated by Labour, less obvious in the British Communist Party than in France or Italy if only because of the complete lack of electoral success here. The ideologies of social democracy and Stalinism no longer dominated the labour movement, but they had yet to be replaced by Marxist ideas and Marxist organizations which had really broken decisively free from the crippling legacy of small group sectarianism. In practice in 1966 groups of Marxists with quite modest and 'sectarian' targets – the formation of a campaign in solidarity with the Vietnamese, the organization of a committee to defend shop stewards, the production of a rank-and-file paper (although it was based only on a handful of workers), even printing one's journal in two colours instead of one – were to prove more successful.

For after the 1966 landslide, the rate of disillusion did accelerate. *Tribune* may have thought that 'socialism is on the agenda again', but *Labour Worker* was probably more accurate when it predicted 'Wilson's "victory" means the end of fig-leaf politics'. Wilson's attempt to please working-class voters as well as the stock market increasingly pleased neither. The incomes policy hardened into a complete wage freeze plus a savage deflation. Thirty or so Labour MPs moved into almost permanent opposition and the TUC begun to make warning noises. Wilson's attempt to straddle this rapidly widening chasm led him to adopt a bluff, no-nonsense, imitation-Yorkshire tone of voice to conceal a certain lack of candour which underlay everything he said. The more devious he was forced to become, the more obsessed he became with his infallible honesty. As he sank lower and lower he developed the fascinating psychological mannerism of repeated self-quotation, until he could scarcely bear to answer a question in the present tense. His cabinet's signposts for the sixties now read 'God save the Pound', 'Soak the Sick', and 'Loyalty! Selectivity! Redundancy!'. In 1967 there were the beginnings of a real political opposition. In July the

Vietnam Solidarity Campaign held a march of a few hundred, but without the platform of Labour MPs, Communist union leaders and progressive vicars which had been obligatory at previous Vietnam marches. In July a rally of several thousand students protested about the raising of overseas students' fees. The Campaign against Racial Discrimination was taken over by black people, to the horror of Julia Gaitskell and other worthies who had hitherto led its deliberations. And in the remarkable year of 1968 there was real evidence of the rebirth of Marxism in the events in Paris and Prague. By 1969 there was a rash of explicitly political national strikes, almost unknown in the British labour movement, and unheard of against a Labour Government.

The end of an era is too often announced. British labour history is littered with premature Marxist obituaries of the Labour Party. And despite them the Party has repeatedly survived the most comprehensive betrayals of working-class interests and remained the main expression of working-class political life. It has retained, however grudgingly, working-class electoral support. Indeed the Labour Party's ability to continue to command the loyalties of those workers which it is obliged to ignore once in power has been a vital element in the stability of British capitalism. And yet Wilson's redefinition of the Labour Party as the modernizer of capital and his inability to deliver the most modest of reforms, although not as spectacular a failure as MacDonald's, may in the end prove more decisive. For it has forced working-class people to bypass the Labour Party in defence of the living standards they have won for themselves in twenty years of full employment. The fight to defend and develop rank-and-file trade-unionism must, after Wilson and 'In Place of Strife', take place independent of the Labour Party. The international traditions of the socialist movement, the continual protest that the Left in an old imperialist country must make against Britain's political and economic subjection of other nations, not only takes place outside the Labour Party but is led, because the anti-imperialist struggles themselves are so led, by revolutionaries. The movement against racialism in Britain is no longer in the hands of liberal well-wishers but the black people themselves, who see official Labour with its vicious record of anti-immigrant legislation as an enemy not a friend.

And although the electoral machinery and the press releases continue to churn out of the top of the Labour Party, its activists are increasingly absent and there would appear to be an irreversible decline in active loyalty to the Party. A recent study of Liverpool showed the local

Labour Parties as a shell with a tiny active membership dominated by more or less middle-class people.* As an older generation of stalwarts die they are increasingly replaced by white-collar workers and professionals who view the Party mainly as a route to the 'professionalized' and totally undemocratic cliques that run our large towns. And although Labour made much fuss about regional subsidies and redundancy payments, support has ebbed too in the traditional centres of Labour's strength in Wales, the north-east and Scotland. In the northern region for example six years of Labour lost 66,000 jobs, despite a net loss of over 30,000 people through migration. The odd poisonous and highly mechanized aluminium smelter or chemical plant, financed by lavish Government subsidies, has not purchased a great deal of loyalty in spots like Sunderland, where eighty-two men were looking for every job by 1969. A handful of perfume factories in the Welsh valleys has failed to revive the miners' once coal-hard loyalty to Labour.† The Labour Left itself is curiously more feeble than it was under Bevan in the fifties or the Socialist League in the thirties. And in Parliament after the October 1969 reshuffle there was not a single minister from a working-class background, while in Attlee's day it was half the Cabinet. That old fraud Ray Gunter had a point when he said, after resigning from the Cabinet in 1968, 'to the ordinary fellow in the workshop, the Labour Party was *our party*. It was the instrument forged to help them in the pursuit of things that they thought were proper. The tragedy is that so many of the people in this country no longer think of it in that sense.'‡

One important result of this process is that the Marxist groups, which had a rather uneasy, compromised and necessarily semi-secret existence in the Labour Party, have felt able to leave it. As early as 1965 the executive of International Socialism passed Mike Kidron's motion that 'The IS Group rejects the Labour Party as an instrument for social change, rejects it as a milieu for *mass* conversion to socialist consciousness; and sees in it primarily an area for ideological conflict and a source of individual recruitment to a revolutionary programme.' In the same year, the SLL decided to leave the Young Socialists and set up an independent organization of the same name, forcing Transport House to rename the official organization the Labour Party Young Socialists, which has had a vigorous if exclusive life ever since. The

*See Barry Hindess, *The Decline of Working-Class Politics*, Paladin, 1970.

†See Dave Peers, 'Depressed Areas: How Labour Subsidizes the Bosses', *Socialist Worker*, 11 December 1969.

‡*Listener*, 11 July 1968.

great entrism debate was solving itself; in Labour Party after Labour Party there was simply nothing to enter. Marxist groups and cadres which dated from the upheavals of 1956 and the Young Socialist battles of the early sixties tended to channel the movements which arose against Wilson and tended to recruit from them. The massive political upsurge of 1968 multiplied the size of all the revolutionary groups, and if the recruits tended to be more middle-class than before they provided the numerical strength to undertake practical activities in the working-class movement. And increasingly the contact between students and workers, once a slogan, then a rather embarrassed and stilted encounter, became a natural alliance on the picket line and in the demonstration, with many young workers much closer in their political attitudes to the students than to the leaders of their own unions. In 1968 the IS paper *Labour Worker* made the highly symbolic change of name to *Socialist Worker* and its circulation soared. There now remained only one Marxist grouping within the Labour Party, publishing *Militant* and committed to the 'deep entrist' position that in revolutionary crisis workers would return to the traditional organizations of the working class and that the Labour Party, if provided with a revolutionary leadership, could itself execute the revolution. (*Militant*'s rivals argued it was simply a case of the protective covering of the Labour Party actually becoming absorbed, by a process of political osmosis, onto their own surface.) A tendency within the RSL, the Selbyites, have achieved the logical conclusion of this approach by now having a Trotskyist MP who is, of course, unfortunately unable to reveal his identity. Whatever else Wilson is seen by history as achieving, an irreversible destruction of social democracy's active working-class following may not be his least important.

Labour's Party:
Mike Kidron

Delegates have a clear choice at Scarborough this year. They can sit tight on their opinion polls and 'leave it to Harold'; or they can try to sketch the guidelines for a future Labour Government – at some risk to themselves from both polls and party managers. The Resolutions suggest that they will choose the first. Perhaps. But it is as well to know at what cost.

There's a lot of unfinished business left over from the last Labour Government, which the present leadership would like to get through. Then, they saw their prime task in adapting British capitalism to the decline of Empire. To do this they had to make good the loss of investment income from abroad by pushing exports from home – 'export or die' ran the Ministerial chorus. To get exports, industry had to be confirmed in the dominance over finance it had attained during the war – and this Labour helped by fostering mergers, takeovers and strong trade associations. Industry had further to be sustained with a substructure of cheap services – hence the nationalization of coal, electricity, gas and the rest. It was a fine legacy for British capital, but not the whole estate that was in Labour's giving. The raised level of exports prevented utter collapse, but the pound remained weak and invited balance of payments crises every second year or so. Concentration of capital was important, but it stopped short of full inducement planning on the French model and well short of any attempt to plan labour. As for nationalization – it needs remodelling to catch up with industry's changed orientation and structure. Given a second term, Labour promises to make good the lapses of its first.

Whether or not a Labour Government contributes to new international currency arrangements – as it says it will; or takes Britain into Europe – as it says it won't but yet might; or does a Beeching not only on the railways but in mining, gas and one or two other industries – as it is pledged to oppose but in all probability will support – whether or not it does these is far less portentous for the labour movement than its obvious determination to plan wages and absorb our organizations into the new state planning apparatus.

Already Wilson has stumped union conferences seeking support for a wage freeze. The giant Transport and General has already given its bureaucratic word not to embarrass our Man at No. 10; the Boilermakers were asked but kept their honour intact. At the same time, by advocating a minor inquiry into profits, the National Income Commission has made it easy for the Labour Party to abandon its uprightness and join in lacing working-class demands into capitalist corsets.

If the present leadership get their way the next Labour Government will be well set to present capital with the greatest prize ever, sought for two hundred years or more, the *voluntary* abdication of their bargaining role by the organs of the labour movement. It is this above all which Conference has the opportunity to condemn.

The pressures against doing so will be immense. It is a pre-election rally, we're already home and dry (or so it seems), the official Left has opted out of politics and into cheer-leading, has let unity take the place of unilateralism. But let it not be said that Social Democracy delivered itself bound *and* gagged to capital. Unlikely though it appears at this point of time in this country, there *is* an alternative to capitalist planning and wage freeze. It is democratic planning under workers' control.

(From 'Notes of the Quarter', *International Socialism*, 14, Autumn, 1963)

Trade Unionism in Despair:
Stacy Marking*

GWYN JONES (fitter in AEUW): If you were to draw a graph of socialist hopes against time, they would level off during Attlee's time, there'd be a temporary improvement in 1964–5, and then it would take a nose dive since Wilson. The Labour have become the party of conformity; they have retained the private sector of industry. They have made no inroads into capitalism. The haves and have-nots are still the same. Nothing has changed.

SID MORGAN (son of miner now working in Cardiff University): People in this area are naturally socialist, it's in the whole history of the valley. The early men in the movement suffered and fought for it. If they are disillusioned now, where can they turn? The conservative solution is no solution here.

GWYN JONES: The Labour majority here in Caerphilly used to be 20,000. The old MP Morgan Jones used to sit in the pub lording it, they are so confident. And this time they got in by a paltry 2,000. It'll be Plaid next, for where can we turn? History has buried the Liberals, and the Tories have had 200 years to get things done.

DAI WALTERS (ex-NUM member and coal-face worker): Three years ago 80 per cent of the men who worked with you would be with Labour, now 60 per cent are against.

DR ALISTAIR WILSON (GP and ex-Communist local councillor): I don't see any progressive alternative to Labour Government. I want to see a Labour Government with a socialist policy.

GWYN PHILLIPS (ex-NUM Lodge secretary and Labour Councillor, now Industrial Representative for East Wales and member of Plaid): I have seen Labour from the cradle until now, almost the grave! But there has been a breakdown in the fabric of democracy. The great debate of the twenties was between democratic socialism and revolutionary socialism. It was against the tradition of Chapel and revivalism – people began to see that Chapel identified with management, and they embraced the religion of politics. The majority went for democratic socialism and embraced the Labour Party. People

*These quotations come from interviews made in 1966 in South Wales by Stacy Marking for the ITV current affairs programme 'This Week', at that time edited by the Labour MP Phillip Whitehead. The programme was neither filmed nor transmitted.

argued, but they really believed they could change the world.

I hoped that the Labour Party would get to grips with this question of the relationship between the individual and government, but it has been taken even further away. Less and less democratic process. They've been no better than the Tories with the sick, the injured, the over-sixties. They have failed in their mission to bring the Government nearer the people. The whole country has been forced under departmental control; coal, hospitals, transport, education, no matter what local objections. And that they should say that they have too much work to do and put some of it into a non-elected body like the Lords is to exacerbate it.

GWYN JONES: Labour was the party that carried the people's hopes; they were going to lead them to the promised land. Now I hear Gunter saying last week 'people must accept a lower standard of living'. Now what did Baldwin say? 'People must accept lower wages!' Now to me that sounds remarkably like the same thing. Barbara Castle talks about this year's economic crisis. Well, in my home there is an economic crisis every week. Every pay packet is an economic crisis. The haves and the have-nots are still the same. Nothing has changed.

BEN DAVIS (unemployed ex-miner): Angela was in flames in her nighty, trying to warm herself at the oven. Of course there are laws against inflammable nighties, but in our family everything has to be passed on or cut down, and it was cut down from her mother's. This Government is a dead loss, they put up their own wages and then stopped everybody else's. What can you believe when Mr Wilson goes on TV and says minimum wages will be £25, when you know that a man at the pit working underground gets £13? Since my attack I've been getting 6d. less than I did when I was working. What kind of standard of living do you get from £13 a week for hard work, and no security?

DR WILSON: The Prices and Incomes policy is producing poverty – the pressure falls on the already depressed. 1,735 out of work in these valleys. The national average is 2.5 per cent but Caerphilly is 9.5 per cent. ICI makes £500 profit per Welsh worker each year, Dunlop makes £225, the Steel Company of Wales £331. And yet still they are declaring redundancies.

DAI WALTERS: The only boom is in unemployment. The only new building in Bargoed is the new Ministry of Labour. At the new factory, Johnson and Johnson, 200 men a week are applying for jobs, and they are taking only six men a month. These are jobs for skilled workers, they are not right for men who have been digging.

SID MORGAN: They claim to have brought jobs to the valley, but look at the jobs, they're not for the over-forties and it's for women, which means that it's cheap labour, just as Wales has always meant cheap labour. We did a survey in the Rhondda valley about what people felt about the Labour Party and it was funny. They'd say that 'the country' in some abstract sense was running well, but anything in their experience was not. They were particularly against the Government's fuel policy, unemployment and the sort of jobs that are brought in.

DR PHIL WILLIAMS: I remember they ran a recruitment campaign while I was at school. There's a safe future in the mines. That's what you were promised – money; and conditions were not good, but at least there was security. The one thing that the Labour Party could be identified with would be the fight against unemployment. But now, by not devaluing they have made it official Labour policy.

GWYN PHILLIPS: Trade-unionism is in despair. There's a withering away of contact between the individual worker and his union. The men's loyalty is to their immediate group, which may clash with union loyalties.

EUART DAVIES (who was awarded two scholarships to the LSE but was too poor to take them up, became a trade-union official and Labour councillor and has now left the Party and runs a pub): The trade-union movement has been caught between the demands of its members and its party loyalty. There's a breakdown through this political loyalty. You can't attend some meeting, or the Congress, unless you are a member of the Labour Party. And yet socialists feel that the Labour Party has left them. For the first time ever a Government has threatened a trade union and its members with gaol if they don't do what they're told. The Government has got so undemocratic I'm afraid Wilson will take matters into his own hands and say No Elections this time.

REG STUART (ASLEF engine-driver): The heart of it should be *elective* unionism. Members must have the power of recall over their representatives. Look at the remoteness of the transport unions. Unionism is upside down; decisions come from the top downwards. Instead they should be formed so that the rank and file decide.

SID MORGAN: Nationalization round here has meant the trains and the coal industry, and look at them. The people here feel totally out of touch with the railways; decisions are not made here. The closures aren't from malice, they're by default, with no consulting or planning with the needs of passengers or any new industry they hoped to bring. Railway people don't even think railways. They had an inspection the other week of this line – the men were brought by car and later picked up by car; they never even thought of coming by train.

GWYN PHILLIPS: The idea of public ownership – it was better than the private old days, when it used to be said they robbed the shareholders and starved the miners – but they let it go to waste. In the first five years there was tremendous good will. Shinwell promised, 'We will not change the brass plates immediately, but we will change the brass faces' and the workmen genuinely thought it would happen. Our wages were the lowest in the country, but we also had the lowest record of absenteeism. Until 1955–6, we began to feel the first chills. The Coal Board offices began to have oil heating. But we thought that with the Labour Government of 1964, stoppages would be arrested. But they have made it their own fuel policy, and begun a rundown regardless of speed. There are many things that they have not done that they could have done. They could have co-ordinated their plans and controlled the rundown simply by being well informed. But they left the provision of incoming private economic forces just like the Tories. They've failed to provide for the interests of individuals. The greatest sufferers have been the older generation. Maybe they have to have a pool of unemployment, but this is chaotic, quite unplanned. It's not really mobility of labour. There are say 150 lads in this valley who could have taken up apprenticeships in coal, but the rundown has been so fearful they won't go into mining.

DAI WALTERS: You are told to put up productivity, but there is a ceiling on productivity. They will only take so many tons of coal a year, so to produce more means closing the mines faster. There was a good opportunity lost with nationalization.

WILF BERRIMAN (power-station supervisor in his late forties): We have a consultative committee at the NBC power-station but it's a carnival. We troop in with our suggestions for efficiency (and we know what we are talking about) but you can see it's a formality, in one ear out the other. They buy ridiculous furnace equipment – they never thought of asking the men who worked it.

DR PHIL WILLIAMS: In effect nationalization made no difference to the men. Alienation between working men and the management was at least as marked. The reasons given for closing the pits are 'absenteeism', but the real reason is the fuel policy – so many pits to close per annum regardless. There is nothing that the men can do about it.

They have never been told if the mine in Bargoed was making a loss or a profit, never, until it's announced it's closing. Why don't they open the books?

GWYN PHILLIPS: Bevan struck a severe blow at democratic socialism with the National Health Service, with committees that are selected not elected. The hospitals here were maintained by subscription, each miner paid 6d. a week, it was his hospital – everyone who attended the Annual General Meeting, and heard the accounts read out. They destroyed that, and with it an area where we could have experimented with workers' control and participation.

DR WILSON: There's been a loss of local power; control has gone from the local councils over gas, electricity, hospitals and education. Funds are cut at a national level, so we don't get a junior school. We need a democracy that works all the way upwards, and where therefore everyone is involved in decisions for their own lives. We need a Labour Government with socialist principles.

Crossman at King Hill:
Solidarity and Socialist Appeal

At this time the Labour Government was making strenuous efforts to maintain its fragile majority by winning the Erith by-election. Their lightweight candidate, Mr Jim Wellbeloved, was being bolstered by frequent visits from Cabinet Ministers.

On 25 October it was the turn of Richard Crossman, Minister of Housing, to visit the constituency. The Minister duly climbed onto the platform of the Erith Girls' Grammar School and beamed at a large audience, blissfully unaware that it contained a dozen or more families from King Hill and thirty or forty of their socialist friends.

Had he known this, he might perhaps have chosen not to address this meeting from behind a poster which boldly proclaimed 'ANOTHER LABOUR PLEDGE FULFILLED — FREEDOM FROM EVICTION!'

However, he began his speech without interruption. It was not until after some fifteen or twenty minutes of unstinting praise for the Labour Party and its fantastic record in housing and protecting tenants, etc., that someone decided to inject a note of reality into the proceedings by asking 'WHAT ABOUT THE HOMELESS FAMILIES AT KING HILL?'

Instead of explaining that he knew nothing whatsoever about King Hill, Mr Crossman chose to ignore the question. More and more of the audience joined in the questioning, until (when it became clear that Mr Crossman had no intention of answering any questions on this topic) the interruptions became constant and angry. The Chairman made repeated appeals and demands for order, promising that the Minister would answer questions later, but the more experienced among the questioners demanded a personal assurance from the Minister that he would eventually answer questions on King Hill, and when this was not forthcoming, even the Chairman, as he later confessed, shared in the general feeling of betrayal.

Amidst continuous uproar Mr Crossman finally sat down. The inept candidate, Jim Wellbeloved (sic!), rose gaily to try and retrieve the situation by delivering a speech about an elaborate and fantastically expensive new town centre he wanted – a speech that had been carefully writtten well in advance to appeal to middle-class voters.

The audience listened for a few minutes with growing incredulity. Then the questions began again, still directed at Crossman! The humiliated candidate tried to dismiss the homeless by inferring that they were irresponsible. He denounced their supporters as 'Trots and anarchists' or even worse 'members of Socialist Action'. It seemed as if the whole meeting suddenly came to its feet at this ludicrous evasion. It was notable that local trade-unionists, who had frowned at earlier interruptions, were now angrily demanding that the legitimate questions of the homeless should be answered. At the height of the uproar, Brian Lomas, one of the husbands who was later to go to prison for refusing publicly to forswear his wife and children, coolly walked onto the platform behind the speakers and placed copies of the King Hill leaflet in front of them. He was grabbed by several stewards who began to manhandle him out of the hall. Other stewards attempted to remove people from the rear of the room, but they held their ground.

At this stage the Chairman gave up in despair. It was clear that the platform no longer had any control over the meeting. A violent situation was only averted when a member of Socialist Action produced a megaphone and called the meeting to order. Before handing it back to the Chairman this speaker explained that they had not come with the intention of disrupting the meeting but solely to ask Mr Crossman if he was aware of what was happening at King Hill. Did he know that women and children were being evicted? Did he know that children were being taken into compulsory care and forcibly separated from their parents? And now that he did know – would he do something about it? The hostel was by no means full. Would the Labour Government stand by and allow the Kent County Council to use police and bailiffs to evict these families?

The Labour Minister still did not answer. Shortly afterwards, he left the hall with a set face, a police escort, and the pleas and jeers of the homeless ringing in his ears.

The following day's papers described the meeting with varying degrees of bias and distortion. According to the *Daily Mirror* 'a pitched battle took place between police, stewards and homeless demonstrators!' In fact the police, for once, did not intervene. The only violence (apart from attempts by the stewards to maintain the Labour Party's democratic image by ejecting its critics) took place when one well-dressed woman, who would have looked equally at home at a Conservative Party Conference, chose to declaim loudly that, as an owner occupier who had come along to hear Mr Crossman, she was not interested in King Hill! Unfortunately, she said this standing immediately behind a mother of four, who for three months had endured the squalor and misery of King Hill. In turning to reprove this affluent exponent of the 'fuck you, Jack' mentality, the mother was seized by one of those moments of speechless exasperation in which emotion takes charge. Instead of words, she delivered a resounding slap.

The Labour candidate, appalled at the introduction of practical issues and human problems into his comfortable ascent to Westminster, made strenuous efforts to prevent any recurrence of this humiliation. At future meetings in Erith there were often more policemen and stewards than audience!

(From 'KCC vs the Homeless', a joint Solidarity/Socialist Appeal pamphlet on the King Hill struggle)

Goodbye Nob:
George Moore

In bidding farewell to my London bus colleagues after seventeen years in the editorial chair of the *Platform*, I am torn with conflicting emotions of sadness and pride. Sadness that the remorseless hand of old Father Time now dictates my retirement – and pride in the integrity and achievements of the little journal I have been privileged to edit over so many years.

I have done this job because I was – I am – and I will always be – a socialist. For forty-six years, within the limits of my capacity and to the best of my ability, I have worked in the trade union and labour movement, adding my tiny quota to bring about a socialist system of society, where, for the first time in his long history, man may finally get up off his knees, rise to his full stature, and live in dignity, decency, progress and peace.

Let me hasten at once to say that the socialist principles and ideas that I uphold are not those daily peddled in the press and on television by the representatives of that alleged 'socialist' government that sits in power today threatening imprisonment of trade-unionists and dispensing wage freeze, rising prices and unemployment as the fruits of socialism and the tokens of human brotherhood.

No, brothers. My socialism is based on a clear recognition that we live in a class society – a society divided into the 'haves' and the 'have-nots' – the exploiters and the exploited – the capitalists and the working class. By its very nature, such a society breeds class war between the two contending classes. The job of the socialist is to play his full part in that class war – and to end it – by finally abolishing classes altogether, and with them, the private-enterprise system itself. Those who play their part in this struggle are socialists. Those who do not, whatever they may call themselves, are, in practice, upholders of capitalism.

Now take a long, hard look at such a quintet as Harold Wilson, Jim Callaghan, Michael Stewart, George Brown and Ray Gunter as the leading Cabinet representatives of today's 'socialist' government. Then honestly ask yourself: What, in even the remotest sense, have such people to do with socialism? Do they not, in fact, out-Tory the Tories in their defence and protection of the private-enterprise system? And is not the abolition of the capitalist system the absolutely fundamental aim of socialism? Is nót the principle enshrined in Clause Four of the Labour Party constitution itself?

Yet there is nothing special or peculiar about this modern bunch. The social democrats have always been the same. The man I knew as Ramsay MacDonald forty years ago is called Harold Wilson today. The late (and very unlamented) Jimmie Thomas now answers to the name of Ray Gunter. The men who betrayed the General Strike of 1926 now threaten to imprison shop stewards in 1966. That is the measure of the advance to 'socialism' made by the Parliamentary Labour Party during forty years.

Similarly, on the trade-union side, in almost half a century I have never yet known a trade-union general secretary who, when the chips were down, truly represented the class interests of his members in struggle with the employers.

When such general secretaries meet collectively to constitute the General Council of the TUC, and, in that capacity, meet Cabinet Ministers of the calibre mentioned above, we get precisely the situation we see today, i.e., the top trade-union brass and the alleged 'socialist' Government, united – all along the line – to preserve the class interests of the capitalists – to the greater glory of the Pentagon and the Swiss banking circles.

It is at this stage that a most nauseating farce is played out. Having climbed to power on the backs of trade-unionists, having financed their very election campaigns with trade-union money, having enacted legislation threatening the very lives and liberties of trade-union shop stewards, having produced massive unemployment, these same hypocrites have the gall to appeal to their very victims for loyalty – to *your* government.

Thus do the leading social democrats – on both the trade-union and political wings – fulfil their role – not as socialists (which they never were) but as upholders of capitalism. The Second World War brought two new words into our vocabulary – Quisling and collaborator. One does not have to look further than the TUC and the Parliamentary Labour Party today for a true definition of those terms.

It is because we have recognized these facts that the *Platform* has always made its appeal direct to the rank and file. We do not believe that the working class will be led into the 'promised land' by a Messiah – not even when he holds a Labour Party card and wears a trade-union badge.

If the working class is ever to be educated, organized and united to establish its own power and build a socialist society, then those tasks must be carried out by the working class itself. And, the principal arena for waging that struggle must always be at the point of production itself, i.e. in the factories, the mines, the mills – and, so far as busmen are concerned – in the garages.

My convictions as a socialist and my faith in the final triumph of our cause remain as firm and undimmed as ever. If I had my time over again I would not wish to change any principle I hold or alter what I have done (except to hope that I might have done a little better).

So – good-bye Nob. To work ceaselessly to strengthen and unite the trade-union movement, to clarify the ideas and political understanding of its members, and to use that united power and understanding to help build a socialist society is a glorious aim. No trade-unionist today can put his hand to a greater cause.

(From the *Platform*, rank-and-file paper of London busmen, December 1966)

The Golden Boys:
Paul Foot

The young reformer comes from far away in the North somewhere, and his father was a staunch trade-unionist in the red old days, who flirted with the I L P and even with the Communists. The young reformer went to a good school and an even better university, and notched a chairmanship or two in university politics. He learnt a little law, and a little less economics, but above all he studied language; the right language; the sort of language which really means something in this harsh, realistic, modern world. And, because he watches the telly a lot, the young reformer learnt to speak the language correctly: that is, in the jerky, didactic tones of Ian Trethowan and Alan Whicker.

Nothing serves the young reformer better than this knowledge of the right language. He has learnt how to express opposition to 'restrictive practices on *both* sides of industry', which he takes to mean keeping Frank Cousins firmly under control. He has learnt, too, the up-to-date epithets to replace the crude, outdated nonsense of the thirties.

Instead of 'equality' he talks of 'increased productivity'; instead of 'brotherhood', 'a more efficient technology'; and instead of 'God', 'growth'. He thinks of himself as radical, progressive, fair-minded, realistic and dynamic; and scientific. He has taken out a subscription to the *New Scientist* and can talk with ease and a little knowledge about radio isotopes and synthetic fibres. He is a keen supporter of liner trains, as a means for facilitating cross-Channel and transatlantic travel. Foreign politics bore him, though he has nothing but contempt for 'disloyalty' – that is, putting the interests of one's own country above those of Great Britain.

The young reformer is totally opposed to all forms of racial discrimination. He has dined, twice, with an Indian doctor, and was overcome by his companion's 'extraordinary intelligence'. He never forgets the crucial phrase: 'regardless of race, colour or creed', which he slots neatly into almost all his perorations. But he moves perforce among lesser men, indeed ordinary men, and he knows all about their weaknesses. It is for *them*, he says, and in *their* interests that we should keep black men out of the country, regardless of race, colour or creed.

The young reformer is an ardent advocate, in private, of homosexual law reform, divorce law reform, abortion law reform and the abolition of capital punishment. Such delicate matters, he is convinced, are for the private conscience, and not by any means to be subjected to the hurly burly of the hustings.

Yes, the hustings. For if the young reformer is not in Parliament, he means to be. Because he loves the place. He loves question time, and the big debates, and the debates in which he speaks and he loves slapping humble constituents on the back in the Central Lobby. He has been known on summer evenings on the terrace over a pint of bitter to quote from Wordsworth and Rupert Brooke, wishing the while that he had the courage to make a pass at the girl who served him.

He is a man of principle, with many beliefs, but above all he believes in communications. He writes articles about rates and the European Common Market in his local paper. He is quite impervious to pressure groups, but he needs to travel, and has visited most European capitals as a guest of the Society for the Advancement of the Common Market. Above all he wants to sweep away the cobwebs of British society; to clear the dead wood out of the boardrooms, to reform the House of Lords and the honours system. His heroes are Sir William Carron, Lord Shawcross and Lord Beeching.

The young reformer does not normally read books; though he has read *The Making of the President* (1960 and 1964) by Theodore White, twice each. He encourages his wife to go to work because he believes in female emancipation and because it leaves him freer for his political duties. He sent his two children to the local comprehensive school, after they failed the Common Entrance. He likes his Wates-built house, within easy reach of Charing Cross, and enthuses about the 'common facilities' in his housing estate, though secretly he prays for a high-walled garden, separated from the neighbours. He goes once a year to the opera, and tells two dirty jokes a year when judging a beauty contest in his constituency.

The young reformer is happy as long as there is work to do; a meeting to attend; a local paper to read; a division to vote in. He is thoroughly bored by his family, his friends and his leisure time, and does his best to exclude them all as far as it is politically possible.

His politics are his life. And his politics are always the politics of his party.

Oh, yes, of *course*, he is a member of a political party. But he cannot for the moment recollect which one.

(From *Town*, 1966)

They're Our Enemies, That's the Key Point: Bob Rowthorn*

Comrades, looking at the resolutions submitted to the conference, it still seems to be the case that a large number of Constituency Parties believe that the Labour leadership is basically all right, but that it's made a few mistakes. They point to one or two things that weren't done, or were done badly, in the first three years of office, and they say, 'well we've still got to face these problems'. In this way they approve, tacitly, the Government's overall policy, but they tell it: 'You've made mistakes.' It seems to me that this is a fundamentally wrong position. I think that the actions the Labour leadership in fact did not take, and the actions they did in fact take, show very clearly what their priorities were.

The situation they faced, when they came to power, was one that any socialist leadership, conscious of the realities of the present day world, should have been prepared for. That situation was the following: that Britain was a country very deeply in debt, on one level, to foreigners; but, on another level, an owner of vast overseas assets. These overseas assets, which run to something like £16,000 million, which comprise factories, mines, oilwells, oil refineries, shares, a vast variety of financial claims: these assets are considerably greater than the debts that Britain owes to foreigners. It's a very widespread idea that Britain is in debt. In fact, we're always told that we've got to pay our way in the world, and we can't afford to be in debt: but the point is that Britain *is not* in debt, Britain *has not been in debt*, as far as is known, at any time in the last 100 years. It's a complete myth.

For example, successive Labour chancellors between '45 and '51 said, 'Well, we've got to pull our socks up now, we can't live on our earnings from abroad because we're now in debt, we lost all our wealth in the war.' This, in fact, was not true. Recent estimates have shown that we were probably, in 1950, just about in balance. Now the point about this, unfortunately, was that these assets were in private hands. Shares, £3,600 million worth in 1964, quite a lot of money that is, were

*A speech made at a teach-in on the eve of the Labour Party Conference at Scarborough 1967 convened by the Mayday Manifesto Group, the Voice Newspapers, the Campaign for Democracy in the Labour Party, organized by the Sheffield Trades and Labour Council and the Centre for Socialist Education and arising from a decision at the Fifth National Conference on Workers Control at Coventry in June 1967. Text of the speeches published by the CSE as *A Future for British Socialism?*, Nottingham, 1968.

held by private British citizens, many of them banks, firms and other corporate entities. So our assets were in private hands, but, unfortunately, most of our debts were public, because, owing to the successive moves towards convertibility – started by the Conservatives, but continued by the present Government (for example, only in April they took a move which made something like another £1,000 million worth of money in Britain convertible when they abolished the security sterling market) – most of these debts are official. The Government is committed to meeting them; something like £9,000 million of money is held in Britain on the short term, which means that foreigners, if they decide that Britain is not a safe place to keep their money, can, by various means, demand that the Government give them gold, dollars, marks, francs or some other acceptable international currency. Britain is committed to doing this. That is: British capital and the City are committed, and the Government agrees to back them up.

What this means is that if a Labour Government, coming into power, does socialist things they can be made to suffer. They did one or two things in 1964 which could, I think, incorrectly have been interpreted (and, in fact, were interpreted) as socialist measures. For example, in Autumn 1964, they announced a corporations tax and a capital gains tax, which caused a stampede in the City. Quite incorrectly this caused a stampede. They were clearly not intended as socialist measures, they were intended as measures of rationalization of the system, which is somewhat different, I think.

Of course, if they'd been really socialist, if they had really said: 'Well, in five years time, the commanding heights of the economy will be totally nationalized, with some degree of workers' control' and all the other kind of socialist slogans one can think of, there would have been a stampede of unprecedented proportions and Britain would have been bankrupted in the absence of any special action on their part. In fact, even if they'd said that they were going to keep the economy growing, if they haven't even been socialist, if they just said: 'To hell with the pound: we're going to grow, and if it means the pound sinks to £15 to the dollar that's so much the worse for the pound, we're not going to put British workers out of work, we're not going to stop the economy from growing!' – if they just said that, there would have been a stampede, because every foreigner with money in Britain would have been convinced they were a gang of economic lunatics, and they would have withdrawn their money.

They wouldn't have sabotaged the economy consciously, in the sense that they would have said, 'We've got to bring this socialist Government down.' What they would have said is, 'Well, we don't care what the British do, they're not doing it with our money', and so they would have withdrawn their money.

In that situation, what would the Government have had to do? The only thing it could have done in that situation would have been to nationalize Britain's overseas assets and sell them off as fast as it could, the vast majority of them. But just think of the political implications of that. They might be able to get away with that one single act: but what would it mean? It would mean the end of the City, bang goes the City.

But if you look on the boards of directors of large British firms, far from being a conflict between financial and industrial capital in England, they're very difficult to distinguish. Chairmen of boards of directors are bankers, this is a very very common pattern. Insurance firms are very powerful in industrial firms. In fact, there's a very close meshing between the City and Industry. So consequently, the Labour leadership, by nationalizing these shares, would have immediately come into political conflict with all the major centres of British capitalism, industrial capitalism.

If you look back, for the last twenty years, at the writings of Labour leaders, and this includes the official party documents, you can find such statements as 'On the whole we think that the big firms are serving the nation well, in this industrial society.' I think earlier documents, under the '45–'51 Government, said very similar things. In fact, it's been a constant theme, 'these people are our allies'. Harold Wilson has pushed this line again and again: 'Away with the dead wood in the boardrooms, but let's leave the live wood.' This is the thing he's after and the point is that their whole strategy has been one of co-operation with the more dynamic sections of private business.

But, unfortunately, the situation in which they found themselves in '64, '66 and in which they still find themselves, is that, to co-operate on a programme of economic growth with these people, they have to attack the City. But to attack the City and certain financial institutions in Britain brings them into conflict with these same people. So they're in a dilemma. They can't make the reforms which would make British capitalism work because by doing so they'd bring themselves into conflict with their allies. They're thus in a situation with only two alternatives. What's happening now is one alternative: or a socialist policy is the other one: and they're well aware of this.

This is no accident. They know perfectly well that they could devalue the pound for example, they could wind up the City, but they also know this is politically impossible for them to do. So what they've chosen, quite consciously, is the alternative of stagnation and deflation, hoping that, somehow or other, they're going to be able to escape the crisis. This is not through lack of nerve: it's because there's a radical discontinuity involved. They either have to go right down the line on a socialist policy, nationalizing the major sectors of British industry and really confronting the class that owns and controls British industry: or, alternatively, they just have to do what they are doing now.

It's no use, therefore, saying, 'We congratulate the Government although they've made a few mistakes.' You have to recognize that it's a leadership which is acting on principle. It's not a leadership acting simply in an opportunist fashion, it's one that's got no choice other than a radical socialist policy: and most of these people do not believe in that. They are men of principle, but they're our enemies. That's the key point.

The Loneliness of the Left:
Nigel Harris

The succession of disasters that has overtaken the Labour Party – the County, the Borough and municipal elections – might suggest that Wilson will leave an indelible impress on the Labour movement: namely, the complete destruction of social democracy and political Labour as a popular movement. Not since the trauma of 1931 have such defeats taken place. Apparently immovable monuments, London and Ebbw Vale, have moved; the landscape is in dissolution.

But one must also recognize that this rejection of Wilson is negative. It is not an affirmation of socialist opposition, so much as marginal resentment among the few (a shift to voting Conservative) and, much more, a gigantic yawn in the face of the gimmicks, the lies and the games played in irrelevant institutions. The market towns have stayed put; the big cities have moved against Labour. But for the solid block of the working class, the change is relatively slight – the reality of local government has at long last begun to overtake the myth, and the Labour Government has only accelerated a process long in train. It will take very much longer for the reality of parliamentary government to approach the myth, and we may well see the Labour vote sustained in future General Elections even though dying at the local level. Again, the emerging pattern is reasonably clear – tiny political cliques, isolated from any popular movement whether organized in local parties or mass trade unions, elected in a five-year ritual that means no more than an individual's meaningless reaffirmation of some residual sense of citizenship: and as the old get older, perhaps the young will not even want to make that slight gesture. Within the ritual, the cliques themselves serve as no more than a gloss on the bureaucracy, the public relations aspect of an independent state administration. All this has been much more clearly evident at the local level than the national – many councillors have long been no more than the façade to City administration; the rise of the City bosses, Newcastle's Dan Smith, is one acknowledgement of the real state of affairs.

Perhaps Wilson will be saved at the next General Election. The tired tactic of taking the brake off the economy so that a little synthetic boom colours an atmosphere of generalized gloom may still do the trick in four years' time, particularly if a new European authority looks like superseding even Westminister and food prices have not escalated.

But if the days of the Parliamentary Labour Party are far from ended, those of social democracy as a movement, the Party militants, do seem numbered. This second process has long been urged by the 'quality' newspapers as the secret of a successful Parliamentary party – devalue the Party Conference, ignore the militants, assert 'strong leadership' and demonstrate the Prime Minister's first responsibility to the 'nation' not to some 'sectional interest'. A Labour Government was required to accelerate the trend so rapidly. Constituency parties are slowly dying, delegates cannot be found for routine conferences, general management committees shrink as wards disappear (dramatically so where there is a Labour MP), just as trade-union branch attendance has shrunk. Council candidates cannot be found to fill the list, and Council Labour groups operate even more as cliques independent of local parties. More and more, to stir any response from many local parties, the attack from the Left has to be pitched from outside the Party since, within, there is no viable context to make such an attack meaningful. The dreary old issue of entrism or non-entrism is being solved by erosion, the Party is dying around its militants, leaving unfettered power in the hands of the professional organizers. The national Party itself acknowledges the trend by its own proposals for a 'reform' of local government – namely, by creating properly undemocratic bodies, experts or 'representatives of local interests' to supersede local authorities through regional government. Rationalization both acknowledges the drift, and puts another nail in the coffin.

Thus, with so little at stake for the ordinary voter, his garden becomes more interesting; for the working-class voter, voting Tory becomes a possible way of expressing resentment. This seepage of popular interest affects the Communist Party as much as Labour, both equally wedded to the existing institutional structure of misrepresentation, and it is this seepage, rather than the immediate electoral defeat, which is the direct cause of the gloom and isolation of the traditional Left. It was a central thesis of social democracy that each extension of state power by the Labour Party, given effective parliamentary democracy, was an extension of popular power, and took place at local and national levels as well as in industry through the trade unions. But if the basic condition for this extension – namely a popular movement behind the Labour Party, acting through the electoral machinery – fails, what is left? Merely the extension of the state, the purposes of which can no longer be identified automatically with popular interests. The state has become autonomous, not merely the instrument of the popular will, nor even 'bodies of armed men', but the supreme expression of the *status quo* and independent of the ritual of party politics. Each past crisis of socialist thought has embodied an immense change of gear in the nature of capitalism, and the current crisis arises from the emergence of state capitalism within the formerly private capitalist countries. Thus, the slogans of the past – extension of state power, nationalization, planning and so on – have two meanings: the first, when such slogans were pitched against the greed and anarchy of private capitalism; the second, when such slogans become the declared aims of a developing state capitalist regime. The first embodied popular revolt. The second embodies the new *status quo*, for it lacks any popular basis to make it meaningful in socialist terms, it lacks at the national level, decisive democratic determination, and at the industrial level, workers' control. ICI, General Motors, the Pharaohs and Eichmann all 'plan'; but it is the purpose to which the plan is devoted that concerns socialists. Nationalization without workers' control means, not socialism, but state capitalism.

Thus, the problem for the traditional Left is not just the lengthening list of errors and omissions by the Labour Government – an 'unfair' incomes policy, curbs on the trade unions, failure to help the poor, brutality in Aden, betrayal in Rhodesia, subordination to the purposes of US capitalism – but the whole meaning of social democracy in the absence of a popular movement. This makes the loneliness of the Labour Left much greater than ever before. Then they could argue, rightly or wrongly, that forces existed within and around the Party that, if only given control of the leadership, could create a new society. But there are no forces there pressing for the new society, and the Left becomes no more than the people of which it is composed, and precious few of them.

Any exit from this dilemma requires a complete reappraisal of the old assumptions about what socialists are trying to do and, indeed, what socialism itself means. Dogmatism and revisionism provide alternative cul-de-sacs for socialists who want to survive while still pursuing the original vision. Some will give up the popular elements of the theory, accepting state power (including, for a few, high office) as a convenient and tangible substitute for the intangible and inconvenient pursuit of popular support – consolation comes from marginal changes in welfare provisions, building new roads, supporting the UN, and so on. Others will accept the dilemma head-on, accept a prospect of increasing gloom, and perhaps withdraw, condemning mankind's corruption as they go. Some may devote themselves to welfare work, a campaign on poverty and community action, under the illusion that they are 'really doing something instead of just talking'. Yet others, a very few, may cling to the false optimism that has in the past provided such a convenient disguise for reality – for the social democrat, things really are getting better and better all the time for there is a Labour Government in power; for the Communist, the perspective is the same, for Russia launches sputniks and even her enemies accept the Soviet Union now. But none of these methods effectively re-links the reality that faces us and the original purposes of socialism: one or other end of the equation, reality or socialism, is violated. To restore that equation requires scrapping the false consciousness, 'Marxist' or otherwise, that has inhibited socialists trying to grapple with the real world.

The class struggle is not over, the battle of the proletariat is not finished, the fight to achieve popular power, socialism, is not complete nor redundant nor 'old-fashioned'. But it is not taking place between embattled cliques on high, trade-union leaders versus employers' confederations, Labour versus Tory, Moscow (or Pekin) versus Washington, but rather down on the ground where it always was, in a thousand isolated places, each at this stage with its own different characteristics. If one is looking for great forests, they have all gone to the timber yards; but if one is searching for the new generation of young saplings, there are many to be seen. And it is here where socialists, whatever their origins, should be, and where they will learn that hope is possible, but only when firmly rooted in real men in real struggle.

(Editorial from *International Socialism*, Summer, 1967)

The Strange Death of Social Democratic England: Alasdair MacIntyre

The most striking piece of news about Britain recently has aroused practically no comment. There are now over half a million unemployed, more than there have been in any June since the war, and since March the average increase in the number of unemployed each month has been 20,000. These facts are surely striking enough in themselves, but when we add to them another fact, that this unemployment has been deliberately created by the Government, we ought all of us surely to be a little more astonished and appalled than we are. Every previous Labour Government regarded rising unemployment as a defeat, as a sign that its policy was not working or that it had chosen the wrong policy. This is the first Labour Government which must regard rising unemployment as a victory for its policies, as a sign that they are working in the way that the Chancellor predicted that they would work. Left-wing critics of Labour Governments have often felt able to accuse them of pursuing not socialist but Keynesian economic policy – a criticism which pays a quite undeserved compliment to former Labour Chancellors and at the same time quite gratuitously insults Keynes. But Mr Jenkins is our first Labour Chancellor whose policies would even have been intelligible and acceptable to those as yet untouched by the Keynesian revolution, and it is well worth asking why Labour has made, and has felt able to make, this total change of attitude. If we are to do so, however, we must remember that a political change on this scale never occurs in isolation. Indeed, I want to go so far as to suggest that what we are seeing is a major change in the social scene, a change which might well be called 'The Strange Death of Social Democratic England'.

It's now over thirty years since George Dangerfield published a book called *The Strange Death of Liberal England*, in which he diagnosed in the years 1910–13 a fundamental change in the assumptions which defined British politics. One can summarize an important part of Dangerfield's thesis by remembering that in the decades before 1910 politics had been played according to Liberal rules, even by the opponents of Liberalism. And then those whom Liberalism excluded or pretended did not exist suddenly rose around it on all sides: trade-unionists in militant strike action, suffragettes, Irish nationalists, Irish Unionists. What would have happened if the German Emperor had not rescued England from internal strife by kindly invading Belgium is a great unanswerable question. But the central moral is clear. When the parliamentary system cannot express the major social conflicts of an age, then those conflicts will be expressed not only outside but against that system. It's some of the consequences of this truth that I want to explore now.

I've suggested that if the years from 1910 to 1913 witnessed the strange death of Liberal England, then the years which we are living through now are witnessing the strange death of social democracy. The basic premises of social democracy were twofold. The first was that class-conflict was genuine, that in the market economy of classical capitalism the interests of the working class ran clean counter to those interests which relied upon the smooth working of the economic system. This premise social democrats shared with a variety of revolutionary socialists, whether Communists, syndicalists or anarchists. But they differed from all varieties of revolutionary socialist in holding that a second premise was true, namely that the political system of parliamentary democracy can at once contain and express that conflict. The classical social democratic belief is that the interests of the working class can be expressed by a political party which would both adhere to the conventions of parliamentary democracy and also accept the fact that the interests of the working class must conflict with the goals which dominate the economic system.

This belief was strongly expressed, for example, in the policies of the Labour Government of 1945–51; the goal of full employment was taken to have overriding importance, and so firmly was the importance of this goal imprinted that in the immediately succeeding years of Conservative rule the impossibility of not pursuing the goal of full employment was taken for granted. The Conservative claim even became that they too could achieve some of the basic goals of social democracy; the political game was being played according to social democratic rules. The contrast between Conservative Government in 1951–5 and Labour Government now could scarcely be sharper, for we are in a situation in which full employment, the level of spending in the Welfare State and the growth of wages are all being sacrificed to those traditional gods of the British economic and commercial system, the exchange value of the pound sterling and the achievement of a surplus on our external trading figures. The political cost of this economic policy is the gradual disfranchisement of the working class, resulting from the insistence that the working class have no specific and special interests in conflict with the interests of others. Consider in this respect the operation of the prices and incomes policy.

The background to any consideration of this policy must be the grotesque degree of inequality which still exists in England. About 7 per cent of the population owns well over 80 per cent of all private wealth. The richest 1 per cent of those receiving incomes receive over 12 per cent of the total incomes received. Furthermore, there has been remarkably little change in recent decades in relative incomes as be-tween different social classes. Middle-class people still often believe in the myth of a period of radical income redistribution during the war and the 1945–51 Labour Government. But no such redistribution occurred. We remain very much where we were in the 1930s, and what John Strachey wrote in 1956 has been true for the whole of this century: 'Capitalism, it has turned out, is a Red Queen's sort of country from the wage-earner's point of view. They have to run very fast for a long time to keep in the same place relative to other classes.'

What the so-called prices and incomes policy does is at least to freeze and maintain this situation of inequality and perhaps to accentuate it. For because of a variety of fringe benefits, of salary scales with auto-matic increments and the like, middle-class incomes simply are not subject to the same degree of restraint that working-class incomes are. Now in this situation of gross inequality, the only institutions which are available to the working class to express their special and conflicting interests turn out to be part of that trade union and Labour Party net-work in which power is held by those operating the very policies which ignore their interests. The Labour Party and the Labour Government have accepted definitions of political reality and political possibility according to which social democracy can no longer exist. And this is something genuinely new.

I am not saying, what some Marxists used to argue, that social democracy must be ineffective in all circumstances in a capitalist society. I am instead asserting that we must recognize that in the period from 1900 to 1955 in Britain, and in differing degrees elsewhere, social democracy could provide a viable expression for interests that the working class were able to recognize as their own. Where Communists have seen social democracy as betraying the interests of the workers, I am asserting that social democracy was often their authentic repre-sentative and voice. But the acceptance of the assumptions of the new technocratic growth-oriented capitalism by the British Labour Party has necessarily severed this link. For in the perspectives of that capitalism no allowance can be made for the special interests of the working class. It follows that the electoral prospects of the Labour Party must be in even graver doubt than they already appear to be. For, if I am right, what we are experiencing in the present run of by-elections is in some part not just another swing of the pendulum, a temporary dissatisfaction, but a permanent shift of the working class, perhaps not merely away from the Labour Party but even from the electoral system.

Yet radical as this is, it still remains at the political level: it scarcely merits the title 'The Strange Death of Social Democratic England', with its strong suggestion of the death of an entire social order. To justify that title, I shall have to ask what it was about the social democratic period in our history which marked its entire social order. And the answer goes far beyond any merely political argument and concerns large changes in the values of society. During the social democratic period a new set of answers was given to the questions of what rights individuals have, of how they may legitimately claim their rights, and of what responsibilities the community has for the fate of individuals.

The particular institutions of the Welfare State, from Lloyd George's social insurance scheme to Aneurin Bevan's National Health Service, were the embodiment of a whole new social climate. For the first time the poor, the unemployed, the ill and the old were recognized as having equality of citizenship at an economic as well as at a political level. The consensus as to these new values was always very far from complete and it was the outcome of continuous struggle by radicals and socialists inside and outside the trade unions. But it was a consensus in striking contrast to the values of Victorian society, being a repudiation both of private paternalism and of the extension of the values of the market into social life. Social democrats may, and often do, overrate the achievements of social democracy, but the rest of us ought not to underrate them. One way not to do this is to realize how the values of social democracy contrast not only with the values of the society that preceded it, but also with the values which have become established now.

I remarked at the outset that what is surprising is not merely the fact that the Government has been actively promoting the growth of unemployment, but also and above all the fact of the astonishing lack of response to its policies. This is important, for it is in the degree of response to political facts of this sort that we find one important clue to the values of a society; and silence may be the most significant response of all. What else are we silent and unresponsive about? Well-grounded predictions which have in fact been made that the collapse of the

National Health Service is imminent would, one might have expected, have brought questions about the nature of that service to the centre of national discussions of social questions. They have not. We no longer treat welfare questions as important questions compared with questions about productivity. 'Production for what?' – the old social democratic inquiry, voiced for example by R. H. Tawney – is not heard.

A social order in which the values of welfare have been removed from those which the established consensus maintains, and in which the working class have been disfranchised from the political system, is one in which an increase in conflict has become inevitable. That increase is made all the more likely by two other facts. The first is a matter of the way in which political agreement over central goals among those within the established parliamentary system may leave those who cannot articulate their dissent, even on marginal issues, with no alternative but to break with that system; and this may be as true of those who are not radicals as it is of the radical.

The strange death of Liberal England was the outcome of a system that could neither accommodate nor come to terms with the trade unions, the Irish or the suffragettes, conservative as many of the leaders of these in fact were. The strange death of social democracy has been accompanied by an unwillingness even to admit the existence of demands for local and regional self-government and of the degree of support which has emerged for Welsh and Scots Nationalism. Moreover, the equivalent to the old hysteria about trade-unionism is the new hysteria about unofficial strikes. The Prime Minister and Mr Ray Gunter have been all too willing to see strikes as led by, indeed devised by, Communists or Trotskyites or whatever. In fact, of course, what they see and what they fear in unofficial strikes is the resurgence of an independent working-class leadership. The most dangerous single threat to freedom in our society is the will to prevent unofficial strikes – that is, to prevent any direct expression of their interests by working-class people which goes beyond the limits set by established institutions.

A second factor which will exacerbate conflict is this. All government depends on the tacit consent of the governed. But it's characteristic of our present-day society, in Britain at least, that government has continuously to appeal in a self-conscious and visible way to the governed, inviting them to collaborate in the operation of those very same social structures in which they are excluded from power. And in the course of doing this, government continuously promises what it cannot in fact perform. Government legitimates itself not merely through parliamentary elections, but through a continuous assurance by every political party, in power and out of power, of rights to employment, to education, to material prosperity, and so on. This deeply embedded appeal to and promise of rights has to coexist, not just with the present facts of inequality which I've described, but with a future in which inequalities of income and status must be maintained, if the economy is to flourish at least in terms that would be recognized by this Labour Government, or any feasible alternative in the parliamentary system. What people are promised as their rights will therefore not be performed. And working-class people will gradually learn that they are still to be excluded, and that in streamed comprehensive schools and expanded universities, it will still be the case that all the advantages lie with the children of middle-class parents. If they learn also that no conventional political remedy can help them, then they will have the choice between a kind of non-political subservience that has been alien to them even at their most apathetic and a new politics of conflict. For my part, I hope that they learn both lessons fast, and if it is said that I've been presenting something akin not so much to a personal view as to a partisan political broadcast, let me point out that I am talking for and of a group that now has no party, the British working class.

(From a broadcast on BBC Radio Third Programme, reprinted in the *Listener*, 4 July 1968)

Chapter 6
Freeze, Squeeze, Then Prod:
The Industrial Struggle 1964-70

The industrial unrest which marked the period 1945–66 was the work of one man known as the Agitator (his real identity was never discovered). His method was to infiltrate the Labour movement and put forward extravagant demands backed by a strike threat. When this failed, he would surround his fellow-workers single-handed and threaten them with violence. This tactic was especially successful with men like the dockers who were noted for their timidity. With the aid of secret funds paid to him by certain foreign powers, the Agitator travelled about the country creating numerous disputes simultaneously. Under various names he got himself elected to key positions in the trade unions. How this was achieved, in view of the traditional good sense of British trade-unionists, is open to conjecture; but hypnotism cannot be ruled out. The Agitator's activities would never have been exposed but for the untiring efforts of the *Daily Mirror*, the Confederation of British Industry and a Labour prime minister whose name has long since been forgotten.

(ROGER WODDIS, *New Statesman* Competition)

Sir, I can take the living stone from the quarry bed and with sharp-edged tools and native cunning build you a shed, or a mansion, or a church in which you can leave the outside world to its own devices, whilst you bring to fruition all those inner yearnings to leave your mark with posterity; or, if you wish I will build with warm red bricks, a factory or a bank or a school, the hive for your swarming desires to accumulate.

I will lay the floors, or nail the highest tile, put in the glass to give your house its eyes; a fireplace where you can dream on winter's night, and cover the bare walls with any type of shell that you may indicate, for you must see before you realize the purpose of your environment. All these, the paint and the stone, and the wood and the glass I hold in my hands and place unscathed precisely where your fancy would have them be.

But this is not art – I am just one of those lay-abouts that won't work on the Barbican site. How does that strike you?

(A. H. BAILEY, Letter to the *New Statesman*)

The Labour Party's economic policy outlined in the party programme 'Signposts for the Sixties' was an eclectic selection from the ideas of technological modernists like Michael Shanks plus a little Kaldor/ Balogh quackery. The few elements of socialism which had survived Gaitskell were re-defined quietly into an obsession with growth (which avoided awkward discussions about distribution and thus power) and a devotion to the pound as some kind of economic phallic symbol. Gaitskell was sufficient of a social democrat to feel unable to omit a dim and faint-hearted commitment to a transition to a different kind of society. The transition to this society was, of course, distant and vague and was to be executed by wise men in Parliament drafting and debating suitable reforms. But there were going to be reforms, and those reforms were to have a human meaning. Education because it broadened horizons of kids, urban planning to make better, happier cities, nationalization even because it extended public control of an otherwise anarchic market.

Under Wilson these aspirations vanished. As he told his audience in the Town Hall, Birmingham, 'Socialism, as I understand it, means applying a sense of purpose to our national life; economic purpose, social purpose, and moral purpose. Purpose means technical skill . . .'* Education was now good because it gave skills, planning was good because it set national targets for growth, nationalization was good for efficiency. The mightiest party of its kind in history had chosen to stop lobbying capitalism with forceful (or more often faint) working-class demands and instead become Capital's sergeant-at-arms. The Labour Party under Wilson decided that it must postpone all reforms which could not be provided free until it had secured adequate 'growth' to pay for them. A working-class party, elected for the first time in the midst of full employment and by a confident class, spent six years paying massive subsidies to private employers, witch-hunting workers' elected representatives, attempting after the sharpest squeeze for forty years to pass savage anti-trade-union legislation. And in 1970 the poor were poorer, the growth rate lower, the dole queue longer and the hate rate higher than the day they had begun. And to this day one can hear the faint dandruffy sound of social democratic economists scratching their heads and trying to work out what went wrong. There is talk of being blown off course, of early devaluations missed, of 'inheritance' and of sterling, or gnomes and wreckers. Some socialists still actually believe Wilson did quite well really, considering, and all the mounds of evidence to the contrary is simply Tory lies or the invention of what

* Harold Wilson, 'The New Britain', speech made at Birmingham Town Hall, Sunday 19 January 1964, reprinted in *Wilson: Selected Speeches*, Penguin Special, 1964.

Michael Foot calls 'incorrigible sectarians'. But Wilson's economic and labour policy developed with a logic which might have been arranged as a text-book demonstration of Karl Marx's ideas on the hundredth birthday of *Das Kapital*. For once Wilson chose to aim at growth and commit himself to what was called an export-led boom within a world market whose rate of growth was slackening, he was bound to find himself tightening the belt of the workers in Britain to keep up his trading pantaloons. And when injunctions to thrift, diligence and self-sacrifice failed to cut workers' proceeds, he was obliged to freeze, squeeze and finally threaten to lock up his trade-unionist supporters who were unenthusiastic about the lowering of their members' wages to give 'confidence' to a distant boardroom of bankers. And Wilson was finally forced to make active use of that vilest of all weapons, unemployment.

The clearest evidence of Wilson's success in eradicating the Labour Party as a popular force is being seen now in the fury of the dockers, the railmen and bus drivers fighting, too late, to recover the jobs they signed away, under Wilson's modernization and redeployment drive, to make way for 'dynamic' one-man buses, streamlined train crews and container depots. For at the time opposition to Wilson's plans and the trade-union leaders he used to transmit them was slow to emerge and reluctant to break the loyalties which have cost the Labour movement so much. Slowly the process has caught up on the Labour Party. And in the labour movement of the seventies it has forfeited its restraining and retarding influence to a politics which once again speaks to the realities of class power and class struggle.

The much-promised first 100 days of the Wilson Government set painstakingly about the task of facing two ways, extending on one hand a humane reforming image while also lavishly courting Capital's goodwill. Political olive branches were generously extended at businessmen's banquets. 'Profits,' said Douglas Jay, 'provided they are earned by efficiency and technical progress and not by restrictive practices or by the abuse of monopoly, are in my view a sign of a healthy economy.' 'We have no prejudices against market mechanisms when they are efficient,' added James Callaghan. 'It is not our job to make it more difficult for you to make a living.' And, ever to the point, George Brown added, 'We in the Government want private enterprise to flourish.' At first the employers were frankly disbelieving. 'There are ominous signs,' thought the Institute of Directors, bewilderedly, 'of the free enterprise system being eaten away without the country's citizens being aware of it.' And Lord Robbins confessed to *The Econo-*

mist that, 'Looking ahead I find the future fuller of perplexity and indeed anxiety than at any time in recent years . . . It is difficult to resist the impression of a deep undercurrent of hostility in high places to the activities of the private sector.'

But he need not have worried. For as promises vanished into the abyss of the balance of payments, Wilson was to remain decisively loyal on one alone. Mercilessly wringing every ounce of sentiment and loyalty from the trade-union leaders, he was to pursue wage restraint with a success which had eluded the Tories. Indeed the Tory essays at wage restraint in 1956–7 and 1961–2 had always been lifted clear of confrontation by renewed phases of boom. But Wilson's determination to modernize and streamline an ailing British economy came at a time when the chronic growth crisis of the British economy had, added to it, an acute and recurrent currency crisis. Wilson's long-term aims, of selling workers an incomes policy on the basis of its social justice and of attacking traditional 'inefficient' job practices with productivity deals, might otherwise have been possible, given the lack of real political opposition on the shop floor and the frank support of the TUC. But this strategy was continually jeopardized by the balance-of-payments crises which required short-term squeeze and deflation and inflamed relations with the TUC, who were obliged to put on a show of militancy to please their members. When Wilson actually wanted to lecture the trade unions on their duties and jolly them into co-operation, he was forced to speak over their heads to the world bankers, using sterner tones. The financial situation developed too fast for him and continually threatened to go out of control. His ability to buy time with wage restraint so as to set about 'rationalization' was continually threatened by 'crises of confidence'. Very quickly it was not just the New Britain, but his Government's very existence which depended on Labour's success in selling their centre-piece, 'prices and incomes policy' or 'a planned increase in wages' or a wage freeze, depending on how you looked at it.

To begin with it looked as if Wilson would have no difficulty. TUC response was rapturous. When Wilson outlined his plans shortly after his election victory, the minutes record that he was welcomed with a standing ovation, his speech was punctuated with repeated applause and laughter, he was hailed at its end with a standing version of 'For He's a Jolly Good Fellow' and Mrs Wilson was presented with a bouquet. Reeling under Wilson's rhetoric about an economy which would be 'dynamic, thrusting and extrovert', the TUC swallowed whole the notion that Labour could administer the controls on prices and dividends that they could clearly exert on wages. 'Planning' by Labour was seen as an alternative to capitalist greed, not simply its modern form. And although National Plans previously had been employed by rulers to the right of even Wilson, like Tutankhamun and Krupp, Brown's Plan was somehow to be magically different.

The myth was deep-rooted. The Draughtsmen's Union, the most politically astute in the TUC, had, for example, rejected the Tory NEDC but pledged full co-operation in a 'socialist equivalent' under a strong Labour Government. *Tribune*'s economic correspondents were to tear a phrase from Marx to celebrate the signing of the National Plan, calling it 'a victory for the political economy of labour'.* The *New Statesman* was to reach the bottom of its Fabian pail when it actually announced that the 1966 wage freeze represented a socialist breakthrough. 'Prices and incomes regulation . . . has true socialist blood in its veins and, properly nurtured, is likely to grow into a powerful champion of social progress.'† George Woodcock even boasted about the TUC's success in cutting wages: 'the increase has been 2½ per cent to 3½ per cent less than it would have been without our efforts. I would say our part in this was fundamental, absolutely indispensable.'‡ When the TUC Chairman, Joe O'Hagan, was sent on his summer tour, the TUC magazine announced that he had received 'great praise from European trade-unionists and the press for his speech on how British unions, committed to planning, were facing up to the allied problem of securing an effective incomes policy'. Wilson had skilfully played on many rank-and-file trade-unionists' abstract belief in planning, dislike of stop-go and preference for real rather than paper increases. He had also reassured unionists worried about the group of anti-union High Court decisions taken in the last years of Tory rule. Special legislation was passed to correct these ambiguities and the Royal Commission set up under Lord Donovan was expected to follow the same lines. When Bill Lindley, the Lightermen's leader and himself a victim of High Court action, attempted to press the TUC General Council to press Wilson for still more decisive laws to establish the right of trade-union membership, George Woodcock was able to simply 'put the General Council's view that the matter was very complicated and best left to the Royal Commission'.

Early attempts to warn the movement of what Wilson had in mind

---

*Michael Barratt Brown and Royden Harrison, *Tribune*, 8 January 1965.

†Paul Johnson, 'How Labour Blundered into Socialism', *New Statesman*, 16 September 1966.

‡George Woodcock interviewed in the *Guardian*, 29 April 1966.

were not well received. Motion 12 at the 1965 TUC Conference moved by the boilermakers and the draughtsmen rejecting incomes policy was heavily defeated. It was the draughtsmen's view that 'a solution to Britain's economic problems will be achieved only through planning for general benefit in a society in which the people have adequate control over the means of production, distribution and exchange. Under such conditions trade-union participation in an incomes policy would be a logical and rational outcome. The Executive Committee sees little evidence of such conditions today.' But outside the TUC, there were already the beginnings of rank-and-file political opposition. On 25 January, the proscribed Lambeth Trades Council (banned because of the dominance of SLL members in its councils) led a lobby to the House of Commons against the effective wage freeze implicit in incomes policy and 3½ per cent wage norm. And on 2 March another lobby organized by four shop stewards' committees attracted 2,500 marchers. Labour Party speakers on the 1965 London May Day march were vigorously heckled on the subject.

Throughout 1965 the real meaning of Wilson's policy towards the unions began to become clear. Most notable was the Prices and Incomes Board, the section of Brown's Department of Economic Affairs which was to vet price and wage increases, As Brown notes, 'the job bristled with difficulties!' It required 'sufficiently a national figure to command respect, sufficiently detached from his judgements to have a fair chance of voluntary acceptance'.* Brown therefore chose a Tory MP who was a director of Guest, Keen and Nettlefolds and chairman of Staveley Industries. And the two figureheads reflected the real nature of the Board. Brown was encouraged to clown around, giving the impression of dynamic bipartisan activity. As Wilson puts it, 'One moment he was banging the table at the bakers who were intent on raising bread prices; the next he was holding the baking unions in check on their wage demands.'† But the real work of the Board and Aubrey Jones was to make pay rises conditional on changes in the organization of work itself, to attack at the work-place the 'old habits, inherited attitudes and institutional arrangements' which had been won in the fifties and placed labour in a commanding bargaining position. In the first report, delivered in July 1966 on busmen's wages, increases were made conditional on negotiated losses in conditions and jobs.

*George Brown, *In My Way*, Penguin Books, 1972, p. 96.

†Harold Wilson, *The Labour Government 1964–1970. A Personal Record*, Weidenfeld & Nicolson and Michael Joseph, 1971, p. 63.

The sophisticated sale of the rule book had long been a Wilson theme. He told the AEF National Committee 'the sooner your rule book is consigned to the industrial museum, the more quickly the union will be geared to the challenge facing industry and the nation'.* The aim of the Prices and Incomes Board was rationalization by the Party of the Nation, its extremely wide-ranging advice was to bully managers into disciplining their work-force, customers not to pass on price increases, unions to steel their members to solve labour shortages by getting the existing labour force to abandon old rules and work. Comparability, the main lever for wage rises, must be replaced by a new system of wage bargaining resting on measured increases in productivity. In short, workers must be put unreservedly at the service of a more vigorous cost-conscious management. The tendency of British capitalism to buy its way out of labour difficulties was to be replaced by a management offensive aimed at weakening working-class institutions, rules and practice. The Prices and Incomes Board was to do what Common Market entry might have done, tighten the slack in management and discipline the directors into disciplining their employees. This logic was spelt out in great detail in the Geddes report on shipbuilding, Devlin's three-stage plan to de-casualize the docks (and in the process abolish the docker) and Beeching's efficient butchery of British Rail's employees and services.

The logical expression of this Government-orchestrated intensification of exploitation was in the Industrial Reorganization Corporation. IRC was, in Wilson's words, 'a statutory body equipped with state funds to help to promote rationalization'. In fact it was a £150 million industrialists' piggy bank. It was established in January 1966 after a summer of monthly dinners at an official flat in Carlton Gardens to which Brown invited leading industrialists, and proceeded to act as both midwife and moneybags to prospective mergers. And mergers there were. An early Labour move had been to strengthen the Monopolies Commission and extend its powers to prevent mergers. But Lord Kearton, the Courtauld takeover champion who headed the IRC, was to produce an unprecedented burst of major mergers. The natural appetite of capital for concentration and centralization was sharpened by the IRC's buccaneering enthusiasm and its massive bank account. In the period of 1965–8 there were 120 mergers within the terms of the Monopolies Commission, three of which were halted. The total expenditure on mergers in 1968 was £1,693 million. Ten years before, the total sum had been just over £100 million. The centralization

*Wilson, op. cit., p. 226.

was particularly marked in engineering, motors, oil, paper, glass, electronics and property. And in the wake of some of these new monsters, like Triplex, GEC–AEI, British Motor Holdings, Burmah Oil and GKN Crankshafts, were to come some of the most vicious labour disputes of the late sixties. And behind all of them stalked unemployment, of a new 'technological' and permanent type, tastefully described as 'shake-out' and 'redeployment' by the mandarins of the DEA but still feeling like plain old dole for the workers concerned.

Wilson's considerable skill at twisting the arms of union leaders in the name of 'Our' National Plan was most vividly shown in his personal interventions in deadlocked strikes.* The NUR, a union which had once been a driving force of the syndicalist movement and still retained in its constitution relics of its commitment to workers' control, was the first union to have a claim legally referred by Wilson to the NPIB. The Board's recommendations of a 3·5 per cent increase was rejected by the drivers on the eve of the 1966 election and a national stoppage planned for 14 February. Wilson absolutely refused to vary the settlement – 'not a penny in amount, nor a day in terms of dating'; instead he gathered the NUR Executive at Downing Street and proceeded to 'try to raise their eyes beyond the immediate grievance ... Here Barbara Castle ... who took an almost parental interest ... with little encouragement spoke for twenty minutes, weaving a web of hope.' In his enthusiasm to create a matey atmosphere Wilson sent police and labour correspondents out to forage for trade-union-style cold sausages, beef sandwiches and beer to replace the dainty snacks provided by the Government Hospitality Fund. The cigars 'kept for elder statesmen' and the contents of Callaghan's bread bin were brandished, and 'all my stocks of whisky and beer were mobilized to help in lubricating the machinery of industrial relations'. This nauseating pantomime was sufficient to swing two or three critical votes and the strike was called off.

Wilson actually chaired the first joint meeting on strings and structure. 'And before long Barbara Castle was once again using her considerable charm and persuasion to break the deadlock over rail containers.' Indeed, as Wilson boasts, the Downing Street agreement did 'bring about a totally new structure and a new deal for Britain's railwaymen, paid for out of higher productivity'. Between 1965 and 1969, one third of railway jobs were lost (from 365,043 to 253,064), all rail-

---

* Wilson personally intervened in a total of five strikes, in each case in effective support of the employers: the February 1966 rail dispute, the seamen's strike in June 1966, the anti-Devlin docks strike in October 1966, the ASLEF dispute of December 1969 and the Fleet Street printers' dispute of June 1970.

men forced into compulsory weekend and evening overtime (averaging nine hours' overtime per week), and yet in 1972 the basic wage rates of 90,000 out of a total of 130,000 wage-grade staff were below the Tory Government's official poverty line with a basic rate of £17·20p., still £4·55p. below what the Post Office workers got after being defeated by the Tories.*

But Wilson's whisky and Castle's webs of hope were only icing. In the seamen's strike, which occurred within four weeks of Labour's return with the second biggest majority in its history, Wilson was to show the savagery which underlay the sweet talk. His handling of this dispute was to mark the Labour Government's tossing aside of any lingering sympathy with the working-class movement. There was not a flicker of hesitation in the choice between the £15 a week seafarers and the enormously wealthy owners. Instead, Wilson, with a finesse which left the Tories gawping with envy, proceeded to deal the seamen a political thumping from which they have not yet recovered. As George Wigg put it, 'Wilson's conduct reached a high water mark . . . Single-handed he smashed a strike.' In February 1966 the shipping owners had received a claim from the National Union of Seamen for a forty-hour week and a 12s. 6d. a month increase. They replied with a three-year agreement, staging reductions in hours, withdrawing the Sunday-at-Sea leave agreement and refusing point-blank to make any cash increase.

A national seamen's strike, the first official one in history, began on 16 May. Very quickly it took on a meaning beyond the relatively modest NUS wage demand. It became a trial of strength of the incomes policy, with Wilson demonstrating to business and banking onlookers that he was quite prepared to sacrifice some of Britain's lowest-paid workers to the altar of the Pound Sterling. And as the economic stakes were higher, Labour was forced to take its attack on the seamen far further than the Tories had dared to venture against the engineers in 1965 or the London busmen in 1959. The seamen got their go from their conditions of work. The seagoers' reserves of resentment had been fuelled by decades of undisguised company unionism, the battering of the rank-and-file seamen who had organized the reform movement within the union, the legal exemption of seamen from the right to strike and the military discipline on board British ships. The Merchant Shipping Act made British shipping a floating prison from the point of view of trade-unionism. The strike was like a gaol break. The Executive

* See 'Goodbye Jobs! British Rail Makes the Going Easy . . .', *Socialist Worker*, 25 March 1972.

of the union was still right-wing and dominated by officials, its President Bill Hogarth, mild-mannered and anti-Communist. But the enthusiasm of the seamen kept pushing them, like the proverbial wheelbarrow, right to the end. Wilson was already advised by ruling-class opinion, dissatisfied by the impact of the $3\frac{1}{2}$ per cent norm on real wages, to attack the unions. 'The only way to achieve an incomes policy in 1966 is going to be by outfacing the trade unions on some big national wage struggle,' said *The Economist*. 'The Central Bankers thoroughly approve the Government's stand against the seamen. They have always urged Mr Wilson to have a showdown with the unions, and indeed this has been the major condition of all the various support operations,' wrote the *Guardian*'s Financial Editor. But he needed little encouragement. On the opening day of the strike, face puffed with paternal ire, he delivered a fireside declaration of war on the seamen. Their strike would be, he said, 'a strike against the state – against the community'. And his own account of the breaking of the strike dispenses with even a show of remorse and instead shows a real pride at his own cunning which certainly surpassed even the high standards of post-war strike-breaking established by Attlee and Bevin.

Wilson took personal responsibility for shortening the strike and isolating the seamen. He mobilized the Navy, declared an immediate emergency and organized the TUC to exert pressure on Bill Hogarth, lobbied the T & G to discourage sympathy action among rank-and-file dockers, arranged – again with willing TUC aid – action to keep oil supplies moving, and set up the usual Government-controlled 'independent inquiry'. In all this he received not one jot of resistance from the Labour Left or the union brass. Frank Cousins sat tight in his Cabinet post throughout, Michael Foot forebore even to clear his throat as the emergency regulations were passed. In fact even the rank-and-file support for the seamen was slow in mounting. The key to victory lay in the docks, but there Communist Party militants miscalculated badly in believing that the docks would clog up of their own accord. In fact the month's notice given to the shipowners by the NUS had been put to good use by the port authorities in reorganizing berthings to prevent just this. And in general the Communists and Labour Left militants remained cautious and constitutional, constrained by their reluctance to admit what Wilson had made clear from the off, the political nature of the strike. The *Morning Star* insisted on declaring, in the face of all the evidence, 'this dispute is not between seamen and the nation. It is between seamen and the shipowners.' Considerable sums were made available to the NUS by miners, foundry workers and the strong shop stewards' committees of the car and air-craft industry, but in the circumstances actually served as conscience money when what was needed was sympathetic stoppages. For real centres of industrial resistance to Wilson had not yet emerged.

The still tiny revolutionary groups had not yet begun to swell with disillusioned ex-Wilsonites. The Socialist Labour League led a deter-mined march and lobby, through the pouring rain, of two thousand, including many seamen from the northern ports conspicuous in white open-necked shirts and shore suits. The march passed from the London docks to Parliament on 25 May, ending however in the Porchester Hall in the usual rambling denunciations of the Communists and the parad-ing of alsatian guard dogs up and down the aisles. A joint Trotskyist and anarchist sign-writing team painted 'Save the Seamen' on a large Oxford wall but the students' only response was to paint out the 'a' in 'Seamen' and add 'New Emissions Policy' beneath. What kept the strike strong was the seamen themselves, whose determination actually grew as more and more docking ships spilled off more men to buoy up the strike. Only at the cross-Channel ports, where summer earnings were the bulk of the year's pay, was there even a sign of weakening. The seamen's singlehanded stubbornness and the strength of their case forced even the Fleet Street press to pay lip service to their cause before going on about what 'the Nation can afford'. But not so Wilson. He now launched an attack on 'a closely knit group of politically motivated men' who apparently had the NUS Executive at its mercy. As a political allegation it was strikingly unsuccessful – a variety of news-papers investigated and disproved it. The Tories disbelieved it and IRIS, the extreme right-wing trade-union surveillance organization which exists to expose Communists, dismissed it. Only the 'radical', 'lively', 'fair' organs of liberalism, the *Observer* and the *Guardian*, stooped to printing it.

But it will live on as one of the most successful political lies ever told. It gave an excuse for the middle-of-the-roaders on the NUS Executive to change sides and still square their conscience. The NUS, four weeks after rejecting the findings of the Pearson Committee, de-cided to 'adjourn' the strike for a year. To the last, sixteen seagoing executive members voted against, and at meeting after meeting seamen showed fury and incomprehension at the return to work.

But in a curious fashion trade-unionists continued to shield them-selves from the politics of their militancy, to hang on to the older local industrial strength and ignore the state's attacks. In January of 1966 a London Industrial Shop Stewards' Defence Committee was founded by trade-unionists in International Socialism and supported by many Communists. A similar committee was established in Glasgow and several publications on incomes policy and industrial struggles were commissioned and distributed by that committee. But its magazine *Resistance* floundered in the lack of real resistance. For even by 1966 there was still considerable passive support for the Government's professed aims and a general scepticism about its ability really to weaken the positions of industrial strength. The promises of an increasing national income, reforms without taxation and cash without a struggle were still attractive, especially to the ill-organized and lower-paid workers who were carefully courted in Wilson's speeches.

But in July an external economic crisis was to tip Wilson off his economic high wire. The balancing act collapsed under the relentless pressure of bankers whom Wilson was committed to pleasing. He was actually tipped over by another balance-of-payments crisis which was at least partly caused by his irrational determination not to devalue the pound and to continue to use troops in the Far East in support of the USA. But this external crisis only emphasized the necessity for a real shift in the balance of power in industry, forcing Wilson into a straightforward declaration of class war, unvarnished by the old verbal formulas. 'The consequence of not earning an honest living is unemployment, and we had better face the fact,' announced Ray Gunter on 8 July. 'To be effective, a policy of wage standstill coupled with severe deflation must hurt,' echoed *The Times*. The complex of commitments which Wilson's economic policy stemmed from, the pound, the City, the export drive, interacted so as to rule out virtually all Labour's historical aspirations and electoral pledges. Promises were postponed to the remote future, in the here-and-now was the biggest single deflationary package in post-war history and a complete halt to wage increases which, unlike dividends, were lost for ever. 'Each well-publicized redundancy announcement will be seen as real evidence that the Government's measures are biting,' wrote the *Guardian* on 11 November 1966. And even then many trade-unionists continued to think it was some kind of a temporary aberration. At the Brighton TUC, to which Wilson read a long sermon on the virtues of docility and announced that 'what was at stake . . . was the ability to turn the vision of a just society into a reality', only two million votes went against the wage freeze. And as the first stage of a total freeze for all claims whose implementation fell between July 1966 and January 1967 merged into six months of severe restraint, the TUC's Conference of Executives was still waffling that 'Incomes policy is to the TUC preeminently a long-term instrument of planning in which the element of restraint, in a selective and purposeful setting, is incidental.' The TUC was still mesmerized by the prospect of labour coming to power; their evidence to the Royal Commission, 70,000 self-righteous words, was headlined in the TUC magazine as 'When trade unions walk down the corridors of power'.

These particular delusions of grandeur were to reach a climax in the 100th anniversary of the TUC when over 900 trade-unionists finally negotiated their way into a Buckingham Palace garden party. At a banquet which expressed 100 years of working-class organization in Britain, Her Majesty the Queen, keynote speaker, announced, 'It is my pride to wish you well on your hundredth birthday and as you cross the threshold of your second centenary to pray that you will flourish and that you will continue to provide the wise leadership on which our country so much depends.' Rising to restate a working-class perspective, George Woodcock insisted, 'It was a mistake to think that trade unions existed simply to increase the money incomes of working people.' As his audience braced themselves for a vigorous restatement of the tasks of trade-unionism in the second centenary, Woodcock continued, 'Trade unions exist to increase the dignity of working people, to give them status.'

But apart from the garden parties and the banquets, it had been a grim end to a hundred years of trade-unionism. At the Square Grip concrete reinforcement company in Lanarkshire, thirty-nine men who had dared to join a union spent eleven months on £4 a week official strike pay while their Lordships pondered over the legal issues raised by the employers' successful court injunction against the blacking of Square Grip products. At Woolf's rubber factory in Southall, Indian and Pakistani workers who endured sweltering heat and non-existent safety regulations ('They like it like that,' said the management) struck against conditions which would have been considered unsavoury 150 years ago. The wage freeze was depressingly successful, the only exceptions being the strike at Morris Radiators against redundancy and the decision of a handful of engineering employers to grant clandestine wage increases to their draughtsmen by upgrading their work status. At Radiators, women strikers sent a telegram to York, 'Have you no guts, Carron? Make our strike official.' But in general the Government had considerable success with the freeze. It did not have its bluff called, was not forced publicly to invoke Part IV, the penal clauses of the prices and incomes legislation. The wage freeze, because punctured on a 'nothing said' basis, remained fully inflated. Instead the initiative was taken by the employers. A succession of hints and winks from Wilson had actually amassed sufficient determination amongst some employers to expose the weakness of trade-union strength. In London a concerted attack was made on those large central building sites whose strong job organization and willingness to spread the butter had made them leaders in the London building industry. The carefully delivered and adroitly timed blows dealt by the employers show every sign of considered joint planning by the companies, the trade-union officials and the police. But for the workers, the struggle at the Barbican, like the seamen's strike, had a ghostly, uninhabited quality. In the centre of London a decisive battle in the modern class struggle was fought, and eventually lost, in a painful isolation. The Joint Sites Committee, which the employers told the courts 'aimed to disrupt the industry by pressing unreasonable demands for workers', was a loose informal meeting of the militants on the London sites in an industry which more than any other relied on the sheer organizing ability of single trade-unionists. Certainly Jack Dash had promised support, Paul Foot wrote pamphlets, socialist students from LSE lent their weight to the picket and stuck up illegal posters in the refectory which aimed, as a spokesman told *The Times*, 'to show a community of interest between us and the strikers'. But the building workers were basically on their own. It was their own leaders, especially Lou Lewis (who had become a Communist while in National Service because he thought too much about the consequences of nuclear testing), who reported back and kept up spirits throughout a summer outside the gate. For the employers were prepared to pay for the unconcreted steel foundations to rust silently through the summer if they could break the Joint Sites Committee and with it the wages of London builders. The end of this strike was a miniature of what the seventies is all about. An 'independent tribunal', under the Scottish judge who had smashed the militant organization at Fords, instructed a return to work, the employers and the union bureaucrats placed a joint full-page advertisement in the London evening papers demanding a return to work and outside the long-silent site a small but desperate early-morning battle was fought between mounted horsemen and 2,000 policemen and the strikers, as a coachload of scabs finally re-opened the job.

This new-found confidence of the employers actually to combine to attack organization was seen throughout 1967 and in the main it was successful. From different directions but with the same intention, shop stewards' organization was attacked by concerted state-employer offensives. In ENV an American manager preferred to close the factory and transfer the work *en bloc* rather than pay well-organized workers. In Stockport a Southern Carolina anti-trade-union employer was encouraged by giant squads of police to keep open his factory until a virtual threat by the local Trades Council to close down the whole of South Lancashire forced him to retreat. The draughtsmen's union was locked out of the shipbuilding industry and only survived by their success in extending the strike to all draughtsmen. And in Liverpool and London a confused and ill-synchronized national unofficial stoppage in protest against the Devlin Stage Two proposals to narrow dock work further was beaten. BMC car shop stewards faced their first major cutback since 1961. And the socialist Minister of Labour made what had become the standard response to visible evidence of class struggle: 'The Communists,' he vouchsafed, 'are planning a winter of disruption.' What was specially sinister about the Barbican, he said, was that Communists and Trotskyists actually combined forces. Wilson, speaking at a wine-merchants' banquet, agreed: 'Everyone here,' he told the bibulous vintners, 'will endorse his words.' And as unemployment in Scotland scaled heights unrecorded for twenty years, Wilson told the Scottish TUC, 'This is your country, work for it.'

On 16 January 1968 the Government announced their package of reforms designed to make the November devaluation 'work'. These abolished the very few reforms the Labour Government had made in its initial days and made deep visible cuts into welfare, including such financially meaningless steps as reintroducing prescription charges, which was in fact a piece of gratuitous nastiness designed to impress the banking audience. The working-class movement was, whether it liked it or not, being obliged to mobilize resistance, to reach out to wider co-ordination, to penetrate the shrouds of its old assumptions, to rejoin the industrial and the political. In 1967 for the first time real incomes failed to rise and unemployment really began to bite. The Communist-controlled Liaison Committee for the Defence of Trade Unions was aroused from its fairly moribund life of the past two years and began to talk of industrial action against Wilson. But by 1968 Incomes Policy had actually moved from the centre of the wages offensive. Increasingly the value of Aubrey Jones was not to cut wages (Jones himself calculates that he deducted only 1 per cent from the real earnings) but rather ideological, designed to create an atmosphere in which unions could increasingly be helped into the straitjacket of the productivity deal. By the end of 1968, over 200 groups of workers per month were taking the first bite at the productivity cherry, causing the *Financial Times* to declare, 'the country's present obsession with productivity probably exceeds the wildest dreams of those who were trying to spread the word five years ago'.

At the Labour Party Conference vote opposition to the Government's policy was increasingly unignorable. Outside the hall the car workers who lobbied in 1967 and the miners who in 1968 burst into the deliberations with banners reading 'Halt pit closures now before it's too late' disturbed the platform's political sleep. For by 1967 Wilson had managed to achieve an increase in productivity per employed person, but at the cost of an unemployment figure which had begun to gallop upwards. And, compared to the last recession in 1961, jobs were being lost more permanently. In 1967 455,000 jobs had gone for good, of which 370,000 were in manufacturing. (In 1961, when the listed unemployed had risen to over half a million, the jobs lost were only 183,000.) On the eve of the TUC meeting at Brighton in 1967 the total unemployed was 594,315, the highest since August 1940. By 1968 the Dyers' and Bleachers' motion condemning TUC wage vetting was very nearly successful. In the winter of 1968, although the expected national engineering strike had been called off, the overseas telephonists had led stoppages in nineteen cities, assembled 15,000 in Hyde Park and got twenty switchboard operators in the Department of Employment and Productivity itself out on a two-hour sympathy strike. Faced with this determination the Government, discreetly, climbed down. 2,500 London firemen too marched on County Hall to deliver their demand for an adequate bonus to cover the extreme under-manning the service was experiencing. For in 1968 there was again a species of stalemate. With the memories of the May events in their minds and the knowledge that British workers had already pulled their belt far tighter than their French counterparts, the Government and employers were reluctant to come to the crunch on a national dispute. And official trade-unionism still kept its fists firmly in its pockets. Between the two of them it was clear that the workers had lost at least the first round of productivity dealing. But compromise was still inadequate for Labour and although the snorting Gunter was replaced by the flexible Castle and the Donovan Report repudiated legal solutions and stressed the long-term perspective of the attack on the shop floor, Wilson still had to press ahead.

'In Place of Strife' proved the sticking point. It had in it teeth that really bit, teeth which could not be camouflaged and it was openly attacked by an emerging leftist wing on the General Council. Although Frank Cousins was still capable of joining a standing ovation to Wilson within hours of denouncing his wages policy, other trade-unionists had by now overcome their schizophrenic loyalty to Labour. On 27 February 1969 the Liaison Committee called the first purely political one-day stoppage since 1926 to lobby the TUC, which was followed by over a quarter of a million workers. They included Scottish and Welsh miners, engineers in Manchester, Glasgow, North London, Slough and Luton, builders in Bristol, London and Merseyside, bus drivers, printers and car workers. And this was followed on May Day by a demonstration of 200,000, in London overwhelmingly print workers from SOGAT, stopping the daily papers and thus becoming unignorable. The NASD and the Lightermen were the only unions to support the stoppage officially, but not only the 28,000 London SOGATs marched, in Sheffield 25,000 came out, with 50,000 marching on Merseyside, and 30,000 car workers stopping for the day. The 5 June Recall TUC proceeded to announce that having beaten off Wilson's legal chains they were about to strap themselves into a harness designed by the General Council itself. As *Socialist Worker*'s report put the shift in the General Council's Programme for Action, 'It accepts the arguments that workers must make the sacrifices, accept the restrictions and work all the harder so as to solve problems in the "National Interest" like so much nasty medicine that must be taken to make us all better. The only question is: who should spoon out the medicine, the Government or the TUC leadership? It is a Battle of the Bureaucracies. It has little to do with the workers' fight against the attacks being launched and everything to do with the details of how the control of workers and their organizations is to be institutionalized.'*

The last year of the Labour Government marked a new mood in the unions or rather an end to the piecemeal, isolated, listless response to Wilson's attack. With the world economy shrinking and the British economy still unable to break out of stagnation of production and investment, Wilson was forced to continue the productivity offensive. The Commission on Industrial Relations, whose staff included George Woodcock and the ex-Communist miner's leader Will Paynter, continued the attempt to implement the proposals of the Donovan Report industry by industry, to erode away shop-floor organization discreetly. But the Government had exhausted its supply of political goodwill among even the most loyal of Labour trade-unionists. At each stage in the progressive collapse of Government strategy – the 1965 Declaration of Intent proposing wage restraint to deal with the Tory deficit, the 1966 freeze to prevent devaluation, the 1968 cuts to make devaluation work – Labour supporters had been forced to surrender more cards.

* *Socialist Worker*, 29 May 1969.

From the work bench Labour looked ludicrous, there was no disguising it. And though Wilson had patched up a formula with the TUC inner cabinet to produce the Programme for Action, it was not only the General Council left-wingers, Scanlon and Jones, but many right-wing leaders who felt that they had better assert their independence within the system, if they were to ride their membership's growing dissatisfaction. For the presence on the General Council of union leaders who, while very far from revolutionary, were prepared to give the nod to political strikes, undoubtedly both reflected and strengthened a new militancy among the rank and file.

Wilson's productivity wizardry (by 1969 over 25 per cent of British workers were governed by some sort of a deal) had begun to reap its own reward. The unofficial miners' strike of October 1969 was essentially a revolt against the National Power Loading Agreement, a national productivity deal signed in 1966. Since the deal, output per man-shift at the face rose at a phenomenal 20 per cent (from 110 cwt in March 1966 to 132 cwt in March 1969). Over the same period 166 pits were closed and 120,000 men lost their jobs, while average earnings increased only 9 per cent. And long after the first cash bait had disappeared into rising prices, the conditions sold were taking their toll. Accidents increased, shift work extended, consultation was dropped. The resentment which was finally to erupt and win the 1972 miners' official strike was already on the boil in 1969. The Fords strike of February 1969 had too a strong political aspect overlying the wages settlement and produced a clear trial of strength between the motor stewards and the union tycoons, on the issue of penal clauses in the settlement. As Timothy Raison, ex-editor of *New Society*, headlined in the *Evening Standard*, 'The real significance of the Ford affair is, will it blow a hole in the Donovan Report?' In settlement after settlement, the cry of 'No strings' was being bellowed from the shop floor as the implications of the first wave of prod deals sank in. The slide-rule negotiator and white-coated time-and-motion expert were becoming new shop-floor bogies.

The whole geology of the labour movement had shifted in such a way that the deepest and deadest layers were able to go into spontaneous combustion. A dispute in Lambeth over dustmen's right to tott saleable bits of salvage out of the refuse ended in a strike of 60,000 municipal workers. An argument over wage-packet errors in the Flat-Drawn Department of Pilkington's St Helens glass factory ignited a strike which stopped a whole town in its tracks, discovered in its shop stewards political abilities they hadn't dreamed of, and for a dazzling moment showed what human wonders lie hidden under words like 'strike' and 'solidarity'. 'What have we won so far?' asked the rank-and-file bulletin at the end of the strike. 'First and foremost SELF-RESPECT – and the respect of the people of St Helens and the rest of the country. We have received an EDUCATION that money could not buy. We have seen the *real face* of Pilkington Brothers and NUGMW.'* For six years of Wilson had been an education. Freeze and incomes policy had, in spite of itself, instilled in the militants of the labour movement a new need for politics which extended beyond the purely industrial. For the purely industrial no longer existed. An unambiguous national attack by a Labour Government on rights and strengths which trade-unionists had come to take for granted forced politics back into the work-place. And it forced trade-unionists, who, in the same plant or industry or town, had become separated into a mosaic of independent centres, to acknowledge once again the general pattern of the movement, the mutual dependence and the common goals. This meant exploring new alliances, discovering perhaps more in common with student socialists who arrived, rather embarrassed, at the picket line than with the whizz-kid negotiator hot from union head office. It meant discovering, or rather re-discovering, as the workers in Injection Moulders, Abbey Wood Construction and GEC–AEI Liverpool did, the arguments for factory occupations. It meant piecing together a political labour movement and overcoming the traditional forces which for various reasons inhibited a general rank-and-file-based opposition to the travesty trade-unionism had become in order to sit down at the Queen's Banquet.

The ideas of the revolutionary Left, seeds carefully if somewhat dustily shielded from the light of twenty years' boom, returned again to the working-class soil from which they had come. The books of Marx and Lenin, of Trotsky and Luxemburg began to find readers again in the movement which thought it had outgrown them thirty years ago. The Institute of Workers' Control, closely modelled on Guild Socialism, began to attract several hundred, then a thousand trade-unionists to its discussions. London printers restarted a Workers' Mutual Aid Association based on the anarchist Kropotkin's plans. *Socialist Worker*'s brisk attacks on Wilson and his works increasingly replaced *Tribune*'s tortuous apologetics as shop-floor reading. The process was slow, the working-class response to Wilson more muted and splintered than defiant and nationally coherent. But by the end of the sixties, in some

* Quoted in Colin Barker, *The Pilkington Strike*, a Socialist Worker pamphlet, 1970.

unions, in a few factories, in a couple of towns, revolutionary trade-unionism had been reborn into a world of immense working-class possibilities. Born not by some intellectual whim but out of realities of the modern class struggle. For by 1970 it was those in the labour movement who believed in the indefinite prosperity of the present system who were the utopians and the dreamers.

To All Seamen

Dear Brother,

This pamphlet is to help YOU to explain the present struggle (to fight for a forty-hour week) to your wife, mother or girl friend, for once the shipowners see just how united we seamen are, as they have done in the past, their newspapers, radio and television will slant their propaganda more and more towards our womenfolk. They know as well as we do just how important it is that our women understand the issue at stake, and how much it means to us that we win this fight.

Before this Official Strike is over the shipowners will try all usual means to break it and maybe think up a few new ones, apart from trying to fill your jobs with outside black labour. These include among others: False reports that the strike is over, that ships have sailed fully manned, when they have not; report of intimidation by strikers to other non-strikers; efforts to confuse the issue (the forty-hour week) by spreading slanders about the members of the Executive Council and the Strike Committee; mis-reporting of events that take place during the strike. And in many other ways they will try as hard as they can to divide us and draw away public support from the British seamen's struggle for their just rights, and so weaken the strike. So let us be very clear what this stoppage is for, that is the forty-hour week, at sea and in port in principle and practice NOW.

If you have any doubts or questions in your mind, we ask you to please come to or telephone into YOUR UNION HALL, to get things cleared up.

We seamen, of all colours, creeds and political beliefs, stand together, united under the banner of the National Union of Seamen, in this fight for the forty-hour week.

Let nothing divide us,
Unity is Strength,
Division is Defeat.

HULL STRIKE COMMITTEE

(Pamphlet of the Hull Branch of the National Union of Seamen, 1966)

Not Wanted on Voyage:
Charlie Hodgins and Jim Prescott

When the unbelievable happened, and the docile long-suffering British merchant seamen came out solidly on strike, the first reaction of the press, TV, Government, was to hammer them for 'irresponsibility'. Then it gradually dawned upon the British people that they were witnessing something which has not happened for many years – a great wave of working-class and labour-movement opinion swung in behind the strikers; increasingly the press had to record this sympathy, increasingly it was the Government which appeared isolated. When the full history of this strike comes to be written, it will be seen that a crucial part was played by the measure of support which the strike won from the British Labour movement. We believe that as the strike enters the phase after the Inquiry, it is of the utmost importance to arrest the confusion which that Inquiry has caused amongst the sympathizers and supporters. Of course, it is clear that certain organs, such as the TUC establishments, and the International Transport Workers Federation, seized on the Inquiry, and its phoney 'compromise' appeal, as a welcome excuse to withdraw support, and to isolate the seamen. The press swung back to open hostility, delighted at the prospect of the labour organizations abandoning the NUS to its fate. We are bitterly resentful of the easy way in which trade-union leaders, in the TUC and the ITWF, have turned their backs upon us, without a decent and honest appraisal of the Inquiry's methods and bias; it seems all too much like 'Black Friday' of ill-famed memory. But we know too, from our meetings up and down the country, that genuine rank-and-file opinion has been confused by the dishonest reporting of the Inquiry's findings. Indeed, it is one of the purposes of this pamphlet to answer those findings, for the benefit of our brothers throughout the trade-union movement, so that they can see that they are making common cause with a JUST FIGHT. Now it is up to the rank and file; they must show by their solidarity that their leaders are wrong, that the battle is still on, that the case has not altered, and that betrayal is unthinkable.

Those who have supported us, and continue to support us, are vast in numbers and spread across the labour scene from one end of the country to the other. It has been said that 'now we are on our own'. We don't believe it. We know that it is not so. Even today after the Inquiry report, resolutions continue to be passed, and collections taken, by trade-union districts, and branches, by Labour Party meetings, and as we prepare this, a great move is on foot to form solidarity committees in every town in the country. The seamen must stand firm and be worthy of this magnificent support. The tide of feeling is turning our way again, despite all efforts of press and TV.

To list all the organizations which have given their support, either in resolutions, demonstrations, or collections, would be almost impossible. The Roll of Honour below is not complete; even as it stands, it is impressive and moving. If the Government now goes ahead with navy and troops into the ports, if official support now fades away as it seeks to do, then we know that the dockers stand ready immediately to take more direct measures in our support. We have not encouraged this desperate turn of events; we do not however intend to disown or spurn that generous support if and when it develops. The responsibility lies firmly with owners and Government, cheered on by their willing servants in the mass communications media. Let them note the weight of support we have mustered.

Organizations passing resolutions and/or collecting money for NUS strike up to 17 June 1966

Annual Conference Fire Brigades Union

Seaman's groups in Denmark, Australia, France, Greece, Holland, Russia, US, W. Germany

Hull dockers unofficial Portworkers' Committee

Irish Council of the DATA

Shorts Belfast Works Committee

S. Wales Miners

ASLEF Executive Committee

Glasgow no. 2 AEU branch

Oxford University Liberal Party

London Labour Party. 400,000 strong

Annual Conference of the AScW

EC of the National League of Young Liberals

Bristol Trades Council

Rover Shop stewards in Solihull and Tyseley

AEU branches at Halesowen and Kings Heath

N. W. London PTU

Kentish Town Bakers Union

Port of London ship repairers

W. India Dock Liaison Committee

Daily Mirror Printers

Wellingborough CAWU

AUF Letchworth

W. London Oil men TGWU

Govan dry dock workers

USB Rutherglen

AEU Sheffield District Committee

ETU Sheffield Central

Leeds University students

Leeds USDAW and ETU branches

Scottish District ASSET

Co-op Women's Guilds
Conference
Airdrie Trades Council and NUR
Scottish Miners Lodges
Lanark strikers
Scottish Plasterers Union
Scottish CWS
AEI Springburn, workers
Clyde Hillington, AEU
S. London AEU District
Greenwich Trades Council
BAC Filton, Bristol workers
London AEU ship repairers
Shop Stewards
NASDU, no. 7 branch
Haringey CP
Cypriot N. London workers
Harrow CP
Glacier Metal shop stewards
Smithfield meat porters
Earls Court branch NUR
Wembley no. 3 and 4 branches
AEU
Wembley branch AUF
Hounslow branch ETU
Merseyside AUBTW
Nottingham Trades Council
Cardiff Trades Council
Hull Trades Council
Hull North Labour Party
Hull West Labour Party
Petrochemical Construction
workers
Bradford Road. Gasworks workers
Sheffield District AEU
Shardlows Sheffield workers
Manchester District ASW
Greenwich and Bermondsey
Trades Councils
University of Sussex Socialist
Society

Hemel Hempstead Labour Party
Young Socialist branches (many)
N. London District AEU
Printers branch London
Bristol Siddeley shop stewards
Harrow Trades Council
Fazakerley (Liverpool) building
site
Co-op Insurance Staff
Conference
Scottish Miners Union
Morning Star
Tribune
The Week
Labour Worker
and many other newspapers of the
labour movement
Islington Tenants and Residents
Association
Ratcliffe Tools workers
Reliant tool draughtsmen
Camden Trades Council
Uxbridge building site
E. W. Bliss Ltd, Derby, workers
BAC Alderstone, workers
Watermen, London
ASW Conference
BMC Tractor and Transmission
plant
Glasgow Trades Council
Liverpool Trades Council
Liverpool Labour Party
Miners at pits in Yorks. area
Nottingham CSE meeting
Hull CSE meetings
West Scotland Insulating workers
Boilermakers and platers in
Scotland
Knightswood bus garage
Teachers at Coatbridge technical
college

Perth Trades Council
150 Members of Parliament
Derbyshire NUM
Northern Committee of Irish TUC
Babcock and Wilcox workers
John Browns workers
Cammell's shipyard
Red Road Building site
Glasgow AEU shop stewards
Solidarity Committees of
   Sheffield and Rotherham
Shop stewards at Chesterfield
   iron coy.
ASSET
Humber car workers
Dunlop workers
Midland District Committee
   TGWU
London NUFTO branch
French Federation of Seamen's
   Unions
W. German Transport Union
AEU works committee at Rootes
Standard Telephone shop
   stewards
BAC Weybridge workers
Merthyr District Committee of
   AEU

Birmingham East AEU
Joseph Lucas factory
Jaguar Daimler shop stewards
Liverpool gas workers
Rootes, Linwood
Scottish television workers
ASSET branch 751
Barbican London, building
   workers
Kent miners
Greater London District
   boilermakers
Vietnam Solidarity Campaign
Northern Drivers Union,
   N. Zealand
Finnish dockers
YCL Branches
ASSET conference
DATA Executive
Humberside Voice
Scottish Commercial Motormen
Boilermakers Union
Immingham BR plumbers
Putney, Stroud and Sydenham
   CPs
Hammersmith 2nd branch ASW
ETU, W. London supply
   Fulham PTU

AND MANY HUNDREDS OF UN-NAMED UNION BRANCHES, LABOUR ORGANIZATIONS AND INDIVIDUALS THROUGHOUT THE COUNTRY.

(From *Not Wanted on Voyage: The Seamen's Reply*, a 16-page pamphlet published in June 1966 as a reply to the Pearson Report by the members of the Hull Strike Committee)

The Struggle at Mytons :
Lou Lewis

(*Fiddles with microphone.*) This is something like Mytons I think, it won't go. (*Mike works.*) Comrade chairman, comrades, I think I've got a difficult problem to try and relate the history of twelve months of dispute, with some of the lessons we've learnt in it, and some of the reasons for it, which I believe it can be seen, come out of the present Government's policy, to say why we're in dispute. Further, the fact that there's not only one dispute in the building industry in London: but there are two disputes. I think that I should outline briefly the beginning of the dispute, because we have had a report from a court of inquiry set up by the Minister of Labour, Ray Gunter, and that report has condemned everyone who has taken part in these two disputes, not only the lads who picketed the job but also the trade-union officials who supported their members in dispute.

The dispute on Mytons: first, we started over a simple issue: three steel fixers were dismissed for allegedly unsatisfactory production; that was in October of last year. As a result we were in dispute for ten days, and then instructed back by our trade union. We returned to work on the instruction of our trade unions. At the time that we were instructed back two unions out of the three involved had declared the strike official. Two days after our returning to work the management sacked the whole site. They then put before the unions a number of conditions for re-opening the site. Firstly, that the local agreements, which we know as bonus agreements, would have to be substantially cut; secondly, that there would be a selective re-employment of those dismissed; and thirdly, that there would be strict control of the rights of shop stewards to operate on that site.

We were then in dispute right throughout November, December, January into February. In February an agreement was arrived at, where the unions involved in the dispute agreed with the management. Firstly, the site would re-open on 20 February. The management were prepared to re-employ on that site everyone with the exception of the three steel fixers over whom the dispute arose, and, secondly, the six shop stewards who constituted the works committee. When the lads met on 20 February to discuss this, they unanimously turned it down. They turned it down because within the agreement there was a clause that the six men could contest the case before the arbitration machinery, which we know as a disputes commission in the industry.

The disputes commission sat firstly, at regional level, and after failure to agree, then at national level. The employer had no charge against the six men as individuals, against either their time-keeping, their record as workers, or their record as shop stewards. But what they did claim was that the six shop stewards who were members of a works committee: 'They were troublesome to us, they acted against all that is good in the interests of the employers, and therefore we demand our right not to re-employ them.'

Unfortunately for the lads in dispute the national disputes commission upheld the employers' claim, not on the basis of our employment on the site, but on the fact that the six stewards had been responsible for organizing a picket on that gate up to the time that the national disputes commission held court, which was from October, when we went in dispute, up to the time of the national disputes commission, which was in March of this year. On the trade unions calling the lads together to discuss whether they would accept the findings of the national disputes commission which was refusing to re-employ the men, it was recommended that they should not be re-employed on the site in the interests of industrial relations on that site. The men discussed the disputes commission findings and unanimously again refused to return. The employer then attempted to re-open this site with scab labour. In trying to re-open this site with scab labour he failed, because of the solidarity of London building workers, who formed a mass picket on the site on 3 April, and as a result the scabs returned from whence they came (I don't know whether that's in the Bible or not).

We then found ourselves in this position. (And I think I'm skipping this very briefly and maybe a bit too quickly, but I find it necessary because I've got to say something at the end.) The Minister of Labour then set up a court of inquiry to look into the circumstances, the causes and circumstances of the dispute on Myton's Barbican and also the dispute that had been running alongside the one at Myton's for the same period of time, that dispute being the Sunley site on Horseferry Road.

At the court of inquiry we held the same position as we had at the national disputes commission; the employers claiming first that the six shop stewards represented a problem to the employer in that they were prepared to fight on behalf of the men and carry out the decisions the men arrived at at meetings held on the site. And the decisions were obviously this, that they wanted better conditions. The court of inquiry also heard from Sunleys that the Sunleys employer provoked a dispute; this was admitted by a director. The firm also said that one of the reasons they provoked the dispute was that a national trade-union official, who is the president of the Federation of Building Unions, agreed that, if they sacked the works committee, he would support them, and see that, when it came to a national disputes commission, the firm would win.

Now the findings of the court of inquiry are known to all. It not only dealt with the two disputes, it dealt with the industry as a whole. It recommended on the Myton's dispute that the six shop stewards shouldn't be re-employed. It recommended that Myton's should take back, or offer employment to, all those dismissed with the exception of the six shop stewards. It recommended that there should be more disciplinary powers for workers on that site, it recommended the appointment of shop stewards, and it recommended also that if any shop steward may dare to represent the men who elected him into that position, he should be disciplined, and removed from holding that position of shop steward.

On the case of Sunley's, the decision was that the firm, having admitted provoking the dispute, be recommended to accept that all workers on that site should be re-employed on the site, but the shop stewards who formed the works committee on that site when it was dismissed should not be allowed to hold office again. The court also attacked the committee called the London Workers' Joint Sites Committee, as a subversive body.

We all know what rank-and-file committees are and what their weaknesses are, and if they are able to do something, they do it because of the support they enjoy. Now I can't deal with all I'd like to have dealt with because the chairman tells me time is up, but I'd like to say this, that we have seen within this dispute a lot of evidence for what has been said from this platform today. An alliance was formed between the employer, the state and right-wing trade-union leaders. We have seen this operating, to the extent that not only do they attack the lads in dispute, they also attack those trade-union officials who are prepared to represent their members. We have had that off the local officials in this dispute.

I think that we have got to be quite clear on the situation confronting us as workers: we have a situation that when we go in dispute we don't have to dump in one big bundle every trade-union official, because what has given us strength in this dispute has been the fact we've recognized those who support us and those that oppose us. We've recognized the employer is the main enemy, and all those that join with him, we also work against them, or attack them.

I make this final point: that as far as the lads are concerned in this dispute, we have to decide one way or the other whether we accept these recommendations. As far as we're concerned no Scottish judge, no employer and no outside trade-union leader is going to tell us that we end a dispute after fifty weeks: but the people who will tell us are the 200 lads that were sacked on this site in November. The strike committee has said it will abide by any decision they arrive at, at a meeting called in accordance with trade-union practice and tradition.

(Speech at the 1967 Scarborough teach-in)

Roberts-Arundel Strike Committee: The Story of the Strike

On Saturday, 18 February, the Stockport and District Trades' Council organized a large public meeting in a square in Stockport, which was followed by a march round the factory. Several thousand trade-unionists took part in this demonstration, which was led by local and national officials of some of the unions concerned. Stewards from several local factories announced at the end of this demonstration that they intended to take the following Wednesday afternoon off and take part in a monster picket at the Roberts-Arundel factory.

The picketing had been growing more active over the previous two weeks or so, and there had been lively scuffles on a number of occasions. One morning one of the scabs pulled a screwdriver out and attempted to stab one of the pickets, and on another occasion scabs hurled bricks and bottles at the picket from inside the factory gates. One morning the personnel manager, Mr Mangham, lost his nerve and refused to go through the picket line. Instead he paced the pavement opposite the gate for an hour, like some ghost on the battlements, while the pickets mocked him.

On the Monday and Tuesday mornings, a number of arrests were made, in an extremely arbitrary manner, and this helped to strengthen indignation against the police. On Monday night a small 'unofficial painting party' visited the factory in the early hours of the morning and used fifteen bob's worth of paint to good effect in painting up slogans and so forth on the walls and gates of the factory. The main intention of this was to let any workers or drivers coming to the factory know that an official dispute was in progress. The management saw the slogans up before the paint had dried properly, however, and called out the fire brigade to wash the paint off. This cost them £60, so the painters felt that at least they had struck not too bad a bargain!

On Wednesday afternoon several hundred workers gathered outside the factory – including a large number from the local firm of Craven Brothers, who had struck for the afternoon to take part. At first there was a feeling of disappointment at the small numbers who had turned up to support the picket, until a cry came from the end of the street: 'They're coming!' Round the corner came a march of hundreds of workers in procession, carrying placards and calling out slogans. The 'Panter Division', as it was afterwards known, had arrived. (Brother

Bernard Panter is the Stewards' Convenor at Shell Chemicals, whose workers had come down in coaches with large numbers of their Brothers from the construction sites next to the Shell plant at Carrington.)

Suddenly, the street, was filled with pickets. Estimates of the numbers vary, but probably there were around 2,000 present. During speeches through a portable loudspeaker, attacking the management, a worker appeared at the factory door with his cards, declaring that he would no longer work for a scab firm. He was welcomed with cheers and cries of 'Get all the scabs out'. The police began to try to push the crowd back from the doors, and the pickets, annoyed by the police behaviour, shoved back. In one charge the factory gates nearly gave way. Missiles began flying about, and a number of the factory windows were broken. (Some of these missiles were provided by a very militant old lady living around the corner, whose tea had warmed the pickets up on many a cold morning!) Three workers managed to get to the factory side door, but they were then cut off from the main body of the pickets by the police, who pushed them into the factory, where they were deliberately beaten up by the scabs under the surveillance of the management.

One of the police, who had been seen kicking workers earlier, was struck in the face with a stone. The police moved forward in anger. When the men pushed back again the Deputy Chief Constable was trapped against the gates by the weight of his own men and his wrist was broken.

More police were brought in from Manchester and other local areas in coaches. Some behaved with great brutality, while others were simply cowed and amazed by the pickets' determination. At 4.30 the AEU District Secretary arrived and asked the workers to call it a day. He had been told by the police that if he did not get the workers to go they would use extreme violence. (More police with batons were waiting round the corner.) After some argument, the majority decided to go. Those who remained were pinned up against the wall opposite the factory by the police, so that the scabs could run home from the factory.

Up to this point, the police had been out-numbered, and, faced with the pickets' militancy, had not dared to make a single arrest. But now they felt that they were on top again, they began to arrest men. In all nine pickets were arrested.

These arrests were carried out in an entirely arbitrary way. This was proved later, when two of the nine men who were arrested appealed against their fines and won. They were fortunate in that someone had been taking photographs during the picketing and they were able to prove that they had been wrongfully arrested, much to the chagrin of the police. Like the earlier arrests, these men were simply arrested because the police felt they ought to arrest *someone* – and anyone would do, it seemed.

The next day all demonstrations and processions near the factory were banned, and for a time the police would not even allow proper pickets to function. Even people living in the street were stopped and had to prove their identities to get home! But gradually the picketing has been picking up again, although so far not with the earlier forcefulness that produced such excellent results. No one likes to use force in a trade-union dispute, but in this particular case it appears that there is nothing else that can bring this management to reason. In the seven months of this dispute, nearly thirty pickets have been arrested, but there is not one of them, or of the strike committee, who feels that he had any choice in the matter, given the attitude of the firm, the scabs and the police to normal methods.

Mr Cox, the managing director, has also been in court. One evening he came out of the factory in a tremendous temper, got into his blue Jaguar and drove down the street outside the factory on the right-hand side. The pickets had stood one of their white boards on a pole in a grating, and Cox drove straight at it to smash the pole. He was so intent on this that he drove straight at one of the pickets, who had to jump for his life; he then continued straight out into the middle of the main road and crashed into a passing lorry. For this extremely dangerous driving he was fined £25 plus costs, but the sympathetic magistrate decided that 'in view of the situation' he would not endorse his licence . . .

There can be no doubt that the picketing has been of the greatest importance in this dispute. The pity is that it has, generally, been carried by only a small proportion of local trade-unionists. The vast part of the burden has been carried by only a few local factories and stewards' committees. In some ways the strike has shown up some of the weaknesses in organization at other factories, and it is to be hoped that future pickets will be able to draw on the support of others who have done less, instead always of having to rely on the same old faces.

The importance of the strike at Roberts-Arundel for the trade-union movement can hardly be stressed too much. If the labour movement allows this management to get away with its deliberate challenge to British trade-union practice and principles, then the labour movement will have shown itself to be a poor thing indeed. Every other management in Britain with reactionary tendencies will take note and will try to get away with the same kind of thing.

Victory at Roberts-Arundel on the other hand will represent an important sign of the continuing strength of trade-unionism in Britain. There is no doubt, whatever the sceptics of the national press may say, that this dispute can be won. But victory requires hard work and an even greater display of the marvellous solidarity that has sustained the morale of the strikers for so long.

This strike is your dispute too. Please do all you can to help bring it to a speedy and successful conclusion.

SUPPORT ROBERTS-ARUNDEL!! DEFEND FACTORY ORGANIZATION!!

(From *Roberts-Arundel, the Story of the Strike,* published by the Strike Committee)

Smash the Freeze,
Fight Unemployment

'Incomes Policy' now finds its logical outcome in a wage freeze. Wilson's brave words on coming to power about a 'planned rate of growth of incomes' gives way to no growth at all. There is no guarantee that the freeze will not be extended past the six months promised by the Government. When the working class are bearing the burdens there is nothing more permanent than the temporary.

Prices will not be frozen

Everyone knows that many prices have increased since 20 July. As the *Financial Times* put it '. . . in fact there is no price freeze. The section on prices in the July White Paper does not amount to anything approaching a universal standstill on prices.' There can be no machinery to ensure that the prices in hundreds of thousands of shops up and down the country are frozen – as we already know to our cost.

The Government's blanket refusal of increases contracted for and agreed months in advance of the freeze contrasts strangely with the exceptions permitted to manufacturers for price increases due to taxation, increased import costs, seasonal changes in supply and increased costs of components. In fact many food prices are excluded from the freeze altogether.

The freeze (like 'Incomes Policy') is a fraud. The effect of price increases without wages following is a planned decrease in wages.

The employers will take the hint

In many cases the employers will find the wage freeze and the credit restrictions an excuse to cut fringe benefits and bonuses. The attack on long-established rights and conditions will be stepped up by the bosses. Short time, and above all unemployment, also mean nothing but a slashing of workers' wages. The Government is creating the framework in which the employers can more effectively fight organized workers.

Unemployment

To justify 'Incomes Policy' Wilson and Brown argued that wage restraint was the necessary alternative to unemployment. Now we are getting wage cuts *and* unemployment. Wilson claims that unemployment will not rise above 500,000 (a situation that must look more comfortable from the front bench at Westminster than a dole queue in Wigan) while at the same time he threatens the TUC with 2,000,000 on the dole if they do not surrender the trade unions to his policy.

William Davis of the *Guardian*, who has good connections in Government circles, claimed that unemployment would probably reach 750,000. Pryke, an ex-member of Wilson's DEA, stated that the figure will reach 1,000,000 by the winter after next. The City keeps its dividends, the bosses keep their profits and the workers lose their jobs.

Cause of the crisis

The real causes of the balance of payments crisis that Britain faces are first, military spending abroad; second, the export of private capital overseas. In the present year the estimated loss on the balance of payments will be about £220 million. The military expenditure abroad – to protect British investments in the Middle East and elsewhere – will be £650 millions; and private capital export will exceed £450 million.

The financial crisis is a crisis of the capitalist system. It is caused by the bosses. *Let them pay for it.*

Smash the wage freeze

To pass resolutions in the trade unions against the wage freeze, as the TGWU and other unions have done, is important, but it is not enough.

We need action, not words.

The employers, the Government, and sterling, could not face up to a prolonged and determined strike by workers in any key section of the economy.

The trade-union leaders who oppose the freeze have to live up to the logic of their opposition. For example, Cousins who agreed to 3½ per cent for the provincial busmen was not serious in his opposition to Government policy. In the ranks of the TGWU there are sections (i.e., tanker drivers) who could beat the freeze hands down. Cousins and his followers in the trade-union leadership must match their verbal radicalism with meaningful and determined action.

State and employers in league

Whenever workers defend themselves – be it the seamen or the printers – they find themselves facing not only the employers but also the state.

Wilson turned the seamen's strike from a purely industrial strike into a battle with the Government. The working class will have to realize that from now on every struggle to improve and defend conditions is a political struggle.

Wilson and the employers want a trade-union movement timid and obedient to state discipline. The fight against the freeze is also a fight for the very future of the Labour movement.

A programme to fight the freeze

1. No sacking, share the work – if the employers claim to be unable to keep a factory open, our reply is that the workers cannot afford to have it closed. Let the state take it over and guarantee that it stays open.
2. State responsibility for work or full maintenance.
3. Full support for all workers engaged in strike action to defend or improve conditions.
4. Action – official if possible, unofficial if necessary – to break the wage freeze.
5. Fight for rank and file control of the workers' organization and against Government intervention in trade-union affairs.
6. Smash the Freeze.

(Leaflet published by the Industrial Shop Stewards' Defence Committee)

May Day – Give Your Guv'nor That Choking Feeling:
Pete Gold

In 1889 the Second (socialist) International decided to start a campaign for the eight-hour day and they called on workers in all countries to stop work on 1 May.

Not only did the International call the strike as the first step in the campaign for the eight-hour day, they intended it to be a day of working-class solidarity, a day for the working class of the world to demonstrate its might.

The first May Day demonstrations took place in 1890. In Germany hundreds of thousands of workers stopped work and took to the streets and in Italy there were mass strikes and demonstrations.

By 1891 all the European countries had adopted May Day as workers' day with the exception of Britain. As far away as Argentina and Bolivia and of course the USA, workers were striking and demonstrating on May Day.

At the present time most countries make May Day a public holiday. In America Labour Day is the first Monday in September.

On that basis, Britain ranks with fascist South Africa as one of the few countries in the world not to make May Day a holiday.

But what of today, seventy-nine years after the first May Day demonstrations?

The Russians use May Day as an excuse to show off their latest weapons in mass murder. The social democrats use it as the day on which to report how many votes they got last year and tell us how they are going to lead the working people out of their misery in 200 years' time.

And yet the call of the Second International remains as clear and relevant as ever. All over the world, working people are struggling, fighting and dying trying to form a society that is not based on a lunatic search for profit.

In Vietnam, in Africa, in America, these people are in the same struggle. We must demonstrate our solidarity with them.

In Britain, working people are being attacked on all sides and are being made to pay for the faults and difficulties of this lunatic system of production for profit. But they are fighting back.

L.B.–15

What the governors would like is a working class which, though well paid, will become another part of the machines. At the moment we are wage slaves, but we are not complete slaves, as the bosses would like.

That is why Barbara Castle's legislation on trade unions is being put through Parliament. Make no mistake, this is not an attack on the trade-union leaders but on the ordinary Herbert on the shop floor who fights for better wages and conditions.

Lined up against the working people are the governors, the Government and most of the trade unions. That's a pretty powerful alliance and that's what we're up against.

Against this background, the London May Day Committee was formed with the aim of re-establishing May Day as a day of protest and defiance. In 1967, 200 workers took part. In 1968, 2,000 people marched through London.

This year we hope for an even bigger turnout, but it will be a demonstration with a difference. We are not marching through London to shout at the so-called citadels of power. Unfortunately there are no Joshuas in the working-class movement and the walls of the stock exchange will not fall down as we shout slogans.

We are marching from Tower Hill through the East End to Victoria Park where we will enjoy ourselves. There will be jazz bands, pop groups and dancing.

As one building worker said at the first meeting, 'My governor is going to be choked when I take the day off. He's going to be double choked if I enjoy myself.'

There is nothing more that the pompous, pious people in power hate more than contempt. If we go to Parliament we attach some importance to these people. It's like lobbying your boss. All they can do is say they will abstain or vote against or jump out of the window. In the words of a wise man appealing is for beggars.

We call on all London workers to stop work on May Day (Thursday, 1 May) and try and get their workmates to do the same.

Let us make this May Day a day to remember. Let it be a day of resistance, a workers' day.

(From *Socialist Worker*, 5 April 1969)

A Day with the Leadership: Jim Higgins

In the last ten years it has been my pleasure to attend conferences organized either directly by the Socialist Labour League or through one of its rapidly changing front organizations. Each conference was hailed as the most important working-class gathering to date, each conference heralded the new revolutionary leadership and at various times the cadre was to be replenished and expanded from dockers, building workers, the 'revolutionary youth', and, most recently, the left MPs.

It is my impression that SLL conferences are not what they used to be. Perhaps time is lending glamour to a failing memory, but the first such event that I attended (the Newsletter Conference of 1958) was the best of the lot. The maturity of the delegates and the quality of their contributions was matched by the ability of the platform, which included Peter Fryer, Brian Behan and Harry Constable (all of them long gone from Clapham High Street).

Measured by this standard, the 3 February conference, held under the auspices of the Oxford Liaison Committee for the Defence of Trade Unionism, was a sad degeneration. The speeches were poor stuff, many of the speakers were distinctly 'revolutionary youth' and a recent levy at that, the numbers were down and the platform speaker who announced 550 delegates should clearly stop counting feet and start counting heads.

Now obviously these are not major questions for complaint. Numbers are not crucial to a successful conference and bad speeches which contain some thought and an attempt to contribute from real experience are always worthwhile. There were, however, only two such speeches – one from a provincial busman and another from R. Hamilton of DATA.

The first gave some indication of the difficulties in the busmen's fight. He explained how an overtime ban that took a third of the buses off the road resulted in far more work for the busmen, while revenue was little affected because more people crowded on the buses that remained on the road. The final decision to strike, with its consequent complete shutting off of revenue, brought the employers to heel in short order. This victory is real even though Cousins's grotesque resort to the courts will obviously squander much of the advantage gained.

Bro Hamilton made a closely reasoned and factual speech on the shipbuilding consortia on the Clyde and the employer/trade-union leader drive for rationalization and speed-up.

That however was the lot and two speeches do not make a conference. For the rest we were treated to a farrago of ill-connected nonsense. The need for leadership renewal ran through the proceedings like Andrews through the alimentary tract. This intangible quality was seen to reside in the queerest places, at one stage it was the SLL, at another the Young Socialists and at another it was being constructed that very day in the deliberations.

The Communist Party came in for its well-merited share of abuse (can it stand much more of this and live?) with some knock-about comedy at the expense of Dick Etheridge, which seemed to go down well with the locals. A new demon on the SLL index of untouchables is, apparently, the 'syndicalists'. At the first intimation of Healy's latest anathema I was puzzled, assuming that the reference was to the few organized anarcho-syndicalists still extant, but by paying close attention I was able to unravel the mystery.

The fractured logic seems to go something like this: syndicalists are anti-politics; the only real politics are SLL politics; therefore if you are opposed to SLL politics you are a syndicalist. As my old schoolmaster used to say, there is a brain at work somewhere.

Another piece of frivolity that had the faithful rolling in the aisles was the suggestion (seriously intended apparently) to reconvene the Labour Party conference. This, it seems, is part of the campaign to expose the Wilson administration; that Wilson can go no further on the road of self-exposure without eviscerating himself seems to be missed by the rising new leadership.

A touch of light relief (and it was needed) came when an unemployed worker told the conference that the only organization to help the unemployed was the 'Socialist Labour Party', a statement that may please the shade of De Leon, but is unlikely to win friends in the Socialist Labour League.

But what comes out of it all in this case is a meaningless committee with pretensions to national leadership firmly under the control of the SLL. The opportunist politics are the same; only the focus has been slightly shifted. The problems half raised and badly analysed at the conference do exist. But the fight against the employers and the Government is not helped by the arrogant assumption of leadership by those who have the greatest difficulty in coherently putting over their policy, particularly when that policy is an attempt to graft on to the actual needs of the situation the special interests of a small but hysterically vociferous organization.

(From *Labour Worker*, March 1968)

The Seymour Hall Conference:
Tom Hillier

Some 700 delegates attended, representing a wide range of industry. Unlike the SLL-sponsored Oxford Conference these delegates were not kids new to industry. Most of them were industrial workers.

Those delegates who weren't Party members expected perhaps that the Conference would give a lead in organizing the defence of *all* trade-unionists under attack. But it soon appeared that some trade-unionists – like some of George Orwell's animals – are more equal than others.

The Conference opened with Bill Jones, a London busmen's leader, in the Chair. He read out the agenda and Declaration of Purpose – but was rudely interrupted by several people standing up and shouting. When the initial shock was over, it appeared that the 'disrupters' wanted to know why a shop steward had been refused entry. The steward in question was Brother Bill Hunter of Joseph Lucas (Fazakerley), a well-known Trotskyist. He was on 'official' strike and had credentials entitling him to attend, but had been excluded on the grounds that he had attempted to distribute strike committee literature in the main hall.

The platform was visibly embarrassed by this false start. Things like this shouldn't happen at 'their' well-orchestrated conferences. You could almost read their minds: 'a few years ago we would have slung 'em out on their ears, etc.'. But, alas, times have changed. The conference secretary, building worker Jim Hiles, proposed: 'Either we let the Brother in to sit at the back as an observer, or he can stay out.' The delegates endorsed this 'democratic compromise'. So much for the defence of trade-unionists on strike, when their politics happen to differ from those on the Platform. A 'Committee to defend trade unions' which prevents a trade-unionist from appealing for support because of disagreement with his politics should consider changing its name.

The Declaration of Purpose was a highly original document. It rejected the wage freeze. It attacked profits and rising prices. It deplored unemployment. It called on the TUC to fight for its own resolutions – including the muddled one simultaneously asking for increased efficiency and productivity (under capitalism) and the maintenance of full employment. It declared its support for resolutions in support of these principles. There wasn't a word about challenging managerial prerogatives or linking up struggles at rank-and-file level.

Delegates from the floor were given five minutes to speak. Being a democratic meeting this rule was relaxed occasionally, *depending* on the politics of who was speaking. Some speakers were allowed fifteen minutes or more, others a bare three minutes.

The first speaker to attack the platform was one Vivienne Mendleson, of the SLL. She claimed (wait for it) that anyone thinking that the policies of the Labour Government could be changed was living in Cloud Cuckoo Land – not long ago she'd have been expelled from her own outfit for such a speech! The young lady then made an unexpected plea for democracy: she pointed out that the Declaration of Purpose left no room for either an alternative set of proposals or for amendment of any kind. Just as she was about to produce more surprises, she was stopped by the platform.

The next speaker vigorously attacked her remarks. He reassured the delegates that the overwhelming majority of workers still had great faith in the Labour Party. Therefore talk of revolution (which no one had mentioned) was out. 'Unity on the broadest basis' was the solution.

The next delegate spoke of the need to give solid support to the brave twenty-four 'Left' MPs who after all had abstained on health charges. Others gargled in the same key.

Several others spoke about the growth of profits and the increase in unemployment – their solution (like the platform's) was a change of leadership. To a man they all clung to the idea that getting the right fellow in as a union official and lobbying MPs was of prime importance. These militants are shackled and stifled by the deadweight of the Party and its reformist policies. They sat like zombies, predictably applauding at the right moment, like a well-trained TV studio audience.

A delegate, worried no doubt that someone might have taken friend Mendleson literally and declined to vote Labour, attacked her remarks about Wilson. Whom did she wish to put in his place? Callaghan? Brown? I glanced at the group of SLLers. They sat silent, but one could observe a nervous twitch on their lips. To a man they seemed to be muttering: 'Healy!'

One old man, white-haired and almost toothless, seemed to think he was at a presentation ceremony. He stuck out his stomach in a proud gesture and told the delegates he'd been a trade-unionist for forty-five years. A great contribution to the conference that was!

The show is never complete without its star turn, and we were not to be disappointed. It turned out to be Jack Dash, the dockers' leader. He denounced those who attacked Wilson and Co. – 'It's the policies of the right wing, that's what's got to be fought!' With his rich cockney voice he yelled into the mike his attack on anyone who dared criticize the sacred Liaison Committee. 'We didn't bleeding well need 'em,' he cried (referring to the dock dispute), 'but they was there and helped us no end, arranging things.' (A pity they couldn't have arranged a link-up between the dockers and the lads at Sunley's or Myton's, but then they had been very busy: a total of three lobbies had been arranged in the two years since the Beaver Hall meeting.) We must, I suppose, pardon the Committee for allowing their 'golden boy' three times the normal speaking period.

Speaker after speaker stressed the need to 'change the leadership' as the only way of bringing about different policies. The parrot-cries 'Nationalize this or that industry' and 'Make the left MPs fight' were heard again and again, just as at Oxford, only this time coming from more mature throats. One might as well have made a tape recording.

The role of the rank and file is apparently not to think for themselves or to act on their own initiative. According to Tony McLelland, Chairman of the Merseyside Defence Committee, the *only* role of the rank and file is to 'develop the power below which will strengthen people like Scanlon for their fight at the higher level'.

Possibly the only speech anything like worthwhile was that of Bernie Panter, who told the delegates that without the help of fellow trade-unionists no struggle could be won.

If the 700 people there had decided to get down to the job of linking up workers' struggles, the conference could have marked an important new phase in industrial struggle. But the conference organizers think that their job is to organize the rank and file into loyal supporters of the 'left' bureaucrats. They are wrong even on their own terms. The 'left' bureaucrats might display a little more militancy if they occasionally saw a rank-and-file movement independent and critical of them.

The delegates spoke of everything bar linking up industrial struggles and organizing the massive strength of the working class. The depressing thing is the thought that the Stalinists can still manage to draw 700 stewards and convenors together to do nothing that will shake the employing class or in any way challenge their rights to push us around. The main and permanent feature of Stalinism today appears to be its utter and complete bankruptcy in ideas and fighting spirit.

The whole affair was so obviously organized to endorse the Party line that it is a moot point whether militants should consider abandoning such conferences altogether, i.e. leaving the dead to bury the dead!

(From *Solidarity*, Vol. 4, No. 12, March 1968)

The Pilkington Strike:
Colin Barker

'The way this strike happened, we could have had the whole town stopped in no time – if we'd just been prepared to go along with what was happening. And it was just so near to this happening . . .'

(A Pilkington shop steward)

The Pilkington strike started in the Flat-Drawn Department, Sheet Works. Around Easter, the stewards found large numbers of discrepancies in the workers' pay slips. When they investigated the matter, they discovered the pay-office had been making mistakes for quite some time. The management promised to set the matter to rights.

But the next week the pay slips were wrong again. The stewards found the management accommodating and apologetic, offering to let two stewards go through the pay cards with the clerk to check the whole thing again. But when the stewards reported to the men on the top floor, they received a very straight answer:

'You can go back and tell the management we're walking off at half past eleven if we don't get the money.'

Back went the morning shift stewards to management. When they came back upstairs at 11.30, the men had come off the machines and the manager was attempting to address them. He invited the stewards to hold a meeting with the men, and get them to elect a delegation to see the management, so management could explain its case.

But it was too late for the Flat-Drawn management. Already, once the action had started, the men were tasting their own strength. Now, suddenly, the word was only, 'We're out for the half a crown an hour!'

The demand for 2s. 6d. an hour on the basic rate had been put forward six to nine months before, through the normal channels, and the GMWU officials had brushed it quietly under the carpet. Now, through very different channels, the demand was voiced again, and in very different tones. The word went around the Department like lightning, up and down the top floor, down the voice-tubes from the top to the operators at the bottom, across to Number Six Tank some 400–500 yards away: 'We're out for the half a crown!'

Even the more militant shop stewards were taken by surprise. Preparation for the strike had been minimal. Over the previous weeks a few more committed men had been arguing the case for sticking close together, saying that if management tried to jump on one section everyone else ought to jump back hard at them, but no one had expected this. Suddenly, unexpectedly, Flat-Drawn was out, solid, all the morning shift. The manager put through a call to the GMWU office, to Harold Norton, the fulltime branch secretary. No answer – he must have gone to lunch. Twelve o'clock, perfect timing!

Meeting outside a pub on the nearby corner, the assembled workers elected a delegation to meet the management, as requested. Or almost: management had asked for eight or so, from the top floor, to discuss their pay slips. Instead a delegation of fifteen, five from each tank, walked back to the Flat-Drawn Department. With them was the senior steward, Bro Irlam, who had seen them in the pub and had come along to see what was going on. In the factory, before they met the management, they held a meeting with Bill Bradburn, senior shop steward for Rolled Plate, and the District official, Harry Plumb. The delegation told Plumb: 'We're out for half a crown an hour!'

'You're what? Now look, I came down here on the understanding that this was a dispute over wrong payment.'

'Well that may be how it started, but it's half a crown an hour now!'

The official and the senior stewards looked shocked. In came three of the management, the senior personnel man, and the managers of Flat-Drawn and Sheet Works. 'Now then lads,' smiled management, 'this problem over the bonus. I've given every assurance . . .' and on and on he went about the pay slips.

And then the bombshell dropped: 'We're not out for that. We're out for half a crown an hour!'

Shock. Amazement. 'What's this, Mr Plumb?'

'I don't know, I came in here like you and now they tell me it's for half a crown an hour on the basic rate.'

Out marched the management, explaining that they couldn't deal with a claim like that, and that the matter could be put to the Joint Industrial Council if there were a return to work.

Harry Plumb just said, 'You'd better decide what you're going to do.' So the delegation discussed, and voted to continue the stoppage till they had the 2s. 6d.

Meanwhile the afternoon shift had turned up, and met the morning shift outside. They stayed outside together. Finally, as it was cold, they all trooped in together to the canteen. There the delegation, plus Harry Plumb, met them. Harry Plumb had the opportunity to address them, but refused to say anything, as 'this is unofficial'. In the view of at least one of the workers, Harry Plumb could have stopped the strike there and then: 'What a goon. He could have got up on the table and told them: "There's nothing we can do locally lads, but you get back to work and I can assure you we'll get negotiations in the pipeline." He might well have carried it.' But instead, a young steward spoke. He told the assembled men that the delegation had voted to continue the strike till they'd got the half a crown. Cheers of approval, and shouts at Plumb – 'Get him, he's never done anything for us.' Then a shout of 'Let's get Rolled-Plate out', and out rushed 200 men to Rolled-Plate.

One of the stewards tried to get some organization out of the chaos. He proposed putting pickets on all the other Pilkington plants in St Helens, to tell the afternoon and night shifts, as they changed over, what had happened at Sheet Works. The first attempts at organization were not especially effective. There was little in the way of experience or traditions among the Pilkington workers, held down for several generations by the combined weight of Pilkington Bros. and Lord Cooper's GMWU. Finally they all agreed that they would meet that evening outside Sheet Works.

That evening 200 or so pickets, from Flat-Drawn and Rolled-Plate, met and a few went up to the Cowley Hill Works. There they spoke to the workers going in and out as the shifts changed: 'We're all out for half a crown an hour! We've been shit on for years and we're not having it any more.' Those who supported them most strongly, and wanted to stay outside with them, they advised to go in. 'Don't stop here with us, lads! Get inside, tell the other men, get your jackets off and let the afternoon turn go home, but don't start work. Get 'em out.'

Fifteen hundred workers turned up for the Cowley Hill Works meeting on Sunday morning. The meeting was opened by Bro Roberts, one of the old-style GMWU stewards. He didn't work, but received his average pay and walked round the factory talking to workers and management. With him were Bill Cowley (a Sheet Works steward) and one or two others.

Bro Roberts, opening the meeting, was very nervous. None of the stewards had any experience of addressing large meetings, and he simply announced baldly, 'We had a meeting yesterday of all the stewards, and we've decided to go back to work. Because you're not going to get owt while you're out.' Had he wished to agitate to keep the men on strike, he could not have made a better speech. There was a great yell of protest from the workers!

Bill Cowley then spoke and told the meeting that in his view they had done magnificently, they had really shaken Pilkingtons. Now, he thought, they should go back to work and let negotiations proceed. But although this was better received, there was again a great roar of disapproval from the crowd. 'Right,' said Bill Cowley, 'we're here to do what you want. But whatever you decide, make sure you are all at Sheet Works' meeting this afternoon, and let them know what's happening so they do the same. Make sure it's a joint meeting.' This was agreed.

Then Bill Bradburn had a go. While he was speaking, a worker near the front shouted at him, 'What's all this about half a crown an hour? Let's go for £25 for 40 hours!' and another cried, 'Yes, I'll second that.'

Bradburn, who really wanted them back at work, said, 'OK, £25 for 40. All those in favour?' And up went a forest of hands! Thereafter, this became the central demand.

The Cowley Hill meeting finally broke up in chaos, but everyone knew they weren't going back to work.

In the afternoon, at the joint Sheet Works/Cowley Hill meeting, there were several thousand workers, and a tremendous atmosphere of excitement. Even the militants among the shop stewards found themselves being abused: 'You union men are all the same, you've never done owt for us. Get down off that box!' And several workers took the loud-speaker, and said what they thought.

'Let me have a go . . . If we go back to work, we'll get nowt. They'll crap on us for ever more.'

'Stuff 'em. We'll stop out till we get it.'

Each worker jumped on the platform, said his few words, then jumped down again. Generally they had no experience of speaking, but were bursting to say their piece.

'Let's get them beggars out at Triplex!'

The next thing, between 2,000 and 3,000 were marching up the road to the Fibre Glass works, one solid mass of workers all the way up the road. At the Fibre Glass gates the mass procession halted.

The crowd opened, with a cheer, to let a single constable in a panda car come through. He drove into the yard, got out of his car, made a great show of taking off his flat hat and putting on his topper, and came back to the gateway. 'Now lads, we don't want any trouble. Stay outside the gates.'

Alone, the constable held the breach, and the marchers sent a man in. A moment later, they saw a worker come out and clock off. Then a batch of men came out, and then a bigger batch. Smiles and cheers.

'Right, let's go to Triplex.'

By this time there were three bobbies there. A steward asked one of the forces of law and order, 'We're going to march to Triplex – which route do you think we ought to take, to keep on the right side of you fellers?'

'Don't ask me, mate,' says the constable, 'I'm only a bleeding hand-rag here. Find somebody with a bit of brass up.'

And so the march, thousands strong, and protected by three constables, marched to Triplex. By now the rain was sluicing down, and there was a great deal of shouting and joking.

At Triplex the workers watched the Triplex men hold a meeting in the yard, and vote to join the strike. More cheers and shouting. 'Right, we're going to City Road.'

And out came City Road.

One or two shouted: 'Let's go to UGB and get them out!' The whole of Pilkingtons was now on strike, and the crowd could easily have marched, thousands of them, to the United Glass works and brought them out too. That they could have stopped UGB, and Fosters too, seems hardly open to doubt. All the next day, according to *Big Flame* (April issue) workers from all over St Helens were ringing up the GMWU offices and asking: 'Do you want us out in support?' Needless to say, the officials didn't. Everything, they replied, was under control.

But that Sunday, so many men had not been seen in the streets since the Saints (the local Rugby League team) won the cup. One worker said: 'It was fantastic, the atmosphere that afternoon. We could have done anything. We could have stopped the world. We didn't give a monkey's, for the rain, the bobbies, Pilkington, the union. It was ... bloody great.'

(From *The Pilkington Strike*, a Socialist Worker pamphlet, 1969)

PILKINGTON BROTHERS' TRUE COLOURS

Bulletin No. 1

Issued by the Rank and File Strike Committee

A changed situation

The situation in St Helens has changed dramatically in the past few days. *Pilkington Brothers have now come out in their true colours.* The bribes have failed to secure a return to work. The lies told to the Press and television have not worked. The people of St Helens have not been deceived. The pressure put on the widows and pensioners has been of no avail. PILKINGTONS ARE FRIGHTENED. *Discipline and determination are needed.*

In the next few days we shall be subjected to tremendous pressures. We still hope to avert violence *because that is not part of our policy.* But the threats being uttered by the firm still produce one answer from us – £5 NOW and *the rest* later!

Provisional Pilkington Trade-Union Committee

Membership application forms for the Provisional Pilkington Trade-Union Committee are now being printed. Membership is open to all interested in improving their wages and conditions. This will be a trade union to safeguard the interests of its members. IT WILL NOT BE THE FIRST STEP ON THE LADDER TO PROMOTION FOR AMBITIOUS MEN as the NUGMW has been in the past. All monies paid in will be vested in a special account and all book-keeping will be vested in a company of Chartered Accountants whilst we negotiate with several interested national trade union bodies for acceptance as members of their organization.

What to do now

We will send in the contracting-out forms. Management must then STOP deducting NUGMW dues from our wage packets. At the same time our solicitor will inform management that any attempt to ignore our demand to stop the 2/6 will result in a Court Action which this Committee ACTING ON LEGAL ADVICE will not hesitate to bring.

KEEP IN TOUCH WITH YOUR REPRESENTATIVE – HE WILL KEEP YOU INFORMED.

Bulletin from Rank and File Strike Committee 13 May 1970

The following lines are dedicated to Lord Cooper, General Secretary of the National Union of General and Municipal Workers.

(You will remember the NGMWU – it used to be the workers union at Pilkingtons. It finished on May the 10th, 1970. R.I.P.)

Little Lord kneels at the foot of the bed
Looks underneath to see if there's a *Red*.
Hush, hush, whisper who dares.
Little Lord Cooper is saying his prayers.

God Bless Lord Harry – I know that's right
With a fellow Lord I never shall fight
For he's so right, and the men so wrong
Oh, God bless Bradburn and make him strong.

If I open my fingers a little bit more
I'll see Caughey's shadow behind the door
And I'll lift my arm, and I'll throw more mud
Oh, God bless Caughey and make him good.

I'll close down the office and stay in my bed
With fibreglass sheets right over my head
And keep wage agreements exceedingly small
And pretend to myself there's no strike at all.

Thank you God, for a lovely day
For long, long hours, and low, low pay
I've missed out something – now what can it be
Ah, now I remember it – GOD HELP ME!

What have we won so far

First and foremost SELF RESPECT

Special Bulletin from Rank and File Committee Sunday 10/5/70

Brothers & Sisters

We have now come to the parting of the ways. The NUGMW no longer serves any useful purpose for the workers of Pilkingtons. Therefore, arising from the general view expressed at last Sunday's meeting, we are issuing the forms for contracting out of the NUGMW. By so doing we rob Pilkingtons of the last argument they have for not conceding our claim, that is, that the NUGMW think their offer 'fair and reasonable'.

For a long time now the NUGMW has served as a vehicle for the promotion of ambitious individuals to positions of management. That is why it has been impossible to get certain shop stewards to reflect the views of the men they were supposed to represent. THEY are FINISHED now.

(Extracts from rank and file strike bulletins)

The Fords Strike:
Jim Lamborne

Now the autumn of 1968: after negotiations Ford Motor Company published their proposals. By one of those coincidences which so amuse the cynical they were published the same day as Mrs Castle's infamous 'In Place of Strife'. The Ford proposals were the first thin end of the Donovan Report wedge.

An offer of £20 a year increase in holiday bonus and lay-off pay was offered in return for employees not being involved in 'unconstitutional action'. I quote here from a Ford management 'Memorandum of definition of unconstitutional action' which defines such action as:

1. withdrawal of labour
2. overtime ban
3. concerted restriction of work output, whether by quantity of work produced, or range of work undertaken.

The vast majority of Ford workers strongly objected to these 'penalty clauses' but, in their naïveté, knowing these proposals had been unanimously condemned by the TUC General Council and by most unions at their Annual Delegates Conferences, they were sure these proposals would be rejected by the full-time officials on the NJNC. The shop stewards, more experienced and less trusting, sent their convenors and branch officers on delegations to their Union Executives to express rank-and-file anger at this encroachment on their liberty.

But Fords called a hurried meeting on 10 February and these proposals were accepted by a 'majority'. Voting was 7–5 with 2 abstentions.

When this news became known there was a great surge of revolt from the shop floor. Les Kealey of the T&GWU, who abstained, was reprimanded in front of his stewards by Jack Jones, secretary designate. Stewards sounded out their members at shop-floor level and resolutions were passed to stop work rather than submit to these clauses.

A total stoppage was voted for on Monday, 24 February, at a meeting of all Dagenham stewards. Halewood had voted to stop on the previous Friday. Ford officials shrugged their shoulders: their attitude was obvious. They would call these stewards' bluff. It was no secret that the PTA, with its history of lay-off and overtime bans, had no heart for the fight, and a couple of small plants, Langley and Swansea, lacked leadership. Friday, the 21st, was a day of tension. There was a meeting of the TU side of the NJNC and it was known that company officials would be available for consultation. Most convenors and branch officers were thronging the meeting-place to assure their officials of their members' feelings. Two-thirds of Ford workers, represented by the AEU and the T&G, wanted new negotiations with no penalty clauses. But Fords had their piece of paper and were sticking to it. The stewards in Dagenham had all the reactionary forces against them.

Let me retail my experience: having heard early on Friday that there was little hope of a solution during my first rest-break I went up and down the eighty members I represent. I reminded them what unofficial strike would mean – no wages, and a complete lack of sympathy from the public guided by a hostile press.

Of my members 60 per cent are coloured immigrants with less than a year's service. I got an almost complete affirmation of solidarity. Then 'supervision' got to work. The hand on the man's shoulder, the soft words, 'There's a job for you Monday. Everybody else is coming in.' My members seldom argue with foremen: that, in their view, is the steward's job. They merely say 'yes'. Cock-a-hoop my management approached me. 'They will all be in Monday.' I told them they would not. During my afternoon break I went round the department again and asked for an honest assurance of support. I got it.

Next thing I knew two dapper young men, foundry personnel officers, were walking up and down my moulding line. 'You don't want to strike, do you? These penalty clauses mean little ... etc.' Come the end of the day my members went in the locker-room to wash. As they went to clock out I stood by the door. I recalled the victories that had been won by them: the number of upgraded jobs in their department; the freedom from petty restrictions enjoyed by a militant department. I pointed out that as I had always had their confidence so they now had mine: and as each man clocked out I asked him to look me in the eye and give me an honest answer to my question: 'Will you give me your support on Monday?' Seventy-eight of them pledged their support and kept their pledge.

Monday the 24th was a cold wet day. In the foundry ninety-three men out of 1,500 worked on day shift. I stood on picket that morning. All the time Ford Motor Company insisted through the press and radio that Dagenham was on normal production. Many people heard this and came to the picket line: some accepted our assurances that the foundry was at a standstill but those who passed the picket line soon came back and realized how false the Ford statement was when they saw a nearly empty foundry.

On Wednesday Ford was still talking about nearly everyone working. By that time the AEU had made the strike official and the Ford lie was crumbling. The T&GWU and some smaller unions followed suit and the struggle was on. In an act of desperation Ford flew to the law. That act closed the ranks.

Much has been said about 'power-crazy' stewards, who to quote one journal are 'bullies, agitators and Communists'. As one of those may I speak of what I know ... the fifty-odd foundry stewards. The majority of these men are dedicated. Each of them does a day's work like everyone else. In his little spare time, he is negotiating conditions, advising on a very complicated pay structure, watching that all safety and factory regulations are observed and, if he has a capable general foreman, always being available for consultation on changes in his department. He must be an encyclopedia of knowledge, on union rules, social security benefits, pension schemes, Factory Acts, Workmen's Compensation Acts and company procedure. To be able to keep his members informed he must attend branch meetings and shop steward meetings. I am not saying all our foundry stewards match up to this, but a good two dozen do and around these the movement is built. It was for this reason that the foundry was solid on 24 February: not because the stewards were 'power-crazy', but because they were leaders: not because they bullied the fit, but because they had always visited the sick.

Another heartening aspect of this strike, in particular in the foundry, has been the blow struck against what little colour-prejudice existed. It has not been lost on the white foundrymen that most of the people who scabbed in this dispute were white, while their coloured comrades, usually with greater family responsibilities, listened, sympathized and supported.

This strike is about control. We, the ordinary workers, want to control our unions. Never again will we allow eighteen stiff-necked bureaucrats to make agreements in our name against our interests. Agreements must be made with a mandate from the shop floor. The floor is represented by the stewards, annually elected and working daily with those for whom they speak.

As the strike enters its third week, in some plants there is a reluctance to hold mass meetings. Some convenors are saying that they have nothing to tell the men ... It does not seem to occur to them that the men might have something to tell them. With my own plant we will be holding a meeting, for we feel that action and expression must be from the rank-and-file and that free interchange of information and views is the cornerstone of our solidarity. We have not revolted against the bureaucracy of union officials to establish a bureaucracy of shop stewards.

(From the *Agitator*, 13 February 1969)

I'd like to Shake the Liver out of Him: Rose Boland*

S. S. Having been encouraged by Jack Scamp's report, the Ford management still refuse to recognize you as skilled workers. Do you see the struggle for C grade (skilled) as a struggle against sex discrimination?

R. B. I do, definitely.

To what extent are the women prepared to fight for the recognition of their skills? And will they go on strike to achieve equal pay?

I don't think the women will go out for the 100 per cent equal pay in the C grade just yet, if they could just get C grade. What we're concerned with is proving that we are skilled workers and the Ford management just won't recognize this.

When we go into the Ford Company, we have to pass a test on three machines. If we don't pass that test, then we don't get a job. So why shouldn't they recognize us as skilled workers?

It's up to the girls to decide what to do, but last week they were really ready for another fight, but only for grade C not for equal pay.

You see, you have to have the support of the girls at Halewood as well, which we did have for C grade. But mention equal pay to the women up there and they don't want to know. They've got a different way of life up there really, up there the man is the boss. Not so much now with the younger generation but more with people my age.

The youngsters of today won't have it, they want to be on an equal basis. Personally I think if a woman does the same type of work as a man, she should be entitled to equal pay.

Barbara Castle herself gets equal pay.

She does, and I don't see why she should hold it from us for seven years. Why doesn't she just say to us, 'Right, the women are doing the same work as the men, let them have equal pay – the same as I get.'

I think the nurses should get equal pay, the same as male nurses get. They do the same work, there's no difference. The nurses have to work so why aren't they entitled to equal pay?

Why do you think women are discriminated against?

I think they are discriminated against because the management employ them as cheap labour. They say a women loses more time than a

---

*An interview between Rose Boland, leader of the Ford women machinists' equal-pay strike, and Sabby Segal.

male, she has time off to have children – but myself, I can't see this because I think a woman works as regularly as a man.

During the June strike the strike committee seemed very active in leading the struggle. How did this come about and what was your relationship with the official union?

Our own union made the strike official directly we came out. Wherever our officials went, so our girls went. We just used to get the coaches out and say to the girls, 'any of you can go tomorrow'.

On the whole, during the three weeks we were on strike all the girls worked hard and they always stuck together. In fact, I don't think I saw my husband or son during the whole three weeks. They never knew whether I was in or out.

When we had the interview with Barbara Castle, we had our strike committee there.

When Barbara Castle said that we could have a public Court of Inquiry I knew there was no chance of C grade, so I just said to the management, 'Women in other car firms get 92 per cent, how about us?'

Barbara Castle said, 'Would you go back to work on Monday if you got 92 per cent?' I said, 'That will be up to the girls whether they go back or not, I'd have to ask them first.'

She said to the Ford management, 'Are you prepared?' They said, 'No, 90 per cent.' I said, '92 per cent or else no talk,' so she said, 'If you're prepared to talk then I'll see that you get 92 per cent.'

Well, we took it back to the girls. They were very reluctant at first to think that they weren't getting their C grade but then we knew that we had this Court of Inquiry coming up so there was nothing we could do in that way. We said, 'We'll give them a chance, we'll see what they're going to offer.'

On the Monday, they came up with the 92 per cent and we accepted it pending the Court of Inquiry. Then again, Jack Scamp wasn't man enough to give a straight answer, was he? He just passed the buck to somebody else.

Do you think there was Government pressure on the Court of Inquiry not to grant recognition of your skills?

I wouldn't say there was Government pressure, but it may have had something to do with Fords. Let's face it, if the women had got C grade, which we are still fighting for, it would have broken Fords' wage structure. There are so many men fighting for upgrading that if Fords gave it to us, they would have to give it right through the firm.

And the men know that if Fords turn round to us and say 'Right, you've got C grade', well, they're going to have a better chance to fight.

Do you also feel you are giving a lead to the millions of other under-privileged women?

Yes. Boots at Nottingham for instance – they started something last week. They're out for more pay. I think the Ford women have definitely shaken the women of the country.

From your experience with the Government, do you feel the Labour Party is still the party of the working class?

I don't think the working class has got any party at all to stick up for it. Let's face it, the Labour Government which we looked forward to, they've just let us down. They're just completely washed out as far as I'm concerned. I don't know what Wilson's trying to do, to tell you the truth. I'd like to get hold of him myself and shake the liver out of him if I could because, to me, he's just put the country in a hell of a mess.

The country was in a mess, but he's put it deeper in the hole. You take the ordinary housewife – when she goes shopping and sees the way prices have gone up.

We can work for a living, but you take the old age pensioners – they've got to go to the same shops as we have to, so when are the prices going to stop rising?

They keep saying, 'We'll have to freeze wages.' It's all right for Barbara Castle, with her £7,000 a year. Well, let her take a cut.

Do you think the working class should vote Conservative in the next election or try and create a new alternative?

No, I don't think they should vote Conservative. I think they ought to try something different. I don't know who else. Let's have this lot out and try another lot. Perhaps the younger generation.

(From *Socialist Worker*, 21 September 1968)

Why Workers' Control:
Walter Kendall

The 1960s are a telling time for socialism. Pits, railways, electricity in Britain have been nationalized for twenty years. Yet whilst as in coal, industrial relations have sometimes improved, the status of the worker, as a 'hired hand', has in no way changed. Faceless bureaucracy has replaced the private employer, at best well-meaning paternalism has replaced barefaced ruthless exploitation.

Twenty years of state ownership in Eastern Europe, fifty years in the Soviet Union, while bringing great *economic* progress, have yet to create the conditions of wide and healthy freedom, which all have wished for. The Russian invasion of Czechoslovakia, because it began to *allow* free expression, is one proof. The shameful silence of public opinion in Eastern Europe, the jailing of the Soviet citizens who dared to speak up against their Government's offence, is another.

Students in Sussex, like those in London, Columbia, Berkeley, Paris and Prague, are urging democratic control of their work-places. Students want university to be more than a degree factory, churning out compliant careerists to rule a new bureaucratic world.

Material prosperity, as the tragic quality of social life in the United States clearly shows, does not of itself create a fuller life. It may only produce a well-fed heifer in a clean and tidy stall and a total disregard for the welfare of one's brethren beyond the pale.

Workers' control is relevant to all these issues. To nationalization in Britain because it proposes self-administration of the work-place instead of control from above; to give men *in the plant* the civil rights and privileges he enjoys outside. To Eastern Europe because it proposes that the workers themselves in the plants shall decide issues and thus end forever the claim of any self-appointed atheistic hierarchy, laying a claim to papal infallibility, to rule on their behalf. Socialism requires workers' rule and this must begin at the work-place if it is to exist through society as a whole.

To students because it accepts in principle the demand for self-determination but at the same time shows it to be part of a general struggle of workers and intellectuals, conscious social forces in both East and West for a common goal.

Yet to leave the call for workers' control at the level of abstraction would be, in effect, no more than demagogy. Workers' control demands constitutional recognized forms, it requires plans and programming. To convince workers and intellectuals that workers' control is practicable and desirable, to reach people in their millions which is what must be done, specific solutions to specific problems have to be provided.

Workers' control is thus neither an abstraction nor an infinitely distant goal. Some steps forward, some erosion of autocratic managerial privilege, can be won by hard trade-union bargaining. Others require social, political, even revolutionary change. Each method must be made to contribute to the success of the other. The outdated reactionary, utopian view, that nothing can be done before everything is done, is not for us.

Workers' control plans to put the flesh and blood into the economic structure of socialism; it is nothing more or less than socialism with its working clothes on.

(From *October*, magazine of the Brighton May Day Manifesto Group, second issue)

The Socialist ABC:
Alex Glasgow

When that I was and a little tiny boy
Me daddy said to me:
'The time has come me bonny,
bonny bairn
To learn your ABC.'

Now daddy was a Lodge Chairman
In the coalfield of the Tyne
And that ABC was different
From the Enid Blyton kind.
He sang:

'A is alienation that made me the
man that I am
and B's for the boss who's a
bastard, a bourgeois who
don't give a damn.
C is for capitalism, the boss's
reactionary creed,
and D's for dictatorship, laddie,
but the best proletarian breed.
E is for exploitation that the
workers have suffered so long,
and F is for old Ludwig Feuerbach,
the first one to see it was wrong.
G is for all gerrymanders like Lord
Muck and Sir Whatsisname
and H is the hell that they'll go to
when the workers have kindled the flame.
I's for imperialism and America's
kind is the worst
and J is for sweet jingoism that the
Tories all think of first.
K is for good old Keir Hardie who
fought out the working-class fight
and L is for Vladimir Lenin who

showed him the left was all right.
M is of course for Karl Marx
the daddy and mammy of 'em all
and N is for nationalization –
without it we'd crumble and fall.
O is for over-production that
capitalist economy brings
and P is for all private property – the
greatest of all of the sins.
Q is for quid pro quo that we'll
deal out so well and so soon
when R for revolution is shouted
and the Red Flag becomes the top tune.
S is for Stalinism that gave us
all such a bad name
and T is for Trotsky the hero who
had to take all of the blame.
U's for the union of workers, the
Union will stand to the end
and V is for vodka, yes vodka,
the von drink that don't bring the bends.
W is all willing workers, and that's
where the memory fades
for X, Y and Z, me dear daddy said,
will be written on the street barricades.'

But now that I'm not a little tiny boy
Me daddy says to me:
'Please try to forget the things I said
Especially the A B C.'
For Daddy's no longer a union man
And he's had to change his plea
His alphabet is different now
Since they made him a Labour M P.

(From *Close the Coalhouse Door*, a play about mineworkers written by
   Alan Plater with songs by Alex Glasgow)

Chapter 7
Make One, Two, Three Balls-Ups:
The Student Left

Look at you
Checking it out,
Look at you, you little hippy,
Your steak ain't no hipper than my pork chop.
Your cadillac ain't no hipper than my bus stop.
Your champagne ain't no hipper than my soda pop.
Look over here,
I'm ready to take care of business.
Have no fear I'm already here,
I tell you I'm qualified.

Your top hat ain't no better than my ginger brown.
Your shark skin ain't no better than my Levi jeans.
The money you've got ain't no better than how you're spending baby.
All I've got is a bit of commonsense.
The best teacher is experience.
I'm qualified.

('Qualified', by Dr John the Night Tripper)

The whole theory of modern education is radically unsound. Fortunately in England, at any rate, education produces no effect whatsoever. If it did, it would prove a serious danger to the upper classes, and probably lead to acts of violence in Grosvenor Square.

(Lady Bracknell, in *The Importance of Being Earnest* by Oscar Wilde)

The student movement of Britain was a puny specimen, a late offshoot of a relatively watertight higher-education system. Up until the Second World War it was still possible for the universities to mince on, imitating Oxford and Cambridge, catering for sons of the ruling class and finishing the polish and arrogance which had been instilled in public school. Varsity was strictly for fun; a comic or intense interlude before the serious business of running the British Empire. The rowing and burning of eights, the perfection of classically parsed love verses, elegant drunkenness, pink silk parasols, and membership of the Communist Party were all possible because none of them mattered. One was encouraged to concentrate on something called 'being brilliant', which in fact consisted of being very rich or very conceited or, very occasionally, very brilliant. The gap between students and the rest of the world was unbridgeable. Socialists were simply more polite to their servants. The humanities were studied as a form of mental arithmetic: to teach the habits of orderly thought, primary sources and good punctuation. Even the study of science was somewhat random; 'pure' physics for the clever, medicine for the hardworking but dim. The system was effectively closed to the working class, most of the lower middle class and the majority of women. It was a private tribal schooling; its amiable, not-so-liberal-now, products still administer much of the higher reaches of Parliament, journalism and 'the arts'.

Post-war capitalism needed more than likeable administrators who could half remember Greek quips. It needed technologists, scientists, systems engineers, professional managers. It required more sophisticated manipulators, ideologues and ad men. It needed a mass expansion of higher education to produce new sorts of intellectual skills to fit an altered brain market. And this required a rapid modernization of the grossly inefficient and heavily class-biased Oxbridge-imitating university system. It was the wartime Tories who had begun, in the 1944 Butler Education Act, to reorganize access to higher education. And post-war economic competition sharpened the demand for skilled industrial and commercial personnel. The Piercy Report (1945) and the White Paper on Technical Education (1956) investigated and complained about the low proportion of the university population in technical education and the imbalance towards humanities and pure science. The Robbins Reports represented the first systematic attempt to marry the structure of higher education to the new needs of a changing capitalism. The economic starting point was quite explicit in Robbins, who commented, commending his report, 'unless we move forward on something like the scale indicated by the recommendations, we are in real danger of being outclassed and undersold'.* Although the traditions of an English liberal education were sunk too many centuries deep to permit higher education to be wholly wrenched round to fit the market's new require-

---

*Lord Robbins in a speech entitled 'Recent Discussions of the Problem of Higher Education in Great Britain'. Cited in *The LSE, What It Is and How We Fought It*, 1967, an Agitator publication.

ments, the very rapid increase in the sheer scale of higher education had important results. The sons of the ruling class became only a small proportion of the total. Universities still dealt with an élite, but it was a wider one, originating in all classes and destined for the middle rather than the top of industry and society. 'The modern multiversity now produces not a thin stratum of mandarins and dilettantes but the most skilled layers of the modern working class. The student revolt is a rising of white-collared apprentices.'*

This expansion of higher education was nothing like as smooth and rational as the meritocrats hoped. It proved very difficult to predict the demand for intellectual labour and to adjust its supply. Graduate unemployment at one end and the jockeying for easy university entry in under-subscribed disciplines at the other arose from this loose fit. And the whole higher-education system was still bisected into the universities, financed nationally by the University Grants Commission, and the high-pressure, low-prestige technical institutions controlled and run by the municipality. The unspoken technological pivots of university expansion were denied on all sides in the name of a liberal education. But after three years of mind-broadening, the reality of job destinations still stared out from the desk of the Careers Advisor. And the practical problems stemming from crash university expansion with quite inadequate finance affected the work conditions of students. They had to cope with cramped and crowded libraries, pillbox student flats and immense cafeteria queues while keeping up the pretence of graceful intellectual living. The new universities, located in various fields near cathedral towns and having nothing in common except that they had all been founded at the same time by a worried Tory Minister of Education, attempted to jerrybuild an elaborate inter-university culture, a sort of twentieth-century Oxbridgeness, based on fibreglass and joint showings of avant-garde movies. But it all turned out as so much gossip in the *Observer* and vomiting in the moat. Behind the self-regarding cultural adventurousness, it was still pin-ball machines and Ready Steady Go that people took seriously. The intense but pointless competitiveness of the modern university is well expressed in 'University Challenge', the quiz game for whizz kids. The sociology of the period, admittedly wretched stuff, records a massive indifference to politics.† The National Union of Students exuded a visible self-satisfaction, careerism was the only worthwhile reason for being involved in it. Student magazines were a catalogue of bicker and titter, produced

---

*Stephen Marks, 'Student Theory', *International Socialism*, 36, April–May 1969.
†See Ferdinand Zweig, *The Student in an Age of Anxiety*, Heinemann, 1963.

to enable their authors to graduate into Fleet Street, there to continue the same thing.

But students have always proved very sensitive and early indicators of ideological instability. The nature of their work encouraged criticism of the conditions of work. At the most mechanical input-output end of higher education, students who were to be teachers in two months' time were expected to sign out when leaving for a weekend, and to conduct their personal relationships according to licensing hours. Student life amounted to a canteen and a debating society. The humiliating *in loco parentis* rule was by now widely disregarded in the old universities but could be rigidly enforced at the bottom end of the binary system. And even the prestige new universities, whose vice-chancellors gave Reith Lectures on the academic community, were unable to satisfy the inquiries their own scrupulous liberalism prompted. The official intellectual ideology was that all questions are complex, all ideologies suspect, all larger passions fanatical. But this painstakingly non-partisan position was actually an ideology in its own right. And the universities' pose of intellectual independence was increasingly compromised as evidence of their close connection, both in personnel and finance, with big industry and the state was uncovered. So not only were students taken through the bottleneck of university at an age and state when their general capacity for outrage and hope was intact. But once they took political action on particular problems within the college they very rapidly began to challenge the authorities' insistence that all problems were administrative and all conflict was regrettable.

An independent student movement in Britain was very late arising. The idea of students organizing collectively over university reform and conditions had been codified in Latin America as early as 1918, when striking Argentinian students drew up the Declaration of Cordoba, which began: 'Up to now the universities have been the secular refuge of mediocrity, the sanctuary of ignorance, the safe hospital for all intellectual invalids and – what is even worse – the place where all forms of tyranny and insensibility have found the chair from which they could be taught.' And after the Second World War, French students, who had been influenced politically in the Resistance, developed the idea of student syndicalism and sought, in the Charter of Grenouille, to make a direct analogy between students and trade-unionists. The Charter's first clause was 'The student is a young intellectual worker', and this approach made the majority French student union UNEF a highly political form. But in Britain not only was the academic climate carefully unpolitical but the structure of higher education itself had been far more successfully modernized than the virtually feudal university systems of France and Latin America. The British set-up, with all its irrationalities, was by comparison relatively democratic, efficient and waste-free. Students were carefully selected according to measured ability rather than class, financially supported by grants through a short university course and had a high success rate in Finals. The hungry student of politics, ruining his sight reading in cafés, always exhausted by part-time jobs and spending years in moving from town to town to gain his qualification, is a classic candidate for revolutionary idealism. The grammar-schooled, grant-aided sociologist with three years in a Hall of Residence and a 2,1 degree is more likely to join Metal Box as a cog with a conscience.

Those students involved in politics until as late as 1966 were either general humanitarians adding their weight to foreign policy campaigns, vague supporters of the Labour Party, or hardened adherents of the Marxist sects hatcheting away in the National Association of Labour Student Organizations. The activity undertaken by NALSO was negligible; its emphasis on working-class politics did not seem to result in any contact with that class, although it did act to excuse the organization from doing much work among fellow-students. The Association only intermittently attained sufficient co-ordination to produce a national magazine. Nevertheless its grasp of what was involved in socialist students taking sides in the modern class struggle compared quite well with many of the subsequent antics by revolutionary students. NALSO was certainly not prone to self-dramatizing vanguardism, preferring instead a rather superior Marxist smile. In fact its interpretation of the first tremor of the student revolt, the Berkeley sit-in, was grudging: 'We sympathize with them as with any fighters against the stranglehold of capitalist and other bureaucracies.' But the skills of Marxist debate acquired within NALSO could after 1964 be applied to the Wilsonite Labour Clubs with great effect. While the Tories were still in power, Marxist students had acted as ideological footpads, able to pick off social-democratic stragglers one by one. Once Wilson came to power, the optimistic illusions that his diffuse radicalism had encouraged were turned inside out and large groups of bitter socialist students moved towards the revolutionary explanations they had ignored the year before. This rejection resulted in Marxist Socialist Societies growing from a handful of experts into the main left-wing university organizations, eating away, at various speeds, the Transport House-supporting Labour Clubs which had dominated the University

Left, with their large if inert membership. NALSO's executive failed to reflect this change, since it had effectively driven out Labour Party careerists years ago, and registered instead the level of interest the Left groups had in arguing with each other at any particular time. As activity on campus grew, interest in NALSO fell away and in 1966 it was, through the indifference of everyone else, and the votes of the Right, taken over by SLL students. In January 1967 Transport House monies were therefore withdrawn and, as if by signal, new federations of loyal Labour Clubs were announced. These bodies, whose initials SALSO and SALUS sounded suspiciously like US Navy nuclear weapons, and NALSO itself were to vanish without trace, almost immediately.

The growth of influence of what had been in the early sixties only a handful of very academically Marxist students can be plotted at the LSE, whose reputation as a centre of revolution is actually out of all proportion to the number of revolutionaries there. In the early sixties there were a tiny group of Marxists, two IS post-graduates, two air-force apprentices who had been court-martialled for their sympathies with CND and had found their way to LSE, a *New Left Review* editor, someone from Solidarity. A Socialist Society formed by them was only able to bypass the 300-strong Labour Society when Wilson's policy towards Rhodesia accelerated the process of disintegration of student social democracy. The Socialist Society published an intermittent magazine, the *Agitator*, held meetings on Rhodesia, incomes policy and the seamen's strike, and conducted semi-permanent seminars theoretically combating bourgeois sociology in a large unpleasant circle in the bar, getting very drunk and pinching bums. NALSO and the NUS were considered irrelevant by them.

In October 1966, the *Agitator* produced a broadly accurate broadsheet on Walter Adams, the LSE's new Director, who had been Director of University College Salisbury. The attack continued the previous year's campaign about Rhodesia and racialism, which had a particular importance in a multi-racial college. The authorities were nonplussed by the genuinely spontaneous questioning of Adams's suitability which followed and fell back on naïve reaction, suspending the South African President of the Union and the American leader of the graduate students for writing to *The Times* on the subject of Adams's appointment. The students reacted slowly, with a one-day 'boycott' in November 1966 and a sit-in in March 1967. Both these were carried out with very broad support fuelled by liberal indignation. The sit-in was moved in the Union by the Tory President, elected in a poll of

1,000 in which the Socialist Society got only 200 votes. But during the sit-in it was Soc Soc leaders, preferring the front porch to the platform, who expressed the real enthusiasm of the committed sitters-in and conflicted openly with the official leadership of the strike. After the success of the sit-in, which once again caught the authorities by surprise, the Soc Soc became a coherent force within the Union, but actually led their new supporters away from College, dismissing the constitutional manoeuvring of the 'Machinery of Government' as 'mere scholasticism' and becoming active, mainly through IS, in the founding of the GLC Tenants Action Committee formed to fight the council rises with a rent-strike, and the Barbican dispute. This shift in activity reflected changes within IS as well as in Houghton Street but could have been possible only if many of the students involved in the relatively successful sit-in had been committed to student politics. Several leading LSE students were active in the Microfaction, a short-lived Lukácsian opposition group in IS named for some reason after a small group of Cuban Stalinists denounced by Castro at the time. At the impressive Marxist education course the Society ran, speakers were always preceded by a collection in a yellow plastic bucket for a current industrial dispute.

Elsewhere in Britain, 1967 was a year of ideological turmoil and political recrimination. Practical activities were enthusiastic, inconclusive and sketchy. NALSO's funeral went unmourned and an alliance between its rump, a leftish caucus in the NUS and the Liberal and Communist student organizers had produced the Radical Student Alliance. The aims of the Alliance were studiously vague, a compromise between Communist students who wanted a mass movement solely to displace the NUS Executive and Liberal students who were enthusiastic about mass movements for their own sake. But this fairly opportunist venture was buoyed up, not by a mass movement, but some very sizeable demonstrations which it got credit for. In the air was the heaviness of general dislike of Wilson, the emergence of a specific student syndicalist wing in NUS's hitherto pristine councils and a growing number of student Marxists. But the Adams affair, the overseas students' fees issue and the growing identification with the NLF in Vietnam all failed to earth the tension. The downpour was still to come.

The academic year of 1967–8 was a short era when local spontaneous outbreaks could initially stand a good chance of success over the matter at immediate issue. The university authorities and the NUS were still taken by surprise by the spread of the LSE tactics of direct action; they were still acclimatized to purely bureaucratic encounters with 'student leaders' when the university's black and the students' white would emerge as a negotiated charcoal. The NUS's flirtation with the idea of student participation in university government, designed to make students the instrument of their own subordination, raised rather than buried the spectre of revolt. In Leicester, for example, the heady liberalism emanating from the NUS and the RSA prompted the Student President to submit a modest proposal to increase the efficiency of the university, arguing that 'it would be of considerable advantage to those committees of university government if they had student members who were to express the students' point of view . . . It is evident that students would have a far greater respect for decisions . . . if they were aware of the logic behind them.' Even the not very radical student paper *Ripple* commented, 'The design of the submission is obvious; its docile acceptance of the administration's dominance makes it quite plain the minor role the union bureaucrats wish to play in decision making.'

The university rejected the memorandum and a Union-sponsored sit-in followed. Its success lay in students' resentment of both the universities' paternalism and their own Union's witlessness. A group of New Leftish students attempted to politicize the sit-in by arguing the creation of de-centralized department 'soviets' with control over curricula, teaching methods and examination system. But this sort of demand for structural change, always dismissed by the LSE Left, led to the Leicester students' defeat and the sit-in dissolving into the morasses of eternal working parties. At both LSE and Leicester, the revolutionary students had ended as little more than a twang at the end of the elastic liberalism of the university political centre. As Peter Sedgwick was to argue, 'Student militancy is faced by a dilemma which appears to be unresolvable within the forces it can control: either to press its main emphasis on the restructuring of the institution – with all the pitfalls of either success or failure in this field, co-option onto the Council or the bureaucratic steamroller; or else attempting to be the spearhead of a revolutionary movement in society as a whole. If it tries the former, it is trapped inside the institution which has more sticks and more carrots at its disposal than any factory management. If it attempts the latter, it is completely dependent on the rhythm of the struggle in other sectors.' The student movement in the late sixties was defined by the absence of a class-wide opposition to the Labour Government in the working class. For although throughout the decade there were sorties when Capital attempted to wrest working-class gains of the past decade from their grasp, only on very rare occasions were the issues of class power which lay at their centre revealed. In general at this time the picture was of a holding operation by freeze and incomes policy while the more subtle and permanent erosion of the strength on the shop floor through productivity bargaining established itself. Students' contact with trade unionists was tentative and mutually uncomfortable until quite late in the sixties.

Student socialists' response to the developing student movement reflected the impasse. The boneheaded sectarians denounced anything to do with students as a diversion from the class struggle; IS students, numerically the biggest grouping, perched uneasily on the horns of the dilemma, becoming known on some campuses for the line of taking students off to the picket line and factory gate and on others for insisting that the political minority could lead mass student movements on liberal issues. The newly formed International Marxist Group, influenced by its French co-thinkers' success in the universities, chose to accept the isolation of students frankly, publishing *Student International*, a bulletin for STUDENT POWER! Maoists argued that one should work to unionize the university catering workers; the Leicester students proposed that their governors should be elected annually by a vote of everyone over sixteen in the town.

The May events upped the stakes of the debate. Students suddenly seemed capable of making revolutions by their own sheer audacity. 'Students; the new revolutionary vanguard,' shrieked the *Black Dwarf* immodestly, though some of the editorial board swore the slogan had gone to the printers with a question mark at the end of it. 'Students of the world ignite,' exhorted the *Agitator*. There was much incendiary talk of long and short fuses, detonators, sultry atmosphere, sparking plugs, sparks and prairie fires. Cohn-Bendit's view that 'We will set up the barricades and the workers will find their own way to them' was of the same dazzling stupidity as Blanqui's statement that 'Communism and Proudhonism stand by a river bank, quarrelling about whether the field on the other side is maize or wheat. Let us cross and see.' But at the time, the atmosphere light-headed with the success of the Vietnam marches and Guevara's imperative 'The duty of the revolutionary is to make the revolution', it proved irresistible.

The veterans of the student Left stood carefully, saying to anyone who would listen that what had happened in May was a brief alliance between rebels against certain aspects of higher education in some French universities and young militant workers, temporarily able to pull in to struggle older militants in the trade-union movement and the mass of French workers outside it. But masses of the students who had been at Oxfam lunches two years before whizzed right past them, believed what they read about themselves in the papers and talked themselves into mild re-re-revolutionary hysteria. Stern bus-loads of militants assembled in a national conference at the LSE and duly founded the Revolutionary Socialist Students Federation, after some hours of haggling about its name and immediately preceded by a very funny but totally vague address by Cohn-Bendit. He had been imported with various rather bewildered-looking German, Japanese and Yugoslavian ex-students to explain about student power to the viewers of BBCTV and arrived at Houghton Street to the great annoyance of the LSE militants. Among their number was a Pakistani drama critic, Tariq Ali, who, although working in the Vietnam Solidarity Campaign, was duly christened by the press 'the leader of Britain's students'.

In the autumn thousands of students assembled at the university of their dreams looking for 'action', sprinkled with a miscellany of postgraduates operating on various sorts of detonator theory. There were American ex-radicals lurching towards Marxism, Marxist mandarins hobbling towards activity, people who called themselves Maoist who liked throwing red gloss paint at Americans, people who called themselves Situationalists who liked spraying sardonic Day-Glo remarks in the staff room and bouncing cheques; all the species but just one politics – confrontation. One spark had set France on fire, so British students devoted themselves to throwing lighted matches and hiding the fire extinguishers. It was fondly imagined that after the bold seizure of a random university building and the subsequent brutal expulsion by police, a political fusion would occur between a red mass of students and a mass of workers of indeterminate politics. A few students could take virtually any 'action', garnish it with anti-authoritarian clichés and some ultra-democracy and then complain about being betrayed. Proponents of the Red Base theory actually elevated students' isolation from the working class into a virtue and congratulated the fragmented student Left on its resemblance to guerrilla warfare. Houghton Street was to become the Yemen of the British revolution, inaccessible not geographically but 'sociologically'. And in a final flourish of mock-Maoism, a body named Up Against the Wall Mother-Fuckers (Marxist-Leninist) and consisting, it was believed, largely of Robin Blackburn, announced in a leaflet to the LSE Soc Soc, 'however vital such general theoretical preparation is, it is insignificant beside the task of rooting out timidity and opportunism in Soc Soc itself during this vital period. Those who reject the strategy of the Red Base and the tactic of the New Year offensive will be in serious danger of becoming the objective allies of social imperialism and social fascism.' Needless to say, in such an atmosphere of torrid self-importance, the slightest hesitation about any tactic would arouse immediate suspicions as to one's devotion to revolutionary principle.

But there was a new sense of what was possible. Students had changed the way they thought about themselves, they were no longer people to whom things just happened. The appalling conformity and petty competitiveness which is the reality of undergraduate life had been momentarily shattered. The student's life of postponed gratification and unacknowledged isolation for moments, at mass meetings or sit-ins, melted into an exultant recognition of solidarity, of human beings' uncrushable ability to climb out of the filing cabinets and computers and multiple-choice questionnaires and book lists they had been put into, and scream, 'I'm human.'

It was in this manic mood that the occupations at Hull and Essex were possible. Relatively slender pretexts could be seized or engineered, the administration could be guaranteed to act with great clumsiness and the mass of students would, now, support direct action. Sit-ins became as obligatory as May Balls used to be. At Hornsey and Bristol years of isolated complaint and grumbling erupted, beautifully. The November RSSF Conference filled the Roundhouse with a real student movement. It also attracted a good selection of the unpleasant, egotistical, the politically insane and the sectarian tyros who are one of the occupational hazards of London political conferences. Discussion on student problems was desultory and local reports were ignored by busy conspirators. Maoist orators repeatedly rose to advocate immediate union with the working class, oblivious to the waves of boredom raking the audience. A speaker from Sussex Labour Club explained about the need to have faith in the working class, like a kindly teacher demonstrating the alphabet to short-sighted kids. The *New Left Review* talked rather disdainfully about the need to transcend bourgeois ideology. Oxford students submitted a blank piece of paper as their manifesto. Another group, abusing the name of Mao Tse-tung, delivered a draft constitution which the Red Army would probably have rejected as top-heavy and over-officered. The conference ended with an enormous Peking fan storming the platform, animal impersonations and Situationalist situation comedy. The chairman's table was busily overturned with cries of 'Freedom' etc. If several people there weren't on the CIA payroll they deserved to be.

The fact that RSSF persevered after that showed how determined many students were to hang on to a non-sectarian organization for revolutionary students. RSSF groups in some campuses replaced the Socialist Society as the forum of the Marxist Left, a precarious office was manned over a sporting goods shop in Fleet Street and it seemed that a new national coherence extending beyond an annual quarrelsome conference had come into being. And it was certainly required. The University vice-chancellors had met nationally in May to discuss the student problem and to canvass new forms of discipline. They had initially relied on a Joint Accord with the NUS but must very soon have realized that the NUS would prove an unreliable accomplice. The NUS's entirely unconstitutional warning to students to stay away from the 27 October Vietnam march, for example, was completely ignored. The revolt itself was beginning to run up against the limitations of its spontaneity now the authorities had been told to take it seriously. As the students conceded, the authorities advanced, and this time they wanted to smash the Left rather than smother it.

LSE, still the victim of its own inflated reputation for super-militancy, became a battleground again, but this time the authorities carefully fought for the support of the student middle ground and the isolation of the revolutionaries. It was no longer possible for the Left to stagger from one freak-out to the next. First 'action' at the LSE was an occupation to provide sleeping accommodation and first-aid facilities during the 27 October Vietnam demonstration. Proposed by American New Leftists, it was carried forward by IS students despite a bitter argument over timing. IS successfully persuaded the Left not to break up Trevor-Roper's speech if he refused to talk about Greece, but students were outmanoeuvred into accepting the authorities' terms completely. The authorities then installed gates at various key points within the building (planned before 27 October) and introduced a new disciplinary code (a result of 27 October). The gates were not only a general symbol of the authoritarian university but the particular policy of repression in LSE. For a week debate raged over them, with the majority of the students clearly unenthusiastic about the obvious showdown the authorities were planning. Eventually the tools which had been sitting all week in a van in Houghton Street were used to prise the gates off the wall after the Union decision, on a re-count and after a calculated rebuff by the authorities, to remove them. Although Chris Harman actually proposed an occupation to forestall the inevitable closure of LSE and disciplinary proceedings, it was clearly impossible.

There was no real basis for the adventurous and aggressive step of gate-removal, although it had to be taken. The Left was not actually strong enough to shape events and yet felt unhappy about fighting defensively. The authorities, as expected, closed the school down and the students then campaigned for its opening after a short-lived 'LSE in exile' in Malet Street. The support fanned by RSSF was confined to a radical minority and, although within an aggressive framework, was essentially token. The Left at LSE were obliged to pursue a defensive course despite the advice of various revolutionary experts from other campuses who flocked down to LSE to denounce its Menshevism the moment anything happened. Gradually the administration regained the middle ground. The Left slithered from an occupation which occurred basically because people were too bored to vote against it, and the recriminations which inevitably arose out of its inevitable failure, through an unsuccessful strike which was really a lecture boycott, towards the heckling of strike-breaking lecturers and a further dwindling of support. The politics of escalation and isolation followed their own logic. The Left was finally proved unable to stop the sacking of the only two lecturers who had supported them openly. IS, still the only coherent grouping except for the consciously incoherent action-faction, were sandwiched between the Student's Union's continual tendency to retreat to retain the support of the bulk of LSE students and the freaks' deep-seated desire to make dashing gestures in keeping with LSE's symbolic role in student-movement mythology.

The student upsurges of 1970, the Warwick files issue and the Manchester University sit-in were on a new scale entirely. Practical activity in support of the Warwick students was taken by a majority of students in half a dozen big centres and a minority in more than a dozen others. But in neither case did a rapidly fading RSSF play a role. It was increasingly operating as a vaguely libertarian sect of its own, defined by its hostility to other student socialist groups. Paradoxically this probably strengthened the actions of Manchester and Warwick and allowed the students there to disperse with the hitherto obligatory revolutionary psychodrama. Increasingly sit-ins had become part of the repertoire of reformist student leaders, neither exactly like a strike nor simply a self-dramatizing freak-out, and socialists had to alter their tactics accordingly. And the Left, though demoralized and fragmented in many of the centres which had led the first wave, was probably spread wider and deeper in higher education as a whole. Important socialist centres were emerging in the hitherto silent sector, the technical colleges like Enfield and Highbury.

So if by 1970 RSSF had largely disappeared and the university Soc Socs were dormant and unable to respond to the spankings that were being handed out, the Tory national attack on autonomy was to revive a far larger movement than LSE or Warwick had ever developed. The strongholds of the extreme Left in the first phase had been shattered and in the wreckage of Situationalist high jinks in Essex, Cambridge and LSE the Communist Party managed to reassemble Student branches.* But nationally NUS was eventually to register the shift to the Left which students had been taking for five years and become a forum for quite general political debate with socialism taken for granted. The remarkable upsurge of 1968, in which the phases of development, from student syndicalism through to revolutionary occupation, which had spread over fifteen years in France were compressed and elided into a couple of years, had gone for good. And the sustaining mythology of academic freedom and a community of scholars had vanished, the 'liberal centre' of university teachers having had to choose, by and large, between doing the dirty work for the administration or finding their contracts smilingly terminated. But this process of political clarification of ideas and activity had left Marxist students dominant in most colleges. And the rest could go back to the serious playing of bar football.

*For an example of the shallowness of analysis and straightforward dishonesty of the Communist Party Student branches compare 'Lessons of the LSE ' by the LSE Communist Party Student branch to the reply of a participant, Martin Shaw. For a libertarian perspective of the LSE Struggle in decline see Bob Dent and Maggie Wellings, 'LSE: A Question of Degree'.

The Politics of Compromise:
Clara Clutterbuck

What's the point of NALSO anyway? The true socialists rightly shun it as just another rotten barnacle on the flabby under-belly of that shark, Transport House, the non-socialists are two-a-penny anyway. Surely, you might say, anyone with really radical sympathies can have as much interest in the present Labour Party as he can in the other side of the moon – both, as Wedgwood Benn says, are barren, arid and dark: they tie as competitors in the race to socialism. So what do we do? Go over to the Communists or contemplate our New Left Navels? Develop the permanent itch of the Trots, or abandon the whole mess and concentrate on digging out the invaluable secrets of the evolution of the diphthong in early ninth-century sermons? All socialists are dinosaurs, anyway, left by the ironic tide of history on a scrubbly beach full of oily puddles. And while we play with the pebbles, the under-developed countries can have revolutions. There aren't any real issues left here, anyway – the old age pensioners will get their mite one day; it will soon be too expensive to have the Bomb; we'll have a fly-over through Piccadilly to ease the traffic; nice ministers will give all the colonies their own bit of flag; profit-sharing for the workers and we can settle down *in perpetuo* to being placid and retired. Or that's what they say, and, after all, the Labour leadership are all nice people who, once they lever themselves into power, can tinker a bit here and there and set us all to rights. As we go to press, Morgan Phillips has just produced his statement announcing that the Parliamentary Labour Party is autonomous, and last year Mr Gaitskell said he would not consider himself bound by Conference decisions, i.e., the Parliamentary group is independent of the Party. So what is there in it for us? We needn't bother any more because even if we wanted to change the Party policy we couldn't. Our more energetic and ambitious members can turn out now and then to traipse from door to door with a bit of glossy pamphlet, telling you all about what the Party will *give* you if only you give them a leg up onto the wall where they can reach the apples. A bright bubbly future; all can gorge themselves. The only snag being that the Party might not get legged up the wall, because the owner of the apple-tree can always offer more than the scrumper. And, anyway, in this affluent mess, who wants stolen apples when they can get 'em free on the Conservative Party Apple Welfare Service?

If you are the Labour Party, what do you do? You *organize* people on images so they *think* they can get more from you than the others, and you have a youth organization to get people young so they'll vote for you for the rest of their lives. But, really, this is a bit of a waste of money, because people may like you when they're young and silly and aren't earning much, but when they're older and wiser and earning more ('responsible citizens'), they will easily see that there's more to be sucked out of the Tories than the miserable underfed Labourites. No, the thing is: get a nice image, write lots of nice leaflets that show you *respect* the voters (even the Tory ones), cross your fingers and hope for the best...

There are ten years to 1970, and in that ten years the face of this country could be transformed – this seedy little ghost, NALSO, can have provided one of the starting-points for such a transformation. We need books that are honest, and we need people to read them – we need ideas *and* organization: there is no time to think in terms of a division of function between 'intellectuals' and 'others' – to think so is to accept yet another variant on the class theme. The task is mammoth, pulling ourselves up by our boot-strings – the Labour Movement stands once again in the position it was in the 1860s, after Chartism but long before the Labour Party. But there is the road, and the only one for NALSO if it is ever to create a real life.

(From *Clarion*, 15, October–November 1960)

The Adams Affair and Student Power:
John Lea and Ted Parker

The real issue to emerge from last Friday's Union meeting is not whether or not Walter Adams is a 'good man' or a 'bad man', it is this: are we to be content with a situation in which the direction and administration of LSE is out of the hands of its members and is held to be none of their concern?

This is the opinion of Sir Sydney Caine, demonstrated in his refusal to allow Dave Adelstein to write a reply to *The Times* to Lord Bridges' letter. In a letter to Adelstein he said that he could not agree that the matter was any concern of the students' union.

The press has reacted similarly. The *Daily Express* on 17 October headed its leader 'None of their concern' and the *Sun* set itself the question 'How big a say are students entitled to in the appointment of University staff – if any?' It provided the prompt answer – 'none'.

It is not by accident that the press has stated such opinions categorically. The issue goes way outside LSE; it implicitly challenges the whole structure of a society in which the vast majority of people have no control over the bulk of their lives, no power over the bosses and bureaucrats that determine their existence. The issue is not to plead that a little more 'say' be given to the majority of us in the selection of our rulers; but that the very existence of these people be called into question.

THUS AS STUDENTS OF LSE WE SHOULD NOT BE BEGGING THE CIRCLE OF GENTLEMEN WHO APPOINT DIRECTORS FOR US AND CONCEIVE OF THEMSELVES AS THE EMBODIMENT OF LSE TO ADMIT A REPRESENTATIVE OR TWO OF THE STUDENTS INTO THEIR CORRIDORS OF POWER. WE SHOULD BE DEMANDING THAT THE CONTROL OF THE DIRECTION AND RUNNING OF LSE BE IN THE HANDS OF THE STUDENTS, TEACHERS AND RESEARCH WORKERS THAT ARE THIS COLLEGE.

(An LSE Socialist Society leaflet, November 1966)

The This-Sidedness of Our Thinking: Laurie Flynn

No longer are we as students in a position to suggest what the issues ought to be; we can, however, move towards an understanding of what the issues are. The divergences in student analyses of the situation are no longer valid, not because one approach has been added to another and then divided by two in consensus amendments at Union meetings, but because the School authorities have formulated their stance. They have intimated that the appointment of a Director is no concern of the students and that the students would do well to remind themselves of this. (It is curious to note that their position is anticipated in the *Daily Express* of 17 October and the *Sun* of 19 October.) Thus the power structure of 'our' School conveys to us that a challenge to one particular appointment can only be construed as a challenge to its overall authority.

Thus the competing student ideologies can no longer content themselves with demonstrating their consumer appeal by the sophistication of their reason or alternatively by their ability to successfully stage-manage and bulldoze student union meetings. They must show the this-sidedness of their thinking. The formulation of the issue is no longer our prerogative, the issue is formulated for us, by the School authorities. Our tactics have to be thought through not in terms of what we think the issues ought to be or in terms of what they once seemed to be.

The Union meeting of Friday last is particularly instructive in terms of the malformation of our reactions. Certainly it is advisable to assess the opponent, but we should never tread in fear of him. It is important to understand that we are no longer the challengers of authority, rather authority now challenges us. It informs us that its authority is self-legitimating and therefore infallible. There can be no challenge to any detail of its authority and so it forces us to challenge it in its totality.

What have we to put in its place, we may well ask ourselves. This is as far as we need go, because this question contains an answer. We can put ourselves – the staff and students – in its place.

(An LSE Socialist Society leaflet, November 1966)

Why We Fought the LSE

There can be no doubt that the decision of the Court of Governors to lift the sentences on Adelstein and Bloom was a victory for the students. By counterposing their power to that of the authorities, the students forced the latter to make concessions. The idea that the authorities are basically on the same side as the students and would come round to their point of view through reasoned discussion – an idea that had previously been virtually unchallenged among student organizations in this country – was proved wrong at every stage of the struggle.

But the situation at LSE was neither purely accidental nor unique. We have attempted to show how the power structure at LSE is intimately tied up with the overall structure of British society. At other universities this may not be so immediately transparent, but at these as well students are denied control over their own life situation: individuals with the same backgrounds and interests as the Governors of LSE are found wielding ultimate power. There is no reason whatsoever why students fighting them should not learn the lessons of LSE. Direct action does work: the monolith *can* be moved.

It would be wrong, however, to believe that students alone can do more than marginally improve their situation. At LSE we have been able to defend our representatives, but we have not been able to remove from the authorities their power to appoint their new Director. The reason is clear. Their connections with the British ruling class give them resources which we as students cannot match. Ultimate success in the student struggle for control over their lives obviously depends on the wider struggle against the power of the ruling class.

For as long as there is a ruling class there will be those who continue to fight it. No one expected such a struggle to break out at LSE. No one can predict where the next flare-up will be. The British ruling class and its fellow oppressors, East and West of the Iron Curtain, are continually confronted by such struggles. On the streets of Budapest, Watts or Aden, in the paddy fields of Vietnam or the tin mines of Bolivia, men have fought and will continue to fight to control their own lives.

Nearer home, albeit in a different form, similar struggles occur. That is why we print an appeal on the back cover of this pamphlet for the strikers on the Barbican building site. They have been on strike for six months for the same reason as the students at LSE: the defence of elected representatives and a minimal control over their own situation. Their enemies are intimately linked with ours.

(From *The LSE: What It Is and How We Fought It*, an Agitator pamphlet, written collectively by Chris Harman, Richard Kuper, Mike McKenna, Laurie Flynn and Steve Jefferies, 1967)

LSE Lecture Guide

It is perfectly possible, and in some departments even desirable, never to attend a single lecture at the LSE. If however you should want to attend some . . .

470. K. Popper: Introduction to Scientific Method. Monday mornings, good for 2 or 3 weeks. No smoking.

593. R. Miliband: Marxism and The State and Society. A little slow but not a bad introduction.

842. J. Westergaard: Social Structure of Modern Britain. Good plus useful statistical hand-outs.

121. R. Titmuss: Introduction to Social Policy. Good handling of difficult material.

839. R. McKenzie: Political Sociology. To be avoided at all costs.

851-3. Gellner: Structure of Ethical Theories, Concepts of Society and Ideology and Conservatism. Always worth having a look at; better 2 years Gellner than 1 Gellner and 1 Newfield.

908. R. G. D. Allen: Basic Mathematics. Good, if a little dull. Better than the book.

Economics, Law, History etc. – don't bother.

(From the *Agitator*, Vol. 2, No. 1, October 1966)

'There's Something Wrong With Essex': Colin Rodgers, Rick Coates, and Mike Gonzales

How many times have you heard people in the University say something like that? We are 'integrated': we are 'democratic'. We have an elected Students' Council and elected officers. Yet nothing happens – nothing ever changes. We're the servants of the administration, and still passively receive education as it is presented to us.

We've got a 'Students' Union'. But how does it help us to understand and change our situations? You must know the feeling of helplessness and frustration that attends anything anyone tries to do in the University. For every minor reform achieved, there are a hundred rejections and disappointments. *Whoever* our representatives are, however keen and active, they are powerless.

In many ways ours is a kind of 'company union'. The University has created a hierarchy *for us*, a complex web of committees and higher committees through which any member of the Union is forced to pursue his demands. *This is the machinery of corporation and not of democracy.* The object, it seems, is always to centralize, to create the inevitable pyramid where peak and base have nothing in common.

With the present framework, it doesn't matter which bureaucratic and hierarchical system we have. All such systems would still perform in the same way. We would still have representatives, councils, committees: all the mechanisms which separate those who make the decisions from those for whom the decisions are made.

We know that the process begins elsewhere and that the University functions in a wider context. It does not teach us to improve our lives, nor to develop our freedom of thought and action. Higher Education in all its forms moulds us to specifications laid down by government and industry. Examinations and the nature of our courses; the grant system and the threat of loans; the divisions within higher education – all these things are designed to ensure that we know our place, and limit us to narrow definitions, forcing us to conform to them.

It is not *we* who determine what our environment should be like, either in the University or afterwards. Control begins in the Treasury; the University merely exercises that control, and puts into effect the decisions made by others, as well as its own. We are not asked what system we would like; we are told what it is to be and occasionally invited to make suggestions as to how it can function more efficiently. The present structure of the Students' Union is a mechanism for ensuring our acquiescence in this process, and our approval of it by default.

We *are* consulted on points of detail. But have we any *real* control of finances, our courses, the *nature* of our organization? These decisions are made *for* us. And all we are offered is a façade of representation; our representatives still remain a tiny and impotent minority who have been carefully absorbed into the structure. The ideology of 'integration' only obscures the fact that we still have no independent expression, no separate identity, and no real power over our own situation.

At the moment we are the cogs in a machine. When people ask, 'is education working?', what they mean is, are we producing enough graduates, and are they correctly prepared? We have to know how that objective is achieved before we can fight it. We need to understand the nature and bias of an examination system. We need to know what changes in courses and teaching will create a community where both staff and students are learning; developing a deeper understanding of themselves and each other, and of the significance of the knowledge they are assimilating. In other words, we don't want to be trained to be new parts in an old machine.

(Duplicated pamphlet by members of the Union Reform Committee, Essex University, January 1968)

Hull Demands 'One Man – One Vote': Dave Collins, Pete Latarche and Paul Gerhardt

On the night of 8 June Hull University students took a major step forward in creating a free, democratic university. We occupied the nerve centre of the institution – the administration building.

The fight had been a long and hard one, with many setbacks. It all began thirteen days before when Tom Fawthrop, a third-year politics and sociology student, arrived back from Paris. Tom contacted a few militant students and an emergency meeting was held in his house. At this meeting Tom spoke of his experiences at the Sorbonne and proposed that a Socialist Society meeting be held in support of the French students' and workers' revolution. He emphasized that if there was ever going to be an issue upon which the Left in Hull would unite it would be in solidarity with the students of France.

A meeting was arranged for Thursday, 30 May. But on the Tuesday Tom Fawthrop ripped up his finals papers in front of lecturers, professors and examinees; it was the climax of his one-man campaign. (His book *Education or Examination* has recently been published by the Radical Students Alliance.)

The resulting publicity made Thursday's meeting the largest in the Socialist Society's history. 300 of us crowded in to hear about the situation in France and went on to discuss our grievances against authority here. Eight demands were drawn up. These included equal executive power for the student body – the most advanced demand made by any student body in this country. Our vice-chancellor has had some cause for self-congratulation in the past for having staff/student liaison committees in an advisory capacity – but we have asserted that, since other Universities are at the point of catching up, now is the time for us to be moving on.

And moving on as far as the students are concerned is moving on to the citadels of academic power: a challenge to the prevailing assumptions of paternalism. If it is hard for many of the Faculty to come to terms with what is at stake – some of our students too find liberty a difficult concept. This accounts for the nerve-wracking days of the campaign – days in which the men who wait for liberty to be handed down, and the men who know that to get it you have to fight, struggled for the soul of the movement. The important point is that the people in the centre of the campaign were 'engaged' in the existential sense of lives tied to the determining of their own possibilities.

After Thursday's token sit-in we were forced to face eight days of verbal diarrhoea and confusion. The 'moderates' stepped in to confuse the issue with requests for negotiations and the 'permeation' of the administration. The failure of the administration seriously to entertain our basic demand, or even seriously to consider it, proved beyond doubt that our only true way to democracy was to show, by our united action, that we could deny the administration the exercise of that power that they had refused to share with us.

In this way we could enforce our demands for equal rights to participate in our own education. Throughout this campaign it has proved difficult to convey the meaning of the principle of democracy, in theory and practice, to some sections of the student body. Our society has tolerated too long the definition of democracy which is content with abstract concepts which deny the reality. We hope that our action may show that the practical application of this principle is not only possible, but is the only basis on which education may meaningfully advance.

We have received support from the socially-aware members of the staff, whose position with regard to executive representation is little better than our own. We are continuing the struggle for reorganization of the University on a democratic basis of one man, one vote – students, staff – everyone who works on the campus, from the oldest cleaner to the youngest freshman. We won't settle for less.

(From the *Black Dwarf*, Vol. 13, No. 2, 5 July 1968)

To Sir, Without Love: Mike Rosen

... for years and years people like us have conditioned their whole lives to passing exams. We took exams because that would help us to 'get on'. To bigger and better facts and bigger and better jobs. And there were people called teachers who did two things: they knew the facts and gave them to us in exam-question-shaped bundles – and they told us that we couldn't piddle on the school field because that would be letting the name of the school down.

Watching people take finals this summer in lunatic sub-fusc is like some grisly *déjà-vu* nightmare to me. For three years we accept syllabuses devised by reactionary old men fifty years ago; eating conditions devised 500 years ago; deans, dons (they look like headmasters) inventing their own little rules and fines (there was a dean in Magdalen who fined someone for going home without collecting the exeat he'd given him); proctors acting as judge, jury, defending and prosecuting councils in order to ruin someone's career and/or life by chucking him out. But this is sickening – not simply because this is a gang of reactionary old men and women putting the screws on. I wouldn't want a gang of *nice* men and women, old or young, putting nice screws on me.

I want to make my own decisions about how I run my life. And I want to reach those decisions by co-operating with a lot of other people doing the same thing. On equal terms. That's student participation in the academic sphere and student control in discipline. To abdicate one's right to participate in the decision-making process is abdicating one's basic right to be.

And in discipline. The whole 'loco parentis' matter is absurd. Forcing people to live in landlady-ridden digs and the pretence that, 'Oh, no we don't know that people f—k but by god we'll make it difficult for them if they do.'

So how? Quite simply you start by saying to the authorities: 'We don't like it. Get rid of it.' They say, 'No. You're too young. It doesn't foster the spirit of inquiry. Let's have a commission. Send your leaders to us and we'll have sherry and a chat.' This just won't do. Students can and must be executors. Not consultants to wary little authoritarians fighting off the spectre of the Sorbonne. Before last Monday at the Clarendon they had us by the short and curlies. If a proctor decided he wanted to punish anyone he just went ahead and did it. If that person felt victimized he had no way of protecting himself. They tried it on Tony Hodges and leafleting. We made them stage at least two big climb-downs because we were united. Victimize one – victimize ninety. If you can't – then remove the rule. That victory means that they'll never be able to behave like that again. The proctors had to argue with us on equal terms that day as they've never had to do before. What we do now is turn to the rest of the university authority and say: do the same. The whole thing has been a massive education to me – reaching decisions in groups, no bureaucracy, no executive committees.

The difficulty getting things going here is of course enormous. The collegiate system fragments opinion. A Union which is everything except a union, summer aesthetes' freak-out, success-chasing up at Bush House. Very few people seem to realize before the third year that one of the main causes for their moments of misery in this place comes from segregated submissive living and studying. By the time they do – they're neck-deep in the exam ritual all over again.

(From *Isis*, Summer 1968)

Notes from an Ex-Pre-Diploma Student: A Hornsey Art College Student

I was conned into Pre-Diploma. I was to be the one to make it, everyone else might fail but I would get there. A grant with my own chequebook, and what a future I would have! A worthless Diploma, no job and a meagre education, if I got a place.

In the second term I would choose a narrow line that would lead me into yesterday. There were lots of us who knew that we were lucky to be at art school but by the time the third year came we would be trying to find somebody to blame. Though now there will be nobody because Hornsey will no longer exist. It may not go out in glory and more than likely it will go out in shame, and it's no use thinking 'I'm all right Jack' because even the innocent are picked out. The world ends with a whimper, not with a bang.

I went to Hornsey with many illusions about art colleges, but almost immediately they were shattered and I was left dejected and disappointed. I strove to go through a system as passively as I could, but being without a visible objective my passivity turned sour to apathy. Yet still I saw art colleges, Hornsey in particular, as being the lesser of many educational evils. Even though I had a place like Summerhill as my ideal. I grew to feel that society treated creative people rather like mental patients, an embarrassment to be contained as discreetly as possible.

In the six weeks of the Hornsey Revolution I had more education than I had ever previously experienced. A new sort of freedom emerged, a freedom to work, learn and develop. A new surge of life. The network system we developed was flexible and humane. We evolved a dynamic house of our own design. A direct democracy where people were informed and given time to make their decisions, good organization without the dysfunctions of bureaucracy, a new language, and primarily control over our own education, our own lives. We had freedom to express ourselves creatively and yet end our isolation from the world, the helplessness of the individual was at an end, we began to realize that art was revolutionary but our aims remained educational.

FIFTY-SEVEN STAFF THROWN OUT IN NOVEMBER
NINE STUDENTS THROWN OUT IN NOVEMBER
FIFTY STUDENTS ON PROBATION

FOUR STAFF THROWN OUT ON SATURDAY

MORE STAFF TO BE THROWN OUT ON 31 DECEMBER

MORE STUDENTS TO BE THROWN OUT AFTER THE CHRISTMAS VAC.

GENERAL STUDIES DEPARTMENT LIQUIDATED

ACADEMIC PANELS SHOWN TO BE MEANINGLESS

NO UNION FUNDS

NO COMMON ROOM

NO REPRESENTATION YET ON THE BOARD OF GOVERNORS

STUDENTS PREVENTED FROM GOING TO UNION MEETINGS, THREATENED WITH EXPULSION

SHELTON ABLE TO THROW STUDENTS OUT AT WHIM

MANY GOOD STAFF RESIGNED OR IN THE PROCESS OF FINDING NEW JOBS

IN VIEW OF THE GRAVITY OF THE SITUATION THERE WILL BE *A UNION MEETING AT TWO PM ON THURSDAY* AND FOR CHRIST'S SAKE DON'T BE INTIMIDATED BY STAFF, WHATEVER THEY MAY THREATEN. *DON'T FORGET – THURSDAY 2 PM, ROOMS A AND B, MAIN COLLEGE ACADEMIC BOARD MEETING – TUESDAY 10 AM, ROOMS A AND B*

(From the Hornsey students' duplicated paper *Revelations*, Christmas edition 1968*)

*This resistance paper was run brilliantly by Tony Carey throughout the effective destruction and purging of Hornsey. He died in hospital in spring, 1973, after a suicide attempt.

Lord Beeching Confronts the Students of Southampton University

STUDENT: Since the Labour Government has been in power, it has ruled consistently in the interests of a small section of the population, in the interests of employers, bankers, industrialists – in general, in the interests of men like Lord Beeching. Unfortunately for Lord Beeching, it has not done this well enough. Lord Beeching would like them to do it even better; he would like to see us under the Tories. In practice, this means ruling against the interests of the working people and this is why Lord Beeching would like to see increased laws against the trade unions, attacks on the right to strike. This struggle between the interests of the people who Lord Beeching is representing here tonight and the interests of the working people of this country will go on always at the expense of the working people of this country until the working people take power – and that means economic power.

STUDENT: As far as I am concerned, Lord Beeching – who earned at some time or other £40,000 a year or £50,000 a year, cutting the railway services of this country – is an excellent, very intelligent, very conscious representative of the employers, bankers and industrialists. And that is why he wants to see attacks on the trade unions, and that is why he wants to see cuts in the social services.

BEECHING: How do you draw this line between workers and people like me?

STUDENT: Workers earn £20 a week if they work very hard in factories and do plenty of overtime. It is not very difficult to tell the difference between the two.

BEECHING: You know, I am a successful worker.

BEECHING: Of course I don't justify the system. I didn't start off by attempting to. I said I thought there was something wrong about it. But I don't want to hand everything over to the workers, because I think, when you've done that, you'll still have to evolve a managerial class and they'll look surprisingly like me. There is a certain difficulty about management; a certain experience and expertise is called for. You don't create managers merely by changing somebody's collar or moving into an office.

STUDENT: A guy who works in the mines will quite likely die early, especially up until recently, from the back-breaking work he's been doing all his life. You're saying: well, we're a bit more responsible, we know a bit more about what happens and we've got terrific mental burdens. But I don't think you're going to die immediately and I think you live a better life and I don't think you deserve it.

BEECHING: You are harking back a bit, when you say 'until recently' all these horrid things happened in the mines. The incidence of heart disease and other stress diseases among managers is a source of concern to a good many people.

STUDENT: They eat too much.

STUDENT: So often you must destroy to create something. It's the rotten system – we've got to get rid of it.

STUDENT: We see a system which is totally corrupt, which for the last fifty years, since its initiation, has always ruled from one particular group. Just change at the top makes no difference – we must destroy it.

BEECHING: There's an air of unreality about so many of the things you say. What is this group that this present government represents?

STUDENT: Five per cent of the population owning 80 per cent of the wealth of this bloody country: this is the group which is being represented.

STUDENT: The only thing I can say about you [Lord Beeching] is that you haven't read any books. You've read nothing, man. You've got nothing up there.

HINTS FOR SPEECHES ON BRITISH GOVERNMENT AND DEMO-CRACY

1. Parliamentary Democracy a myth.
2. Real power concentrated entirely in the hands of a few international bankers, industrialists, and owners of shares and capital.
3. Once every five years, British workers are only able to choose whether they want to be exploited under a Tory or a Labour government. Both Labour and Tories rule against the interests of the vast majority of the British people – the working class.
4. Eighty per cent of wealth in the country is owned by five per cent of the population. This hasn't changed since 1890. Wages may have gone up since then, but profits and the standard of living has soared.
5. This will never alter until the power of the rich is broken. This cannot be done through Parliament but only by the people themselves.
6. It is time for a genuine political movement of the workers *themselves*.
7. The ultimate aim of this movement must be the take-over of factories and industry, where the *real* power lies, by the workers themselves,

and the smashing of the bankrupt, played-out Parliamentary machine and the power of the rich. A government of *really* democratic workers' councils is the only way to replace it.

PS. These are only hints. Please do not repeat verbatim, but use as a guide to your own speech.

(An abridged transcript of a 'University Forum' discussion between Lord Beeching and Southampton University students on the proposition that 'We are in danger of discrediting the democratic principle by using a government structure which is ineffective', with a copy of student speakers' notes)

The Academic Cripples Fight Back: Black Dwarf

This letter was sent to Dwarf by several comrades who prefer us not to print their names. They wish to avoid being connected with a resourceful individual who daubed an anti-exams slogan on a Cambridge pub and is now being sought by the City police.

Comrades

So far the exams campaign in Cambridge has consisted of thousands of copies of six fairly lengthy leaflets, mass distribution of posters, slogan-painters, one mass meeting, meetings in several colleges and faculties, and the 'March of the Academic Cripples', complete with bandaged heads, burning gowns, street theatre, and a fire-hose employed by an unfriendly porter (which burst the ear-drum of one comrade). After two weeks, 250 attended the mass meeting, which, though fewer than expected, was not bad for an exam term, and we succeeded in putting over some fairly complex political arguments. A fair number of students have boycotted prelims and a smaller number Part I and Part II of the Tripos, thus facing degree-less expulsion. This small boycott is not visualized as the end product, however, but as a means of propaganda towards a mass boycott (perhaps 1,000 of 9,000 students) next year or the year after.

The campaign was begun because we saw it as the most valid *offensive* political move we could make. Examinations and assessment are the key instruments of ruling class hegemony in the university:
(1) They illustrate and propagate the evils of university education – single, examinable 'disciplines', teaching principally what is assessable, education ostensibly for a critical approach to individual life, in fact for capitalism, instead of education for a critical approach to *social* life.
(2) They act as the principal end of higher education, and judge the correct status for the examinee's future 'career'.
(3) They are a direct expression of class warfare – 'keeping the buggers down' and ready for mastication in the jaws of the ruling class.

Hence a campaign against assessment is a political offensive on a revolutionary stand: a total negation of the authorities' position rather than an opposition to its inconsistencies (the basis of the LSE struggle – clearly not to be denigrated). But such a campaign, whose strategic aim is to reveal that the strain of revision is class oppression at work, needs a great deal of time, propaganda attacking exams from within the university and from outside it, and above all it means breaking down the mistrust of the left élite and of its often transparent (and hence incorrect) tactical manoeuvres, which is felt by the moderates, potential revolutionaries.

The possibilities of such a campaign, and the importance of the strategy outlined above is, we think, illustrated by last term's events in Manchester where, after a lot of publicity, a motion to occupy until the three-hour written paper was abolished was defeated by 2,400 votes to 1,600. The vote indicates considerable success, but by moving too soon, much of the impetus of the campaign was destroyed.

We would also argue as to the correctness of the demands. A large and politically-led boycott against *assessment* would not give the authorities the opportunity to compromise with committees or continuous assessment, and thus drive the left to start all over again, but leave them with two 'impossible' alternatives: to accept our demands or to send 1,000 students out into the world without degrees, either of which would mean a considerable defeat for ruling-class education. Because *all* students are consciously fucked up to some extent by exams, because the most unlikely people have been working with the campaign, such a mass boycott is clearly on the cards even for next year – given that we can muster enough energy and commitment on the left to sustain the campaign.

> Yours fraternally,
> (name and address supplied)

(From *Black Dwarf*)

Manifesto for a Political Programme: The Revolutionary Student Socialist Federation

Commits itself to the revolutionary overthrow of capitalism and imperialism and its replacement by workers' power, and bases itself on the recognition that the only social class in industrial countries capable of making the revolution is the working class.

Opposes all forms of discrimination and will lend its support to any group engaged in progressive struggle against such discrimination.

Commits itself on principle to all anti-imperialist, anti-capitalist and anti-fascist struggles and resolutely opposes all forms of capitalist domination and class collaboration.

Will lend its support to any group of workers or tenants in struggles against the wage freeze and price and rent increases.

Constitutes itself as an extra-parliamentary opposition because its aims cannot be achieved through parliamentary means.

Extends to all left students and organizations the invitation to co-operate with it in supporting and organizing for its aims, and extends fraternal greetings to organizations abroad already doing so.

Recognizes that the trend of modern capitalism to the increasing integration of manual and mental labour, of intellectual and productive work, makes the intellectual element increasingly crucial to the development of the economy and society and that this productive force comes into sharpening conflict with the institutional nature of capitalism. The growing revolutionary movement of students in all advanced capitalist countries is a product of this. To organize this vital sector as a revolutionary ally of the proletariat and as an integral part of the building of a new revolutionary movement, RSSF resolutely opposes ruling-class control of education and determines to struggle for an education system involving comprehensive higher education, the abolition of the binary system, public schools and grammar schools; the transformation of this sector requires the generation of a revolutionary socialist culture.

Believes that existing political parties and trade unions cannot either structurally or politically sustain revolutionary socialist programmes. It affirms that it is neither meaningful nor valuable to attempt to capture these organizations. While retaining support for their defensive struggles, it believes that new, participatory mass-based organizations are required to overthrow capitalism.

Believes that students will play a part in the building of such organizations and in the linking of struggles of existing militant groups. It sees its particular role as developing socialist consciousness among youth.

Believes that the institutions of higher education are a comparatively weak link in British capitalism, and that the ruling-class field of action can be severely restricted by correctly waged struggles for student control and universities of revolutionary criticism.

RSSF will build red bases in our colleges and universities by fighting for the following Action Programme:

ALL POWER TO THE GENERAL ASSEMBLY OF STUDENTS, STAFF AND WORKERS. ONE MAN ONE VOTE ON THE CAMPUS.

Abolition of all exams and grading.

Full democracy in access to higher education.

An end to bourgeois ideology – masquerading as education – in courses and lectures.

Abolition of all inequality between institutions of higher education – against hierarchy and privilege.

Break the authority of union bureaucracies and institute mass democracy.

(Adopted by 2nd RSSF conference – London, 10 November 1968)

Chapter 8
1968*

A socialist theory finds the causes of working-class discontent more deeply and surely than any other; which is why the workers assimilate it so easily; *if* this theory does not capitulate before spontaneity and *if* it learns to apply spontaneity to itself.

(V. I. LENIN)

An empty head is rather a high price to pay for a broad mind.

(BERDHOLT LUBETKIN, Constructivist architect)

'"We have to be absolutely clear about this," said Chris Harman from the platform of the LSE Old Theatre, as he always said when starting a speech. A groan went round the theatre and Harman brandished his moped crash helmet. "We must be quite clear what's happening. 1968 is a year of international revolution no less than 1793, 1830, 1848, 1917 and 1936. We are experiencing the re-birth of the international Marxist movement after over thirty years of defeat and hibernation." The audience of prematurely hard-bitten student lefties gathered to in-augurate the Revolutionary Socialist Students Federation looked impressed. Harman, although fairly widely disliked, was also widely respected as a Marxist intransigent. When he started evoking the Paris Commune, the Russian Revolution, the Barcelona uprising, he meant it. Militants were to be seen conferring about what did actually happen in 1830.

'There was much rustling of copies of the newly issued *Black Dwarf*

*1968 was a particularly politically unruly year to write about. It defies all attempts to be tidied away. I have instead tried to give a sense of its messiness by using memories, reminiscences, diaries, bits from capitalist and socialist papers, accounts of events and leaflets. Unattributed extracts are taken from personal diaries and tape recordings (including my own).

The year ended raggedly. The surge of spontaneity which the May Events had initiated spread from the French working class around the world. Its impetus was sustained without a falter well into 1969. The extracts at the end of this chapter therefore form a kind of epilogue. For only when the mood of 1968 had crumpled in the audience; the headline screeched "Don't Demand, Occupy". An Irish printing worker who had arrived with a donation of £50 from his union branch was almost speechless with the drama of things and although he concluded, rather unfortunately, that his branch were confident the RSSF would do nothing with the money that would give students a bad name, he was clapped and cheered to the echo. The previous day, as a curtain warmer, Danny Cohn-Bendit and Alan Geismar, two anti-leaders of the Paris students, in London by courtesy of the BBC's current-affairs department, had talked in rotation to packed lecture theatres in the LSE. Both looked exhausted and utterly unclear about where they were. Geismar, looking especially grim, was asked by a Labour Party lecturer, also worried in case students might give themselves a bad name, if it was really wise to allow tramps and petty criminals, some of whom might have been mercenaries, into the Sorbonne. After all they might get up to anything. Geismar looked witheringly at his questioner. "Those people you talk of, they are victims of the same system which oppresses us in the universities. The capitalist system has destroyed those men like it begins to destroy us. When we talk of revolution, it is such people we think of." The questioner smiled a Fabian smile to himself – the man was completely mad, even if the BBC had paid for his plane fare. At London airport the previous day a knot of lefties had waited to receive Cohn-Bendit in the customs lounge. It had been rumoured that he would be banned from Britain. Richard Kirkwood, one of the reception committee, sprang onto a green-leather lounge seat and proceeded to address the masses on the right to travel freely. The right of political asylum was given to Marx himself, to Lenin and to Trotsky. So why is the Government so afraid of Cohn-Bendit? The masses walked past grinning, and newly suntanned.'

Whatever the economic successes of this system – whatever its technological and material achievements – the ideology of this system is bankrupt. The *Black Dwarf* exists to expose this emptiness, to expose

a little, turned in on itself and subsided into mere antics, did the deeper consequences for working-class politics become apparent. May 1968 turned the key in a lock which had been rusted solid for nearly thirty years. Only through its chaos was it possible for (some of) the revolutionary groups to revolutionize themselves, to emancipate themselves from their political ghettos and the self-consoling delights of sectarianism and begin serious, organized growth in size and influence. Out of the sweet, came forth the strong.

the shoddiness and secretiveness of capitalism and the hypocrisy and arrogance of its rulers. To expose its mean and dehumanized prospects for the future, and above all to expose the terrible crimes it constantly commits in order to keep its hold on the peoples of the underdeveloped world and our own people here at home.

The renewal of revolutionary politics which undoubtedly took place throughout the world in 1968 seemed to have a slightly unreal quality. In the May events in France a temporary alliance of student militants and young industrial workers had pulled the established trade-union movement into what was at times a revolutionary general strike. In Czechoslovakia, yet again a liberalizing leader's need to weaken the artistic intellectual bureaucracy was turned to advantage by the working class, who had so threatened the state that it required the forcible entry of Russian tanks to prop it up. The Prague Spring, as the intellectual re-awakening imprecisely became known, was, far more than the Hungarian Revolution, due to impetus from above. But as the parade-ground of Stalinist society sub-divided into smaller organizations at the work-place, responsive to the authentic wishes of their members, so the Kremlin trembled. Although some of the impetus for the formation of workers' councils was actually provided by Dubček's own need to create a counterweight to the very rapid growth of organizations among the white-collared working class, 'anti-Soviet soviets' were once again pungently in the air.

And in Vietnam, the stubborn resistance of the Vietnamese peasants to the power of the most powerful state in history declared to the world that imperialism could be beaten back. De Gaulle, the Kremlin and Lyndon Johnson all looked suddenly vulnerable. It was, as the year advanced, as if a gigantic demonstration of revolutionary theorems, for so many years guarded in small groups and little-read pamphlets, was being laid on by history. It was as if everybody's possibilities had been altered, that a new defiance was possible against the authorities which had seemed utterly to dominate daily life.

Patrick Wall meeting in Hull. Opens with resounding chorus from revolutionaries of 'God Save the Queen'. Streamers, balloons, confetti; all the weapons of academic thuggery out in force. Imperialist and racialist speech lost in the ryhthmic drumming of many feet.

Be Realistic — Demand the Impossible

How can people with a lot of skills and creative energy devote their talents fruitfully? In 1968 there was an upsurge of the revolutionary Left which was not being channelled into existing organization. The Vietnam movement was the best expression of this new approach.

In May 1968, through the initiative of CAST (a small guerrilla theatre group playing to left audiences with an acidic, refreshingly self-critical style), a meeting was called of left-wing people with skills and ideas. As a result they set up, using a private house with a phone, offering to any left group, irrespective of their ideology, their political and cultural skills and started to build up a huge list of active people in the London area.

At this time organizing was started for the 20/21 July Vietnam demonstration. The idea was that the political groups should create imaginative propaganda, and that culture was not for consumption, and that the movement should control its own media. From the planning committee arguments evolved and it seemed that for the Radical Booking Agency to make its own event was to make its own politics. So they went ahead, having changed their name to Agitprop (Agitation and Propaganda – memories of Bolshevik Russia in the twenties). The 20 July event took place with a political happening in Trafalgar Square, with pop groups, poets, street theatre, and huge inflatables.

From this, Agitprop continued in the cultural field, forming its own street theatre group which played at the Fords Dagenham strike and continues to play to the tenants' organizations. In 1969 Agitprop for the second time organized its own demonstration. The Centre Point demo at Tottenham Court Road emphazised the housing problems and the waste of private property. For several hours a street event was held using masked figures, banners, leaflets and street theatre.

(TONY REYNOLDS, *International Times*, April 1970)

'Met an old friend in a pub by accident, cursing and banging the table. "The bastards, the bastards." He had been reading in the *Evening Standard* how Mayor Daley had beaten down demonstrators against

Nixon's Death Party in the stockyards of Chicago: demonstrators as pathetically unprepared and politically trusting as the civil rights students in Derry or the French university radicals. The bastards were everywhere, reacting to the first tentative challenges to their power with a casual brutality.'

Pour a Gallon of Petrol over Your Baby
Set Light to It

Watch it burn. Then you'll know what it feels like to be a parent in Vietnam. Because that's what napalm *does*. Napalm is used by the American forces in Vietnam. Yesterday, today, tomorrow. While they talk of peace in Paris. The Korean peace talks lasted three years. A lot of people die in three years.

20 July is the anniversary of the signing of the Geneva agreements on Vietnam. The main points were: 1. Removal of all foreign troops and bases from Vietnam. 2. Free elections to unite Vietnam by 1956. Among those who signed the Vietnamese liberation forces, France, USSR, China, Britain. The US did not. It is now clear why.

The Vietnamese people have fought for their independence against the Chinese, the French, the Japanese and now the US. They want to sort out their country in their own way. We want them to win that battle. We want *you* to help us. Why us? Because although Britain signed the treaty, our Government is supporting US policy in Vietnam. What can *you* do? In our 'democracy' not a lot. But there is something. On 20 July at 2.30 p.m. we are meeting in Trafalgar Square to let people know about 21 July, when at 2.30 we will meet in the Square to go to the US Embassy to deliver a petition. We will also send medical supplies, bikes, radios, etc. People are dying for your help.

So if you care, be there.

(Agitprop leaflet)

'It seemed to be happening everywhere but here. For a month, I rushed out every morning to read the *Financial Times* reporting of the NLF sweep towards Saigon. Socialists wandered about with transistor radios, listening to the news reports from Paris, hearing tape-recordings of the

CRS charges and riotous missiles. Across the room, the television news suddenly showed the RUC outside the railway station in Derry, the crack of their batons deafening.'

The underlying fears and frustrations of everyday living which prompted Thoreau's sombre dictum are responsible for bringing sleepless patients to the surgery today. Far from being dispelled by higher living standards the same human doubts and disappointments are indeed amplified by the modern standards of impersonal comfort blamed for phenomena such as 'high flat neurosis'. Faced with a problem which taxes sociologist, psychologist and cleric, the physician must often be content to restore sleep. But now more than ever the choice of method is critical. Recent emphasis on the qualitative as well as quantitative aspects of sleep has made Mandrax an increasingly common choice as a method of encouraging normal sleep patterns. By providing a restful night and a refreshed awakening, Mandrax helps you restore to those who need it, the resilience to cope with the changing challenges of everyday life.

mandrax for your
new sleepless patient

(Drug company's advertisement to doctors)

A soft lob encouraged her. The mandrax had hit me and I was enjoying the initial explosion of sensual sleep. Ah that's what her lips are good for. Those parson-nose pouts suited my weapon well. He rose like a stallion and stormed into the back of her throat. She slipped off and lay back.

'Fuck me.' Alright.

She came again and I was tired. Those fucking pissed and pilled-up bastards had started freaking again. Lock the door. Now she wanted a cuddle. I wanted peace. All this cuddling makes me hard again. Listen to the rain.

'I'm licking your ear.' Not anymore!

'I knew you'd fuck me to a standstill.' This bird is obviously a horse, all her good living, baths, regular food, soft bed, they make the mandrax a stimulant. Her head is swaying, her mouth parted and moaning.

'Have another mandrax it's good for your box.'

(From *The Guttersnipe*, the autobiography of the Newcastle upon Tyne claimant-poet Tom Pickard, City Lights, 1971)

'If you are capable of trembling with indignation every time that an injustice is committed in the world then we are comrades.'

CHE GUEVARA

The orthodox left, which had appeared as indomitable and everlasting as de Gaulle and the CIA, was actually running for cover. For a while it was hard to find a Communist who would defend the Party's attacks on the French students and closing down of the general strike, and the Party leadership was forced, for the first time, publicly to disown the Russian invasion of Prague. The Labour Party appeared to have vanished from public places. An early faltering of loyalty was hardening into a deep hatred for Wilson's desire to lick the bootstrings of American power. But the fury and the passion was still close to the phony. The re-awakened Left was always slightly unreal; unable to break out of its own deeply felt isolation with the political forces at its disposal. For although the mood of the student soviet at the Sorbonne and the sheer bravery of the Tet offensive in South Vietnam made quite a sharp impact on some workers, official trade-unionism still had its fists firmly in its pockets.

WANTED

ONE HAROLD WILSON

FOR THE FOLLOWING CRIMES:

Gun running to Lagos: terrorizing and black-mailing British workers and students: colluding with racists Smith, Vorster, Callaghan, Nixon.
Height: none.   Nationality: Scillian.
Distinguishing features: smug expression and a sanctimonious whine.

(*Black Dwarf*)

'I hate the Labour Party because they are a bunch of aristercrats having a good time on the expense of the working class.'

(Essay, London Transport Apprentice, 1968)

If it was a time of possibility, it was also a time of helplessness. For no sooner had the new forms of action been demonstrated – the factory occupations and councils of action in France, the civil rights movement in Northern Ireland, the renewed upsurge against Stalinism in Czecho-slovakia – than they were smothered. Revolutionaries were in an agonizing position. Understanding exactly what was going on, having longed for it and predicted it, and now triumphantly saying I told you so. But they were still unused actually to taking responsibility for their ideas when they become peopled, clothed, three-dimensional.

There are groups of socialist revolutionaries who spend their time sighing for the type of opportunity which was presented to the Left in Northern Ireland after 5 October 1968. Suddenly there was an audience tens of thousands strong, shocked out of its old attitudes, bewildered and excited by what was happening, looking for explanations, asking to be led. The Left proved incapable of taking the opportunity.

(EAMONN MCCANN)

Some managed to give the impression they actually rather resented all these new people becoming involved. A march in solidarity with the French students in London ended in fighting between groups demon-strating, with the organizers shopping fellow-marchers to the police. The largest single march under revolutionary slogans in London since the Chartists was welcomed at Hyde Park by representatives of the Socialist Labour League, who handed out a message from their Central Committee explaining they were refusing to have anything to do with a march in solidarity with the Vietnamese revolution because it had been organized by 'Fleet Street paper tigers'. But even if the vanguard had not yet noticed it, a revival of Marxism and a forced rejuvenation of revolutionary politics was abroad. A political Pandora's box had been opened, and ideas which had been tidied away out of politics for forty years were in the air again.

Why the Socialist Labour League is not marching

The 27 October demonstration organized by the Vietnam Solidarity Campaign has been transformed by the capitalist press, the BBC and television into an orgy of inflated publicity for a number of nondescript leaders whose record of struggle against the employers, the labour bureaucracy and the government on behalf of the working class is nil.

During the eighteen months' campaign against the Prices and Incomes Act becoming law they were nowhere to be seen except perhaps hiding out in the tired, dwindling ranks of Stalinism.

Taking advantage of the suffering and persecution by American imperialism of the Vietnamese workers and peasants, these relatively unknown people have been overnight transformed by the press lords and the mass media into the most over-publicized paper tigers in the Fleet Street zoo.

Naturally, when confronted with such 'opponents', the Home Secretary, Mr Callaghan, can well afford to put up a show of 'fair play' by the police.

This is just a diversion for whitewashing the authorities. After deliberately building up the VSC 'phonies', they now generously offer 'democratic rights' as if people such as Tariq Ali threaten anything or anybody.

Those many well-meaning students who march on the demonstration should take note that the whole thing is deliberately publicized in order to whitewash the police and, at the same time, engage students and others in the kind of irrelevant protest activity which separates them from the working class . . .

The Socialist Labour League refuses on these grounds to participate in the demonstration. Our task is to direct all young workers and students towards serious consideration for the theory and role of Trotskyism and the Fourth International towards the building of the revolutionary party . . .

(Socialist Labour League pamphlet, 25 October 1968)

*

But in Britain, the new English Jacobins who solidarized with the Vietnamese revolutionaries, who flew over to Paris and who pasted over their bathroom mirror Che's imperative injunction 'The duty of a revolutionary is to make the revolution', were troubled. While events in foreign parts sprouted wild plumage, the struggles in Britain were a determined mufti. The brightly coloured Cuban posters and the visionary eyes of Guevara which stared out of so many bathrooms didn't quite fit with the bus queues and grumbling of a British working class still much closer to Wilson and the World Cup than shoot-ups in Mexico City and gun-downs in Bolivia.

What must be emphasized and re-emphasized is the immense gulf that separates the working class's revolutionary potential and our revolutionary ideas. There are no short cuts to overcoming this. No amount of verbal euphoria or frenetic activism will do this – especially if confined to the university ghetto. What is required is not the heroic gesture or the symbolic confrontation (any more than the perfect resolution); nor is it vicarious participation in the self-activity of others (whether they be in Hanoi or Paris); rather we have to be where the various sections of the working class are as they begin to work out new ways of dealing with the new problems, in the factories, in the unions, in the estates and the localities, criticizing existing ideas and the conceptions of action that flow from them, suggesting alternatives and linking these to a coherent revolutionary socialist world view. The task is not easy or glamorous: but without it the fire next time can still sputter out.

('1968 – The Ice Cracks', *International Socialism*)

Group Working

For speed, it's a good idea to have one person operating the squeegee (who will also lift the screen at the end of each pull), someone removing the prints, and a chain of others passing the prints to the drying rack, which can't always be close to the printing table. Have sufficient ink mixed ready for length of run (especially if same colour is important). Keep stock of paper handy to put new pile under screen.

(Agitprop 'How To Do It' manual)

Early AGITPROP Event

'Somehow sponsored by the unlikely YCL to send white bicycles to Vietnam but with heavy hippy overtones like Pete Brown audible from 500 yards and still incomprehensible at five yards, and Mike Farren bawling something about 'the revolution isn't just about Vietnam – it's about being able to go out in the evening and have a good screw without having any hang-ups' or something equally unconvincing. Gentle singing by the audience of

> "Do, do, do, do, do you remember
> Gro, Gro, Gro, Gro Grosvenor Square?"

A laughing and sniggering policeman drawing a penknife to start slashing and lunging at a large inflatable. A small puppet box to which all the left-wing groups had been invited to send spokesmen. Sure, sure, Tony Cliff had said, but the only one to turn up was the mad Maoist, Adolpho, who refused to get into the puppet box and predictably began to denounce the whole proceedings. "Very imaginative for the YCL," thought next week's *Freedom*, the anarchist paper. The coconut shy made up of US soldiers carefully constructed in the Agitprop studio in Islington got lost, and the organizer appeared to have collapsed somewhere in Piccadilly from a poisonous boil in her calf.'

This chronicle is a day and night journal of the squat at Ilford. We want to make it an objective and authentic record of all that is happening, for this particular squat has an immediate and we hope historic importance.

It is a struggle which the families of this neighbourhood must be aware of. As we write the day-to-day diary, copies will be left at every door on Woodlands Road, Ilford, so that people will know every stage of our action and be able to follow every phase of our thoughts.

We are writing this by a roaring wood fire. Candles flicker on the mantelpiece, as we have no electricity. We moved in on 21 June 1969.

We have since replaced the floorboards on the top floor. We have left the open joists below and made the house impregnable from any assault other than artillery from air or ground. Our intention was and still is to repair this building and to hand it over to a family in need. We made no decision who this family should be and wanted no payment for our work. We could have finished our job in another week. But the Council acted swiftly. They hired a gang of known thugs, Mr Barry Quartermain's private detective agency, to violently evict us from this house and to stop us doing our work. Quartermain came, whooping, hollering, leading his cronies with stones and iron bars. We were ready. Quartermain did not succeed. He will come back, perhaps again and again. But we will always be ready.

We are squatting occupiers, and not trespassers, according to both ancient and common law handed down by previous generations. The bit of ground we hold now is protected not only by law but by a common feeling that there should be land available to all. Our neighbours on Woodlands Road are aware of this. We want to thank them for their support. They have given us supplies, bread, butter, coffee, and more than a few warm words.

Now it is quiet in this room. People are hunched up in sleeping bags on the floor from wall to wall. The only sound is the spitting and gurgling of the fire. A few squatters stand by the window keeping guard, smoking, thinking. They have come from all over London to help in the struggle. This is the sixth day of the siege. We have repulsed the attackers Monday and Wednesday. It seems they need an intervening day to lick their wounds. A chill breeze whips in through the paneless windows, shattered by the Bailiffs. We huddle closer together around the fire and silently wonder whether they will come tomorrow.

('The Squatters', *International Times*, 60, 18 July)

Undoubtedly the intellectuals were registering a shift which was to open gaps wide in working-class life in the seventies, but in 1968 talk of general strikes and the coming battles was unreal. The set-piece confrontations between labour and capital which were to dominate the first three years of Tory Government, though near, were still far off. In 1968 the engineers' union carefully backed down from the national strike which had been mooted for October, almost as if to deny the connection between the gigantic Vietnam March and the emerging working-class industrial militancy. The lefty films and magazines of the time harked on the distance still to be crossed, the ironies of the revival of the revolutionary movement in the West, the torment and guilt of the middle-class revolutionary. Films like *Far From Vietnam* and *US* screamed with the pain of not being in pain. Magazines started up with titles like *Only Connect, Thinking is Linking, Escalate* – as if to bridge the gap by mental agility alone. The RSSF produced an incendiary poster 'Students of the World IGNITE'. The *New Left Review*, now a small coterie of expensively educated intellectuals specializing in a Marxism of a kind, or rather after a fashion, which prided itself on its utter non-involvement with socialist activity, invented a theory about red bases which sought to congratulate left-wing universities on their similarity to peasant guerrillas and elevate their isolation into a tremendous virtue. There was a rise of cultural, or rather anti-cultural, activism with the sudden revival of a propagandist art of posters and street plays and public readings themselves desirous of explaining how sensible revolutionary ideas actually were. Agitprop, Cinema Action, Poster Workshop, the *Black Dwarf*, all stemmed from the desperate desire to communicate the intensity of the possibilities suddenly released. What can only be seen now as a colossal and wonderful spasm of ultra-leftism ricocheted around the world, where exhilaration and bathos kept bumping into each other.

Everyone was just starting to settle in/talking to each other/thinking about the coming night's playful exploration of the desolate academic labyrinth *when the platform bureaucrats took over finally and irrevocably*. From then on imagination and creativity were out. Frozen talk/frozen responses were the rule – hecklers mauled – the lot. A tyrannical discussion (speaker versus audience) followed, providing the framework for the professional revolutionary to enact the parliamentary power game and administer in the safest way possible the functioning of the building. Lenin's little homily was pasted up . . . 'guard as the apple of your eye your tools etc.' therefore 'guard the LSE etc.' – a statement which may have been relevant fifty years ago but which is desperately inappropriate to technological regression and the conditions of a claustrophobic consumerism. What do we want to guard . . . teaching as a commodity totally removed from life? No one suggested fighting against the irrelevancy of what they were being taught – maybe burning a few files, facts, statistics or whatever. Instead we were entertained with seminars. 'The sociology of the revolution' etc. (WOW!) *We* were occupied – by the phantoms of an alienated education system – the situation was created in the name of revolution and yet the relationships, language, and bodies were the reincarnation of the authoritarian ghosts who have buggered us all once already. How often must it be said that any true expression of a revolutionary libido *now* must necessarily involve a subversion of the 'tools': tools devoted today largely to the creation and maintenance of false needs and desires. A building as dry and cold as LSE under such revolutionary circumstances would be radically deranged, charred, fucked etc. in the process of cathecting with a liberated psyche ... On reflection, this may have been *deep down* what the Committee of Public Safety feared ... perhaps they too realize soccer hooligans are the most militant group within the British working class.

(Situationalist diatribe, LSE 1968 Vietnam Occupation)

I used to do a great deal of travelling round the universities. I virtually packed it in two years ago when I had rather an unpleasant experience at Essex University, at their so-called Revolutionary Be-In. I regard this as being my personal failure, not what they were like, but my sudden slump afterwards. Well, you know, fuck it, if they don't want to talk, if they just want to have 'happenings' and scrawl slogans from Plekhanov to Régis Debray all over the walls and burn a car in the campus ... One lad came up to me – I was with John Arden – and they threw this smoke-bomb in the auditorium, and this kid said, 'That is a more meaningful event than anything either Arden or you could say.' So Arden diffidently said, 'What does it mean then?' and he replied, 'It means what it means, man.' Arden and I rather shiftily ambled out.

(DAVID MERCER, *Theatre Quarterly*, 1973)

WELL, LET'S GET DOWN TO DISCUSSING NEXT YEAR'S STRATEGY ... SOME COMRADES HAVE PRODUCED THIS PAPER 'TOWARDS TOTAL STRATEGY '...

We can't start talking about that until we know who the chairman and secretary are.

CAN WE HAVE A LITTLE ORDER PLEASE?

There are three criticisms I would like to make of this paper. At the top it says 'Abstract', and that seems fairly true of the whole paper. The second criticism is that it doesn't mention ... and the third is that ...

SHUT UP!

We've read your thing, so why shouldn't you listen to him?

BECAUSE HE'S BORING!

(*General confusion, disconnected voices from numerous parts of the hall*)

The dialectic is the only myth we have and we mustn't misuse it. This is OK but it's worthless, in its own terms it's OK, but the terms are useless.

It's all a question of language.

Well, what do you want to say about language?

Man, it's all fucking dialectic – movement – verbs and nouns and things.

WHAT YOU SHOULD HAVE SAID IN YOUR PAPER, I MEAN, THE REAL TROUBLE WITH IT IS THAT IF YOU WANTED TO SAY ANYTHING YOU SHOULD HAVE TALKED ABOUT YOURSELVES, HOW YOU WORKED TOGETHER ... THIS WOULD HAVE BEEN FANTASTIC A YEAR AGO BUT IT'S OUT OF DATE NOW.

Why do you think it's important to walk on the grass?

WHY DON'T YOU WALK ON THE FUCKING GRASS?

Well, what's the fucking grass got to do with it?

BECAUSE THEY'RE GETTING AT YOUR MIND ... WHEN YOU FIRST COME HERE YOU THINK IT'S A DRAG. BUT AFTER THREE WEEKS YOU'RE USED TO IT...SO...

Stealing. I don't see what stealing's got to do with revolution. Theft is only the mirror image of capitalist acquisition. It just depends what you're knocking off and what you're using it for.

THE REAL TROUBLE WITH YOUR PAPER IS THAT YOUR TURGID NLR LANGUAGE DENIES EVERYTHING THAT YOU'RE TRYING TO SAY.

You couldn't tell the difference between revolution and the back of a bus, that's what socialism's about, the difference between cars and buses.

We must make sure we go round all the local factories, to explain to the workers what the student revolt is about.

LOOK MAN, YOU CAN'T TALK TO THE WORKERS WITHOUT ANY SELF-RESPECT.

Can we have one person speaking at a time. You can't have a meeting when everyone's trying to speak at once.

WHEN I GO DOWN TO THE ADDENBROOKES BUILDING SITE AND I TALK TO THE WORKERS THERE AND THEY TALK ABOUT THEIR EXPERIENCE OF STRUGGLE AND I TALK ABOUT MY EXPERIENCE OF STRUGGLE AS A STUDENT AND I THINK THAT'S ALRIGHT. ISN'T IT?

Sure, man.

That's a load of shit.

What we need is a good issue.

Why don't we have another campaign on the Town Council.

There was a lot of us, and we decided to have a competition to see who was the most freaky, and I was the second most freakiest!

I MAY BE THICK, BUT ALL I KNOW IS THAT THERE WAS A GUY CALLED MARX AND HE WROTE A BOOK CALLED 'CAPITAL', AND THAT MEANS MORE TO ME THAN ALL THIS CRAP.

We must develop course critiques in the faculties.

Nobody could give a fuck about course critiques. Bourgeois historical scholarship is only one stage worse than Marxist historical scholarship. It's all a load of shit. Cambridge history is about historical scholarship. It should be about historical consciousness. That is understanding ourselves as historical individuals and becoming aware of history in those terms.

YOU'RE TALKING ABOUT COURSE CRITIQUES AS ACADEMIC PRODUCTS, COMPLETE AND CONTAINED IN THEMSELVES, AS WRITTEN ON PIECES OF PAPER, AND WE'RE TALKING ABOUT LIVING COURSE CRITIQUES, OUR IDEAS IN ACTION – GROUP EDUCATION.

That was why the exams campaign was a failure, there wasn't enough theory, research behind it.

SOME FAILURE, EVERYONE'S TALKING ABOUT IT AND HAVING TO JUSTIFY THEMSELVES.

There are only two women here and they're both on the same side, so they're bound to win.

Look comrade, you don't understand the principles of Marxism-Leninism, where's your analysis?

We've got to talk about organization, we've got to get organized.

LOOK AT THE EXPERIENCE OF SOC. SOC.

NO! NO! No horror stories mate!

You don't have to have a long face to be serious.

After the revolution you'd put us all in concentration camps, and you'd be the camp commander, wouldn't you?

ALL THIS IS ALL VERY WELL. BUT WE'VE GOT TO THINK ABOUT THIS WHOLE CAPITALIST SOCIETY, THE WORKING CLASS COULDN'T GIVE A DAMN ABOUT YOUR HANG-UPS.

What you guys needs is a trip and a fuck. When did you last have a fuck?

What the hell has fucking got to do with socialism?

WHAT HAPPENED IN FRANCE HAPPENED BECAUSE SOME GUYS FELT THAT THEY DIDN'T LIKE BEING TOLD WHEN THEY COULD AND WHEN THEY COULDN'T HAVE A FUCK.

NO, CAN'T YOU SEE THAT THE CONCRETE REALITY IS THE CAPITALIST SOCIETY, AND STARVATION, AND WORKERS GETTING EXPLOITED ...

But that's not immediate to our situation and we've got to work from our own situation.

But students are a grossly overprivileged group.

NO WE'RE FUCKING WELL NOT. IT'S JUST THAT WE'RE RE-PRESSED DIFFERENTLY.

What do you mean, you're repressed?

I MEAN, I KNOW WHAT I'M MEANT TO BE, WHAT THEY WANT
ME TO BE, AND I KNOW THAT I DON'T WANT TO BE IT, AND
THAT FUCKS YOU UP BEFORE YOU CAN EVEN START TO THINK
ABOUT ANYTHING ELSE. THEY'RE DENYING MY FREEDOM, MAN,
JUST LIKE THEY DENY THE WORKERS' FREEDOM, BUT IN A
DIFFERENT WAY . . .

. . . and that's why so many people crack up, and that's why the mental
hospitals are full, man, because people are forced into stereotypes by
this system, and they can't take it.

It's all quite simple, you see, this side of the room wants to be liberated
and the other side wants to liberate someone . . . so why don't you get
together. All you've got to do is smash the right, get a backlash, and
there you are.

Oh man, it's not as though there were two sides, the situation we're in
affects the emphasis of our politics, it's not enough to take up a position
blindly.

WE'VE BEEN TALKING FOR THREE HOURS NOW, AND WE
HAVEN'T MADE A SINGLE DECISION ABOUT WHAT WE'RE GOING
TO DO NEXT YEAR.

Yes we have, we've arranged six meetings, and we've had some elections.

So what about this theoretical magazine?

(Transcript of a Cambridge Revolutionary Socialist Student Federation
meeting, 1968)

General Meeting, Second Meeting on the Camp Itself

The specific 'provocation' for this meeting was the removal of the
ladies' toilet tent in order to erect it as a communal meeting place,
instead of meeting, as had hitherto been the case in the evening, either
around the fire if it was dry, or in the café if wet. This removal was
done *without reference to the wishes of any kind of general meeting*, on
the purely individual initiative of a few comrades. In this apparently
trivial affair (though not, no doubt, to the ladies!), there was at least
one important principle – whether decisions regarding the camp could
or should be taken on purely individual initiative without reference to
the rest of the camp. Other incidents which needed discussion were the
non-payment of camping fees by certain friends and also an outbreak

of 'stealing' ... and whether the latter was in fact possible in an 'anarchist' camp! The suggestion was made that all property should be pooled for the duration of the camp – after some discussion this idea was rejected with some reluctance as being impractical given that everyone would have to return home at the end of the camp and either returning with different gear, or the problem of having to sort out, i.e. decommunalize, gear at the end of the camp would prove extremely inconvenient not to say impossible. There was also discussion on the mundane everyday affairs of running the camp, especially with regard to the fact that the same people were doing the work all the time, or seemed to be. It was suggested that the most vocal critics of the administration of the camp never did anything anyway ...

Discussion at this point hopped from one topic to another so quickly that, while many useful points were raised, no decisions were made on any of them. Though perhaps this did not really matter and was even, perhaps, all to the good.

(From *A Report of Speeches and Discussions from the Anarchist Summer Camp, Cornwall, England, 1969*, a Kropotkin Lighthouse Publication)

'A tool for counter-information, at the service of the class struggle: solidarity with industrial, student and tenant strikers, and liberation fronts all over the world. You are invited to participate with information, ideas, slogans, archetypes, designs, and the actual printing of the posters in silk screen. The projects will be voted upon by the assembly on the spot.'

This 'manifesto', which was the first thing to appear on the walls of the Poster Workshop, describes the essence of the activities of our studio at 61 Camden Road, London NW1. Groups for whom the workshop has made posters include: Dozens of tenants' associations, nurses, many squatters groups, Angry Arts, 'community action groups', Bernadette Devlin, several strikes such as Fords, Black Arts Group, Anti-Apartheid, many colleges and universities, many Vietnam posters, Agitprop, Stop-It, Left Convention, several left periodicals such as *Black Dwarf*, CP and YCL, PAC and ANC, UCPA, Biafra, various boycotts, firemen, Open Films, Persia, Régis Debray (except he doesn't know it), King Mob, Schools Action Union, Anguilla, Royal Group of Docks Campaign, Spain, Greece, etc. We have also helped many demonstrations which would have looked depressingly bare had it not been for the fact that the Poster Workshop produced placards: 1,500 for example, for 27 October last year.

The workshop also makes general agitational posters, e.g. 'We Are All Foreign Scum', 'Unite Against Imperialism', and some against the White Paper. We distribute these through as many contacts as we can.

(*Black Dwarf*, July 1970)

'In your work, you're just a nameless number'

(France, May 1968)

Only it wasn't quite so simple

I have been a socialist all my life since the age of fourteen. I know a little at first hand about revolution and I lost an eye fighting Fascism. Socialism to me means a society where people are no longer crippled and depraved emotionally and morally by the pressures of capitalism, and where for the first time human relationships will be honest, open and moral in the real sense of that word.

In your Vietnam issue you devote space to some doggerel by Mick Jagger, an unfortunate nothing whom the world could do well without, and more disgusting still, you couple his name on your front page alongside Marx and Engels; something which will surely make any sincere socialist want to vomit.

Almost as bad as this, you waste valuable space on a letter of condolence to John Lennon as if this poor confused drug experimenter was of any importance in the fight for socialism.

The private standards of individuals are most certainly their own affairs but do not debase a noble cause by enlisting the 'help' of amoral bums, looking for a cheap band-wagon. The great revolutionaries of history, men like Conolly, Lenin and Trotsky, and the humble people too, such as the Spanish anarchists, were shining examples of integrity and honesty in their personal lives which were indeed merely another aspect of their political beliefs. That is what socialism means in practice.

May I say finally that the layout, the typography and much of the content of the Vietnam issue was of a very high standard indeed.

> Sincerely,
> Pat McVeigh
> East Lothian, Scotland

*

The Editor,

If the *Dwarf* persists in publishing such drivel as the correspondence between Lennon and Hoyland it will lose the few readers it has. Mr Hoyland should be told that bourgeois like Lennon are cured not converted. There is not anything in Lennon's thinking that hunger and a few weeks in Fidel's canefields would not correct.

Rather than waste your time with such trash, devote another page to the ideas of intelligent socialists. For example, print excerpts from Venceremos. 'Strawberry Fields' and 'A Day in the Life' sure as hell were not part of what made Che Guevara into the kind of socialist he was.

yours faithfully,
R. Sentes

'Every man has a right to where he belongs So declare yourself and tell me where you are from'

(PRINCE BUSTER)

A New Left Review Conversation Piece

'What is your ideological formation?'
'Fish and chips.'
'That sounds like workerism.'
'Is it quicker if I plead guilty?'
'Can you give a theoretical justification for your position?'
'I want to have a beer before the pubs shut.'
'Hooliganism.'
'Oh, why can't you leave people alone.'
'Economism.'
'Pardon. I don't understand what you're on about.'
'Naturally. That means you can't play in my revolution.'

'Meany. It's not fair . . . What are the rules?'

'Correct, of course.'

'Who's going to win? Is it rigged to start with? Tell us the odds.'

'Comrade, you're consumed with petty bourgeois cynicism.'

'Well, how long will it take to win then?'

'Utopian adventurist. Anarchist ultra-leftist. Hippy.'

'Well, I can see it could be dodgy. But as long as it's worth it all at the end. Still, with all your ideological formations behind us we're bound to be all right, aren't we? There they all are, ranks and cadres of personal pronouns.'

'The philistine attitude of certain comrades to the theory we kindly accumulate up here merely serves to demonstrate that the English tradition is fundamentally one of fabianism, reformism, empiricism, chauvinism, hypostasization and conflation . . .

'Are you trying to tell me all I can do is wank?'

'Vulgar psychologism.'

'Don't you ever have a laugh?'

'Why haven't you built the revolutionary party? The initial form for the revolutionary culture is to be seen in the student movement.'

'I hate forms – they always come with officials. Anyway, who's going to fill it up for you? You can't go around telling us we're a lot of wankers and then expect us to fill your forms up for you.'

'You have obviously no conception of the role of the proletarian vanguard.'

'What's it look like – is it stripy or plain? Does its tail wag? Is it nice to know? No chance of sex appeal anywhere in it, is there? What's it do the rest of the time? Does it come here often? Why don't you meet more of them? Isn't it too popular?'

'The role of the proletarian vanguard is on top or out front, whichever way you care to look at it.'

'Cor blimey, rather you than me. Bit exposed, isn't it? I mean personal pronouns and ideological formations are all very well but I wouldn't rely upon them.'

'The role of the proletarian vanguard is to bash coppers, according to the correct ideological formation. From this unity of theory and practice in the moment of confrontation it will be revealed to all those lacy telly-watching embourgywhatitworkerswot we're on about.'

'BUT YOU NEVER EXPLAIN TO ANYONE WHAT IT IS YOU'RE ON ABOUT. PERHAPS YOU'VE NO IDEA AT ALL. PERHAPS YOU'RE JUST AFRAID TO LET ON THAT YOU DON'T REALLY KNOW

WHAT TO DO. AND YOU CAN'T LET DOWN YOUR DAD BE-
CAUSE HE TOOK US THROUGH THE WAR AND YOU CRIED IN
YOUR SIREN SUIT AND IT'S AWFUL BEING GROWN-UP,
ESPECIALLY IF YOU'RE A MAN AND MIDDLE CLASS, BECAUSE
PEOPLE ARE ALWAYS EXPECTING THINGS OF YOU AND NEVER
GIVING YOU EXCUSES LIKE WOMEN'S LIB. AND WHAT NOT.'
(Message – get it? – oppression of white middle-class anglo-saxon
male accounts for owlishness manifested in extreme snootiness.)
'It's completely clear you're a Menshevik and we disagree 100 per
cent.'

A Trendy Party Conversation Piece

Kenneth Tynan, an artistic director of the National Theatre and ex-
Leftist (with grandiose flip of right wrist): 'Now you're not going to
go on and on about the working class.'
Frank Campbell, UCATT shop steward and IS executive member (in
strong Glasgow accent): 'Yes I fucking am.'

Mick (named after Michael Collins) is nineteen years old, born and
dragged up in Liverpool. Left school at fifteen; went to work on the
docks with his Dad and thought he was pretty lucky to have got the
job. Somehow he found out about the existence of the 'underground':
he read his *IT* and discovered that in London there were communities
where people genuinely cared about one another, a whole new life-
style was being evolved, an explosion of happiness, energy and ecstasy.
It seemed a good idea. So he came down to London, carefully dressing
himself up for the occasion: unfortunately, it was the wrong uniform.
The North might be swinging, but it's not outrageous! You can't buy
kaftans and crushed velvet flare-lines in Mick's town. Still, he came
from a long line of 'it doesn't matter if your boots are falling apart,
lad, as long as they're *clean*!' So he had his best brown suit dry-
cleaned, polished his Clarks-for-Men, put on a clean white shirt, and
was off down to the Smoke.
   He arrived at the old Arts Lab. Nobody said hello: they were all far
too Frigidaire for that. Nobody even pointed or giggled: that's not
their style. They simple used their cool to freeze him right out. He just

didn't exist. He stood around for a bit and watched. Remembered all that advice about 'other people are shy too; someone's got to make the first move', but when he approached a group and tried to talk to them he was very firmly told to 'Fuck off, man!' So Mick fucked off – back to Liverpool. Now he works on the assembly line at Fords. It's hard work but better money than on the docks.

That was twelve months ago. The Arts Lab thing's happening in Liverpool now – it was probably happening then but he didn't know where – but it's too late for Mick.

'A worker is he who has no power over how he lives and knows it'

(France, May 1968)

Education and the Worrying Class (Indoors Play)
John Barker and Jim Greenfield

There are two actors.
One is planted in the audience in a focal position. The other marches round in a circle rhythmically chanting 'Ed-u-ca-tion and the Worrying Class'. Having circumscribed a circle (a motif in the piece – 'going round in circles' etc.) he goes up to the planted actor and awards him a B.A.: the other replies 'baaaaaaa' and follows around the circle also chanting.

1. The first scene was an attack against the antithetical, dualistic method of teaching which usually deals with worn-out antitheses, trying to create some false emotional adhesion to one side or the other. A blackboard with one half white is a useful prop. The teacher stands on a table/chair and the pupil sits crosslegged on the ground with his back to the audience. The teacher begins with 'we will *discuss* . . .' – the example we used was Napoleon. The teacher shouts out various antitheses which overlap and even contradict:

   Pragmatist not a Platonist
   Strategist not a Pragmatist etc.

   The pupil's head goes from side to side, faster and faster, like at a

tennis match, with each antithesis, with the teacher shooting out his arms first one side then the other to stress the points. It gets faster and faster and more and more banal: 'fat not thin, short not tall' ... until the teacher's arms are so fast that he is making a circle and meaningless noises; this becomes a helicopter blade (pupil pull away chocks) and slows down into:

2. The teacher is miming a clock with both arms, clicking his tongue on the hours. The other actor under this clock mimes out a routine day – which can be of worker or student – eating, reading paper, drinking in pub, travelling etc. A 24-hour cycle is presented.

3. The actor playing the clock comes off his table still clicking and his head goes in circles. And becomes a 'neurotic student' who confronts his 'liberal' tutor, When the student comes in threatening suicide in a very hysterical way, the tutor responds in a bland and banal way. The student works up a terrific hysteria, telling the tutor what a shit he is, then tells the tutor to put on the gas fire, without lighting it and leave. The tutor plays along, trying to ingratiate himself, comes back later. Student switches off gas, pretends he is dead. Tutor trying not to panic. Tension. Then student leaps up and starts laughing very loud, tutor takes it up until he too is rolling around the floor, laughing like a hyena, trying desperately to prove he understands. Student gets up, looks quizzically at audience: 'See, they're all fucking mad, here.' ...

12. The Museum of Revolutions:

Gullible tourist-archetype with camera being dragged round, getting increasingly bored. The museum guy treats them very aesthetically. 'Wat Tyler, very inconclusive, hardly worth including really, more a rebellion I'd have said, though some specialists have put forward a strong case for it as an early example of a people's uprising. Local, though.' Gets excited about the American Revolution as he sees an important trend i.e. the mixture of a revolution about ideals and one of national liberation, which he keeps stressing about 1870, Vietnam etc. Treats the French and Russian revolutions as absolute classics (means and ends), at the end sells Che buttons and posters and NLF flags, for the kiddies. The tourist takes the lot; as he is bored he'll do anything to get out ...

16. The piece finished with a scene about historicizing our meagre 'revolutionary' experience. This was prompted by the kind of things liberals were saying after we had a sit-in in Cambridge, the piece was performed shortly afterwards.

'Wasn't it fantastic? First time they've had a sit-in in 600 years, you know' etc., etc., concluding with 'wasn't it fantastic when we marched out with all the T V cameras pointed at us, reading all about it next day, front page?' and the climax line, said by both (they are waltzing around in ecstasy together now), 'SOLIDARITY WITH LSE' – the people at the sit-in had needed the excuse, they had no reality of their own. They fantasize wildly about the future of the movement: 'Soon, we'll be taking over the universities', 'running our own alienation', they croon dreamily.

Monday, 13 May 1968

6.15 a.m. Avenue Yves Kerman. A clear cloudless day. Crowds begin to gather outside the gates of the giant Renault works at Boulogne Billancourt. The main trade-union 'centrales' (CGT, CFDT and FO) have called a one-day general strike. They are protesting against police violence in the Latin Quarter and in support of long-neglected claims concerning wages, hours, the age of retirement and trade-union rights in the plants.

The factory gates are wide open. Not a cop or supervisor in sight. The workers stream in. A loudhailer tells them to proceed to their respective shops, to refuse to start work and to proceed, at 8 a.m., to their traditional meeting place, an enormous shed-like structure in the middle of the Île Seguin (an island in the Seine entirely covered by parts of the Renault plant).

As each worker goes through the gates, the pickets give him a leaflet, jointly produced by the three unions. Leaflets in Spanish are also distributed (over 2,000 Spanish workers are employed in Renault). French and Spanish orators succeed one another, in short spells, at the microphone. Although all the unions are supporting the one-day strike all the orators seem to belong to the CGT. It's their loudspeaker . . .

6·45 a.m. Hundreds of workers are now streaming in. Many look as if they had come to work, rather than to participate in mass meetings in the plant. The decision to call the strike was only taken on the Saturday afternoon, after many of the men had already dispersed for the weekend. Many seem unaware of what it's all about. I am struck by the number of Algerian and black workers.

There are only a few posters at the gate, again mainly those of the CGT. Some pickets carry CFDT posters. There isn't an FO poster in sight. The road and walls outside the factory have been well covered with slogans: 'One day strike on Monday', 'Unity in defence of our claims', 'No to the monopolies'.

The little café near the gates is packed. People seem unusually wide-awake and communicative for so early an hour. A newspaper kiosk is selling about three copies of *l'Humanité* for every copy of anything else. The local branch of the Communist Party is distributing a leaflet calling for 'resolution, calm, vigilance and unity' and warning against 'provocateurs'.

The pickets make no attempt to argue with those pouring in. No one seems to know whether they will obey the strike call or not. Less than 25 per cent of Renault workers belong to any union at all. This is the biggest car factory in Europe.

The loudhailer hammers home its message: 'The CRS have recently assaulted peasants at Quimper, and workers at Caen, Rhodiaceta (Lyon) and Dassault. Now they are turning on the students. The regime will not tolerate opposition. It will not modernize the country. It will not grant us our basic wage demands. Our one-day strike will show both Government and employers our determination. We must compel them to retreat.' The message is repeated again and again, like a gramophone record. I wonder whether the speaker believes what he says, whether he even senses what lies ahead.

At 7 a.m. a dozen Trotskyists of the FER (Fédération des Étudiants Révolutionnaires) turn up to sell their paper *Révoltes*. They wear large red and white buttons proclaiming their identity. A little later another group arrives to sell *Voix Ouvrière*. The loudspeaker immediately switches from an attack on the Gaullist government and its CRS to an attack on 'provocateurs' and 'disruptive elements, alien to the working class'. The Stalinist speaker hints that the sellers are in the pay of the Government. As they are here, 'the police must be lurking in the neighbourhood'. Heated arguments break out between the sellers and CGT officials. The CFDT pickets are refused the use of the loudhailer. They shout 'démocratie ouvrière' and defend the right of the 'disruptive elements' to sell their stuff. A rather abstract right, as not a sheet is sold. The front page of *Révoltes* carries an esoteric article on Eastern Europe.

Much invective (but no blows) are exchanged. In the course of an argument I hear Bro. Trigon (delegate to the second electoral 'college' at Renault) describe Danny Cohn-Bendit as an 'agent du pouvoir' (an agent of the authorities). A student takes him up on this point. The Trots don't. Shortly before 8 a.m. they walk off, their 'act of presence' accomplished and duly recorded for history.

At about the same time, hundreds of workers who had entered the factory leave their shops, and assemble in the sunshine in an open space a few hundred yards inside the main gate. From there they amble towards the Île Seguin, crossing one arm of the river Seine on the way. Other processions leave other points of the factory and converge on the same area. The metallic ceiling is nearly 200 feet above our heads. Enormous stocks of components are piled up right and left. Far away to the right an assembly line is still working, lifting what looks like rear car seats, complete with attached springs, from ground to first-floor level.

Some 10,000 workers are soon assembled in the shed. The orators address them through a loudspeaker, from a narrow platform some forty feet up. The platform runs in front of what looks like an elevated inspection post but which I am told is a union office inside the factory.

The CGT speaker deals with various sectional wage claims. He denounces the resistance of the government 'in the hands of the monopolies'. He produces facts and figures dealing with the wage structure. Many skilled men are not getting enough. A CFDT speaker follows him. He deals with the steady speed-up, with the worsening of working conditions, with accidents and with the fate of man in production. 'What kind of life is this? Are we always to remain puppets, carrying out every whim of the management?' He advocates uniform wage increases for all (augmentations non-hiérarchisées). An FO speaker follows. He is technically the most competent, but says the least. In flowery rhetoric he talks of 1936, but omits all reference to Léon Blum. The record of FO is bad in the factory and the speaker is heckled from time to time.

The CGT speakers then ask the workers to participate *en masse* in the big rally planned for that afternoon. As the last speaker finishes, the crowd spontaneously breaks out into a rousing 'Internationale'. The older men seem to know most of the words. The younger workers only know the chorus. A friend nearby assures me that in twenty years this is the first time he has heard the song sung inside Renault (he has attended dozens of mass meetings in the Île Seguin). There is an atmosphere of excitement, particularly among the younger workers.

The crowd then breaks up into several sections. Some walk back over the bridge and out of the factory. Others proceed systematically through the shops, where a few hundred blokes are still at work. Some of these men argue but most seem only too glad for an excuse to stop and join in the procession. Gangs weave their way, joking and singing, amid the giant presses and tanks. Those remaining at work are ironically cheered, clapped or exhorted to 'step on it', or 'work harder'. Occasional foremen look on helplessly, as one assembly line after another is brought to a halt.

Many of the lathes have coloured pictures plastered over them: pin-ups and green fields, sex and sunshine. Anyone still working is exhorted to get out into the daylight, not just to dream about it. In the main plant, over half a mile long, hardly twelve men remain in their overalls. Not an angry voice can be heard. There is much good-humoured banter. By 11 a.m. thousands of workers have poured out into the warmth of a morning in May. An open-air beer and sandwich stall, outside the gate, is doing a roaring trade.

Monday, 13 May, 1.15 p.m.

The streets are crowded. The response to the call for a twenty-four-hour general strike has exceeded the wildest hopes of the trade unions. Despite the short notice Paris is paralysed. The strike was only decided forty-eight hours ago, after the 'night of the barricades'. It is moreover 'illegal'. The law of the land demands a five-day notice before an 'official' strike can be called. Too bad for legality.

A solid phalanx of young people is walking up the Boulevard de Sébastopol, towards the Gare de l'Est. They are proceeding to the student rallying point for the giant demonstration called jointly by the unions, the students' organization (UNEF) and the teachers' associations (FEN and SNEsup).

There is not a bus or car in sight. The streets of Paris today belong to the demonstrators. Thousands of them are already in the square in front of the station. Thousands more are moving in from every direction. The plan agreed by the sponsoring organizations is for the different categories to assemble separately and then to converge on the Place de la République, from where the march will proceed across Paris, via the Latin Quarter, to the Place Denfert-Rochereau.

We are already packed like sardines, for as far as the eye can see, yet there is more than an hour to go before we are due to proceed. The sun has been shining all day. The girls are in summer dresses, the young men in shirt sleeves. A red flag is flying over the railway station. There are many red flags in the crowd and several black ones too. A man suddenly appears carrying a suitcase full of duplicated leaflets. He belongs to some left 'groupuscule' or other. He opens his suitcase and distributes perhaps a dozen leaflets. But he doesn't have to continue alone. There is an unquenchable thirst for information, ideas, literature, argument, polemic. The man just stands there as people surround him and press forward to get the leaflets. Dozens of demonstrators, without even reading the leaflet, help him distribute them. Some 6,000 copies get out in a few minutes. All seem to be assiduously read. People argue, laugh, joke. I witnessed such scenes again and again.

Sellers of revolutionary literature are doing well. An edict, signed by the organizers of the demonstration, that 'the only literature allowed would be that of the organizations sponsoring the demonstration' (see *l'Humanité*, 13 May 1968, p. 5) is being enthusiastically flouted. This bureaucratic restriction (much criticized the previous evening when announced at Censier by the student delegates to the Coordinating Committee) obviously cannot be enforced in a crowd of this size. The revolution is bigger than any organization, more tolerant than any institution 'representing' the masses, more realistic than any edict of any Council Committee.

Demonstrators have climbed onto walls, onto the roofs of bus stops, onto the railings in front of the station. Some have loudhailers and make short speeches. All the 'politicos' seem to be in one part or other of this crowd. I can see the banner of the Jeunesse Communiste Révolutionnaire, portraits of Castro and Che Guevara, the banner of the FER, several banners of 'servir le Peuple' (a Maoist group) and the banner of the UJCML (Union de la Jeunesse Communiste Marxiste-Léniniste), another Maoist tendency. There are also banners from many educational establishments now occupied by those who work there. Large groups of lycéens (high school kids) mingle with the students as do many thousands of teachers.

At about 2 p.m. the student section sets off, singing the 'Internationale'. We march twenty to thirty abreast, arms linked. There is a row of red flags in front of us, then a banner fifty feet wide carrying four simple words 'Étudiants, Enseignants, Travailleurs, Solidaires'. It is an impressive sight.

The whole Boulevard de Magenta is a solid seething mass of humanity. We can't enter the Place de la République, already packed full of demonstrators. One can't even move along the pavements or through adjacent streets. Nothing but people, as far as the eye can see.

As we proceed slowly down the Boulevard de Magenta, we notice on a third-floor balcony, high on our right, an SFIO (Socialist Party) headquarters. The balcony is bedecked with a few decrepit-looking red flags and a banner proclaiming 'Solidarity with the Students'. A few elderly characters wave at us, somewhat self-consciously. Someone in the crowd starts chanting 'Op-por-tu-nistes'. The slogan is taken up, rhythmically roared by thousands, to the discomfiture of those on the balcony who beat a hasty retreat. The people have not forgotten the use of the CRS against the striking miners, in 1958, by 'socialist' Prime Minister Guy Mollet and his role during the Algerian War. Mercilessly, the crowd shows its contempt for the discredited politicians now seeking to jump on the bandwagon. 'Guy Mollet, au musée,' they shout, amid laughter. It is truly the end of an epoch.

At about 3 p.m. we at last reach the Place de la République, our point of departure. The crowd here is so dense that several people faint and have to be carried into neighbouring cafés. Here people are packed almost as tight as in the street, but can at least avoid being injured. The window of one café gives way under the pressure of the crowd outside. There is a genuine fear, in several parts of the crowd, of being crushed to death. The first union contingents fortunately begin to leave the square. There isn't a policeman in sight.

Although the demonstration has been announced as a joint one, the CGT leaders are still striving desperately to avoid a mixing-up, on the streets, of students and workers. In this they are moderately successful. By about 4.30 p.m. the student and teachers' contingent, perhaps 80,000 strong, finally leaves the Place de la République. Hundreds of thousands of demonstrators have preceded it, hundreds of thousands follow it, but the 'left' contingent has been well and truly 'bottled-in'. Several groups, understanding at last the CGT's man-oeuvre, break loose once we are out of the square. They take short cuts via various side streets, on the double, and succeed in infiltrating groups of 100 or so into parts of the march ahead of them, or behind them. The Stalinist stewards walking hand in hand and hemming the march in on either side are powerless to prevent these sudden influxes. The student demonstrators scatter like fish in water as soon as they have entered a given contingent. The CGT marchers themselves are quite friendly and readily assimilate the newcomers, not quite sure what it's all about. The students' appearance, dress and speech does not enable them to be identified as readily as they would be in Britain.

The main student contingent proceeds as a compact body. Now that we are past the bottleneck of the Place de la République the pace is quite rapid. The student group nevertheless takes at least half an hour to pass a given point. The slogans of the students contrast strikingly with those of the CGT. The students shout 'Le Pouvoir aux Ouvriers' (All Power to the Workers): 'Le Pouvoir est dans la rue' (Power lies in the streets); 'Libérez nos camarades'. CGT members shout 'Pompidou, démission' (Pompidou, resign). The students chant 'de Gaulle, assassin', or 'CRS – SS'. The CGT: 'Des sous, pas de matraques' (Money, not police clubs), or 'Défense du pouvoir d'achat' (Defend our purchasing power). The students say 'Non à l'Université de classe'. The CGT and the stalinist students, grouped around the banner of their paper *Clarté*, reply 'Université Démocratique'. Deep political differences lie behind the differences of emphasis. Some slogans are taken up by everyone, slogans such as 'Dix ans, c'est assez', 'A bas l'État policier', or 'Bon anniversaire, mon Général'. Whole groups mournfully intone a well-known refrain: 'Adieu, de Gaulle'. They wave their handkerchiefs, to the great merriment of the bystanders.

——As the main student contingent crosses the Pont St Michel to enter the Latin Quarter it suddenly stops, in silent tribute to its wounded. All thoughts are for a moment switched to those lying in hospital, their sight in danger through too much tear gas or their skulls or ribs fractured by the truncheons of the CRS. The sudden, angry silence of this noisiest part of the demonstration conveys a deep impression of strength and resolution. One senses massive accounts yet to be settled.

At the top of the Boulevard St Michel I drop out of the march, climb onto a parapet lining the Luxembourg Gardens, and just watch. I remain there for two hours as row after row of demonstrators march past, thirty or more abreast, a human tidal wave of fantastic inconceivable size. How many are they? 600,000? 800,000? A million? 1,500,000? No one can really number them. The first of the demonstrators reached the final dispersal point hours before the last ranks had left the Place de la République, at 7 p.m.

There were banners of every kind: union banners, student banners, political banners, non-political banners, reformist banners, revolutionary banners, banners of the Mouvement contre l'Armement Atomique, banners of various Conseils de Parents d'Élèves, banners of every conceivable size and shape, proclaiming a common abhorrence at what had happened and a common will to struggle on. Some banners were loudly applauded, such as the one saying 'Libérons l'information' (Let's have a free news service) carried by a group of employees from the ORTF. Some banners indulged in vivid symbolism, such as the gruesome one carried by a group of artists, depicting human hands, heads and eyes, each with its price tag, on display on the hooks and trays of a butcher's shop.

Endlessly they filed past. There were whole sections of hospital personnel, in white coats, some carrying posters saying 'Où sont les disparus des hôpitaux?' (Where are the missing injured?). Every factory, every major work-place seemed to be represented. There were numerous groups of railwaymen, postmen, printers, Métro personnel, metal workers, airport workers, market men, electricians, lawyers, sewermen, bank employees, building workers, glass and chemical workers, waiters, municipal employees, painters and decorators, gas workers, shop girls, insurance clerks, road sweepers, film studio operators, busmen, teachers, workers from the new plastic industries, row upon row upon row of them, the flesh and blood of modern capitalist society, an unending mass, a power that could sweep *everything* before it, if it but decided to do so. My thoughts went to those who say that the workers are only interested in football, in the 'tiercé' (horse-betting), in watching the telly, in their annual 'congés' (holidays), and that the working class cannot see beyond the problems of its everyday life. It was so palpably untrue. I also thought of those who say that only a narrow and rotten leadership lies between the masses and the total transformation of society. It was equally untrue. Today the working class is becoming conscious of its strength. Will it decide, tomorrow, to use it?

I rejoin the march and we proceed towards Denfert-Rochereau. We pass several statues, sedate gentlemen now bedecked with red flags or carrying slogans such as 'Libérez nos camarades'. As we pass a hospital silence again descends on the endless crowd. Someone starts whistling the 'Internationale'. Others take it up. Like a breeze rustling over an enormous field of corn, the whistled tune ripples out in all directions. From the windows of the hospital some nurses wave at us.

At various intersections we pass traffic lights which by some strange inertia still seem to be working. Red and green alternate, at fixed intervals, meaning as little as bourgeois education, as work in modern society, as the lives of those walking past. The reality of today, for a few hours, has submerged all of yesterday's patterns.

(From a Solidarity pamphlet, 'May 1968', by 'Martin Grainger')

Cathy Come to Centre Point: It's Empty!

This building is a public scandal! Like hundreds of others it has stood empty for two years – while thousands of people in this country are homeless or live in slum conditions. There are 8,000,000 square feet of empty office space in Greater London alone – enough to house *all* of Britain's 10,000 homeless families in one go.

These families are in the care of local councils, some living in appalling conditions. At one hostel visited eighteen women and children were living in one room with only twelve beds and one cot between them. This is only the tip of the iceberg. Look at these figures:

1,800,000 houses in the UK 'unfit for human habitation'.

4,700,000 houses 'seriously in need of repair'.

3,000,000 families living in slums.

BUT BUILDINGS LIKE CENTRE POINT STAY EMPTY. WHY?

Because the longer a building is held empty, the more profit made by the speculator who built it. For example, it pays a business man who put up a building in 1965 to wait five years before letting it. By this time the current rent will have increased by 25 per cent (5 per cent per year). At such a rate the businessman will soon have covered his cost – and will be making a vast profit. In other words, while 160,000 people wait on the housing list in Greater London, rich profiteers build sprawling office blocks and speculate on rising rents and building costs.

WE DEPLORE A SYSTEM WHICH ALLOWS A FEW RICH MEN TO MAKE MONSTROUS PROFITS IN THIS WAY WHILE SO MANY ARE DEPRIVED OF THEIR BASIC NEEDS.

(Agitprop leaflet)

Capitalism = Empty Homes + Homeless People

A small group of socialist street actors and artists paraded outside the empty thirty-four-storey Centre Point building in London yesterday to protest against property speculators and housing conditions in Britain. In mummers' costumes and masks, the group, calling themselves Agitprop (Agitation and Propaganda), attempted several times to perform a protest play on the pavement outside the building which stands at the junction of Oxford Street and Tottenham Court Road, but were prevented by police.

A rather disorganized march was led by Mr John Hoyland, an artist, who wore a giant black and red mask and carried a placard bearing a slogan in the shape of a speaker's bubble in a cartoon. The group unfurled 25-ft-long banners declaring 'Cathy Come to Centre Point'.

Mr Bob Rowthorne, a lecturer in economics at Cambridge, said the group did not want to see homeless people accommodated in Centre Point but wanted to protest over the money wasted on the skyscraper. He added, 'When this building was completed two years ago, office rents were almost £3 a square foot. If it had been let at that time it would have been worth £11 millions. Now office space is worth £5 a square foot, making the block worth £18 millions.'

Mr Hoyland said Agit-prop was formed eight months ago to provide left-wing groups with propaganda experts. The group included designers and poster painters as well as actors and artists. A street play was staged in Dagenham by the group during the Ford strike. 'We are all dedicated to using our talent for radical social purposes,' he said.

(From the *Guardian*)

'Phone up about a new issue of the newspaper of the GLC Tenants Action Committee who are campaigning on the London estates for a rent strike against the increases. After discussing it for a bit, Judy Roberts says, "Do you know the Russians have done it?" "Done what?" "They've sent the tanks into Prague." Although it had been on the cards, it was shocking, although Judy was much more interested in the GLC tenants and didn't seem very perturbed. "What, today, into Prague?" It was specially shocking because it was something my political views had led me to expect, curiously like a *déjà vu* or a dream that becomes true. Skip off work and go over to Kilburn to write a leaflet, which seems like a rather ineffectual act, more of a political reflex action than a real way of influencing things. A leaflet giving the views of the Angel Islington branch of the International Socialists is duly printed after some testy exchanges, as someone typing out a new version of C. L. R. James' *State Capitalism and World Revolution* is persuaded to vacate the typewriter for a few moments. Listen to the radio while slicing the pages in half. Prague is being occupied with frightening efficiency, capitalist spokesmen chortle. Stalinists interviewed are either disconsolate or cheerful. Go on the tube train to Covent Garden after delivering most of the leaflets, to meet Eleanor Thornycroft in the Lamb and Flag. As we go round the corner, George Matthews comes out of the King Street headquarters of the Communist Party to deliver a statement of the British Party on the invasion. A group of market porters and passers-by watch respectfully from the Moss Bros side as TV journalists crowd round him. Matthews looks physically shaken like an insect, pinned against the glassy green stone-proof walls of the CP by the antennae of the TV cameras and jabbing shorthand pencils. Something about "a violation of socialist legality". Obviously even they can't defend the Russians this time. Matthews changes from an insect into a victim of a firing squad, ill, exhausted and tortured-looking. Must have been quite a meeting inside the green glass. Horrified to find myself feeling sorry for him. I go across and present him with a newly minted leaflet giving the views of the Angel IS on the class nature of Russia, the ambiguous role of Dubček, the way forward for the Czech working class. He puts it in his pocket.

'Outside the Czech Embassy there was already a largish gathering of socialist demonstrators blazoning red flags and hammers and sickles in front of the elegant building which occasionally emitted a smooth limousine. Further down the road, a rather dejected group of émigrés and some younger students with Personality Posters of Dubček gathered, looking with hostility at the Embassy and with slightly greater hostility at the socialists. All the left-wing groups have arrived with their leaflets and slogans and busily compare notes on each other's analyses. Their distributors all look somewhat dazed that such a crucial moment in world working-class history should be taking place in such an elegant sun-dappled Kensington street, and clutch their statements on the situation which give the impression of being designed more to reassure themselves than to persuade others. Through the midst of the demonstrators strode a single figure armed with a single eloquent portrait of Trotsky, which he carried aloft like a religious icon. From a distance the picture appears to have a life of its own, wafting backward and forward like some kind of fairy godmother over the tousled heads of the revolutionaries. Much later the march drifts off towards Earls Court Road where there is a Russian Trade Fair. The few policemen in attendance, already utterly bemused by all the hammer and sickles being virulently shaken at the Ziz saloons, gave up completely when the march announced it was going to the East European motor show. After much confused navigation through Notting Hill Gate backstreets, boutiques and Indian restaurants, a large red combine harvester sitting outside Earls Court was reached. The gates had been firmly locked. A scout on a moped arrives from the new IS Printshop in Tottenham with a printed leaflet condemning the invasion. Those with merely duplicated sheets look duly respectful. Several speeches outside the combine harvester. Tariq Ali blusters, John Palmer in belted blue mac demonstrates what we must be absolutely clear about, somebody from the Militant proceeds to take the first two speakers to task for completely failing to deal with the question of something or other. The émigrés set light to red flags and sing hymns, the reds shout abuse at them and take the tube train home.'

Appeal for Support for the International War Crimes Tribunal

For several years Western news media have unwittingly documented the record of crime committed by the United States in Vietnam, which comprises an overwhelming *prima facie* indictment of the American war. The terrible series of photographs, and accounts of torture, mutilation and experimental war has impelled Bertrand Russell to call us together to conduct an exhaustive inquiry into the war in all its aspects. Scientists, lawyers, doctors and world renowned scholars will serve on commissions investigating the evidence. Witnesses will be brought from Vietnam to give their first-hand testimony. Investigating teams will travel throughout Vietnam and Indochina, gathering data on the spot. The documentation published in the West and elsewhere will be relentlessly examined. . .

We command no state power; we do not represent the strong; we control no armies or treasuries. We act out of the deepest moral concern and depend upon the conscience of ordinary people throughout the world for the real support – the material help, which will determine whether the people of Vietnam are to be abandoned in silence or allowed the elementary right of having their plights presented to the conscience of Mankind.

(Bertrand Russell Peace Foundation)

Hippies didn't like Vietnam very much . . .

Last Sunday 5,000–6,000 leftists, Communists, socialists, professional discontents and black-power advocates – that mixed-bag of the so-called humanitarian Left – had still another demonstration against British Government support of American policy in Vietnam. This particular outing culminated in fights, arrests and the destruction of the beautiful green lawn at Grosvenor Square. Nothing more was accomplished!

Oh yes, something more: a catharsis for a lot of people who would rather march and talk about it than think and act effectively... *International Times* favours Design Revolution, Spiritual Evolution, Ying-Yang Uprising, Inner Space Adventure, Work Democracy, a Release of Man's Extraordinary Potential and the Transformation in the Myths that direct Life and Thought.

If you really want to travel why can't you just transfer yourself – by changing your matter into energy and back again? Why can't you? What's stopping you from doing it?

The answer is in your head!

(From *International Times*, 27 October 1967)

Commitment was too complicated . . .

LAING: Quite a few years ago I was in a position where, for many reasons, I wanted to affiliate myself... I wanted to join the Communist Party, and I talked to a friend who was, I gathered, well informed, who told me: 'You know, there's very little point, since the party has been infiltrated by government agencies, up to a considerably high level, even to the point of being able to determine or affect policy decisions.' I think that if there were a sufficient number of cool clear heads, but they would have to be 100 per cent very very clear, a good start would be to become policemen, infiltrate the police force. It would take some time, but it is likely that using their intelligence, they could reach high levels quite quickly, and eventually help to transform the police force, by working within it. But they would have to be very clear, sufficiently clear . . .

(*International Times*, 4-17 July 1969)

'The March Vietnam demo – for me (and others, I know) – was a great turning point. We went on that in the same spirit of CND-ism, some people even had kids with them, prams, girls in sandals. And we were ASTONISHED, AMAZED – couldn't believe it was really happening, HERE IN ENGLAND – when the police started to surround the crowd packed into Grosvenor Square, started to push us in on three sides, so lots of people panicked. Many people hurt just because they were so

UNPREPARED – their feet were crushed, girls' bare legs under mini-skirts were scratched and bruised, men lost their sandals or gym-shoes. People fell over because they'd NEVER BEEN IN A DEMONSTRATION LIKE THAT, PACKED TOGETHER, BEING PUSHED BY THE POLICE, REALLY FRIGHTENED, PANICKING. I remember vividly being pushed up, accidently, to the very front, and being shoved against a line of policemen, with linked arms. Behind them another row. I felt I was going to faint, I was so completely squashed between policemen at least a foot taller than me and – from behind – the pressure of thousands of demonstrators pushing into the square, they were oblivious to what was happening at the front. Even then we were so naïve, so pre-1968, in our thinking. I remember looking up at the nearest policeman, my face being pushed into the front of his jacket, and smiling, saying, "You'll have to let us through somewhere, I mean we simply can't get out any other way – you must see that we can't move back now?" And he looked at me with very hard eyes, and kicked me in the shins! I wasn't so much angry, I just couldn't believe it ... even after all our ravings about the "fascist pigs" ... I couldn't believe an English police-man had deliberately kicked a girl so much smaller than him, so obviously helplessly caught in the situation. He didn't know I was political – I could have been any innocent bystander caught up in the thing. I wasn't surprised at his "brutality" (as I'd so often heard it described), I think it was his "lack of gallantry", even at that late stage I think we still felt the English police *weren't* like those in America and Europe. We didn't realize that once a scared ruling class chose to make them play that role, they would have no choice. Remember clearly sitting at home that evening, watching the demo on the news, nursing bruised legs, swearing never to go on a march again without wearing boots, jeans, and being prepared to defend myself (a vow we probably all made to ourselves sometime in that year). Felt stunned, and very lucky that somehow, through pressure somewhere else, nearer the Em-bassy, the police cordon *had* broken and somehow I'd stumbled through it along with a few others. A numbing experience, that one.'

The meetings went on and on . . .

The debate over the nature of the demonstration was taken up again at the Liaison Committee on 10 September. From this point on, at national level, the tempo of organizing began to decline, with smaller numbers at meetings, most of which were boring (i.e. concealed the real feelings of people and thus avoided struggle), with dissension, rumours and muttered hostilities. Every 'faction' had internal dissension. A compromise solution with which no one can fully identify does not inspire, though everyone tries to interpret it in accordance with his or her own philosophy. The YCL/CP were also preoccupied by the Czech situation over which there was an internal split.

We had to organize the meeting on 17 September. Ernie Tate said discussions about how we hoped to hold the streets were useless, it was a minor technicality. To ask the demonstration to set itself a task and thus develop revolutionary consciousness was absurd, this was something only a revolutionary party could do. The important thing was how many people would come? Chris Harman, indicating the development of IS, opposed him. We had a responsibility to know what we were trying to do. Political level could be raised by a common purpose and the unity it engendered. Numbers and slogans were important but not everything, we had to have a list of demands – to stop a particular firm involved in war production, to stop Dow, to shut down the South Vietnamese Embassy, and campaign to get this done. The demonstration was part of the campaign.

Because of the need to make the demonstration a conscious act, the mass meeting on 18 September must also set itself a task in preparation for 27 October. If it was to be a success, it could not be formless, a meeting should be designed to answer a question through collective discussion. Platform speeches which gave an expert view or a 'lead' inhibited discussion – as did the inclusion of notable figures (TU bigwigs or 'left' MPs). The movement had grown past this stage. Despite Ernie's pessimism that 'meetings happened, we had to make the best of them', the liaison committee agreed that five speakers would pose the questions we needed to have answered and thus give form to the meeting. A meeting must not only permit, but actively encourage, the majority of people present to take part, not just the professionals. People must stick to the point, try and understand what others have said and develop this, and avoid destructive behaviour or set speeches which merely assert their own general world view. Five opening talks, not more than ten minutes each, were agreed, myself (VSC), Chris Harman (IS), Emrys Thomas, Pat Jordan (IMG) and Barney Davis (YCL). The questions would be 'Why we demonstrate, how will this demonstration help to build a mass movement against US aggression in Vietnam?' and 'Whom do we organize, and how?'

On 17 September, the large hall in the Conway Hall was packed in

both senses, over 300 people there, and a British Vietnam Solidarity
Front contingent of about sixty. We pinned up 'Why do we demonstrate?' in large letters on computer paper, perhaps an ironic presence.
Dave Slaney heroically held the chair. Ed Guiton as secretary briefly
reminded us of the need to be democratic in making decisions, and to
remember this was only London – other parts of the country had to be
considered. The demonstrations must build a movement. I spoke on
the need to see our demonstrations as developing as an alternative
form of political life to parliamentary politics. It was our thing, which
we decided on and controlled, and not an appeal to the Government.
The strength of our demonstration rested on an increasing recognition
of the corruption and oppression of capitalist society, and the need to
confront it directly. It was because the Vietnamese were doing this that
we saw their victory as our victory, and the war as a common struggle
against a common enemy. I laid stress on the need for continuous
campaigning, building local groups, and the need to sustain the unity
of the demonstration before and after, to build a movement which
identified in the day to day life of its members with a revolutionary
struggle ... I was interrupted by cries of 'Grosvenor Square!', an
ominous rumble. Chris Harman related the demonstrations to developing revolutionary politics, the need to involve wider sections of
the population and the foolishness of attacking the police, who are
only instruments of the ruling class and not the class itself ... We must
defend ourselves against such a bodyguard, but we had to defeat
capitalism politically. The interruptions, cat-calls and shouting increased. Emrys Thomas, Pat Jordan and Barney Davis made similar
contributions, stressing the need to mount bigger and bigger mobilizations, to increase support for the Vietnamese, to unite wider sections
of the Left; and to make this a legal demonstration ... Already the
emotional temperature was rising, and the themes slipping away to a
hostile debate on where do we go. I cannot summarize the contributions
from the floor. They were mostly from BVSF people, and based on
the assertion that not to go to Grosvenor Square was betrayal and
cowardice. People not of their view were shouted down mercilessly.
Most of our contributors answered in similar vein, defending the ad-
hoc committee route, rather than asserting our aims, and accusing the
BVSF of mindlessness (true, but insufficient). Richard Kuper on the
other hand spoke quietly and to the purpose on the problems of
building a movement, and was listened to with few interruptions.
Someone right at the back, with false modesty, said this was his first
experience of politics in this country and he felt sure that if this was

how the Left behaved, people would be turned off for life. A plague on both your houses. Bob Purdie accused the BVSF of having organized a separate committee for a separate demonstration and of being splitters. Bateson admitted this, saying they were forced to it by the actions of the VSC/YCL bureaucratic clique. The important thing was where you do it not what you do (as the actress said to the bishop). Finally a vote was insisted on this motion: 'That the demonstration on Saturday, 26 October, go to Downing Street and on 27 October to Grosvenor Square.' Peter Cadogan of the defunct Committee of 100 interrupted with his resolution: 'Recognizing that there are two demonstrations we should work for the success of both with close liaison between.' This got no votes for or against. As Dave Slaney said from the chair: 'Does anyone give a shit?' BVSF, defeated 70 to 116 on the first motion, left in a fury as 10 p.m. struck. A victory for us but a meaningless one. Until we learn to use meetings to plan activity as part of an ongoing movement, and not as a propagandist substitute for that movement, parasitic minorities will always be able to paralyse us by exploiting the amorphousness of our structure.

(From 'End of a Tactic' by Geoff Richman)

Comrades! Your meetings are unbearable! You are riddled with inhibitions which you have to release as aggression against comrades who say something stupid or something you already know. These aggressions are only partially the result of insight into the stupidity of the other side. Why don't you at least admit that you are exhausted from the strain of the last year, that you don't know how to bear the stress any longer, that you consume your physical and intellectual energies without getting any pleasure from them? Why don't you discuss, before you plan your campaigns, how they can be carried out? Why do you all buy Reich? Why do you speak *here* about the class struggle and at *home* about the difficulties of orgasm? Is that not a subject for the SDS?

(Helke Sanders, German Women's Liberation)

27 October 1968

1 p.m. on the Embankment beneath Waterloo Bridge. A grey day, not cold, and the rain will probably hold off. Already the banners are being

propped up, waiting, hundreds are milling round the assembly point at Charing Cross. A dozen of us gather to give out the official leaflet 'Street Power', with our extra strength footwear and semi-protective clothing (here a duffle coat, there a padded cap). After four months of interminable committee meetings, what will happen? Will it be a success or a fiasco? What criteria could we adopt to judge the demonstration?

At 1.15 p.m. we start to give out the leaflets, hampered by dozens of sectarian organizations selling their own papers and giving out their own literature (from the Socialist Labour League 'Why We Are Not Marching, a message from the Political Committee' – to 'Why Israel is Important'). The (tiny) breakaway British Vietnam Solidarity Front is well in evidence, advising people to go to Grosvenor Square. For them, the test of success is easy: can they persuade people not to go with the main march? Thousands begin to pour down Villiers Street and around Charing Cross Station before 2 p.m., the scheduled time of start. They are of all ages and types – certainly not just students. The majority are here out of political conviction, or because their friends have told them about it. They accept our leaflet eagerly – 'Stay with your friends – you may need them today', 'Find a group and keep in it'. There are no marshals, no stewards, no orders. The organized contingents, assembled elsewhere, come up, singing the Internationale or chanting Victory to the N L F. Police are scattered about plentiful as wormcasts on a bourgeois lawn, making no attempts to intervene. They had however stopped some of the coaches entering London and searched people. Late Sunday morning all cars on roads from some of the outer London suburbs which had young people (under-thirties are all subversive) were stopped, including delicious and astonished debs. The head banner with '27 October Ad Hoc Committee' is well up towards Temple Station according to plan, though there are scuffles about who should keep the head, the anarchists and the B V S F attempting to push in and even take the banner. Eventually the front is taken by a motley crowd, with the banner thirty yards behind, accompanied by the loudspeaker van appealing to demonstrators to link arms and keep together.

By 2.15 we have given out 20,000 leaflets to about one in two of the unorganized entering the march. Thousands are still coming onto the Embankment, and will do so, until about 2.45 p.m. The contingents had already been mailed a duplicated version, and so were not leafleted. Allowing 10,000 for the last-mentioned section, we have 50 to 60 thousand as a first provisional figure.

The march was now under way, occupying the left side of the Embankment. All traffic had been diverted, the police kept well away. Scattered groups began to take over the right hand side of the road, and when the Kentish Town VSC contingent (some thirty strong) came up against a line of police just before Ludgate Circus, expecting the confrontation at last – the police fell back amiably. After Ludgate Circus the entire road was occupied and swinging into Fleet Street it was filled, packed from end to end, and side to side. The shouts of 'US Out!', 'Ho Ho Ho Chi Minh' echoed between the freshly boarded-up windows of the press offices and banks and other buildings which had been hurriedly barricaded the previous day.

From the number of marchers to the yard in Fleet Street across the road, about 100, and its total length, we get about 80,000 as a provisional figure. The march came up to Australia House and halted momentarily. The Australian flag was burnt by the 'Australians and New Zealanders against the war in Vietnam'. The march swept along the Strand, contingents doubling up along the right-hand side of the road to keep it filled. The contingents kept together, self-disciplined, linked arms, changing pace to keep the march cohesive. Thousands of onlookers lined the streets, almost all sympathetic. The television caused more obstruction than the police. Towards Trafalgar Square we began to slow down and halt for minutes at a time. We feared trouble, but it was only the physical configuration of onlookers surrounding the Square and the need to turn sharp left down Whitehall that slowed us. Confusion here could have been disastrous. BVSF spokesmen ran up and down trying to draw people off – and uniformed demonstrators might have gone, not knowing what was involved. The police tried to clear the crowds back, to allow free egress from the march. Some of the contingents' internal stewards set up the cry 'Whitehall', 'Turn left' (luckily), but it was essentially the self-discipline of the marchers – and the leaflets – which prevented trouble. About 500 to 1,000 ran off up the east side of Trafalgar Square towards the US Embassy; the rest, chanting 'Whitehall', kept to the agreed route.

Whitehall was filled, but not packed, and when the head was well out and into Victoria Street, the tail had not yet entered it. 100,000 will pack Whitehall, so again 80,000 is a probable figure. Groups of anarchists with their black and red flags halted at Downing Street throwing crackers at the police, hissing and booing. We clapped rhythmically in sympathy, but moved on. Wreaths on the Cenotaph were destroyed. Past Parliament Square: 'Disembowel Powell' – 'We are all foreign scum'. Up Victoria Street, Grosvenor Place, swarming over the walls and green at Hyde Park Corner, up Park Lane. A small group of fascists waved a Stars and Stripes. We felt a small prick of anger and felt we should tear it down; most of the march moved past, but a group eventually captured it.

To Speakers Corner where an endless list of speakers harangued a large passive crowd, after a group of fascists who had tried to seize the microphone had been dealt with. The crowd consisted of some thousands at the head of the march and thousands already in the Park. Suddenly the vast mass of the march began to arrive – and the speeches had to be given all over again.

The contingents stood around their banners, discussing tired feet and a sense of frustration. We had started off apprehensive of chaos from police attacks, provocateurs and disruption from those wanting to go to Grosvenor Square. We had none of these, we had kept together, we had filled the streets, our numbers were enormous. CND and police 'unofficial' counts were as high as 100,000 (the BBC in a news report said one tenth, about 6,000, went to Grosvenor Square – a slip, as they claimed only 2,000). We had linked arms, though swamped often by older people, by those unaware of our need to remain cohesive and so ambling along in and around our lines. We had proclaimed a clear solidarity line, though nearly half the people there were uncertain as to its meaning (the *New Society* survey of 270 demonstrators said 42 per cent favoured a compromise peace, 53 per cent victory for the NLF). Yet we were curiously unfulfilled. As press reports came in, commending our good behaviour, applauding us and the police for the pacific nature of the events, it became clear that we had defrauded ourselves.

Meanwhile from 5.30 p.m. thousands drifted off to Grosvenor Square to witness the fighting. Three separate groups had gone there, perhaps 2,000 in all – dissatisfied VSC supporters such as Notting Hill Gate VSC, or the Essex contingent who felt a peaceful march inadequate, various anarchist groups, and BVSF. There were pushes and charges at the powerful police cordons, who easily resisted them, while confining their own attacks to the occasional beating, and throwing the demonstrators back into the crowd (there were only 44 arrests, 4 police and about 50 demonstrators injured, compared with over 250 arrests in March, when 25,000 demonstrators were enraged and attacked by police cordons obstructing the march). A number of NCCL observers were attacked and their notebooks taken by the police. One TV cameraman threw missiles at demonstrators and attempted to film their response as some sort of dramatic action. But on the whole it was very good-natured. After three hours of pushing and shouting the crowd broke up and went home, the BVSF leaders singing Auld Lang Syne in unison with the police.

(From 'End of a Tactic' by Geoff Richman)

It appeared that the ruling class was taking notice . . .

So much controversy and confusion surrounded the events and personalities of 27 October that we believe they deserve observations by a commentator of Miss Mary McCarthy's stature.

(*Sunday Times*)

The Demo: How Newsmen Planned for a Revolution

After Sunday's demonstration march it wasn't just the police who were patting themselves on the back. Fleet Street is positively purring with self-congratulation. 'Our planning went off so successfully we now know that if there is a revolution we can cope,' said Mr Denis Holmes, planner of special projects, who master-minded the *Daily Mail's* comprehensive coverage.

(*Campaign*, 1 November 1969)

How Sunday's Demonstration Was Reported: Newspaper Treatment of Events Under Criticism

Offensive weapons
Sir – After the behaviour of some thugs in Grosvenor Square, isn't it time flag poles and sticks for carrying banners were classed as offensive weapons?

Children who wave flags for the Queen would have to be considered but maybe there can be a way round this.

Yours faithfully,
W. T. Pattinson

*

... and finally for every person who is a socialist, and in this context every socialist is an extremist, it is a system 'sufficiently strong and relaxed' to allow seven and a half million people to live in wretched poverty, to expropriate the wealth of the majority of people in this country, and to underwrite the war of the United States in Vietnam. In fact it is an inequitable and panic-stricken capitalist system. That is why, in your dim Manichean world of 'the public' and 'extremists', you will never be able to understand either the aims or the actions of socialists, and why they will always greet your efforts to do so with derision and contempt.

> Yours faithfully,
> Alexander Cockburn

Tribute to police

Sir – Those of your readers wishing to demonstrate their admiration for the Metropolitan Police may like to know that contributions to their welfare fund may be sent to the Commissioner of Metropolitan Police, New Scotland Yard, Broadway, SW1.

> Yours &c.,
> Margaret Croft

20 Parks Road, Oxford

As a supporter of capitalism who took part in the demonstration purely on the issue of Vietnam I was horrified and disgusted to read the violent, distorted nature of the reports in the national press.

> Yours faithfully,
> Graham Bell

Loughborough University of Technology

The boost did come on Sunday from the main march. While you concentrated on 2,000 people involved in a piece of knockabout farce in Grosvenor Square – it ended with the police and demonstrators singing Auld Lang Syne – 100,000 (repeat 100,000) were marching in determined, disciplined manner to their target. Here was the real threat to the system – the fact that such an enormous body of people could accept the aims of the organizers, could link arms and march that distance without being deterred by disrupters, uniformed or otherwise. Here is the force that is going to make the link between the demonstration and the growing struggle of the industrial workers. When that link is forged, we hope we will not disappoint you with our revolutionary potential.

Yours faithfully,
Roger Protz

(Five letters from *The Times*, 30 October 1968)

Last summer I took a class of young GPO workers to the Stock Exchange. We were shown a film about the delights of Big Business and the world of money. We were smiled at and talked to by pretty girls in smart uniforms. There was nothing in the papers next day about the indoctrination the GPO boys had been subjected to.

A few Thursdays ago I had a class of London Electricity Board apprentices. I teach the boys Liberal Studies – which means, amongst other things, current affairs. The topical issue today is student protest. I want the boys to get a first-hand impression of what it's all about, so I ask them if they'd like to go to the University of London Union to see what's going on – and, if possible, talk to some LSE students. They agree enthusiastically.

At ULU we go to the information desk and ask if there are any LSE students about. They find one for us. We all go into the hall, and the LEB boys ask him questions for about half an hour. When the discussion is over, we go back to college and talk about what the LSE student has said. The boys are critical, but glad they've had the chance to see for themselves.

While still at ULU, though, I have met an old friend of mine, Rodney Tyler. He has asked me what I'm doing these days – and more particularly what I'm doing at ULU. I tell him. He then tells me he is now a reporter on the *Daily Mail*.

By midnight the first edition of the *Daily Mail* is out. Mr Tyler's information about his friend has proved very interesting to his bosses. It seems, in fact, that my Liberal Studies class is the most important event that has taken place in the entire world that Thursday. It occupies over 100 column inches on the front page under the heading 'Lesson in Revolution'. There is also a photo – across seven columns.

The minute the first edition appears, the jackals of Fleet Street are on to me. The *Express* understands that I might not want to make a statement, but wonder if I have anything to say 'off the record'. (Is anything you say to the *Express* ever off the record?) An *Express* reporter is there in person banging on my front door at 1 a.m. And the phone keeps ringing till 4 a.m.

I lie awake, convinced that they'll hound me out of my job, having absurd fantasies about the things I will say if they give me a fair chance.

At about 8 a.m. the baby wakes up. As I fetch her from her bedroom, I see two eyes staring at me through the letter-box. It is a reporter: whom I tell quite reasonably to go away. Although I'm standing twelve feet back from the door, this conversation is described in the *Evening Standard* as me shouting 'go away' through the letter-box when reporters call at my house.

At 9 a.m. I try to phone my college Principal. But the phone isn't disconnecting when I put it down, and there's an *Evening Standard* reporter at the other end. So whenever I pick up the phone, there's this voice:

'Mr Hoyland?'

In the end I'm screaming at him:

'Get off the line! Will you get off the line! LEAVE ME ALONE!'

By now I've realized the golden rule: don't have anything to do with them. No statements, no photos, nothing. Because they're incapable of conducting themselves with the minimum standards of integrity, and they'll use anything you do or say against you.

Not only the papers. The BBC tricks County Hall into going on The World at One by telling them I've agreed to go on myself – which I haven't. And during the afternoon a female BBC reporter sees fit to stand in front of my house, peering into the window and describing what she can see into a tape-recorder. This monologue is later broadcast on the South-East News, because it is very important that the British Nation should know how my kitchen is decorated.

My liberal studies class is big news now. All the papers are on to it, so is the television and radio. When I go out, reporters chase me in taxis. There are reporters at college, reporters at County Hall. I feel impotent. The whole thing is weird and scaring and unfair. But the teachers at college are very nice and stick by me, and in the afternoon papers I see that some of my students have said they'll have a sit-in if I'm sacked. They send a note of support to my house. Beautiful. I almost weep. Solidarity isn't just an idea – it's love in action, a human and humanizing experience . . .

The LEB boys are fantastic, too. On the TV they say all the right things. Almost certainly, they save me my job. For in the end, nothing happens. Because for all the *Daily Mail*'s scare-mongering I've done nothing wrong – except that I've failed to get permission from the head of department before taking the students out.

But then, I didn't do that when I took the students to the Stock Exchange either. Nobody seemed to mind then. I wonder why.

(*Black Dwarf*, April 1969)

Kids certainly noticed . . .

How many of your friends or family who are at work would put up with this sort of treatment?

'You boy! Stop talking! Come here. What is that you're wearing? Jeans! How dare you come to school in jeans! You're a disgrace. And look at your hair. It's far too long. Who the hell do you think you are?'

Well, who the hell do you think you are?

It's pretty clear what a teacher who talks to you like that thinks you are. Many people treat animals more kindly. That teacher obviously does not think that you are human. Or if he does, he does not think that you are as good a human as he is.

But this is all part of a plan. The schools are run by the state, and the state dictates what sort of school there should be. The schools of today train young people to be the citizens of tomorrow. It is pretty obvious what sort of citizen it wants. It wants literate citizens, maybe, it wants educated citizens, maybe, but above all it wants obedient citizens. Citizens who all through their younger years have been trained to obey authority; authority in the form of teachers and headmasters.

All pupils are subjected throughout their school life to a constant barrage of petty restrictions on their freedom, which are designed with one thing in mind – to make them obedient. You are told to wear uniforms, punished if you do not. Yet there is no law which says you must. You are told to get your hair cut, keep to your own side of the playground, not to enter school during the playtimes. Of course you can't go to the toilet. Who do you think you are? Above all you must never tell a teacher he is wrong, because remember that all teachers are always right.

By the time the pupils reach the fifth year, they have been so conditioned to authority that they readily become members of it as prefects, petty officials that are often more vicious than authority itself.

Well, who do you think you are? Are you some kind of robot? Daleks who can only mumble 'we obey', or are you individuals with your own ideas?

Are you human?

Are you free?

(The above leaflet was handed in by a group of schoolboys in an East Ham, London, school. Distribution was followed on 24 July this year by a two-hour sit-in at the school)

I want to see a band who can scream and shout about the dangerous thoughtlessness of the great grey society, about the brutality of our cops and the stupidities of our laws. I want to see a group inciting a riot. I want to see some action. This summer is the time, the mood is right for us to fight politics with music in the same way as the press and tele can (but rarely do) fight it, because rock is now a media. Sure it's basically a recreation, a pastime, for most people but because we've now applied new rules to the way it's run – it's also a weapon. Let's use it.

(*International Times*)

'Living School was meant to be what school and learning could be like, about real things with interesting, interested people talking and not talking down. Someone in the Government found out that it was going to be held in the LSE and banned it. So it had to be transferred to Conway Hall in complete confusion, which was not helped by spending most of the morning arguing about whether Living School should attempt to re-take the now locked LSE. There was a film about squatting and the perennial puppet show with Barbara Castle as the wicked aunt and a puppet shop steward, hitting the policeman instead of Punch. John Berger sat in one corner carefully explaining things and Steven Sedley gave a long talk about industrial law and when Ernie Roberts got tired of being shouted down he went off for a cup of tea with the organizer who was by now reduced to simply making a long list of what was happening in which room. In the meantime, there was a brisk schoolkids' demonstration against their eviction from LSE and a tiny bannerless crowd foiled the police completely by weaving up and down Fleet Street and finally nipping in to the *Daily Express* to hold a quick sit-in. Everyone had a great time.

The second Living School was organized entirely by the schoolkids. It was awful and consisted mainly of bossy little male chauvinist boys from the International Marxist Group and the Maoists expelling each other.'

Folkestone, recently. School comrades were distributing *Vanguard*, the Schools Action Union paper, outside the girls' grammar school. They were given a lift in a car by some comrades who are not at school. Sex, male; age, 23. They were seen by one member of the local police force whose wife is a teacher at the school. Symbolic relationship. The following week, parents of six of the girls received a letter from the headmistress of the grammar school. She could not understand what interest twenty-three-year-old men could have in thirteen-year-old girls. It was clear to her that their daughters were being used, and not just for political reasons. She warned parents that the girls 'may' have been taking drugs and that they were associated with people who did take drugs. No evidence, of course. But to the Folkestone authorities, legal, educational and parental, it is self-evident that the demand for increased democracy within schools could only come from sex-maniacs, drug addicts and Communists. A mother of one of the girls told one of the undesirables that her daughter was 'one of the sheep' and it was obvious nobody could be interested in her except for sexual reasons. The girls involved have been kept under parental house arrest. 'Undesirable' literature is banned, which includes the Penguin on Risinghill and Victor Serge's memoirs. One girl was forced to tear up a copy of *Vanguard* in front of her parents. Interest in the Vietnam war was described by other parents as unnatural. Folkestone comrades are described by parents as being 'undesirable twenty-three-year-old men'.

Ironically, in fact, the forces of Folkestonian law and order are providing a beautiful object lesson in authoritarianism. For once they are really educating. And the lesson isn't being ignored. Not only has a school action group been formed, but suddenly everyone is becoming undesirable, twenty-three, and VERY DETERMINED.

(*Black Dwarf*)

'A load of us always seem to get down to Hyde Park for the Free Concerts. I think a lot of the trouble is because quite a lot of the hairy music gets boring to listen to after a bit and people get restless and then there's trouble – not always our fault either.

'But what we say is why not have a free Reggae and Soul Concert at Hyde Park? The trouble is some of the artists and agents are too poor to afford to play free, and others are too bothered about getting money and couldn't give a fuck about us. But surely a record company could sponsor it, and get loads of publicity for doing it. Just imagine sitting in a boat on the Serpentine, listening to the Upsetters or the Niyah Shuffle. Could be pretty good!'

The People Band are men of few words. They appear to distrust words, especially written down words. It is as if they feel words have and will ultimately and inevitably let them/you down. They like interviews even less.

'Tell me Mr People Band how do you know what notes to play next?'

'How do you know what words to write next?'

In the beginning was the grunt. Then came the division of labour. The grunt became word and sound. This was the origin of the original misunderstanding.

The People Band deny both the principle of division and the discipline of labour. At the time of the great divide, music was allocated the experience that didn't fit into words. The People Band reject completely this historical restriction. The gap has grown very wide. People who throw themselves as connections over abysses are asking for trouble. In translating the noise the People Band make into words I certainly am. It's like spelling out 'I LOVE YOU' letter by letter just before you come.

'Tell me Mr People Band how do you relate to the revolution?'

GRIN. 'We are the revolution.'

I am talking about the People Band in words because I wanted to find out what kind of revolution they were on about.

The following is the result of some considerable time spent disentangling with the People Band. All clumsy distortions in translation are my responsibility not theirs.

They play the most extraordinary music. They manifest their music. Aspects of experience combine, interact, communicate, conflict. They are continually jumping out of their own shape, like mocking jack-in-the-box poltergeists. You couldn't categorize the music into any style. The sequence could be called random – which means nothing much except that its not arranged beforehand. With the People Band there is the minimum of arranging beforehand. It's rather random who ends up doing the gig when they get there. They have an osmotic relationship to the audience. Indeed watching them play you sometimes wonder if the People Band is there at all. They disappear playing red trumpets through doors of retreat into corners or just sit down and have a rest. As you listen to them you realize that they appear to be celebrating something. The words that leap to mind are joyous, exulting. Not words that come particularly easily these days. Not with any honesty anyway. Whatever else they are doing the People Band are certainly not having you on. But in my revolution it seems that hatred, despair or mourning are frequently the only genuine emotions around. Everything else is too often hot air and the mirror image. But the People Band can make you laugh and laugh. They make people crawl on all fours and bang and grin and shout. Sometimes you are in a green ocean exploring great valleys and mountains you never thought existed before, or a kid filthy and exhausted after the most tearing roaring wrestling romp that ever was when the grown-ups forget completely to organize. You might very well be next on the road to Shangrila, or Chicago or the pub in Pudsey where the man plays the piano, or anywhere. There are plenty of artistic dealers in discord around. But the People Band do something more. They admit chaos frankly. Then they move around in it freely without fear and make their own patterns. All walls, all boundaries inside and outside are liable to continuous transformation. But that's no reason to lose your head close up and become conservative or sectarian. You just keep your eyes very open and your ears flapping in the wind.

The People Band aren't hiding they're revealing aspects of a manifold dis-appropriation. Capitalism has manufactured the most distorted people. Whole parts of us are deaf, dumb and blind. At this rate most of us are going to be so numb and paralysed we won't be even able to imagine anything different never mind change it.

There is a great robbery going on of the ability to feel. Sense – experience is fetishized and marketed as 'the most sensational thing'. There are whole realms of experience for which in the language of common sense there are no longer any words. Such experience is regarded as dangerous. It is always contained in one way or another. One brand of containers are labelled as 'art'. Art is licensed out to an élite who congratulate themselves on their sensitivity or coolness as the case may be. The art dealers and hip merchants like a good return on an investment. They go for nice tidy packages and they've got the market parcelled out.

The People Band don't fit in here at all. They've been called the most uncommercial band in the world. In communicating disappropriated experience they won't let themselves be appropriated as art. They resist packaging and labelling of all kinds. They are far too busy extracting from what is happening. They are too intent on playing. Because the process of extraction is so concentrated it leaps over into glimpses of what could be. They are not just describers but explorers and suggesters. Revolution in brightly coloured socks can dance happy and gloriously down the streets in joyous dignity. Part of what they are doing is not just in the playing, not just in the noise they make. It is how they make it. They challenge not only with music that can't be capsulated, but they break out of being a band. It's not enough to try and make what you do unmarketable. If you don't want them to absorb you you have to be sure they are not conning you into thinking you're somehow more precious than everyone else because you're not out on the open market. Otherwise you're still part of their division of labour. You're a professional failure.

Much later part of the People Band became part of Kilburn and the High Roads. They weren't as good but they were still brilliant.

Dear Mr T. Fawthrop:

Further meetings of the Senate were held last week at which it has been agreed:

1. That you presented yourself in May 1968 for Part II of the Final examination for the B.A. Joint Degree in Political Studies and Sociology;
2. That you be now re-admitted to the University;
3. That you be allowed to take Part II of the Final examination in Political Studies and Sociology on one further occasion in June 1969;
4. That you be deemed not eligible for the award of honours when you take this examination.

Yours sincerely,
(signed) W. D. Craig, Registrar

'When I was at school, just because I didn't like metalwork the teachers used to tell me to empty the dustbins and sweep the floors. So I thought that the best thing to do was to leave school and I would be able to do something better, but here I am in a little printing firm sweeping up the rubbish, as usual.'

'When I was at school I was having an argument with one of the teachers and he turned on me and beat me up and ever since then the slightest thing I did wrong, he either sent me out or sent me to the Head Master. Some teachers listen to you and understand your problems but the majority of them are bastards.

'And now me and Col have left school and hang about in a gang, the coppers come up to us just like the days at school, and pick on us by telling us to move on or threatening to nick us if we hang about in a gang.'

'Today's Marxists are concerned only with adults: reading them one would believe we are born at the age when we earn our first wages.'

J.–P. SARTRE

It also appeared that the working class was taking notice . . .

Message to the Living School: Why We Are on Strike at Punfield Barstows

You are here because you are involved in an area of struggle that has only recently come to the forefront. That is the fight against an educational system that is socially unacceptable and whose prime objectives are teaching people respect for authority, discipline, obedience and an unquestioning acceptance of the destinies our 'betters' have decided to channel us towards.

The struggle in industry is a lot older but it is not completely separate. Both are challenges to the ruling élite and their right to make the decisions that affect us all.

*

Comrades:

Ford Shop Stewards Committee, on behalf of all their members, the rank and file at Fords, would like to express their feelings to the students who supported us throughout our Strike by saying 'thank you' and by giving their support to all the good work the students are doing.

Brian Wood
(on behalf of the Joint Trade Union Strike Committee)
Ford Motor Company, Dagenham, Essex

Claimants' and Unemployed Workers' Union

A message to the sick and disabled, to the unemployed and all people who have become forced to rely on social security benefits for their standard of living.

Because of government economic policies, industrial mergers, more and more people are being made unemployed. Putting people on the dole, forcing more and more elderly people to retire early, is becoming an ever increasing part of government and big business policy. On the grounds of so called economies, nearly a million people have been robbed of their right to a job. So long as they are not actually starving, who cares?

The old anti-working-class ideology about having it good on the welfare state will be increasingly encouraged by a government and selfish people who want to fob off their social responsibilities.

With every industrial merger, with every productivity deal, more factories are closed and a few hundred more workers are PAID OFF. It's not so bad while the money lasts, but after a while, when prospects of a new job fade, paid-off workers soon learn what *redundancy* means.

Because of their age, or 'worked-out' physical condition, many of these chaps are doomed to permanent unemployment. ENFORCED RETIREMENT with an ENFORCED DRASTIC REDUCTION in their living standards. A WANTON WASTE OF VALUABLE HUMAN ASSETS.

If the economic policies of the government and big business mean that people have to be made unemployed, then we must demand full compensation, AN ADEQUATE STANDARD OF LIVING FOR ALL DURING THE PERIOD OF UNEMPLOYMENT.

We must put an end to the PHASED LOWERING OF LIVING STAN-DARDS, which is attractively called 'earnings related benefits', but which are only payable for six months and is put there to hide the consequences of unemployment.

THE TIME HAS COME FOR THE WORKLESS TO BE GIVEN AN ORGANIZED VOICE – A VOICE THAT CAN DEMAND AND SECURE A WELL-PAID JOB FOR THOSE ABLE TO WORK – A VOICE THAT CAN DEMAND AND SECURE A GOOD LIVING BASIC FAMILY INCOME FOR THOSE UNABLE TO WORK.

Unorganized, your living standards are at the mercy of politicians; what you receive is regarded as charity, to be lowered or raised according to the political opportunities of the day. Unorganized, your living standards become dependable upon charitable organizations where you can see ALLEVIATION from your acute POVERTY, but never put an end to it.

ORGANIZED, you can put an end to your poverty YOURSELVES. Organized, you can have a say in deciding your standards of living. Organized, you can make officials your servants and not your masters.

Long experience has taught the working man that he can only get his just claims met by COLLECTIVE ACTION. That is why you should join us, so that through your collective strength, you can provide the living standard you deserve.

YOU HAVE A VOICE – YOU HAVE STRENGTH – ORGANIZE AND USE THEM

To get what is rightfully yours – let this be your purpose, along with us.

(JOE KENYON, leaflet of the Barnsley Claimants' and Unemployed Workers' Union)

Certain connections were being made . . .

1. Building workers are lobbying at their local town hall about some breach of the health regulations on their site. TURNED AWAY by some municipal bureaucrat, they troop down the steps, re-form, link arms and charge past the astonished clerk shouting 'Ho, Ho, Ho Chi Minh'.
2. American soldier drunk in a bar in Hong Kong to British merchant seaman: 'When the hell are you Limeys going to start fighting in

Vietnam?' British sailor: 'Well, the Viet Cong haven't asked us yet.'
3. At South London tenants' meeting. Member of the committee, a veteran Communist, advocates caution. Tenant at the back disagrees: 'We've got to fight them with everything we've got, like them bloody Viet Congs do.'

Horace Cutler, hated and goateed boss of London GLC Housing, wrote to the *Daily Mirror* after a columnist had supported squatting. 'If his incitement is followed,' wrote Cutler, 'we may expect to see mobs breaking into the shopping centres to get free food and no one will dare to sell his house lest squatters break in ... Squatters are stealing ... Please don't support this irresponsible line or you may find your car, your house or even the Editor's chair grabbed.'
WHAT YOU CAN DO: When you see an empty house, waiting drearily till some bureaucrat gets around to renting it, organize a Squat. Don't believe Government sabotage like the Minister of Housing claiming a housing surplus by 1973. There are over a million homeless people in England. If a Squat already exists in your neighbourhood, go round and lend a hand. Squat is happening! It's fact. Spread the word. RE-PEOPLE THE GHOSTLY HOUSES!

(SARAH, *International Times*)

How much does it cost to leave a man alone?

IT COST £54,000 to evict squatters from Piccadilly. (900 policemen, £60 each)
IT COST £12,000 to evict squatters from Bloomsbury. (200 policemen, £60 each)
IT COST £18,000 to evict squatters from Holborn. (300 policemen, £60 each)
IT COST Mr Lyon £1,000 to show his gratitude to the police for looking after his property rights.
IT COSTS ratepayers £85,884 17s. a year in unpaid rates to have Centre Point empty.
IT COSTS £100 to take a man to Court.

IT COSTS £15 a week to keep a man in jail.

IT COSTS £33 billion to go to the moon.

IT COSTS £16 13s. a week to keep a man, wife and 2 kids on Social Security.

IT COSTS Kensington and Chelsea Council £3 million to build a luxurious new Town Hall, although they already have three with all the gold fittings.

IT WOULD COST VERY LITTLE to house all the homeless in Britain.

It costs nothing to leave a man alone.

IT COST Redbridge Council £3,000 to take up floor boards and ruin a perfectly good Council house, so that people should not live in it.

HOW MUCH DID IT COST Redbridge Council to employ Quartermain and his fellow thugs to try to evict squatters at Ilford when the Council had no need to do so?

HOW MUCH DOES IT COST the GLC to evict 5,000 tenants, employing bailiffs, police and the ensuing court charges? It would be cheaper and more realistic if every working man and woman with or without children were to demand NOW that every empty house and office block be filled and/or converted for the thousands of families living in slums, cramped conditions or half-way houses. In this way all these would be put to good use rather than left empty and neglected. The councils would not be in debt to the professional moneylenders, but provide their own interest from their own investments, and the country as a whole would have a more humane rather than inhumane housing plan. Profiteering would be stopped, the poor would be better off with a decent roof over their heads. We say use all the empty houses of which there are hundreds of thousands.

USE EMPTY HOUSES NOW. TAKE OVER EMPTY OFFICES FOR THE HOMELESS.

WE WILL NOT WAIT.

*

Squatters seized an empty five-storey office block in London's Brixton Road on Saturday, 29 March. About a dozen squad cars, black marias and motor cycle police surrounded the building just before 9 a.m., minutes after the 'invasion squad', otherwise known as the South London Squatters, had got in through a back way.

A detachment of police headed by an inspector from the nearby Brixton police station and a plain-clothes man clambered over a ten-foot hardboard fence at the back of the concrete and glass building and tried to get the squatters to leave quietly. They refused. A few minutes later large banners appeared over the balconies of the block reading: 'Homes not offices' and 'Enough room here for eighty families'. Plus a red flag.

The building is next to Brixton Register Office. Astonished wedding guests watched as police tried to get the squatters out. According to a leaflet handed out by supporters outside, the building – 40,500 sq. ft of it – has been empty for three years. 'Why can't Cathy come home to this?' the leaflet asks. 'We have occupied this building to expose the housing shortage. A building this size could be converted at only £1,000 a unit to house eighty homeless families. Eight million sq. ft of office building stands empty in London alone – enough to house all the homeless in Britain.'

The operation, the first carried out by the group, was surprisingly simple. The glass in a door at the back of the building was cut and Hey Presto! The next they heard were the sirens.

Said Ray Gibbon, travel agency manager and father of two, of Shakespeare Road, Herne Hill, 'We intend staying here until 5.30. Then we'll leave quietly after we've made our point.'

The squatters, all local people, passed their time listening to the radio, playing football and putting records on a record player they'd brought with them. At lunch-time fish and chips and bottles of beer were hoisted up by rope from outside. Rubbish was put in a Lambeth Council paper sack they had brought in with them. 'We want to be as tidy as possible,' said Mr Gibbon.

During the day, the squatters gave out over 7,000 leaflets in the Brixton shopping centre. One West Indian bus conductor said, 'Give me a heap man. I'll give them out to the lads when I get to the garage at Croydon.' The leaflet said: 'Some people try to blame immigrants for the housing shortage but we know we had lousy houses in Britain long before we ever saw a black face or heard an Irish accent. The real reason for the housing shortage is that a small group of people make millions of pounds out of our need for a decent home.'

(*Black Dwarf*)

In the 1940s a judge denounced the squatters as a 'bunch of ignorant busybodies going about making confusion'. Well, here we are again:
IGNORANT . . . because we don't believe in the law of the judges and the privileged class.
BUSYBODIES . . . because we care what happens to other people.
MAKING CONFUSION . . . as much confusion as we can because we know that that is the only way to get things changed.

We, the Edinburgh Squatters, encouraged by successes in London, organized a token squat to demand that this high-rent housing be made available to people on the waiting list. We sneaked into one of the flats before dawn on the morning of Monday, 17 March (the police are still trying to find out how we got in). After an hour the first policeman arrived, contacted headquarters and soon there were four. They banged on the door, ignoring others giving out leaflets in the street, and announced that they were the police. The squatters inside agreed that they were, but didn't open the door. The morning then passed quietly with two plump constables marching up and down (to check that no breach of the peace occurred) and we discovered that they were quite sympathetic. A lady from the corporation visited (she was a housing visitor!) and demanded to know what right we had to be there. We explained politely and she left. The reactions from local people were really encouraging. They had been upset about the corporation's housing twelve to fifteen sharing a toilet. One old dear explained that 'The Duke of Edinburgh doesnae want nae common council hoose tenants aside his palace'. Workers from a nearby building site visited and gave their approval but were moved on by the police, though the police had made no attempt to interfere with our movements.

(Bob Finlay, *Black Dwarf*)

*

From the Minutes of the United Tenants Action Committee

Mrs Rosenberg, NUT member, spoke on behalf of the teachers in their present dispute. Reported on new militancy of the teachers, and the urgent need for wide support from the rest of the working class. Asked that resolutions be put to trade union branches and tenants' associations, and also Parent Teacher Associations if possible. Brought along 5,000 leaflets explaining our case and 5,000 on meeting in Hackney next Monday. Asked that everyone try to come to the meeting.

The meeting fully endorsed and supports the teachers' action.

Policy discussion

GEORGE BAKER: Cutler has come out with his March increase. We have to decide what we're going to do.

SCRIV.: Have anticipated this meeting with posters for rent strike. First thing is to have mass meeting of GLC and borough tenants.

BOB DELEW: If we call total rent strike straightaway will not get the tenants who have paid this time. Suggest we withhold increase for first six weeks to get the people in and give them confidence, then call total strike.

J. LUCK: Samuda was one of the most awkward estates to organize, but people on my estate will not pay at all next time.

JIM RUTTER: Whether rent increase or total rent strike, we will ultimately be faced with eviction – so let's do it the quickest way.

JOHN KIMBER: Before we do anything it's essential to organize. Two enemies – the GLC and the newspaper. Scriv.'s poster premature. If we reorganize for rent strike we won't get anywhere – should organize first and then put the question.

DAVE ANDREWS: We're under-estimating the tenants' militancy. Whatever we withhold next time will be outside the law. Anything less than a full rent strike in week 1 of the increase and we may as well all go home.

GEORGE HARRIS: Compare this with fight in factory for wage rise. Lot of negotiations, then workers get fed up and go out on strike. Press never report what leads up to strikes. Been talking to people paying increase – said we'd have been better off with total rent strike.

It's got to be thought over and talked over. Got to have everybody behind us – including trade-unionists.

TERRY CONNOLLY: People who paid look down their noses at us – in many cases could afford it. These are the kind of people we are confronted with.

GEORGE BAKER: This is discussion only – we want solid and firm decision to be taken by the tenants.

MICK O'LEARY: Endorse total rent strike. How we do it is the important thing. Get everyone in, and about a month before hold mass meeting to take policy decision. If decision here, some estates would say yes and some no. Main thing is how we implement the policy.

HELEN LOWE: The people most difficult to organize last time were the people who could not afford to pay it, on the older GLC estates where incomes are low.

SCRIV.: Start the rumour now. Keep feeding the people with the word rent strike. That's what that poster means now – it's only the beginning of it.

SID BRISTOW: I believe the Government is making the future for us very easy. Bus fares up 32 per cent today. Grocery bills going up. Future policy for wages will not cover bus fares let alone rent increases. Don't think there's a hall large enough – need Trafalgar Square, or Victoria Park, Tower Hill or Hyde Park. Only we can do this. We need more propagandists. The people are getting fed up seeing the same faces. Times are now changing – many who paid it now find they can't afford it. Disagree with Chairman that it should be only the rent – should stop the lot.

MICK HOULIHAN: Suggestions that we go back to tenants ridiculous. We must recommend a policy to the tenants. If we go into next one again withholding the increase the GLC can afford to let us stew. No policy but a total rent strike – if we don't do this we may as well go home. People want to become involved now, not just go to meetings.

JUDY ROBERTS: Finished revised version of Not a Penny on the Rent. All the new stuff handed round tonight. All the rest people here have seen. Like people to read it this week and have suggestions for next Sunday. Like to have it ready for sale by Christmas.

GEORGE ASHTON: Like to know what we're going to do after we successfully conclude a rent strike. We must be able to provide alternatives. Mass meeting must be on the cards for February next year. Porter at LSE investigating use of their hall. We're still guarding the prefab – we've had overtures from new District Officer.

MICK O'LEARY: Move we go away from here tonight to campaign for a total rent strike from week 1 of the rent increase. (Seconded Manny Lane, agreed unanimously.)

After Discussion on Demonstration Sub-Committee report, it was agreed that the Mystery Tour for 14 December be cancelled and all efforts be directed at getting mass demonstration to County Hall for 16 December when the GLC will be ratifying the next increase.

The Government have referred the GLC rent increases to the Prices and Incomes Board. Tenants should be under no illusions that this is going to mean anything other than a postponement, or slight adjustment, of the rent increases. Petitions and lobbies will only have the same effect.

IN THE LAST RESORT ONLY A RENT STRIKE BY GLC TENANTS WILL EFFECTIVELY STOP THE RENT INCREASES: OTHERWISE THEY WILL GO THROUGH. LOBBIES AND PETITIONS WHICH ARE NOT BACKED BY STRIKE ACTION WILL BE LARGELY IGNORED. Lobbies, petitions, meetings and poster parades, however, are all extremely important forms of activity, particularly in the early stages. They enable contact to be made and organization to be built. By bringing tenants together, they create confidence and solidarity, without which no further action is possible. But if the ultimate aim of this activity is to stage a mass lobby of Parliament, and nothing further, it might as well not be undertaken. If the GLC rent scheme is going to be stopped this will not be done by Parliament or the Labour councillors at County Hall.

IT WILL ONLY BE DONE BY THE TENANTS THEMSELVES, THROUGH THEIR OWN RESOLUTION, ACTION AND ORGANIZATION.

* Discuss the rent rises continuously with your friends and neighbours – this is the way solidarity grows.
* If there is a tenants association on your estate, join it, and go along to its meetings. Don't leave it to do all the work. Tenants associations depend on their members.
* If there is no tenants association, get together with your neighbours and form one.
* Contact the GLC tenants action committee:
  We can help with

LEAFLETS

POSTERS
PETITIONS
SPEAKERS

* Many GLC tenants are in the trade union movement. We must get our trade union branches, trades councils, shop stewards committees, etc. involved in this campaign.

* Organize: Petitions, Lobbies, Demonstrations, *but* let's remember: These seldom force any authority to retreat.

OUR ONLY REAL WEAPON – THE ONLY ONE THE TORY GLC (AND THE LABOUR OPPOSITION) ARE REALLY WORRIED ABOUT – IS A RENT STRIKE.

RENT STRIKES ONLY SUCCEED THROUGH MASS ORGANIZATION AND SOLIDARITY.

SO ORGANIZE NOW!
DON'T RELY ON OTHERS TO FIGHT OUR BATTLE.

(From *Not a Penny on the Rent*, by Ian McDonald and Ken Lowe, GLC Tenants Action Committee)

Comrades,

On Thursday, 20 February, some 2,000 marched through London to Westminster. GLC tenants protesting. Obligingly 'protected' by three busloads of police – cocky, arrogant and safe. The people on the march were predominantly 'middle-aged', men and women of 40–50 years, some older, some younger, some infirm – but all united against the fascism of a council that can decide to increase house rents by as much as 30 per cent sitting on its fat conservative arse without knowing what 30 per cent means to tenants in Tower Hamlets and Poplar.

When will our movement realize that this is where we need to be? OK – spend a few hours at Claridges – make a smell for Nixon – but in the end realize that the smell doesn't *destroy* profits – it just makes them a little harder to collect. We must support, but support, the GLC tenants – the Ford strikers – the 'Royal' dockers. All right, it's not easy to involve yourself in things out of your immediate orbit. But we know that these are different facets of the same malaise – the same system. Without our support for them, how can we expect their support for us?

Trowbridge, and Kingshaven and Explorers, and Warwick, and Yeading Green and Ravenor Park won't rise up and suddenly discern in LSE's struggle the same cause that forces them to declare in their militant fashion – 'Not a penny on the rents'.

R. Allen, London, SE6

(Letter to *Black Dwarf*)

This was the BIGGEST WORKING-CLASS DEMONSTRATION London has seen for many years. Another interesting point was the fact that the average age of demonstrators was much closer to 50 than 20. Women outnumbered men by at least a 3:2 ratio and this marks an upsurge of militancy in working-class women that could well surprise the most optimistic observer. The virtual press blackout the following day and the total absence of TV coverage about the demonstration is very instructive to those of us who are used to the barrage of nonsense which follows Vietnam marches. No stories of hooliganism, Communist subversion or secret plots. In fact nothing at all! 1,500 SDS demonstrators in Germany got approximately 100 times the publicity in the press, so much for objective reporting!

Dockers March to Back Powell

I remember Nigel walking into the room with this *Evening Standard* headline. Big and black and two inches high. He looked as if his best mate had just this moment snuffed it. We were just completely shocked numb. It was predictable in so many ways and yet still quite shocking. You suddenly realized how little influence the Left really had, how the roots of the political organizations like the Communist Party had been rotting in the soil. How pathetic the squabbling between groups all was. Just how urgent things had become. It did more to me than the May events and Czechoslovakia rolled into one. I seemed to spend the next few days leafleting solidly and I'll never forget the look on the faces of the Pakistani postmen when they read the leaflets and found out they weren't fascist. For those few days after Powell, they were petrified. But so was I.

*

The Vacuum on the Left

The first draft of this editorial was framed in the early part of May. It began: 'the ability of the Government to ride its Prices and Incomes bill roughshod over any objections from Labour MPs or trade-union leaders underlines how little it depends upon these supporters for survival, and therefore how powerless they are. The local government elections more dramatically bear witness to the speed with which local Labour Parties are disintegrating. The legacy of a political working class is in ruins. And the speech of Enoch Powell, seeking to blame the immigrants (more narrowly, the coloured immigrants) for the Government's failure to improve housing, hospitals, and schools, evoked scarcely any response from what is left of the old labour movement. Resolutions from a few union executives, Ministerial asides deprecating Powell's impoliteness (let's take immigration out of politics, for we have no answer to the racialists which will stand up in the light), these tired gestures are all that remain. Alarmingly, the old labour movement has become a paper tiger.'

All that remains true, yet it is a mark of how rapidly the situation is changing that it is only half the truth. The magnificent revolt in France has answered Wilson and Powell much more effectively than could have been foreseen. It has also answered all those who believed that the working classes of industrialized countries were politically finished, bribed or bamboozled into permanent apathy. Whatever the outcome of the French revolution of 1968, an answer has been given to the dockers. With great clarity and astonishing speed, the vulnerability of Western capitalism has been demonstrated, and the strength and creativity of the French working class exhibited. France is not Britain, yet there are lessons to be learned – and the British ruling class will learn them, if the Left does not.

(*International Socialism*)

'Actually I'd been in political retirement for some time, absorbed in more internal things. I was wrenched out of this retreat by seeing the dockers clustered round Westminster. I'd just come out of the Tate Gallery. They were waiting to cheer Powell when he came out of

Parliament. I felt a lot of things all at the same time, but mainly a kind of shame at seeing this group of working-class men who had got little enough out of capitalism for themselves standing about with an awkward dignity on that dull wet afternoon waiting for Powell. Because Powell combines so many qualities that manual workers are both alien from and yet held down by – intellectual authority and arrogance – the classical quotations, nob embellishments of a lost empire – and a particularly lower-middle-class capacity to nip down dark alleys of the mind.

'I felt as though my political retreat, weary with meetings and leafleting, although small and unimportant in itself, was a desertion. My own immediate responsibility was brought back to me when a class of Port of London messenger boys greeted me the next morning with Hail Enoch fascist salutes when I went to teach them for liberal studies. The lesson that followed was stormy. I said the obvious things, about Powell's attitude to unemployment and the health service, about how the Right had always used the same arguments against the Irish and the Jews. In an East End class the names read like an immigrant's itinerary, Greek, Italian, Irish, German, French.

'They were too angry and worked up to listen much. Though one boy who was unusually like Sleepy in the Seven Dwarfs – he told me he had felt sleepy ever since he had failed his 11-plus – said "Thank goodness you've given us some facts. I've been arguing my head off on the docks with no evidence. I knew Powell couldn't be right." In the circumstances he was a kind of hero – though he never realized it.

'I was to have the same argument again and again. But as the week went by, they became less and less keen to stick by Powell, more angry about unemployment and tended to veer over to oppose him.

'Powell had entered a vacuum. The dockers were already pissed off with Labour. They had no traditional loyalties like their parents. They were fairly cynical about unions but extremely class-conscious. The Left had no influence on them. Later, I knew some engineering apprentices who were really deeply affected by politics by the end of '68. Powell somehow opened them up to some kind of commitment. Some of the militants in the docks today, it was Powell that started them thinking about politics.

'He certainly shook me up. I suddenly realized that my politics, which I'd got by osmosis after many meaningless meetings, were not a token affair of sitting in the back waiting for someone to take decisions. I had to do something.

'Even me doing things could affect things. Not to do things was to desert completely the people who had otherwise only the normal capitalist stuff about immigrants being hurled at them. Perhaps I was slightly turned by events – and more so as '68 went on. But it was really a time when extreme voluntarism was needed and seemed to work. Anyway it needed a shock to jolt us out of the peace and love and breadfruit and tiny troubles of the mind of '66–'68.

'The *Black Dwarf*'s first sheet was brought out in time for the Powell demo. It had a picture of him and information about his political record on the back. This was a blow-up of an IS leaflet. We carried it on a demonstration, the route of which I don't quite remember clearly, but then I never remember routes. It was a chaotic jumbly demonstration that suddenly turned a corner and came and found itself in front of Parliament with the dockers, angry and in small groups, grabbing the occasional student and doing them over. But, like all situations like that, with the odd docker talking to another group of students. I remember one oldish man in a cap saying, "I'm not against the blacks but it's like a cup. It can only hold so much," with an excessively polite Indian graduate with an upper-class English manner, explaining patiently his class interests to him.'

We shambled by – not a march any more by now, clusters shuffling past clusters of dockers. The main clump of dockers were hemmed in by the police. I crossed with another girl to give them leaflets. They surged forward – held back by the police. Someone spat in my face and we beat a hasty retreat.

In the tube a man with long grey hair and a posh voice was mouthing his contempt for the dockers. He had carried a banner from Notting Hill. I felt intense dislike for him. He was so obviously delighted at having some deeply held hurt against the working class opened up for a sniff of violence with a gloss of self-righteousness: 'I'm in the right, these crude vulgar men are in the wrong.' There was something nasty that went into some of the left politics that came out of '68. Something quite as nasty as Powell himself – like all nastiness it has left a bad taste which has still not gone quite.

There was anyway something fishy – that spontaneous demonstration.

Terry Barrett, one of the very few left-wing dockers who actually tried to stop the march, told me afterwards that it wasn't spontaneous at all. Not only did the small group of fascists who normally had no influence play on the dockers' fears about their jobs (very legitimate fears, as it has turned out), but they didn't lose their pay when they went down to the House of Commons and they were allowed by the police to carry their banners to Parliament. Usually demonstrations have to put them down by the wall. And the conflict at Westminster wasn't just between Right and Left, it was a clash between the new student Left and a very traditional sector of the working class.

Postscript: A year later I was in Victoria Park and met a docker who had been marching against 'In Place of Strife', Barbara Castle's White Paper. He asked me why the students had changed sides and were now supporting them when a year ago they'd called them racialists. He'd been on the dockers' march a year before. He was out on an industrial/political issue with us the following year.

It shocked the left towards a kind of unity . . .

The Urgent Challenge of Fascism

The outburst of racialist sentiment and activity since Enoch Powell's Birmingham speech marks the beginning of a new phase in British politics. A section of the ruling class (although not yet by any means the dominant section) is resorting to the crudest forms of prejudice in order to confuse, divide and divert workers from the real struggle. It does so in a situation where British capitalism is forced to cut real living standards, keep unemployment at a relatively high level, and raise rents and prices, while fearing that its rule is no longer guaranteed by the mass complacency of the fifties and early sixties. Powell thinks he can overcome these problems by developing a mass following on a racist programme. The ready response to his speech has revealed the prevalence of racialist ideas among workers, which had been inculcated by centuries of capitalism and imperialism. Paradoxically it also indicates the extent to which people are fed up with existing society. They are disillusioned with established politics and have lost faith in the succession of leaders who have betrayed their trust. But instead of blaming actual enemies and looking for the real source of their frustrations, they blame the immigrants.

The traditional organizations of the Left have totally failed either to offer real, socialist alternatives to capitalism or to combat the racist upsurge. The Labour Left has completely lost touch with the mass of workers. The Communist Party, despite its many individual militants, responded to the racism too little and too late. Internationalist propaganda did not immediately appear. Counter-demonstrations were not organized. As for the bulk of trade-union officials, with a few honourable exceptions, their chief concern seems to have been to avoid any responsibility, hoping that the upsurge would die of its own accord.

The events of the last few weeks have exposed the extreme isolation and fragmentation of genuinely anti-racialist forces. Many a militant in industry found himself quite alone when confronted with the racist tide, despite his success in leading purely economic struggles in the past.

An urgent reorganization of these socialist forces is necessary if the onward march of racialism is to be checked and any long-term fascist development fought against. (Previous differences have to be subordinated to the struggle against the common threat.) Socialist alternatives to frustrations and anxieties created by capitalism must be presented and linked to systematic anti-racist propaganda on a massive scale. A SINGLE ORGANIZATION OF REVOLUTIONARY SOCIALISTS IS NEEDED TO FIGHT THESE NEW AND URGENT BATTLES.

We invite all those who agree with the following programme to come together in trying to build this:

1. Opposition to imperialism; for the victory of all genuine national liberation movements.
2. Opposition to racism in all its forms and to controls on immigration.
3. Opposition to state control of trade unions; support for all progressive strikes.
4. Workers' control of society and industry as the only alternatives to fascism.

If you are interested in discussing possible sorts of action, contact International Socialism at the addresses overleaf.

(*International Socialism*)

But unity is hard to get and harder to keep . . .

'The Ho Chi Minh memorial meeting took place to commemorate the death of Ho Chi Minh. There had been two massive demonstrations on the subject of Ho Chi Minh. The first of which had occasioned a conflict in Grosvenor Square which outraged and shocked the bourgeois press and at the same time greatly cheered those who participated provided they didn't have to go through it all over again. On the second Vietnam demonstration great precautions were made by the bourgeoisie to prevent the seizure of state power. But the revolutionaries organized in such a way that they spent most of their time stewarding the march to prevent people breaking the law, like a large number of sheepdogs chasing each other into tidy shapes. The memorial meeting was effectively an epitaph on the solidarity campaign as far as I was concerned.

'A large number of people who had come into VSC had, after those two marches, decided either to piss off back home and play their records or alternately to join a political organization. Some did both. The death of Ho Chi Minh provided the last gasp of opportunity for the VSC to call a meeting with some hope that it would gather people from quite a wide political spectrum and drag back the various warring elements within the VSC. These were effectively the International Socialists and the International Marxist Group. Around these two groups was a whole number of small Maoist organizations and on one edge and feeling very unhappy was the Communist Party.

'Everybody agreed that the death of Ho Chi Minh was a bad thing. It was not particularly surprising that Jack Woodis as the representative of the Communist Party took the chance to reappear on a VSC platform. Nor was it surprising that a representative of the North Vietnamese Embassy should be there too. This in fact suited everyone because it convinced Jack Woodis that he was part of the young aware radical generation or something and it suited the IMG's belief that they were part of some world-wide movement striding to victory after victory in Indo-China and elsewhere. It suited me because I had to dish out leaflets for the Irish Civil Rights Solidarity Campaign, which was considered at that time a going concern, and this was a very handy concentration of lefties to do it. Also there were Maoists who had broken away from the great Vietnam demonstration-that-never-was to go to Grosvenor Square and now felt their hair might fall out if they went inside the Conway Hall and so stood outside failing to flog stuff. Inside the score was about 40 per cent IS, 30 per cent IMG, 30 per cent CP, Maoist etc. Most of the meeting was taken up with various people saying that the death of Ho Chi Minh was a great loss to the revolutionary movement throughout the world. Which is probably true but got a bit repetitive. Chris Harman got up for IS and made a speech showing no sign that he might be addressing other than an IS meeting. He addressed the meeting with a certain lack of style but no more than one would expect and proceeded in fairly forthright terms. He dealt first with Ho Chi Minh's contribution to the world revolutionary movement. And everybody sat there soaking up the usual collection of left-wing platitudes to which they had been well accustomed in the Conway Hall. Left-wing audiences are aware of the times that they gather together to clobber hell out of each other and they are aware of the times they gather together to indulge in mutual self-congratulation about the strength of the Left. The latter occasion is rare, but when it comes people thank god for it and think how great it is to be part of the united left against Fascism or the Spanish Civil War or something.

'After a while Harman proceeded to get on to the question of Ho Chi Minh's contribution to killing off the Trotskyist movement in North and South Vietnam. He expanded on various themes and pointed out that from the International Socialists' point of view, though they supported fully the Vietnamese people's struggle against American imperialism and had done a great deal practically in Britain on this theme, it was crucial to realize that Ho Chi Minh and the regime he had headed were not the answer to North Vietnam or Vietnam as a whole and what was eventually necessary was a workers' republic which would have to get rid of the present set-up. This went almost unnoticed by the audience. I regarded all this as fairly sound stuff which I'd heard before anyway hundreds of times. Anyway, Harman finished his speech and a lady aged about 55 to 60 got up and marched to the front and said that it was absolutely outrageous that people should just sit there and vegetate when somebody had just made a totally slanderous attack on the leader of the Vietnamese Revolution who had just died. Whereupon there was thunderous applause from the 60 per cent of the audience who weren't in IS. Harman looked slightly surprised and slightly grieved and slightly pleased by the reaction to his address. Tariq Ali looked very unhappy indeed because he could see his meeting falling apart in front of him. At the back of the hall a Maoist shouted "Washington spy!" at Chris Harman, which seemed to please him further. The audience now became somewhat heated. The Communist Party started to denounce the IMG, the IMG in its turn started to denounce the IS. The IS stood there looking grieved in some cases, sheepish in others and quite pleased with themselves for causing so much fuss and bother among the other groups. One Communist came up to the IS contingent and said "You're always like this. You were like this during the thirties. You'll try and wreck anything." By this time the platform was somewhat depleted since half of it had stormed off. The IMG speaker then proceeded to make a declamatory speech that no one could understand.

'Harman had wandered off the platform for some reason and Tariq Ali was left making occasional remarks about the IS letting the side down. The IS shouted at Tariq, "So you support the Communist Party, when did they ever join the VSC?", "Opportunist" etc. People at the back shouted at each other. The general atmosphere that came over for anyone who took a slightly detached view of the proceedings was one of a collection of nutters screaming at each other, and achieving very little. The IMG seemed quite pleased, however, to have photographs of the IS failing to stand up or sit down, whichever the case may be, during the Vietnamese national anthem. This created considerable problems because they seemed to be playing the Red Flag at the same time and I was not sure whether you should stand for either or both or leave, since my reaction since childhood has always been that whenever a national anthem gets played I walk out of the room as fast as possible. All IS being rude meant to me was that instead of dying a quiet private death three weeks later, VSC died in Conway Hall. But because the IS actually said that after all Ho Chi Minh wasn't such a good thing, the VSC got off its bed and ran around for a couple of minutes before collapsing in two minutes in a dead coma.'

An Anti-Fascist Conversation

Stan Newens, Labour Member of Parliament, to girl marcher: 'Walk quickly.'
GIRL MARCHER: 'Who are you?'
s.n.: 'I'm Stan Newens, Labour Member of Parliament.'
G.M.: 'So what?'
s.n.: 'It's people like you who are ruining this demonstration.'
G.M.: 'With people like you it's no wonder people are disillusioned with Parliament.'
Maoist shop steward holding banner of Islington YCL: 'Typical of the Labour Left, persecuting a poor girl.'

Cinderella Organizes Buttons:
Sheila Rowbotham

A year ago *Black Dwarf* declared 1969 the 'Year of the militant woman'.

A lot has happened in 1969. There has been action by women at work ranging from the lavatory attendants who struck against the White Paper, to the women at Industrial Mouldings plastic plant in Coventry who secured the same rate as the men. In jobs like nursing and teaching where women are very numerous, there has also been an important and determined militancy. Apart from local agitation, the National Joint Action Campaign for Women's Equal Rights organized a demonstration in the summer which included women from the potteries, buses, GPO and engineering.

In the student movement the secondary role women play was raised at the RSSF conference in the spring. Since then there has been discussion within all the left socialist groups as well as the Communist and Labour Parties. Various women's liberation and socialist women's groups have started, and two papers have appeared, *Socialist Woman* and the *Shrew*.

Our weaknesses are apparent: lack of communication, lack of empirical information, lack of theory and lack of confidence. Our strength is our willingness to work with one another and our determination to base any analysis on the actual situation of women now. For many women the simple discovery that they were not alone has been important. It has given us the confidence to argue and to act without feeling we were freaks. Here the stand taken by Lil Bilocca and the fishermen's wives in Hull, the sewing machinists' strike at Ford's, helped, as did the news of the women's liberation movement in America and Germany, and less directly the impetus from the experience of Black Power.

EMERGENCE OF DISCONTENT

Discontent has emerged from very different situations.

Consequently it reflects different emphases, different preoccupations, and looks to different objectives. Working-class women have complained about their pay, about the way jobs are graded, about lack of training, lack of creche facilities, about the difficulty of combining work and housework, about lack of representation in union positions, about being regarded as a decoration at conferences. Young educated middle-class girls, often students or ex-students, are particularly sensitive about their sexual situation. They know that contraceptives have brought them the possibility of enjoying sex without worrying. But this hasn't really affected the way they see themselves as people or the way men see them. Before you were wrapped up and traded to the highest bidder, your virginity hopefully intact. Now you're 'free' to circulate on the open market. The protective wrapping of your 'niceness', your 'spirituality', is stripped off. You're on the sex nexus. You're still a commodity. For socialist women there is a great irony; amidst all the talk about people controlling their lives, and counting equally and developing fully, it never seems to be applied to them. They are beginning to demand that it should. Young working-class girls are in a similar, often more contradictory position. An alternative is less clear to them but they're asking awkward questions. 'Why is it always naked women on the tube, why aren't there naked men?' 'The Pope must be bent. He doesn't like women, does he? He's against the Pill.' 'I'd like to take boys out in a car late at night in the rain and push them out in the road and make them walk home.' 'Every boy in this place is a raving sex maniac, and yet they say they want to marry a virgin.' There are stirrings too amongst older women who are housewives and don't work. They feel the isolation and trivialization of their lives. They resent their confinement inside. They feel pushed on one side. They are told that they're failures if they can't adjust. They are complaining about the false choice they are forced to make between neglecting their children or dropping all the things which they were interested in before they were married. They see right through the hypocrisy which mutters piously about motherhood and does nothing to make their lives easier. They are absolutely essential to the community as producers and consumers. But they don't produce things and they don't get paid, so capitalism does not value them.

EMPHASIS OF DISCONTENT

Despite these different emphases the basic assertion is the same. It's the demand for self-definition, recognition and human beingness. Instinctively women's groups stress everyone speaking, distrust leaders and figures. It's important to understand every aspect of the very different ways all women experience subordination in capitalism. There's a tendency to try and restrict it to particular groups and particular areas. Middle-class women are described as experiencing psychological oppression, working-class women economic oppression.

Discussion of non-economic oppression is seen as diversionary. Well, you can't zone off oppressions and then stick them mechanically together with a percentage and say this = exploitation, and leave it at that. If you do, you'll end up with an identikit, not a person. You'll find the spheres of oppression overlap and interact so much that you either go round in circles, locating the origin of one oppression in another, or you'll disentangle them but produce an abstracted clarity which doesn't express what it feels like. Both these miss the way particular experiences merge and particular oppressions reinforce one another. They ignore the way groups interact on one another. Young middle-class girls could be encouraged to look at their own situation differently by the action of working women. A group they start could be important in involving more working women.

COMBINATION OF DISCONTENT

Think how subordinations combine in the situation of the working-class woman. She suffers straightforward economic exploitation, she gets something like half the average wages of men. She exists in what amounts to a permanently underdeveloped section of the working force. She is a transient, denied training opportunities and consequently access to skilled work. Both the reason and justification of this are not simply that she is a member of the working class, but that she is a woman. Because she is a woman her main commitment is seen to be making a 'success' of her family. If the family breaks up, if the children are difficult, if his shirt cuffs are frayed or the washing-up not done, she blames herself, other women blame her, the family blames her, the advertisers, the sociologists and psychologists and everyone blames her. There's no way out of the guilt. It's consequently very difficult for her to put effort and responsibility into her work. She'll go for a job which isn't too demanding, which allows her to think about her other preoccupations. Undoubtedly the money's important. The bit of economic independence is valued as well as the change. But so much of the work is boring, the pay so poor, that to think of it as emancipatory is starry-eyed. Some work obviously can be, but most of it, and most of the kind women do, is just crushing. The two spheres, work and home, invade each other. There's the remembering, the sheer practical difficulty of quite little things like shopping, collecting children when you're on shift-work.

Amidst all this, it's a very exceptional woman who takes on the extra job of shop steward or union work. It's also a very exceptional husband who'll encourage her. Not only will his comforts suffer. He'll have to face his friends. Eyebrows are still raised about wives who are always nipping off to conferences and summer schools and meetings, and leaving men baby-sitting. The man is partly seen as a sucker; partly felt to be hardly done-by. To stand out against this pressure, men have to be very convinced and rather brave. There's still the feeling, give them an inch, they'll take a yard. Men still mutter to one another about giving them a few kids so you know they'll stay put.

The individual working woman isn't just stuck in these ways. She's stuck in the memory and experiences of her own past and the past of other women. Dolls, not soldiers, toy hoovers, not cowboy outfits, little girls can cry but they can't get dirty. Little girls do not climb trees, jump off high walls, fight. They are not allowed to be a full member of the gang. There is the whole mystery of menstruation, the bewilderment of puberty, 'pull your skirt down', the separation of bras and make-up. There is still too the double standard, reputation – easy-old slag. Remember that factory girl sentenced to a remand home in Kidderminster last summer because she had an affair with a married man. Seven hundred girls are sent off to approved schools each year for being attracted sexually to men, or for being assaulted by men.

There are no myths and no connecting ideas which can communicate an alternative for the individual working-class woman. She can either sit like Cinderella taking it all, complaining masochistically to Buttons from time to time, and wait for the prince to come and take her off to a shiny comfortable world. Or she can dress up like a boy and go off to sea in her imagination, and pretend she's a boy. But she'll always be sent off home again to be a woman as soon as she's discovered. No one ever heard of Cinderella organizing Buttons into a trade union, or undisguised girls capturing and occupying boats. If they did you can bet there'd be no prince or pirate king who'd look at them. Who wants to give up the definite possibility of princes and pirate kings for unpleasant struggles of doubtful outcome and no history?

Women are conditioned to leave the external world to men, to 'go helpless', be suspicious, and regard all other women as poachers. The whole conscious world of articulation and organization belongs to men. It's not surprising women often let themselves be pushed around – they're trained to – or don't stand up for themselves – they're not expected to. It's true there is an implicit solidarity. But it doesn't have words to describe itself, much less concepts to situate itself. It exists only in particular experiences, it is flashed between women in a look. It understands pain, humiliation, persecution, menstruation, abortion, being hit, ridiculed, the subject of dirty jokes and dirty postcards and dirty actions. It has its own strength, its own toughness and its own code. 'They're all the same', 'just like children', 'they don't half go on', 'they're like that' or simply 'Men!' Behind the stock phrases there's the feeling 'If we ever had a chance', an affirmation of ability, worth, importance. But the feeling is always accompanied with a shrug. What's the point of fighting? Whoever heard of winning? It's loaded in their favour. You just lose what you've got now – cling on to it. It's always been this way. It's just being a woman.

GENERALIZATION OF DISCONTENT

That's why Lil Bilocca's so important, and Rose Boland and Kath Fincham and Daisy Nolan and all the women you never hear about. They break through all the hopelessness, all the fatality, the resignation, the passivity. They make possibilities. Not only is their situation and action generalizable to all women; it can be extended to all men. We are all entrapped in these interconnecting oppressions. We are all separated and afraid. We are all unable to be fully ourselves, to act consciously and creatively in the world. We are all passive victims. We are all devourers.

(From 'Year of the Militant Woman', *Black Dwarf*)

On from Grosvenor Square (Part 73):
Nigel Fountain

The Cambodia demonstration of 10 May was, it was concurred, a
fiasco. That Saturday a meeting took place at the University of London
to work out what went wrong, how things could change. How students
could organize, their role in revolutionary struggle . . . An optimistic
meeting, three papers were to be prepared and a meeting was arranged
for the following Saturday afternoon.

One o'clock at ULU, a big open lounge, a sunny day. Only about
thirty people to start with, mostly from SOAS but the numbers grew.
The discussion begun with the students, how they could organize, their
role in revolutionary struggle . . . It was like a ping-pong game where
the balls, filled with hot air, floated into the roof. A girl from SOAS
said they weren't here for post-mortems but decisions on how the
movement was to be built, develop, what it was to do. A French militant
argued that in talking of the 'demonstration', one had to realize that
the media could theatricalize the event purely in their own terms, that
its impact on the mass of the population was negligible, and that new
methods of demonstration to overcome this kind of weakness had to
be found.

Someone said that the discussion had to get to the grass roots and
someone else said this was an abstraction. The girl from SOAS
claimed that one had to separate action and theory and it was pointed
out that there was a dialectic between the two. A turning point came
when a paper from Chelsea and Bedford Colleges was read by Phil
Sirokin. This, after a potted history of the last ten years of the British
Left, came down to certain specific points. IS was denounced for its
role at the LSE, where it was claimed they had been dealing as a
parliamentary opposition and had spoken in irrelevant abstractions,
leaving a demoralized student movement. 'It took a couple of Americans to get the picket lines going,' it was alleged. The British Left was
unorganized, there was no link up of the various 'ideological' groups.
A new type of student movement *doing* something was needed – militant, united on a 'broad programme', working as unionists in the
unions they could join, revitalizing the NUS and taking the initiative
from Jack Straw. Concretely, a national student strike based on the
demand for a 50 per cent grant increase. This was ill-received, grant
strikes took the student movement back into the dark ages, thought

David Triesman. A broad-based campaign, liberal (if it was broad-based it had to be), with militants in control back at the GRASS ROOTS, that was what was needed on an issue like binary higher education. 'There is an immense tactical gain if we can use a liberal movement,' said Triesman.

Sirokin was asked how his proposals differed from those that had launched the RSSF. Individuals not groups were launching it he said. Why should individuals, who could apparently agree on nothing at the meeting, form the basis of a new movement? No answer was immediately forthcoming, but it was suggested that if the others could not agree, then Sirokin and Co,. even if only eight in number, would go off and form their own organization. Which took the whole thing neatly back to the fragmentation of the British Left.

Robin Blackburn pointed out that militancy did not have to be rooted in uniformity of political views. That massive demonstrations had been organized by disparate tendencies. 'This country has more political groups perhaps than any other advanced capitalist country. But we have no method of intervening. They have to get themselves together on an ad-hoc basis.' A strong London student movement could do a good job of disrupting the forthcoming election. Which then reverted the discussion to *why* one was disrupting, what it meant in terms of the media. The French comrade stressed that unless the Left could find some way of translating actions into a language the working class, the 'public', could follow then it would prove counter-productive.

A Dutchman said that in Holland they had attempted to get through to the workers by showing them pornographic films they had made and talking about them. John Birtwhistle asked if this was really necessary. The meeting laughed.

The discussion had threaded on for three hours, a cameo of the English Left, no topic could be discussed adequately, none was. The fact that the cast changed frequently helped the discussion to revert, also the habit of some of the participants of going into a noisy conclave as soon as anybody began to ask them a question. Eventually the meeting lost all trace of its original orientation and concentrated on the nature and form of demonstration. The Frenchman argued that situations where demonstrators just went out and got arrested were a waste of time, the purpose would be totally inexplicable and would be regarded with hostility by the masses – 'It is not the duty of a revolutionary to get arrested'. At this point the obligatory nut Maoist denounced this revisionist position and said that one could not talk about the isolation of the British Left, 'you can't be isolated from the masses – you're so isolated you've reached saturation point'. So from this point the argument was a Blackburn/Maoist one that any act which inflicted a blow on US imperialism was valid; even if the reduction of the US Embassy to rubble drove the working class a few degrees to the right this was worthwhile, after all it had got them thinking. This was not well received. Blackburn proclaimed a 'faith in the masses' but how this long-term 'faith' was to be realized when one was busy shifting them up the wrong end of the political spectrum was not explained. Of course, he argued, other comrades would be working in the factories and so on through their membership of IS etc. but one had also to see the validity of his tactic. One didn't. The French comrade couldn't see how the approach was to break out of the clutches of the bourgeois media's interpretation. Those confronted with the problem of attempting to make revolutionary politics meaningful to the working class could not see how isolated violence would make the task easier.

'That meeting was a perfect advertisement for joining one of the groups,' said the French comrade. All cohesion had vanished, the previous weekend's hopes had vanished as discussions about correct tactics for hypothetical demonstrations meandered into nowhere. Some things were clear, the idea of a core of hard dedicated militants who *knew what they were doing* was laughable. The poor bastards who get arrested are those least capable of organization – outraged liberals, the periphery, those who've been in it for the last fortnight.

Later that day the reporter went to see a comrade who was in hospital, having lost four teeth, had his nose broken and been effectively kicked over. 'Colour-blind paki-bashers,' he suggested, 'I'm moving towards the law and order lobby.' Later still the reporter talked to four Scottish/Irish workers in a pub. They were reds, they said, and thought that students were a load of playboy layabouts.

(From *Idiot International*, 6, June 1970)

The Festival of the Oppressed:
Nigel Fountain

The Festival of the Oppressed was based on the Arbour Square Squat. Arbour Square is just off the Commercial Road, in Stepney, London E1. Two years ago the local Labour Council cleared the tenants out of a late forties block of flats on the pretext of renovation. New tenants would soon be admitted. Having done so, and with one of the largest housing waiting lists in London the council then left the flats. The conditions in the Stepney half-way house are appalling and the move by local squatters to take over the flats met with a desperately eager response from the local homeless families. They are now confronted with the closing stages of a High Court action.

The squatters decided to hold a festival. This fell into three parts: a meeting at the Roundhouse the Sunday before the election to 'come together'; a march on the Stock Exchange on Election Day; and a party in Arbour Square in the evening, with a party for the children in the afternoon.

Act I, at the Roundhouse, was a disaster. The organizers had gone to great trouble *not* to invite the established left groups (who they feared might take it over). Had they done so it would have been the occupation of a blancmange. The usual inflatable swiz-prick and the massed hippies of London. The amplification didn't work, so Tom Fawthrop addressed the audience through a fuzzed megaphone.

Three old ladies were sitting at the back. 'There are going to be some political speeches *we* were told. Can't hear anything. I thought Barbara Windsor was going to be here. We were here from 11 o'clock and the Hemel Hempstead Brass Band were coming I was told. It looks like it's for young people . . .'

The hippies danced. 'We are here,' said a speaker, 'to express our utter disgust. We are going to organize here together in a movement which is going to challenge the system in our terms, not theirs.'

The hippies danced. 'People! Don't just freak! Break through at the grass-roots level! What sort of society do you want? You LONG-HAIRED FREAKS! All you can do is dance.'

'Well you lot don't do any better,' said a strangely articulate hippy. 'All you got is 1917 and that didn't work out and Cuba. You old leftists don't know. You organizers want to use this lot as troops for your aims.'

The meeting had turned into a perfect example of people not got together. One man ran around screaming. Occasionally an organizer would make an incoherent address through the megaphone and a small crowd, like a rugger scrum sharing a private joke, would gather round him. A rock group on stage refused, it was alleged, to allow their amplification to be used. People were pretty unhappy about that. The group didn't look too pleased either. They denied the charge, they had the wrong plugs or something.

The hippy-left were most unhappy. When one organizes a meeting and entices the hippy-freaks along, then their behaviour is a parody of their petit-bourgeois class origins. Each couple erects a small semi and a garden, dances in it and ignores any concept of a community at all. Which they did.

The feeling by half past five was close to that of a Labour supporter the following Friday morning. Nothing had been got together, none of the promised speakers (Trocchi, Blackburn, Pilkington striker . . .) had spoken, assuming they had arrived and the general atmosphere was very bad vibes indeed.

Act II, Election day, sunny midday at Aldgate. The March of the Oppressed was to go from nearby Itchy Park to the City via Brick Lane and Spitalfields. A friendly local newspaper seller smiled as he misdirected the oppressed down Commercial Street to a churchyard where they sat with the methies for half an hour.

Itchy Park is a dusty hill/field, with trees on top and methies scattered around the periphery. About four hundred people gathered round the trees, the Edgar Broughton Band was going to arrive soon, it was rumoured. Outside the park the locals gathered.

'They give the impression on this bright and sunny afternoon, to me at any rate' – an amiable office worker deliberating – 'that they are a lot of layabouts. I could be mistaken of course.'

'What are they doing it for? They are protesting about not having free radio, you've got a blockage by the BBC haven't you?' said a youth. 'I'm all in favour of that.'

'Harold Wilson is a gentleman, is a very clever man.' (Drunk).

At this stage of the day (two o'clock) all the worst features of the Festival were showing. Nobody was attempting to explain to the passers-by what they were doing. A lady ate an Indian take-away in the dust, using Embassy packets as spoons. Whenever the beautiful people gather it always becomes reminiscent of the Asian countryside, as Dylan on the Isle of Wight so disastrously exemplified. Then it improved.

Some skinheads came up on the Hill and having denounced the march, 'this isn't going to achieve anything – bullshit load of Bongo drums,' stood round and watched.

'We are going to march,' said Tom Fawthrop 'through the East End and into the City. To show people what we think of the election. To involve them.' So, replete with bongo drums the march, around three hundred strong, moved off. When they returned Edgar Broughton might have arrived. It was announced that his generator had broken down and he had gone off to buy a new one.

The reaction in the East End around Brick Lane varied. Some were openly hostile, some totally confused. An old Jewish tailor said he would put them in labour camps, 'they *live* on us, *we* work! They should do *forced* labour. They don't deserve to live.' The workers weren't too keen, the general reaction being that if anyone should march it should be them, and the marchers could take over the factories. A masterpiece of British tolerance really. A policeman with a moustache: 'they are free to do what they like. It is the Law of the Land and I uphold it, that is what I am paid for, eight hours a day.'

'They should chuck a fucking bomb at them,' suggested a foreman.

'They are marching because they believe there is no choice in the Election!'

'There isn't any. We should go out and join them. Ha Ha.' He, and workers, retired inside.

In the flats around Fashion Street they hardly noticed. Those flats are evil. The people are so immersed in their own appalling conditions that a collection of freaks straggling by just merge into the scenery. 'They class people by numbers, you know,' said a lady. 'Children put rubbish through my letterbox. Terrible things go on, you know. They class people by numbers, people here only three years get maisonettes, I've been here seventeen years. They haven't given *me* a maisonette.'

In Brick Lane a group of nubile young men in shorts above a betting shop took photos and laughed. They looked very odd. A homosexual bordello? Rather ill located, one would have thought. The reaction in the City was different. Pure hatred. Dark narrow streets, office workers in small rooms, pig-faced stockbrokers swearing. They were really shocked. 'The nastiest looking rabble I have ever seen. If they're students then we should be ashamed of ourselves. They *can't* be students. Power lies with the Stock Exchange. Bollocks!'

There were a lot more police. One marcher got busted and disappeared white faced into a van. Bank messengers swore and talked to the police.

'You want to get in there,' said a policeman to an angry onlooker. They both laughed.

Edgar Broughton hadn't appeared when they got back. The marchers laughed like they had got back from stealing apples. 'They were all stuck in their little minds. That was the first march for this area – it was good.'

'They liked the message even if they didn't like the people,' said a squatter. 'They've got mistrust against students down here. You've got to work with them, they remember the students fighting them in '26.'

Much of the march was a self-contained party, a collective ego-trip. But it did have good elements, it was different and happier than the Vietnam shows, it may have made little sense to the public but worried them more than the bi-annual parade down Oxford Street. If there was some more effective way of communicating to the public they might even be valuable.

But the feeling on the day was that it was a gesture against an inevitable Labour victory. Now it begins to resemble a wake for the easy days of sellout Labour rule. A ghost for the sixties.

Act III. The party was in Arbour Square. The families squatting stayed guarding their flats. Other local people gazed at the freaks dancing. The freaks lit a fire. The Fire Brigade put it out. Another fire, they put that out too. The local children enjoyed that. The Edgar Broughton Band was to arrive about nine.

Some East Enders moved in among the hippies and common hostility to the police coupled with the rarity of anyone doing any entertaining on that barren piece of wasteground created some links.

'It's all right if Edgar Broughton comes isn't it?' Skinhead. They lit a third fire.

Edgar Broughton was to come at ten but didn't actually make it.

(From *Idiot International*, 7, July 1970)

The Arbour House Squat:
Tony Mahoney

When the Redbridge squat was initiated, the major premise of those who organized it was that the housing situation being so bad, a large squat which had some hope of success would act as a catalyst to a series of such struggles in every city in England. Such a dream was never realized. But the participants of the Redbridge squat were so enthused by the support which that struggle obtained, that other campaigns were begun without the analysis necessary for future development. Thus in Lewisham and East London the tactics of these campaigns have been dictated almost completely by the attitude of the local authorities, and by the motivating principles of the squatters.

When *Idiot International* asked the East London Squatters to write an article, we thought it a good opportunity to present a tentative appraisal of our position. What we have tried to do is bring the mistakes to light so that they can be discussed. A chronology of events is included in this article. We propose to comment on the most important of these, in order that a total picture can be built up of the strategy of the campaign. We would like in return helpful criticism from *Idiot International* readers; we would prefer comments from activists rather than ideologists. We should mention that as a group we are not experts on Marxist theory. We have read our basic texts, and have tried to apply what we have learnt to the situations presented to us. We did not abandon fundamentals, as is common in New Left circles; rather we kept hold of such ideas as the necessity of a vanguard, the need for organization and discipline, and decisions arrived at by majority vote (we were suspicious of spontaneity). We do not however apply these ideas in any received way – we try to avoid dogma. This is because we feel most deeply of all that socialism, in order to remain true to itself, must radically break with its history. Only in this way does it remain a historical movement.

Last October, the East London Squatters seized an empty block of flats in Stepney owned by the London Borough of Tower Hamlets. This block, Arbour House, had remained empty for two years before we occupied it. We felt that this was a good opportunity to highlight the hopelessness of an authority that has implemented the principles of Social Democratic government for something like thirty years. Indeed, we thought that Tower Hamlets – for so long a refuge for soporific socialists – would answer the challenge of our trumpeting and the walls come tumbling down. They didn't. What happened was that everyone yawned and turned over, usually farting in our direction as they did so. An instance: Solly Kaye, a Communist Councillor, solemnly declared that by encouraging families to ignore the waiting list, we were guilty of dividing the unity of the working-class struggle. This statement surpasses all credibility in a borough that has nine thousand families on a closed waiting list, 58,000 families in privately owned slums, and a housing deficit which has brought a confession of bankruptcy from the housing department.*

Three reasons are apparent to us for our failures. (1) the isolation of our struggle, (2) the lack of support from local left groups and the left movement generally, (3) our own inability to raise the consciousness of the families and the surrounding area to any perceptible degree. These failures are inseparable from each other, and have made the squat what it is. The isolation is probably the most important factor. Young revolutionists who come to the squat – and they still come – and say, 'Man, this is fantastic' continue to surprise us, because, Man, it's not fantastic. In fact it is a struggle gasping for life. The only way it can be given life is by association with other struggles. We never wanted to be told we were fantastic, but that we were part of something fantastic. Unfortunately it rarely happened.

The realization of our isolation occurred when the first batch of writs were issued. One particular family had an astonishingly good case which we thought was worth publicizing in court. We never led anyone up the old garden path about victory through the capitalist courts, but we did think it worth while to use them as platform from which we could disturb the complacency of the authorities yet again. We went to the Stepney Neighbourhood Law Centre and asked for the assistance of a solicitor. We should explain that this Law Centre is based on the American model and is meant to give legal assistance to oppressed sections of the community. They received us coldly, but we were able to see a solicitor. After we had briefed him, we were told that we could not return to any of the Monday evening weekly sessions, because our case was taking up too much of their time. We felt pretty crushed by this, but decided to continue with their solicitor. Then bread, bread, bread, was all that mattered. We were informed that counsel would cost at least 200 guineas, and that the legal aid department considered that we were not eligible for financial assistance. So we were completely

* Figures taken from an independent survey undertaken by members of the work force of the housing department, 1968.

taken up with finding bread. Every rich lefty we approached told us that all his money was going either to Brazil, or South Africa, or Northern Ireland, etc. Which confirmed our belief that most lefties in this country just don't believe that England can make it; it's not a good investment. We didn't get the bread, so we didn't get counsel. Some families panicked, and left the squat. Our constant inability to show the families that they are part of something much larger than our own squat has been a major setback.

We have also noted among some leftists that homelessness is inevitably associated with the 'lumpen'. It seems that many middle-class theorists do not believe that the appalling poverty in all our cities can be attributed to the market. Instead, they have swallowed hook, line and sinker the propaganda of capitalism that no one in our beautiful Welfare paradise need be without any of the consumer delights of postwar prosperity. An afternoon at any office of the department of Employment and Productivity should dispel any such illusions. Yet these illusions linger and that is why, we think, some have not supported us. The biggest blow occurred however when the United Tenants Action Committee debated whether or not they should support us if any evictions took place. The discussion was, understandably, heated. But our amazement grew as we realized that an influential section of UTAC's theorists regarded us as a positive intrusion in the tenants' struggle. Well-known opponents of the Communist Party, who have time and again criticized the Party for refusing to show a lead in uniting struggles, stood up and boldly stated that the struggle of homeless families could not be entertained as part of the tenants' struggle. The debate ended with UTAC refusing to give its support to our struggle, but recommending that any of its associations who wanted to help off their own backs could do so. We feel we understand partly why UTAC has failed so dramatically to keep the support of GLC tenants. On the other hand, among the people who have helped us, Jim Bailey, of the National Association of Tenants and Residents, stands out because of his constant support and comradeship. He is a London Transport worker and was himself homeless for eighteen months. His advice, which comes from twenty years as a revolutionary, has been for the Campaign a constant source of revitalization.

In Tower Hamlets itself the reason for lack of support springs from two main sources: the Labour Party and the Communist Party. The New Borough is made up of three old areas, famous in the past for their militancy, both on the Left and on the Right: Stepney, Poplar and Bethnal Green. It was this area which produced such leaders of the

Labour movements as Lansbury, who, working through the Labour Party, created a radical consciousness which was associated with the Party. Such a radicalism has not outlived the death-throes of Labour, and thus the mystifications of socialist struggle through the Labour Party are intensified. On top of this, 'The British Road to Socialism' has produced within the Communist Party an inertia which shows particularly in such an area as East London where the Party has traditionally controlled the political thinking of certain sections of the working class. Unlike such areas as West London and Brixton, Tower Hamlets has never, until very recently, been influenced by the developing ideas of the Left. This has meant, among other things, that the old Left has had no comparisons by which it can assess its own position. They are therefore unable to understand the new theory that is thrown up to meet new problems. Instead, they view such movements as potential dangers to their entrenched positions. Furthermore, they use their long-established influence in the traditional organs of the working class to suppress new thinking. This is not only true of the squatters movement; such groups as the Pakistani Workers, 'the Wappingite' and the opposition to the St Katherine Dock Scheme have all found the Council and the Communist Party unable to understand the essential correctness of their political position. When in April we invaded a Council meeting, only two Labour Councillors supported our cause, and again Solly Kaye made the day by telling us that we should have waited until the 'lawful' business of the Council was completed before we made representation to them. The 'lawful' business of the Council consists mainly in rhetorical declamations about how much more wonderful London would be if the G L C was controlled by such stalwarts of socialism as the Members of Tower Hamlets Council. Other left groups in the area seem to have a blinkered loyalty to the Labour Council because 'they are not the enemy'. We maintain that the apparatus of the State is not the enemy, but the class in whose interests the apparatus is worked. We have been bemused by these left supporters of Labour, because their theoretical standpoint seems to imply a belief that the apparatus of the state is worked in the interests of the oppressed when in the hands of the Labour Party.

By about February it was obvious that the squat would not be able to rely on much help from the locally based left groups and the articles which were appearing in many underground left papers seemed to imply that squatting was last year's scene and did not deserve any longer the attention which it had received in Redbridge. As well as this, an irrevocable split had occurred between the Lewisham Family Squatters and the East London Squatters over the conditions by which the Lewisham Squatters came to an agreement with the local Council over the use of their empty houses.

We felt at the time, and still do feel, that the agreement produced a situation whereby the Lewisham Squatters became an appendage to the Welfare services provided by Lewisham Council, and in no way advanced the breaking up of control which the Welfare system has over the lives of the oppressed.

The reason why we have laboriously charted these external events is because they bear directly upon everything which has happened up till now within the Arbour Square squat. Left to our own devices, and without the physical presence of any opposition, we felt our main task to be raising the consciousness of those involved in the squat. By that we mean families, campaigners and the surrounding area. However, the problem which confronted us and still confronts us is what is meant by 'raising consciousness'? Obviously, during a struggle in a factory where workers and management are in physical opposition to one another, or again during the Redbridge squat, where the presence of the bailiffs needed no words to explain the situation, the raising of consciousness is a natural development. The task of a vanguard in such a situation is to direct that consciousness towards the final end of breaking the power of capitalism and in the short-term to show those engaged in the struggle the enormity of the task. We were in the somewhat cosy position of developing the largest squat in London with the apparent acquiescence of the Council. (At least two families have been directed to the squat by Council officials.) At the same time, the problems within the Tower Hamlets area are fast rising to the surface. As we have said above, racial conflict, redevelopment of the docks, lack of jobs, and community control are issues which now begin to bite into the flabby flesh of the ruling bureaucracy. A correct strategy should be able to unite all these issues, and create a common front through which a radical opposition might be developed. We have learnt that such a development is not yet possible. Not only ourselves, but also such groups as the East London Claimants Union and community workers in the Wapping area have up till now been unable to interest those with whom they work in anything but the immediate problems of their particular campaigns. Within the squat, the families show a great suspicion towards the political thinking of the Left, and refuse to engage in any political discussions with us. That is not to say, of course, that there are no political attitudes within the squat. In the last analysis, the Council is still seen as the means by which the families are to be given the homes that they require. This does not come from the sophistication of realizing that in a non-revolutionary situation all action is necessarily reformist, but because they do not believe there is any alternative to the present structures. There is also the commonly held view that the problems of homelessness and lack of jobs and overcrowded schools are due to coloured immigration. No amount of discussion seems to change this view. Faced with these problems, the campaign had the alternatives of vulgarizing the issue and putting forward the commonly held thesis that life was about Us versus the Pigs, or to seek out the best families within the squat to take up some sort of position as a central committee.

This is an emotive phrase; what we mean in this context is that the issues which were necessary to be discussed and voted upon at the weekly family meetings were first discussed by an elected committee of ten who presented the problems at the family meetings in a way that did not create the confusion which was so apparent at earlier meetings and was the direct result of complete political illiteracy. This has alleviated to a certain extent the feeling which the Campaign had, after numerous failures, come to accept, that the squat could not hope to have any other objective than the re-housing of some forty families; but it is still true that very little headway is being made in being able to produce the political implications of the squat in a manner which is understood and accepted by the majority of the families.

The politicization of the squat was the cause of a major split in the Campaign. Throughout the development of squatting, there has been a large and influential anarchist element whose work, in terms of fruitfulness, compares favourably with any other tradition that has been associated with the movement. It was however inevitable that the problems which we have mentioned would create a division between them and the socialists. The anarchists were adamant that we should pursue a policy of non-politicization, and that there should be no organized committees with overall responsibility for any actions undertaken in the name of the whole squat. They proclaimed a policy of 'do your own thing'. They saw any opposition to this attitude purely in terms of personality conflicts. When the crisis deepened over the question of which direction the squat should proceed internally, they began to attack the socialist elements of the Campaign at unofficial family meetings to which the socialist campaigners were not invited. When the matter was brought up at a family meeting, a savage exchange of views took place, after which they left the Campaign.

The time at which the split occurred was during the preparations for

L.B. – 23

the 'Festival of the Oppressed' which occurred in June. The Festival had a political purpose which was to unite struggles in and around London and to give a direction to those people who came to participate in it. The anarchists in the squat considered the Festival to be an imposition on the families and that the struggle would be used as an opportunity for large numbers of people to enjoy themselves at the families' expense. The families were not averse to the idea of the festival, but became confused when they were allowed to see how great and unnecessary a split it was causing within the ranks of the Campaign. In the event, the Festival could best be described as an interesting experiment. But it caused none of the violence nor discomfort to the families which the anarchists had predicted. We feel there are important lessons within this event. It became quite clear that as long as it is necessary to have outside influence in any struggle, whether it be of an anarchist or socialist tinge, this influence must have an agreed policy to present to the people with whom it is working. We have found from our own experience that it is simply untrue to believe that the masses living in a bourgeois society are able to demystify themselves without the assistance of those who have set themselves the task of understanding the workings of capitalist society. We feel that to believe differently is to negate the necessity of a revolution.

The present situation of the squat is that we control two blocks of flats in Stepney: Arbour House and Burrell House, a small block of twenty flats owned by the GLC which we seized at the beginning of August. This block is to be demolished together with a much larger one so that a road may be widened as part of the new Highway scheme associated with the redevelopment of St Katherine Dock. The health of the squats is conditioned by the factors which we have mentioned above, and the problem that we face is connecting our struggles with the others of the surrounding area and furthermore making strong links with groups in other parts of the country who are motivated by the same concerns as ourselves. We are ready to admit that we have not come to grips with the problem of showing ourselves as a worthwhile group to the community at large. During the length of time that we have been working in the area, we have tried on numerous occasions to involve the larger community in what we are doing. Such projects as adventure playgrounds, community poster workshop, street theatre and the like, have been initiated but were abandoned because of the problems that constantly beset us within the squat itself. If we had had more people working with the campaign, these projects could possibly have taken on a life of their own. As it is, we feel we have still only created the skeleton of a struggle.

It is still not possible to see under what terms these squats could end. The fact remains, however, that the sort of life-style which a squat creates for the families who are involved in it demands that there must be some sort of end in view. 'A home is a right' is one of the slogans under which we are fighting this campaign. Yet the implications of that slogan are such that without the concretization of such a hope through total revolutionary action it remains a liberal design which can occupy enormous space in the colour supplements.

In all cities in this country, a home is still a privilege, granted or not according to the condition of the market. The homes which are being produced today for the working class are virtual slums even before they are ready for occupation. Environment and ecology are as important as bricks and mortar. Politically, therefore, the main purpose of a squatting campaign is to lay the groundwork necessary for an understanding of how it is possible to defeat the workings of the present structure. The success of a squat cannot be determined by the number of people who are housed through its activity. At the same time, having committed ourselves to aiding certain people in their struggle for a home, within the context of welfare capitalism, we have a duty to do all in our power to achieve that end. These two objectives create a tension within the struggle which is by no means destructive. On the contrary, one of the most important lessons it produces is the necessary humanism in revolutionary activity. The Campaign is often haunted by the realization that one is playing with men's lives. If we're around on the Great Day, when the chains of capitalism are broken, we hope we won't have forgotten this lesson.

We have, during this Campaign, helped to create in East London the beginnings of a new type of activity, and we feel that the Council is aware of this in a way that the local established left groups are not. The families are prepared to negotiate with the Council on condition that the appalling welfare slums are not the accommodation which is offered them. We for our part, as a campaign, are eager to discover the long-term implications of our activity. As this continues to be an ongoing struggle, we cannot predict what tomorrow will bring, but one thing that we are certain of is that in the future our direct action will come from activity within the community. We feel that the distance between the New Left and the working class, both at home and at work, is nowhere near being bridged. Until this occurs through the unrewarding work connected with the immediate needs of working-class people the large-scale demonstrations in support of other people's revolutions will continue to be a liberal substitute for our own.

(From 'The Squatters of Arbour Square: An Obituary', *Idiot International*, 9, October 1970)

Nothing So Romantic:
Tony Cliff

Nick Walter: Your name is not in fact Tony Cliff; why do you find it useful to use a pseudonym?

Tony Cliff: I worked for thirteen years in illegal conditions in Palestine under British rule and there we had to use pseudonyms and I think it just became habit-forming.

N.W.: It isn't part of the Bolshevik tradition, this use of pseudonyms?

T.C.: No, I don't think it came from that, nothing as romantic.

N.W.: You mentioned Palestine. Would you like to say briefly what your personal background was before settling in this country?

T.C.: I was born in Palestine in 1917 to a Zionist family, but from very early youth I was disgusted by the terrible conditions of the Arab children. I was from a middle-class family with quite good educational opportunities and quite a good standard of living whereas the Arab children were very poor with no chance of education. I became, very early on, anti-Zionist and anti-imperialist.

N.W.: You are now best known in this country as one of the leading members of the IS groups; would you like to say what the origins of the group are and what its position is now and how it is distinguished from other British political groups?

T.C.: Central to our position is the statement that the emancipation of the working class is the act of the working class – which many only mouth on May days and other occasions of celebration. This statement is for us the beginning and the end of all our analysis. And if you put the working class at the centre of the arena, then socialism cannot be established except through the expression of the potentialities of the working class.

N.W.: As a group which emphasizes the central role of the working class, IS does seem to be a group which has a very large proportion of intellectuals in its membership. Would you like to explain this?

T.C.: I think that the picture that people have about IS from outside is not exactly correct; even members of IS are sometimes misled about our social composition. Out of about 1,000 members we have just over 200 manual workers, and because they have a base in industry are much less known in national terms, but are much more important for the organization. It is very bad that we still have such a small minority of workers in the group but this is largely because militant workers

have traditions of their own and are very often in their own organizations. They are not ready to accept us and it takes a much longer time
for them to accept us than for intellectuals who are playing with ideas
and not really facing the problems of life.

*N.W.: How do you stand in relation to the Hungarian revolution of
1956 and to the liberalization movement in Czechoslovakia in 1968?*

T.C.: The Hungarian revolution threw forward the form of the workers'
council, the most democratic form of organization of the working class
and it is thus in the same tradition as the Paris Commune and October
revolution and we wholeheartedly supported it. The Czech events were
different – merely an effort by part of the Czech bureaucracy to bring
reform from above in order to prevent a revolution from below.

*N.W.: You began your political career by rejecting Zionism; what is
your present attitude towards the Middle East, with regard to Israel and
with regard to the semi-socialist Arab countries?*

T.C.: The term semi-socialist is absolutely wrong; one would have to
speak of middle-class state-capitalist regimes in Egypt, Syria and Iraq.
Naturally we support unconditionally the Arab revolution against
imperialism and Zionism, and I believe that this struggle will never be
won unless the struggle of the Arab peasant for land is connected with
the struggle against Zionism. That is why the struggle against Dayan
cannot be separated from the struggle against Feisal, Hussein, Nasser
and the Ba'ath. Therefore, the only two organizations we support in
the Middle East are the Democratic Front and Maatzpen within Israel
itself.

*N.W.: Do you think that there is any practical prospect of an inter-
national movement to overthrow all of these regimes in the Middle East?*

T.C.: The trend is there – each time the Arabs are defeated, they become more radical and the challenge to the Arab regimes is increasing,
regardless of the ways in which Arafat and El Fatah try to limit the
struggle. You can't defeat Dayan without expropriating the oil companies, and this is what the Arab workers and peasants are beginning
to learn.

*N.W.: To move much closer home. You have written about France in
1968; what do you think of the events of 1968 and the position since then?*

T.C.: For twenty years the myth existed amongst some so-called
'Marxists' that the working class in Western Europe was completely
integrated by washing-machines and televisions and that they had
therefore lost all their revolutionary potentialities. Many people looked
to anyone but the workers of W. Europe – students, peasants in Bolivia,
or anyone – but not the working class itself. The French events proved

such people completely wrong. For twenty years we had said so and we were proved right: the working class is the only real agent for social change. But the French events also proved something else. They proved that even with the biggest strike in world history, without the organization to link up the different sections of the working class, the ruling class in its centralization will triumph. Thus the French events confirm the working class as the agents of social change and also confirm the need for a revolutionary party.

N.W.: Would you still agree that it needed the intellectuals to detonate the revolution or would you say that it was coming anyhow?

T.C.: It is easier for students to act because a minority of students can act on their own to start with. Workers cannot go on strike in a minority; for students it is much easier to act. But their impact is far more limited and therefore students rise like a rocket and fall like a stick. They are manic-depressive, whereas workers, once they move, are much more effective – there is no question about that.

N.W.: But didn't the students' movement continue after the workers' movement had subsided?

T.C.: I think as a matter of fact that the student movement declined after the May events; there was fantastic dissension and bitterness and a feeling of hopelessness leading to adventurism and the search for short-cuts and the lesson is really quite simple. You can't lead the working class from outside: you need an organization that is part of the class and not superimposed from outside.

N.W.: Doesn't this contradict Lenin's theory of the consciousness of the working class?

T.C.: Here you are wrong; it is true that in 1902 he said that consciousness can only come to the working class from outside, but in 1905 he wrote, 'The working-class is instinctively and spontaneously social-democratic' (in those days that was the name of the revolutionary party), or again he wrote, 'The special condition of the proletariat in capitalist society leads to a struggle of the workers for socialism.' A union of them with the socialist party burst forth with spontaneous force. And he was not an élitist; in the act of the revolution he knew that the workers had to be organized in mass revolutionary organizations.

N.W.: From which one learns that Lenin must be treated with great care.

T.C.: From which one must learn that Lenin as a Marxist knew that Marxism is a guide to action and that action depends always on the concrete situation.

N.W.: Isn't there a danger that the party which tries to organize the workers will suffer the same degeneration as the Communist Party of France?

T.C.: There are two conceptions of the vanguard party – one is of the party that stands in front of the class, the other is that the most advanced sections of the class are organized in a party. This second concept is the Marxist concept and if you say that any organization is bound to degenerate, then really you have to accept the pessimists' conception of original sin, and if you accept this pessimistic conception then you can say goodbye to socialism. There is nothing inherently bad in organization. If there is, then there is no future for socialism.

N.W.: To move to Northern Ireland, there have been great difficulties amongst left groups as to what position to adopt towards Northern Ireland. What is the IS position?

T.C.: Our attitude has two elements to it: first of all we argue that only the working class of Ireland, both Catholic and Protestant, can emancipate themselves nationally and socially. But at the same time we argue that for whole historical reasons a Catholic worker doesn't identify himself with a Protestant worker, and vice versa, and therefore our attitude towards the Catholic is like our attitude towards black rebels in America. We are for black and white uniting and fighting, but we are for the black rebels acting for themselves without waiting for the white worker to catch up. Therefore we support the civil rights movement in Northern Ireland even though it is Catholic, and at the same time we believe that the civil rights movement can never win unless the bread and butter questions of jobs, houses etc. come to the front so that Catholics and Protestants unite and fight.

N.W.: But didn't IS support the introduction of British troops into Northern Ireland?

T.C.: Absolutely not. We never supported this idea. But let me give you an analogy, if there are 50 fascists and 5,000 of us, and 100 police between us, then we say 'get the police out of the way, we want to smash the fascists'. But if there are 5,000 of them and 50 of us then we don't say 'get the police out'. We never welcomed British troops, we recognized that their role is to stabilize British imperialism in Northern Ireland, but we couldn't ask Catholic workers in Belfast to demand the right to be pogromed against.

N.W.: What is your relationship to the Labour Party at the present time?

T.C.: The Labour Party is a capitalist party; it carries capitalist policies but it does this with the consent of many workers who believe that it is not a capitalist party. Therefore our job is to do two things: first of all to expose the truth about what the Labour Party is – that it carries out capitalist policies on things like unemployment, immigration, imperialism etc., etc., etc., and this is the most important job. No one should ever tell lies to the class and we should tell them that in the real world this is what the Labour Party is like. The Labour Party is not a socialist alternative to the Tories and therefore there is *no* alternative at present. That's the first thing to say; but on election day we have to say in all honesty that if the Tories win, the ruling class that identifies itself with the Tory Party, and has done so for hundreds of years (after all big business gives subsidies only to the Tory Party, not to Labour), and their pleasure is enough to say, 'We must wipe their smiles off their faces even if we have to use such a bastard as Harold Wilson.'

Secondly, Wilson in opposition would take out the little red book of the sayings of Nye Bevan that he keeps in his pocket, and Anthony Greenwood, instead of murdering the Adenese workers, would be chairman of the Movement for Colonial Freedom. We prefer to have that hypocrite in office where he cannot hide behind his left face. Therefore from the standpoint of exposure of both parties, it is better to have Labour in power. Or as good old Lenin put it: 'We will support the Labour Party like the rope supports a hanging man.' Therefore, tactically when the election comes we will continue to attack the Labour government's record of a capitalist government and at the end we will say, because we have no other alternative, it is tactically better to have Harold Wilson than Ted Heath.

N.W.: Would you go further than this and say that IS should work inside the Labour Party as actual members of the party?

T.C.: Because we have no respect at all for the Labour Party, our attitude *vis-à-vis* entrism into the Labour Party is like that of someone going poaching. If it helps in poaching to get a licence, then you do it. That is our attitude *vis-à-vis* the Labour Party. If we were in Nazi Germany we certainly would have been in the Arbeitsfront. One decides such questions upon the concrete reality of the day. At the moment it would be pointless to become members of the Labour Party.

N.W.: What is your relationship towards the Communist Party of Great Britain?

T.C.: The CP has a dual role: on the one hand it is a community of militants, mainly industrial militants, that join the Party because they don't want to be isolated at their place of work; on the other hand the leadership is an agency of the foreign policy of the Russian bureaucracy and the result is, of course, that every time Stalin sneezed, Harry Pollitt got his handkerchief out of his pocket. We oppose consistently the policies of the Party and the leadership of the Party, especially now that the CP has become such a right-wing social-democratic party, supporting the parliamentary road to socialism, very soft on trade-union bureaucrats like Jack Jones and Scanlon. But at the same time we collaborate with rank-and-file industrial members of the CP in various joint activities.

N.W.: Do you think it would ever be worthwhile to use entrism into the CP?

T.C.: Entrism into the Communist Party is impossible because the Communist Party won't accept from Bolshevism the need for revolution. Once Stalinism came that revolutionary element disappeared.

N.W.: Ideally you would like to see a revolutionary socialist party of your own?

T.C.: Yes, of course. We believe that the vanguard section of the class, in other words the most advanced section of the working class, the 200,000 shop stewards of this country, should be organized not only industrially but also politically. There should not be individual shop stewards like individual marbles in different shops, but a shop stewards' movement that will have also political life of its own, and this will be the revolutionary party.

N.W.: How do you see the revolutionary party as being organized?

T.C.: Because the working class has to emancipate itself, the revolutionary party must reflect the class. But which section of the class is it to reflect? There is an unevenness of consciousness in the class, therefore the party must reflect the consciousness of the more advanced section of the class.

It must be extremely democratic because the only way in which you can reflect the mass of the people is by having a great deal of internal democracy. It is not true that the working class has one cohesive point of view. The revolutionary party would reflect that lack of cohesion, of course. And therefore, if you speak in terms of dialogue with a class, the class itself has different views, and therefore this democracy is necessary. Centralism is necessary for obvious reasons. The ruling class is highly centralistic, and we can't fight the enemy unless we have a symmetrical organization to it and every strike is centralistic. The worker goes to work as an individual; when he goes on strike he acts as a collective. Revolution is the most centralistic thing in the world, and that is why in time of revolution you speak about Paris 1789, you don't speak about 5 million Frenchmen; when you speak about Russia you don't speak about 200 million Russians, you speak about Petrograd.

N.W.: Do you see no contradiction, for example, between the two million of Petrograd and the much smaller numbers of the military committee of the Bolsheviks in Petrograd who actually carried out the revolution? Can there be no contradiction between the centre of the party and its base in any particular area?

T.C.: Revolution comes because there are contradictions. If the whole working class had one level of consciousness there would not have been any need for revolution, there never would be any need for a strike, there wouldn't have been any need for a picket line. There is a picket line because workers act differently. In every revolution there are millions on the revolutionaries' side. Because of that, if there was no unevenness in the level of consciousness we wouldn't have needed a workers' government or the organizations of the proletariat, because there wouldn't have been anybody to suppress. To fight millionaires you don't need a picket line, because the duchess never crosses picket lines. Workers cross picket lines. To fight the reactionary labourers in Russia you didn't need a Red Army, you need a workers' state. That's why in reality we need revolution, strikes, picket lines, a workers' government – the uneven level of consciousness.

N.W.: But nevertheless, this does seem to suggest that the centralism of your democratic party, the militancy of the class, the militancy of the party seems to be directed not so much against the class enemy – since you suggest this will fade away in a revolution – as against the less advanced sections of the working class.

T.C.: The answer is this: up to now, with every strike, the fight is never between the workers and the employers, because the employers never did anything for themselves in their lives – they didn't fight imperialistic wars, they sent workers to fight imperialist wars; they didn't break strikes themselves, they sent workers to break the strikes. And if you want to say that every strike is a fight between workers and workers, it is absolutely true. A section of workers are serving the ruling class. It is the same in Vietnam: it is not a war between the South Vietnamese peasants and American multi-millionaires – on the contrary, the American multi-millionaires are not drafted; it is a struggle between Vietnamese peasants and American workers in uniforms.

N.W.: This seems to suggest a rather interesting development in Marxism, where you no longer have classes acting out their destinies separately. You are suggesting that the working class is divided between those who are serving their real interests and those who are serving the interests of the ruling class. In a sense, the ruling class scarcely seems to exist in this analysis.

T.C.: No, on the contrary. Even in 1789 the bourgeoisie didn't make its own revolution; it was the sans-culottes of Paris who had to make the revolution; the capitalist never did anything for himself, by definition he never does anything for himself, he uses other people. In a revolution it is always the poor that are being used. It is the class struggle: the struggle between the workers and the capitalist class is always reflected in the struggle between the section of the working class which is under the influence of the capitalist class and the section which is opposed to the capitalist class.

N.W.: I am still quite worried about some of your remarks about the party's function. I should like to ask you more carefully: before any revolutionary situation, how should the party consider its relationship to other organs, either Marxist or non-Marxist, but still revolutionary organs none the less?

T.C.: We are against substitution, but we are also against saying let's wait until everyone is ready to march. You have to stand up and say when we want the majority to march; if the majority accept it they will march then; if not, you stand there as a minority and you stick to your position. The same applies to the revolutionary party; the revolutionary party cannot substitute for the class. The working class must emancipate itself; the emancipation of the working class is the act of the working class.

The role of the revolutionary party is to come forward and explain to other workers what the party thinks the correct policy should be. The only way the strike committee can win is by the members of the strike committee proving themselves more consistent, more loyal to the interests of the majority, etc., etc., etc. They have to be put to the test and therefore we are absolutely for the freedom of all socialist parties to stand in competition, with the real hope, of course, that if we are correct 99·9 per cent of workers will vote for us, and ·0001 per cent will vote for Harold Wilson. But we have not arrived at that yet . . .

N.W.: Let's take a concrete example. In Russia after the Bolshevik revolution there were democratic elections against which one can raise many objections, but nevertheless there was a majority in favour of moderate peasant socialism and a very small minority vote for the Bolsheviks. In such a situation what do you think the Bolshevik party or any other vanguard revolutionary party should have done?

T.C.: The basic tragedy of the Russian revolution – and this is really a tragedy – is that the Russian working class was such a small minority. And therefore in the Russian revolution we had a combination of two revolutions: a working-class revolution which was aiming at socialism and a peasant revolution which was aiming basically at what the French revolution of 1789 achieved. Now the French peasant, once he got the land, became a conservative element that smashed the 1848 revolution, that smashed the Paris commune of 1871, because the peasant had something to conserve. Now the Russian Bolsheviks knew that this was the situation in Russia, and assumed that the German revolution would come to their help to get them out of the dilemma. But German Social Democracy smashed the German revolution of 1918–19 and the Russian revolution remained in isolation. Once the Russian revolution remained in isolation the working-class power base became very very narrow. Moreover the Russian working class practically disintegrated in the course of the civil war. There were 3 million industrial workers in 1917; there were only 1 million in 1920. Under such conditions you couldn't speak about the possibility of a democratic set-up. The Bolsheviks were really faced with a terrible tragedy. Their only mistake, if they made a mistake, was that quite often they made a virtue out of necessity.

N.W.: If such a situation recurred as in France in 1968, when there were elections despite the massive strikes and the enormous social mobility, there was yet again a majority for social democracy and indeed for Gaullist democracy. Again, what should a revolutionary party do if it had the power to upset such elections?

T.C.: So long as the majority of the workers don't support the revolutionary party, the revolutionary party has no alternative but patience to go on trying to get the confidence of the mass of the workers. You can't make revolution behind the back of the working class. We don't believe in the minority acting for the class, we are not terrorists – in other words liberals that despise the working class and suggest that a minority should use a bomb – the liberal with a bomb – that's what a terrorist is, and that's basically what the anarchists are, you know, because they really don't believe in the working class or in action. If the majority of workers are supporting the Communist Party you have to go on and on explaining and showing in practice through the day-to-day struggle that they are wrong.

N.W.: To go further with the revolutionary party, being democratic it will come to decisions in a democratic way; being centralist, how will it carry out such decisions if there is dissension?

T.C.: If a majority of workers decide on a strike, and even if you think this specific strike is wrong, you don't cross the picket line. You accept the decision. For example – I will go to the extreme – the workers are going on strike on racialist grounds, I would not cross the picket line; I would stand next to the picket line and condemn the strike – I'll say it is a wrong strike, that it is a reactionary strike, but I am not going to break democratic decisions of workers. Therefore there is no question about it; if a majority decides on it the minority has to obey it, the minority of course has to have complete guarantee that it will have all the time, the opportunity to express its views and influence the views of the majority – and not in secrecy, but in open debate in the face of the class.

N.W.: What happens when a minority refuses to accept?

T.C.: If the minority decides to cross the picket lines the majority are absolutely right in trying to stop them.

N.W.: What do you think of the many groups active in this country who consider that the revolutionary situation is above all abroad?

T.C.: Of course, I do not say that the revolutionary situation is at home. We are not yet there. But we are in a long transition towards a big convulsion and there is no question that the seventies will be the red seventies – if they are not the red seventies they will be the black seventies. We are not going to repeat the disorganization of '48 onwards. And my attitude to the other groups; I believe the majority of them, because of many, many years of frustration, and isolation, in the end turn to the game of sour grapes. They accept their impotence, accept their weakness, and therefore they get vicarious pleasure from people struggling elsewhere. And so they are absolute experts about the Paris commune – every one of them will tell you what the Paris communards should have done. They are experts about Bolivia; they are experts about Vietnam; they know absolutely clearly everything that Lenin said to Plekhanov. But they know very little about British working-class history, they know very little about the British working class, they care very little about the struggles in this country.

And why? Because in reality they are beaten! They are beaten, they are demoralized, because they really don't believe Marxism is a guide to action; they believe that Marxism is a description of reality, instead of a factor in changing reality . . . If the only thing you are aiming at is not to fight the elephant but to make a picture of the elephant, there is no reason why you and I shouldn't collaborate in picturing the elephant – you can picture your elephant and I can picture my elephant. Similarly you can kill your capitalism and I can kill my capitalism; you can smash Wilson today and I can smash Wilson tomorrow. And this way we don't have to unite; if we have to fight with the existing real elephant we have to unite forces, and therefore sectarianism is the by-product of all this substitutionism, of giving up the real struggle.

N.W.: You don't feel at all incongruous as a non-member of the working class with almost the whole of your political philosophy directed towards the working class? You yourself, in a sense, are substituting, surely?

T.C.: No, on the contrary, nothing of the sort. If you look at my book on productivity I don't hide the fact at all that not one idea of it was created at the university, not one idea was created in the library, not one idea came from my own blooming brain. Everything came from experience of the class, everything came from experience of workers, and it came from the past.

It was the workers of Russia who created the Soviet, and it was Lenin who understood how marvellous an organization it was. It was the workers of Paris who created the Paris commune and it was Marx who understood the great importance of this type of workers' government. You learn from the workers to the workers, from their struggle to the struggle. And that is why I don't feel a substitutionist at all.

(From *Idiot International*, 6, June 1970. Interviewer Nicolas Walter)

Chronology
Compiled by Dave Phillips

This chronology of events between 1956 and 1968 is not intended as a fully exhaustive account of all relevant happenings. It is an attempt to list the significant events from the viewpoint of left socialists, as well as giving a roughly representative impression of the period. The Labour Research Department's *Diary of Events* and Richard Hyman's list of principal stoppages 1960–71 in the 1973 *Socialist Register* were a great help.

1956
January
24 Rotax: Strike of 2,700 at Beaconsfield, Willesden and Hemel Hempstead when eight men sacked at Beaconsfield, including convenor and two shop stewards. Men reinstated on 6 February after seventy London factories black all Rotax work.

February
14–20 USSR, Twentieth Congress of CPSU: 'peaceful coexistence' to be Russian policy. In secret session Khrushchev gives detailed account of Stalin's purges and 'cult of the personality'.

March
15–27 Print dispute: Federation of Master Printers lock out typesetters in provincial, then Fleet St, papers in dispute over basic rate. Lock-out broken by typesetting unions signing individual agreements with printers outside the master printer's association.

April
26–13 May Standard Motors: 11,000 strike against 2,600 redundancies. Final settlement a defeat – sacked men, including many union militants, receive £15 redundancy handshake.

30 Norton Motors: Thirty-week strike begins against twenty-eight redundancies.

June
11 Standard Motors: Overtime ban in long dispute to get work-sharing instead of sacking of further 1,150.

27 BMC gives three days' notice of 6,000 redundancies. Complete walk-out at Austins, Longbridge, on 29th; worker participation and consultation over redundancy proposals demanded.

1956 *contd*

28–29 Poland: Workers at Zispo locomotive factory, Poznan, strike for overtime pay. Demonstration becomes violent insurrection, with 113 killed and 270 wounded. Marked end of 'Polish spring' liberalization, when Stalinist leaders were removed from power following Khrushchev's speech.

July

Right-wing W. J. Carron elected AEU president by 83,847 votes to Reg Birch's 35,400. Shop stewards are sacked and strikers ordered back to work before Carron retires to the Lords.

23–10 August BMC at total standstill. TGWU and NUR black movement of all BMC goods. Settlement favours strikers – BMC agrees to redundancy payments, reduction in number to go and worker consultation over any future redundancies.

25 Briggs Motor Bodies, Dagenham: 12,000 walk out when 2,400 get dismissal notices due to hold-up in bodies caused by BMC strike. Notices withdrawn three days later.

26 Nasser announces nationalization of Egyptian-built Suez Canal.

September

1 Covent Garden: 2,000 porters ban Saturday working for five-day, forty-hour week. Given forty-four-hour week with Saturday bonus rate when Ministry of Labour intervenes.

4 UK Optical, Mill Hill: USDAW members strike for union recognition, but firm will negotiate only with individual workers. Letters sent out to each member are returned in one package on 10 October.

October

10 Avro, Cheshire: End of seven-week strike by aircraft workers over piece-rates for work on new Vulcan bomber.

23 Hungary: Anti-Russian demonstration in Budapest attacked by political police.

24 Insurrection in Budapest. Workers' councils set up as organs of self-government with delegates from factories, colleges and army units. Giant statue of Stalin hauled down.

30 Suez: Eden launches Anglo-French bomber offensive against Egypt in Suez Canal Zone, the day after Israel attacks Egypt in the Sinai; British paratroops land in Port Said.

November

1 5,000 Russian tanks invade Hungary under pretext that workers' rising has been organized by 'reactionary counter-revolutionary circles'. 200,000 Russian troops needed to suppress provisional government of Imre Nagy and install Kadar regime. 28,000 die in the fighting and reprisals that follow.

2 Israel occupies Sinai. Soviet tanks seal off Hungarian border with Austria.

4 Russians re-enter Budapest after withdrawing to city boundaries. Fierce fighting as working-class districts are shelled.

6 Suez: Britain orders cease-fire. UN forces are sent into the Canal Zone.

8 Russian military commander in Budapest orders workers back to work.

14 China issues statement supporting Russian invasion of Hungary.

21 Budapest Workers' Council calls forty-eight-hour general strike which lasts a month. Eden goes to Jamaica for three-week holiday from 'severe overstrain'.

December

9 Hungary: Martial law declared throughout the country and all workers' councils banned.

12 N. Ireland: IRA launches new campaign against British rule across the border.

23 Egypt: Last British troops pull out of Port Said.

1957

January

9 Eden resigns. Macmillan appointed Prime Minister the following day.

15 Egypt nationalizes British and French banks.

18 IRA blows up police barracks at Dungannon, N. Ireland.

25 Briggs Motor Bodies: Five shop stewards suspended following month of work-to-rule against redundancy threats and speed-up. Plant comes out on strike. On 29th Johnny McLoughlin, one of the militant five, victimized and sacked. Men return on 4 February when Court of Inquiry is set up. McLoughlin never gets his job back.

February

3 Glacier Metals, Kilmarnock: 800 strike over eight suspended shop stewards.

11 Cyprus: One-day general strike called against British rule.

19 Welfare service cuts: school meals and milk to cost more; Health Service contributions raised.

March

15 Holborn Hall: First meeting of London Socialist Forum demands release of Hungarian Marxist George Lukács from prison in Romania; further meetings of this Marxist discussion group announced.

16–4 April National shipbuilding and engineering strike for rise in basic wage. Ends when second Court of Inquiry set up; but on Merseyside employers withdraw local 33s. bonus pending result of Inquiry; boiler-makers therefore remain out until 29 April.

April

27–28 Wortley Hall: Conference of Socialist Forums. First national meeting, after Hungary, of ex-Communists and other socialists resolves to form 'an organized movement of the Marxist anti-Stalinist left'.

May

First issue of the *New Reasoner*, edited by John Saville and E. P. Thompson, the journal of 'Britain's largest unorganized party – the ex-Communist Party'.

1957 *contd*

10 First issue of the *Newsletter*, set up at Wortley Hall, edited by Peter Fryer.

17 Metal Box, Crawley: Four-week strike ends with reinstatement of steward sacked for 'insolence'.

22 Kenya: UK authorities order compulsory tape recording of all African political meetings.

27 'Call-up' for National Service in the armed forces is ended.

28 AEU inform Johnny McLoughlin that attempt to get him reinstated at Briggs Bodies has been given up. He gets £150 compensation plus £8 a week for next six months

June

6 Rent Act becomes law: large number of rented homes decontrolled and rents go up.

July

15–19 August Porters at Covent Garden, Spitalfields and Borough produce markets strike in dispute over terms of employment. Police escort lorry convoys into docks while employers try to keep markets going, but dockers black the produce. When port employers threaten sackings, 6,000 dockers strike on 12 August. Cousins fixes up hasty settlement on his return from holiday: market men vote on 14th to return on 19th. Dockers offer to return on 14th if not asked to handle blacked goods. Port employers will not accept; dockers also stay out till 19th.

20–29 Nationwide company bus strike settled for tribunal award of 11s. rise. Pirate coach services blocked by picketing busmen.

21 British troops sent out to help Sultan of Oman crush first of many revolts. RAF bombs village tribesmen armed with muskets.

August

12 Council on Prices, Productivity and Incomes ('Three Wise Men') set up to deal with inflation and administer Chancellor Selwyn Lloyd's first credit squeeze.

18 Morris Cowley, Oxford: 5,000 out of 5,500 work-force unionized after vigorous campaign, including lightning walk-outs for union recognition.

September

19 Selwyn Lloyd raises bank rate to the then unprecedented level of 7 per cent to deal with economic recession; Labour demands recall of Parliament.

November

7 UK explodes its first megaton H-bomb on Christmas Island.

15 White City building site: 400 working on the new BBC TV studios strike when twenty-four shop stewards sacked for holding a meeting in working hours. They are reinstated, but site strikes again when building workers' Federation steward is victimized for collecting union dues four days later; this time all twenty-four stewards dismissed.

21 Soviet Union: Communist Party leaders from twelve countries issue declaration of intent to pursue 'peaceful road to socialism'.

1958

January

6–16 British Cycle Corporation, Birmingham: Strike of 3,000 when firm breaks redundancy agreement and sacks eighty workers without shop-floor consultation. Ends with new redundancy procedures guarantee by the firm.

14–20 BMC: Strike of 600 vehicle builders at Morris, Cowley, in support of twenty-eight semi-skilled workers claiming skilled status grading.

22 BMC: Internal transport men strike for £2 increase at Fisher & Ludlow body-works.

February

1 S. Wales: 7,000 in Welsh protest march against unemployment.

3 BMC: Storemen at Austin, Longbridge, stop work when only some of their number are paid a negotiated increase.

10–21 Armstrong-Whitworth, N. Shields: Strike of 200 when convenor at this pneumatic tool plant victimized. Ends in his reinstatement.

11–14 Steel Co. of Wales, Abbey works: 550 on strike in demarcation dispute, and again from 2 to 4 March over same issue.

12 BMC: 300 men in tractor and transmission plant strike when firm put three members of breakaway organization (National Association of Toolmakers) into 100 per cent trade-union shop.

17 Campaign for Nuclear Disarmament launched at packed meeting at Central Hall, Westminster and four overflow meetings.

28 Harland & Wolff, Belfast: 600 steel-platers strike for parity with English shipyard rates.

March

14–4 April 300 Strike at Yorkshire Engine Co., Sheffield, for reinstatement of convenor, sacked for allegedly threatening progress chaser with violence.

24 Harland & Wolff, Clyde: Strike when management refuses short-time working instead of sacking eighty-six men.

April

4–7 CND hold first fifty-mile march from London to Atomic Weapons Research Establishment at Aldermaston, which 10,000 marchers reach at the end of Easter weekend.

13 12,000 attend Trafalgar Square demonstration organized by the Labour Party, against atomic bomb tests.

19–22 June Smithfield Market and London Docks: Strike of 1,700 hourly-paid meat-lorry drivers at Smithfield, when employers turn down a 15 per cent pay increase bid submitted to make up their wage packets following the raising of speed limit for heavy goods vehicles from 20 to 30 mph. 600 meat porters laid off on 26th; on 11 May 6,500 inside workers at Smithfield strike in sympathy with the drivers. The next day workers

1958 *contd*

at riverside cold stores refuse to handle frozen meat for Smithfield and are sent home. On 13 May, dockers at Tooley St refuse to load blackleg lorries escorted into the docks by police; the dockers are locked out, and by 18 May 3,700 are idle. On 21 May some dock employers use unregistered labour at Blackfriars and Tooley St – an offence under the Dock Labour Scheme – and 9,300 dockers strike the next day in the Pool of London. By 5 June 20,000 dockers out and entire London docks at a standstill over use of unregistered labour. After nine-week strike, Smithfield drivers vote to return pending Court of Inquiry into their wages. They return on 22nd, as do 7,000 other Smithfield men and 20,000 dockers, who also successfully claimed a pay rise during the strike.

28 Pressed Steel Co., Swindon: Strike of 1,500 car body workers for hourly increase of 8d. skilled, 6d. semi-skilled, 4d. unskilled. By 8 May, 10,000 car workers at Birmingham, Coventry and Oxford laid off. Return on 29 May after month-long strike, settling for 2d., 1½d., 1d. increases.

May

1 St Pancras council raises the Red Flag on the Town Hall. Nineteen people, including Labour councillors, arrested at open-air May Day meeting.

4–21 June London Transport: 50,000 bus crew members strike for 10s. 6d. across-the-board increase for all busmen – an attempt to break government's pay freeze. Strike solid for eight weeks, with oil-refinery workers blacking distribution of oil supplies to private coach depots. Official Tribunal argue that TGWU demand 'would set in motion leap-frogging claims'. Union settle on 21 June with most busmen getting 8s. 6d. rise, but cuts in services mean 10 per cent fewer buses on the roads, and redundancies.

15 NUR accepts 3 per cent rise after threatening national rail strike.

20 9,000 in mass CND lobby of Houses of Parliament.

21 John Lawrence, St Pancras Labour group leader, is suspended from membership of Labour Party.

June

17 Hungary: Imre Nagy and comrades in October Provisional Government quietly executed.

July

23 Cyprus: Widespread rioting in Nicosia and Famagusta for independence; 1,300 arrests.

25–5 August South Bank Shell building site (McAlpines): 1,200 construction workers strike for appointment of full-time safety officer, following death of a foreman – third death on the site in three months.

August

13 Peking: Khrushchev and Mao issue joint pledge of support for national independence movements; call for an immediate summit conference and withdrawal of US and British troops from Middle East.

September

2 'Notting Hill race riots': fifty-eight arrested in gang fights. Two weeks later nine white youths jailed for four years for 'nigger-hunting'.

15 McAlpines, South Bank: Ninety steel-fixers strike when two men, one non-union, break overtime ban. McAlpines claim they were re-phasing the site on the 25th, closing it down and sacking 1,250, in bid to smash militant site organization. Amalgamated Union of Building Trade Workers does not back men. On 2 October the Civil Engineering Conciliation Board declares that no dispute exists on the site and that McAlpines can recruit new men, although the site is being picketed by 1,000 workers at the time. The next two weeks see repeated battles between pickets and police, and by 17 October McAlpines have succeeded in getting 300 un-skilled scab workers on site. Building unions issue more back-to-work orders; on 29 October the AUBTW suspends all members of South-East London District Committee for supporting the pickets.

30 Cyprus: two-day general strike in opposition to British partition plan.

October

13–21 BOAC maintenance engineers in successful strike for pay rise and reinstatement of five sacked militants. Mass meeting on 20th calls for resignation of Jim Mathews, trade union representative on Committee of Inquiry, after he has attacked militant union members on TV pro-gramme.

17–20 January Belvedere Power Station, Kent: Construction site blacked and closed down for fourteen weeks after 240 men sacked; 110 re-employed, but most of the stewards victimized.

31 Aden: British police fire on crowd demonstrating for independence.

November

10 Cyprus: 3,000 Greek-Cypriot workers sacked from British air bases and NAAFI canteens as security measure. Call goes out for patriotic English volunteers.

16 First national industrial rank-and-file conference called by the *Newsletter* presents draft charter of workers' demands.

December

6 Direct Action Committee against Nuclear Weapons (DAC): forty-six in first non-violent demonstration at North Pickenham rocket base, Norfolk. Several protestors thrown in pools of cement by builders on the site and two are detained in hospital.

19–20 More demonstrations by DAC supporters at the Thor rocket base, Pickenham, result in forty-five arrests.

1959

January

1 Cuban revolution. Dictator Batista flees as Castro's forces occupy surrounding countryside, before entering Havana the next day.

15 Fords, Doncaster: First strike since factory opened seventeen years ago

1959 *contd*

starts when worker is sacked for eating a meat-pie two minutes before mid-morning break. Reinstated the next day.

20 Twenty-three St Pancras councillors surcharged £200 each after voting for council to pay Rent Act increases on decontrolled houses.

February

22–24 10,000 on strike at Steel Co. of Wales plant at Port Talbot when a clerical worker is sacked without notice, in breach of redundancy procedure agreement.

March

18 Kenya: Inquest opens on eleven African detainees who died at Hola 'irrigation scheme' camp.

April

8–28 Handley Page, Cricklewood: Strike of 2,000 when convenor given one hour's notice for 'insubordination'. 2,000 more come out in sympathy at Radlett on 10th and work on the Victor bomber is halted.

May

6 Kenya: Coroner finds that eleven detainees at Hola camp were beaten to death by British guards. On 19th, British government votes to pay £120 compensation to dependants of each dead man.

17 West Indian Kelso Cochrane stabbed to death in North Kensington race fight.

June

19–31 July Seven-week print dispute for 10 per cent increase and forty-hour week starts in provinces. Federation of Master Printers locks out typesetters and compositors. Fleet Street eventually brought to a halt when supplies of printing ink are blacked. Wage freeze broken by $4\frac{1}{2}$ per cent increase agreed at end of July.

23–25 Devon Colliery, Clackmannan, Scotland: sixty-six miners stage a 'stay-down' strike against threatened closure of the pit. They surface when Scottish NCB agreed to discussions, by which time forty-three pits and 20,000 men are out in the Scottish coalfield. The pit is finally closed on economic grounds.

July

16–12 August Morris Motors, Cowley: Strike of 3,000 when BMC sack chief TGWU shop steward Frank Horsman for 'obstruction, insubordination and insolence over many years' and 'assuming the prerogatives of management'. Ministry of Labour intervenes when eleven unions back the strike.

August

10–20 Short Bros. & Harland, Belfast: Strike of 8,000 against threatened 1,500 redundancies at this aircraft firm after cancellation of vertical take-off plane contract. Return when management suspends further sackings.

September

5 Peter Fryer resigns editorship of the *Newsletter* 'for reasons of ill-health'.

28–6 October British Oxygen: 900 tanker drivers at ten depots strike over pay-claim delay. Other industries, particularly motors, were quickly halted and lay-offs began almost immediately. TUC General Council condemn the dispute during the national conference, and all depots return after a week. On 21 October the NUGMW suspends 112 of its members for six months for participating in the strike.

October

8 General Election: Macmillan defeats Gaitskell in the 'You've never had it so good' election by the largest popular majority since the Tories beat Attlee, to the dismay of Labour Party and the *Daily Mirror*, which had waged unusually vigorous election campaign in its columns.

December

29 Britain signs 'outer seven' trading pact with EFTA countries, in face of competition from Common Market.

1960

January

First issue of *New Left Review*, theoretical Marxist journal, edited by Stuart Hall.

3 Eighty-two arrested at DAC demonstration at Harrington rocket base.

11 Aircraft industry merger: Vickers, English Electric and Bristol Aero combine to form British Aircraft Corporation.

17 50,000 in London march against anti-semitism after outbreak of swastika-daubing on synagogues in Germany and London.

February

3 Macmillan addresses South African Parliament on rise of African nationalism: 'The wind of change is blowing through the continent. Whether we like it or not, this growth of national consciousness is a political fact.'

28 Trafalgar Square demonstration against apartheid: many thousands out to support a boycott of South African oranges and other goods.

March

21 South Africa: Massacre at Sharpeville. Police fire on African crowd demonstrating against new 'pass laws'. Seventy killed, 150 wounded.

April

13 'Blue Streak' missile cancelled after £100 million spent on developing this delivery system for Britain's H-bomb.

17 Anti-apartheid demonstration: 800 turn out to boo the arrival of South African cricket team.

20–15 May Engineering apprentices: National strike for higher pay of 35,000 apprentices in engineering and shipbuilding.

28 New credit squeeze announced: hire-purchase controls brought back after eighteen months, 20 per cent deposits on HP sales.

1960 *contd*

May

First issue of *International Socialism* published by group of revolutionaries in Trotskyist tradition, many from the old *Socialist Review* readers' group.

2 Thirteen anti-bomb demonstrators arrested at Foulness Atomic Weapons Research Establishment. Sentenced to six months when they refuse to give undertaking not to enter Defence Ministry property.

June

13 Robens becomes chairman of NCB to preside over closure of half Britain's pits and massive redundancies.

July

First ever productivity deal signed at Esso Oil Refinery, Fawley, Hants: workers to get immediate 40 per cent pay rise in return for increase in productivity and four-year wage standstill (by which time it was to be one of the lowest-paid refineries in the country).

6 Death of Aneurin Bevan, left-wing Labour Party stalwart.

August

10–26 September Seamen's strike begins on Merseyside and spreads to other ports. The National Seamen's Reform Movement formed during the struggle, to break the power of O'Leary on the NUS Executive. The strikers are denounced as 'subversives' by both employers and union, and eight men jailed under punitive clauses in the Merchant Shipping Act. Strike finally collapses, but rank-and-file opposition to the leadership established in the union.

24 TUC decides to hand over publishing control of *Daily Herald* to Odhams Press.

28 Don Cook, secretary of St Pancras Tenants' Association, served with eviction order for refusing to pay 28s. a week rent increase, prepares for a state of siege with other tenants.

September

15–18 November Shipwrights and Burners, Port Glasgow and Greenock: 550 strike for pay rise, resulting in 2,800 lay-offs when agreement finally reached.

20–15 October Strike of 1,600 tally clerks in London and Tilbury docks against transfer of other dockers onto clerks' register, which they see as attempt to dilute labour force and create pool of unemployed dockers. Dock Labour Board, TGWU, and Court of Inquiry all condemn the strike.

22 End of St Pancras rent strike by 2,000 tenants. A force of 800 police supporting twenty-eight bailiffs succeed in evicting tenants' leaders Don Cook and Arthur Rowe, barricaded in their flats for over a month. State of Emergency declared in St Pancras by Home Secretary Henry Brooke and all public demonstrations in the borough banned. 1,000 police cordon off the Town Hall from 14,000 marching tenants, striking railwaymen and building workers.

October

3 Scarborough: Labour Party conference votes against the platform in favour of unilateral nuclear disarmament; Gaitskell declares that he will 'fight, fight, and fight again' to get this motion reversed.

18 *News Chronicle* and *Star* cease publication on Fleet Street – 4,000 printers and journalists made redundant.

November

14 US Ford Motor Company in take-over of British Ford Motors.

December

5 Standard Triumph Motor Co. and British Leyland in merger.

1961

January

16–15 May Merseyside ship-repairing: Engineering workers in five months of stoppages at various firms demand a special 22s. bonus; a bonus increase eventually agreed.

February

15–11 March Strike of 70,000 Yorkshire coal-miners for 10 per cent increase in contract prices and guaranteed shift rate.

18 Newly formed Committee of 100 opens campaign of direct action when 4,000 sit down outside the Ministry of Defence. Bertrand Russell pins H-bomb denunciation on the door. In Glasgow, CND march is supported by 10,000, protesting at decision to site US Polaris submarine base at nearby Holy Loch.

March

16 Parliamentary Labour Party withdraws whip from five left-wing MPs for voting against the defence estimates: Michael Foot, Sidney Silverman, Emrys Hughes, S. O. Davies and William Baxter all opposed to Britain's nuclear deterrent.

28 USA: Biggest arms budget since the war ($44 billion) is announced, with massive spending on Polaris and Skybolt missiles.

April

3 32,000 CND marchers from Aldermaston and Wethersfield met by crowd of 100,000 supporters in Trafalgar Square.

6–12 May Pressed Steel, Swindon: Strike of 1,200 skilled workers for extra 9d. an hour without official AEU support. 10,000 workers in the car industry have been laid off after a month, and firm threatens strikers with redundancy if they stay out. A drift back in absence of union support, and many militants victimized by the company and sacked.

17 Hearing begins into allegations of 'ballot-rigging' by Communists on the Executive of the Electrical Trades Union, made by Les Cannon and Frank Chapple (ex-members of the Communist Party).

16–20 Bay of Pigs: CIA-backed invasion and bombing of Cuba by force of exiles rapidly defeated.

1961 *contd*

22–3 May Strike of 15,000 London dockers when Dock Labour Board permit an employer to use unregistered labour for occasional unloading work.

29 Whitehall: 2,000 on first mass 'sit-down' organized by Committee of 100: 826 arrested.

June

27–30 Fords, Dagenham: Strike of 25,000 in protest when management refuse (on grounds of government pay policy) to negotiate until September on a claim submitted in May.

July

25 Selwyn Lloyd announces further credit squeeze accompanied by a 'pay-pause'; bank rate put back to 7 per cent; teachers' pay rise cut; price of cigarettes, drink, petrol and household goods all rise as purchase tax is increased. TUC condemns measures as inflationary.

31 Macmillan announces that Britain is to seek membership of the Common Market.

August

13 East Germany: Ulbricht's security forces seal off East Berlin and build a continuous wall across the city. A general hotting-up of the 'cold war' in the months that follow and much diplomatic activity over the 'Berlin crisis'.

30–29 November British Light Steel Pressings, Acton: Combine committee at this Rootes subsidiary calls a strike when management refuse to discuss rumoured redundancies. AEU Executive orders a return, ignored by the strikers. By October car production at Rootes virtually halted. A drift back when firm threatens sackings. Eventually strike committee recommends a return, but most are sacked as company takes opportunity to victimize leading militants.

September

US and USSR both resume atmospheric testing of nuclear warheads.

12 Thirty-three members of Committee of 100, including Bertrand Russell and his wife, jailed for seven days after refusing to be bound over with regard to further anti-Polaris demonstrations.

13 Home Secretary Brooke invokes Public Order Act to prohibit demonstration organized by Committee of 100 for the following Sunday.

13–28 October Steel Co. of Wales, Port Talbot: Three bricklayers suspended after refusing certain duties when management unilaterally changes the pay structure. Staff carry out the bricklayers' work (repairing blast-furnace linings). Remaining furnace maintenance workers refuse to work with them, bringing works to complete shut-down. A return eventually agreed pending negotiations.

17 12,000 Committee of 100 supporters demonstrate against the bomb in Trafalgar Square, despite official ban; 1,314 arrested. At Holy Loch, 351 arrested on a sit-down at the Polaris sub-base.

28 Chancellor Selwyn Lloyd proposes the establishment of a National Economic Development Council (NEDC).

October

2–7 November Building workers: Nationwide stoppages over differing interpretations of the 'refreshment break' clause in national construction agreement. Local settlements negotiated.

18 Many thousands at Commons on CND lobby for 'No War over Berlin'.

30 Russia explodes biggest and most radioactive bomb ever in the Arctic – 50-megaton warhead.

December

6 Police raid Committee of 100 offices with warrant issued under the Official Secrets Act. Two days later five members arrested.

9 6,000 take part in anti-bomb sit-downs at Wethersfield NATO base, Ruislip USAF headquarters, and in Manchester, Bristol, York and Cardiff. 860 arrests.

1962

January

24 TUC decides to co-operate with government and sit on NEDC.

February

5 Nationwide one-day strike called by Confederation of Shipbuilding and Engineering Unions in pursuit of national pay increase.

25 Trial of the 'Wethersfield six' arrested during December Committee of 100 sit-down; five men get eighteen months, the woman is jailed for one year.

March

5 Further one-day national strike called by Engineering Unions. Subsequent ballot shows a 3–2 majority against an indefinite strike. Agreement reached on a 3 per cent increase. (This was the last annual national engineering pay claim: in November the AEU National Committee approved the principle of long-term pay agreements.)

23–31 Merseyside docks dispute: Strike of 10,000 TGWU men against employment of members of the breakaway 'blue' union of Stevedores and Dockers. Employers eventually agreed to TGWU closed shop; TGWU men refuse to co-operate in management-organized union-card checks.

April

2–9 Austins, Longbridge: Various groups of workers in week-long strike for 36s. increase in bonus rate. Work resumed pending productivity dealing.

23 Aldermaston march ends with rally of 150,000 addressed by Hiroshima victims in Hyde Park. Two days later, US starts a new series of nuclear bomb tests on Christmas Island.

28 10,000 nurses march to Trafalgar Square in protest against their low pay.

May

27 110 tenants of Greencoat Properties march twenty-six miles from Bethnal

1962 *contd*

Green to council chairman's home, protesting at exorbitant rent rises and demanding compulsory purchase of the flats.

June

28 UN General Assembly calls on Britain (by 75 to 1) to formulate a new constitution for Southern Rhodesia providing for one man one vote, restoration of freedom of political activity to non-Europeans, and release of all political prisoners. (In the same month, FRELIMO and PAIGC formed to fight Portuguese colonialism in Mozambique and Guinea.)

July

1 Commonwealth Immigrants Act becomes law, restricting right of entry to UK of coloured British citizens: fourteen refused entry on the first day. National Socialist Movement led by Colin Jordan holds fascist meeting in Trafalgar Square under heavy police protection. Nineteen arrested as crowd attacks speakers.

22 Attempt by Mosley's Union Movement to hold Trafalgar Square meeting stopped by anti-fascist demonstration after fifteen minutes and fifty-five arrests.

31 Crowd of several thousand stop Oswald Mosley speaking in Ridley Road, Dalston.

August

10 British guided missile 'Blue Water' to be scrapped – 2,000 English Electric workers to be made redundant.

14 £1,400 million banking merger between National Provincial and District banks.

Ministry of Works bans all Trafalgar Square meetings planned by Union Movement, British Nazi Party and other fascist groups. On 17th, Jordan, John Tyndall and two others arrested and eventually jailed for controlling a 'quasi-military' organization called 'Spearhead'.

September

16 Fighting in Ridley Road, Dalston, when Mosley makes snap appearance and is knocked out. Fourteen arrested.

October

3 One-day rail strike called by NUR brings out 285,000 men in protest at cuts in services and closure of twelve railway workshops.

9 Bethnal Green Council takes over 1,018 flats of Greencoat Properties, after militant tenants campaign against rent increases.

17–29 Fords, Dagenham: 1,400 walk out on strike after leading shop steward, Bill Francis, is sacked for holding meeting during lunch break. Unions order a return which strikers agree to. Fords send out letter stating that only workers who agree to its rules will be accepted back, and seventy 'troublemakers and wreckers' are victimized. Unions waver and in months that follow the firm takes the opportunity to break existing shop-floor organization; by May the number victimized has been reduced to seventeen, while Fords pushes through the introduction of three-shift working.

22 Cuban missile crisis: Kennedy announces US blockade to prevent shipment of Russian missiles and threatens 'further action'. Third World War seems very close.

November

28 TUC demands meeting with Chancellor Maudling to discuss unemployment: wants cuts in purchase tax, lower bank rate, lower national insurance contributions.

December

20 Number out of work highest December figure for twenty years – 603,077.

29 Blizzards sweep southern England. Worst winter conditions since 1947. Arctic weather lasts three months. Many power cuts; factories shut down and many laid off.

1963

January

14 Common Market: De Gaulle vetoes Britain's application to join.

18 Hugh Gaitskell, leader of Labour Party, dies of lung infection.

24 Winter unemployment reaches 860,580.

February

14 Harold Wilson elected leader of Labour Party by 144 votes to George Brown's 103.

March

26 10,000 unemployed workers lobby Houses of Parliament.

27 Beeching's plan for the railways published: many lines and services to be axed; large-scale redundancies forecast.

April

12 11,000 start out on CND march from Aldermaston. 'Spies for Peace' publish documents revealing details of 'Regional Seats of Government' (bomb-shelters for the ruling class) and results of NATO exercise 'Fallex' held previous September simulating nuclear war.

June

5 Profumo affair: Minister of Defence admits he lied in statement to Commons about his relationship with Christine Keeler and call-girl circle. Big security scandal; Stock Market slumps on 10th. *The Times* declares 'It *is* a moral issue' and press embarks on a witch-hunt of everyone involved.

9 King and Queen of Greece on state visit are booed by demonstrators protesting at assassination of left-wing MP George Lambrakis the previous May. Police make ninety-four arrests. A year later, Det. Sgt Challenor is found 'insane' after planting bricks in demonstrators' pockets to help him in his inquiries.

August

3 Stephen Ward, doctor on trial for running call-girl ring involving Profumo, the Russian cultural attaché, and property racketeer Rachman, commits suicide.

1963 *contd*

8 Great Train Robbery: £2½ million liberated from the Royal Mail. In April 1964, seven of the gang get jail sentences of thirty years.

19–24 Selective one-week strike called by National Federation of Building Workers in support of more pay and shorter hours; implementation over a three-year period agreed by employers.

October

10 Macmillan enters hospital for prostate gland operation and resigns as PM, reportedly broken by Profumo events.

19 Earl of Home, hitherto unknown Scottish landowner, emerges as PM.

23 Robbins report on higher education published, arguing for expansion of universities, related to needs of industrial technology and commerce.

November

22 Kennedy assassinated in Dallas. Police arrest ex-Communist Lee Harvey Oswald, shot dead by Jack Ruby during live TV coverage two days later.

December

23–2 February Steel Co. of Wales, Port Talbot: AEU demand for £5 increase for maintenance workers coupled with action of seven craft unions for three-week annual holiday result in closure and 10,000 laid off. TUC intervention leads to AEU men getting pay rise with productivity strings after lengthy inquiry.

1964

January

14–8 April Raleigh, Nottingham: 300 toolroom workers strike for three months against redundancies, demanding work-sharing instead. Redundancy agreement finally accepted.

20 Tanganyika: African troops mutiny against British officers for more pay and promotion.

24 Inquiry begins into allegations that Ferranti Co. is profiteering on government contract for 'Bloodhound' missiles.

February

8 Portsmouth: 20,000 council tenants march against new rents scheme involving £2 weekly increases.

10 TUC sells off its holding in the *Daily Herald* to International Publishing Corporation.

March

28 Committee of 100 sit-down outside Ruislip USAF base ends with 302 arrests.

29 Clacton: Police arrest ninety-seven teenagers in fight between 'mods' and 'rockers'.

April

13 Ian Smith becomes Rhodesian PM; three days later Nkomo and other nationalist leaders are jailed.

May

2 600 British troops sent as reinforcements to Aden, bringing garrison total to 2,000.

June

4 US Chrysler to have 30 per cent interest in Rootes Motors, leaving only BMC free from control of American capital. Heath says this is in the best interests of the car industry.

July

8 Announcement that Britain's share in costs of producing supersonic air-liner, Concorde, will rise from £85 to £140 million. First of many such announcements.

10–16 Postal workers: 100,000 come out on a one-day stoppage and numerous unofficial walk-outs finally result in a 6½ per cent pay increase, breaking the government's 4 per cent wages norm.

August

5 Incident in the Gulf of Tonkin, when US frigate provokes North Vietnamese shelling, provides pretext for USAF bombing of North Vietnam.

October

15 General Election: Labour voted into power with majority of five MPs in the Commons. Wilson becomes PM. Patrick Gordon Walker defeated in Smethwick by the Tory Peter Griffiths in a racialist campaign. Wilson provoked to describe Griffiths as 'parliamentary leper' in first session.

26 Labour announces first economic measures to deal with £800 million balance of payments deficit: 15 per cent import tariffs and tax rebates for exporting industrialists.

November

11 Autumn Budget: Income tax up 6d.; petrol up 6d. a gallon. Callaghan proposes to introduce capital gains and corporation taxes at a later date.

16 MPs award themselves pay rise from £1,750 to £3,250 a year.

20 City reaction to Labour government: share prices down and currency crisis as international financiers unload sterling holdings on to the market.

December

2–3 Mass occupation of Sproul Hall, Berkeley, California, follows suppression of pro-civil rights Free Speech Movement on the campus. 800 police break up what turned out to be the start of 'the student revolt'.

1965

January

16–15 May Company busmen in wave of one-day unofficial strikes starting in the Midlands, for national pay claim. Committee of Inquiry finally recommends 15s. increase and forty-hour week.

February

4 Labour announces introduction of further legislation to restrict Commonwealth immigration.

1965 *contd*

7 Vietnam: US B47 aircraft commence saturation bombing of North Vietnam, hitting civilian targets with high-explosive, napalm and anti-personnel fragmentation bombs.

24 Sir George Bolton, Bank of England director, attacks Labour for 'doing liitle to make the City – meaning finance and industry – feel happy about the present or the future'.

March

1–12 BMC, Longbridge: Strike of 300 maintenance fitters-mates for a rise in their percentage of the craft rate. After 18,000 lay-offs, agree that their pay review be advanced from October to June.

29–14 April Pressed Steel, Oxford: Strike of 750 toolroom workers for 'substantial' increase. Firm will negotiate only with plant unions jointly over any agreement, so AEU Executive advise them to return. Men finally agree to 'suspend' their action in face of hostility from other unions.

April

8 Government White Paper on Prices and Incomes Policy calls for voluntary wage restraint.

19 150,000 at CND rally in Trafalgar Square at end of Aldermaston march. Some contingents carry anti-Vietnam war slogans.

May

26 Australia and New Zealand send military detachments to fight in South Vietnam. One month later, Wilson proposes a Commonwealth peace mission to Vietnam.

July

9–22 October Motor industry, Birmingham and Coventry: Midlands car-workers refuse to implement engineering package deal of December 1964, which allowed five-shift night-working. Shop-floor demands have been for four ten-hour night-shifts to make up the forty-hour week; at many plants workers boycott the Friday night short shift for a longer weekend. Eventually, the four-night shift week is agreed nationally.

August

4 Devlin report on docks published: recommends 'decasualization' of labour force, but hints at closures, rationalization and productivity deals to come.

19 Fords announce short-time working: 10,000 on four-day week starting in a fortnight.

October

3 Start of a general strike in Aden. More British troops flown in.

November

4 Labour gives Fairfields shipyard £1 million loan and on 8 December government takes over this Clyde yard, which specializes in defence contracts, setting up a works council (in name only).

9 Queen's Speech opening Parliament announces legislation for 'improved' industrial relations, controlled wages and prices.

11 Rhodesia: Unilateral Declaration of Independence made by Rhodesian Front Government, representing 5 per cent of the population. Africans organize strikes and demonstrations. Wilson announces economic sanctions which will restore the situation 'in weeks rather than months'.

1966
January

Industrial Shop Stewards' Defence Committee formed by trade-unionists in the International Socialists, with support of some Communist Party members, in North London area.

17 Establishment of Industrial Reorganization Corporation (IRC) announced – 'a statutory body equipped with state funds to help to promote rationalization'. Lord Kearton, having recently taken over Courtaulds, heads this body, which proceeds to finance mergers and the creation of giant industrial monopolies with tax-payers' money.

25 Parliamentary lobby against the Incomes Policy $3\frac{1}{2}$ per cent wage norm, sponsored by Lambeth Trades Council and supported by Socialist Labour League and Young Socialists.

March

1 4,000 trade-unionists in first parliamentary lobby organized by Liaison Committee for the Defence of Trade Unions (LCDTU).

31 General Election: Labour voted back with increased parliamentary majority.

April

21 Queen's Speech announces nationalization of steel industry.

25 Communist Party changes name of the *Daily Worker* newspaper to the *Morning Star*.

25–13 June BMC Engines, Coventry: 230 machinists involved in series of stoppages over piece-rates; 7,500 laid off on two different occasions.

May

3 Budget introduces Selective Employment Tax, a tax on man-power in the service industries designed to redeploy workers from non-essential to heavy industries. (In fact it led to higher prices, redundancies, or both.)

16 Start of national seamen's strike for reduction of the standard working week from fifty-six to forty hours without loss of pay. The shipowners, with full support of the Labour Government, resist what they call an 'inflationary demand'. As ships dock at the end of voyages, the number of seamen on strike swell to 30,000.

23 Labour declare a State of Emergency because of seamen's strike, though less than half NUS membership are actually striking, with many still at sea.

June

20 Wilson speech in Commons launches red-scare attack on the moderate Seamen's Executive who are, he claim, under the influence of 'a tightly

1966 *contd*

knit group of politically motivated men'. NUS leaders pressurized into accepting a half-way compromise and the six-week strike ends 1 July.

29 Wilson regrets US bombing of Hanoi and Haiphong but reaffirms general British support for US policy in Vietnam.

July

National Power Loading Agreement introduced in the coal mines, with shift from piece-work payment to measured day work. The ending of 'payment by results' means less control of miners over the size of their pay packets.

3 Frank Cousins resigns from Labour cabinet, in opposition to Prices and Incomes policy.

Thirty-one arrests in Grosvenor Square at demonstration outside US Embassy against bombing of Hanoi and Haiphong.

13 Trade deficit doubles; another currency crisis puts pound under pressure.

20 Wilson brings in new economic measures to protect the pound: six-month wage and prices freeze; ban on dividend rises and rise in surtax. 'What is needed is a "shake-out" which will release the nation's manpower, skilled and unskilled, and lead to a more purposive use of labour for the sake of increasing exports . . . This redeployment can only be achieved by cuts in the present inflated level of demand.'

30 England wins the World Cup at Wembley.

August

8 Home Secretary Jenkins changes the jury system, allowing majority 10–2 verdicts in criminal cases.

22 ICI announce 1,000 redundancies among nylon workers.

24 ENV, Willesden to close, making 1,450 redundant. Very strong shop-floor organization has run this gear-producing factory for six years under virtual 'workers' control'.

September

26 BMC announce 11,000 redundancies by November. 5,000 on short-time working at Vauxhalls, Luton.

October

1 Compulsory wage freeze introduced.

20 Number unemployed rises by 100,000 in a single month.

21 Mytons, Barbican site: 230 out on strike after six men, including the site convenor and Federation Steward Lou Lewis, are victimized in attempt to break the London Joint Sites Committee of building stewards. All unions involved refuse to back the locked-out strikers, who then picket the site for thirty weeks while the foundations rust and crumble.

London School of Economics: 750 copies of Socialist Society's *Agitator* report on Walter Adams, LSE's new director, sold out in ten minutes. Campaign grows among students to resist his appointment.

24 Sunleys, Horseferry Road: 300 down tools and join the painters who walked off this Westminster site a month ago. Another long dispute provoked by

the building employers on a municipal contract, when they introduce a new bonus scheme and hours which would mean a longer day for no extra pay. Seen as further attempt to victimize and blacklist trade-union militants in the building industry.

November

3 100,000 idle in car or component firms because of economy measures or strikes.

22 White Paper on the economy outlines a 'period of severe restraint'.

LSE: One-day lecture-boycott by 1,500 students when authorities suspend students' union leaders for writing to *The Times* on union instruction outlining opposition to Adams, without permission of school administration.

December

1 Wilson ('I would not sit at the same table as a racialist') holds talks with Smith about Rhodesia on board the cruiser *Tiger*.

Additional investment grants to industry of £120 million over next two years announced by the Treasury.

3 First conference of 700 rank-and-file trade-unionists organized by LCDTU.

6 Roberts-Arundel, Stockport: Start of seventeen-month official strike by 145 AEU men against redundancies and attacks on union organization, after firm is taken over by US bosses. Movement of firm's products and machinery blacked at local docks and airports.

21 Thomson take-over of *The Times* gets government approval.

1967

January

15 'Peace with Rhodesia' rally in Trafalgar Square brings left out in force to drown speeches by Duncan Sandys, Patrick Wall, Biggs-Davison and other prominent Smith supporters.

17 US Chrysler Corporation finally takes over Rootes Motor Group, with Labour's approval.

19 Unemployment figures pass 600,000.

21 National Union of Students begins campaign against doubling of university fees of students from overseas.

February

3 Wilson, speaking at Swansea Labour meeting: 'the price of freedom from crisis, from "stop-go", is the abandonment of free-for-all incomes'.

21 Socialist Labour League and Young Socialists organize parliamentary lobby 'To make the Left MPs Fight'.

22 NUS day of protest, with lobby of Commons against raising of overseas students' fees.

Roberts-Arundel: Mass picket of over 2,000 workers from local Stockport factories in running battle with police, when US management tries to bring scab labour across picket lines.

1967 *contd*
March

7–12 May Two weeks after Tyneside draughtsmen strike for higher pay, Shipbuilding Employers' Association lock out all 1,400 DATA members in the industry. Lock-out abandoned after two months with slight improvement in wage offer.

12 LCDTU and other trade-union bodies sponsor anti-incomes policy lobby of Commons.

13 LSE: First British student occupation, lasting six days and involving more than 2,000, starts after student leaders Adelstein and Bloom are suspended for writing letter to *The Times*. Opposition to 'pedagogic gerontocracy' leads to wider demands for 'academic freedom'.

22 Disclosures that Bristol Siddeley have profiteered on government contracts for servicing aero-engines.

29 Barbican: Mytons tries to bring in non-union labour onto the site; met by a mass picket joined by all the workers on neighbouring Turriffs and Laing sites.

May

1 *May Day Manifesto*, intellectual socialist critique of Labour Government, edited by Raymond Williams, Stuart Hall and Edward Thompson, launched at Central Hall meeting.

2 Wilson announces that Britain is applying to join the Common Market.

June

5 Second Prices and Incomes Bill published.

Israel starts the 'Six Day War' against Arab neighbours and proceeds to occupy large parts of Palestinian desert, driving out many Arabs to refugee camps.

19 Brown announces heavy spending on defence in Arabia, following Aden's independence in January 1968.

July

3 Aden: Fierce battle wages as NLF occupies small town of Crater while the Argylls try to blitz them out.

15–29 International Congress of Dialectics of Liberation at Roundhouse, Camden Town. London intelligentsia are addressed by group of radical intellectuals, including Lucian Goldman, Herbert Marcuse, Ernest Mandel, Stokely Carmichael, and R. D. Laing, in 'a unique gathering to demystify human violence in all its forms'.

20 Highest summer unemployment figures for twenty-seven years released – over ½ million out of work.

24 Prices of school meals and welfare milk raised. Further cuts in Government spending on social services and benefits, accompanied by resignation of Mrs Margaret Herbison, Minister of Social Services.

September

4 Britain offers to negotiate with NLF in Aden following collapse of South Arabian Federal Government set up by Britain eight years before.

7 Cameron Report into Barbican and Horseferry Road disputes white-washes the employers and attacks the militant shop stewards on the two sites, recommending that building unions take powers to discipline or disqualify site stewards.

18–27 November Liverpool and London dockers involved in separate disputes arising from reorganization of dock labour following implementation of Devlin proposals: Merseyside strike for higher piece-rates; London strike against transfer of men to different employers and from one dock to another.

25–29 Vauxhalls, Luton: 16,000 workers laid off by management in response to overtime ban and work-to-rule for an improved pay offer.

28 GEC, headed by Arnold Weinstock, in successful take-over bid for AEI for £150 million.

October

21 USA: 50,000 demonstrators march on the Pentagon against Vietnam war.

21–23 December Municipal busmen in five towns strike for implementation of national TGWU claim for £1 a week increase, which had been frozen by the government wage standstill. Eventually receive increase in December 1968, backdated one year.

22 Grosvenor Square: Vietnam Solidarity Campaign organizes demonstration in support of National Liberation Front, marching to US Embassy from Trafalgar Square; 5,000 involved in fights with police cordons, when prevented from delivering message of protest.

November

Barbican: Employers and unions place joint advertisement in London evening papers calling for a return to work along recommendations of Cameron Report. Fifteen scabs enter supported by a force of 2,000 police, including mounted police, to break picket line.

9 Robens, NCB chairman, says manpower in mining industry will drop from 387,000 to 65,000 by 1980 if current policies are pursued.

14 Trade deficit and currency crisis: pound slumps and Government hastily borrows £90 million from Swiss bankers.

18 Pound is devalued by 14.3 per cent against the dollar. Bank rate up to 8 per cent; cuts in Government spending and credit squeeze announced.

29 British troops leave Aden after 128 years' colonial rule.

1968

January

5 Wilson informs TUC that maximum wage rise norm of 3½ per cent is to operate for next twelve months.

16 Cuts in spending on education, housing and health – 'to make devaluation work'.

17 BMC and Leyland merger creates British Leyland, aided by £25 million government loan from the IRC.

1968 *contd*

26 National Provincial and Westminster Banks in merger forming National Westminster Bank.

30 Vietnam: Start of the Tet offensive. NLF launches hundreds of guerrilla attacks throughout the South on provincial capitals, US and other military bases. Ends one month later when city of Hué is finally recaptured by US marines and ARVN forces in some of fiercest fighting ever.

February

1 Following recent merger, GEC–AEI announce plans to close Woolwich factory, making 5,500 redundant, and sack 500 laboratory workers elsewhere.

4 4,000 march in Wolverhampton protest against Sikh busmen not being allowed to wear turbans on duty.

5 Third Hull trawler in three weeks, *Ross Cleveland*, sinks with loss of nineteen lives, overturning in Icelandic waters with iced-up rigging. Lil Bilocca leads militant campaign of trawlermen's wives for improved safety conditions in the fishing industry.

11–2 **March** British Steel Corporation, Shotton: 1,700 maintenance craftsmen ban overtime in support of weekend pay claim; 7,000 production workers laid off.

20 Secondary school milk to be cut; National Insurance contributions to go up.

22 Home Secretary Callaghan introduces new Immigration Bill restricting entry of Commonwealth immigrants holding UK passports to 1,000 a year.

25 3,000 march to Downing Street against Immigrants Bill.

March

1–25 **May** 3,200 Liverpool busmen stop work when local 23s. wage agreement frozen by Prices and Incomes Board. Return when PIB finally approves the rise.

17 Solidarity demonstration by 20,000 in support of NLF outside US Embassy, Grosvenor Square. 300 arrests as mounted police are used to break up the demonstration.

18–5 **April** Strike of 7,000 road haulage drivers on Merseyside for a local claim for £16 weekly basic. Returned pending negotiations with individual employers.

April

15 25,000 in Trafalgar Square at end of CND march from Aldermaston. Breakaway demonstration marches on the German Springer press office in the IPC building, Holborn, in protest at the shooting the day before of Rudi Dutschke, SDS leader and subject of constant vilification by Springer's network of papers.

20 Enoch Powell makes racist attack on immigrants: says that nation is heaping its own funeral pyre and 'like the Roman "I seem to see the River Tiber flowing with much blood" ', forecasting race wars in future.

23 1,000 London dockers march to House of Commons, downing tools in support of Powell, after Heath sacks him from shadow cabinet.

May

Black Dwarf, a non-sectarian newspaper taking its name from a satirical weekly widely read by London workers and artisans in the early nineteenth century, published.

1 Anti-Powell demonstration by students and some workers clashes with another dockers' march in support of Powell.

3 France: Students occupying the Sorbonne violently attacked by the special riot police (CRS).

6 CRS attack Sorbonne students again, this time using CS gas; many students savagely beaten.

7 Police and dogs called to Essex University after students break up meeting addressed by chemical warfare expert.

8 GEC–AEI announce another 2,700 redundancies, bringing total sackings to 10,000 since merger six months before.

10 Cecil King, *Daily Mirror* editor and Bank of England director, calls on Wilson to resign in front-page article, and talks of grave financial crisis threatening country. The pound slumps again.

10–11 Paris: 'Night of the Barricades': Violent battle takes place between CRS and students in the Latin Quarter after the Sorbonne is closed. On 11th, police are withdrawn, arrested students released and Sorbonne reopened.

13 French trade-union organizations call general strike against police violence and for educational reform. A million workers march through Paris streets. Students reoccupy Sorbonne.

13–7 June Rootes, Linwood: 4,000 laid off when 200 AEU press-shop workers strike against productivity deal accepted by other unions. A further 550 refuse to work the new conditions. Work resumes pending inquiry into the agreement.

14 France: First factory occupation takes place as workers take over Sud Aviation, Nantes.

15 National one-day strike by $1\frac{1}{2}$ million engineers for £2 weekly increase with no productivity strings.

16 Ronan Point, block of flats put up by Taylor Woodrow in East Ham, collapses. Five killed after gas blast sets off a 'progressive collapse' caused by faulty design.

France: Renault car-workers occupy factories at Rouen and Flins.

22 France: Ten million workers now on general strike for improvements in pay, hours and working conditions. Until the end of May hundreds of factories and colleges are occupied by workers and students. Councils of Action set up and demand of 'workers' control' raised. Troop movements on the outskirts of Paris.

28 Hornsey Art College: Start of a seven-week sit-in following victimization of progressive members of the teaching staff.

L.B.–25

1968 *contd*

June

1 International Socialist's paper *Labour Worker* becomes *Socialist Worker*.

7–28 Fords: Small number of women sewing machinists reduce whole of Dagenham works to a standstill in demand for parity classification with male wage rate, bringing demand for equal pay for women back onto the shop-floor. They finally settle for 92 per cent of equivalent male rate.

8 Hull University occupation against examination system starts when student tears up his papers and walks out of exam hall.

10 Labour Government reintroduces prescription charges after abolishing them when they first came to power.

17 France: Last factory occupation ends when Renault workers vote to return to work.

27 Prices and Incomes Bill, containing penal clauses, passed in the Commons.

July

2 Labour announces further aid to Federal Nigeria, while civil war with secessionist Biafra continues.

11 *Pravda* expresses alarm at liberalization in Czechoslovakia, where Dubček is introducing 'socialism with a human face' and economic reforms to make the economy more efficient. One week later, Warsaw Pact leaders say Czechoslovakian situation is unacceptable in a socialist country, while Czech workers talk of greater participation in decision-making.

21 London: 15,000 march in 'solidarity with N L F' Vietnam demonstration.

25 9,000 G L C tenants march on County Hall against rent increases. Arrive to discover Tory council entertaining lords and ladies at the chairman's reception ('So that's where our money goes').

Injection Moulders: Eighty-five machine operators, mainly Indian and Pakistani, hold sit-down, refusing to operate new shift system, and are forcibly evicted by police from this North London factory.

August

1 Government report on the building industry refuses to end the system of 'lump' labour sub-contracting.

20–27 Czechoslovakia: Tanks from Russia, Poland, Hungary and East Germany invade in the early hours. Workers and students offer passive resistance, telling tank crews to go home, though some are set ablaze. Dubček spends a week in Moscow accused of right-wing revisionism before returning looking pale. Country is to remain occupied until situation is 'normalized', and hard-liners in Czech Communist Party are set up in power.

28 Chicago: Mayor Daley's police violently attack young demonstrators outside Democratic National Convention.

September

2 100th T U C opens at Blackpool.

6 GEC–AEI announces merger with English Electric, which gets government approval.

7 *Socialist Worker* becomes a weekly newspaper.

11 Robens announces another 25,000 redundancies in the coalfields.

19–13 November Morganite Carbon, London: Strike of 1,700 workers for an extra 6d. an hour, the management demanding they give up their tea break in exchange. Workers get increase when firm backs down.

24 MCC cancels cricket tour of South Africa over D'Oliveira.

October

3 Ulster: March organized by Northern Ireland Civil Rights Association against anti-Catholic discrimination in jobs and housing is banned by Minister for Home Affairs, William Craig.

5 Londonderry: Police attack civil rights demonstrators with clubs and water cannon; thirty people are taken to hospital. The next day, the RUC go into the Bogside, breaking into houses and attacking Catholics: another twenty end up in hospital, two dying in weeks that follow.

8 Wilson has further talks with Smith on board *Fearless*, in which he drops 'no independence before majority rule' pledge on Rhodesia.

26 Birmingham: 600 rank-and-file trade-unionists attend inaugural conference of All Trades Union Alliance.

London: 1,000 students occupy LSE in preparation for VSC demonstration.

27 100,000 march peacefully past barricaded shops and offices and large contingents of police from Embankment to Hyde Park Corner, on biggest demonstration organized in support of the NLF against US imperialism in Vietnam. A breakaway group skirmishes with police in Grosvenor Square.

28–29 Lorry and tanker drivers in national forty-eight-hour strike against Government proposal to introduce 'spy in the cab' meters which would log drivers' hours.

November

4 Labour abolishes free school meals for the fourth and subsequent children of large families, saving £4 million for the Exchequer.

5 1½ million building workers have pay rise frozen after increase of 10–12s. had already been negotiated. Turriffs lock out 400 men for working to rule on Ivy Bridge housing development site at Isleworth, Middlesex.

17–19 Civil rights strike and demonstrations by Londonderry workers against police brutality and victimization of Catholics.

19 Thousands of GLC tenants march against 7s. 6d. rent rise to County Hall, demanding 'Not a Penny on the Rent'.

22 The *QE2* sets sail on Clyde, and 600 men who built it are made redundant. As compensation, John Brown's bosses open up the liner's bar for the sacked men, who smash up the luxurious Royal Suite in anger.

1968 *contd*

December

1 London squatters open campaign for housing homeless families when fifty people occupy roof of half-empty block of luxury flats at Snaresbrook.

5–16 Bristol University sit-in: 800 occupy Senate building demanding the expansion of student union facilities and access for students from the neighbouring art and technical colleges at poorer end of the binary higher education system.

13 Fords, Dagenham: 1,000 assembly-line workers hold a one-hour sit-in at the administrative block in protest against lay-offs. Action goes unreported in the Fleet Street Press.

Glossary

This glossary is aimed to give basic factual and political information on left-wing groups and publications between 1956 and the early seventies. Length of entry reflects my level of interest and information, not the organization's importance. The comments of Val Clarke, who typed the manuscript, are worth printing as an editorial warning to those using the glossary. 'It *will* be helpful to those who don't understand what the difference between the groups are, since it indicates how these differences arise from, and affect, the way in which theories are put into practice. So even though there will be adverse reaction to the detailed attention you've given to (sometimes) extremely obscure sects, the total impression is that the numerous splits, so confusing to a "beginner" who sees them as irrelevant, *are* explained in a way which answers the naïve but understandable question "Why can't you stop arguing and all get together to fight for socialism, because after all you're all supposed to be on the same side?" My only real reservation is the amount of attention paid to the student and/or "intellectual" (and I use the quotation marks advisedly!) left – I am inclined to think that you have given it more importance than it deserves, and that certain individual front-runners will have had their egos boosted yet again. I sometimes wonder when reading the history books if some of these "famous leaders" of the past were maybe the mere shouters, writers and unaligned interferers that we still see today – always there at the front, always first to act as spokesman, but in reality nothing whatsoever to do with either the action or the ideas behind it. Not from lack of commitment (they've got that, which is to their credit), but from a complete ignorance and misunderstanding about life as it is lived by ordinary people. They actually *believe* they are in touch, and that they *are* listened to and influential. Sometimes in your book – for all your snide remarks – it seems as if you think they've played a pretty big part too.'

Agitator   The theoretical and muck-stirring magazine of the London School of Economics Socialist Society. In 1966 published the background of Walter Adams, the School's ex-University College of Rhodesia Director, whose appointment led to the first mass student sit-ins in Britain. Published the pamphlet *The LSE: What It Is and Why We Fought It*. Appeared briefly as a national socialist student magazine. Contributors included Steve Jeffereys, Martin Shaw, Mike McKenna, Ted Parker. In 1974 revived as journal of National Organization of IS Student Societies.

AgitProp   Founded in May 1968 as a radical booking agency by Sheila Rowbotham, then in the International Socialists, and Roland Muldoon, originator of the street theatre group CAST (◊ Cartoon Archetypal Slogan Theatre). The name came from the thirties memories of an ILP veteran. Organized a surrealist Vietnam demonstration in Trafalgar Square in July 1968. Set up a street theatre group and actors' workshop which produced plays on the rent strike and Ford's battles (incorporated in the Red Ladder Mobile Workers' Theatre). Organized a demonstration outside Centre Point in 1968. Attempted to become a non-sectarian co-ordinating centre for the left, distributing left publications, producing monthly *Red Notes*, how-to-do-it manuals and a *Directory of Organizations*, and involved in the National Convention of the Left. In the seventies dwindled to a radical bookshop in Bethnal Green and a political diary in a London entertainment weekly. Eventually incorporated into the Rising Free bookshop and research centre and a gay community commune, Bethnal Rouge, which folded in 1974.

All Trade Union Alliance   ◊ Socialist Labour League.

Anarchist Federation of Britain (AFB)   Federalist co-ordinating body of British anarchists which was inherited by the syndicalist faction after the Great Split in 1945 between ◊ *Freedom* and the Socialist Workers' Federation. Inert but periodically reconstituted, most successfully in Bristol in 1964.

Anarchy   The anarchist pocket review brilliantly edited by Colin Ward from 1961 to 1970 which pioneered many ideas on education, architecture and art which were to become Leftist commonplaces by the late sixties. A second, scruffier series was commenced in 1971 by younger anarchists who severed the journal's connection with Freedom Press Group.

Angry Brigade   Name adopted in late sixties by a libertarian group who ignited small bombs outside political targets, scorching Robert Carr's front room and Biba's dress shop. Issued melodramatic communiqués to the underground press and *The Times*. Of the group eventually arrested after the biggest police search of the decade, the majority were acquitted at the Old Bailey. Jake Prescott, Jim Greenfield, John Barker, Anna Mendelson and Hilary Creek were imprisoned for lengthy sentences on conspiracy charges.

Anti-Internment League.   ◊ Irish Civil Rights Solidarity Campaign.

Artery   Cultural review devoted to prolonging 'socialist realism', produced by Communist Party members and advised by Alan Bush and Hugh McDiarmid. Breathtakingly pompous and genuinely Stalinist.

Association of Communist Workers   Tiny Maoist group of prolific publishers based in Hemel Hempstead. Control the Union of Women for Liberation, who single-handed persist with the Women's National Coordinating Committee and issue histories of how sham socialists, Trotskyists and revisionists have betrayed the women's movement.

Bertrand Russell Peace Foundation   London anti-imperialist body sponsored and financed by Russell and associated with the Vietnam War Crimes Tribunal. Became centre of private communications system through which

Russell and his various assistants cabled advice to world statesmen. Published *London Bulletin* (1967–9) which was incorporated into the political review *Spokesman*, edited by Ken Coates with an advisory board including various non-aligned intellectuals and union full-timers. Russell participated in setting up *Spokesman* in his last months and, according to the *Spokesman* editors, 'wanted the journal desperately in order to be able, the better, to organize support in all the various battles in which he was engaged'.

Big Flame A local working-class newspaper founded in February 1970 as a non-sectarian newspaper by and for the working class on Merseyside with the support of local shop-stewards' meetings and help from the ⟡ International Socialists. Evolved into a libertarian Marxist sect heavily influenced by the Italian Lotta Continua group. Produces factory and docks bulletins in Liverpool and spawned a London group based on ex-students working around Fords, Dagenham. Published pamphlets and 'fact folders'. Moving toward vanguard politics with Guevarist overtones in tow of Chilean and Italian mentors.

Black Dwarf Revolutionary newspaper set up by socialist poets and journalists in June 1968, adopting the name of Tom Wooler's early nineteenth-century broadsheet. (The first issue, in 1968 was headed 'Est. 1817, Vol. 13, No. 1'.) Multi-sectarian editorial board including Tariq Ali, Sheila Rowbotham, Bob Rowthorn, Clive Goodwin, Adrian Mitchell and Fred Halliday. Pioneered photomontage, direct reportage and Marxist sensationalism. Emphasis on young people, culture, alienation, anarchy and the Third World. In 1969 ⟡ International Marxist Group members began packing the board and advocating *Dwarf* readers' groups as the basis of a new youth movement. After a botched takeover, IMGers split to start ⟡ *Red Mole*, and most of the independents resigned exhausted. The *Black Dwarf* rump, dominated by *New Left Review* editors, proved incapable of producing either a popular youth paper or light entertainment for intellectuals and the paper sank in September 1970 as the 1968 wave finally ebbed.

Black Flag 'An anarchist bulletin published in the interests of a working-class revolution', issued almost monthly since 1970. Edited by Glasgow anarcho-syndicalist Stuart Christie, and by Albert Meltzer, veteran anarchist, boxer and auto-destructive artist. Associated with the anarchist Black Cross, a welfare organization for political prisoners especially in Spain, headed by Miguel Garcia Garcia. Black Cross members have been singled out particularly for police attention: 'Pino' Pinelli, secretary of the Milan Black Cross, was pushed out of a police station window, and Georg von Rauch shot by police in the street.

Black Panther Movement Brixton and Islington-based black revolutionary group. Several members prosecuted in the Mangrove Trial in 1971. Published *Black Peoples' News Service*. Became Black Workers' Movement in 1973.

Black and Red Outlook Monthly paper of the Anarchist Syndicalist Alliance, a small northern grouping based on working-class syndicalists and armed-love hips organized in 'industrial networks'.

Black Unity and Freedom Party   A London-based working-class black Marxist-Leninist grouping. Some following in Stoke Newington and the Brixton area. Publishes *Black Voice* and associated with INSLF.

Black Voice.   ◇ Black Unity and Freedom Party.

Brent Group   ◇ *Marxist, The.*

British-Vietnam Solidarity Front   ◇ Manchandra Group.

Building Workers' Charter   Communist Party-controlled 'organ of rank-and-file building workers' founded in July 1970. Successor to the Manchester paper *Rank and File*. Holds large annual supporters' conferences. Published intermittently and not at all during thirteen-week builders' strike in 1972.

Campaign Against Racial Discrimination (CARD)   White benevolent anti-racialist organization controlled by liberals, Fabians and 'race-relations experts'. Taken over by blacks in 1967 and soon ceased an independent existence.

Campaign for Democratic Socialism (CDS)   Parliamentary pressure group of Labour Right: fervent Gaitskellites. Dedicated to changing the party's aims from 'class' to 'national' purposes and then to overturning the influence of unilateralism at Conference and in local parties. Subsequently characterized by a fierce loyalty to the Common Market; some of its supporters, e.g., Roy Jenkins and W. Rodgers, survive relatively unchanged.

Campaign for Nuclear Disarmament (CND)   Formed in 1958 to demand unilateral nuclear disarmament by Britain. Organized the Easter Aldermaston March and publishes the monthly peace paper *Sanity* (1961–   ) Has episodic youth and university organizations.

Cartoon Archetypal Slogan Theatre (CAST)   Original (indoor) street theatre group based on Unity Theatre actors around Roland Muldoon, who began to present a sequence of mobile plays concerning the adventures of Harold Muggins in 1967 to VSC and student audiences. Produced revolutionary roadshow with poets and rock bands in 1968. Associated with ◇ AgitProp and later the ◇ International Socialists. Have produced an unreleased film concerning Muggins' visit to the Planet of the Apes. A minority tendency, Kartoon Klowns, absconded in 1973.

Case-Con   Journal of revolutionary socialist social workers founded by International Socialist members in 1970 and associated with NALGO Action.

Centre for Socialist Education   Founded in 1967 to set up local socialist study groups nationally federated and headed by a steering committee of worthy figureheads from socialist groups and the University Left, who proceeded to do virtually nothing. Such publishing work as it promised was largely undertaken by the ◇ Institute of Workers' Control. One of the last flings of the academic left.

Challenge   ◇ Young Communist League.

Chartist   ◇ Revolutionary Communist League.

Cinema-Action Socialist film group established in 1968 to use film directly in the class struggle. Made several feature-length films on the industrial struggle including film of the UCS work-in, and 'Arise Ye Workers', on the Pentonville Five.

Clarion Oxbridge-based student magazine of the ⟡ National Association of Labour Student Organizations (NALSO) in late fifties. Founded by Ken Coates, edited by Nigel Harris.

Club, The The name given to the Healy–Lawrence minority faction of the ⟡ Revolutionary Communist Party who were licensed by the ⟡ Fourth International to operate independently within the Labour Party from 1947. Able to dominate the British Trotskyist movement after the RCP voted to dissolve itself and enter the Labour Party too in 1949. Notorious for its organizational robustness, briskly expelling the invididuals who were to regroup in the ⟡ *Socialist Review* and the ⟡ Revolutionary Socialist League. Produced the paper *Socialist Appeal* until Healy and Lawrence themselves fell out in 1953.

Cogito The theoretical and discussion journal of ⟡ Young Communist League. Appears occasionally and published part one of the three-part analysis on Trotsky by Monty Johnstone, which went into two editions, and a special issue on Czechoslovakia.

Comment ⟡ Communist Party.

Committee of 100 Nuclear disarmament group formed in 1960 by Bertrand Russell and Michael Scott, influenced by American student Ralph Schoenman, to combine methods of Direct Action Committee Against Nuclear War and members of Campaign for Nuclear Disarmament. Began with list of named celebrities to sponsor massive civil disobedience demonstrations organized by working group of obscure militants, but after series of large-scale sit-downs during 1961 devolved into several autonomous committees all over the country, and celebrities gradually withdrew. Declined during 1962 with imprisonment of six leading activists and failure to respond to Cuba crisis; briefly revived by Spies for Peace and Greek Week episodes during 1963, but soon declined again and was finally dissolved in 1968. Influential during early 1960s in spreading non-sectarian libertarian ideas and activities.

Committee to Defeat Revisionism, for Communist Unity (CDRCU) Inner party opposition established within the Communist Party in the early sixties by the Etonian Michael McCreery on the basis of a return to factory branches, a reassertion of the classical Marxist theory of the state, approval of the Scottish and Welsh national movements and support for the Community Party of China against the Russians. Associated Johnny James, a West Indian from the Stoke Newington Communist Party Branch, later Secretary of CARD, and Ken Houlison, founder of the Workers' Party of Scotland. In November 1963 from 'the Lucas Arms meeting' they issued an 'Appeal to All Communists from members of the CPGB' and were promptly expelled. Between February 1964 and McCreery's death from cancer in 1965, published *Vanguard*. In 1964, McCreery polled over 800 votes against Harold Wilson in the Huyton constituency. Never more than thirty members and sustained by McCreery's private wealth. (◊ Evans, A. H.)

Communist Federation of Britain   ◊ Joint Committee of Communists.

Communist Organization in the British Isles   Split from ◊ Irish Communist Organization believing in the indivisibility of the British Isles and the Socialist Labour Party, a sectarian precursor of the Communist Party inspired by Daniel De Leon. Strict conditions of membership include reading knowledge of at least one foreign language. Publish *Proletarian*.

Communist Party (CP)   Founded in 1920 by the amalgamation of the existing revolutionary groups, inspired by the Russian Revolution. Successfully dominated the Marxist Left in Britain for forty years. Programme is 'The British Road to Socialism', personally approved by Stalin and adopted in 1952. A masterpiece of ambiguity, but hinged on a parliamentary strategy, and annually more reformist and nationalist. The British Communists' transformation from a Bolshevik past into a modern left social-democratic electoral party is no less pronounced than that of the European Parties, but is obscured by the sheer lack of success. Operates an effective electoral machine in the trade unions and provides a tradition and a community for rank-and-file industrial activists who even if they operate independently have an enduring loyalty. Paper membership was fairly stationary at about 35,000 throughout the sixties but activity and attendance is fairly low and many branches are surprisingly middle-class. Has an extensive organizational façade whose maintenance absorbs much time. Once one of the most obedient and orthodox of the European Communist Parties but became officially anti-Stalinist in the sixties and condemned the Czechoslovakia invasion in 1968, because it 'violated sovereignty'. Retains strong Stalinist factions. Underwent some intellectual revival in the early seventies partially because its lack of theoretical perspective and low level of commitment made it attractive to the theoretically inclined. Publishes the daily paper the *Morning Star* (incorporating the *Daily Worker*), the fortnightly review *Comment*, and the monthly *Marxism Today*. Associated with ◊ *Labour Monthly, Labour Research* and the Marxist publishing house Lawrence and Wishart.

Communist Party of Britain (Marxist-Leninist)   Largest and most proletarian of the Marxist-Leninist groups, endorsed by China and Albania. Founded on the initiative of Reg Birch, a veteran engineering militant, full-time AUEW official and Executive Committee member of the Communist Party, who was expelled in 1967 for 'being in correspondence' with foreign Marxist-Leninist leaders, it was launched fairly abruptly, on Birch's return from China in September 1967. Published *The Worker* monthly from January 1969, based on North London engineering workers, but appears to have made little inroad in the industrial North-West, Scotland or Wales.

Communist Party of England (Marxist-Leninist)   Small, rich Maoist sect which has attained a certain eminence by publishing an unreadable daily bulletin, *Workers' Daily* (All The News That Serves the Proletarian Socialist Revolution), and making lunatic attacks on police cordons.

Community Workers' Unity Organization (Marxist-Leninist)   Maoist fragment based in London and Grimsby which proposed unity to the other Marxist-Leninist groupings, spurned by all but the Marxist-Leninist Workers' Association.

Connolly Association   Communist Party controlled Irish Republican organization publishing the *Irish Democrat* edited by the historian G. D. Greaves.

Counter Information Service   Modern Marxist research group publishing investigations into the corporate giants. Associated ◊ International Socialists.

Correspondence   ◊ Johnson-Forrest Tendency, The.

Cuddons Cosmopolitan Review   A curious Dadaist political review with cartoons by anarchist bus-driver Arthur Moyse.

Direct Action   ◊ *Freedom.*

English Student Movement   Tiny Maoist religious grouping which flourished in Sussex University in the late sixties. Marxist-Leninist Children of God whose guru is Hardial Bains, a Canadian 'Internationalist'. Produced *Words International* and *Art and Revolution.*

Evans, A. H.   Welsh founder member of the ◊ Committee to Defeat Revisionism, for Communist Unity. Obsessional polemicist. Prints and publishes idiosyncratic Biblically written studies of science, psychology and art and Maoist rhymes, including *On Khrushchev, Fertilizer, the Future of Soviet Agriculture, An Anthropological View of Engels, Down with Falsehood in the Name of Science, What's Wrong with Peter Selfman* and *The Danger of Irrational Thought in the Marxist Movement.* Collaborated briefly with a student at Sussex University, John Hoffman (author of *Brecht: Socialist or Sewer Rat*) until they fell out (see *The Correspondence of A. H. Evans and John Hoffman. Their fundamental quarrel on: the position of women in our society; the place of the bourgeois intellectual; the monist view of history*).

European Marxist Review   ◊ Revolutionary Workers' Party (Trotskyist).

Fife Socialist League   Independent Marxist party in the Fife coalfields 1957–64, led by Lawrence Daly and loosely associated with the ◊ *New Reasoner.* Organization decided to dissolve into the Labour Party 'in view of the changes in the leadership of the Labour Party and leftward trends in its policy (due, to some extent, we believed, to the influence of the New Left)'. Springboard for Daly's career as Scottish and then National Secretary of NUM.

Flashlight   A not very lively attempt to re-group Communist Party electricians and establish a Broad Left within the ETU after the 1962 trials had died down.

Forum   Anti-revisionist magazine published inside the CP in mid-sixties by Marxist-Leninists who had declined to leave in 1963 with the McCreery group (◊ Committee to Defeat Revisionism, for Community Unity). Known as 'Selfmanites'.

Fourth International (FI)   Formed by Leon Trotsky in September 1938 as new revolutionary International to supersede Stalin's Comintern. Evolved from the Left Opposition (1923–8), a reform grouping inside the Russian Communist Party, and the International Communist League (1928–38), but still had negligible support outside Spain and Greece. After Trotsky's assassination in 1940, its headquarters was maintained in Europe by the Greek and Belgian intellectuals Michael Raptis (◊ 'Pablo') and Ernest Mandel ('Germaine'), appointees of J. P. Cannon and Sam Gordon ('Stewart'). Disorientated when the Second World War ended in an expansion of Stalinism in East Europe and a prolonged economic boom. Initially Mandel, the FI's theorist, argued that the 'buffer states' were state-capitalist, even 'police bonapartist', but, after Tito's break with Stalin, declared, at the 1951 Third World Congress, that Yugoslavia and the Easter bloc were, in fact, 'deformed workers' states' and that the official Communist parties could, after all, lead socialist revolutions. Eventually, when Michael Pablo's supporters took his position to its logical conclusion and left the Trotskyist groups to enter the Socialist Party in America (Cochrane), the Communist Party in France (Le Mestre) and the Labour Party in England (Lawrence), the Fourth International split, on the initiative of the American Socialist Workers' Party's 'Open Letter' issued in November 1953, into the Paris-based International Secretariat and the SWP-orientated International Committee.

Fourth International (1) English-language version of *Quatrième Internationale*, the quarterly of the ◊ Unified Secretariat of the Fourth International since 1948. (2) A bootleg version of above founded by the ◊ Socialist Labour League and the ◊ International Committee of the Fourth International in Spring 1964 as the successor to ◊ *Labour Review*. Quarterly, edited by Tom Kemp and Cliff Slaughter, university lecturers in Hull and Leeds respectively, with 'an Editorial Board which includes the most advanced international thinkers in the movement today'. Mainly attacks on rival Trotskyist groupings, and Trotsky reprints.

Freedom The anarchist weekly newspaper originally founded by Peter Kropotkin and Charlotte Wilson in 1886. The editor, Thomas Kell, was imprisoned for opposing conscription in 1916 and three editors, Vernon Richards, John Hewetson and Philip Sansom, went to jail at the end of the Second World War for advising soldiers to retain their weapons. Split along class lines in 1945 with Tom Brown (who left the Communist Party in 1926) and Ken Hawkes (a sports writer on the *Sunday Citizen*) taking most working-class anarchists into the Anarchist Federation of Britain/ Socialist Worker's Federation. During the sixties *Freedom*'s gentle and eclectic version of anarchism appealed neither to the Marxist-minded nor to student libertarians and the paper came close to collapse when the squatters of 144 Piccadilly, having been offered shelter, stole and sold the antique press's lead. Editors since Vere Richard's departure in 1965 include Jack Robinson, Jack Stevenson, Peter Turner and John Rety.

Frendz Notting Hill Gate music paper which started as an English edition of *Rolling Stone*, and transmogrified into *Friends of Rolling Stone*, *Friends* and *Frendz*, becoming consistently poorer and more political until it folded in 1972 in the throes of establishing a new distribution system.

Gay Liberation Front (GLF) First revolutionary homosexual organization in Britain, started by male gays in London in 1969. Published *Come Together* and developed national organization based on conferences and autonomous local groups.

Germs Eye View Duplicated rank-and-file hospital trade-unionist paper originating in Manchester and spawning a London edition based on the Royal Free Hospital. Dissolved in 1972 into *Backlash*, a national magazine established to co-ordinate the 1972 unofficial strikes which itself was superseded by the *Hospital Worker* in 1973.

Gunfire The late-sixties magazine of the Young Liberals at the height of their radicalism.

Heatwave A pioneer sixties anarcho-poetic journal of provocation. Edited by Chris Gray.

Hod Pioneer schools magazine produced in Leeds in 1968.

Hustler An independent revolutionary newspaper produced by blacks in Notting Hill Gate in 1968. Short-lived.

Idiot International A non-sectarian paper of the revolutionary Left funded by a giant donation made to Douglas Gill, a one-time editor of *Black Dwarf*, by a French princess. Edited in Shoreditch by Hugh Brodie, Nigel Fountain and Neil Lyndon during 1970. Most of the issues did not leave the distributors' copious basement.

Independent Labour Party (ILP) Rich remainder of the party which once dominated the Labour Party. Largely content to vegetate in abstract utopianism, but post-1968 developed a revolutionary socialist tendency. Subject to periodic attempts by left-wing sects to syphon off its alleged fortunes. Publishes the newspaper *Labour Leader*.

Indian Workers' Association (IWA) Formidable national welfare and political organization for Indian workers. Strongly involved in British trade-unionism but tends to be politically aligned according to the divisions in the Indian Left. Local branches differ dramatically, some active in the socialist movement, others dominated by local businessmen whose left-wing rhetoric conceals Asian and class conservatism. Has repeatedly split, so that rival IWAs often co-exist in the same towns.

Industrial Shop Stewards' Defence Committee North-London, Manchester, Newcastle and Glasgow based grouping of shop stewards including ◊ International Socialists and dissident Communist Party members campaigning against Wilson's wage freeze and incomes policy. Published *Incomes Policy, Legislation and Shop Stewards* in 1966 and a bulletin, *Resistance*. Involved in lobbies against anti-trade-union legislation and local meetings.

Largely incorporated into the ⬦ Liaison Committee for the Defence of Trade Unions, a national Communist-Party-led body who called successful strikes against 'In Place of Strife' and 'A Fair Deal at Work'.

Ink A messy, multi-coloured attempt at a 'professional' underground weekly founded by Richard Neville of *Oz*, Ed Victor, ex-director of Jonathan Cape, and Andrew Fisher, underground businessman-journalist in April 1972. After an abysmal start the largely ex-Fleet Street staff vanished (Alex 'Mad Mitch' Mitchell to join the ⬦ *Workers' Press*, Andrew Cockburn to *Frendz* and Marsha Rowe to found ⬦ *Spare Rib*). After two transitional issues on repression, edited by John Gerassi, reverted to an anarchist collective who produced a robust fortnightly until, after the '*Ink* In Love' issue of February 1972, the bailiffs entered.

Inside Story A professional libertarian news magazine edited by Wynford Hicks 1972–3, specializing in the media, Ireland, prison and women.

Institute of Workers' Control (IWC) Grouping of socialist academics and trade-union officials who began in 1964 acting as a publication and research centre and as a convenor of national and industrial groupings of trade-unionists to discuss workers' control. The first conference in April 1964 was sponsored by the 'Voice' group of newspapers (⬦ *Voice of the Unions*) and *The* ⬦ *Week* and attracted eighty people. It was followed by a London seminar organized by the Co-op Political Committee. A Manchester conference in 1965 set up local study groups of Sheffield steelworkers and Hull dockers, and annual conferences mushroomed in size, with over 1,000 people attending the 1969 Sheffield conference and 1,300 at the Birmingham Bull Ring in 1970. The original conception of a discussion meeting built around self-regulating industrial seminars became increasingly obscured by platform speeches from eminent trade-union officials. The organizers' determination that the IWC should not itself take direct political initiatives increasingly led to conflict with socialists who wished to commit the conference to action. Although constitutionally pledged to 'the unification of workers' control groups into a national force in the Socialist movement', in practice the IWC were reluctant to do more than convene conferences, publish a mass of literature and submit evidence. In October 1973 a monthly bulletin commenced (edited by Steven Bodington and John Jennings). Benn's Tribunites.

Intercontinental Press ⬦ Unified Secretariat of the Fourth International.

International Committee of the Fourth International (ICFI) Established in 1953 by the American ultra-orthodox Trotskyist group, the Socialist Workers' Party, to oppose the European leadership of the Fourth International. The abrupt split was sparked when the American supporters of Michael ⬦ Pablo, the Cochranites, boycotted the 25th Anniversary Banquet of the Socialist Workers' Party. The ICFI was supported by the Canadian group led by Dowson, the Argentinian Moreno group, the Chilean Vitale group, and the French and English Trotskyists led by Pierre Lambert and Gerry Healy. The IC asserted the orthodox critique of Stalinism against

Pablo but retained the basic Pabloite position on the nature of the Stalinist states. In 1963 the SWP voted for re-unification on the basis of the recognition of Cuba as a workers' state and a Parity Commission designed to squeeze Pablo out of the leadership. The majority of the ICFI followed the SWP back into the ◊ Unified Secretariat (USFI). The rump of the ICFI, the Lambert and Healy groups, met again in September 1963 and April 1966 but itself divided in 1971.

International Marxist Group (IMG) Official Trotskyist section of the USFI (◊ Unified Secretariat) in Britain. Emerged in 1968 from the forty-strong group who produced *The* ◊ *Week*. Devoted mainly to Vietnam solidarity work, maintaining the remnants of entry work in the Labour Party, with a few small college outposts. Negligible working-class following. Acted as a faction within the multi-sectarian ◊ *Black Dwarf*, splitting in 1970 after failing to take it over, to establish another front paper, the ◊ *Red Mole*, which was itself dissolved into the official IMG organ *Red Weekly* in 1973. Expanded quite briskly among students in early seventies by a fairly literal application of the methods of the French youth section of the USFI, plus the oratory of Tariq Ali and Robin Blackburn. Active within the Women's Liberation Movement around the Nottingham-based journal *Socialist Woman* and its local readers' groups. Also active in Irish, Indo-China and Ceylonese solidarity campaigns, none of which have reproduced the success of the ◊ Vietnam Solidarity Campaign. Internationally continued *The Week*'s starry-eyed lack of discrimination, adept at detecting socialist mirages in Cuba and Libya and extending their political blessing to the Provisional IRA and various urban guerrillas and hijackers. Scandalized, however, when Ho Chi Minh was criticized in passing in VSC. Essentially Pabloites minus Pablo. Consider themselves highly 'political' in respect of other left groups. Short existence and the predominance of ex-students has led to a rather bombastic, short-winded and often sectarian super-Trotskyism. Have attained some factory bases by 'industrializing' their student members.

International Marxist Review ◊ Revolutionary Marxist Tendency.

International Socialists (IS) Continuation of the ◊ *Socialist Review* group who regrouped as International Socialists in 1962 with about 250 members. Main recruiting field was young people in ◊ YS and ◊ CND. Produced *International Socialism*, edited by Mike Kidron, advancing a classical Marxist critique of many Trotskyist orthodoxies and developing Marxist economic analysis. Ran a monthly industrial paper, ◊ *Labour Worker*, based on supporters' groups and calling for support for unofficial strikes and outright opposition to incomes policy, Stressed self-activity and spontaneous shop-floor revolt, and critical of orthodox Trotskyism's self-importance and leadership fetish. Dominant force in the Labour Party Young Socialists' paper ◊ *Young Guard*, recruiting groups of apprentices in Glasgow and Birmingham *en bloc*. Ceased systematic work inside the adult Labour Party by 1965, mainly active independently in local struggles over redundancy, victimization, housing and racialism. Although it began organized rank-and-file work in NUT in 1965, set up the SSDC in January 1966 and led the LSE student occupations, its first mass campaigning was in the London rent strikes of 1968–9 and in the Vietnam Solidarity Campaign. Moved from a federalist national structure in 1968 with about 800 members, spurred by the May Events and after two special conferences and five separate factions. In 1968–70 it executed 'The Turn to the Class', aimed at utilizing the entire group's resources to establishing a substantial industrial base, through the systematic sales of two booklets, *Incomes Policy, Legislation and Shop Stewards* and *Productivity Deals and How to Fight Them*, the production of regular factory bulletins using information from sympathizers within plants, and the establishment with other socialists of democratic rank-and-file papers for particular industries. Profited from the Communist Party's unwillingness to take initiatives and lack of enthusiasm of those they took. Associated Pluto Press. The largest of the far-left groupings with 3,000 members evenly divided between industrial workers and white-collar workers, students, teachers and housewives. Tend to regard themselves as a development of the Leninist tradition rather than as Trotskyists. Known for their members' sense of humour except when people laugh at *them*.

International Socialist Journal English edition of the Italian bi-monthly *Problemi del Socialismo*, which went international sponsored by independent socialists in France, Britain, Italy and Belgium, influenced by the ◊ Unified Secretariat of the Fourth International. Published prestigious general theoretical articles and reliable political and trade-union studies. English contributors Ken Coates, Michael Barratt-Brown, Jim Mortimer; the editorial assistant in Rome was Jean McCrindle, ex-Communist Party, ex-secretary of Left Clubs.

International Times (IT) Pioneer London bohemian fortnightly, set up by Americans 'bored with Marxism' late in 1966 and finally expiring in 1974, having passed through about twelve different editorial teams all deeply committed . . . to everything from organic baking to leather fetishism and cocaine. Revived in 1974, unsuccessfully.

Internationalism Sophisticated international ultra-left theoretical journal of state-capitalist, council-Communist persuasion. English edition incorporated into the quarterly *World Revolution* in May 1974. Attitude to trade unions drawn from the Spanish Trotskyist Grandizio Munis's *Unions Against Revolution*.

Internationalist, The Duplicated bulletin published monthly in Nottingham in early sixties to put the views of the ◊ Unified Secretariat of the Fourth International after the collapse of *Workers' International Review*.

Irish Civil Rights Solidarity Campaign Founded in 1968 by London Irish, ◊ Irish Workers' Group ex-members and International Socialists in support of the Northern Ireland civil rights movement and the People's Democracy, based on local branches initially in Islington, Hammersmith, Fulham,

Glasgow and Coventry, established by meetings addressed by Bernadette Devlin, M P. Held marches and raised money. Largely wrecked by the ⟡ International Marxist Group's insistence on turning it into an anti-imperialist campaign in solidarity with the Provisional I R A, which led to the eventual withdrawal of the Clan-na-h-Eirean and International Socialism. Largely merged into the Anti-Internment League, a federation of socialists and Irish groups which held two massive London demonstrations and had many local branches. The rival Irish Solidarity Campaign, 'neither an Irish organization in Britain, nor a movement of British people in solidarity with the Irish struggle: it is an attempt to combine the two and make use of the links between them to grease the slope of British imperialism's decline', succeeded in April 1972, published an independent newspaper, the *Irish Citizen*, and swiftly redissolved back into the Anti-Internment League, itself largely superseded by Troops Out movement.

Irish Communist Organization A proletarian Irish Maoist grouping founded by six people in November 1965 centred on Brendan Clifford, an associate of McCreery (⟡ Committee to Defeat Revisionism, for Communist Unity). Published *Irish Communist* and the North-London based *The Communist* with branches in London (where it is known as the Communist Workers' Organization), Bangor, Dublin, Belfast and Cork. Strict Stalinists. In 1969 adopted a Marxist variant of Bonar Law's 1912 theory of Ireland as 'two nations' and campaign for the Ulster protestants' right of self-determination. Notorious for theoretical nitpicking and polemical virtuosity. Compulsive pamphleteers with a special emphasis on reprints from Irish history and exposing the crimes of Leon Trotsky. Expelled a founder member who ceased to support Two Nations theory in 1971, who now publishes the 'theoretical quarterly' *Communist Worker*. ⟡ Communist Organization in the British Isles.

Irish Liberation Press Marxist-Leninist newspaper emphasizing the Irish struggle, with a circulation of several thousand. Edited by Ed Davoren, associated with the Irish Liberation Solidarity Front, 'a broad front with Marxist-Leninist leadership and most definitely proud to be just that', associated with the ⟡ Black Unity and Freedom Party through the 'Anti-Fascist Revolutionary Coordinating Committee of National Minorities'. Mixed clear agitational articles with Marxist crosswords and slabs on the counter-revolutionary role of Trotskyism. 1970–72: incorporated into *Voice of the People* after ILSF splintered.

Irish Liberation Solidarity Front (ILSF) ⟡ *Irish Liberation Press*.

Irish Militant ⟡ Irish Workers' Group.

Irish Workers' Group Very hierarchical, fractious and small Irish Trotskyist group founded in 1964 and disintegrating in 1967. Leading members included Gerry Lawless, Sean Matgamna and Sean Morrissey; its leading rank and file included, at times, McCann, Farrell, Tobin and other leaders of the civil rights movement in the North. Published the newspaper *Irish Militant* and the intermittent theoretical journal *Ad Solas* (later *Workers'*

Republic). Notable for its capacity for giving birth to disputes and its influence on ⟡ People's Democracy.

Joint Committee of Communists   A federation of autonomous local groupings of Marxist-Leninists who left or were expelled from the Communist
Party in the mid-sixties. Formed in April 1967 with bases in Camden,
Bristol, Coventry and Glasgow. Concerned to undertake extensive pre-
paratory analysis before the organization of a suitable party, therefore refused to join ⟡ Communist Party of Britain (Marxist-Leninists) in 1967.
Became Communist Federation of Britain in September 1969, launching a
monthly newspaper, *Struggle*, and a quarterly journal, *Marxist-Leninist
Quarterly*. Relatively sane Maoist grouping which has grown steadily.
Committed to the destruction of social democracy, revisionism, Trotskyism
and the CPB(ML). Founders, with ⟡ International Socialism, of 'narrow
left' in TASS, the technical section of the engineers' union.

Johnson-Forrest Tendency   The Detroit-based split from mainstream American Trotskyism led by C. L. R. James ('Johnson'), a West Indian journalist,
historian, literary critic and cricket-lover, who had been active in the
Marxist Group (forerunners of the ⟡ Revolutionary Communist Party) in
London and had developed the Socialist Workers' Party analysis of the
black question, and Raya Dunayevskeya ('Forest'), Marxist philosopher
and ex-secretary of Trotsky. Published critiques of Shachmanism in the
Balance Sheet in 1947 and orthodox Trotskyism in the *Balance Sheet Completed* in 1951, and a developed theory of global state-capitalism, rejecting
the vanguard party conception, emphasizing the young Marx (they published an American translation of *The Philosophical and Economic Manuscripts* in 1947) and shop-floor organization as the seed of the organization
of the future socialist society. Produced the newspaper *Correspondence*
from 1953 from which *News and Letters* split in 1955, emphasizing the car
industry, the black movement and the woman question. James was to return
to Trinidad to edit the newspaper of Eric Williams' party and later to lend
support to Nkrumah and Castro. English publications group 'Facing
Reality' had some influence in the black and women's movements.

Labour Leader   ⟡ Independent Labour Party.

Labour Monthly   An 'independent' Communist-Party-controlled monthly
review founded in 1921, edited since then by R. P. Dutt, an Anglo-Indian
foundation member of the Communist Party. Orientated to 'Labour left'.
Its editorial board is said to be 'not a political organ, but a group of
eminent representatives in a wide variety of fields, trade-union, socialist,
Labour Party, Communist and independent, embracing a variety of viewpoints and united in a common devotion to the cause of the working class,
socialism and Left unity.'

Labour Party Young Socialists (LPYS)   Official Labour Party youth movement organized by Transport House in 1960. Its National Committee published *New Advance* (1960–64). Initially a mass working-class youth movement until the expulsion and defection of the 'Keep Left' in 1964, had a

full complement of socialist groupings active. Declined steadily, until by 1970 only the Militant group and the Young Chartists remained, to inherit the organization. (◊ Revolutionary Socialist League.)

Labour Research Department   Marxist research body for the Labour Movement since the First War, specializing in company information and background on industrial law, insurance and health. Publish the monthly 'Labour Research' and numerous pamphlets. Associated Communist Party.

Labour Review   Theoretical quarterly of The ◊ Club founded in Manchester in 1951, edited by Joe Pawsey. First issue stated: 'This review, published by active members and supporters of the Labour Party, is launched at a fateful juncture for the people of Britain, and especially its working class. The Tory electoral victory amidst the continued collapse of the British Empire not only guarantees higher prices and more scarcities but also brings closer the prospect of atomic war. Never was there greater need for plain and fearless speaking on behalf of Labour and the struggle for socialism.' No mention of independent grouping, instead a 're-invigorated LP can rescue England from capitalist reaction and war'. Despite the claim to a 'serious approach to the problem of socialist theory', contents were boring, predictable and almost wholly written by G. Healy. Enlarged and greatly improved in 1957 under the editorship of John Daniels, a Nottingham University extra-mural lecturer, and Bob Shaw, an NUR member. Appeared bi-monthly 'not as a sectional, Trotskyist journal. We wish to make it the main journal for conducting the principled discussion of every aspect of revolutionary theory.' After Daniels was expelled from the Socialist Labour League in 1959, it declined rapidly and was incorporated into the quarterly ◊ *Fourth International* in 1964.

Labour Worker   The monthly industrial paper of the International Socialism group (originally named *Industrial Worker*) edited by Karl Dunbar, Paul Foot 1962–4, Roger Protz 1964–74 and Paul Foot 1974– . Incorporated into the fortnightly *Socialist Worker* in July 1968.

League for Democracy in Greece   Group campaigning for democracy in Greece and the release of trade union political prisoners especially Tony Ambetielos. Associated Communist Party.

Liaison Committee for the Defence of Trade Unions   Rank-and-file trade-union committee founded by Communist Party members in March 1966 to lobby against anti-trade-union Parliamentary legislation. Organized unofficial national stoppages against 'In Place of Strife' in February and May 1969 and led the 1971 strikes against the Industrial Relations Act. Failed to act over the imprisoned dockers or the engineers' entanglement with the National Industrial Relations Court. Has proved reluctant to elect an organizing committee, allow resolutions from the floor or set up local liaison committees for fear of conflict with the official machine. Secretary, Jim Hiles of the London Joint Sites Committee, Chairman Kevin Halpin, victimized in 1962 at Dagenham and an unsuccessful Communist Party parliamentary candidate.

London Street Commune   A youth mob in the city centre who tried to be something more. Very loose alliance of working-class drop-outs (the Dilly Scene) and post-graduate drop-outs (the LSE Bar). Occupied the Pronto Coffee Bar (1968), 144 Piccadilly (December 1969) and 114 Endell Street (1970), making attempts to promote sub-cultural unity between skinheads and hippies in East London. Associated with *Yell, Aggro, Rubber Duck, Y-Front* and other political comics.

Manchandra Group   Small, all-sorted Asian Maoist group centred on a portly Pakistani, Alberto Manchandra. A fervent supporter of the ◊ Communist Party of Britain (Marxist-Leninist) and a member of its Provisional Committee, he has subsequently materialized at great length in the ◊ Vietnam Solidarity Campaign (where his supporters walked out of the founding meeting to a room, previously booked, to found the British-Vietnam Solidarity Front), the ◊ Revolutionary Socialist Students' Federation, the Socialist Scientists' Group (whom he lectured on the nature of Chinese science) and Women's Liberation. It was the abusive behaviour of one of his supporters at the 1970 Skegness Women's Conference which led to male observers finally being barred from the national meetings.

Marx Memorial Library   Communist-Party-run library, archive, meeting place and publications centre in a house on Clerkenwell Green frequented by Marx and Lenin, long associated with the London Left. Houses an unparalleled collection, only partially catalogued.

Marxism-Leninism   The polite word for Maoism. Used variously by supporters of the Chinese Communist Party, old Stalinists, partisans of the French philosopher Louis Althusser, and critics of the Communist Party leadership's reformism and the British Road to Lost Deposits.

Marxism Today   ◊ Communist Party.

Marxist, The   Lavish theoretical monthly of Marxism-Leninism financed by businessmen engaged in trade with China as focus for the anti-revisionist movement in November 1966. A general forum for non-sectarian articles on history, economics and the tenants, and industrial struggle. Declined in the late sixties as its editors decamped to start their own papers. Now produced occasionally by a nucleus of North London engineering workers, the Brent Group, who are embarrassingly frank about the industrial irrelevance of most other Mao-groups.

Marxist-Leninist Organization of Britain.   Microscopic Maoist sect founded in September 1967 out of the Manchester-based Hammer and Anvil group. Profuse publishers of duplicated material and socialist-realist art (*Red Front, Red Vanguard, Class against Class*) and run poky East London gallery. Exposed Mao's thought as 'essentially revisionist and anti-Marxist-Leninist in character' in January 1968. Its leader, Mike Baker, is known as 'Britain's Khrushchev'.

Marxist-Leninist Quarterly   ◊ Joint Committee of Communists.

May Day Manifesto Bulletin Organizing bulletin started in Summer 1967 to service the mass movement which was supposed to come out of the National Convention of the Left. Organized working groups, some of which later became autonomous socialist specialist groupings, and began a pamphlet series which included *Women's Liberation and the New Politics* in 1969. Otherwise nothing.

Microfaction, The A faction inside ◇ International Socialism in 1968 questioning the turn to democratic centralism on the grounds that it was an unsuitable structure to express modern working-class consciousness. Mainly comprised of LSE post-graduates. Named, humorously, after the pro-Russian Escalante group in Cuba purged by Castro.

Militant International Review ◇ Revolutionary Socialist League.

Mineworker ◇ Revolutionary Workers' Party (Trotskyist).

Movement for Colonial Freedom National Communist Party/Labour Left/ liberal alliance against British colonialism figure-headed by Lord Brockway and organizing publications, research and protest. Eclipsed in the late sixties by more militant anti-imperialist groups. Changed its name to Liberation without altering its politics much.

National Association of Labour Student Organizations (NALSO) The national student body affiliated to the Labour Party and publishing *Labour Student*. Used to groom Labour Party careerists (Walden, Price, Hattersley) in early sixties. Dominated by various Marxist sects thereafter. In both cases a shell organization. Periodically disaffiliated.

National Council for Civil Liberties (NCCL) An independent body concerned to give advice and prepare recommendations on legal and police matters.

National Federation of Claimants' Unions Skeletal national structure for local Claimants' Unions which co-ordinated the unemployed, single mothers, disabled and others dependent on Social Security against officialdom. Fiercely decentralized. Prolific publishers in a distinct, well-illustrated style. Organized one, very successful, national campaign against SS snooping on single mothers to enforce the Co-habitation Clause. Dominated by an informal elite of libertarian ex-students who, despite their own efforts, carried the organization until they, mostly, lost interest *circa* 1973.

National Joint Action Campaign for Women's Equal Rights An equal-rights organization established after the 1969 Dagenham seamstress's strike by ◇ Institute of Workers' Control, Labour Left and Communist Party supporters with a rank-and-file of women from the revolutionary groups and from Women's Liberation which emerged simultaneously. Organized a very successful trade-union Equal Pay march in September 1969 but disintegrated through the platform's inertia and Marxist-Leninist sectarianism.

New Advance ◇ Labour Party Young Socialists.

New Left Review ◇ Bibliography, pp. 510–15.

New Reasoner Halifax-based New Left quarterly of socialist humanism.

Published ten issues between Summer 1957 and Autumn 1959. Preceded by the *Reasoner*, an internal Communist Party opposition bulletin, and succeeded by the *New Left Review*.

News and Letters ◊ Johnson-Forrest Tendency, The.

Newsletter ◊ Socialist Labour League.

Organization of Revolutionary Anarchists A national anarchist federation with a working-class orientation founded in Leeds in November 1971 by student anarchists from York impressed by ◊ International Socialism's growth, to bring together libertarian Communists and active anarchists demoralized by isolation. Produced *ORA Newsletter*, alternating production between local groups, in 1963 the national newspaper *Libertarian Struggle* and in 1974 the theoretical *Libertarian Communist Review*. In 1974 Keith Nathan and other founder members left the group and applied to join the Workers' Revolutionary Party (◊ Socialist Labour League). Associated French and Swedish ORAS.

Northern Star ◊ People's Democracy.

Pablo, Michael (Michael Raptis) Greek revolutionary who became secretary of the ◊ Fourth International in 1943. Drafted the theses for the Second and Third Congresses of the FI and, while Mandel and the FI majority still held the orthodox view that the East European 'buffer states' were state-capitalist, developed theory of the 'new reality': that Stalinist Communist Parties had been compelled to lead revolutions and that, since a global war with a highly revolutionary character was imminent, the FI ought to enter Communist Parties to steer them in a revolutionary direction. In 1952, with the active support of the ◊ Socialist Labour League and the Socialist Workers' Party, expelled the dissenting French majority grouping. Considered the 'epicentre of world revolution' had passed from the European working class to the Third World peasantry. Acted as 'economic adviser' to Ben Bella's Algerian government and was arrested in Amsterdam in 1962 for running documents, money and weapons to Algeria. Re-elected to the FI executive while in prison but went into a minority during the Seventh World Congress and was expelled in 1964 for refusing critical support to Mao and criticizing the Holden Roberto group in Portuguese Angola in the journal of the African Bureau *Sous le drapeau de socialisme*. Now a partisan of 'self-management'. (◊ Revolutionary Marxist Tendency.)

Peace News The veteran pacifist weekly which became a forum for nonviolent revolutionary thought in the mid-sixties. Retreated to a fortnightly Nottingham-based magazine in 1974. Wide range of contributors and reports and information. Pulls off regular coups, exposing G.B. 75 in 1974, a year early.

People's Democracy Student-based civil-rights grouping which re-opened the Irish Question in 1968. Briefly linked to ◊ International Socialism and the ◊ Irish Civil Rights Solidarity Campaign. Published *PD Voice* monthly from July 1969 and after internment the fortnightly *Unfree Citizen*, as well as a discussion journal, *Northern Star*. Many Irish members entered Northern Resistance with the Provisional IRA. Since 1970 has had independent London supporters' group.

Poster Workshop An independent silk-screen poster studio mainly concerned with the GLC tenants' rent strike but open to any left-wing group wanting help. Run by Bert Scrivener and the two Sarahs. Various locations in Camden 1968–9. Inspired by the Paris Atelier Populaire and the posters of the May Events.

Race Today The establishment journal of 'race relations' produced by white academics, moved sufficiently leftwards to have the business grants to the parent Institute of Race Relations rescinded. Eventually parted company with the Institute and was edited and produced by a black Marxist. Inspired by *éminence noire* C. L. R. James.

Radical Students Alliance A pressure group within the National Union of Students run by student members of the Liberal and Communist Parties in 1966–7. Superseded by the ◊ Revolutionary Socialist Students' Federation.

Rank and File A rank-and-file union paper started by International Socialism and ex-Communist Party London teachers in Spring 1968 to campaign for industrial action by teachers, against 'professionalism' and for democracy inside the union, notably breaking its domination by head teachers. Succeeded in leading strike action in 1969 through the Ad-Hoc Salaries Campaign Committee. Largely overtook the Communist Party magazine *Education Today and Tomorrow* as the main organizer of the Left. In 1969 a group succeeded to produce the short-lived *Militant Teacher*. In 1974 the magazine turned to a newspaper format.

Reasoner ◊ *New Reasoner*.

Rebel 'A democratic journal of the young socialists' founded as a successor to ◊ *Young Guard* in July 1966 as 'the beginning of a revival of socialism in the YS branches'. Run by quarterly readers' meetings with an elected editorial board, dominated by ◊ International Socialist members. Notorious for its disrespectful cartoon 'SuperTrot'. Foundered in 1967, although some readers' groups persisted. New edition of bimonthly restarted in November 1971, outside the Labour Party, on the initiative of Manchester Rebel supporters, who had produced a local duplicated magazine. Despite a circulation of several thousand and eight local groups and national readers' meetings, this too collapsed in March 1973. Edited by Charlotte Brunsden (Schools Action Union activist), then Louis Lemkow.

Red Ladder Mobile Workers' Theatre ◊ AgitProp.

Red Flag ◊ Revolutionary Workers' Party (Trotskyist).

Red Mole Fortnightly political newspaper firmly controlled and financed by the ◊ International Marxist Group but with a coalition editorial board including refugees from the ◊ *Black Dwarf*. Provided a transition between the IMG exodus from *Black Dwarf* and the launching of the official IMG weekly *Red Weekly* (1 May 1973). Awkward blend of hippy typography and Trotskyist prose. Published occasional broadsheets.

Red Rag Socialist feminist theoretical magazine started unofficially by Communist Party feminists and expanded to include libertarian, International Socialist and non-affiliated Marxists. Sold mainly within Women's Liberation. Named after sanitary towels and bull fights.

Red Weekly ◊ *Red Mole*.

Resistance ◊ Industrial Shop Stewards' Defence Committee.

Revolutionary Communist League An orthodox Trotskyist fragment, obsessed with the Transitional Programme. Founded by workers who absconded from the ◊ International Marxist Group and entered discussions with French Trotskyists about the significance of the May Events. Took over the ◊ Socialist Charter movement and published a newspaper aimed at the ◊ Labour Party Young Socialists, the *Chartist*, equipped with a 'revolutionary programme for the Labour Party', and since January 1974 a quarterly duplicated theoretical journal, *Chartist International*.

Revolutionary Communist Party United British Trotskyist organization founded by the fusion of the ◊ Workers' International League with the smaller and fissiparous ◊ Revolutionary Socialist League in 1944. Its leaders were prosecuted for supporting the 1944 strike of Tyneside engineering apprentices. Jock Haston, the RCP General Secretary, stood as a candidate in the 1945 Neath by-election, where he polled 1,781 votes. A minority tendency, The ◊ Club, led by Gerry Healy, officially entered the Labour Party in 1948. The following year the RCP voted to dissolve itself and rejoin the Healy Group inside the Labour Party.

Revolutionary Marxist Tendency Small grouping around the current ideas of Michael ◊ Pablo, the wartime secretary of the Fourth International, expelled with the 'African Bureau' in 1964. Supporters of the 1967 document *Marxism in Our Time*, stressing self-management and a rejection of hierarchical and substitutionalist forms of leadership. Have moved from regarding themselves as a Trotskyist tendency wrongfully expelled from the ◊ Unified Secretariat of the Fourth International to an autonomous revolutionary grouping linked through an International Alliance of Revolutionary Marxists. In 1968 launched duplicated discussion quarterly *Bulletin for Marxist Studies* edited by Ken Tarbuck and Chris Arthur, in Staffordshire, followed by the *Bulletin for Socialist Self-Management*, which became monthly 'in response to the growing wave of sit-ins, takeovers and work-ins by workers'. Since June 1971 have collaborated in the English-language Pabloite journal *International Marxist Review*.

Revolutionary Socialist League The name of the original section of the British Fourth International, a hasty fusion of several groups dominated by 'The Militant' group, whose leader D. D. Harber was, with C. L. R. James, British delegate to the founding conference in 1938. Restarted by Ted Grant, the South African senior theorist of the ◊ Revolutionary Communist Party, when his supporters were ejected from The ◊ Club in 1951. Exponents of 'deep entry' into the Labour Party, predicting that a massive left-wing movement, expressed within the Party, will either, having adopted a Marxist programme, lead the revolution or give rise to a split, which will leave the RSL installed at the head of the revolutionary opposition. Therefore works as a loyal secretive opposition within constituency Labour Parties and the Young Socialists arguing for 'a Marxist current'. Afforded the official British franchise of the International Secretariat of the ⟡ Fourth International in 1957 when it launched the bi-monthly *Workers' International Review* in a brief association with members of the Nottingham Group. Since 1964 have issued the staid *Militant, for Labour and Youth* and since 1969 the quarterly *Militant International Review*. Also dominated the Sussex University Labour Club in the late sixties and used the club's magazine *Spark* as an RSL vehicle. Have made some inroads into the apparatus of the Labour Party and gained formal control of the Young Socialists in 1972.

Revolutionary Socialist Students' Federation National revolutionary student organization with individual membership and federated local branches. Founded in Summer 1968, it finally petered out in 1971.

Revolutionary Workers' Party (Trotskyist) A small furtive British grouping supporting the Latin American ⟡ Fourth International based in Uruguay and led by Jean Posadas. Posadas led a joint faction inside the International Secretariat with ⟡ Pablo (1959–61) against the 'Europeans', but then denounced Pablo, and stormed out of the International with the majority of the Latin American Trotskyists. Pro-Chinese and in favour of the USSR launching a nuclear war to ensure the victory of socialism. Publishes sweeping appeals to the masses in the paper *Red Flag* and torrents of J. Posadas's thoughts as duplicated bulletins. Associated with *European Marxist Review*. Supporters produce *Student Red Flag*, the Newcastle-based young socialist paper *Socialist Revolution* and the *Mineworker*.

Rocket Mid-sixties bulletin of Marxist art criticism publishing poets and painters of the 'Scottish (socialist realist) Renaissance' and edited by Alan Bold.

Sanity ⟡ Campaign for Nuclear Disarmament.

Seaman's Charter Rank-and-file paper in the National Union of Seamen founded after the 1966 strike. Devoted campaigner for the election of Jim Slater to replace William Hogarth, but has continued despite achieving this success.

Selfmanites ⟡ *Forum*.

Shilling Paper, The Weekly eight-page revolutionary paper produced by student Left in Cambridge and edited collectively by Neil Lyndon.

Situationalism Species of Marxist cultural and political criticism propounded by L'Internationale Situationaliste, a tiny group of intellectual terrorists formed from the fusion of the Romanian Surrealist Isidore Ison's Mouvement Lettriste with other nihilist and anti-cultural avant-gardists in 1957. Influenced by the Trotskyist Surrealists Breton and Péret, as well as Lefebvre, de Sade, Lautréamont and Lewis Carroll. Specialists in staccato, sarcastic and heavily Hegelian denunciations of the Spectacle, art, advertising and consumption. Operated first (1957–62) as anti-artists, believing modern art to be the most alienated of human activities. In 1966–7, Situationists led by Mustapha Khayati took control of the treasury of Strasbourg University students' union in order to publish a denunciation of 'student poverty considered economically, politically, psychologically and sexually'. Published the review *Internationale Situationaliste* (reprinted by Van Gennep, Amsterdam, 1970), Guy Debord's *The Spectacular Society*, Raoul Vaneigen's *Totality for Kids*. Vulgarized in England by *Oz*, *Frendz* and the post 1968-student Left in Cambridge and Essex. In its simplified form became a rationale for 'action' and the propaganda of the deed during the decline of the student Left. Its executive has had British members, including the Scots novelist and junkie Alex Trocchi, but they have usually been swiftly expelled.

Socialisme ou Barbarie Split from French mainstream Trotskyism in 1949, producing between 1959 and 1964 a remarkable body of theory consistently evolving and associated with a parallel factory organization. Adherents of the bureaucratic-collectivist analysis of Russia, and associated with the ◊ Johnson-Forrest Tendency in America, they connected their critique of the Soviet bureaucracy with a trenchant analysis of the stratified bureaucracies governing in Western society, including the workers' movement, emphasized unofficial strikes (actually relatively rare in France), spontaneous shop-floor activity. In reaction to orthodox Trotskyism, Stalinized Leninism, and Communist Party economism, stressed 'young Marx' and the Council Communist conception and capitalism's success in overcoming its economic contradictions. Leading figures Cornelius Castoriadis (alias Paul Cardan, alias Pierre Chaulieu), Claude Lefort, Daniel Mothe. In 1960, when the majority of the group moved towards a non-Leninist organization, an anarchist minority seceded to form Informations Correspondance Ouvriéres, which in turn recruited sufficient student anarchists from the 1968 movement, 22 Mars, to lead to small pro- ◊ Solidarity split in 1973.

Socialist Appeal ◊ Club, The.

Socialist Charter Pressure group of Labour Left, *Tribune* and trade-union leaders around a new 'charter'. Taken over by members of the ◊ Revolutionary Communist League active in the Young Chartist movement at a convention in August 1972 (which twenty-three attended) and now produce the *Chartist*. Known as the Lunar Marxists in view of their way-out inconsistency.

Socialist Current A monthly Marxist journal of Labour opinion put out by a tiny indomitable and friendly group of London Trotskyist workers. Independent continuous publication commenced when they seceded from the ◊ Revolutionary Socialist League in 1955. Turned into a bi-monthly duplicated newspaper in September 1970, 'not least owing to the fact that our old machinery has got in the state where it was no longer repairable'.

Socialist Labour League Orthodox Trotskyist group founded in May 1959 supported by many Communists who left the Communist Party over Hungary, but firmly controlled by The ◊ Club. General Secretary, Gerry Healy, Irish veteran of the Communist Party, ◊ Workers' International League, ◊ Revolutionary Communist Party and ◊ Socialist Outlook. Published ◊ *Labour Review* and the fortnightly bulletin the *Newsletter* with accessory pamphlets and 'specials', edited by Peter Fryer and then Michael Vander Poorten ('Banda'). Originally involved in the strike wave of the late fifties, switched to work in the ◊ Labour Party Young Socialists after 1960 and proceeded in annual bursts of campaigning, on racialism, Profumo, Vote Labour, Against Wilson's Wage Freeze, Make the Left MPs Fight, Vote Labour, General Strike to Kick Out the Tories, etc. Regular pattern of spring demonstration, May Day March, Labour Party Conference Lobby, Summer Camp, Autumn 'celebration', and Winter demonstration, plus miscellaneous memorial and anniversary meetings. Traditional local adult support in Liverpool, Oxford, South London, Swindon, Leeds, Hull and Newcastle. Despite the insistence that 'the SLL does not require a separate industrial-front type of organization within the factories and trade unions' (G. Healy, *Newsletter*, 14 October 1967), launched an 'industrial arm', The All Trade Union Alliance, in 1969, based on the Oxford Liaison Committee established by SLL car shop stewards. Holds rallies and achieved some following in the actors' and film technicians' union; campaigned vigorously in support of the Pilkington glass workers. Since 1953 a member of the International Committee of the ◊ Fourth International and after 1972 virtually its only member. Gave support (critical) to Messali Hadj's Algerian MNA and the Red Guards. Regard East Europe as workers' states (deformed) but insist Cuba is still capitalist.

Established the first ever Trotskyist daily, the *Workers' Press*, in September 1969 and transformed itself into the Workers' Revolutionary Party. Fielded nine candidates in the 1974 election, all losing their deposits. Although boastful about their grasp of Marxist method and ability to 'train the youth in dialectical thinking', operate according to a rigid and static theory based on the letter of Trotsky's final writings. Catastrophist economic perspective, regarding mass unemployment as imminent since 1952 and explaining the survival of post-war capitalism solely by the treachery of the Communist Parties and the Bretton Woods agreement. Highly exclusive, working with no other left group except on its own terms. Somewhat despotic internal regime and rather uncomradely in political style. Regards ◊ International Socialism as 'a specialized anti-Trotskyist detachment of the ruling class' and 'an excrescence of imperialism'; the ◊ International Marxist Group a 'revisionist cancer'; the ◊ Vietnam Solidarity Campaign as 'a carnival of middle-class confusion and politically impotent protest'; and the ◊ Institute of Workers' Control as 'an unprincipled farce', but consider 'the greatest day in the history of British Trotskyism' was a rally in the Empire Pool in March

1973 when a forty-foot enlargement of G. Healy was projected on a screen. Predominantly working-class membership whose number is known only to the General Secretary (probably under 1,000), but can organize rallies of over 10,000. Members tend to look aggressive and tense.

Socialist League   An organized Marxist-influenced pressure group founded in 1932 from ex-members of the Independent Labour Party, socialist academics and trade-union bureaucrats within the Labour Party. Expelled in 1936 after its entry into a united front with the Communist Party and ILP, it then went into rapid decline.

Socialist Outlook   Founded December 1948 as a monthly 'paper of Labour's Left Wing' edited by Bermondsey print-worker John Lawrence, with a board of Tom Braddock, Jack Stanley and Gerry Healy, and a loose association with Ellis Smith's Socialist Fellowship. Fortnightly from May Day 1950, weekly from November 1952. Although politically indistinguishable from *Tribune*, uncritically parliamentarian and pro-Bevan, and silent about Stalinism, it was actually a 'deep-entry' organ of the ex-Revolutionary Communist Party Trotskyists, The ◊ Club. Proscribed in 1951 and bankrupted by a libel action taken by Godfrey Phillips Tobacco Ltd in 1953 thanks to information published by the Communist Party. The majority of the *Outlook*'s readers drifted away, while The Club took to setting up *Tribune* readers' circles. Linked with quarterly ◊ *Labour Review.*

Socialist Party of Great Britain   Small fundamentalist grouping established in 1904. Indefatigable, old-fashioned propagandists of the virtues of socialist society. Many local branches and groups, main activity meetings and street speaking. Publish the monthly *Socialist Standard.* 'Calls on the members of the working class in this country to muster under its banner to the end that a speedy termination may be wrought to the system which deprives them of the fruits of their labour.' Denounced the Russian Revolution as state-capitalist within hours of hearing of it.

Socialist Review   An immediate regroupment of 1951 expellees from The ◊ Club based around the conception of Russia as state-capitalist and a rejection of the economic analysis and internal regime of The ◊ Club. First met with thirty-three overwhelmingly working-class members in September 1950, produced 350 copies of the first issues of *Socialist Review* (subtitled 'Neither Washington nor Moscow but International Socialism'), which continued as a monthly (with occasional bouts of fortnightly publication) until 1962 when it was incorporated into *International Socialism.* Members operated in the Labour Party and the trade unions, Geoff Carlsson, a founder member of the *Socialist Review* group and a North London engineer, polling 5,615 votes in the 1959 AEU presidential election. Editors have included Pat Jordan, Peter Morgan, Terry Gallogly and Mike Kidron. Contributors included Tony Cliff, Henry Collins, Jim Higgins, Seymour Papert and Eric Heffer.

Socialist Revolution   ◊ Revolutionary Workers' Party (Trotskyist).

Socialist Standard   ◊ Socialist Party of Great Britain.

Society for Anglo-Chinese Understanding (SACU) Non-sectarian educational and travel body spreading information about modern China. Publishes *China Now*. Periodically invaded and denounced by Marxist-Leninist groups.

Solidarity   Libertarian Marxist group with industrial perspective founded by ex- ◊ Socialist Labour League members in 1960. Influenced by the ideas of Paul Cardan and the French group, ◊ Socialisme ou Barbarie. Committedly anti-Leninist, anti-Trotskyist, anti-anarchist, anti-syndicalist, enthusiasts for the Workers' Opposition, whose history they have done much to uncover and publicize. Initially a loose association of sympathizers around a publishing centre in London with groups in Aberdeen and Glasgow. Re-groupment in 1967 around the statement 'What We Stand For', when their aversion for organizational pyramid building was overcome sufficiently to introduce formal supporter status and subs. Influential in the anti-nuclear-war movement, early tenants' struggles and with a consistent involvement in decentralized working-class struggles involving job control, notably in Fords and Vauxhall. Insist they are not a leadership but simply help those in conflict, generalize experience and raise consciousness. Between 1969 and 1972 autonomous local groups published their own magazines but the North London edition remained the group's official mouthpiece. Generally hostile to post-1968 student libertarians, who in return regard Solidarity as somewhat old-fashioned. After the departure of a Marxist faction in 1973 into an alliance with the Merseyside council Communist grouping ◊ Workers' Voice, became more explicitly critical of Marxism. Loosely linked to the surviving Dutch council Communist grouping Daad en Gedacht (Thought and Action), the Belgian grouping Liaisons, and Informations Correspondance Ouvrières. Membership never more than sixty, but its pamphlets and booklets have reached considerable numbers. Mascot is a hedgehog; small, prickly and doesn't like being interfered with.

South West Worker   Duplicated socialist magazine which evolved out of the upsurge in industrial disputes in Devon and Cornwall, notably the strikes at Centrax and Fine Tubes. Later became *West Country Worker*.

Spare Rib   Feminist monthly started in June 1972 to put Women's Liberation on the newsstands. Muddled start, got more collected, collective and political, became most successful survivor of that era of left-wing journalism.

Spartacus League   Youth vanguard group set up 'in political solidarity with the ◊ International Marxist Group'. Student-vanguard smash-everything politics, actually did very little between its founding conference (120 people) in July 1970 and its fusion with the IMG in May 1972.

Spokesman   ◊ Bertrand Russell Peace Foundation.

Struggle   ◊ Joint Committee of Communists.

Student Red Flag   ◊ Revolutionary Workers' Party (Trotskyist).

Subversion   Occasional anarchist-situationalist agitational magazine.

Syndicalist Workers' Federation   ◊*Freedom.*

Synic   Monthly news-sheet and diary run by radical Young Liberals drifting left between 1968–70. Strong on Third World liberation movements and 'information'.

Tribune   'Labour's independent weekly', the press of an organized Labour Left caucus in Parliament, distributed mainly through constituency Labour Parties and newsagents. Politics range from straight reformism to a species of social-democratic Marxism. Privately owned, organized annual rallies at Labour Party conferences and poetry readings. Read mainly for its letters, book reviews and adverts. Several of its leading lights prominent in the 1974 Wilson Government. According to its editor, Richard Clements, 'the brightest beacon which has shone in the British press in the last three decades'.

Trotskyist   Applied strictly, an adherent of a section of one of the four rival Fourth Internationals. More loosely, the acceptance of Trotsky's criticisms of Stalin and application of them to Moscow's subsequent rulers, the refusal to countenance united fronts with bourgeois parties, a commitment to independent revolutionary politics on an international scale and along Leninist lines, and a stress on the leading role of even a numerically small working class in the colonial and ex-colonial nations. In practice many orthodox Trotskyist groups violate the essence not only of Trotsky's work, but of Marx's as well.

Unfree Citizen   ◊ People's Democracy.

Unified Secretariat of the Fourth International (USFI)   Largest of the internationals claiming continuity with Trotsky's ◊ Fourth International. Produced by the 1963 re-unification of the International Secretariat and the International Committee. Since unification has suffered the secession of the Latin American Bureau led by the pro-Chinese megalomaniac Juan Posadas into the ◊ Revolutionary Workers Party (Trotskyist) and Michael ◊ Pablo, ex-Secretary of the FI, departed into the ◊ Revolutionary Marxist Tendency. Involved in Castro's Organization of Latin American Solidarity. Has undergone substantial growth based on students since 1968. British sections were the ◊ Revolutionary Socialist League (1956–64) and ◊ International Marxist Group (1966–   ). Publishes weekly news review *Intercontinental Press* in New York and a Brussels-based rival, *Imprecor*.

United Coloured People's Association (UCPA)   A Caribbean-based Black Power organization with some following in West London.

Vanguard (1)   The 'official national journal of the Schools Action Union' evolving from the duplicated London Region SAU fortnightly started in January 1969. Published local reports of organization in schools. Taken over by precocious Maoists and eventually swamped by the National Association of Schools Students. (2) ◊ Committee to Defeat Revisionism, for Communist Unity.

Vietnam Solidarity Campaign (VSC)   Anti-imperialist Vietnam campaign initiated by the ◊ International Marxist Group, financed by Bertrand Russell, and founded in January 1966 in opposition to the Communist

Party-controlled British Council for Peace in Vietnam. The ⟡ Manchandra Group and the ⟡ Socialist Labour League both walked out of founding meeting. Active membership IMG, ⟡ International Socialist and non-aligned. At first argued for a solidarity position within the Left, 500 attending a dispirited march to Transport House to protest against Labour Party involvement in 1966. Rejected lobbying marches to Parliament. Demonstration to the American Embassy on 22 October 1967 amazed police and the press by laying siege to the Embassy and virtually storming it. Throughout 1968 grew locally with local independent branches and central support from the ⟡ Cartoon Archetypal Slogan Theatre, ⟡ AgitProp, Stop-It (a militant group of Americans living in London). Attacked by the Communist Party for bringing revolutionary themes into the 'peace movement' and slogans which make 'not a call for unity but a call for disruption'. Held a march of 10,000 to Grosvenor Square on 17 March 1968, anniversary of the first Saigon demonstration against the Americans, and, in October 1968, 100,000 marched in London, calling for the 'Defeat of US Aggression in Vietnam', 'Victory to the NLF and the Vietnamese Revolution', and an 'End to Labour Complicity in the War'. Declined in 1969 but continued to campaign on Indo-China, resisting suggestions to turn into an all-purpose revolutionary youth group. Published *VSC Bulletin*, *Vietnam* and *Indo-China*.

Voice of the People ⟡ *Irish Liberation Press.*

Voice of the Unions Left Labour industrial newspaper founded in January 1963 campaigning for workers' control and union democracy (⟡ Institute of Workers' Control), sponsored by Labour MPs and union officials. Edited by Frank Allaun and then Walter Kendall. Organizer for the 'Broad Left'. Produced Voice Broadsheets. Spawned regional and industrial papers including *Steelworkers' Voice*, *Shopworkers' Voice*, *Voice of Fords' Workers*, *Humberside Voice*, *Merseyside Voice*. Sued by the ETU in 1973 for libel.

Week, The Weekly news analysis for socialists published in Nottingham between January 1964 and March 1968, subsequently incorporated into *International*. Edited by ex-miner and adult education tutor Ken Coates and LSE post-graduate Robin Blackburn, and sponsored by just about everyone from Perry Anderson to Konni Zilliacus. The unofficial organ of the Nottingham Group, who, minus Ken Coates, were to become the official British section of the ⟡ Unified Secretariat of the Fourth International. Capitulated regularly to union bureaucrats, refused unconditional support to incomes policy and hailed the Zanzibar revolution as 'classic in conception and execution', and the Algerian as 'developments in self-management'. Important early organizers of Workers' Council seminars and published the proceedings of the London, Manchester and Nottingham conferences.

Women's Liberation Workshop Loose federation of sixty autonomous Women's Liberation groups in London set up in 1969. Publishes weekly *Newsletter* and the occasional *Shrew*, edited in rotation by local groups.

Generally non-sectarian until 1973, when office control passed to separatist radical feminists.

Worker, The   ◊ Communist Party of Great Britain (Marxist-Leninist).

Workers' Broadsheet   ◊ Working People's Party of Great Britain.

Workers' Fight   Duplicated magazine published in Manchester by small group of ex- ◊ Socialist Labour League and ◊ Revolutionary Socialist League orthodox Trotskyists in 1967–8. Entered ◊ International Socialism in 1968 as a permanent faction, 'The Trotskyist Tendency', where they continued to publish *Workers' Fight* and factional statements. Viewed IS as a group veering between reformism and Marxism. Argued for the partition of Northern Ireland. 'De-fused' at a Special Congress in December 1971, and members asked to decide whether they would join IS or WF. Continued to publish *Workers' Fight* as a printed fortnightly newspaper, the Phoenix pamphlet series and a journal, *Permanent Revolution*. Support the ◊ Unified Secretariat of the Fourth International although rejected by it; probably have a bigger industrial base than the official section. Produce a steelworkers' paper *Real Steel News*, Teesside-based, and a dockers' paper, *The Hook*, based on the Manchester docks.

Workers' International League (WIL)   A pioneer British Trotskyist grouping formed by Jock Haston in Paddington in 1936. Declined to attend the foundation of the ◊ Fourth International. Major constituent of the ◊ Revolutionary Communist Party.

Workers' International Review   ◊ Revolutionary Socialist League.

Workers' News Special   ◊ Workers' Voice.

Workers' Party of Scotland   A working-class Maoist party established in Glasgow and Edinburgh in 1968 around anti-revisionist veterans Ken Houlison and Val Sutherland. In March 1972 three members were sent to prison for a total of eighty-one years for their part in alleged bank robberies. They were convicted on the evidence of a witness who claimed to have identified them, wearing masks, from a distance of forty feet through stained glass. William McPhearson's sentence of twenty-six years was the highest ever meted out by a Scottish court.

Workers' Press   ◊ Socialist Labour League.

Workers' Revolutionary Party   ◊ Socialist Labour League.

Workers' Voice   Merseyside grouping of working-class revolutionaries in the council Communist tradition; anti-parliamentary, critical of Leninism, interested in Sylvia Pankhurst and the KAPD, 'ultra-left' offshoot of the German Communist Party. Since 1970 published a duplicated monthly, and historical pamphlets. London sympathizers broke off to produce *Workers' News Special* standing for 'an independent, revolutionary workers' party'.

Working People's Party of Great Britain   Tiny Maoist group formed in May 1968 consisting of the remnants of the McCreery grouping (◊ Committee to Defeat Revisionism, for Communist Unity), who as the London Workers' Committee had published the duplicated monthly *Workers'*

Broadsheet. Based on five organizational principles: serving the people; uniting all who can be united against the main enemy; active members only; maximum initiative for members; all officials subject to immediate recall by members. Secretary, Paul Noone, a founder of the Junior Hospital Doctors' Association and prominent member of the Medical Practitioners' Union.

World Labour News ◇ *Freedom*.

Young Communist League (YCL)   Communist Party's youth organization. Publishes the newspaper *Challenge* (founded 1935), and the very occasional discussion magazine ◇ *Cogito*. Decimated in 1956, revived through CND, but remained persistently small, although solidly working class, through the sixties. Cause of much worry to the adult party.

Young Guard   Young socialist revolutionary paper dominated by ◇ International Socialism resulting from the merger of the local Young Socialist papers *Rally* and *Rebel*. Active in the Labour Party Young Socialists 1961–6. Editor elected by readers' meetings.

Young Socialists (YS)   Young workers' organization controlled by the ◇ Socialist Labour League. Based on the 'Keep Left' group who walked out of the ◇ Labour Party Young Socialists in 1964 to form an autonomous independent movement after the witch-hunting, manhandling and expulsion of individual 'Keep Left' supporters by Transport House. Campaigned for Victory to the Viet-Cong since 1965, carrying the banner of an NLF soldier who told the Americans 'You may shoot me ... but others will come against you', followed by placards stating 'We Are Those Others'. Sent a delegation of 800 to a ◇ Unified Secretariat of the Fourth International demonstration in Liège, Belgium, against NATO and the Vietnam war in 1966. Contested the Swindon by-election with a middle-aged YS candidate in 1969, polling 446 votes. Campaigned against Wilson's visit to Nixon in 1970. In 1972 mounted marches of unemployed young workers from Glasgow, Swansea, Liverpool, Deal and Southampton to a rally of 8,000 at the Empire Pool, Wembley, to 'force the Tories to resign and to defend the right to work'. Holds regular conferences, 'Keep Left' Annual General Meetings and summer camps. Strict discipline and sports.

Zilliacus, Konni   Labour MP active as a left-wing speaker and writer on Cold War questions. His starry-eyed partiality towards the East European Stalinist regimes went with a special fondness for Titoist Yugoslavia: consequently he was denounced as a spy of British intelligence in the Prague show-trials of 1952. Disciplined by the Labour Party and boycotted by the Communist Party, he won his way back into favour of both in the Cold War 'thaw' and died an unrepentent admirer of both Harold Wilson and N. S. Khrushchev.

Bibliography

1: The Double Exposure: Suez and Hungary

A good popular account of the Suez invasion is available in *The Day Before Yesterday*, edited by Alan Thompson (Panther, London, 1971). The inside story is contained in Rt Hon. Sir Harold Anthony Nutting's *No End of a Lesson: The Story of Suez* (Constable, London, 1967). Nutting's subsequent biography, *Nasser* (Constable, London, 1972), has interesting material on the tensions between the Arab leaders.

Relevant Marxist analyses of oil and modern imperialism are contained in Tony Cliff's *The Struggle in the Middle East*, issued as an International Socialism pamphlet in 1967 and re-published in the otherwise weak anthology *The New Revolutionaries* (Peter Owen, London, 1969), and Michael Kidron's 'International Capitalism' and 'Imperialism: The Highest Stage but One' (first published in *International Socialism*, 9 and 20, reprinted in *International Socialism*, 61).

Eyewitness accounts of the Hungarian Revolution include Peter Fryer's *Hungarian Tragedy* (Dobson, London, 1956), Basil Davidson's *What Really Happened in Hungary?* (Union of Democratic Control, London, 1956), and the beautifully written account of the Polish novelist, Wictor Woroszylski, *Diary of a Revolt* (Segal & Jenkins, London, 1956). The Stalinist view is presented in *The Counter-Revolutionary Forces in the October Events in Hungary* (Information Bureau of the Council of Ministers of the Hungarian People's Republic, Budapest, 1956) and in R. Palme Dutt's 'Notes of the Month' in *Labour Monthly*, notably in December 1956 ('. . . the only organized force ready to exploit the situation [were] the armed gangs of counter-revolution, with key forces previously trained in the West'), and in such assemblages as Andrew Rothstein's 'Workers' Power: A Postscript' (*Labour Monthly*, March 1957), which attempts to prove that the Hungarian workers' councils 'were a travesty of the title; the general pattern was one of armed gangs raiding the factories and forcing on the bewildered workers "Councils" consisting of former Horthyites'. The unreliability of Rothstein's anecdotes is devastatingly illuminated by comparison with Balaza Nagy's scrupulous history 'La Formation du conseil central ouvrier de Budapest en 1956' (in *Études sur la révolution hongroise*, Imre Nagy Institute for Political Research, Brussels, 1961, reprinted in a translation by Colin Barker and Olivia McMahon in *International Socialism*, Autumn, 1964). *National Communism and Popular*

Revolt in Eastern Europe, edited by Paul Zinner (Columbia University Press, New York, 1956), is a comprehensive collection of documents from the uprising. *Stalinism in Britain* ('Robert Black', New Park, London, 1970) also contains some documentary material which is accurate despite the banality of its general analysis.

Tracts published by British revolutionary groups in support of the revolution included *Revolution and Counter-Revolution in Hungary*, a *Newsletter* reprint including a November 1956 article, 'The Workers' Councils in the Hungarian Revolution', by Gerry Healy, *The Hungarian Workers' Revolution*, published by the Syndicalist Workers' Federation, and Andy Anderson's Solidarity booklet *Hungary 56*, which includes a full chronology and bibliography. Cliff's *Russia, a Marxist Analysis* (IS, London, 1955; revised 2nd edn, London, 1964) and *Stalin's Satellites in Europe* (published under the name of Ygael Gluckstein, Allen & Unwin, London, 1952) contain background on Eastern Europe, as does Chris Harman's *Bureaucracy and Revolution in Eastern Europe* (Pluto Press, London, 1974). Other sources are G. Mikes's *The Hungarian Revolution* (André Deutsch, London, 1957), H. Dewar and D. Norman's *Revolution and Counter-Revolution in Eastern Europe* (Socialist Union of Central-Eastern Europe, London, 1957), *L'Insurrection hongroise*, published by the French post-Trotskyist grouping Socialisme ou Barbarie, and Dora Scarlett's *Window onto Hungary* (Broadacre Books, Bradford, 1959).

On the splits in the Communist Party, *Communism and British Intellectuals* by Neal Wood (Gollancz, London, 1959) is a fairly accurate account by a well-endowed US academic who finds Marxism inconceivable, Ian Birchall's 'The British Communist Party 1945–64' (*International Socialism*, 50, 1972) is sound, if dry. The most comprehensive political account of the 1956 debate in the British Party is in Julian Harber's unpublished study, sadly lacking material from a world-wide influx of supporting letters received by E. P. and Dorothy Thompson. The best public source for local details on branches and details of resignations is the *Newsletter* for 1957–8. For an extended statement of the dissidents' analysis see *Hungary and the Communist Party: An Appeal vs Expulsion* by Peter Fryer (published by the author, London, 1957), 'Why We Left the Communist Party', the eight-page statement of the Nottingham Marxist Group (Nottingham, 1956), and the duplicated opposition bulletin, the *Reasoner*. A review of the impact in the American Communist Party is in Hershel D. Meyer's *The Khrushchev Report and the Crisis in the American Left* (Independence Publishers, New York, 1956). The less dramatic impact of 1956 on the French Party is covered in Jacques Roussel's deadpan history of French Trotskyism *Les Enfants du prophète* (double issue of the monthly review *Spartacus*, Paris, January-February 1972) and Richard Gombin's perky but lightweight *Les Origines du Gauchisme* (Éditions du Seuil, Paris, 1971).

For connoisseurs, material on the 1959 expulsions from the Socialist Labour League is contained very funnily in Behan's *With Breast Expanded* (Mac-

Gibbon & Kee, London, 1964), ironically in Solidarity pamphlet no. 4, *By Their Words Ye Shall Know Them*, selected correspondence, fully annotated, between the National Secretary and certain ex-SLL members, and sensationally in the infamous bulletin, *The 1959 Situation in the SLL*, containing documents by Coates, Fryer and Cadogan, who were informally grouped in the Stamford Faction (so called because they met in a park near Stamford) and who were promptly served writs by G. Healy.

2: Don't You Hear the H-Bombs' Thunder?

The standard history of CND is Christopher Driver's *The Disarmers: A Study in Protest* (Hodder & Stoughton, London, 1964), which, as befits a *Guardian* journalist, is accurate, snide and apolitical; but Nicolas Walters' review in *Solidarity*, vol. 3, no. 7, p. 11, unearths a few factual errors. Herb Greer's CND history *Mud Pie* (Max Parrish, London, 1964) is right-wing and unreliable, informed by 'a cold recognition that ideals cannot be carried unaltered into practical politics. An apparent attempt to do so causes these ideals to appear ridiculous and erodes the values they have as ideals.' It is spattered with spectacular mistakes. Frank Parkin's retrospective study of constituency Labour Parties is a more canny reconstruction of the battles that ebbed and flowed in Labour wards (*Middle Class Radicalism: The Social Bases of the British CND*, Manchester University Press, 1968). Another interesting academic survey is L. J. Mcfarlane's 'Disobedience and the Bomb' (*Political Quarterly*, October-December 1966, pp. 366–77). As for the leadership, Peggy Duff's political biography (*Left, Left, Left*, Allison & Busby, London, 1971) is lively reading, although portraying herself as more revolutionary in intention than she was in reality. Canon Collins' autobiography is predictably self-righteous and tedious. The terminal *Black Dwarf* contained Russell's 'Last Testament', commenting critically on the Committee of 100 and Ralph Schoenman, the organizer who became his aide (5 September 1970). David Boulton's anthology *Voices from the Crowd* (Peter Owen, London, 1964) shows the breadth of CND's support and includes the speeches of the defendants in the Wethersfield conspiracy trial. Much of Boulton's material is taken from CND's papers *Sanity* and *Youth Against the Bomb*. The Committee of 100 produced a lively 'independent magazine', *Resistance*, which grew out of a circular which the London Committee Secretary used to send to Working Group convenors called 'Action for Peace'. An insider's account of the Spies for Peace action was published in *The Spies for Peace Story* published jointly by Solidarity, members of the Syndicalist Workers' Federation, the London Federation of Anarchists, the ILP and the London Committee of 100 in June 1963 and republished as a special issue of *Anarchy* in July 1963. A fuller account, including the sectarian confession that boxes used in the publication were dumped in the waste bin of the *Morning Star*, was published (*Inside Story*, no. 8, March/April 1973). For the Committee of 100 at its more melodramatic, see Nicolas Walters' 'Damned Fools in Utopia'

(New Left Review, 13–14, p. 119, 1962) ... 'Right now the Committee leads the Maquis of the British section of the Third Force in the Cold War'. Over-optimistic socialist analysis of CND is to be found regularly in the *Reasoner* and *New Left Review*.

More sober criticism is to be found in Chris Farley's 'CND after the Election' *(New Left Review*, 1, pp. 18–19), Dave Peers' 'The Impasse of the Campaign for Nuclear Disarmament' *(International Socialism*, 12), Tirril Harris, et al., 'Labour and the Bomb' *(International Socialism*, 10, 1962) and Peter Sedgwick's report on the Defence Ministry sit-in, 'The Direction of Action' *(Socialist Review*, May 1961). Solidarity, the revolutionary grouping most deeply involved in the Committee of 100 and especially its industrial sub-committee, published prolific attacks on the pacifists and reformists in CND's unrepentently undemocratic leadership with such titles as 'Canon Balls', 'Beyond Counting Arses', 'Jail House Rock' and 'Empty the Gaols'. Their political perspective on the anti-nuclear movement is presented in 'From Civil Disobedience to Socialist Revolution' and 'Civil Disobedience and the Working Class' (vol. I, 8 and 9). For the CND leadership's drift to the right, see 'The Bomb and You', the Executive's 'revised statement' of CND policy (London, July 1962) and Stuart Hall's 'The Cuban Crisis: Trial Run or Steps Towards Peace' in *War and Peace*, CND leadership's shortlived 'theoretical journal' (vol. I, no. 1, January 1963). An account of the impact of CND among rank-and-file workers is given by Jim Arnison in 'Peace in Our Time' *(Labour Monthly*, April 1960): 'Imagine a meal break on a building site, men with parcels of sandwiches, drinking tea from tin lids, not very advanced in conditions from the scenes described in *The Ragged Trousered Philanthropists*. The dialogue however is very different. They are discussing Neville Shute and in particular that author's stand against nuclear horror. From that discussion comes the demand to me as the Federation Steward that their shop stewards should organize a public demonstration in support of disarmament.' Arnison was to become one of the Communist Party's finest industrial reporters and writers.

The mood of Aldermaston is probably best conveyed in David Mercer's TV trilogy *The Generations* (published by Calder, London, 1964) and Mike Horovitz's pioneering poetry magazine *New Departures*. A good collection of CND songs was published in 1960 by Hackney YCND and YS called *Songs of Hope and Survival*.

3: The Two New Lefts

The history of the New Left is essentially one of the undemocratic dancing of its intellectual leadership in various editorial formations. *New Left Review*, which served as the central organ of the New Left intellectuals between 1960 and 1963, itself resulted from a merger between *Universities and Left Review* and the *New Reasoner*. *ULR* was a political review for university student socialists founded in 1957 by a nucleus of ex-Communist Party Students around Raphael Samuel and *Oxford Left*. By 1959 *ULR* had risen on the CND surge to a circulation of 8,000 copies three times a year. Although its appeal was (probably intentionally) woolly and unselfconsciously middle-class ('Without CND supporters, Anti-Ugly protesters, Africa demonstrators, Free Cinema and the Society for the Abolition of the Death Penalty we would be nowhere'), its editorial core were hard enough to produce such classic studies as *The Insiders*, a special issue on the internal structure of the British ruling class. The *New Reasoner* was a Yorkshire-based quarterly with a circulation of about 4,000, which had originated from the duplicated internal bulletin the *Reasoner* which carried Marx's injunction 'To leave error irrefuted is to encourage immorality'. It specialized in extended feature articles of Marxist analysis of colonial policy, economics, welfare and labour history but also emphasized poetry and drawings, regular international reports, news on the growth of the Left Clubs and CND, and Edward Thompson's breezy notes of the quarter. The *New Reasoner* was explicitly in the Communist tradition and saw itself consciously echoing the more reputable intellectual heritage of the Communist Party, notably of the cultural and scientific review *Modern Quarterly*, which had published such writers as Hyman Levy, F. D. Klingender, Christopher Hill, George Thompson and W. E. Le Gros Clark in the late thirties. The *New Reasoner* took a special and, as it transpired, rather indiscriminate interest in the writers of the East European thaw, published the stalwarts of the British anti-Stalinist intellectual Left like Hill, Hilton, Hobsbaum, Kiernan, Lindsay, Meek and Berger but extended its editorial compass sufficiently to attract contributions from such as J. T. Murphy, G. D. H. Cole and Cedric Belfrage.

During 1959 the two journals collaborated in an industrial conference in Yorkshire (a *Reasoner* initiative) and the joint publication of a 64-page pamphlet entitled *A Socialist Wages Plan* by John Hughes and Ken Alexander (New Left Pamphlets, 1959) which pioneered the rationale for direct state wage control utilized so destructively by the Wilson Government. This publication, one of the very rare New Left statements of direct relevance to working-class politics, was vigorously attacked at the time, especially by the *Socialist Review* group. The controversy was reprinted, *en bloc*, as Part II of the anthology *A Socialist Review* under the title 'Reform or Revolution' (pp. 83–106).

In January 1960, after prolonged negotiations, the two journals were successfully merged into *New Left Review*, edited in a London office by Stuart Hall, and surrounded by an immense, eminent and, as before, over-whelmingly male editorial board. The editorial platform was stout enough to hold together the cultural journalism of the university New Lefties with the anti-colonialist and unilateralist commitments the Reasoners had inherited from their Communist past (this blend of concerns was interpreted by bourgeois observers as humanistic undergraduates being taken for an intellectual ride by wiley Bolsheviks, although in fact exactly the reverse was to happen). It insisted on taking seriously its political responsibilities to its readers and

Bibliography 511

used the pages of the journal to organize and sustain a national network of Left Clubs which aspired to give organizational structure to attitudes of the New Left. Several editorial board members contributed to a publishers' *pot pourri*, *Conviction* (ed. Norman Mackenzie, MacGibbon & Kee, London, 1958), and Thompson edited the only 'official' New Left anthology, *Out of Apathy* (Stevens & Sons, London, 1960), which contains the two most outstanding essays of the late fifties' crop, MacIntyre's 'Breaking the Chains of Reason' and Thompson's 'At the Point of Decay'. But political strain and personal exhaustion mounted as the editors were variously absorbed into the bureaucracy of CND, involved in pre-election policy fights within the Labour Party, attending to the left discussion groups and the attempt to combine socialist showmanship with Marxist scholarship. As Thompson puts it, 'One's responsibilities as an intellectual workman became forgotten in one's tasks as an impresario' ('Open Letter to Leszek Kolakowski', *Socialist Register*, 1973). For the relations between the *NLR* and the Trotskyist groups, see 'Revolution Again!' by Edward Thompson, *NLR*, 6, and Mike Kidron's letter of reply in *NLR*, 7.

In January 1963, in circumstances which remain mysterious, the journal was purchased by an old Etonian who proceeded to dismiss the entire editorial board and change the journal in all but name. The commitment to political involvement characteristic of at least the core of the old *NLR* was completely jettisoned and in the first year of the new regime more space was devoted to tenor saxophonists playing in New York than to the British working class in its entirety. After a brief editorial interregnum which was responsible for such curios as Barbara Castle on 'The Lessons of French Incomes Policy', the restyled *NLR* launched a breathtakingly pretentious series of pocket histories ('The Origins of the Present Crisis', 'The Anatomy of the Labour Party', 'The English Working Class') which apparently amounted to 'the central concern of the *Review*, the fundamental recasting of our thought about British society and British socialism, in terms adequate to the problems they pose us'. The essays were republished alongside some routine apologetics from the Labour Left and not-so-Left in *Towards Socialism* (Fontana, 1965). The Anderson–Nairn theses were dismantled, like an elaborate but obviously defective motor-mower, by Edward Thompson (in 'Peculiarities of the English', *Socialist Register*, 1965, pp. 311–62). The Anderson response, 'The Myths of Edward Thompson', was published in *NLR* 35, whose cover was portentously emblazoned 'Storm over the Left'.

Anderson's *NLR*, with its board augmented with protégés from the Oxbridge student glossy *New University*, proceeded through a sequence of infatuations with various figures of European Marxism who were accorded their 'due international currency' – by publication in *NLR* and exegesis in a usually incomprehensible explanatory gloss. Variously 'La Critique de la raison dialectique' by J.-P. Sartre was 'the massive treatise that dominates Marxist discussion today', 'La Politique et la lutte des classes' by Nicos Poulantzas was 'perhaps the first systematic work of Marxist theory since the war', and 'Reading Capital' by Étienne Balibar and Louis Althusser was 'perhaps the most significant recent contribution to Marxist philosophy'. Although the ostensible aim of these analytic imports was to raise the lamentable theoretical level of British Marxism, the educational operation was carried out with such pomp, pretentiousness and deliberate obscurity that it probably served to retard, distort and discredit Marxist thinking, and was indeed positive incitement to philistinism.

The *NLR*'s super-Marxism was uncontaminated by suggestions as to what Marxists might actually do. Although the old *NLR*'s editorials were prone to pomp, they seriously attempted to link the Marxism of the journal to the problems of such mass movement that existed. The post-1963 board permitted themselves only the most occasional editorial pronouncements and were consistently wrong. In 1964 a considered editorial statement announced that 'The Labour Government is condemned to act radically or perish. Fortunately Wilson understands this. Where Gaitskell would have sought "moderation" at all costs ... Wilson will be more ready to follow the logic of the situation ... British capitalism will find the administration of the same ideas by a party of the working class a different, less comfortable experience.' In 1965, in the course of a promotion for Régis Debray, perhaps the most catastrophically inaccurate Marxist of the sixties, it was explained that 'as a strategy, guerrilla war weds revolutionary practice to an adequate social analysis so that even temporary setbacks and reversals can make clear the way to final victory'. In 1969, the *NLR* reached the height of fatuity with a series of 'tactical' articles by Editorial Board members on the student movement, one of whom, 'James Wilcox', advocated with a straight face that socialist students should abandon old-fashioned concerns with strikes and propaganda and seize some, any old, university building which was 'sociologically inaccessible' as a 'Red Base' (or, as another Editorial Board member thought, 'Latin Quarter') which should be prepared for immediate fusion with a mass of workers of indeterminate politics.

This is not to say that *NLR* remained aloof from political activity. Members lent themselves to the founding committee of the Vietnam Solidarity Campaign and a small band were to be seen prancing about in both Grosvenor Square and Hyde Park Corner during the October 1968 Vietnam March under an *NLR* banner. Junior members of the *NLR* functioned as an élite clandestine grouping in the student movement and succeeded at one point in gaining control of the Revolutionary Socialist Students' Federation national apparat (to the dismay of students actually struggling; see Merfyn Jones on RSSF London Office's behaviour during the Warwick Files struggle, *International Socialism*, 44, p. 42).

A similar ineptness dogged a long-planned and short-lived venture into political journalism, *Seven Days* (1971–2), undertaken by *NLR* board members (Stedman Jones, Cockburn, Barnett, Halliday) with various non-aligned and much-abused Marxists. As Sue Vicary's early letter of resignation from the *Seven Days* working party put it, 'The politics of the paper are fatally confused ... It reeks of educated-middle-class preoccupations, detached irony, dilettantism, opulence and Marcusean pessimism. We are not militants, we have no roots ... yet we fancy ourselves as a revolutionary general staff, who have an overview and can generate "information" for different sectors of the battle' (24 March 1971).

The *Review* had effectively been transformed from a popular forum of socialist activity and theory into the paper emporium of a coterie of Marxist swots at the mercy of their own intellectual crazes, and prizing theory more as evidence of their own cleverness than for its possible relevance in the struggle for socialism. Underlying the apparent sophistication of the analyses was the extraordinarily arrogant belief that it is the role of the intellectuals to make the theory, the job of the workers to make the revolution and that what is wrong in Britain is that the latter are too backward to understand the former's instructions.

Consistently unable to create new options within itself, the *Review* splintered in the early seventies into neo-Stalinist and orthodox Trotskyist tendencies. Ben Brewster, a Cambridge geology prodigy who went to study post-graduate politics at LSE and who, after the first wave of Anderson–Nairnery had subsided, increasingly became the intellectual powerhouse of the *Review*, resigned in 1971 in protest against a mild *NLR* rebuke of tacit Chinese support for the Bandananaike government's suppression of the Ceylon Uprising in April 1971. As Brewster correctly points out, 'to argue in this way is to reject the principles of what was originally called the theory of "socialism in one country"' ... and about time too.

He was to found *Theoretical Practice*, an Althussarian philosophical review which took the *NLR*'s taste for theory without practice into the higher realm of the theory of theory. *Theoretical Practice* was briefly the centre of a network of graduated Stalinist study cells but itself disintegrated in 1973. After a prolonged flirtation with the Unified Secretariat of the Fourth International, Quintin Hoare, the managing editor of *NLR*, becoming the editor of the International Marxist Group's occasional theoretical journal *International* and Robin Blackburn joining the political leadership (*Red Weekly*, 1 May 1972, made the recruitment front-page news!), Blackburn continued to work with New Left Books, founded in 1972 to produce high-priced hard-backed translations of Marxist scholarship. Other editorial personnel were Bob Rowthorn, an ex-CND, ex-IS, ex-*Black Dwarf* economist and since 1971 a leading member of the Communist Party Economics Commission, Tom Nairn, who played a consistent and admirable part in the 1968 art students' movement, and David Fernbach, active in GLF and a founder editor of *Gay Marxist*. For further material on the history of the New Left see the special issue of *People and Politics* (pp. 211–17) on 'The Condition of England Question' by Stuart Hall, Mike Rustin and George Clark (1967), Laurens Otter in *International Socialism*, 18, p. 22, and Peter Sedgwick's 'Theory at the Hour of Wilson' (*International Socialism*, 22, p, 19). Clancy Sigal's novel *Weekend in Dinlock* (Secker & Warburg, London, 1960) has a thinly disguised portrait of Dorothy and Edward Thompson, Dennis Potter's *The Glittering Coffin* (Gollancz, London, 1960) is the socialist playwright's first and fiercest New Left polemic, and Peter Sedgwick's 'Pseud Left Review' (*International Socialism*, 26, p. 18) an appropriately disrespectful parody of new Left prose. Raymond Williams published a rather damp account of the old New Left entitled 'An Experimental Tendency' (*Listener*, 3 December 1970) and Jonathan Ree an only slightly intimidated review of E. P. Thompson's Kolakowski Letter (*Radical Philosophy*, Winter 1974, pp. 33 ff.). For a teddy-girl's encounter with the New Left see Val Clarke, 'It was PEOPLE that made me a socialist' (*Socialist Worker*, 1 December 1973).

4: That Was the Affluence That Was

Chronological details of industrial disputes can be found in *Labour Research*'s monthly strike notes and the TUC's *Industrial News*, which served as a weekly briefing for the editors of trade-union papers. On a day-to-day basis a blending of the *Daily Worker* and the *Financial Times* is the most informative combination. *Labour Monthly* is the best source for the views of left-inclined union leaders, while *Socialist Review* and the *Newsletter* attempted to publicize the shop stewards' viewpoint. The duplicated monthly *Solidarity* (which appeared first in 1960 as the *Agitator*) has a well-deserved reputation for descriptive reports from the shop floor, notably in engineering and the car industry (a full index to *Solidarity* was published in 1972). Official union newspapers open to rank-and-file opinion and letters included the weekly *Railway Review*, the *Draftsman*, published by DATA and edited by Jim Mortimer, and the shop-workers' monthly *New Age*. From 1962 onward, under the sponsorship of a group of Left Labour MPs and edited by Walter Kendall, *Union Voice* was launched to serve the 'broad Left' of the trade-union movement, and has since developed regional and industrial variants stressing workers' control in a fairly dilute 'guild socialist' guise. Publications of joint shop stewards' committees themselves are intermittent and hard to trace but included the *Powerworker*, *Portworker's Clarion*, *Platform*, the *Voice of Ford Workers* and the *Metalworker*, publication of the Engineering Shop Stewards' National Council. Industrial shop stewards' groupings also published occasional pamphlets such as *Blow You Jack, We Were Right*, a forceful reply to the Jack Court of Inquiry into the London Airport strike of 1958 published by the BOAC shop stewards (interestingly reviewed by Wal Hannington in *Labour Monthly*, April 1959). Some regional industrial information can also be gleaned from Trades Councils publications such as Birmingham's *Journal*, edited by Peter Morgan. Recently, histories of trades councils such as Liverpool, Swindon and Bristol also contain useful material on the post-war labour movement, despite the sometimes dramatic decline in importance and activity of the councils in the fifties and sixties. See also *Industrial Relations in the British Printing Industry*, humorously subtitled 'The Quest for Security', by John Child (Allen & Unwin, London, 1967), and for a fascinating account of flying picketing and police support for Edward Martell's scab daily during the 1958 national newspaper stoppage, see Fred Gallaway, 'Printers, Police and Picketing', *Labour Monthly*, September 1959.

Worthwhile post-war studies on particular industries are equally scanty, but include the outstanding *Coal is Our Life* by Norman Dennis, Fernando Henriques and Clifford Slaughter (Eyre & Spottiswoode, London, 1956), Graham Turner's *The Car Makers* (Eyre & Spottiswoode, London, 1964), David Wilson's *The Dockers and the Impact of Industrial Change* (Panther, 1972), Jim Fyrth and Henry Collins, *The Foundry Workers* (Amalgamated Union of Foundry Workers, 1958) and John Mathew's *Ford Strike: The Workers' Story* (Panther, London, 1972). On the docks, Bob Pennington gives a history and analysis of the emergence of the Blue Union (the National Association of Stevedores and Dockers) in Liverpool in 'Docks: Breakaway Unions and Unofficial Movement' (*International Socialism*, 2, p. 5) and similar pro-NASD material is in the pamphlet *Hands Off the Blue Union* written by Bill Hunter and produced by the Socialist Labour League, who championed the northern dockers' cause. The NASD was also supported by *Tribune*, about the last time the paper was ever to clearly side with the rank and file against the union bureaucracy. Jack Dash's autobiobraphy *Good Morning Brothers!* (Lawrence & Wishart, 1969; Mayflower, 1970) gives a London Communist's view of the NASD's foundation – 'brothers or cousins who happened to be on opposite sides, each loyal to the policy of his own union, would walk past each other like strangers'. The background to forced redundancies in the docks is contained in the *Devlin Report* ('Final Report of the Committee of Inquiry under the Right Hon. Lord Devlin into Certain Matters Concerning the Port Transport Industry', Cmnd 2734, August 1965). For a port-workers' reply see 'The Anti-Devlin Report' drafted in 1965 by London and Hull dockers and *Humberside Voice* supporters (reprinted *International Socialist Journal* March-April 1966).,

On Engineering, see *What Next for Engineers* by Ken Weller (Solidarity pamphlet no. 3), *The Standard Triumph Strike* by Tom Hillier, Jim Petter and Ken Weller and introduced by the Secretary of the Strike Committee (Solidarity pamphlet no. 5), 'The BLSF Dispute' by Ken Weller, an account of a long unofficial strike at British Light Steel Fittings, North London (Solidarity pamphlet no. 8). On aspects of the fight against the late fifties redundancies, see Harry Finch's account of the Birmingham Norton factory closure, 'The Fight Against Redundancy', published by Norton Motors Strike Committee, September 1956, reprinted in *Industrial Democracy in Great Britain* by K. Coates and T. Topham (MacGibbon & Kee, 1968), Paul Foot's *Socialist Review* pamphlet *Unemployment*, and 'Lancashire Fights Back' by the General Secretary of the Burnley Weavers' Association, Harold Dickenson (*Labour Monthly*, May 1959).

Accounts of the London transport workers' strikes in 1958 are to be found in 'London the Battlefield' by two London Communist Party organizers of the old school (*Labour Monthly*, June 1958), Mike Kidron's survey 'The

Economic Background for the Recent Strikes' (*International Socialism*, 1, p. 57) and Palme Dutt's 'Strike Strategy' (*Labour Monthly*, June 1958). The full story of the Scottish bus strike of April 1964 is in the pamphlet *Glasgow Busmen in Action* by Bob Potter and rank-and-file Scots busmen (Solidarity pamphlet no. 17, London 1964). Donald McLaren's account of the Clydeside apprentices' strike ('My First Strike', *Labour Monthly*, April 1960) is unfortunately one of the few written reports of this famous baptism of a generation of post-war Clyde militants including Ross Pritchard, Bobby Cambell, Jim Scott and Frank Campbell. 'Boys who had never uttered more than three or four consecutive sentences became budding public speakers holding forth to thousands of apprentices, arguing a direct and sincere case . . . the Propaganda Committee storming Clydeside with their leaflets, whitewashing teams, and factory gate meetings . . . The Finance Committee handling hundreds of pounds with the ease of Wall Street bankers . . .'

The internal affairs of the ETU, which suddenly became the subject of a newly discovered concern for labour movement democracy, are outlined in C. H. Rolph's account, *The ETU Trial* (André Deutsch, London, 1962), with a self-righteous introduction by John Freeman. See also *Defend the ETU: against Fleet Street and King Street* by Peter Fryer (a *Newsletter* pamphlet, London, 1958). On the pioneer Fawley power station productivity deal, see Allen Flanders, *The Fawley Productivity Agreements* (Faber & Faber, London, 1964), and for an early, overlooked socialist analysis see Tony Topham's 'The Importance of "Package Deals" in British Collective Bargaining' (*International Socialist Journal*, September-December 1964). Tony Cliff's indispensable study *Productivity Deals: What They Are and How to Fight Them* (Pluto, London, 1970) also contains material on the first round of productivity deals.

For the comprehensive story of the St Pancras rent strike and its industrial support (against a St Pancras Tory differential rent scheme which prefigured the Housing Finance Act) see Dave Burn's *Rent Strike St Pancras 1960* (published by Pluto Press for Architects Radicals Students Educators, London, 1972), and Ian MacDonald's 'Housing: The Struggle for Tenants' Control' (*International Socialism*, 33, p. 7). Don Cook's account, 'The Siege of St Pancras', must be one of the most exciting reports by a participant ever written. It starts, 'I write this from my barricaded top floor flat at Kennistoun House, St Pancras, where we are reaching the climax of a long struggle against rising rents. In the courtyard below the guard on the gates is maintained by a mass picket, twenty-fours hours a day, made up of tenants and local trade-unionists, many of them ex-service men and women. A rocket stands mounted ready to fire an alert which will bring hundreds of neighbours rushing to the defences within minutes from the blocks of council flats and private dwelling houses, whose roofs I am looking down on from behind our barricades' (*Labour Monthly*, October 1960).

For material on the shop stewards' movement in the fifties and early sixties, see Colin Barker's 'The British Labour Movement: Aspects of the Current Experience' (*International Socialism*, 28, p. 12, reprinted in *International*

Socialism, 61, special double issue), which echoes the general analysis pioneered by the widely read booklet *Incomes Policy, Legislation and Shop Stewards* by T. Cliff and C. Barker with a dissenting introduction by Reg Birch, published by the London Industrial Shop Stewards Defence Committee (London, 1966). Sections of Topham and Coates' anthology *Industrial Democracy in Great Britain* (MacGibbon & Kee, London, 1968) contain very interesting material with good introductions. Chapter 7 of Michael Kidron's *Western Capitalism Since the War* (revised edition, Penguin Books, Harmondsworth, 1970) deals succinctly with changes in trade-union organization and consciousness in the fifties.

A series of *Labour Monthly* views on the modern shop steward's role stimulated by the TUC General Council's renewed attack on joint shop stewards' committees illuminates the divided loyalties of many Communist Party stewards who valued the movement variously because of its support for the bureaucracy ('They alone can mobilize workshop strength in defence of *real* leaders', Norman Dinning, 'In Defence of Shop Stewards', November 1959); their public service ('the quiet and steady unpaid service which the shop stewards constantly render for trade unionism day by day', 'Vulcan', 'The General Council and the Shop Stewards', February 1960) or for their revolutionary potential ('in dingy little workshops, back street buildings and huge well laid out factories, in every place of toil, sweat and profit, bonded together with common aims and future political action', Martin Guinan, 'The Industrial Vanguard', March 1970).

See the academic studies, A. L. Marsh and E. E. Coker, 'Shop Steward Organization in Engineering' (*British Journal of Industrial Relations*, June 1963), and H. A. Clegg, A. J. Killick and Rex Adams, *Trade Union Officers* (Basil Blackwell, Oxford, 1961).

On union amalgamations and structure, see J. E. Mortimer, 'The Structure of the Trade Union Movement' (*Socialist Register*, 1964), and John Hughes, 'British Trade Unionism in the Sixties' (*Socialist Register*, 1966). For material on the increasing state role in wage bargaining, see V. L. Allen, *Trade Unions and Government* (Longmans, 1960), and Michael Harrison, *Trade Unions and the Labour Party since 1945* (Allen & Unwin, London, 1960). For a refreshingly curt account of the conflicting strands in Tory industrial policy see Nigel Harris, *Competition and the Corporate Society: British Conservatives, the State and Industry 1945–1964* (Methuen, London, 1972), elements of which are published as 'Tories and Trade Unions' (*International Socialism*, 7, p. 5).

For light amusement, see the late fifties craze for putting the working class's house in order (later to develop into straight union-bashing) as Eric Wigham's Penguin Special *What's Wrong with the Unions* (Harmondsworth, 1961), complete with twenty-five cures, or Michael Shanks' *The Stagnant Society* (Penguin Books, Harmondsworth, 1961). Shanks (the Royal Artillery and the *Financial Times*) was worried that 'trade unions are failing to adjust themselves to the changing pattern of industry and society. This gives them an increasingly "period" flavour. The smell of the music hall and the pawn shop still cling to them', and that 'shop stewards' organizations have been acquiring all too much power in recent years, and that this is unhealthy for the unions'. He was also alarmed that there had been 'no Winston Churchill of the TUC', an organization which also 'badly needs its Walter Reuther', lest it 'fell into the wrong hands'. Perhaps the most sloppy example is *The Peril in Our Midst* by Woodrow Wyatt (Phoenix House, London, 1956), who has continued to make an excellent living out of witch-hunting. The virtually identical examples of 'evidence' quoted by Wigham, Shanks and Wyatt might lead the conspiracy-minded reader to wonder if they all got their briefing from the same anti-Communist espionage organization.

For more reliable material on the shop-floor mood in the late fifties, see Alan Sillitoe's Nottingham novel *Saturday Night and Sunday Morning* (W. H. Allen, London, 1958) ('No more short-time like before the war, or getting the sack if you stood ten minutes in the lavatory reading your *Football Post* – if the gaffer got on to you now you could always tell him where to put the job and go somewhere else'); Colin Barker and Joyce Rosser's careful account of a militant factory 'The ENV Story: A Working Class Defeat' (*International Socialism*, 31, p. 21) and the late Dennis Butt's report on the Midlands car industry, 'Men and Motors' (*NLR*, 3, pp. 10–18).

5: Let's Go with Labour

There is no decent account of modern social-democratic theory, which is by no means as empirical as its founders or most Marxists believe. Ralph Miliband's classic, *Parliamentary Socialism* (Allen & Unwin, London, 1961, revised edn London, 1973), is indispensable but actually disappointingly sketchy on modern Labourism. See also T. Cliff's analysis of Miliband's material, 'The Labour Party in Perspective' (*International Socialism*, 9, p. 4), Michael Barrett-Brown's *From Labourism to Socialism* (Spokesman Books, Nottingham, 1972) and Tom Nairn's 'The Fateful Meridian' (*NLR*, 60), the most convincing of this author's continuing elaborations of an analysis which attributes the distinctiveness of the Labour Party to its 'late' formation.

Attlee's reassertion of collectivism in *The Labour Party in Perspective* and the apparent if partial success of the first wave of post-war nationalization, which could still be seen by working-class Labour supporters as the first instalment in some longer-term socialist transformation, provided the background to the pluralist revisionists of the fifties, notably C. A. R. Crosland's *The Future of Socialism*. Gaitskell's own thought was consciously ethical, anti-Marxist and anti-working-class, influenced in particular by the 'democratic socialist' Evan Durbin (see Gaitskell's *Recent Developments in British Socialist Thinking*, London, The Cooperative Union, 1956, and the key Gaitskellite programme *Industry and Society*, finally adopted in 1957). There is nothing approaching a Marxist biography of Gaitskell. What is possible is indicated in Peter Sedgwick's delicate survey of the development of *Socialist*

Commentary, the leading theoretical organ of the Gaitskellite Right through the career, from crypto-Leninism to state-corporation, of its editor Allan Flanders (see 'The Origins of Socialist Commentary', background paper to the Balliol seminar in the series 'The Theory and Practice of Socialism', 10 March 1972; also *Idiot International*, 'On Flanders Fields', July 1970, p. 9). The standard account is *Hugh Gaitskell*, by a disciple, Bill Rodgers (Thames & Hudson, London, 1964). A convenient volume of extracts, mainly from official Labour Party policy, is gathered by Frank Bealey in *The Social and Political Thought of the British Labour Party* (Weidenfeld & Nicolson, London, 1970). Marxist criticism of Gaitskellism is contained in *From MacDonald to Gaitskell* by Alasdair MacIntyre (SLL Pamphlet, London, and Plough Press), of modern social democratic 'planning' his 'Labour Policy and Capitalist Planning' (*International Socialism*, 15, p. 5). See also Chris Harman's superb history of left social democracy in 'Tribune of the People' (*International Socialism*, 21 and 24). The probable role of CIA conduits in financing parliamentary and trade-union revisionists is referred to in *Socialist Worker*, 17 March 1973 ('How Dollar Spy Men Back Labour's Far-Right') and *Solidarity* 'Foundations and Empire' (vol. 6, no. 8).

The policy of Wilson's Government is to be extracted from *The New Britain: Labour's Plan Outlined by Harold Wilson* (Penguin Books, Harmondsworth, 1964); *Planning for Progress: A Strategy for Labour* by Thomas Balogh (Fabian Tract 346); *An Incomes Policy for Labour* by Michael Stewart and Rex Winsbury (Fabian Tract 350); and, in a starry-eyed idealistic version *Why Labour?* by Jim Northcott (Penguin Books, Harmondsworth, 1964), which makes an interesting contrast to Roy Jenkins' feeble *The Labour Case* (Penguin Books, Harmondsworth, 1959).

The principal critiques of the Labour Government in power included *May Day Manifesto* (first published by May Day Manifesto Committee in 1967 and republished in an expanded version by Penguin Books in 1968), Paul Foot's *The Politics of Harold Wilson* (Penguin Books, Harmondsworth, 1968), the same author's 'If Wilsonism Means Anything' (*Socialist Worker*, 28 September 1968), his review of the Labour record in 'How to Fight the Tories' (*Socialist Worker* pamphlet, London, 1970, pp. 4–7), Ralph Miliband's polemic in 'The Labour Government and Beyond' (*Socialist Register*, 1966) and 'Vietnam and Western Socialism' (*Socialist Register*, 1967). As Wilson progressed, the critics were even joined by liberal academics and the Labour Centre and Right; see Anne Darnborough 'Labour's Record on South Africa' (London Anti-Apartheid, no date), *Matters of Principle: Labour's Last Chance* (London, 1968) and *Beyond the Freeze: A Socialist Policy for Economic Growth* edited by Charles Feinstein with a foreword by Russell Kerr (London, 1966). For a fascinating example of an ex-Trotskyist repelled by the Labour Party but quite unable to conceive of existing outside it, see Ken Coates in *The Crisis of British Socialism* (subtitled *Essays on the Rise of Harold Wilson and the Fall of the Labour Party*) (Spokesman Books, Nottingham, 1971), and 'Socialists and the Labour Party' (*Socialist Register*, 1973).

For controversy on Marxists' electoral attitude to the Labour Party in 1970 see 'Let It Bleed: Labour and the General Election' by Robin Blackburn (*Red Mole*, 15 April 1970), Pat Jordan's 'The Labour Party Debate Continued' (*Red Mole*, 1 June 1970), and Roger Protz and Peter Sedgwick on electoral strategy in *International Socialism*, 43, p. 10; also 'Labour's Left in Crisis' by Ted Grant in *Spark*, March 1968 (London W1R Publications). For a betrayal by betrayal account of the 1964–70 government, see the horse's mouth, Harold Wilson, on *The Labour Government 1964–1970* (Weidenfeld & Nicolson and Michael Joseph, London, 1971; Penguin Books, Harmondsworth, 1974). For laughs, there is George Brown's account *In My Way* (Penguin Books, Harmondsworth, 1972).

For popularist political refits and revamps after the Tory victory in 1970 see A. Wedgwood Benn, *The New Politics* (Fabian Society, London, 1970), Stephen Haseler and Gyford, *Social Democracy: Beyond Revisionism* and Anthony Crosland's essays on Labour's need for a 'limited programme of radical measures which do not promise more than we can actually perform' (*Socialism Now*, Cape, London, 1974).

6: Squeeze, Freeze, Then Prod

General background is to be found in the *Morning Star*, the *Workers' Press*, *Socialist Worker*, *The Week*, *Solidarity* and the publications of the Institute for Workers' Control. General background can be found in *Can Workers Run Industry?* edited for the IWC by Ken Coates (Sphere, 1968), *Industrial Democracy in Great Britain*, edited by Coates and Tony Topham (MacGibbon & Kee, London, 1968), *British Capitalism, Workers and the Profit Squeeze* by A. Glyn and R. B. Sutcliffe (Penguin Books, Harmondsworth, 1972), Tony Cliff's *The Employers' Offensive: Productivity Deals and How to Fight Them* (Pluto, London, 1970), and *The Incompatibles: Trade Union Militancy and the Consensus* edited by Robin Blackburn and Alexander Cockburn (Penguin Books, Harmondsworth, 1967). First-hand accounts of industrial life can be found in Bob Leason's collection of interviews *Strike: A Live History 1887–1971* (Allen & Unwin, London, 1973), and *NLR*'s 'Work' series of personal accounts edited by Ronald Fraser, republished in two volumes by Penguin Books (Harmondsworth, 1968–9). Journalistic narratives of industrial relations at the top are contained in Peter Jenkins' *The Battle of Downing Street* (Charles Knight & Co., London, 1971), Steven Fay's *Measure for Measure: Reforming the Trade Unions* (Chatto & Windus and Charles Knight, London, 1970), and Eric Heffer's *The Class Struggle in Parliament* (Gollancz, London, 1972).

Socialist analyses of particular industries include 'Taking London for a Ride', the busmen's case as put by a group of London rank-and-filers associated with *Platform*, *Aircraft Industry and Workers' Control* by the Bristol Siddeley Engines Shop Stewards' Committee, *The Power Game* by Colin Barker, which deals with the impact of work study and productivity dealing on the electricity supply industry (Pluto, London, 1972), 'The Merseyside Building Workers' Movement' by Martin Barker (*International Socialism*, 32), 'The Docks' by Terry Barret (*International*, vol. 1, no. 3), which explains just how Devlin was pushed through, and *Stop Devlin Now* by Jack Gale (SLL, London, 1967). Jim Allen's television play *The Big Flame* deals brilliantly with the resistance to Devlin on Merseyside. 'Grading and the Contracting Sparks' by 'Thurso Berwick' (*Labour Worker*, London, 1967), John Charlton's *Productivity Dealing and the Miners*' *Next Step* (Pluto, London, 1971), *The Crisis in the Machine Tool Industry* (*Socialist Worker* pamphlet, Coventry, 1971), Vincent Burke's study *Teachers in Turmoil* (Penguin Special, Harmondsworth, 1971), and Nick Hillier's *Farmworkers*' *Control* (IWC, no date). See also *Rank and File* and the *Building Workers Charter* for the building industry, *Flashlight* 'rank-and-file reform paper' for the ETU, and *Rank and File* for the teachers.

For accounts of disputes see *No Bus Today: The Case of the East Yorkshire Bus Strike* (10/15a Branch TGWU, Hull, 1966), the *Rank and File* pamphlet *The Anti-Cameron Report* by Paul Foot for the details of the conclusion of the Barbican dispute, and 'Barbican Postmortem' (*Solidarity*, vol. IV, no. 10, p. 26). Paul Foot's account of the seamen's strike, admittedly plundered from the Hull seamen's 'Not Wanted on Voyage', which he describes as 'one of the most devastating documents ever produced by British workers on strike', is in *The Incompatibles* (see above); see also Nick Howard's comments in 'The Seamen's Strike' (*International Socialism*, 26, p. 4). A short history of the NUS is in 'The Seamen's Struggle' (*International Socialism*, 55, p. 7). Jim Arnison of the *Morning Star* wrote a lively account of the Roberts–Arundel dispute, again much helped by the publications of the Strike Committee themselves, in *The Million Pound Strike* (Lawrence & Wishart, London, 1970, with a tough-talking introduction by Hugh Scanlon). Colin Barker's delicate and beautifully written pamphlet *The Pilkington Strike* (*Socialist Worker* pamphlet, London, 1970), marred only by a rather indecisive attitude towards breakaway unionism, is greatly superior to the lengthy but academically flat-footed *Strike at Pilkingtons* (Fontana, London, 1971). On Pilkingtons, see also 'GMWU: Scab Union' ('Mark Fore', *Solidarity*). For details of the first unsuccessful attempt at a work-in, at Liverpool GEC–AEI, see *Socialist Worker*, 25 September 1969, 'Behind the Mersey Defeat: Lack of Grass Roots Support and Lure of Government Redundancy Handout', *Anarchy*, no. 108, 1970, and *Solidarity*, 'GEC: The Balance Sheet' (Vol. 6, no. 2).

On disputes involving predominantly immigrant workers, see 'What Happened at Woolfs' by Chris Davison, a crisp account of strike action among Pakistani rubber workers in Southall, and 'The Injection Moulders' Lockout' by J. Higgins and J. Deason (*Socialist Worker* pamphlet, London, 1968). For the politics of the left wing of the TUC General Council (which are naturally nowhere near as left as they themselves, Fleet Street and King Street believe), see *The Way Forward for Workers*' *Control*, the text of a speech given by Hugh Scanlon to the Sixth National Workers' Control Conference in 1968 (IWC pamphlet series No. 1), and 'The Role of Militancy' (*NLR*, 46), an extended interview in which Scanlon describes his youth in Metro-Vickers, Manchester, and his views on Parliament: 'if we could build up wider unity on the Left within the trade-union movement, this of itself would give far greater scope for more effective Left opposition in Parliament'. Margaret Stewart's *Frank Cousins: A Study* (Hutchinson, London, 1968) has some illuminating quotations from Cousins' predictable career in Parliament. For the equally predictable drift of an ex-Stalinist to the right see *The Road from Wigan Pier* by Olga Cannon and J. R. L. Anderson (Gollancz, London, 1973), the official biography of Les Cannon of the ETU, and an illuminating and honest interview made before Cannon's death by Nicholas Woolley (*Listener*, 28 January 1971). For the official TUC rationale for its involvement in state labour laws, see 'A Hundred Years of Trade Unionism – George Woodcock on the TUC's Anniversary' (*Listener*, 13 June 1969).

For shop stewards' opinions see the published reports of the National Workers' Control Conferences, especially the Fifth and Sixth, and *In Place of Strife Out*, probably the most pungent attack on the Labour legislation in the form of quotes from the Bill with comments (and produced by the North West Shop Stewards' Action Committee which was sponsored by stewards from Shell Stanlow, Shellstar, Warrington Gas and Fiddlers Ferry, Ellesmere Port, 1967). *Workers' Control* by Ernie Roberts (Allen & Unwin, London, 1973) is one of the best and clearest products of the IWC supporters, but still hedges on the concrete problems. For the Communist Party viewpoint see *Incomes Policy: The Great Wage Freeze Trick* by Bert Ramelson (London, 1967) and Ramelson's debate with the IWC. See also the unrestrained controversy between Ray Challoner and the IWC organizers (*International Socialism*, 37 and 40), the ILP's *Which Way for Workers' Control* (by Alistair Graham), the IMG's *Theories of Workers' Control*, and Peter Sedgwick's 'Workers' Control' (*International Socialism*, 3, p. 18). For more anarchic viewpoints, see 'Workers' Mutual Aid' (London, 1968), 'Law and Order on the Shop Floor' (Coventry Workshop Books, 1969), and the 'Workers' Control' issue of *Anarchy* (vol. 1, no, 2, 1961).

A very useful review with an industrial chronology of principal stoppages from 1960–71 is 'Industrial Conflict and the Political Economy' by Richard Hyman (*Socialist Register*, 1973). The *Trade Union Register 1969–1970* has material, mostly rather thin whenever it is written for workers by sympathetic union full-timers rather than by the participants themselves, on the Leeds clothing strike, 1969 Fords strike, provincial busmen and the revolt of the lower-paid.

7: Make One, Two, Three Balls-Ups: The Student Left

For a history of NALSO see the analysis of an ex-National Chairman, Ian Taylor's 'Student Left in the Sixties', first published in *Durham Left* and reprinted in two parts by *Guerilla*, the fortnightly magazine of Manchester University Socialist Society, in October 1968, Bruce Bebington's 'The Decline and Fall of NALSO' in *Student International*, nos. 2 and 3 (Glasgow, 1969), and the letters column of *Tribune*. For NALSO's changing attitude towards student unions see 'Socialists in Students' Unions' by Martin Loney, NALSO Vice Chairman, in *Labour Student*, 7, January 1966. For the political views of those SLL students who finally found themselves bearing the corpse of NALSO, see the *Marxist*, the magazine of Leeds University Union Marxist Society, vol. I, no. 2 ('Marxists versus Revisionists'). On early radical student politics, see 'The New Student Revolt' (special issue of *U* inter-university and college mazagine, vol. 3, no. 8, November 1965), *Gunfire*, the Young Liberal magazine, *Snap*, the duplicated newsletter of the NUS opposition in the mid-sixties, and the interminable history of the RSA in D. Widgery's 'NUS – The Students' Muffler' (in *Student Power*, edited by Robin Blackburn and Alexander Cockburn, Penguin Books, Harmondsworth, 1969). For a disdainful Marxist view on these organizations see Richard Kuper in *Agitator* (May 1968), the occasional magazine of the LSE Socialist Society ('The Times They are a-Changing'). For the first exposure of the NUS leadership's involvement in the CIA funding of anti-Communist student organizations, see the notoriously ill-duplicated RSA pamphlet 'ISC, CIA and NUS' by David Widgery, Adrian Perry and David Triesman (RSA, London, 1967). For details of the first Vietnam teach-in organized by Tariq Ali, David Caute and Steven Lukes at Oxford in 1965 and attended by a schoolmasterly Michael Stewart and a grim Eric Hobsbawm, see 'Boos to the Left, Hisses to the Right of Him, Into the Jaws of Death Rode the Foreign Secretary' by Nicholas Tomalin (*Sunday Times*, 20 June 1965). RSA publications included Tom Fawthrop's *Education or Examination* (RSA and Narod Press, London, 1968) and David Adelstein's duplicated anthology *Do It Yourself Student Power* (RSA, London, 1968).

For accounts by participants of student struggles see *University and Revolution*, a duplicated pamphlet published by Leicester RSSF (Leicester, 1968), *The Hornsey Affair*, by students and staff of Hornsey College of Art (Penguin Education Special, 1969), and Tom Nairn, 'On the Subversiveness of Art Students' (*Listener*, 17 October 1968), which argues blithely that 'a few North London crackpots achieved more than the working class of this overwhelmingly proletarian country, after a century of development', *The 13½ Days That Shook the University*, Manchester IS Students (Manchester, March 1970), and *Warwick University Limited*, edited by Edward Thompson (Penguin Books, Harmondsworth, 1970). See also 'Trouble in the Valley' and 'Students Revolt: In Search of Positive Selfconsciousness' (on Essex University) in *Solidarity*, vol. 5, nos. 7 and 8, 'Hull: The Way Forward' by Pete Latarche and 'Regent Street Poly: Sociologists in Crisis', by Edward Ludd, in *Black Dwarf*. The LSE has spawned two fairly inaccurate books by visiting postgraduates, *Academic Freedom in Action* by Paul Hoch (Sheed & Ward, 1970) and *LSE: The Natives Are Restless* by Vic Schoernbach. Much more valuable are 'The LSE: What It Is and How We Fought It', produced by the Open Committee of the Socialist Society, 'Jill West's' inside story of the collapse of the liberal staff in 'Thugs and Wreckers: The Case of the LSE' (Mayday Manifesto Special Bulletin No. 1, March 1969), 'Lockout and After: London School of Economics' by Martin Shaw (*International Socialism*, 36, p. 9), 'Revolt at LSE' by Brewster and Cockburn (*NLR*, 43) and 'LSE in Retrospect' by Dave Slaney (*Black Dwarf*, 1 October 1969). 'Lessons from LSE: A Communist Perspective', produced by the LSE Student Communist Party Branch which duly materialized out of the defeats, is unreliable to the point of dishonesty.

See also 'The Ascent to Naked Repression', a national RSSF leaflet, two LSE special editions of *Socialist Worker* in January 1969, *What is to be Done with the LSE*, a Spartacus League pamphlet, Robin Blackburn's analysis of the school's social-imperialist foundations ('The Great Tradition of the LSE: Reaction, Racism and Imperialism', *Black Dwarf*, 14 March 1969), and *LSE and Liberalism* by David Adelstein (LSE Graduate Students' Association, London, 1970).

For general background to the student movement see the national coverage of *Black Dwarf* and the political magazines *Essex Left*, *Labour Student*, the *Agitator* (which produced three national issues in Spring 1969), *Guerilla* from Manchester, Hornsey's *Revelations*, *Spartacus*, published by the Oxford and Cambridge University Labour Clubs, *Oxford Left*, *Sinistra*, and *Forward*, magazines of the Cambridge University Labour Club, succeeded by the weekly Cambridge *Shilling Paper*, and Birmingham's *Red Base*. For a laugh, see such examples of student bumptiousness as the ill-duplicated *Escalate* (a pirate RSSF 'theoretical journal' produced in Brighton – 'The title is not chosen for an *effect* (aesthetic, humorous, etc.) exterior to its political function; it evokes the whole tradition of revolutionary politics not as the living death of a tradition, a past lived in the absence of a present . . .'); for student incomprehensibility, the Althussarian science review *Hundred Flowers*, concocted by the Chelsea College Philosophical and Ethical Society; for student irrelevance, *Students Red Flag*, 'The bulletin of the student fraction of the Revolutionary Workers' Party (Trotskyist)'; and for straightforward charlatanism 'MacIntyre, The Game is Up' by Robin Blackburn (*Black Dwarf*, 16 January 1970, p. 11), which elects to expose the 'idealist pseudo-empiricism lying beneath MacIntyre's Coronation Street Marxism'. For a typical example of self-important sexism which passed for British situationalism, see 'King Mob: Two Letters on Student Power'.

RSSF National Office produced regular bulletins in 1969, a special paper on the struggle in Ireland (May 1969) and bound collections of local leaflets and article reprints (Red Texts), and some local branches and specialist groups produced their own material, such as Manchester RSSF's pamphlet *The Concept of a University*, and *Red Scientist*, a magazine originating from an RSSF scientists' conference in Manchester in 1969. Contrary to bourgeois belief, H. Marcuse did not greatly inspire the British student movement;

bestsellers on the LSE bookstall in 1966 were instead *The Autobiography of Malcolm X* (Hutchinson, London, 1968), Hal Draper's *Berkeley: The New Student Revolt* (Grove Press, New York, 1965) and Isaac Deutscher's anthology of Trotsky, *The Age of Permanent Revolution*. The most generally read publications were probably *Education, Capitalism and the Student Revolt* by Harman, Kuper, Shaw, Clark and Sayers (IS, London, 1968), the first extended Marxist analysis of the student revolt to appear in Britain, David Fernbach's widely reprinted 'Revolutionary Strategy and the Student Movement' (*Spartacus*, no. 5), Tom Falthrop's 'All Power to the Campus Soviets' (*Black Dwarf*), Ernest Mandel's speech at the Sorbonne, and eventually the New Left Review Penguin Special *Student Power* (Harmondsworth, 1969), originally commissioned as an RSA NUS-orientated anthology and hastily supplemented and revolutionized after the May Events to the justified distress of Communist Party students like Alan Hunt and Digby Jacks, whose contributions were dumped.

In general 'student power' was a description which most student militants disliked but couldn't avoid being labelled with. As David Triesman wrote, 'Student Power is a horrible expression. Not only does it convey remarkably little – it is obviously meaningless to most students – but what it does appear to convey is the intention to fight for a sectional interest, intent on increasing the advantages available to itself, when it is already, probably, the second most privileged sector in the industrial set-up in this country' (*Student Power: The Long March*, Essex, January 1968).

The Communist Party student organizer was scarcely able to conceal his dislike for the 1968 upsurge when apparently 'the real problems of real students disappeared' ('Student Perspectives' by Fergus Nicolson, *Marxism Today*, October 1969), whereas the Maoist views were in general to demand an immediate fusion between students and the working class which ought to commence with the college catering staff (see Joint Committee of Communists, *Towards a Worker/Student Alliance*, Sussex, 1969). In general, the Marxist-Leninist groups who actually had worker-members stayed well clear of student politics. For a pretentious review of the positions taken by the main organized socialist groupings in RSSF see *The Political Theory of the Student Movement – Notes for a Marxist Critique* (Liverpool, March 1971), working notes produced by an RSSF rump of sectarian anti-sectarians whose professed theme that 'quite simply, the sects have been trampling Marxism to death for too long' is ill justified by their own plodding prose.

For other background articles see Rudi Dutschke, *The Students and the Revolution* (Spokesman pamphlet no. 15, Nottingham, 1971), an *Observer* report datelined Paris, 18 May, 'Soviets on the Campus' ... 'this is revolution ... it is a total onslaught on modern society ...' etc. etc. (Neal Ascherson, *Observer*, 19 May 1968), Hal Draper, 'The Mind of Clark Kerr – Behind the Battle of Berkeley' (Independent Socialist Club, Berkeley, no date), Phil Goodwin, 'Higher Education in Capitalist Society' (*Marxism Today*, September 1970), Steven Marks, 'Student Theory' (*International Socialism*, 36,

April-May 1969), John Cowley, 'The Strange Death of the Liberal University' (*Socialist Register*, 1969), J. and M. Rowntree, 'The Political Economy of Youth', which fortunately had a far smaller influence in Britain than in the USA (*ISJ*, 25 February 1968), Ernest Mandel, *The Revolutionary Student Movement: Theory and Practice* (Merit, New York, 1969), Eric Heffer, 'The Student Movement, the Labour Party and the Road to Socialism' (*Tribune*, 26 July 1968), R. Palme Dutt, 'World in Movement: France and Students' (*Labour Monthly*, July 1968), Peacock and Culyer, *Economic Aspects of Student Unrest* (Occasional Paper 26, Institute of Economic Affairs, London, 1969), and the Select Committee's Report on Student Relations for its learned liberal incomprehension.

8: 1968

For liberal opposition to the Vietnam war see the monthly magazine of the British Campaign for Peace in Vietnam, which depended on Labour MPs, clerics, and ex-CNDers for its platform and the Communist Party for its local organization. *Report*, a fortnightly résumé of developments in the war published by the York Vietnam Group, reprinted much press comment. For the liberal conscience see the *Guardian*'s infamous editorial 'Commitments in South East Asia' (6 June 1966), published after the paper's editor returned from an extensive US-advised tour of South Vietnam. The history of the movement in solidarity with the NLF is given in *End of a Tactic* by Geoff Richman (duplicated, London, 1969) and in the Bulletin of the Vietnam Solidarity Campaign, especially its conference reports July 1966, May 1967 and June 1968. VSC's most important publications were *Why Vietnam Solidarity*, *The Dirty War and Mr Wilson* and *Vietnam and Trade Unionists*. It also distributed material from the Bertrand Russell International War Crimes Tribunal which met in Stockholm in 1967, especially Russell's *Appeal to the American Conscience*. This last magnificent chapter to Russell's life is fully documented in *Prevent the Crime of Silence: Reports from the Sessions of the International War Crimes Tribunal*, edited by Ken Coates, Peter Limqueco and Peter Weiss with a foreword by Noam Chomsky (Allen Lane, London, 1971). For an account of a local VSC group which was involved in everything from street market stalls and wall newspapers to Sunday volleyball in Parliament Hill Fields beside NLF flags and which took its own internal organization extremely seriously, see *Red Camden*, 'collectively produced by Camden VSC to communicate to the people of Camden'.

For comment on the first successful VSC demonstration in Grosvenor Square see Jeremy Bugler, 'Solidarity with Violence' (*New Society*, 21 March 1968) – 'Sunday's main message may be the first sign that the British tradition of compromise and polite politics is past' – and with similar sentiments and much greater gusto *The Death of CND as Performed by the Grosvenor Square Demonstrators under the Direction of Themselves Alone* (Solidarity pamphlet no. 28, 1968). For reprints and replies to Stalinist, anarchist and pacifist criticism of VSC's demonstration style and slogans, see 'Vietnam and the Left: An Answer to Some Critics' (*The Week*, vol. 9, no. 11, 13 March 1968) and general comment Rachel Matgamna ('Vietnam Solidarity Campaign' in Survey, *International Socialism*, 35, p. 9). The scandalized views of M Ps complete with Tory demands for deportation of the mythical alien agitators are to be found in *The Times* ('Grosvenor Square Violence Angers M Ps', 19 March 1968). For a detailed study of Fleet Street techniques during the October 1968 demonstrations, when the press first promoted a scare that the march was a cover for a violent uprising and then jeered at the demonstrators for failing to seize power, see *Demonstrations and Communication: A Case Study* by Halloran, Elliott and Murdock (Penguin Books, Harmondsworth, 1970). For a more sophisticated version of the same technique by an ex-Leftist, see 'On the Demo' by Mary McCarthy (*Sunday Times* Colour Magazine, November 1969). For a thyrotoxic complaint that the demonstration betrayed everyone by not going to get bashed over in Grosvenor Square – 'the October revolution had sold itself out after three hours. For most of the freaks in the crowd, the flirtation with the conventional left was over' – see Mick Farren and Ed Barker's *Watch Out Kids* (Open Gate, London, 1972). For views on politics of mass demonstrations see post-march editorial of *Socialist Worker* (2 November 1968), VSC Bulletin nos. 19 and 20 ('End of a Tactic'), and John Berger's 'On the Nature of Mass Demonstrations' written for *New Society* and reprinted in *International Socialism*, 34 and his Penguin *Selected Essays and Articles*. Harmondsworth, 1972).

For anti-imperialist analysis of the Vietnam war critical of the Hanoi regime see *Vietnam* by Bob Potter (a Solidarity pamphlet with 'useful background information on all the participants'), *Vietnam: Stalinism v. Revolutionary Socialism* by Richard Stevenson (A Chartist International Publication, London, November 1972) and 'Washington nor Moscow – but Hanoi?' (*International Socialist Journal*, 32, 1968). For the Communist Party position on the war and the Vietnam solidarity movement see *Ultra-Leftism in Britain* by Betty Reid (Communist Party, London, 1970), especially pp. 47–57. For a local case history of how the Communist Party fulltimers eventually and ham-fistedly attempted to muscle into the solidarity campaign after years of denouncing it, see *Ad Hoc Ad Nauseam* (Sheffield VSC), a detailed account of the 1 March 1969 demonstration in Sheffield when Party stewards sided with the police and tore down banners.

For analysis of the May Events, see *The Beginning of the End*, a starry-eyed collaboration by an English *New Left Review* editor and an Italian situationalist (Panther, London, 1968), *Paris: May 1968*, a widely read eyewitness account (Solidarity, London, 1968), *France: The Struggle Goes On*, which stresses the absence of revolutionary organization in the defeat of the May movement (T. Cliff and I. Birchall, IS Publications, August, 1968), a special issue of *New Left Review* (no. 52) with a breathy editorial: 'For years the Left in Europe has been writing "Letters from Afar", attempting analysis, expressing solidarity, discussing strategy. Now the struggle has suddenly arrived at home.' For the orthodox Trotskyist version see Ernest Mandel, *The Lessons of May 1968* (IMG Publications 1968, reprinted 1971) and for a denunciation of everyone in France except the AJS, a Trotskyist grouping which contrived to be at the factories when everyone was on the streets and on the streets when everyone else was at the factories, see Tom Kemp's *French Revolution Betrayed* ... mysteriously hard to obtain since the SLL and the AJS have fallen out.

A belated defence of the tactics of the French Communists is to be found in 'France – Lesson in Unity' by the *Morning Star*'s (loyalist) French correspondent, Lance Sampson (*Labour Monthly*, July 1968). The anarchist view was widely read in Cohn-Bendit's *Obsolete Communism: The Left Wing Alternative*, whose title is a pun on Lenin's *Left-Wing Communism, an Infantile Disorder* which didn't survive translation (Deutsch, London, 1968; Penguin Books, Harmondsworth, 1969).

For material on the Czech invasion see *Russians – Out of Czechoslovakia* (*Socialist Worker* Czech crisis special issue), *Czechoslovakia: Revolution and Counter-Revolution* with a foreword by Raya Dunayevskaya and Harry McShane (published jointly by *News and Letters* and the Glasgow Marxist Humanist Group, Glasgow, 1968). For a masterpiece of selective advocacy, pseudo-impartiality and self-justification see R. Palme Dutt, 'Czechoslovakia' (*Labour Monthly*, October 1968) and the heated correspondence including the resignation of the magazine's Arts Editor, Stuart Douglas, in *Labour Monthly*, November 1968. *Labour Monthly* editors report 75 per cent of letters received supported the editorial.

On Powell's first speech, see *Wanted for Intent to Fool the People*, a London Young Communist Anti-Racialist Broadsheet (Challenge Publications, London, 1968), *The Rise of Enoch Powell* by Paul Foot (Penguin Books, Harmondsworth, 1969), *Enoch Powell* by Andrew Roth (Macdonald, London, 1970), and the first issue of *Black Dwarf*.

For an appeal for a single organization of revolutionary socialists to 'meet the urgent challenge of Fascism' see *For Left Unity Now* (leaflet, London, 1968), containing 'Proposals for Action' to the National Convention of the Left. The Convention, which was arranged by individual members of the Communist Party, IS, the Young Liberals and independent socialists associated with May Day Manifesto and the Haslemere Declaration as a discussion forum, was somewhat overtaken by the events of 1968. In response to the momentary panic that working-class support for Powellism induced, IS, quite unconstitutionally, proposed to the Convention that it convene a unity commission consisting of representatives from all interested organizations, with representation in proportion to their membership, to set up a new socialist organization. Invitations were to be issued to all interested socialist, immigrant and trade-union bodies including shop stewards' committees to participate. IS argued that 'the revolutionary Left can have credibility in the eyes of a growing number of working people and others (including youth) who are in conflict with the system – given a number of conditions. That the revolutionary Left creates a united organization. That it seeks on the basis of its commitment actively to defend reforms and civil liberties and supports struggles in the fragments to help build connections between the fragments (between factories, between shop stewards, between tenants and squatters etc.). That it develops a programme of demands, on the basis of uncompromising but elementary socialist principles, for all those engaged in confronting the capitalist state. That it develops a healthy intellectual life, which can create a living theory and a real unity between theory and practice.' Although the appeal undoubtedly caught the mood of many local Communist and Labour Party branches and trade-union delegates to the Convention, there was still a great deal of suspicion of IS's motives from other groups. The IMG issued a well-hedged statement suggesting adding 'solidarity with the Cuban Revolution' as an entrance qualification, and suggesting a national Left 'liaison committee'. Eventually the only group to respond was the tiny but lively orthodox Trotskyist grouplet 'Workers' Fight', which entered IS in 1968 and departed an unhappy three years' later, slightly less tiny. For a sardonic comment by old-timers, see 'Unity of the Left – For What?' (*Socialist Current* Special, 1968). For a patronizing account of the *Black Dwarf v. Tribune* debate at the Central Hall Westminster when Michael Foot and Eric Heffer faced Tariq Ali and Bob Rowthorn, and the political hopelessness of the Tribunites was only mitigated by the political unpleasantness of some of the 'revolutionaries' in the audience, see D. Jones, 'Small Papers' (*Listener*, 30 January 1969), and *Black Dwarf*, 14 February 1969, p. 5. Trevor Griffiths' much touted melodrama *The Party* (produced by the National Theatre at the Old Vic in December 1973 and published by Faber & Faber, London, 1974) is an account of the everyday life of Marxist trendies in 1968 based on a discussion group for artistic intellectuals set up by the SLL in 1968.

For attempts of the freak Left to promote a British Situationalism see Chris Gray's Heatwave, 1966 translation of Raoul Vaneigen, published as *The Totality for Kids*, various pirate mistranslations of *The Poverty of Student Life* and the output of King Mob Echo, The Bash Street Kids and the Dublin New Earth group. For socialists' criticism of the freak Left see E. J. Hobsbawm's 'Shocking the bourgeoisie is, alas, easier than overthrowing him' (in *New Society*, 22 May 1969: 'The Revolution is Puritan'), Norman Fructer's 'Movement Propaganda and the Culture of the Spectacle' (*Liberation*, New York, May 1971), John Hoyland and Jane Nicolson's critical account of a meeting, or rather quarrel, between socialist and hippy newspaper staff, 'A Solipsistic Cricket Match' (*Black Dwarf*, 7 July 1970) and David Widgery's 'Whistle While You Wank?' (*Oz*, 32, January 1971) and 'Underground Press' (*International Socialism*, 51, p. 3). For a complicated meditation on the freak Left inspired by the AgitProp Grosvenor Square demonstration see Raymond Durgnat's 'Why I Kicked My Underground Habits' (*IT*, 37, 9 August 1968) and for a sardonic tale of local relations between hippies and socialists in Rochdale see 'The Great Aspidistra Mob' (*IT*, 82, 3 July 1970): 'Bleak warehouses, quiet drunks, Heinz baby ads, greasy transport cafes, fat

chintzy sofas and the flicker of Hughie Green through the living-room cur-
tains. In the pub The Radicals are drinking to the Revolution and the dialectics are flying.' For fascinating material on the AgitProp techniques used
in the thirties see Ewen McColl interviewed by Fred Woods in *Folk*, May
1973, and McColl on John Littlewood's work with the Red Megaphones in
pre-war Manchester ('The Workshop Story', *Theatre Quarterly*, January
1973). For modern material see *Radical Arts*, an anthology of late-sixties renewal of street theatre, edited by Bruce Birchall, and the magazine *Culture
and Society*. For early advocacy of squatting see *Anarchy*, vol. 3, no. 23,
'Squatters' (London, 1963) and vol. 8, no. 83, 'Tenants Take Over' (London,
1968). Socialist analysis of the American New Left, largely non-existent in
the Movement's heyday, has become voluminous since its collapse. James P.
O'Brien's laconic chronology *The New Left 1960–68* (published in 'Radical
America' in three parts between May and December 1968 and subsequently
issued as a pamphlet by the New England Free Press) cites most of the published literature and was updated in another bibliographic review, 'Reading
About the New Left' by O'Brien and Allen Hunter, in *Radical America*,
July-August 1972. The most comprehensive source of source material is
edited by an Italian veteran of the student Left Massimo Teodori: *The New
Left: A Documentary History* (Bobbs-Merrill, New York, 1969). The skin-
deepness of SDS's overnight conversion to Marxism in 1968 can be judged
from the heroic banality of the positions of the two main contenders in the
1969 split contained in *Revolution Today: USA*, the analysis, if that's not too
strong a word, of the Progressive Labor Party (Exposition Press, New York,
1970) and Harold Jacob's *Weathermen* (San Francisco Ramparts Paperback,
1970). Two fascinating political novels, without exact parallel in Europe, are
Harvey Swades's account of the anti-war agitation of the Worker's Party
Standing Fast and Clancy Sigal's *Going Away*, a terrifyingly bitter portrait of
an ex-Communist attempting to escape his political memories. Todd Gitlin's
collection of political poetry *Campfires of Resistance* (Bobbs-Merrill, New
York, 1971) is the only sixties' equivalent and marvellously displays the Movement in all its gusshiness and self-absorbtion as well as its bravery and
candour.

SOCIALIST HISTORY

Material on the recent history of the movement can be found, with various
degrees of reliability, in these accounts.

Trotskyism

An administrative history of the Fourth International by Pierre Frank, a
veteran partisan of the USFI is *The Fourth International: A Contribution to
the History of the Trotskyist Movement* (Maspero, Paris, 1970), English translation available in *Intercontinental Press*, vol. 10, 13 March to 29 May 1972).

Critical accounts are Duncan Hallas's two-part series 'Against the Stream', studying the gyrations of the post-war F I (*International Socialism*, 53 and 60), and Tim Wohlforth's 'The Struggle for Marxism in the United States', written by an American adherent of Healy but despite this a serious attempt to place the Socialist Workers' Party in the context of native American radicalism and a well-informed inside history of factional disputes useful to contrast with J. P. Cannon's *History of American Trotskyism* (Pathfinder, New York, 1970). Wohlforth is something of a closet state-cap. Accounts of revolutionaries in the French car industry are contained in D. Mothé's *Militant chez Renault* (Paris, 1965) and P. Bois's *La Grève Renault d'arni-mai 1947* (Paris, 1971).

Jim Higgins' 'Ten Years for the Locust' (*International Socialism*, 14) is the standard history of British Trotskyism by a fine (amateur) Marxist historian based on the texts but enhanced by personal friendship with the veterans. It concludes: 'the history of Trotskyism in Britain is a history of failure, but it is a history of struggle and high endeavour ... it is on this we can build.' Reg Groves' *The Balham Group: How British Trotskyism Began* (Pluto, London, 1974) is a warm and delightfully told account of South London working-class opposition to King Street in the early thirties, with documents and correspondence appended. A short but vigorous speech by Harry Wicks, another working-class Trotskyist rebel, is to be found in 'British Trotskyism in the Thirties' (*International*, vol. 1, no. 4, 1971). Duncan Hallas's anthology *The Fourth International: Stalinism and the Origins of the International Socialists* looks at the political issues which lay beneath the disintegration of the British movement in the early fifties from an IS vantage point (Pluto, London, 1971).

Other material throwing light on the decline of the Fourth International in the early fifties are Michael Pablo's *The Fourth International. What It Is and What It Aims At*, the text of a lecture given at an ILP summer school in 1958, Lucy St John and Tim Wohlforth's *Towards a History of the Fourth International* (Bulletin Pamphlet Series no. 10, New York, 1972), Gerry Healy's *Problems of the Fourth International* (*Newsletter* pamphlet, London, 1967), John Walter's 'Some Notes on British Trotskyist History' (*Marxist Studies*, vol. 2, no. 1, Winter 1969), 'The History of the Johnson-Forrest Tendency' (an appendix to 'Facing Reality', *Correspondence*, Detroit, 1958), and 'Some Notes on the Origins of the Revolutionary Marxist Tendency' (*International Marxist Review*, no. 1, June 1971).

The Socialist Labour League has developed a department of polemical literature to itself. Its version of world history is to be found in *A Balance Sheet of Revisionism* by Cliff Slaughter (*Newsletter* pamphlet, London, February 1969) and *Who Are the International Socialists?* (*Workers*' *Press* pamphlet, April 1971). *In Defence of Trotskyism* (SLL, London, 1973) is apparently the philosophical rationale for the split between the French and British sections of the ICFI, another version of which is to be found in 'The Statement of The International Committee of the Fourth International (Majority)' in the *Workers*' *Press*, 5 November 1971.

Attacks on the S L L in rough order of sophistication include Tony Whelan's

The Credibility Gap: The Politics of the SLL (IMG Publications, London, 1970), *Healy 'Reconstructs' the Fourth International*, with a preface by Joseph Hansen (SWP, New York, 1966), Ernest Germain's *Marxism versus Ultraleftism. Key Issues in Healy's Challenge to the Fourth International* (The Fourth International (USFI), Paris, 1967), Tony Polan's sharply written *The SLL – an Autopsy* with an appendix by Sean Matgamna attacking Duncan Hallas (Workers' Fight, Manchester, 1969), and 'Building the Leadership' by Duncan Hallas (*International Socialism*, 40, October 1969). The SLL has published a reply to each of these publications, usually in pamphlet form. A sour Communist Party view of the entire revolutionary Left is to be found in the sixty-page pamphlet *Ultra-Leftism in Britain* by Betty Reid (Communist Party, London, 1969), a rather paltry survey which elicited from the SLL a reply consisting of a 440-page book *Stalinism in Britain* by 'Robert Black' (New Park Publications, London, 1970).

A specialist literature also exists on Marxist critiques of the Soviet Union. A historical review is given (from an SPGB viewpoint) by W. Jerome and A. Buick in 'Soviet State Capitalism' (*Survey*, January 1967) and R. Maille's *Le Trotskyisme et l'USSR* (Pouvoir Ouvrier, Paris, 1965).

Marxist-Leninist

Historical background can be found in 'Revisionism and the Anti-Revisionist Movement' by 'T.M.' in *Marxist-Leninist Quarterly*, no. 3, Winter 1972, which dwells on the circumstances surrounding the foundation of the CPB(ML). Material on McCreery's Group is in 'Sincerity Is Not Enough' (*Struggle*, May 1972) and a reply *Michael McCreery, the Workers Party of Scotland and the Communist Federation of Britain* by Paul Noone (Workers Broadsheet, vol. 6, no. 7). George Thayer's highly inaccurate *The British Political Fringe* (Blond, London, 1966) does contain an interview with McCreery.

Anarchist

Accounts by participants in the post-war anarchist movement include George Woodcock's *The Source and the Stream*, dealing with Herbert Read's role in the 1945 Regulation 39A Prosecution and the Freedom Defence Committee, Ethel Mannin's *Comrade, O Comrade* (Jarrolds, London, 1947), a fictional account of the 1945 split in the AFB, and Marie Louise Berneri's *Journey Through Utopia* (Routledge & Kegan Paul, London, 1950). 'What's Wrong with Freedom?' by Jerry Westall is a cheerful personal reminiscence of eminent anarchists (*Anarchy*, new series, no. 12, 1972) and *Towards a History and Critique of the Anarchist Movement in Recent Times* is a stern account by Colin Williams, R. Atkins and Keith Nathan of the organizational failings of the anarchist movement (ORA pamphlet no. 1, York, 1970). For the problems of the underground press see Marsha Rowe's 'Workin' for the (underground) man' (*Open Secret*, issue 2, 1970) and Andrew Cockburn's 'The Day the Underground Went Overground' (*Frendz*, November 1971).

Communist

The historical accounts of the modern Communist Party are either by right-wing liberals pretending shock (N. Pelling, *The British Communist Party*, or Neal Wood, *Communism and British Intellectuals*, or Trotskyist scissors and paste jobs ('R. Black', *Stalinism in Britain*). K. Newton's *The Sociology of British Communism* has some interesting figures and Ian H. Birchall's *Workers Against the Monolith* some clearly told facts. From the people who make up the Party there is silence.

FILMS

Many documentary and newsreel films were made in the thirties by socialists in groups like the American Workers' Film and Photo League and the British Workers' Film Society movement. These films, ignored by the film historians, expunged from the filmographies and, in the case of Kino, physically destroyed, are only now being rediscovered. Stanley Forman presented a programme at the National Film Theatre, entitled 'Treasures from an Archive', of his own collection of British films made by socialists. It included slightly comic material like the visit of a team of socialist ballerinas to the Red Dean, Dr Hewlett Johnson, but had also historically priceless fragments of film of the mammoth May Day 1937 London demonstration, the 1938 Communist Party Congress, the St Pancreas rent strike and Harry Pollitt's 1955 election address which was shown by mobile film units in the areas with Communist candidates. There were also shots of Bob Stewart, J. B. S. Haldane and Claude Cockburn in Spain, Tom Mann, Paul Robeson, Fenner Brockway and James Maxton.

In postwar Britain a similar movement has arisen. Cinema Action pioneered the modern use of documentary film making and showing their films in direct collaboration with trade-unionists. They have produced material on the struggle against the Industrial Relations Act, the Upper Clyde struggle, the release of the Pentonville Five and the resistance in Derry. The Berwick Street Film Collective have made an extended feature on the campaign to unionize London night cleaners and the Women's Film Group has material on the Equal Pay Act, the miners' strike and the Industrial Relations Act. Ivor Montagu has produced a feature on the Communist Party seen through the ideas of *Labour Monthly* called 'Fifty Fighting Years'.

BIBLIOGRAPHIES

Useful bibliographies in print include the extended radical reading list in *Counter Course* edited by Trevor Pateman (Penguin Education, Harmondsworth, 1973), *Marxism Versus Sociology: A Guide to Reading* by Martin Shaw (Pluto Press, London, 1973), *Reading Politics: A Guide to Intelligent Inquiry*, compiled by Leslie Bridges (duplicated, Ipswich, 1968), *Pacifism: A Selected Bibliography*, compiled by John Hyatt (Housmans, London, 1972), Sheila Rowbotham's *Women's Liberation and Revolution: A Bibliography* (Falling Wall, Bristol, 1972) and Leonora Lloyd's *Booklist for Women's Liberation* (Socialist Woman, London, 1971). The *New Left Review* has an index in issue 23 and a list of golden hits in their tenth birthday issue (No. 60, 1970), *International Socialism* published an author index in issue 61 (June 1973) and *Solidarity* published a duplicated index of the magazine, including their other pamphlets and books, in August 1972.

Collections of radical literature are to be found in The Public Library (an annex of the London libertarian bookshop Rising Free), The Marx Memorial Library, the Institute of Race Relations' excellent catalogue of local radical newspapers, Warwick University's Modern Records Centre, the London School of Economics Library and the International Institute of Social History in Amsterdam.

Index

More about Penguins
and Pelicans

Penguinews, which appears every month, contains details of all the new books issued by Penguins as they are published. From time to time it is supplemented by *Penguins in Print*, which is a complete list of all titles available. (There are some five thousand of these.)

A specimen copy of *Penguinews* will be sent to you free on request. For a year's issues (including the complete lists) please send £1 if you live in the British Isles, or elsewhere. Just write to Dept EP, Penguin Books Ltd, Harmondsworth, Middlesex, enclosing a cheque or postal order, and your name will be added to the mailing list.

In the U.S.A.: For a complete list of books available from Penguin in the United States write to Dept CS, Penguin Books Inc., 7110 Ambassador Road, Baltimore, Maryland 21207.

In Canada: For a complete list of books available from Penguin in Canada write to Penguin Books Canada Ltd, 41 Steelcase Road West, Markham, Ontario.